Topics in Practical Halacha

Vol. 3

Selected topics in practical Halacha from the four sections of Shulchan Aruch in accordance to the rulings of Shulchan Aruch Harav, Chabad Custom, and other Halachic authorities

Compiled by: Rabbi Yaakov Goldstein

Topics in Practical Halacha Vol. 3
Second Edition
Published and copyrighted © by
Yaakov Goldstein
Bar Yochaiy Safed, Israel
For orders, questions, comments, contact:
Tel: 050-695-2866
E-mail: rabbiygoldstein@gmail.com
www.shulchanaruchharav.com
Available on Amazon.com
All rights reserved. No part of this publication may
be reproduced in any form or by any means,
including photocopying, without permission in
Writing from the copyright holder

5781 • 2020

ISBN: 9781073189427

Shulchanaruchharav.com is a state-of-the-art Halacha website that contains the largest English database of detailed Halacha available on the web. A Halacha database has been established to help the learner research a Halacha and have it available on his fingertips. For further information visit our site at
www.shulchanaruchharav.com
Please support us!
Our website is available free of charge and is dependent on subscription of our site members! Please see our website for member options!

Approbations for the Authors previous work of "A Semicha Aid for Learning the Laws of Shabbos"
Reprinted with the explicit permission of the Rabbanim

ב"ה

RABBI MENACHEM M. GLUCKOWSKY
CHABAD RECHOVOT
12 HAGANA ST. RECHOVOT ISRAEL
Tel: 08-9493176 Fax: 08-9457620 Cel: 050-4145770

מנחם מענדל גלוקובסקי
רב קהילת חב"ד ברחובות
מען: רח' ההגנה 12/1 רחובות 76214
שרד 08-9493176 פקס. 08-9457620 נייד 050-4145770

Elul 577

I have seen the valuable Sefer "A Semicha Aid for Learning The Laws of Shabbos" written by Rabbi Yaakov Goldstein. The purpose of this Sefer is to assist students learning Semicha in learning the material from the Alter Rebbe's Shulchan Aruch, as well as for them to come out with a valuable and large database of knowledge in practical Halachic questions dealt with in contemporary authorities. It excels in its clear presentation, concise language and thorough summaries in all the relevant laws covered in the Shulchan Aruch of Admur.

It can also serve the general English public in giving them the opportunity to learn the Laws of Shabbos faithful to the opinion of the Alter Rebbe.

Mention must be made, as writes the author in his foreword, that one is not to use this Sefer, amongst all Sefarim of Melaktim, to Pasken for himself. One must rather address all matters which require clarification to a qualified Rav.

I bless the author for his work and wish him much success.

Menachem Mendel Gluckowsky

Approbations for the Authors previous work of "A Semicha Aid for Learning the Laws of Shabbos"
Reprinted with the explicit permission of the Rabbanim

בס"ד

RABBI B. YURKOWICZ
CHABAD LOD

ברוך בועז יורקוביץ
רב ומד"א דשיכון חב"ד לוד
אה"ק ת"ו

The book "The laws of Shabbos" written by Rabbi Yaakov Goldstein is a comprehensive compilation of the laws and customs of Shabbos, up until the many Poskim of today's time, which discuss the practical applications of the laws. Sefarim of this nature are very important and will certainly strengthen the proper observance of Shabbos.

I thus come here with words of blessing and praise to my dear acquaintance, the author, who brings merits to the masses through this important work.

As the author himself has mentioned in his foreword I reiterate that which is known that the layman cannot use this Sefer to Pasken for himself even after learning it in whole, but must rather address all their questions to a qualified Rav.

I am confident that in the merit of this spreading of the laws of Shabbos, on which the Sages state "If the Jews guarded Shabbos they would be redeemed", it will hasten the coming of our righteous Moshiach speedily in our days.

Rabbi Baruch Jurkavitch

Important Notice

The Halachas provided in this book are intended to serve as an aid in understanding Halacha and as a resource of practical Halachic questions and sources for the English reader. It is not meant at all to take the place of a competent Rav, Moreh Horaah or one's own personal research of a Halacha.

Foreword

Acknowledgement:

First and foremost, I give thanks to the Almighty which has blessed me to be able to compile this work. I thank my wife, My Eishes Chayil, Shayna, which if not for her support this book would have been impossible to accomplish. I thank all the Rabbanim and Rosheiy Yeshivas which have given me advice and support regarding the project, and of course my students in which through teaching them many insights have been added to the laws written here, following the dictum of the Sages "And from my students more than all". A special thanks to Rabbi Roberto Szerer and his wife who have graciously given their support throughout the course of the writing of this Sefer, The merit of the masses rests on their shoulders. I also thank Rabbi/Dr. Kenneth Trestman and his wife for their monthly support throughout the course of the writing of this Sefer, as well as each and every member of shulchanaruchharav.com who with their support fulfill the dictum of the Sages "If there is flour [$] there is Torah" and allowed me the time to write this book.

The importance of learning Halacha:

It is known and evident the importance that the study and knowledge of Halacha plays in the role of the life of a Jewish man and woman. As is known, the Rebbe lived and preached that one must be a Shulchan Aruch Yid, a Jew which every movement of his life is dictated by the directives of the Shulchan Aruch. To such extent was the knowledge of Halacha in the forefront of the Rebbe's eyes, that he pleaded and suggested in a talk of Yud Shvat 1955 that in today's times the Yeshivas are not to begin the accustomed deep analytical studies in Talmud until the students have been taught the fundamental principles of Jewish belief and the laws which are written in Shulchan Aruch. The Rebbe continued, "If the situation continues the way it is, then in a number of years from now there will not be a Rabbi which will know a simple law regarding a Jew's daily life, such as a law in the laws of Muktzah. Yes, he will know maybe a law in Nezikin or Choshen Mishpat from the Talmud which he learned, but he will be ignorant of the simplest of laws brought down in Shulchan Aruch".

<u>Ruling of Shulchan Aruch:</u>[1] In the laws of Talmud Torah the following ruling is given: The learning of practical Halacha takes precedence over learning other fields of Torah. Only after one is clearly well versed in practical Halacha and knows the detailed laws relevant to his daily life, is he to study other parts of Torah in depth. One is to learn majority of Orach Chaim and selected sections of Yoreh Deah, Even Haezer and Choshen Mishpat.

<u>The opinion of the Chassidic Rabbeim:</u> The Baal Shem Tov and Maggid state that the evil inclination tries to persuade a Jew not to learn practical Halacha and tells him to spend all of his days learning the Talmud and its commentaries. This is done in order so the person does not serve G-d properly according to His will.[2] The Alter Rebbe distanced people from learning Torah simply for the sake of Pilpul and emphasized the necessity of learning in depth for the sake of practical Halacha.[3] The Mittler Rebbe decreed that every community is to set a study session to learn the entire Alter Rebbe's Shulchan Aruch on the section of Orach Chaim.[4] The Rebbe Rashab writes that every Chassid is obligated to learn the Alter Rebbe's Shulchan Aruch Orach Chaim from beginning to end and that every person is to establish a daily learning session to learn and review these Halachos.[5] In today's generations one must especially have Mesirus Nefesh not to swerve from even one letter of Shulchan Aruch.[6] The Rebbe Rayatz reiterates this by saying that every Jew must establish a daily Torah session in Halacha, each person on his level; Shulchan Aruch or Kitzur Shulchan Aruch.[7]

---

[1] Hilchos Talmud Torah 2:9-10; Shach Yoreh Deah 246; Hakdama of Mishneh Berurah; Toras Menachem 13 p. 236
[2] Tzivas Harivash 117; Or Torah of the Maggid 221
[3] Beis Rebbe p. 32
[4] Hakdama of Mittler Rebbe in Shulchan Aruch Harav
[5] Kuntrus Hatefilah 17
[6] Sefer Hamamarim "Ein Hakadosh Baruch Hu Ba Betrunya" 1888
[7] Sefer Hamamarim 1926 p. 263

The directives of the Rebbe:[8]

<u>Learning Halacha as part of the Yeshiva schedule</u>: The Rebbe stated that a revolution is to be made in the learning curriculum of the Yeshivas, for it to include the section of Orach Chaim and practical Halacha. The Rebbe stated that if the Yeshivas don't desire to change the curriculum of the regular study hours, it should at least be encouraged when the students are on break.[9] The Yeshivas are not to begin the accustomed deep analytical studies in Talmud until the students have been taught the fundamental principles of Jewish belief and the laws which are written in Shulchan Aruch.[10] This applies even to the Yeshivos Gedolos, as we see that the knowledge of the Yeshiva students is very minute amongst the laws found in Orach Chaim.[11] If I had the power I would establish that every Mosad, beginning from the kindergartens and through the Yeshivos and Kolalim, establish a Shiur in these practical laws.[12]

<u>The importance of being an expert on the laws in Orach Chaim</u>: Elsewhere the Rebbe stated: Unfortunately, we see amongst many students that the more they expand their knowledge in Talmud and its commentaries the less they know the laws relevant to their practical life. The laws in Orach Chaim are extremely necessary for one to be constantly well versed in them, as the questions that arise in these subjects in many instances do not give one the time to ask a Rabbi or look in a Sefer for the answer.[13] This especially applies to the laws of Birchas Hanehnin; Hefsek in Tefilah; Muktzah and laws of the like of which the ignorance in these topics is appalling.[14]

<u>Establishing Shiurim in practical Halacha in all communities</u>: If I had the power I would establish that every community has a Shiur in these practical laws.[15] These Shiurim should take place in the local Shul.[16] Thus each community, and even each individual, is to include within his Torah Shiurim a set time for learning and reviewing practical Halacha.[17] One is to have a Shiur in these Halachas every single day, even for a few minutes.[18] For this purpose it is not necessary to learn specifically from the Shulchan Aruch [which can take much time] but rather to learn from compilations of Halachas such as those found in Derech Hachaim, Kitzur Shulchan Aruch and other compilations.[19] The Rav giving the Shiur is to then give over any extra information that the listeners need to know, that is not included in the compiled Halachas.[20]

Summary:
Every Jew is to have a set learning session every day in practical Halacha, even for a few minutes a day. One is to use this time to learn practical laws from available Halacha compilations, and not necessarily from the actual Shulchan Aruch.

The goal of this Sefer:

This Sefer comes in continuation of our series of Sefarim catered to the English-speaking public on the Shulchan Aruch. Our goal is to cover all the sections of Orach Chaim and the practical sections of Yoreh Deah, Even Haezer and Choshen Mishpat, in faith to the Alter Rebbe's rulings and customs of Chabad Lubavitch. Our previous Sefarim covered specific topics in Halacha, giving our readers a full and complete treatise on the subject topic. This Sefer however is the third in a series within our general

---

[8] See Shulchan Menachem 4 p. 238-244 for a compilation of letters and Sichos on this topic.
[9] Sichas Tzav 13th Nissan found in Toras Menachem 13 p. 236
[10] Sichas Yud Shvat 1955
[11] Igros Kodesh 16 p. 116
[12] Igros Kodesh 10 p. 270
[13] Igros Kodesh 10 p. 130
[14] Igros Kodesh 10 p. p. 130; p. 192; p. 270; p. 355
[15] Igros Kodesh 10 p. 143
[16] Igros Kodesh ibid based on the saying of Chazal [Brachos 8a] "Hashem loves the gates of Jewish law more than the Shul and Batei Midrash."
[17] Igros Kodesh 7 p. 238
[18] Toras Menachem 7 p. 114; Learning the Halachas every single day will help one remember also the Halachas he learned the day before. [ibid]
[19] Igros Kodesh 7 p. 238; Igros Kodesh 10 p. 144; Igros Kodesh 11 p. 281; Igros Kodesh 13 p. 24; Toras Menachem 7 p. 114; "This does not refer to Tur and Beis Yosef, but rather to Shulchan Aruch and Beir Heiytiv. However one who has time for more is praised." [ibid]
[20] Igros Kodesh 13 p. 24

Halacha series, and does not cover any one specific subject in Halacha but rather encompasses various practical Halachic topics throughout all sections of Shulchan Aruch. It is meant to provide the reader with a clear summary of practical subjects in Orach Chaim, Yoreh Deah, Even Haezer, Choshen Mishpat. It provides a clear, and concise, organized essay on Jewish law. In addition, it contains a wealth of practical Q&A that is not dealt with in Shulchan Aruch and gives the reader a clear background of the Rabbinical opinions on the subject. In addition, it provides a wealth of information in the footnotes, which include sources, reasons, overview of the rulings of other Poskim, and clarifications. Thus, the goal of this Sefer is on the one hand to give the English speaking public clear guidance of answers to Halachic questions, and at the same time hand him vast background knowledge of the subject at hand, thus fulfilling the Rebbe's instructions that every Jew is to be wealthy in knowledge of Torah. Many of the Halachos printed in this Sefer have featured on our Daily Halacha email and WhatsApp messages in written and audio format.

Understanding the format of the Halachas provided within this Sefer and the Poskim they are based on:

The rulings provided in the Sefer are faithful to the rulings of the Shulchan Aruch Harav, otherwise known as the Alter Rebbe's Shulchan Aruch, in all cases of conflict with other Poskim. The Chabad customs are mentioned in their relevant places. The other opinions applicable, such as the opinion of the Michaber, Mishneh Berurah, Kaf Hachaim and other opinions, are mentioned in the footnotes. The above only applies to those areas of Halacha in which we merited to have the writings of the Alter Rebbe, which is Orach Chaim and a minority of Yoreh Deah and Choshen Mishpat. However, the majority of Yoreh Deah, Choshen Misphat, and the entirety of Even Haezer we did not merit to receive the writings of the Alter Rebbe, and therefore in these Halachas we followed the rulings of all the classical Poskim who voiced an opinion, and in cases of dispute the dispute is mentioned. The Halachas provided are split into three sections:

1. The Halacha Section: The Halacha section is the main section written in the non-boxed area. In general, only those rulings recorded in the Shulchan Aruch of Admur or Michaber/Rama/Shach/Taz are brought and summarized within this section. Many times, there are additional explanations, stipulations and clarifications of a Halacha which is brought in other Poskim. All these additions are brought in brackets or footnotes. This allows the reader to maintain an understanding of the Halacha as written by the Shulchan Aruch without the additional comments of later authorities, but at the same time gain from their necessary additions.
2. The footnotes: The footnotes provide the reader with a number of different points of information. They provide the sources for each statement written, as well as additional explanations and opinions of a given Halacha. Many footnotes serve to delve into the wording of the Shulchan Aruch in a given Halacha, his intent and the background of his rulings.
3. The boxed area: The boxed area which follows each Halacha serve to provide a concise summary of the Halacha and additional practical Q&A that have been dealt with in contemporary Poskim and relate to the given subject. The Q&A section does not include Halachas that are explicitly ruled in the Shulchan Aruch, as these Halachas have already been written in the Halacha section of the book. The Q&A section lends the learner a greatly needed base knowledge for practical application of the resulting law learned within a topic. Many times, even after one has sifted and comprehended the final ruling of Admur, its influence within practical cases remain obscure. This is besides for the fact that researching a question amongst the sea of Poskim is both time comprising as well as not always practical. We therefore have compiled many major practical Halachic questions which connect with a given Halacha that was learned. The answers given have been compiled from various sources, as noted in the footnotes. In cases where a dispute amongst Poskim is recorded we have not given final rulings, being that we are not in a position to rule for the public like which Posek one is to follow. In these cases, one is to consult with his personal Rav and receive guidance for what he is to do. **It is of importance to note that the ruling of one's personal Rav takes precedence over any dissenting opinion brought in the book,**

whether or not this opinion is known to the Rav. Furthermore, even those which are in Rabbinical position of giving rulings are not to base their rulings on opinions brought in this book without first studying and verifying its source. As is known, one may not base a ruling on summarized Halachas [Melaktim, a compiler of opinions] but is rather to discern this for himself in the sources that are brought. [See Piskeiy Teshuvos Vo. 3 in the approbations of Gedolei Yisrael, and the introduction there.]

Historical background of Shulchan Aruch Harav:[21]

The Shulchan Aruch Harav, also known as the Alter Rebbe's Shulchan Aruch, or Shulchan Aruch Admur Hazakein; was written by Rav Schneur Zalman of Liadi.

Its initiation: The Maggid of Mezritch was encouraged by the heavenly courts to search amongst his students for a proper candidate to compile a new Shulchan Aruch.[22] The Maggid of Mezritch chose the Alter Rebbe to write this compilation.[23]

When was it written: It was written anywhere between the years 1765-1775.[24] Some[25] prove that the section of Orach Chaim was written in the years 1771-1772. The Rebbe Rayatz writes[26] that the Maggid asked Admur to write the Shulchan Aruch when he was 21 years old.[27] The other sections of the Shulchan Aruch were written at a later time. An exact date has not been historically proven.[28]

The laws of Tzitzis-Amongst the first sections to be written:[29] Amongst the first subjects to be compiled by the Alter Rebbe were the laws of **Tzitzis** and the laws of Pesach, which were written while he was in Mezritch, prior to the arrival of the brothers Rav Shmelka of Nickelsberg and Rav Pinchas Horowitz. When the holy brothers saw the work of the Alter Rebbe on these two subjects, they praised it tremendously and blessed him to merit completing his work.

How long did it take to write?[30] The section of Orach Chaim was written by Admur in a span of two years.

When was it printed? The Shulchan Aruch was first printed in its entirety after the Alter Rebbe passed away, in the year 1816.[31] Certain sections of the Shulchan Aruch were printed beforehand. Hilchos Talmud Torah was printed in Shklov in the year 1794.[32]

The name "Shulchan Aruch Harav": The source for this name "Shulchan Aruch Harav" is seemingly based on the title of "Rav" that was given to Admur by the students of the Maggid and the Maggid himself. The following is the story related to the giving of this title:[33] The Maggid once told Reb Zusha "write to our Gaon Reb Zalmana Litvak to come here". Upon the students hearing that the Maggid referred to the Alter Rebbe as our Gaon, they gave him the title "Rav". When Reb Avraham Hamalach

---

[21] See the following resources for historical background of the Shulchan Aruch Harav: Hakdama of Shulchan Aruch Harav, written by the children of Admur; Sifrei Halacha Shel Admur Hazakein; Sefer Hatoldos.

[22] To note that the Gr"a also intended on writing a Shulchan Aruch with all of his final rulings, bringing only one opinion. However this did not come into fruition being the Gr"a testified that he did not have heavenly permission to do so. [Hakdama of Biur Hagr"a written by his children] However the Maggid received Divine consent and motivation to write a new Shulchan Aruch. [Sifrei Halacha Shel Admur Hazakein p. 7 footnote 1; Talpiyos 4:1-2 p. 184 in name of the Admur of Radzin]

[23] Igros Kodesh Admur Hazakein [printed in Maggid Dvarav Leyaakov Hosafos p.47]; Hakdama on Shulchan Aruch Harav, written by the children of Admur. The Maggid stated that the four cubits of Halacha are dependent on the Alter Rebbe and that even the first thought of the Alter Rebbe in a given topic is a glimmer of Divine spirit [Ruach Hakodesh]. [Letter of Maggid printed in Sefer Hatoldos p. 36]

[24] It is unclear as to exactly which year Admur began writing the Shulchan Aruch. The above years are the estimated years of when it was written. [See Sifrei Halacha Shel Admur Hazakein p. 9] Many say that the writing of the Shulchan Aruch was begun by Admur at the age of 25. Accordingly, the beginning of the writing of the Shulchan Aruch would have been in 1770. This is five years after the Alter Rebbe arrived in Mezritch. [He arrived in Mezritch for the first time at the age of 20 -Hakdama of Shulchan Aruch written by the children of Admur; Igros Kodesh Admur Hazakein 2:32; See also Beis Rebbe 2:1; Likkutei Dibburim 3:483.] The year that the Alter Rebbe arrived in Mezritch was 1764. [Rebbe in Haggadah Shel Pesach "Bedikas Chametz"]

[25] Footnote 16-17 in Hakdama of new Kehos printing.

[26] Sefer Hasichos 1929 Sukkos brought in Sefer Hatoldos 3 p. 161

[27] Accordingly it was written in the year 1765-1767. Vetzaruch Iyun

[28] See Sifrei Halacha Shel Admur Hazakein p. 9-10

[29] Hakdama of Shulchan Aruch written by the children of Admur

[30] Hakdama of Shulchan Aruch Harav, written by the children of Admur.

[31] Prior to that time the Chassidim had many hand written copies of the Shulchan Aruch. However it was not printed in a formal book. [Piskeiy Hasiddur introduction]

[32] Sefer Hatoldos p. 33

[33] Likkutei Dibburim 1 p. 100-101

told this over to his father the Maggid, the Maggid replied "The Chevraya Kadisha have projected the truth in this statement. A name has meaning and the Halacha is like Rav. The **Shulchan Aruch of the Rav** will be accepted within all of Jewry."

Following the rulings of Shulchan Aruch Harav versus other Poskim:[34]
Chabad Chassidim have accepted the rulings of the Shulchan Aruch Harav for all matters, whether for leniency or stringency. This applies even if majority of codifiers argue on his opinion. This is similar to those who follow the opinion of the Rambam [or Michaber] and do not divert from his opinion. The Maggid stated that the four cubits of Halacha are dependent on the Alter Rebbe and that even the first thought of the Alter Rebbe in a given topic is a glimmer of Divine spirit [Ruach Hakodesh].[35] His rulings and arbitrations are considered as if they were given on Sinai.[36] The Tzaddik, Reb Levi Yitzchak of Berditchev writes[37] as follows: I testify heaven and earth that if the Alter Rebbe were alive in the times of the Rif and Rambam he would be considered like one of their contemporaries etc. His "words of gold" is literally like the words of the Rif and Rambam of blessed memory."

---

[34] Hakdama of Ketzos Hashulchan; See Divrei Nechemia Yoreh Deah 1
[35] Letter of Maggid printed in Sefer Hatoldos p. 36
[36] Letter of Maggid printed in Maggid Dvarav Leyaakov Hosafos p. 100
[37] Brought in Piskeiy Hasiddur ibid

About the author:

Rabbi Yaakov Goldstein currently lives with his wife Shayna, and eleven children K"H, in Tzfas, Israel. Rabbi Goldstein received Semicha from Rabbi Schneur Zalman Labkowski of the Tomchei Temimim headquarters in 2005 and served as a chaplain in the Lotar/Kalatz and K9 unit of the IDF from years 2005-2008. He is also a certified Shochet, and has performed Hashgacha work in slaughterhouses. Rabbi Goldstein is the director of Shulchanaruchharav.com, the world's leading web-based Halacha database, and is the director of the Home Study Semicha Program, a self-study web-based Semicha program. He is a prolific author of over 30 Sefarim studied by a wide range of readers throughout the world, which is used regularly in Semicha programs around the globe. He is a world renowned Posek, answering questions to a web-based market, and serves as a local Posek, Rav, and Lecturer, in the Tzemach Tzedek community Shul in Tzefas, Israel. His many classes can be heard both from his website, Vimeo and YouTube channel. Students can join live to classes given in the Tzemach Tzedek Shul, through the " בית חבד צפת Chabad Tsfat" YouTube channel.

Other works by the Author

The present author has written books on various subjects in Shulchan Aruch. Some of these sections are not yet available to the public in a published format although all currently available **free of charge** on our website Shulchanaruchharav.com. In order for these subjects to become available on the bookshelf, and in order to add more subjects to the website, we are in need of funding. If you or anyone you know would like to sponsor a Halachic section to become available in print or on the web, please contact the author and the merit of spreading Halacha, and the merit of the Alter Rebbe, will certainly stand in your favor!

The following is a list of other subjects currently available in print:

*All books are available for purchase on Shulchanaruchharav.com & Amazon.com

1. The Chassidishe Parsha-Torah Or-Likkutei Torah
2. The Weekly Parsha Summary
3. The Tanach summary series-Sefer Yehoshua-Shoftim
4. Topics in Practical Halacha Vol. 1
5. Topics in Practical Halacha Vol. 2
6. Topics in Practical Halacha Vol. 3
7. Topics in Practical Halacha Vol. 4
8. Awaking like a Jew
9. The Laws of Tzitzis
10. The Laws of Tefillin
11. The Laws of Tefillin-Summary Edition
12. The Laws & Customs of Kerias Hatorah
13. Kedushas Habayis-A comprehensive guide on Siman Reish Mem
14. The laws & Customs of Rosh Chodesh
15. The laws & Customs of Pesach
16. The Pesach Seder
17. The Pesach Seder--Summary Edition
18. Between Pesach & Shavuos
19. The laws & Customs of Shavuos
20. The Laws & Customs of the Three Weeks
21. The Laws of Rosh Hashanah
22. The Laws & Customs of Yom Kippur
23. The Laws of Sukkos-Summary edition
24. The Laws & Customs of Chanukah
25. The Laws of Purim
26. A Semicha Aid for Learning the Laws of Shabbos Vol. 1
27. A Semicha Aid for Learning the Laws of Shabbos Vol. 2
28. The Laws of Shabbos Volume 3
29. The Practical Laws of Meat & Milk
30. The Laws and Customs of Erev Shabbos and Motzei Shabbos
    - The laws of Shabbos-Workbook
31. A Semicha aid for learning the laws of Basar Bechalav
    - Basar Bechalav-Workbook
32. A Semicha aid for learning the laws of Taaruvos
    - Taaruvos-Workbook
33. A Semicha aid for learning the laws of Melicha
    - Melicha-Workbook
34. The Laws & Customs of Mourning Vol. 1
35. The Laws & Customs of Mourning Vol. 2
36. The Laws & Customs of Mourning-Summary Edition

Daily Halacha Subscription:
To subscribe to our websites mailing list please visit www.shulchanaruchharav.com **on your desktop** or tablet [not available on phone webpage] and look for the subscription bar on the right side of the page to enter your email to subscribe.

The subscription is free and includes a daily Halacha topic sent to you via email and/or WhatsApp, and a weekly Parsha email with a Parsha summary, Chassidic insights, and more. Likewise, you will be kept updated on all of our future publications.

Online Home Study Semicha Program
Under the Auspices of
Rabbi Yaakov Goldstein, Director of Shulchanaruchharav.com & Author of the "Semicha Aid" and "Halacha Aid" series

About
Shulchanaruchharav.com runs an international Home Study Semicha Program, H.S.S.P., catered for those who desire to study the Semicha curriculum and receive Semicha certification although do not have the ability to do so in a Yeshiva setting. A home study program is hence available for students of all ages to become efficient in Halacha and receive Semicha certification from the comfort of their home, in accordance to their time and leisure. For more information on this program please see our website shulchanaruchharav.com.

The purpose of our Semicha program:
The purpose of our Semicha program is to provide Jewish men throughout the world the opportunity of learning practical Halacha within a Semicha curriculum. The entire idea behind today's Semicha is, as explained by the Lubavitcher Rebbe, to increase one's knowledge of practical Halacha in order to be aware of possible Halachic issues involving day to day occurrences. Often one is unable to turn to a Rav to verify the answer for a Shaalah and hence prior knowledge is necessary. Through this program one will gain knowledge in various topics of practical Halacha. The student will be tested and receive certification for his accomplishments. We provide learning textbooks for each subject. These textbooks are meant to accompany the student throughout his home learning and afterwards whenever a question comes up. This allows students who are unable to learn in an actual Semicha institute to also learn the curriculum, gain the knowledge, and receive certification.

What is the difference between your Semicha program and other online Semicha programs that already exist?
Baruch Hashem, we have seen the sprout of many different Semicha programs which cater to different types of students and a variety of settings. Some online Semicha programs currently available, offers the student an online Yeshiva setting of learning Semicha with live online classes. Other programs do not provide set online classes by a teacher, but rather allow the student to learn the material on his own or with a Chavrusa at his own pace, with assistance from the Rabbinical staff. Our program offers both tracks. One can choose the **self-study track**, in which he follows the course module and completes the study of material, and assignments on his own, using the literature that we provide. A second track, the **Yeshiva track**, allows students to join an online classroom platform which includes live Shiurim by Rabbi Goldstein, who will escort the student in his learning throughout the course. Another aspect of our program which has not yet been seen in other Semicha programs is that we offer a large variety of practical Halachic topics for study within the Semicha curriculum. Another novelty of our program is that it caters also to those who do not have background in Hebrew and are unable to learn from the original text. We offer our own Semicha text which is made available in English.

For further details visit shulchanaruchharav.com!

Table of Contents

Table of Contents

- Chapter 1: Orach Chaim..25
- Chapter 2: Yoreh Deah..135
- Chapter 3: Even Haezer 199
- Chapter 4: Choshen Mishpat 227
- Miscellaneous..255

FOREWORD — 6

TABLE OF CONTENTS — 15

ORACH CHAIM — 25

------------------Morning Conduct------------------ — 27
1. May one learn Torah or recite blessings in face of the morning washing water? — 27
2. Wearing the shirt tucked into one's pants versus sticking out: — 28
   A. Introduction-Not to be dressed sloppy: — 28
   B. The law: — 28
3. Does placing a hand on one's head suffice in place of a Yarmulke? — 29
   A. Introduction: — 29
   B. The Law: — 29
4. Is one to stand while reciting the morning blessings [i.e. Birchas Hashachar]? — 30
5. Until when during the day may one recite Birchas Hashachar? — 31

------------------Tzitzis------------------ — 32
6. Wearing a Tallis Gadol properly-Making sure the Tallis covers at least one square Ama of the body: — 32
   A. Introduction: — 32
   B. The Law-How much of the body must the Tallis cover: — 32
7. Making sure the Tallis Katan covers the entire chest area, from below the neckline: — 33
8. May/should one have a separate pair of Tzitzis to wear at night while sleeping? — 33
   A. Background: The obligation of Tzitzis during nighttime and to night garments: — 34
   B. The Law: — 34
   C. Epilogue-The Mitzvah to sleep with Tzitzis at night: — 35
9. Is a blessing said in the morning over a Tallis Katan that one wore at night? — 36

------------------Tefillin------------------ — 37
10. Placing the head Tefillin [i.e. Shel Rosh] by the hairline: — 37
11. May the straps of the Tefillin that are wrapped around the arm touch each other, or overlap? — 40

----------------Davening-General Laws------------------ — 41
12. Writing, text messaging, Whatsapping, during Davening: — 41
    A. Introduction: — 41
    B. The ruling: — 41
13. Yawning, burping, and sneezing during Shemoneh Esrei: — 42

------------------Pesukei Dezimra------------------ — 43
14. The verse of Poseiach Es Yadecha & its relevant laws: — 43
15. Skipping Pesukei Dezimra in order to Daven Shemoneh Esrei with Minyan: — 45

------------------Shema------------------ — 47
16. Sof Zeman Kerias Shema-Until what time may the morning Shema be recited-Understanding the Luach of Sof Zman Kerias Shema: — 47

------------------Shemoneh Esrei------------------ — 51
17. What is one to do if he is in unsure as to which blessing in Shemoneh Esrei he is holding by? — 51

Table of Contents

A. Introduction:	51
B. The ruling:	51
18. What is one to do if he heard Kaddish, Kedusha, Barchu or Modim in middle of Shemoneh Esrei:	52
-----------------Aleinu Leshabeiach-----------------	55
19. Aleinu Leshabeiach-The origin & Purpose of the prayer:	55
A. The origin of the prayer:	55
B. The purpose and greatness of the prayer:	55
20. Saying Aleinu Leshabeiach together with the congregation:	56
21. Spitting by Aleinu:	57
-----------------Kerias Hatorah-----------------	58
22. Should one stand during Kerias Hatorah?	58
23. What is one to do if he is in middle of Shemoneh Esrei, and the congregation began to read Kerias Hatorah?	61
-----------------Beis Hakeneses-----------------	62
24. Bringing small children to Shul:	62
-----------------Netilas Yadayim-----------------	63
25. May one wash hands for bread with a Band-Aid/bandage?	63
--------------Birchas Hanehnin-General-----------------	65
26. What is one to do if he began chewing on a food, or drinking a liquid, and then remembered that he did not say a blessing?	65
27. Saying a blessing or Davening with food, or other item, in one's mouth:	67
--------------Bracha Rishona-----------------	68
28. Which blessing should one precede-Hadama or Haeitz?	68
29. The blessing on Matzah:	69
30. The blessing over onions:	70
--------------Bracha Achrona-----------------	71
31. Sitting during the recital of an after blessing:	71
-----------------Birchas Hamazon-----------------	72
32. Kavana in Birchas Hamazon-Understanding the words of Birchas Hamazon & The preferred language it is be said in:	72
33. Are women to perform Mayim Achronim?	74
34. Covering the knife during Benching:	75
35. How many people must eat together to be able to make a Zimun of ten with Elokeinu?	76
----------------Miscellaneous blessings-----------------	77
36. Which blessing is said first over a new fruit-Shehechiyanu or the blessing over the fruit?	77
37. Rainbow: Saying a blessing upon seeing a rainbow:	77
38. The blessing over an earthquake:	80

Bedtime

39. Making an interval [i.e. eating; drinking; talking] after saying Kerias Shema Sheal Hamita/Hamapil: 82

Shabbos-General

40. May one invite a non-religious guest for Shabbos if he will desecrate Shabbos in order to come to you? 85

Shabbos-Melacha

41. Making and filtering Turkish/ground coffee on Shabbos: 85
- A. The cooking prohibition-Mixing it with hot water: 86
- B. The dyeing prohibition: 87
- C. Filtering the coffee liquid from the ground powder: 88

42. How to remove dirt [i.e. dust, hair lash, insect] from your food on Shabbos: 90

43. Cutting items on Shabbos, such as a tablecloth, garbage bag, paper towel, piece of tinfoil, and toilet paper? 92

44. May one open or close a folding table or folding chair on Shabbos? 94
- A. Introduction: 94
- B. The law: 94

Shabbos-Muktzah

45. Are flowers in a vase Muktzah on Shabbos? 95
- A. Background: 95
- B. The law: 95

46. Are pets [dogs, cats, birds, fish] Muktzah on Shabbos? 96

Hadlakas Neiros

47. Extinguishing the match after lighting candles, before saying the blessing: 97

48. Davening Mincha after candle lighting on Erev Shabbos: 99

49. May one eat or drink after candle lighting? 99

Kiddush

50. Must one cover Mezonos foods that are on the table during Kiddush? 100
- A. Background: 100
- B. The ruling: 101

Havdalah

51. May one drink water before Havdalah? 102

52. Saying a blessing of Besamim upon smelling a tea bag: 103

Rosh Chodesh

53. *Sof Zman Kiddush Levana-Until what day of the month may Kiddush Levana be said?* 105

Pesach

54. Must one check books/Sefarim for crumbs of Chametz? 108
- A. Background: 108
- B. The Law: 109

Table of Contents

------------------Sefiras Haomer------------------ ... 111
55. Why we celebrate Lag BaOmer/Did Rashbi pass away on Lag BaOmer? ... 111

------------------Shavuos------------------ ... 115
56. Eating dairy on Shavuos & the reason we wait six hours after meat but not after milk ... 115

------------------Yom Tov------------------ ... 116
57. May one remove food from the freezer on the first day of Yom Tov on behalf of the second night meal? ... 116
A. The general law: ... 116
B. May one remove food from the freezer on the first day of Yom Tov on behalf of the second night meal? ... 117
C. May one place drinks in the fridge or freezer on the first day of Yom Tov on behalf of the second day? ... 118

------------------Chol Hamoed------------------ ... 118
58. May children, or adults, draw pictures and make paintings on Chol Hamoed? ... 118
A. Background: ... 118
B. The law: ... 119
59. May one go fishing on Chol Hamoed? ... 119

------------------Bein Hametzarim------------------ ... 120
60. Music therapy-May one listen to music during the three weeks for emotional and mental health purposes? ... 120
61. May one continue wearing Shabbos clothing on Motzei Shabbos which is Tisha Beav? Are they to be switched after nightfall before Maariv? ... 120

------------------Fast Day------------------ ... 121
62. When does the fast begin-Which Also is one to follow? ... 121
63. The secret fast day of the 9th of Teves and its uncovering of the origin of Christianity: ... 122

------------------Rosh Hashanah------------------ ... 123
64. From what age may a boy/Bochur blow Shofar for others on Rosh Hashanah? ... 123
A. Background: ... 123
B. The law: ... 124
65. May one eat garlic on Rosh Hashanah? ... 125

------------------Yom Kippur------------------ ... 126
66. May one use Maaser money for Kaparos on Erev Yom Kippur? ... 126
67. May one take medicine on Yom Kippur? ... 126

------------------Sukkos------------------ ... 127
68. Entering pots into a Sukkah: ... 127
69. Aravos-The Kashrus status of an Arava with missing leaves: ... 128

------------------Chanukah------------------ ... 129
70. May one make/use a Menorah of seven branches? ... 129

----------------Purim---------------- 130
71. Must the two foods of Mishloach Manos be of two different blessing? 130
72. May a woman write a Megillah? 130
73. May a woman read the Megillah on Purim on behalf of herself or others? 131
A. Reading on behalf of men: 131
B. Reading on behalf of other women or on behalf of oneself: 132

YOREH DEAH 135

----------------Kashrus-General---------------- 137
1. May one enter a non-Kosher restaurant? 137
2. Does fish oil require a Hashgacha: 137
3. The Arlah fruits of a gentile and matters to beware when purchasing fruits even in the Diaspora: 138

----------------Kashrus-Blood---------------- 139
4. The law of blood found in an egg: 139
A. Fertilized egg [Mufaros]: 139
B. Unfertilized egg [Muzaros]: 140
C. Status of eggs today: 140
5. May a child check eggs for blood? 141

----------------Basar Bechalav---------------- 141
6. If one is in doubt as to whether a certain vessel is dairy, meat, or Pareve, what is the law? 141
7. Am I Fleishig-If one tasted a meat food must he wait 6 hours prior to eating dairy? 142
8. Onion problems-The law if a Davar Charif was used with meat and milk utensils: 143
A. If one cut an onion [or any other Charif] with a meat knife and then cut the same onion with a dairy knife, what is the status of the onion and dairy knife? 143
B. What is the law if one cut onions with a dairy knife and fried them in a meat pot? 144
C. What is the law if one cut onions with a dairy knife and cooked them in a meat pot together with water or other foods? 145

----------------Machalei Akum---------------- 147
9. The bread and cooked food of a non-religious Jew? 147
10. May one drink Kosher coffee brewed by a gentile? Is coffee considered Bishul Akum? 147
11. Bishul Yisrael by candies and cereals: 148
A. The general law: 148
B. Must non-Mezonos cereals, such as cornflakes, be Bishul Yisrael and what is the status of Kellogg's? 149
C. Must Twizzlers and other candies be Bishul Yisrael? 150

----------------Machalei Sakana---------------- 151
12. May one cook fish in a clean meat pot? 151
13. Peeled eggs, onions and garlic left overnight: 152

----------------Tevilas Keilim---------------- 155
14. May a child be trusted to immerse a vessel? 155
15. May one use a new vessel one time without immersion? 157

Table of Contents

-----------Kashrus-Kashering------------	158
16. Koshering a Microwave & May the same microwave be used for meat, milk and Pesach:	158
------------- Sakana & Superstitions-------------	159
17. Not to blow out candles with one's mouth:	159
18. The mystical danger of stepping on eggshells:	159
19. May one sleep with his feet or head towards the door of the room?	160
------------- Avoda Zara-------------	160
20. Is Christianity considered Avoda Zara?	160
21. May one greet a gentile on the day of his holiday?	161
------------- Haircuts & Shaving-------------	162
22. Men shaving armpit and pubic hair:	162
23. Men trimming/shaving their legs, arms, chest:	164
------------- Chukos Hagoyim-------------	165
24. Wearing red colored clothing:	165
------------- Niddah-------------	167
25. Bedikos-The amount of Bedikos needed to be done during Shiva Nekiyim and the law if one missed a Bedika?	167
A. Lechatchila- The amount of Bedikos that are initially required to be done	167
B. Bedieved-The law if a Bedika was not done on a certain day:	168
26. If she did not check herself on the 7th day, how is the Shiva Nekiyim calculated?	171
Case A: Five days passed without a Bedika-Checked herself exactly seven days prior [i.e. 2nd & 8th day]:	171
Case B: Six days passed without a Bedika [i.e. she checked herself only on the 1st day and 8th day]:	172
Case C: Did not check herself seven days prior, but checked herself prior to seven days [i.e. on 1st day] and within seven days, and on 8th day:	172
------------- Hataras Nedarim-------------	173
27. Women performing Hataras Nedarim:	173
A. Severity of vows and its definition:	173
B. Women performing Hataras Nedarim on Erev Rosh Hashanah:	173
C. How to do Hataras Nedarim throughout the year-Men & Women:	174
------------- Talmud Torah-------------	176
28. Learning Chumash and Tanach and being an expert in its content:	176
------------- Tzedakah-------------	179
29. Giving Maaser money to relatives?	179
30. Must one take Maaser off the value of a present that he was given or inherited?	179
31. May one use Maaser money to purchase a seat in a Shul, or to pay for membership?	180
32. May one pay for an Aliyah, or other Kibud, using Maaser money:	182
------------- Sefarim/Genizah-------------	182
33. Writing בס"ד or ב"ה on a letterhead:	182
A. The Custom:	182
B. The Halachic debate and practical directive:	183

----------------- Mezuzah ----------------- 185
34. May a woman put up a Mezuzah or is only a man to do so? 185
A. Introduction: 185
B. The law: 185

----------------- Medical ethics ----------------- 186
35. The Lubavitcher Rebbe's opinion on vaccinations: 186

----------------- Cemeteries ----------------- 193
36. Pregnant wife of Kohen and other pregnant women visiting cemeteries: 193
37. Burying in a Shomer Shabbos burial section: 193
38. May a body be buried in an over ground structure [i.e. Mausoleums; Kevurat "Komot"; Rama, Sanhedrin cave burials]? 194

----------------- Mourning ----------------- 196
39. Until when is Kaddish recited? 196

EVEN HAEZER 199

----------------- Marriage ----------------- 201
1. Marrying a Kohenes: 201
2. Parents of Chasan and Kallah share the same names: 202

----------------- Castration ----------------- 203
3. Is a gentile prohibited from castrating a human/animal as part of the Noahide laws? 203

----------------- Shemiras Eiynayim ----------------- 203
4. Are women commanded in the laws of Shemiras Eiynayim? 203
5. May one walk in areas in which there are women who are not modestly dressed? 204

----------------- Tznius-Arayos ----------------- 205
6. Woman visiting a male doctor/Gynecologist: 205
7. Talking and flirting with the opposite gender: 205
The Law: 206
8. Educating one's children against predators, pedophiles, and molesters: 207
A. May a man have Yichud with another man? 208
B. Matters to beware and educate children in: 208

----------------- Covering hair ----------------- 211
9. Must a divorcee, or widow cover her hair? 211

----------------- Tznius-Clothing ----------------- 211
Wearing red colored clothing: 211

----------------- Yichud ----------------- 212
10. May a man and a group of women be alone together? 212
A. Stringent approach-Sephardim: 212
B. Lenient approach-Ashkenazim: 212

11. Yichud between a brother and sister:	214
12. Yichud with a woman and her mother/daughter in-law:	215
------------------Wedding-----------------	216
13. Must a Kallah cover her hair during the Chuppah/wedding:	216
14. How many people amongst the Minyan must eat bread in order to be able to recite Sheva Brachos?	218
------------------Kesuba----------------	220
15. Using a Kesuba of a Besula for a Beula:	220
------------------Divorce-----------------	222
16. Child support-Until what age is one Halachically obligated to support his children?	222
17. Must one divorce his wife if he has been married for 10 years without children?	224

CHOSHEN MISHPAT — 227

------------------Beis Din-----------------	229
1. Must a guilty defendant pay for court expenses and litigation fees according to Halacha?	229
------------------Loans-----------------	230
2. Lending money to a person who has no means of paying back:	230
3. Repossession-Collecting possessions of a debtor in order to collect a debt:	230
------------------Neighbors/Bein Adam Lechaveiro-----------------	231
4. The prohibition to create and continue a Machlokes/dispute:	231
How many times must one attempt to end a dispute?	232
5. The law if a neighbor's tree is encroaching onto one's property:	233
6. The confidentiality of a conversation:	234
7. Reading another person's mail or emails:	235
8. Jewish manners-Acknowledging the greetings of another:	236
------------------Business-----------------	237
9. Hasagas Gevul in Torah education and occupations-Can an infringement claim be brought against a new Torah class, new Yeshiva, new Rabbi in town, and new Chabad house?	237
10. Is a signed document legally binding if one was unaware of its content?	239
11. Tips and Gratuity fees-Is one Halachically obligated to give a tip for a service he received, [i.e. waiter, cab driver, bartender, mover, etc.]?	240
A. Legal background:	240
B. The Halacha:	241
------------------Hashavas Aveida-----------------	242
12. Returning lost money that one found:	242
------------------Renters-----------------	243
13. Paying rent on time:	243

------------------Borrowing------------------	**244**
14. Using or taking someone's item without permission:	**244**
15. Using someone's Sefarim without permission:	**246**
16. Borrowing a Shul's Sefer:	**247**
------------------Stealing------------------	**248**
17. Paying owed bus fares in Israel:	**248**
------------------Bal Tashchis------------------	**248**
18. The laws of Bal Tashchis:	**248**
A. The prohibition:	248
B. The exceptions:	248
------------Niszkei Haguf Vihanefesh------------	**250**
19. Destroying a tree:	**250**
A. Destroying a fruit bearing tree:	250
B. Destroying a tree that cannot bear fruit:	251

MISCELLANEOUS — **255**

1. How to say Hashem's name when in reference to false gods, such as in the words "Elokim Acheirim:"	**257**
2. May one visit the Temple Mount?	**257**
3. Living or visiting Egypt?	**260**
4. Teaching your children to swim:	**261**
------------Bas Mitzvah------------	**262**
5. Bas Mitzvah-Making a celebratory meal and party:	**262**
6. Customs associated with the day of the Bas Mitzvah:	**264**
A. Tzedakah:	264
B. Davening with extra intent:	264
C. Tehillim:	264
D. Learning Torah:	265
E. Choosing a Mitzvah:	265
F. Presents:	265
G. Shehechiyanu:	265
H. Baruch Shepatrani:	265
I. Doing an act of Ahavas Yisrael:	265

Orach Chaim

------------------Morning Conduct----------------

See our corresponding Sefer "Awaking like a Jew" for the full digest on all Halachos related to this section!

1. May one learn Torah or recite blessings in face of the morning washing water?

According to the Zohar, it is forbidden to learn Torah prior to washing hands in the morning upon awakening, due to the impure spirit that resides on the hand.[1] Now, this water used to wash hands upon awakening, although it removes the impurity from one's hands, it itself now contracts this impurity and becomes impure.[2] Accordingly, many Poskim[3] rule it is forbidden to learn Torah or say blessings in presence of this water, just as it was forbidden to study Torah or say blessings while the impurity was on one's hands. However, some Poskim[4] argue and rule that it is permitted to learn Torah and pray in the presence of the impure water, and the above learning and prayer prohibition only applies if the impurity was not washed off one's hands. Practically, one who is lenient to learn Torah and pray in the presence of the impure water has upon whom to rely[5], although many are accustomed to being stringent.[6]

Avoiding the controversy: There are a number of methods of how one can avoid the controversy, and allow learning Torah and praying even in the presence of the water: 1) If one covers the water, he may learn Torah and pray in its presence even according to the stringent opinion.[7] 2) Likewise, if one spills a Revius of clean water into the impure water, one may learn Torah in its presence.[8] [Thus, one can simply make sure to leave a Revius of water in the washing cup after washing, and then spill it into the water. In the event that one is unable to remove the water, or cover it, or pour water into it, or go to a different room, then heaven forbid for him to abstain from learning Torah due to this.[9]]

---

[1] Admur Basra 1:7; Siddur Hilchos Netilas Shacharis [However, in Kama 1:7, Admur does not mention the learning prohibition as one of the differences between the Talmud and Zohar; See also Kama 4:3]; Mahram di Lunzano in Derech Chaim; Or Hachama [Avraham Azulai]; Birkeiy Yosef 4:8; Zechor Leavraham 4:50; Yifei Laleiv 47:9; Nemukei Orach Chaim 4:1; Kaf Hachaim 4:107; M"B 4:61; Rama 47:13 in his Lechatchila opinion; Sefer Haminhagim p. 4 [English]

Ruling of Talmud and Codifiers: According to the Talmud and Codifiers if one slept in his clothing, he may speak words of Torah prior to washing. [Basra 1:7 and Siddur Hilchos Netilas Shacharis; See Kama 4:3; Michaber 4:23; The Graz of Vilna [brother of Rav Chaim Volozhin] followed this opinion and would hence sleep with gloves in order to be able to learn Torah as soon as he awakens, before washing hands, and so writes Yosef Ometz 198]

[2] See Admur Kama 4:9 [based on Zohar brought in Kaf Hachaim 31-32] *"The water that was used for the morning washing is forbidden to be used for any purpose, as **this water is forbidden in benefit due to the impurity that resides on it**. Therefore, one may not leave the water lying in his house and he may not spill the water on the ground, or any other place where people pass by, as perhaps a person will touch the water and get injured."*; See Kaf Hachaim 4:29 in name of Zohar, that is therefore forbidden to give this water to anyone who asks for it, as certainly they intend on using it for sorcery.

[3] Birkeiy Yosef 4:4, brought in Shaareiy Teshuvah 4:8; Moreh Baetzba 2:57; Kesher Gudal 1:5; Shalmei Tzibur 4:74; Zechor Leavraham 4:50; Mishmeres Shalom 1:6; Ben Ish Chaiy Toldos 9; Ketzos Hashulchan 2:5 [in name of Kesher Gadol]; Kaf Hachaim 4:33; Halichos Shlomo 20:7

Opinion of Chida: The Chida writes in Birkeiy Yosef ibid *"It is the custom of G-d fearing Jews to avoid doing so and so was the custom of the great leader Rav Chaim Abulafia"*. In this source, he does not write that it is forbidden to do so, and that simply is the custom of G-d fearing Jews. However, the Kaf Hachaim and Ketzos Hashulchan ibid record in the name of the Chida from his work called Kesher Gudal that it is indeed forbidden. On the other hand, see the next footnote that some Poskim received a tradition that the Chida retracted his earlier ruling and later ruled that it is completely permitted to Daven and learn Torah in the water's presence.

[4] Siach Yitzchak 2 in name of Chasam Sofer; Piskeiy Teshuvah 2; Toras Yekusiel 2 in name of Divrei Chaim that the Chida and Shaareiy Teshuvah retracted their ruling and hence the entire source of the prohibition has fallen, and so concludes the Toras Yekusiel that he received that in Tzans they were not careful in this at all; Beir Moshe 8:39

[5] Beir Moshe 8:39

[6] See Toras Yekusiel 2

[7] Moreh Baetzba ibid

Placing the basin under the bed: Regarding if it suffices to place the basin of washing water under the bed, if the bed frame on which the mattress rests, or the side ledge, reaches within three Tefach [24 cm] from the ground, seemingly it is considered that the water is covered, and it would be permitted for one to learn Torah according to all. If, however, the ledge and bed frame which supports the mattress is higher than three Tefachim from the ground, then it is considered uncovered. [See Admur 87:4 for a similar ruling regarding feces and urine under a bed; M"A 87:4]

[8] Ruach Chaim 77 brought in Kaf Hachaim 4:33; Toras Yekusiel 2; Beir Moshe 8:39 mentions nullifying in majority; See Admur 77:1 and Brachos 25b for a similar ruling regarding nullifying urine with a Revius of water

If two people washed: If two people washed hands, then one requires two Revius of water to nullify it. [Kaf Hachaim ibid]

Other Opinions: Some Rabbanim rule that even adding water does not help to nullify it. [Toras Yekusiel ibid in name of some Rabbanim]

[9] See Admur 1:7 that even in a case that one did not wash hands due to there being no water available, he is to learn Torah as rules the Talmud and Poskim. Hence, certainly in this case in which there is a dispute in the root of this stringency, one is not to abstain from Torah learning due to the water.

2. Wearing the shirt tucked into one's pants versus sticking out:
A. Introduction-Not to be dressed sloppy:[10]

A Jew is to dress and look decent in order, so he does not appear degrading in the eyes of others. This especially applies to a Torah scholar, or individuals who are viewed as representatives of Torah observance.[11] [The Rebbe once instructed his Shluchim to Eretz Yisrael that they are to place due effort in the look of their dress, so they look respectable as fitting for their mission.[12] The Rebbe Rashab once instructed the students of Tomchei Temimim to not wear their Tzitzis on top of their clothing, but rather under it, as it looked very sloppy in his eyes.[13] With that said, Chassidim would naturally not place **overdue** attention to their appearance and look, due to the philosophy of ignoring the external/Chitzoniyus and focusing on true service of G-d.[14] Nonetheless, a basic descent dress code must be kept, as stated above.]

B. The law:[15]

Wearing a **dress shirt** out of one's **dress pants** is viewed by many in society as a sloppy way of dress and is hence not to be done, especially by those who appear as representatives of Torah.[16] Despite the above, some are particular to wear their shirt out of their pants under one claim or another.[17] Practically, these claims do not have any real basis, and certainly not of the caliber to negate the above said law, which requires a Jew who represents Torah to be dressed appropriately.[18] Thus, one is to wear his shirt tucked in

---

[10] See Kama 2:2 and Basra 2:3 and Michaber 2:3 [regarding wearing a shirt inside out]; 53:32 [regarding the clothing of a Chazan]; Shabbos 114b *"Any Torah scholar who wears a stained garment is liable for death as the verse states Kol Misaneiy Ahavu Maves"* [see there also regarding wearing shirt inside out]; Kitzur Shulchan Aruch 3; Ketzos Hashulchan 3:3

[11] The reason: As otherwise he will be included within "All my haters love death" [Mishlei 8:36], as people [who see him dressed sloppy] will say "How degrading Torah learners are". [Kama ibid; Basra ibid; Perisha 2:3; Shabbos ibid; See also Admur 53:32] It is thus to be done in order not to be included within "My haters" Chas Veshalom. [Basra ibid]

[12] Sicha said on Night of Gimel Tammuz 1956 to the Shluchim to Eretz Yisrael

[13] The following was related by Rav Eliyahu Landa Shlita, Rosh Hayeshiva of Tomchei Temimim Kfar Chabad [Free translation]: *"The following story occurred in the city of Lubavitch. The Bochurim in Tomchei Temimim would wear their Tzitzis on top of their shirts [similar to the custom today of other Chassidic groups]. One day, the Rebbe Rashab told his son the Rebbe Rayatz, who was the official director of the Yeshiva, that upon looking out the window he saw the Bochurim Shleping their Tzitzis which was flying in all directions, and he does not like this at all. The Rebbe Rashab then said that the Bochurim should do one of the two; either to wear a long coat to cover the Tzitzis, or to tuck the Tallis Katan under their shirt. The Bochurim understood that the Rebbe Rashab preferred the first option and hence from that day and onwards the Bochurim in Lubavitch wore long coats."*

[14] Many Chassidic stories are recorded on this matter, such as: 1) Rav Shmuel Munkus dirtying the couch of Rav Pinchas Reitzis, and then belittling him for making an issue of it; 2) The Rebbe Rayatz related that in Petersburg there lived a wealthy man by the name of Shmuel Michel Treinin. He did business with the aristocrats and was very put together by nature. He was particular that his clothing be buttoned, each button in its proper place. One time, R' Michoel Bliner, otherwise known as Michoel Der Alter, went to him on behalf of freeing a Bachur from the army. Treinin needed to go with him to one of the nobles who could have influence over the issue. Upon going there, they had to walk down the main street of Petersburg-Leningrad. R' Michoel would walk in Petersburg the same way he walked in Lubavitch, and his buttons were not fastened properly. Treinin said to him carefully [since he was afraid that R' Michoel would chastise him]: Since we are walking on the main street, which was called Nevsky Prospekt, perhaps you should fasten your buttons. R' Michoel gave him a look and said: Gevald R' Shmuel Michel, what are you immersed in? [Rebbe in Sicha of 13 Tammuz 5715, printed in Toras Menachem 14 p.193; The Rebbe in that Sicha points out how a certain Bochur who was walking around in an unorganized manner, with his Tzitzis and Peiyos flying around, managed nevertheless to make a good impression on another Jew, and thus retold the above story emphasizing the negation of being overly immersed in ones looks.]

[15] Heard from Rav Eli Landa Shlita, Rosh Hayeshiva of Tomchei Temimim Kfar Chabad, and son of the famous Gaon and Chassid Rav Yaakov Landau Zatzal; Rav Leibal Groner replied to the author that he did not hear anything either way from the Rebbe on the above said subject; The students of the famed Mashpia, Rav Zev Greenglass of Montreal, tell over that he would constantly tell the Bochurim to tuck in their shirts

[16] See here http://www.executivestyle.com.au/should-you-tuck-or-untuck-your-shirt-ghtt6; http://blog.fashionmetric.com/tucked-or-out

[17] Some do so under the [false] claim that so is the Chabad custom. Others to do so under the claim that the Rebbe was once witnessed in his private study to wear his shirt out of his pants. Others do so under the claim that it helps them with their Tzitzis so it does not fold, and so the Tzitzis hits the corner. See next for the negation of these claims.

[18] Negating the first claim that so is the Chabad custom: This is only a recent development in Lubavitch and was not the original custom in Tomchei Temimim. Rav Eliyahu Landa Shlita relates that in his days in Tomchei Temimim [the 50's and 60's], under the Mashpia Rav Shlomo Chaim Kesselman, the Bochurim all wore their shirt tucked in and the prevalent custom of today was not to be seen.
Negating the second claim that so did the Rebbe: The Rebbe was never seen in public with his shirt sticking out, as he always wore a closed Kapata covering it. Thus, even if true that the Rebbe was once witnessed with his shirt sticking out, it was in his **private** study when his Kapata was off. Obviously, this cannot serve as any precedent for Bochurim today to wear the shirts out **in public**.
Negating the third claim that doing so assists with proper Tzitzis wearing: It is simply incorrect to state that the Tallis Katan is more securely spread opened by not tucking it in, as the Tallis Katan are more guarded from folding if they are tucked in. Likewise, the "Gumi" elastic is worn by many for this purpose. Rav Eli Landa and Rav Leibal Groner likewise negated this latter point. Another claim that is negated is that when the Tallis Katan is worn tucked in, it is possible that the strings will not touch the corners, and thus we wear the Tzitzis sticking out. In truth, the requirement for the Tzitzis to touch the corners is not a requirement on the strings but on the knots, and this is automatically fulfilled by wearing a Chabad Tallis Katan which has the first knot begin with the two adjacent corner holes, and there is no further need for any more touching to

his pants and not look sloppy. Furthermore, wearing one's shirt tucked in has the advantage of keeping one's Tzitzis in place and prevents it from folding.

The custom in Lubavitch:[19] The original custom in Tomchei Temimim of Lubavitch was to wear the Tzitzis on top of the clothing. However, after the Rebbe Rashab negated this practice [see above], the custom became to wear a long jacket, which would thus cover the Tzitzis. Later the custom became to wear short jackets and tuck the shirts inside the pants.[20] It is only in more recent years that some Bochurim became accustomed to wearing the shirt out. As stated above, this should not be done and Bochurim are to look representable and tuck their shirts into their pants.

3. Does placing a hand on one's head suffice in place of a Yarmulke?
A. Introduction:
In today's times[21], it is forbidden for men to sit, walk[22], or say a blessing[23] without a head covering. This is due to several reasons, including for purposes of modesty and in order not to appear like a gentile.[24] The following will discuss whether placing a hand on one's head is considered a valid head covering in a situation that another covering is not available:

B. The Law:[25]
One's own hand: Placing one's hand on one's head suffices in place of a Yarmulke with regards to being able to sit and walk.[26] [Thus, if one does not have a Yarmulke, or other head covering, he is to cover his

---

take place, aside for the fact that it usually automatically takes place even when tucked in. [See Admur 11:34 and Siddur Admur; Also elaborated in our corresponding Sefer "The Laws of Tzitzis" and website article https://shulchanaruchharav.com/halacha/positions-of-tying-the-tzitzis/]

[19] Related by Rav Eli Landa Shlita

[20] So was the custom in Tomchei Temimim in Eretz Yisrael at the time of Rav Landau's attendance.

[21] In previous times, it was only obligatory to wear a Yarmulke upon reciting Hashem's name or, according to some opinions, when inside a Shul. It was a mere act of piety to wear a Yarmulke during other times. [Admur Basra 2:6; Kama 46:2; 91:3; M"A 2:6] However, today it is an obligation to wear a Yarmulke at all times. [Basra 2:6; Taz 8:3; M"B 2:11]

[22] See Admur Basra 2:6; Kama 27; 46:2; 91:3; Measef Lechol Hamachanos 2:21; Yabia Omer 9:1; Piskeiy Teshuvos 2:9; See Piskeiy Dinim Tzemach Tzedek 1-8 For a thorough analysis on the obligation

The following Poskim rule wearing a head covering is required from the letter of the law at all times: Admur Basra 2:6 [unlike his ruling in Kama below]; Taz 8:3 [always; however see Taz Yoreh Deah 242:11 that implies only when walking four Amos is it required]; M"B 2:11 [always]; Mateh Yehuda 2:10; Nivei Shalom 2:4; Yad Ahron;

The following Poskim rule wearing a head covering is required from the letter of the law if one plans to walk four Amos: Implication of Admur Kama 2:7 [unlike his other sources above and below]; Implication of Michaber 2:6 and Beis Yosef 46 [as learns Piskeiy Dinim ibid; M"A 2:6 and M"B 2:11; Unlike understanding of Machatzis Hashekel 2:6 in Michaber ibid] Kitzur SH"A 3:6

The following Poskim rule wearing a head covering is always a mere act of piety: Admur Kama 91:3 and implication of 46:2 [unlike his final ruling in Kama and Basra ibid]; Admur Basra 2:6 regarding previous times; Bach; Olas Tamid 2:5; Machatzis Hashekel ibid; Mamar Mordechai 91:5; Birkeiy Yosef 2:2. The Kaf Hachaim 2:15 concludes like the Zohar that for layman walking with a head covering is an act of piety.

Other opinions: Some Poskim rule that it is not necessary from the letter of the law to cover one's head when he is under a roof. [Rashal Teshuva 72, brought in Beir Heiytiv 2:6] Others write that walking four Amos with a head covering is a requirement only for Torah Scholars. [Kaf Hachaim 2:15 in name of Zohar]

[23] Admur Basra 2:6; 91:3; 206:7; Michaber 91:3 in name of Yeish Omrim; Beis Yosef 91 that so is the Halacha; Rabbeinu Yerucham 16:7; Misechos Sofrim 14:15 in name of Yeish Omrim; Levush 91:3

[24] The reason: In earlier times it was very common for the majority of people to at times walk around bare headed due to the heat. Hence, it was [only] an attribute of piety to not walk four cubits [6 feet 4 inches] without one's head covering, [and was not required by law.] Today, however, that it is common for everyone to cover their head, it is always forbidden to walk or even sit with one's head uncovered as by doing so one reveals an area of the body which is commonly covered, and this is immodest. Furthermore, in today's times that the gentiles walk bareheaded while the Jews which are holy cover their head due to modesty, certainly it is an obligation for one to cover his head, and one who walks or even sits without a head covering transgresses the command of "In their statutes do not follow". [Basra 2:6]

[25] See Admur 91:4; Basra 2:6; So rules: Machatzis Hashekel 91:4; Ketzos Hashulchan 3:6; M"B 2:11-12; Kaf Hachaim 2:20 based Misgeres Hazahav; 91:20

Background: There are two reasons for requiring a skullcap; one is for modesty, while the second is [an act of holiness that is necessary] in order to utter G-d's name, when one comes to say a blessing, or pray. Regarding modesty, covering one's head with one's hand suffices. Thus, one may walk more than 4 cubits if he covers his head with his hand. However, when saying G-d's name, it does not suffice to use one's own hand as will be explained.

[26] Admur Basra 2:6 "*However, if he places his hand on his head to cover it, it suffices as a recognition, although he may not mention Hashem's name*"; Taz 8:3; Elya Raba 91:5; Machatzis Hashekel 91:4; M"B 2:11; Kaf Hachaim 91:20;

The reason: As the purpose of the Yarmulke is to cover the normally covered areas and as a sign of modesty, and Jewish identity. Thus, placing a hand on the head suffices as recognition for this matter, as the onlooker sees that he is changing from the ways of the gentiles by placing his hand on his head. [Basra ibid; Taz ibid; Machatzis Hashekel ibid]

Other opinions: Some Poskim rule that when one is outside, it does not suffice to place one's hand on one's head. [Peri Megadim 2 M"Z 5, brought in M"B ibid]

head with his hand and may then walk for even more than four cubits.] However, he may not say a blessing, or any of Hashem's names, if his head is covered merely by his own hand.[27] [However, one may place the sleeve of his arm over his head, and this suffices as a head covering even regarding the saying of blessings.[28]]

Another person's hand:[29] If another person places his hand on one's head, then one may be lenient to consider it a valid covering [for all matters, and one may thus even recite a blessing with G-d's name in such a situation[30]]. [Accordingly, if one would like to merit a non-religious Jew with saying a blessing over a food, or over a Mitzvah and the like, and a yarmulke is not available, one may simply place his hand over his head and have him say the blessing.]

4. Is one to stand while reciting the morning blessings [i.e. Birchas Hashachar]?

Letter of the law: From the letter of the law, one is only required to stand when saying blessings which involve commands [i.e. Birchas Hamitzvos], such as when saying the blessing over Tzitzis, and Tefillin.[31] However, blessings of praise do not require standing.[32] This especially applies to Birchas Hashachar which was initially instituted to be said in the process of awakening, and hence many of the blessings were said in a sitting or lying position.[33] [Thus, in the morning blessings, from the letter of the law one is only required to stand for the blessings of Al Netilas Yadayim[34] and Birchas Hatorah[35] being that they are

---

[27] Admur 74:3; 91:4; Basra 2:6; Michaber 91:4; Terumos Hadeshen 91:10; M"A 91:4; M"B ibid; Chayeh Adam 1:9; Chesed Lealafim 91:2; Ben Ish Chaiy Vayishlach 14; Ketzos Hashulchan ibid; Kaf Hachaim 2:20 and 91:20

The reason: As one's hand and body are one entity, and the body cannot be used to cover itself. [Admur 74:3 and 91:3; Kaf Hachaim 91:20]

Other opinions: Some Poskim rule that it is valid for one to cover one's head even with his own hand, even for the sake of saying blessings, as it is uncommon for one to do so, and is hence its use as a covering is readily apparent to the onlooker. [Rashal Teshuva 72 brought and negated in Admur 91:4 in parentheses and M"A 91:4; See Machatzis Hashekel ibid] Some Poskim permit to rely on this opinion in a time of need. [Elya Raba 91:4, brought in P"M 91 A"A 4; M"B 2:12; Shulchan Hatahor 2:1; 91:2] However, this position is negated in Kaf Hachaim 91:20 who rules that from the Poskim ibid it is evident that one may not be lenient even in a time of need. Vetzaruch Iyun according to Admur if he would allow one to be lenient in a case of need like the Rashal, just like he rules regarding another person's hand that even initially one may be lenient like the Rashal.

[28] Bach 91; Kneses Hagedola 91:3; Olas Tamid 91:2; M"B 2:12; Kaf Hachaim 91:20

[29] Admur 91:4; Michaber 91:4 that so is implied; Beis Yosef 91

[30] So is clearly implied from 91:3-4 and is also evident from Basra 2:6 which refers the reader to 91:3, when stating that one's own hand cannot be used as a covering to utter blessings;

The reason: (As the Rashal ibid is completely lenient) [91:4] This means to say as follows: The Rashal rules that one's own hand is a valid head covering even when reciting a blessing. Hence, in a time of need, one may be lenient to consider another person's hand a covering even regarding saying a blessing.

[31] Admur 8:3; M"A 8:2; Beis Yosef 8:1 in name Orchos Chaim Tzitzis 27 based on *Yerushalmi* "*That which it states in the Yerushalmi that all blessings are to be said standing, it refers to Birchas Hamitzvos*"; Haittur Zohar Tetzaveh brought in P"M 8 M"Z 1; P"M Pesicha to Hilchos Brachos 202:18 "*We hold that Birchas Hamitzvos must be said standing*" [however, see P"M 432 M"Z 3]; M"B 8:2 "*All blessings of Mitzvos need to be done standing*"

The reason: This is learned from Sefiras Haomer which is required to be said, and blessed on, in a standing position. [M"B ibid; See Kol Bo p. 16, brought in P"M 432 M"Z 3]

Cases of exception: The above rule is with exception for the blessings made over Shechitah and Challah, being that these two Mitzvos don't hold the same weight as other commands, as they are done merely for the sake of being able to eat the food. [Admur ibid; M"A 8:2] Vetzaruch Iyun according to this ruling why we are accustomed today to sit by various blessings of Mitzvos, such as "Al Achilas Matzah"; "Leishev Basukkah" and others. See P"M Pesicha to Hilchos Brachos 202:18 who explains that since these Mitzvos involve eating, they may be said in a sitting position; See Bach 8; Pnei Yehoshua Megillah 21a; Mor Uketzia 8; Piskeiy Teshuvos 8:4 who differentiate between **Mitzvos** that are performed standing versus sitting.

Other opinions: Some Poskim rule that the blessings of Mitzvos are not required to be said in a standing position, with exception to those Mitzvos that must be performed standing. [P"M 432 M"Z 3 "*Chazal instituted the blessing similar to the performance if it is done standing*"; Artzos Hachaim 8:1 states it is only a Mitzvah Min Hamuvchar to stand; Bach 8 only requires standing for Mitzvos that have no bodily benefit; See Pnei Yehoshua Megillah 21a; Mor Uketzia 8 that depends it if the Mitzvah is accustomed to be performed standing; Piskeiy Teshuvos 8:4]

[32] P"M Pesicha to Hilchos Brachos 202:18 "*Blessings of praise may be recited in a sitting position, except for Birchas Halevana*"; P"M 432 M"Z 3 "*Birchas Hanehnin may be said sitting, and it's possible that this applies likewise to blessings of praise*"; Implication of Rambam Brachos 10:17; Abudarham Dinei Birchas Hashachar p. 45; Birchas Habayis 1:78; Piskeiy Teshuvos 218:1; 227:5

[33] See P"M Pesicha to Hilchos Brachos 202:18; See Admur 46:2 for a list of blessings that were said prior to standing up from bed

[34] So is understood from Admur and Poskim in previous footnotes, as one is obligated to wash hands in the morning upon awakening. This is unlike the law regarding washing for **bread** in which its blessing may be said in a sitting position. [See Admur 8:3; Piskeiy Teshuvos 158:2; Seder Netilas Yadayim of Rav Elyashvili footnote 47 that so was custom of Rebbe]

[35] So is understood from Admur and Poskim in previous footnotes, as one has a constant obligation to learn Torah, and so is the custom of Jewry to stand; See Maarah Kohen 3:3; Yaskil Avdi 8:3 that this is similar to the standing of Bnei Yisrael on Har Sinai.

Other Opinions: Some Poskim rule that Birchas Hatorah may be said while sitting. [Aruch Hashulchan 47:7 and Rameh 102; Beir Moshe 5:17; See there for a lengthy discussion on this matter]

commands and not blessings of praise[36], however one is not required to stand for any of the other morning blessings, which are merely blessings of praise.] Nevertheless, some Poskim[37] argue and rule one is to stand even for blessings of praise.

Custom: Practically, the custom amongst Ashkenazi Jewry is to say all the morning blessings in a standing position.[38] However, Sephardic Jewry is accustomed to sit while reciting the blessings in order to increase concentration.[39] [In a time of need, such as one who is week or sick, or in midst of traveling, it is permitted for even those of Ashkenazi origin to sit while reciting the morning blessings, especially for the blessings of praise.[40]]

Summary:
One is only obligated to stand for the blessings of Al Netilas Yadayim and Birchas Hatorah. Nevertheless, the Ashkenazi custom is to stand for all the morning blessings, unless it is a time of need. However, the Sephardic custom is to sit while reciting the morning blessings.

Q&A
Are women and girls to stand for Birchas Hatorah?
Yes. Women and girls of Ashkenazi origin are to stand for the entire Birchas Hashachar, just as is done by men. This especially applies to the blessings of Birchas Hatorah and Al Netilas Yadayim, as explained above. There is much confusion in the girls learning institution regarding this matter, with different teachers instructing different areas of where they should stand.[41] Those who accustom the girls to sit for Birchas Hatorah and Al Netilas Yadayim, and stand for the remaining blessings are performing a confused custom, as stated above that specifically those blessings require standing. Practically, it is upon the teacher to educate the girls in her class to stand for all the morning blessings, as is the Ashkenazi custom.

5. Until when during the day may one recite Birchas Hashachar?

Initially, one is to recite Birchas Hashachar early in the morning, in close proximity to awakening.[42] If one did not do so, the blessings may be said throughout the entire day [up until sunset].[43] Furthermore, some Poskim[44] rule it may be said even at night, up until one goes to sleep. However, some Poskim[45] argue that it may not be said the entire day and conclude that it may only be said until the 4th hour of the

---

[36] Are women obligated to stand for the blessing of Al Netilas Yadayim and Birchas Hatorah? Yes, as they are obligated in these Mitzvos. [See Admur 47:10 regarding Birchas Hatorah; Chapter 4 regarding Netilas Yadayim that no differentiation is made in the Poskim between men and women; See also Bach 4 who explicitly negates any difference] However, perhaps since their obligation is not similar to men [as they are exempt from Talmud Torah, and according to some are exempt from Shacharis] therefore some are accustomed not to stand. Vetzaruch Iyun.

[37] Siddur Yaavetz *"I must teach you the following rule: All blessings of praise and thanks are to be said in a standing position"*; See Piskeiy Teshuvos 218:1

[38] This is done to suspect for the Yaavetz ibid who rules that all blessings of praise of Hashem are to be said standing. This is especially understood from the fact that the 18 blessings of Birchas Hashachar correspond to the 18 blessings of Shemoneh Esrei, as explained in Shaar Hakolel 1:6-11.

[39] Kaf Hachaim [Falagi] 9:7 *"One is not to recite Birchas Hashachar while getting dressed…rather he is to sit in his place in seclusion and concentration in order to say Birchas Hashachar"*; Yechaveh Daas 5:4

[40] See Admur 94:6 that one who is traveling on a ship [or plane or car/bus] and fears to stand up may say Shemoneh Esrei sitting, and certainly this applies to the morning blessings. Likewise, see Admur 94:7 that one who is weak or old or sick may Daven Shemoneh Esrei sitting, and certainly this applies to the morning blessings.

[41] So was discovered through a survey of girl students in various institutions and classes, that there were discrepancies amongst teachers and classes.

[42] See Admur 46:2-3; 71:1; Sefer Hasichos 1904 p. 20; Igros Kodesh 19:390; 18:277; Shulchan Menachem 1:6

[43] Setimas Kol Haposkim who mention no limit [Biur Halacha 53:1 "Kol Habrachos"]; Machatzis Hashekel 71:1; Ketzos Hashulchan 5:7 based on Admur 52:1 which does not differentiate in this matter; Mamar Mordechai, Nehar Shalom and Gr"a, brought in M"B 52:10; The M"B ibid concludes that one who relies on these opinions is not to be protested.
The reason: As the custom today is to recite the blessings based on the pleasures of the world [and not one's individual pleasures] and there is thus no reason to limit these blessings to the morning. [See Biur Halacha ibid]

[44] Gra in Maaseh Rav, brought in M"B ibid

[45] Derech HaChaim Onen 4 based on M"A 71:1, brought in M"B ibid and negated in Biur Halacha 53:1 "Kol Habrachos"

day [i.e. Sof Zman Tefila]. Other Poskim[46] conclude that it may at the very least be said until midday, and those who say it until sunset are not to be protested. Practically, one is initially to be careful to recite the blessings as early as possible[47], and in the morning, although if this time was missed the blessings may be said up until sunset.[48]

-----------------Tzitzis-----------------

*See our corresponding Sefer "The Laws of Tzitzis" for the full digest on all Tzitzis related Halachos!

6. Wearing a Tallis Gadol properly-Making sure the Tallis covers at least one square Ama of the body:

A. Introduction:

<u>Shiur Tallis-Practical size of a Tallis</u>:[49] The Tallis is to be a minimum size of 1 Ama by 1 Ama [49 x 49 centimeters[50]] on each the front and the back side of the Tallis. Thus, the Tallis is to be a total of two Amos [98 cm] long, and one Ama [49 cm] wide.

<u>The obligation for the Tallis to cover the body</u>:[51] The Tallis Gadol must be worn in a way that it covers one's actual body. Those who cover with their Tallis only their head and around their neck, and are not particular to cover their body, are to be protested.[52] [One who says a blessing on such a wearing is saying a blessing in vain.[53] Likewise, those who wear the Tallis in a way that it is folded and draped over ones shoulders, with the strings of the two right corners resting on ones right chest, and the two left corner strings resting on one's left chest, do not fulfill the Mitzvah and are to be protested.[54]]

B. The Law-How much of the body must the Tallis cover:[55]

The Tallis Katan and Gadol[56] must be worn in a way that the Shiur Tallis, which is the width of at least one Ama [49 cm] of material, and the total length of at least two Amos [98 cm], is spread open and covers

---

[46] Mishneh Berurah 52:10 that initially it should not be delayed past the 4th hour, although Bedieved it may be said until midday, as so is proven from many Achronim [Levushei Serud, Chochmas Adam, Shulchan Shlomo, brought in Biur Halacha ibid], and those who are lenient even past Chatzos are not to be protested

[47] M"B ibid; See Admur 71:1

[48] See Biur Halacha ibid who at first writes that one may/should be lenient even after midday, but then concludes that only one who is lenient after midday is not protested. Practically, from the Setimas Haposkim one may be lenient until sunset.

[49] Siddur Admur; Sefer Haminhagim p. 6 [English]; Artzos Hachaim 16 "so is the custom of Chassidim" in name of Siddur Admur; M"B 16:4 "Custom of Anshei Maaseh" in name of Artzos Hachaim regarding length [does not mention size of width]; Ashel Avraham Tinyana 16; Chazon Ish 3:3 [however according to his Ama it is to be 58 x 58 cm]; See Shiureiy Torah p. 264; Piskeiy Dinim 3:3; Tehila Ledavid 16:1

<u>Background</u>: The Gemara and Poskim ibid do not mention and actual size of measurement for the Tallis and rather suffice with a general description of it needing to cover the body of a child. Nevertheless, later Poskim measured this size and concluded to give it a set measurement.

<u>Other opinions</u>: **1)** Some Poskim rule it suffices for the Tallis to be one Ama by one Ama [in total] [Peri Haaretz 1 brought in Birkeiy Yosef 16:1 and Shaareiy Teshuvah 16; Chesed Lealafim 16:5; Many Poskim in Kaf Hachaim 16:2 agreed to this opinion; Shulchan Hatahor 16:1 states there is no need to be stringent that it be one Ama on each side] **2)** Other Poskim rule the width must be at least 1.5 Amos. [See Lev Chaim 99] **3)** Other Poskim rule it suffices for the Tallis Katan to be 3/4 of an Ama in length [36 cm] and half an Ama in width [24 cm]. [Peri Haaretz 1 in name of Derech Chochmah, brought in M"B 16:4 and Kaf Hachaim 16:2] Many however negate this opinion, stating it has no source from the Talmud. [Machatzis Hashekel 16; Artzos Hachaim 16; M"B ibid; Kaf Hachaim ibid concludes with this opinion] **4)** Some Poskim conclude that at the very least it must be a total of one Ama in width on both sides and 3/4 of an Ama in length on both sides. [M"B 16:4; Rav Chaim Felagi in Mesamchei Lev; Ben Ish Chaiy Lech Lecha 12; Rav Poalim 2:6; Chazon Ish 3:31] **5)** Some Poskim suggest that the Tallis Katan of today does not need to be any minimum size and is hence obligated in Tzitzis even if it does not meet the above sizes that are based on the Gemara. [See Aruch Hashulchan 16:5; Hisorerus Teshuvah 1:7; Igros Moshe Y.D. 3:52; Tzitz Eliezer 20:8; see also Eretz Tzevi 1:1; Halef Lecha Shlomo 1:4]

[50] Shiureiy Torah p. 249

<u>Other opinions</u>: Some Poskim rule that an Ama is 58 cm. [Chazon Ish]

[51] Admur 8:8; M"A 8:2; Beis Oved 27; Shalmei Tzibbur p. 32; Kaf Hachaim 8:9

[52] <u>The reason</u>: As according to all opinions, the main "wearing" of a Tallis is when one is wearing the Tallis over one's body. The argument brought in Admur 8:5 is only regarding if the Tallis must <u>also</u> be placed over one's head, however covering the head alone without covering the body, according to all does not suffice to be considered clothing at all. [Admur ibid; See 10:20 regarding a scarf, that for this reason it is exempt from Tzitzis.]

[53] See Shaareiy Teshuvah 8:3

[54] M"A 8:2; Masas Binyamin 48; Poskim in Kaf Hachaim 8:9; See Nehar Mitzrayim 1 which says that most Egyptian Jews would wear the Tallis this way and they are to be taught to wear it properly, at least for the time of the blessing.

[55] Siddur Admur [4 and 11 in Raskin] "*This entire measurement of the width and length of the Tallis Katan needs to be entirely spread open, and clothe the person throughout its entire measurement, as the verse states "Asher Tichaseh Bah". This teaches us that the above required measurement must cover the person and may not be folded or dented in any amount, being that the folded and bent area is not included in the measurement.*"

<u>Other opinions</u>: Some Poskim rule that the folded areas are included within the Shiur of the Tallis, being that the folded area is meant to be spread open, and hence it is not necessary to prevent the Tallis Katan from folding. [Beis Yaakov 106; Beir Heiytiv 16:1; Bnei Chayi 16; M"B 16:4; See also Michaber 10:6; Admur 10:13; Tehila Ledavid 16:2] The world is not accustomed like this opinion of Admur in his Siddur. [Piskeiy Teshuvos 16:3]

the person's body.[57] The folded areas of the Tallis is not included in the above size. [Thus, those who role the sides of the Tallis Gadol in a way that the Tallis does not cover 49 cm of the width of the back body, or 98 cm of the length of the body, are mistaken and do not fulfill the Mitzvah.[58] There is no justification to roll the sides of the Tallis in a way that it loses its Ama width even if one desires to cover the black stripes of the Tallis so they do not show. This is aside for the fact that in truth it is not necessary at all to hide the black stripes of the Tallis Gadol upon wearing it.[59]]

7. Making sure the Tallis Katan covers the entire chest area, from below the neckline:[60]

According to Halacha, there is no requirement for the Tallis Gadol or Katan to cover the chest area, below the neckline, so long as it covers the body in the measurements described above, in the previous Halacha. Nevertheless, based on Kabala[61], the Tallis Katan is to cover the entire chest area [up until the neck]. Hence if one has a V neck Tallis Katan [as is customary amongst many Polisher Chassidic groups] he is to sew, or button, the sides [so that the flaps do not uncover the neck]. [If one has a non-V neck Tallis Katan with a hole in the middle, as is the Chabad tradition, he must be careful that it does not slide down below the neckline of the chest. Due to this reason, the custom is not to make the neck hole very large, and it is rather made large enough to simply enter the head, in order to ensure that the entire chest remain covered.[62] Seemingly, due to this requirement to cover the entire chest, the Chabad custom is not to wear a V neck Tallis Katan but rather to make a small neck hole, as described above.]

8. May/should one have a separate pair of Tzitzis to wear at night while sleeping?

It is customary amongst Chassidim and the pious and the righteous to wear Tzitzis when sleeping at night, [See C]. In order to be allowed to say a blessing on the Tzitzis the next morning [for those who are not married and do not wear a Tallis Gadol] it is necessary to have two pairs of Tzitzis which are switched for the sake of the next day's blessing [See Halacha 9]. Some who do so are accustomed to have a separate pair of night Tzitzis designated for this purpose which they wear prior to going to sleep and remove each morning. In general, they do not wear this Tzitzis during the day. Others are accustomed to not have a designated night Tzitzis and simply sleep with the Tzitzis they wore during the day, and switch it the next morning. Others switch the Tzitzis at night and wear it until the next night, when it is switched with the second pair. The question is asked regarding which of the above is the correct custom, and may one have a pair of Tzitzis designated only for sleeping use. This subject enters the question of whether a night garment is obligated in Tzitzis [see A] and thus which of the above customs is correct [See B].

---

[56] This Halacha in Admur in the Siddur is stated regarding the Tallis Katan, although he repeats the same concept also regarding the Tallis Gadol in letter 12 [in Siddur Raskin] *"However one must beware that also during the Atifa the Tallis Gadol covers his front **the width of an Ama that is spread open**."*

[57] Must the Ama in width and length cover the body both in front and back? Admur ibid [Siddur 4] does not explicitly mention whether the Shiur Tallis must cover both the front and back, or if it suffices to have it all in the back. By a Tallis Katan, there is no other choice, and hence both the front and back must be covered one Ama in both length and width, as only then is one's body covered for two Amos. However, by a Tallis Gadol, perhaps it suffices to have two Amos cover from one's shoulders until the back. Perhaps it is due to this that when we wear the Tallis during Davening we are not particular that the front be covered by an Ama, and hence allow to fold the Tallis on the shoulders. However, in letter 12 [in Siddur Raskin] of the Siddur Admur states *"However one must beware that also during the Atifa the Tallis Gadol **covers his front** the width of an Ama that is spread open."* Likewise, in Siddur letter 11 [in Siddur Raskin] Admur writes that even according to Nigleh *"it is proper that the main Atifa not be only in the back **but also in the front until below the chest** in order so one be surrounded by Mitzvos"* Vetzaruch Iyun Gadol why we are not accustomed to cover an Ama in the front of the body, despite Admur explicitly requiring also the front to be covered an Ama, as explained from the Siddur

How much of the back should the Tallis cover? Some Poskim write that one is not to have the Tallis drag all the way down the back but is rather to cover until slightly below the waist [for at least one Ama]. The reason for this is because until the chest is the aspect of the Tallis while from there and onwards is the aspect of the Tzitzis. [Asara Mamaros; Shaareiy Teshuvah 21:5; Kaf Hachaim 21:18]

[58] Pashut; Heard from Rav Eliyahu Landa

[59] Rav Eliyahu Landa Shlita; Regarding why the Rebbe was seen to do so, Rav Eliyahu Landa explains that this was so the Tallis does not slip.

[60] Siddur Admur; Artzos Hachaim 16 in name of Admur; Kaf Hachaim 16:3

[61] Peri Eitz Chaim Shaar Hatzitzis 1-3; Nagid Mitzvah

[62] Kaf Hachaim 16:3; Piskeiy Teshuvos 16:3

A. Background: The obligation of Tzitzis during nighttime and to night garments:

The Mitzvah of Tzitzis does not apply at night, to night garments.[63] The definition of a "night garment" is disputed amongst the Poskim.

First opinion-Nighttime: Some Poskim[64] rule that the above exemption refers to the actual period of nighttime, and hence the law means to say that the Mitzvah of Tzitzis does not apply to any garment that one wears at night, even if it is a garment that is normally worn during the daytime.[65] [On the other hand, according to this opinion, when wearing a garment during the day, then one is obligated to attach Tzitzis to it and say a blessing upon wearing it, even if in general this garment is designated to be worn only at night.]

Second opinion-Night garment: Other Poskim[66], however, rule that the above exemption refers to a garment that is designated to be worn only at night, and hence the law means to say that a night garment is not obligated in Tzitzis even if on occasion one wears it during the day.[67] On the other hand, according to this opinion, when wearing a garment that is designated to be worn only during the day, or is designated to be worn by both night and day[68], then one is obligated to attach Tzitzis to it and say a blessing upon wearing it even if one wears it at night.[69]

Final ruling: Practically, due to lack of arbitration in the above mentioned dispute, one is to be stringent like both opinions.[70] Thus, one is to have Tzitzis on all garments that are designated to be worn during the day, or during the night and day, even if he is wearing them at night. Likewise, one is to tie Tzitzis onto all garments that are worn during the day, even if they are garments that are worn only during the night.[71] [However, a garment that is designated to be worn only at night, is exempt from Tzitzis according to all when worn at night. Hence, night-only garments may be worn at night without Tzitzis.[72]] The above stringency is only regarding the obligation to place Tzitzis on such garments, however regarding the blessing, one is not to say a blessing over Tzitzis unless he is wearing it during the day and it is also a garment that is designated to be worn during the day, or during the night and day.[73]

B. The Law:

Although it is proper for those who sleep with a Tallis Katan to have two pairs of a Tallis Katan in order to be able to switch the Tzitzis daily upon awakening and hence recite a new blessing [See Halacha 9], nevertheless one should not designate one of these pairs to be worn *only* at night.[74] This applies even

---

[63] Admur 18:1; brought also in 8:27; Michaber 18:1; Menachos 43a

The reason: As the verse states "Ureisem Oso/That you shall see it" thus coming to exclude night garments. [Admur ibid; Menachos ibid]

At night near light: Some Poskim write that a four-cornered garment is obligated in Tzitzis at night if it is in an area near a candle/light, and hence can be seen. [Pardes of Rashi Tzitzis 36; Hagahos Chasam Sofer 18; See Har Tzevi 1:12]

[64] First opinion in Admur and Michaber ibid; Rambam 3:8

[65] The reason: As in their opinion, the verse is excluding garments that cannot be seen while it is worn. [Admur ibid]

[66] 2nd opinion in Admur and Michaber ibid; Rosh Hilchos Ketanos Tzitzis 1 [p. 40]

[67] The reason: As initially the garment was made to be only worn at a time that it cannot be seen. [Admur ibid]

[68] Admur ibid; Levush; Olas Tamid 18:1 and 3; Tzemach Tzedek Piskei Dinim 18; Ben Ish Chaiy Lech Lecha 16; Kaf Hachaim 18:8

Other opinions: The Bach rules that if it is designated for day and night use, it has the same status as a night garment. The Poskim ibid negate this opinion.

[69] The reason: As these garments were made to be worn at a time when they are visible. [Admur ibid]

[70] Admur ibid and 19:2; Darkei Moshe; Olas Tamid 18:2; M"A 18:3 as explained in Machatzis Hashekel; Elya Raba 18:1; Ben Ish Chaiy Lech Lecha 16; Kaf Hachaim 18:9

Other opinions: In the Beis Yosef, the Michaber rules like the Rambam. Nonetheless, the Sephardi custom follows the ruling in Admur, as Safek Brachos Lihakel is said even against Maran. [Birkeiy Yosef 7:3; Kaf Hachaim 18:7]

[71] Why does the wearing of such Tzitzis not constitute Baal Tosif according to those that exempt it from Tzitzis? As whenever one fulfills a Mitzvah due to doubt it is not considered Baal Tosif. See Siddur Admur *"Doing so does not involve the prohibition of Baal Tosif being that there are opinions that state one is obligated to wear Tzitzis on a day garment even if it is worn at night."* See also Admur 31:2 regarding Chol Hamoed and 34:4 regarding Rabbeinu Tam Tefillin and why it does not transgress Baal Tosif

[72] Regarding if wearing such a garment at night together with Tzitzis constitutes Baal Tosif-see Q&A!

[73] Admur ibid and 19:2; Rama ibid

The reason: As Safek Brachos Lihakel, and hence one must suspect for both opinions. [ibid]

[74] Piskeiy Dinim Tzemach Tzedek 3:2; Ketzos Hashulchan 7 footnote 23; Ashel Avraham Butchach Tinyana 21; Rav Akiva Eiger 121:2; Toras Chaim Sofer 21:5; Darkei Chaim Veshalom 38; Implication of custom of Arizal brought in 21:15

The reason: As according to all opinions, a night Beged that is worn at night is exempt from Tzitzis and hence one is not fulfilling the Mitzvah according to any opinion. [Poskim ibid]

though one wakes up in the morning wearing the night pair, so long as he is not accustomed to continue to wear it throughout the day.[75] The reason for this is because one who has a night Tzitzis which he wears only at night is not fulfilling the Mitzvah of Tzitzis at night according to any opinion, as explained in A. Also, one who has a designated pair of night Tzitzis, according to some opinions would not be fulfilling the Mitzvah of Tzitzis even during the day, if he were to wear this garment during the day, as explained in A. He would thus not be allowed to say a blessing on such Tzitzis even when worn during daytime.

The options: There are several options available to avoid the problem of having only night Tzitzis: **1)** Never switch Tzitzis, and continue wearing the same pair by both night and day [although in such a case, he cannot say the blessing in the morning, as explained in D]; **2)** Switch a pair every morning and continue to wear it at night when one sleeps, until the next morning. **3)** Switch a pair every night and continue wearing it into the day. [However, it is better to follow the option of changing the pairs in the morning as opposed to at night in order to avoid entering oneself into a Safek Bracha.[76]] **4)** Have a designated night Tzitzis but making sure to designate it to also wear **during the day** on occasion. When one occasionally wears these Tzitzits also during the day, as he designated, then it is considered a night and day garment, which is obligated in Tzitzis. It is unclear however how often one must wear the Tzitzis during the day to consider it a day garment.

Summary:
One should not designate one of these pairs to be worn <u>only</u> at night. There are several options available to avoid the problem of having only night Tzitzis:
1. Never switch Tzitzis and continue wearing the same pair by both night and day.
2. Switch a pair every morning and continue to wear it at night when one sleeps.
3. Switch a pair every night and continue wearing it into the day.
4. Have a designated night Tzitzis but making sure to designate it to also wear during the day.

C. Epilogue-The Mitzvah to sleep with Tzitzis at night:
The scrupulous are particular to sleep with a Tallis Katan.[77] The Arizal severely warned that one is to wear the Tallis Katan at all times, even at night.[78] Practically, the custom of Chassidim is to be careful to sleep with a Tallis Katan.[79] One may even initially put on the Tzitzis at night for this purpose.[80]

Other opinions and customs: Many are accustomed to have a Tallis Katan which they only wear upon sleeping at night. Some Poskim justify this custom, stating that the Segulos involved in wearing a Tallis Katan apply even if it is not Halachically obligated to have Tzitzis, being it is a night garment. [See Birchas Habayis 37:4; Baruch Taam on 21; Shevet Halevi 6:50; 10:2; Kinyan Torah 4:1; Piskeiy Teshuvos 21:5 footnote 74]

[75] Implication of Admur 18:5 and M"A 18:3 regarding blankets which are worn into the morning, and at times by day, that it is a dispute if they are required to have Tzitzis, hence implying that according to all they are defined as a Kesus Layla! Hence, when one wears it by day, he cannot say a blessing, as according to the opinion that a Kesus Layla is exempt from Tzitzis, this garment is not obligated to have Tzitzis. Furthermore, if one did not remove this Tallis in the morning and then re-wear it, perhaps even according to the Rambam it is exempt from Tzitzis, and hence one is not wearing Tzitzis according to any opinion. [See Elya Raba ibid; implication from Siddur ibid, brought in previous footnotes]

[76] The reason: As if one changes the pair at night, he enters himself into a Safek Bracha, as some opinions rule one is to recite a blessing over day Tzitzis that are worn at night. Thus, it is better to change the Tzitzis by morning rather than at night even if he plans to wear the Tzitzis until the next night, and then switch it again. [See Taz 581:2; Mateh Ephraim 581:14; M"B 581:6; Piskeiy Teshuvos 18 footnote 16 in name of Maharshal 68 that it is forbidden to do a Mitzvah without a blessing See Tehila Ledavid 18; Piskeiy Hasiddur 42] In a reply from Harav Y.L. Groner I was told he did not receive any set directive in this matter; as to when one is to switch the Tzitzis, by night or by day. A similar reply was received from Harav Y.S. Ginzberg.

[77] Siddur Admur "The scrupulous are accustomed to sleep with a Tallis"; Ketzos Hashulchan 7:7; Darkei Chaim Veshalom 38
The reason: One is to sleep with a Tallis Katan in order so 1) If he awakens after daybreak, he will not be unclothed without Mitzvos. 2) So, he does not need to place the Tallis Katan on prior to washing hands, and thus transgress the holiness of the Zohar, as explained in the laws of Hashkamas Haboker. 3) Based on Kabala, there is a Mitzvah to wear a Tallis Katan also at night. [Siddur ibid]
Ruling of Admur in Shulchan Aruch: It is implied from Admur 8:20 and 30 that the custom of those times was not to sleep with a Tallis Katan.
Belittlement of the Tallis: There is no prohibition to sleep with a Tallis, even a Tallis Gadol [during the day], as doing so is not considered a belittlement to the Mitzvah. [21:4; Rama 21:3; See Halacha 17E!]
Other customs: Some were accustomed not to sleep with a Tallis at night. [Shaareiy Teshuvah 8:1 that so was the custom in previous times; Poskim brought in Piskeiy Teshuvos 21 footnote 67]

[78] Arizal in Shaar Hakavanos Derush Arvis "One must be very careful not to remove the Tallis Katan. Not by day or by night"; Peri Eitz Chaim Shaar Hatzitzis 1 "Do not remove the Tallis Katan at any time, even when sleeping, with exception to the bathhouse."

The Segulos: Sleeping with Tzitzis is a Segula to be saved from impurities and evil spirits.[81] It is a great form of protection for the body and soul.[82] Wearing a Tallis Katan helps reduce inner fear that one may experience.[83]

9. Is a blessing said in the morning over a Tallis Katan that one wore at night?[84]

> Example: One said a blessing on his Tzitzis yesterday and slept with that Tzitzis at night. One plans to wear this Tzitzis also today. Is he to recite a blessing over it?
> Example: One said a blessing on his Tzitzis yesterday and remained awake throughout the night wearing this Tallis Katan. Is a blessing said over it in the morning?

If one did not remove his Tallis Katan at night [and he had worn it that day with a blessing[85]], a blessing is not to be recited over this Tallis in the morning.[86] This applies even if the Tallis Katan is a day garment; one's day pair of Tzitzis that he happened to wear throughout the night. [This applies even if one removes the Tzitzis and re-wears it in the morning, unless a validating interval was made, as explained in "The Laws of Tzitzis" chapter 2 Halacha 15.[87]]

Saying a blessing on another Tallis:[88] Despite the above, it is proper for one to recite a blessing on a different pair of Tzitzis and have in mind to include within the blessing also the pair that he slept with and is still wearing.[89] [Alternatively, he is hear the blessing over a Tallis from another person.[90] If one wears a Tallis Gadol for Davening, such as one who is married, then upon saying the blessing over the Tallis Gadol he is to intend to exempt the Tallis Katan.[91]]

Summary:
One who wore a Tallis throughout the night is not to recite a blessing over the Tallis in the morning. However, he is to try to include the blessing of this Tallis within a blessing said over another Tallis.

---

[79] See Igros Kodesh 13:29; 18:436 *"Regarding what you write in my name of leniencies regarding sleeping with a Tallis Katan at night, I do not recall ever having said such things."* See Shulchan Menachem 1:40-41

[80] Siddur Admur
The reason: Doing so does not involve the prohibition of Baal Tosif being that there are opinions that state one is obligated to wear Tzitzis on a day garment even if it is worn at night. [Siddur ibid]

[81] Or Tzadikim 26:11; Chida in Tziparon Shamir 8:20; Shaar Hakavanos p. 52b

[82] Mishmeres Shalom 3:5

[83] Likkutei Sichos 33:273 [printed in Shulchan Menachem 1:41]

[84] Admur 8:27; 494:3; Tur 8; Bach; Taz 8:15; M"A 8:21; Elya Raba 8:18; M"B 8:42; Custom of Arizal [as brought in Kaf Hachaim 8:61]; Chesed Lealafim 8:7; Ben Ish Chaiy Bereishis 2; Kaf Hachaim 8:61
Background: There is a dispute regarding if there is an obligation to have Tzitzis on a four cornered garment at nighttime, as explained in Halacha C. According to those which hold that there is an obligation of Tzitzis at night, then one cannot make a blessing upon awakening. The reason for this is because there was no time interval between the previous blessing made and his current fulfillment of the Mitzvah, as there was no span of time in which the garment was exempt from Tzitzis. Hence, the nighttime is not considered an interval at all and is rather like one long day. However, according to those which hold that at nighttime there is no obligation to place Tzitzis on a four cornered garment, then the blessing is to be repeated in the morning. The reason for this is because the garment went through a time period of exemption, which serves as an interval. Now, although he physically wore the Tzitzis throughout the night, nevertheless since it was exempt from Tzitzis during that time, it is considered as if he was not wearing the Tzitzis at all throughout the entire night. There is thus a long interval between the previous Bracha he made and his fulfillment of the Mitzvah in the morning, and a new blessing is therefore required. Practically, in compliance with the rule that when there is a dispute regarding the saying of a blessing, the blessing is not said, the blessing may not be said on the Tallis that he has woken up wearing. Nevertheless, in order to satisfy also the stringent opinion, one should try to wear another Tallis and upon saying the blessing on it have in mind also the Tallis that he is wearing. [8:27]
Other opinions: Some Poskim rule that one who slept with a Tallis is to recite a blessing over it upon awaking in the morning. [Michaber 8:16] The Poskim ibid, negate this opinion, and so rules Admur, and so is the Sephardi ruling, unlike the Michaber, as Safek Brachos Lihakel. [See Kaf Hachaim ibid]

[85] If however he did not wear the Tallis Katan with a blessing the previous day, such as he forgot to say it, or he switched his Tallis Katan at night and thus did not make a blessing on it [due to the night] then obviously a blessing may be said in the morning.

[86] The reason: To suspect for those opinions that rule an interval from the previous blessing has not been made and hence a blessing is not required. [Admur ibid; see Background]

[87] See there that when replacing within three hours a blessing is not repeated unless one had decided not to wear it again until later and then changed his mind. [See M"B 8:42]

[88] Admur ibid; M"A 8:21; Chayeh Adam 12:8; M"B ibid; Chesed Lealafim 8:7; Ben Ish Chaiy Bereishis 2; Kaf Hachaim 8:61

[89] The reason: To suspect for those opinions that rule an interval has been made, and hence a blessing is required. [Admur ibid; see Background]

[90] Ketzos Hashulchan 7:7

[91] Ketzos Hashulchan ibid

Q&A

If one changed his Tallis Katan at night, may he recite a blessing over it in the morning?
Yes. If one switched his Tallis Katan at night and thus did not make a blessing on it [due to the night] then a blessing may be said in the morning after shaking the Tzitzis. *See our Sefer "The Laws of Tzitzis" chapter 2 Halacha 4B and Halacha 11!*

If at night one slept with his Tzitzis and is wearing it the next day, may a blessing be recited after Mikveh or after taking a shower?
No, as explained in our Sefer "The Laws of Tzitzis" chapter 2 Halacha 15!

------------------Tefillin----------------

10. Placing the head Tefillin [i.e. Shel Rosh] by the hairline:[92]

The entire Bayis of the Tefillin Shel Rosh must rest in the area where hair grows.[93] This means that [even] the bottom end of the Titura must rest on the area where the hair first begins to grow on the forehead.[94] [One who is not careful in this matter and allows the Tefillin to breach below the forehead, does not fulfill his obligation of wearing Tefillin.[95] This applies even if only a minute part of the Tefillin reaches below the hair.[96] Unfortunately, many stumble on this prohibition and mistakenly think that the upper end of the Tefillin is to be placed in the area where the hair starts, while the main bulk of the Tefillin is to be placed on the forehead. Such a person transgresses the Biblical command of wearing Tefillin, as the entire Tefillin must be in an area with hair.[97] Likewise, if they said a blessing, the blessing is considered to have been said in vain.[98] Accordingly, the many individuals who are not careful in this matter, are to be made aware, and each person is to remind his friend.[99] If one ever feels that the Tefillin has fallen out of place, he is to immediately return it.]

---

[92] Admur 27:14 [omitted in Siddur]; Michaber 27:9 *"The area for placing the Tefillin Shel Rosh begins from the area that hair grows on one's forehead"*; Tur 27:9; Rambam Tefillin 4:1; Rosh Tefillin 19; Menachos 37a "Bemakom Sheoseh Karcha"

[93] Admur ibid; Taz 27:10; All Poskim in next footnote

[94] Admur ibid; Taz 27:10 as understood by some Poskim; Beis Yaakov 131; Elya Raba 27:10; Divrei Yosef 63; Yad Ahron on Hagahos Hatur; Soles Belula 27:3; Shalmei Tzibur p. 37; Birkeiy Yosef 27 Shiyurei Bracha 1; Kesher Guda 3:10; Siddur Beis Oved; Mamar Mordechai 27:8; P"M 27 M"Z 10; Shaareiy Teshuva 27:15; Kitzur SHU"A 10:3; M"B 27:33; Kaf Hachaim 27:38; Divrei Chaim 2:6; Likkutei Maharich; Maharshag 1:7; Os Chaim Veshalom 27:15 [see his wording brought below in negation of the other opinions]
Other opinions: Some Poskim rule that only the Ketzitza [Bayis] must be placed above the hairline while the Titura may be placed below the hairline. [Taz 27:10 as understood by Beis Yaakov 131, although argues on the Taz; Gan Hamelech 153; Olas Tamid 27:8; Implication of Elya Raba 27:10, brought in P"M and Kaf Hachaim ibid; Daas Kedoshim 27] Other Poskim rule that if majority of the Tefillin is above the hairline, it is valid. [Birchas Habayis 38:18; Devar Yehoshua 4:11 that so was custom of some Tzadikim; Ashel Avraham Butchach 27 in his initial suggestion, although does not conclude this way] See Os Chaim Veshalom ibid and other Poskim ibid who completely negate this approach. In the words of the Os Chaim Veshlaom ibid *"It is true that one must be very careful in this, as it is a stumbling block to the public, and the action of the Yetzer Hara to cause people to become Karkaftas that have not worn Tefillin, as the previous Poskim have protested this custom of the masses who wear the Tefillin almost on the forehead, or even slightly below the hairline. However, I have seen that due to our great sins that even Torah scholars and Rabbanim Gedolim wear Tefillin like this below their hairline, and if so, they have never fulfilled the Mitzvah of Tefillin Shel Rosh in their lifetime. They should bemoan the fact that they are sinners and causing the masses who copy them to sin. May G-d save us from their punishment."*
Opinion of Taz: The Taz ibid records *"The end of the Ketzitza is to be where the hair begins to grow."* Some Poskim understand the Taz to mean that the Titura may be below the hair, and only the actual Bayis must be by the hair. [Beis Yaakov 131; Elya Raba 27:10; Yad Ahron on Hagahos Hatur; Shalmei Tzibur p. 37] Other Poskim, however, learn the Taz to mean that the entire Tefillin must be above the hair. [Mamar Mordechai 27:8; P"M 27 M"Z 10; Shaareiy Teshuva 27:15; Kaf Hachaim 27:38]

[95] Taz 27:10; Shiltei Giborim on Mordechai Shabbos; Kneses Hagedola 27; Olas Tamid 27:8; Elya Raba 27:11; Soles Belula 27:4; Tefila Ledavid p. 20; Shalmei Tzibur p. 37; Chesed Lealafim 27:7; Kaf Hachaim [Falagi] 10:20; Shesilei Zeisim 27:23; M"B 27:33; Kitzur SHU"A 10:3; Ketzos Hashulchan 8:10

[96] Taz ibid; Chayeh Adam 14:10; Ben Ish Chaiy Chayeh Sarah 1; Kaf Hachaim 27:40; Poskim ibid

[97] Taz 27:10; Chesed Lealafim 27:7; M"B 27:33 *"One who is not careful in this is included in Posheia Yisrael Begufan and is a Karkafta who has not put on Tefillin...It is as if the Tefillin is in his pocket."*

[98] M"B 27:33

[99] Yifei Laleiv 2:2; Shevet Hamussar 20 p. 51; Soles Belula 25; M"B 27:33

Summary:
No part of the head Tefillin may rest below the hairline of the forehead. One is to make others aware of this matter if he sees their Tefillin crouching below the hairline.

Q&A

If one is bald, or has a receding hairline, where is the Tefillin to be placed?[100]
It is to be placed in the estimated area from where the hair originally grew. This can be clearly identified, as there is a difference between the area where the hair grew and other areas of the forehead.

If one grows hair on his forehead, where is the Tefillin to be placed?[101]
The Tefillin is to be positioned in the normal area where the hair grows by most people.

Must also the sides of the Tefillin be on an area that grows hair?
If one has a receding, rounded, hairline [i.e. widows peak], in which placing the Tefillin at the exact area where the hair begins will cause the sides of the Tefillin to extend past the area where hair grows, then some Poskim[102] rule the Tefillin is to be placed higher up, so the entire Tefillin rests on the hair. Other Poskim[103], however, rule the Tefillin may be placed in the area where the hair begins to grow.

Is the Tefillin to be positioned exactly by the hairline?
Some Poskim[104] rule the Tefillin is to be placed slightly above the hairline.[105] Other Poskim[106] rule the Tefillin is to be placed exactly by the hairline, and not above it, and so is implied from Admur.[107] Those who wear large Tefillin [such as the 4x4 Tefillin worn according to Chabad custom] are most certainly to place it at the beginning of the hairline.[108]

If one wore the Tefillin past the hairline, must he replace it with a blessing?[109]
If he removed it with intent to not wear anymore, then it is to be replaced with a blessing of Al Mitzvas Tefillin. He is to repeat Kerias Shema while wearing the Tefillin.

The Rebbe's Tefillin:
The Rebbe did not contain hair in the front portion of his head, and hence, when he wore his Tefillin, it appeared to many as if it were below the hairline, reaching into the forehead. Various unsubstantiated statements have surfaced as to the Rebbe's remarks regarding this. Of these, the Rebbe is quoted to have remarked after being questioned, that in truth he does keep his Tefillin at the right area, and it is just that his hairline is not apparent due to lack of hair. In addition, the Rebbe is quoted to have stated that at times the Tefillin slides down and he constantly lifts them back up. In a recently published letter to Mr. Dov Lent, the Rebbe writes these exact claims that a) He has a receding hairline, and b) He checks it constantly, although at times it slips from its position. The original letter is included below,

---

[100] Ben Ish Chaiy Chayeh Sarah 1; Kaf Hachaim 27:38; See Eretz Tzevi 1:12; Os Chaim Veshalom 27:15; Piskeiy Teshuvos 27:18
[101] Peri Hasadeh 3:149; Levushei Mordechai 1:110; Beir Moshe 3:7; Piskeiy Teshuvos 27:18
[102] Misgeres Hashulchan on Kitzur SHU"A ibid in name of Shulchan Shlomo; Tiferes Adam 3:4; Imrei Yosher 2:2-3
[103] Chakal Yitzchak 1; Tzur Yaakov 1:163
[104] Shlah; Soles Belula 27:4; Chesed Lealafim 27:2; Shesilei Zeisim 27:23; M"B 27:33; Biur Halacha 27:9 "Ad Sof"; Kaf Hachaim 27:38
[105] The reason: The Tefillin is to be surrounded by hair, as in play of the verse "Vesevivo Nisara Meod." [Shlah ibid] Alternatively, in order so if it slides, it does not slide down below the hairline. [M"B ibid]
[106] Biur Hagr"a 27:25; Maaseh Rav 26, brought in Biur Halacha 27:9 "Ad Sof"; See Piskeiy Teshuvos 27:18
[107] Implication of Admur ibid *"This means that the beginning of the Tefillin is to be placed at the hairline,"* thus implying that it is not to be placed above it. This is unlike the simple wording of the Michaber 27:9 who implies it may be placed even initially anywhere between the hairline and the area of the baby skull.
[108] As otherwise the end of the Titura may extend past the skull area of the baby's head, and the entire Tefillin must be within that space.
[109] See Ashel Avraham Butchach 27

and as related by the son of Mr. Lent, it was in reply to why the Rebbe's Tefillin appears to be below the hairline. Rabbi Leibal Groner relates[110] that the Rebbe was once questioned as to whether one may be lenient to allow the Shel Rosh to go beneath the hairline, based on the fact that they see at times that his Shel Rosh falls below the hairline. The Rebbe responded to the questioner that he should follow the rulings in Shulchan Aruch, as stated above.

Letter of Rebbe

Mr. Dov Lent

The location of the Tefillin on the head is, of course, explicitly given in the Shulchan Aruch. If you have noticed that a certain person seems to have placed the Tefillin lower than the original hairline, it is undoubtedly because the hair of that person had receded, and from a distance it would have been difficult for you to determine actually where the original hairline was. On the other hand, it is also possible that at that particular time the Shel-Rosh had slipped unknowingly to the person, although he usually frequently checks the position with his hand as required by the Din.

The Tefillin of the Belzer Rav:
It is said of the Belzer Rav, Rav Ahron of Belz, that he would his Tefillin would extend below the hairline. I heard the following story relating to this from an old Shamash at the Batei Rand Shul in the Nachalaot, Jerusalem neighborhood:[111] It was on a certain occasion that the famed Gaon of Tchebin, Rav Dov Berish Weinfeld was invited to a daytime wedding in which the Belzer Rav attended. Upon seeing the Belzer Rav's head Tefillin out of place, below the hairline, the known Gaon approached him and respectfully admonished him for wearing the Tefillin below the valid area. The Belzer Rav replied that indeed according to Shulchan Aruch it is not in the valid place, but that is how he received from his Chassidic masters that the Tefillin should be worn.[112] A certain Chassid of the Belzer Rav who had witnessed the conversation, could not hold back his fury at the Tchebiner Rav for admonishing his Rebbe, and when the Tchebiner Rav put down his hat on a chair, the Chassid quickly made the hat disappear out of vengeance for his Rebbe's honor. Eventually, the Tchebiner Rav noticed his missing hat and asked for it to be returned. He added, that if the Chassid who stole his hat does not return it: "Lo Yotzi Shenaso/He will not survive the year." When the Chassid heard this curse from the famed Gaon of Tchebin, he immediately returned the hat, and later on had an audience with his Rebbe, the Belzer Rav, to discuss a Tikkun for his sin, and curse which he received. The Belzer Rav replied "You don't understand what he said. He did not say that you will not survive the year, but rather that your Shenaso, which also means sleep, meaning to say that you will never be satisfied from your sleep." Indeed, this Chassid would fall asleep everywhere he went, and never became satiated from his sleep, as interpreted by the Belzer Rav. This Chassid Davened in the Batei Rand synagogue in Nachalaot and passed away around 2010.

---

[110] Through personal correspondence with the author
[111] As in all stories, especially those heard second hand, not all details may be accurate, although the general story is reliable.
[112] See the "other opinions" brought in previous footnotes.

11. May the straps of the Tefillin that are wrapped around the arm touch each other, or overlap?

Touching on sides: The wrapping of the Tefillin straps around the forearm [between the bicep/upper arm, and the wrist] is done due to custom, and not due to a Halachic requirement.[113] Accordingly, there is certainly no prohibition, or invalidation, involved if the straps of the Tefillin that are wrapped around the forearm, touch each other by the sides. Furthermore, there is also no recorded source, neither in Halacha or Kabbalah, which mentions an adherence of being careful that the straps should not touch each other, and to thus make a space between each one.[114] [Nonetheless, it is a widespread worldly custom to be particular upon wrapping the straps around the arm that the straps remain a distance from each other, and do not touch by the sides.[115] This was likewise the witnessed custom of the Rabbeim.[116] It is unknown as to why the custom is to do so.[117] If later on during Davening, the straps become loosened and touch each other, the custom is to refasten them in a way that they are distanced from each other.[118] During Shacharis, the Rebbe was witnessed to undo and refasten the straps, making sure that they were each some distance from each other, if they became loosened and began touching each other.[119] Practically, Minhag Yisrael Torah Hi, and one is to initially adhere to this matter.[120]]

Overlapping: In addition to there being no issue with the straps touching each other by the sides, without there being a space between them, there is also no prohibition of Chatzitza, or other invalidation, involved if the straps of the Tefillin overlap each other, such as if one of the lower straps is wrapped partially over an upper strap.[121] Accordingly, many Sephardim are accustomed to wear Rashi and Rabbeinu Tam Tefillin simultaneously, and to specifically have the Rashi straps bound on top of the Rabbeinu Tam straps, on the arm.[122] Nevertheless, some Poskim[123] rule it is initially proper to be stringent and not have the straps overlap each other, due to the issue of Chatzitza.[124] Practically, as stated above, the Minhag Yisrael is to initially space the forearm straps away from each other, and certainly to avoid having them overlap.

---

[113] Admur 27:12; Michaber 27:8; M"A 27:13; Kisvei Arizal, Peri Eitz Chaim Shaar HaTefillin 10

The reason: See Peri Eitz Chaim ibid that the seven straps represent seven Naaros.

[114] There is no recorded source amongst the Poskim, or Sefarim of Nigleh or Nistar [that I am aware], which require that the straps of the Shel Yad Tefillin on the arm be surrounded by skin, and that they not be allowed to touch each other on the sides; There is also no reason or basis to find issue with the straps touching each other, even by the other parts of the arm. See all Sefarim quoted below which rule that the straps of the Rashi arm Tefillin are to overlap the Rabbeinu Tam straps, and thus certainly the touching of the sides would not pose any issue either.

[115] I have not found any discussion on this custom in Sefarim

[116] See Ishkavta Derebbe p. 31 footnote 19

[117] See Ishkavta Derebbe ibid "*I do not know and have not heard the reason of the custom of the Rabbeim to at all make space between the straps wrapped on the forearm.*" However, perhaps the following suggestions can be made: **1)** The straps all represent parts of Hashem's name, as written in Peri Eitz Chaim ibid, and just as the letters in a Sefer Torah may not touch each other, so too the straps. [See Ishkavta Derebbe ibid for a similar explanation regarding why we leave a space between the sets 2 and 4 of the straps] **2)** The straps each represent a different level of "Naarah", as writes the Arizal ibid, and these Naaros are to be separate from each other.

[118] This, however, seemingly was done in order to properly fasten the straps on the arm, and not merely because of a touching issue.

[119] See here: https://www.youtube.com/watch?v=P2WbWz3YkVc

[120] Many of the customs, and even Halachos, that we keep regarding Tefillin are "customs" with no source in the Talmud. See for example Rashba 827, brought in Rama 27:4; and M"A 27:5, regarding Chatzitza, that the Rashba gave a final ruling based on the custom he saw done.

[121] See Rama 27:4; Admur 27:7; Taz 27:4; M"A 27:5 that there is no Chatzitza invalidation by the straps of the Tefillin [Rama ibid], especially if they are by the forearm [Admur and Taz ibid], and especially if it is only a small amount [M"A ibid]; See Admur 651:5; Rama 651:1; Tur 651; Sukkah 37b that we never apply the rule of Chatzitza by Min Bemino, which is two items of the same species. The same applies regarding Tefillin. [Revid Hazahav, brought in M"B 27:14; Shulchan Hatahor 27:2; Maharsham 4:137] Accordingly, even if the law of Chatzitza would apply to these straps, leather would not be viewed as a Chatzitza between the straps/Tefillin and the skin; See all Poskim in next footnote regarding wrapping Rashi over the Rabbeinu Tam straps; See Piskeiy Teshuvos 27 footnote 90; 34:3

If the straps have loosened: If the straps have become loosened and have fallen downwards, on top of one of the lower straps, then seemingly it is to be fixed and fastened, otherwise it may not be considered strapped around the arm. Vetzaruch Iyun

[122] See Arizal in Peri Eitz Chaim Tefillin 10; Ben Ish Chaiy Vayeira 21; M"B 34:5; Yabia Omer 1:3; 5:5 Vayeishev Hayam 4:3 [of Rav Yaakov Hillel]; Piskeiy Teshuvos 34:3

[123] See Shraga Hameir 6:80 [See there that he rules it is better for one with a cast to wrap a minority of the straps over the cast, which is a real Chatzitza, then to wrap all the straps on top of each other, in the area of skin that precedes the cast; However, he records the M"A 27:5 that there is no Halachic issue in having only have a small part of the straps overlap each other.]

[124] The reason: As some Poskim rule that by Tefillin even Min Bemino is a Chatzitza. [Birkeiy Yosef 27:1 who compares it to Bigdei Kehuna; Levushei Serud 27; M"B 27:10 and 14 that initially one is to be stringent like this opinion; See Machatzis Hashekel 34:5; Shut Hastam 50; Rav Poalim 3 Sod Yesharim 8; Doveiv Meisharim 2:37; Piskeiy Teshuvos 27 footnote 90; 34:3] Likewise, some Poskim rule that even the straps should not have a Chatzitza under them. [Peri Megadim 27 M"Z 4; Doveiv Meisharim ibid; Cheshev Haeifod 1:21; Teshuvos Vehanhagos 2:26; Piskeiy Teshuvos 27:9]

> **Summary:**
> From the letter of the law, there is no Halachic issue with having the forearm straps touch each other, or even overlap, although the custom of Jewry is to be careful to separate each of the straps from each other with a space, and to fix them in the event that they loosen, and a Jewish custom is Torah.

----------------Davening-General Laws----------------

12. Writing, text messaging, Whatsapping, during Davening:

A. Introduction:
It is forbidden to talk during Davening, from Baruch Sheamar, until after Shemoneh Esrei.[125] The question is raised regarding the status of writing, and if it is likewise forbidden to write, or send text messages, during Davening, just as it is forbidden to speak, or if writing is considered of lesser stringency, and is hence permitted to be done.

B. The ruling:
During Shema:[126] It is forbidden to make an interval during Kerias Shema even if he will not be saying any words, unless it is for the sake of a slight Mitzvah in which case, if he is past the first paragraph of Shema [i.e. in Vehayah and onwards], he may make a non-verbal interval. [Accordingly, it is forbidden to stop during the reading of Shema for the sake of writing or sending text messages through SMS or WhatsApp, unless doing so contains a slight Mitzvah and he is not within the first paragraph.]

Past Baruch Sheamar-During other areas of Davening:[127] Initially, one may not make an interval during any part of Davening [past Baruch Sheamar], even if he will not be saying any words.[128] Accordingly, one is not to stop in middle of Davening for the sake of writing [or sending text messages through SMS or WhatsApp].[129] However, in a time of real need, one may write during Davening, past Baruch Sheamar[130] [so long as he is not in the midst of the first paragraph of Shema[131], or in Shemoneh Esrei[132], or between Goal Yisrael and Shemoneh Esrei[133]].

> **Summary:**
> Initially, one is not to write or send text messages during Davening unless it is a time of real need, and he is not within the first paragraph of Shema, Shemoneh Esrei, or between Goal Yisrael and Shemoneh Esrei.

---

[125] Admur 51:4 and 53:3; Rama 51:4; Levush 51:5
[126] Admur 63:7; Michaber 63:6; Yuma 19b
[127] See Salmas Chaim 49; Yagel Yaakov 10; Betzel Hachochma 4:88; Beir Moshe 2:7 [there he permits writing with exception to 1st paragraph of Shema]; Yabia Omer 9:10; Teshuvos Vehanhagos 2:40; Shevet Hakehasi 1:77; Piskeiy Teshuvos 51:8; 66:1
[128] Beis Oved 51:3; Makor Chaim 51; Kaf Hachaim 51:17; See Admur 63:7
[129] The reason: As although writing is not like talking regarding its quality of interval [See Admur 47:3 regarding Birchas Hatorah], and thus does not receive the same level of severity, nevertheless, initially, one is not to make any interval during Davening, even if it does not involve speech, just as is the law regarding Shema. [Beis Oved 51:3; Makor Chaim 51; Kaf Hachaim 51:17; See Admur 63:7]
[130] The reason: As the main prohibition of Hefsek is specifically regarding speech. [See Admur 51:4] And thus we rule that one may stop to make non-speech intervals even during Kerias Shema, after the first Parsha, if it is for the sake of a Mitzvah [Admur 63:7] even though one may never make an interval for speech even if it is for the sake of a Mitzvah, even in Pesukei Dezimra. [Admur 51:4] Certainly, then this non-verbal interval allowance for the sake of a Mitzvah applies likewise during Pesukei Dezimra. [Beis Oveid ibid] Likewise, this allowance also applies in a time of need. [Poskim ibid]
[131] Admur 63:7; Vetzaruch Iyun if the Heter of a time of need applies to the 2nd paragraph of Shema or only if it contains a slight Mitzvah, as rules Admur there.
[132] See Admur 96-97; 104
[133] Admur 111:1

13. Yawning, burping, and sneezing during Shemoneh Esrei:[134]

One may not burp[135] or yawn[136] during Shemoneh Esrei. If one willingly burps or yawns during Shemoneh Esrei, he is considered to be amongst the haughty individuals.[137] If one gets the urge to yawn [and is unable to control it[138]], then he is to place his hand over his mouth, in order so his open mouth will not be apparent to others.[139] [According to some Poskim[140], the same applies if one has the urge to burp and is unable to control it, that he is to place his hand over his mouth. Other Poskim[141] however rule that by a burp, one is not required to cover his mouth.[142] Practically, one is to be stringent.[143]]

Sneezing during Davening:[144] One who sneezes during Shemoneh Esrei, it is a good sign for him.[145] [Nonetheless, it is common etiquette to always cover one's mouth upon sneezing.[146]]

Summary:
One is not to yawn or burp during Davening, and if he feels an urge to do so, he is to cover his mouth.

Q&A

May one burp or yawn in the parts of Davening that precede Shemoneh Esrei?
The above prohibition against burping or yawning is in reference to Shemoneh Esrei. There is no recorded prohibition against doing so during other parts of Davening, even though it may not be appropriate.

Does one need to cover his mouth during a yawn or burp if he is Davening in private?[147]
Yes.

May one continue saying the words of Davening in middle of yawning?[148]
No.

Which hand is one to use to cover his mouth?
Some[149] say he is to use his right hand.

---

[134] Admur 97:1; Michaber 97:1; Braisa Brachos 24b; Kitzur SHU"A 18:9; Ketzos Hashulchan 20:9
[135] Literally *"Yigaheik, which refers to air that is expelled from one's body into one's mouth as a result of satiation."* [Admur ibid; Taz 97:1; Elya Raba 97:1; Rashi Brachos 97:1; See Kaf Hachaim 97:1]
[136] Literally *"Yipaheik, which refers to opening the mouth like a person who desires to sleep or has awaken from sleep."* [Admur ibid; Taz 97:1; Rashi Brachos ibid; See Kaf Hachaim 97:1]
[137] Admur ibid; Tur ibid; Brachos ibid
[138] Aruch Hashulchan 97:1-2, otherwise it is not considered an Oness, under duress, and he must control it. Vetzaruch Iyun from Brachos ibid.
[139] Admur ibid; Michaber ibid; Brachos ibid; Rashi Brachos ibid; Rosh Brachos 3:39; Yerushalmi Brachos 3:5
[140] Tur 96 "If one needs to do **them**"; Maharsha Brachos ibid; Levush 97; Soles Belula 1; Implication of Chida in Kesher Gudal 12:27; Beis Oved 43; Kitzur SHU"A 18:9; Aruch Hashulchan 97:1; Kaf Hachaim 96:2
[141] Implication of Admur, Michaber ibid, and Brachos ibid, who write only the case of "Yawn"; Elya Raba 97:1; Mamar Mordechai 97:1; Nehar Shalom 97:1; P"M 97 M"Z 1; M"B 97:1
[142] The reason: Some Poskim rule one is not required to cover his mouth in middle of Shemoneh Esrei, if he has a desire to burp, and only by a yawn, in which one stretches his mouth open very much, is covering the mouth required.
[143] Kaf Hachaim ibid
[144] Admur 103:3; Michaber 103:3; Brachos 24b
[145] The reason: As sneezing is pleasant for a person, and just as G-d is giving him a pleasant pleasure down here, so too He is giving him blessing above, to fulfill his will and requests. [Admur ibid; Rav Zeira Brachos ibid and Rashi ibid]
[146] See Yerushalmi Brachos 3:5 *"I saw that when Rebbe yawned and sneezed, he covered his mouth"*
[147] Tiferes Shmuel on Rosh ibid; Kaf Hachaim 97:3
[148] Makor Chaim 97
[149] Orach Neman 97:1; Piskeiy Teshuvos 97:1

------------------Pesukei Dezimra----------------
14. The verse of Poseiach Es Yadecha & its relevant laws:

The meaning: The verse of Poseiach Es Yadecha is a praise to Hashem for overseeing His creations and providing them with sustenance.[150] [In Chassidus it is explained that this verse is a request from Hashem that He enter into one's heart His Divine will and a desire that Hashem be King over him.[151]]

Concentration:[152] One must [especially[153]] concentrate upon saying the words Poseiach Es Yadecha, on the meaning of the words that he is saying. [One is to also concentrate on the fact that the Roshei Teivos of the words spell the Divine name פא"י and is the Gematria of the names Havayah and Adniy. Likewise, one is to concentrate that its Sof Teivos spell the word Chatach, which is the Divine name authorized over the giving of Parnasa.[154] One is however not to concentrate on the deeper Kabalistic intents, unless he is of proper spiritual level to do so.[155]]

If one did not concentrate:[156] If one did not concentrate on the words, then he must repeat [the verse of Poseiach Es Yadecha[157]] with concentration.[158] [If one remembered that he did not concentrate on the verse prior to completing Ashreiy, then he is to go back to the verse of Poseiach Es Yadecha and repeat from there.[159] If, however, he remembered only after he finished Ashreiy, but in the midst of Pesukei Dezimra, then he should say the single[160] verse of Poseiach Es Yadecha.[161] It is to be said in whatever area of Pesukei Dezimra he remembers, and he is afterwards to continue praying from where he left off.[162] Nonetheless, it is best to repeat it between the paragraphs [i.e. Bein Haperakim].[163] It may also be said between Yishtabach and Birchas Shema, although may not be said once one begins Birchas Yotzer Or.[164]

---

[150] Admur 51:8; Tur 51; See Piskeiy Teshuvos 51 footnote 141 for various explanations of the word Ratzon

[151] See Likkutei Torah 54a

[152] Admur 51:8; Michaber 51:7; Rabbeinu Yonah Brachos 32a in name of Gaonim

[153] This is in addition to the generally required concentration upon saying the Psalm of Tehila Ledavid, as one merits Olam Haba due to the recital of this Psalm. Nevertheless, upon saying the verse of Poseiach Es Yadecha, one must add in even more concentration. [Tur 51; Levush 51:8]

[154] Kaf Hachaim 51:34; Piskeiy Teshuvos 51:17

[155] Kaf Hachaim ibid; Chayeh Adam 18:2; However, see Ben Ish Chaiy Vayigash 12

[156] Admur 51:8; 101:1; Michaber 51:7; Rabbeinu Yonah Brachos 32a in name of Gaonim

[157] Implication of Admur ibid and M"A ibid in next footnote "since in this case he is only required to repeat one verse"; Elya Raba 51:6; Birkeiy Yosef 51:5; Kesher Gudal 7:42; Shalemi Tzibur p. 69b; Beis Oved 51:3; P"M 51 A"A 6; Mor Uketzia 51; Derech Hachaim; Ben Ish Chaiy Vayigash 12; Toras Chaim Sofer 51:5; Ketzos Hashulchan 18:4; Kaf Hachaim 51:32
Other opinions: Some Poskim rule he is to repeat the entire Psalm of Tehila Ledavid. [Levush 51, brought in Birkeiy Yosef and Kaf Hachaim ibid] Other Poskim rule he is to repeat from the verse of Poseiach Es Yadecha until the end of Ashreiy. [Chayeh Adam; M"B 51:16; Igros Moshe 2:16; Piskeiy Teshuvos 51:17]

[158] The reason: As the main reason the Sages established reciting the Psalm of Tehila Ledavid daily is due to the praise recited in this verse. In this verse, we praise Hashem for supervising His creations and providing them with sustenance. [Admur ibid; Tur ibid; M"B 51:15] Now, although in today's times we do not generally require one to repeat a prayer due to lack of concentration, as it is probable that even if we require him to repeat it, he will not have concentration during the repetition, as explained in 101:1, nevertheless, since in this case he is only required to repeat one verse we therefore require him to repeat it, as it is easy for one to concentrate on one verse if he so desires. [Admur ibid; M"A 51:6; Soles Belula 51:32] Alternatively, the reason is because in Shemoneh Esrei, if we were to require one to repeat the blessing in case of lack of concentration, and he does not concentrate during the repetition, then it is considered that he a said a blessing in vain. [P"M 51 A"A 6; Soles Belula ibid; Kaf Hachaim 51:32]

[159] M"B 51:16; Implication of Derech HaChaim and Ketzos Hashulchan 18:4

[160] See Poskim in previous footnotes who rule only this verse is repeated and so is the final ruling, however, see other opinions mentioned there who require repetition of the entire Mizmor, or from Poseiach Es Yadecha and onwards.

[161] Derech HaChaim; Ketzos Hashulchan 18:4; M"B 51:16 regarding if he has time to stop and repeat
Other opinions: Some Poskim rule he is not to make an interval and repeat the verse in Pesukei Dezimra, being he can make it up in Ashreiy of Uva Letziyon or of Mincha. [Kaf Hachaim 51:33 based on Tiferes Yisrael Brachos 5:6 who write that the Sages only required Tehila Ledavid to be said once a day, and the reason it is said three times is just in case one did not concentrate.]

[162] Igros Moshe 2:16; Piskeiy Teshuvos 51:17
The reason: As the Seder of the Psalms do not invalidate. [ibid]
Other opinions: Some Poskim understand that according to the M"B ibid [who says repeat "Al Haseder"] one is to go back to Poseiach Es Yadecha and repeat from there in all cases that he remembered after finishing Ashreiy. [Igros Moshe ibid in his understanding of M"B ibid; See Piskeiy Teshuvos ibid footnote 134]

[163] Yabia Omer 6:5; Piskeiy Teshuvos 51:17

[164] See Admur 51:4; 53:3; 54:3 that one may make an interval for the sake of Mitzvah, and that the laws of Hefsek between Yishtabach and Yotzer is more lenient than within Pesukei Dezimra. Hence, if one can make an interval to say Poseiach Es Yedecha in middle of Pesukei Dezimra then certainly he may do so in between Yishtabach and Yotzer; See also regarding the allowance to say Shir Hamalos Mimamakim during the 10 days of repentance that the Magen Avraham 54:2 questions as to whether reciting this psalm during prayer constitutes an interval and the Degul Merivava 54 answers the question of the M"A ibid by stating that the prohibition of an interval is only applicable regarding matters irrelevant to prayer and not with regards to words of praise. So also answer the Aruch Hashulchan 54:2; Toras Chaim Sofer 54:2 against the question of the M"A.

If one did not repeat the verse during Davening, such as he remembered only after he began Birchas Shema, then he is to repeat it after Davening.[165]]

> **Summary:**
> One must especially concentrate on the meaning of the words that he is saying upon saying the words Poseiach Es Yadecha. If one did not concentrate on the words and he remembered prior to completing Ashreiy, then he is to go back to the verse of Poseiach Es Yadecha and repeat from there. If, however, he remembered only after he finished Ashreiy, but prior to beginning Birchas Shema, then he should say the single verse of Poseiach Es Yadecha upon remembering. It is best to repeat it between the paragraphs [i.e. Bein Haperakim]. If one did not repeat the verse during Davening, such as he remembered only after he began Birchas Shema, then he is to repeat it after Davening.
>
> **Q&A**
> **If one did not concentrate upon reciting the verse of Poseiach Es Yadecha in Ashreiy of Uva Letziyon or Mincha, is the verse to be repeated?**[166]
> Yes.[167]
>
> ### *Related customs*
> **Touching Shel Yad and Shel Rosh:**[168]
> Some are accustomed to touch the Tefillin Shel Yad upon saying the words Poseiach Es Yadecha [in Pesukei Dezimra and Uva Letziyon] and to touch the Tefillin Shel Rosh upon saying the words Umasbia Lechol Chaiy Ratzon.[169] This is the Chabad custom.[170] Some, however, are accustomed to touch the Tefillin with the straps and not directly with their hands.[171]
>
> **Raising the eyes towards Heaven:**[172]
> Some are accustomed to raise the eyes towards Heaven upon saying the verse of Poseiach Es Yadecha.
>
> **Raising the hands:**[173]
> Some Sephardic communities have the custom to open the hands towards Heaven upon saying the words Poseiach Es Yadecha.[174] [This is not the Chabad custom.] One who follows this custom is to beware not to lift the hands above his head.[175]
>
> **Giving charity:**[176]
> Some are accustomed to distributing charity upon saying the verse of Poseiach Es Yadecha. [This is not the Chabad custom.]

Other opinions: Some Poskim rule once Yishtabach has been recited the verse of Poseiach Es Yadecha may only be said after Shemoneh Esrei. [Ben Ish Chaiy Vayigash 12]

[165] Levush 51; Chayeh Adam, brought in M"B 51:16
[166] Kaf Hachaim 51:33
[167] The reason: As the Sages instituted that one recites Tehila Ledavid three times a day, as whoever does so merits the world to come. Now, as stated above, the main reason the Sages established reciting the Psalm of Tehila Ledavid daily is due to the praise recited in this verse and hence seemingly the law of repetition would apply to any of the three Ashreiys.
[168] Taamei Haminhagim Likkutim 177
[169] The reason: This is to emphasize that the reason we ask for Parnasa is so we can perform Hashem's Mitzvos. [ibid]
[170] Igros Kodesh 18:265; Sefer Haminhagim p. 9 [English edition p. 22]
[171] Igros Kodesh ibid
[172] Sefer Chareidim chapter 4
[173] Ben Ish Chaiy Vayigash 12; Torah Leshma 31; Makor Chaim of Chavos Yair 51:7
[174] The reason: This is done in order to make a physical vessel for the blessing. [ibid]
[175] Ben Ish Chaiy ibid
The reason: As according to Kabala, one is never to raise his hands above his head, with exception to Netilas Yadayim and Nesias Kapayim. [Ben Ish Chaiy ibid]
Other opinions: Some Poskim rule one is to raise the hands above his head when reciting Poseiach Es Yadecha. [Yad Yosef p. 15, brought in Ben Ish Chaiy ibid]
[176] Likkutei Maharich in name of Seder Hayom and Mavor Yabok

15. Skipping Pesukei Dezimra in order to Daven Shemoneh Esrei with Minyan:[177]

Letter of law:[178] [From the letter of the law] one who arrives late to Shul for Shacharis is required to skip Pesukei Dezimra in order so he be able to Daven Shemoneh Esrei with the congregation.[179] This, however, [does not come to negate the importance of Pesukei Dezimra, which was instituted by the Geonim[180] and recorded by all Rishonim[181] and Achronim[182] and hence] only applies Bedieved if one already came late. However, initially, every person is obligated to do all in his power to come to Shul with enough time so he will not need to skip any paragraph, and will still be able to Daven Shemoneh Esrei with the Minyan [and heaven forbid to belittle this matter[183]].[184]

Ruling of Kabbalah: According to the teachings of Kabbalah, one who skips parts of Pesukei Dezimra is considered to have jumbled the channels [of blessing and G-dliness that result from prayer].[185] Therefore, one is to be careful to come to Shul early, so he can recite the entire Pesukei Dezimra and still Daven Shemoneh Esrei with the Minyan.[186] Furthermore, some Poskim[187] rule based on this that one may not skip Pesukei Dezimra even for the sake of Davening Shemoneh Esrei with the Minyan [unlike the opinion brought above]. Practically, due to this, many meticulous individuals are accustomed not to skip any part of Pesukei Dezimra even if one came late to Shul and will not be able to Daven Shemoneh Esrei with the Minyan unless he skips.[188] This is the widespread custom of Chassidim in general and Chabad Chassidim in particular.[189] However, some Poskim[190] negate this understanding, and rule that even according to Kabala it is better to skip Pesukei Dezimra so one can Daven Shemoneh Esrei with the Minyan.[191] Each community is to follow their Rav and custom.

---

[177] See Halacha Berura [Yosef] chapter 52 for the full details of this subject

[178] Admur 52:1-2

[179] Admur 52:1; Michaber 52:1; Tur 52 in name of Rav Neturai Gaon 12; Rabbeinu Yona Brachos 32a; Rosh Brachos 5:6 in name of Rav Amram Gaon; Semak 11; Semag Asei 19; Aruch Erech Tefila; Hagahos Maimanis Tefila 7 Nun in name of Rav Moshe Gaon; Rashba 3:285 in name of Gaonim; M"B 52:1 concludes to follow ruling in Shulchan Aruch; Ketzos Hashulchan 14:1 and 18:13; Rebbe in Igros Kodesh 7:139 writes that there are 91 Poskim who rule this way

The reason: As the prayer of a Minyan is always accepted and received by G-d, as the verse [Iyov 36:5] states "Kabir Lo Yimas" and [Tehillim 55:19] "Padah Beshalom Nafshi Mikrav Li Ki Berabim Hayu Imadi." [Admur ibid; Rambam Tefila 8:1; Braisa Brachos 8a] Therefore, one who comes to Shul and finds the Minyan at the end of Pesukei Dezimra is to skip Pesukei Dezimra, as Pesukei Dezimra itself was only instituted for the sake of the Shemoneh Esrei, so that it be well received and accepted by G-d, through first organizing the praise of G-d and then Davening Shemoneh Esrei. Accordingly, it is better [to skip Pesukei Dezimra and] Daven Shemoneh Esrei with the Minyan, as then one's prayer is certainly accepted above. [Admur ibid]

[180] Rav Amram Gaon; Rav Sadya Gaon; Rav Natrunaiy Gaon; Rav Moshe Gaon

[181] Rif; Rabbeinu Yona; Rashi; Rambam; Rashba; Ramban; Semag; Semak; Tur

[182] Beis Yosef; Rama; Bach; Levush; Taz; M"A

[183] Rebbe in Igros Kodesh 1:229, printed in Shulchan Menachem 1:71

[184] Admur 52:2; All Poskim brought next regarding the Kabalistic ruling; Rebbe ibid

[185] The reason: As each part of the prayer contains mystical meaning and deep spiritual effects and is like a step on a ladder to reach the next part. For example, Pesukei Dezimras corresponds to the world of Yetzira, and hence how can one reach Shemoneh Esrei which is Atzilus if he does not go first to Yetzira.

[186] Maggid Meisharim Parshas Behar as a warning from the Maggid to the Beis Yosef, brought in Elya Raba 52:5; Soles Belula 52:1; Beir Heiytiv 52:1; Siddur Arizal; Yosef Ometz and Shalmei Tzibur, brought in Shaareiy Teshuvah 52:1; M"B 52:1; Kaf Hachaim 52:2

[187] Pesach Hadevri 52 in name of many Poskim and that so is his opinion, brought in Kaf Hachaim 52:2; Yosef Ometz and Shalmei Tzibur, brought in Shaareiy Teshuvah 52:1, conclude that if one will not be able to ever say Pesukei Dezimra because he always comes late, then he should say the regular order [or at least Baruch Shemar, Ashreiy and Yishtabach] and not skip; Minchas Aaron 12:13; Rav Poalim 2:4 concludes "I am not fond of the skipping, as is known to those with knowledge of Kabbalah, and there is no need to lengthen on this." Ben Yehoyada Rosh Hashanah 35a; Igros Kodesh 18:81 "In addition to the fact that some Poskim prohibit it"; Yaskil Avdi 1:2 "So rule all Achronim"; Or Letziyon 2:7-2; See Poskim in next footnote

[188] Custom recorded in Beir Heiytiv 52:1, M"B 52:1 [although they conclude like the stringent Poskim brought next]; Siddur Arizal p. 35; Soles Belula 52:1 that so he witnessed done by many Gedolei Yisrael; Yifei Laleiv 52:1; Kaf Hachaim 52:2 and 236:22 regarding Maariv; Ketzos Hashulchan 27 footnote 27 regarding Maariv

The reason: As in these generations, the main Tikkun is through prayer [Tanya Kuntrus Achron] and thus we must place greater emphasis on the Avoda of Tefila. [Maaneh of Rebbe recorded in Shulchan Menachem 1:218] Alternatively, once they start skipping it teaches them a belittling of the prayer, and hence it is better not to skip at all. [Igros Kodesh 7:139]

[189] Rebbe in Toras Menachem 2:134 "Although the ruling in Shulchan Aruch is to skip, the Rabbeim direct that one is not to do so, but is rather to Daven the entire prayer in order"; Toras Menachem 18:282, printed in Shulchan Menachem 1:218; Igros Kodesh 7:139 that the Rebbe suggested the Bochurim not to skip; Igros Kodesh 15:170 "Despite the allowances, we do not do this"

[190] Peri Chadash 50; Chacham Tzvi 36, brought in conclusion of Beir Heiytiv ibid, M"B 52:1 [and so is final opinion of M"B]; Shalmei Tzibur and Mamar Mordechai, brought in Shaareiy Teshuvah and M"B ibid, rules this applies even if one usually Davens in private and never skips, that if he is with a Minyan, he is to skip for the sake of Davening Shemoneh Esrei with them

[191] The reason: As even according to the Zohar, the intent was not to negate the ruling of the Poskim, but rather to say that when one is Davening alone, he should never skip parts of Davening even if he is in a hurry etc. However, when Davening with a Minyan, even the Zohar agrees that one should skip for the sake of Davening with them. [Chacham Tzvi ibid]

Saying Pesukei Dezimra quickly in order to Daven Shemoneh Esrei with the congregation:[192] One is not allowed to recite Pesukei Dezimra at a fast pace. It must be said slowly, word for word, in order so one can have proper concentration. Those who say it quickly are not doing a proper thing, as they are shortening the praise of G-d in order to ask for their own needs.[193] This applies even if one's intent in saying it quickly is on order so he can Daven Shemoneh Esrei with the congregation.[194] [Thus, one who came late to Shul is to rather skip parts of Pesukei Dezimra than to read the prayer quickly.[195] If he is accustomed not to skip, as stated above, then he is to recite it in his normal slow pace.]

Summary:
Initially, one must come to Shul on time, so he can recite all the parts of the prayer slowly and without skipping and Daven Shemoneh Esrei with the congregation. If one came late to Shul, then the Halachic ruling is that he should skip part, or all, of Pesukei Dezimra, in order to Daven Shemoneh Esrei with the Minyan. It is better for him to skip Pesukei Dezimra than to say it quickly. However, according to Kabbalah, and so is the custom of Chassidim and meticulous individuals, one is not to skip any part of the Davening, and is certainly not to say it quickly, even if due to this he will be unable to Daven Shemoneh Esrei with the Minyan.

Q&A

What should one do if he Davens at a slower pace than the Minyan, and even if he begins Davening on time, he will be unable to reach the Minyan for Shemoneh Esrei?
The entire Halacha above is only regarding latecomers. However, one who comes to Shul on time, and Davens at a slower pace than the Minyan, may continue to do so without skipping any part of Pesukei Dezimra, or quickening his pace, even though this will cause him to be unable to Daven Shemoneh Esrei together with the Minyan.[196] In such a case he is to begin the prayer with the congregation and then Daven to the best of his ability, and if he is behind the Minyan so be it.[197] He is, however, to make sure to answer Kaddish, Kedusha, and Barchu together with the Minyan.[198] Nonetheless, some Poskim[199] write that it is best in such a case for him to come to Shul early and begin Davening before the Minyan, in order so he reach Shemoneh Esrei together with the congregation.

If a Minyan of six Shemoneh Esrei Daveners will not be available unless one skips Pesukei Dezimra, is one to do so despite the fact that he generally follows the Kabalistic ruling not to skip?[200]
In such a case, the person is to skip Pesukei Dezimra for the sake of establishing the Minyan, and it is only in a scenario that the Minyan will in any event take place that one is allowed not to skip.

---

[192] Admur 51:13; Michaber 51:8; Orchos Chaim Meah Brachos 33 in name of Hamachkim; Levush 51:9

[193] Admur ibid *"Those who say it quickly are not doing a proper thing, as they are shortening the praise of G-d in order to ask for their own needs. Is there any ruler who would agree to this?"*

[194] Admur ibid in parentheses *"When there is a Minyan"*; Beis Yosef in name of Orchos Chaim ibid; Ketzos Hashulchan 18:3 and footnote 12 explains this wording of Admur and Orchos Chaim to mean as stated above that they are not to hasten Pesukei Dezimra even for the sake of Davening with the Minyan; Lechem Chamudos Brachos 5:16; Derech Chaim

[195] Ketzos Hashulchan ibid; Aruch Hashulchan 51:9; Piskeiy Teshuvos 52 footnote 3
The reason: As reading it quickly is a more apparent shortening of Hashem's praise [Ketzos Hashulchan ibid], as well as that it is better to recite a small amount with concentration than a large amount without. [Aruch Hashulchan ibid]

[196] Shaareiy Teshuvah 52:1; Ketzos Hashulchan 18 footnote 401; Igros Kodesh Rayatz 14:398 *"If there is a Minyan without him then he is to Daven on his own pace and not with the Minyan"*; Igros Kodesh 18:81, printed in Shulchan Menachem 1:218
The reason: As the main purpose of prayer is Kavana [i.e. the concentration] and the fact he started with the congregation is similar to Davening with a Minyan, although just similar. [Rebbe ibid]
Other opinions: Some Poskim of today negate relying on this ruling of the Shaareiy Teshuvah, as we have very little concentration today, and hence it is always better to Daven with the Minyan. [Piskeiy Teshuvos 52 footnote 3]

[197] Igros Kodesh 18:81

[198] Shaareiy Teshuvah ibid; Rebbe Rayatz ibid

[199] Shulchan Hatahor 52:3

[200] Pashut as the establishing of Minyan is the greatest of the positive commands, and overrides even the negative command of freeing a slave, as recorded in Admur 90:17, and hence if one will cause the Minyan to break up by not Davening with them, and they will not wait for him, then one is to skip for that purpose; See also Igros Kodesh Rayatz 14:398 *"If there is a Minyan without him* then he is to Daven on his own pace and not with the Minyan"

Should one skip Karbanos in order to be able to Daven with the minyan?
From the letter of the law, one is certainly to skip Karbanos and all the parts said before Hodu in order to Daven Shemoneh Esrei with the Minyan.[201] However, those who follow the Kabalistic ruling, do not skip any part of Davening, even the sections said before Hodu, and so is the custom of Chassidim.[202] Vetzaruch Iyun regarding the Karbanos of Mincha.

------------------Shema-----------------

16. Sof Zeman Kerias Shema-Until what time may the morning Shema be recited-Understanding the Luach of Sof Zman Kerias Shema:[203]

It is a Biblical command upon men[204] to recite Kerias Shema every morning.[205] The morning Kerias Shema [Biblically[206]] must be recited within the first three hours of the day.[207] Thus, one must be very careful during days that have an early sunrise, and/or less daylight hour, to hurry and recite the Shema on time.[208] [Once the end of the third hour of the day has arrived, one has forfeited the Biblical command of reciting the morning Shema, and it can no longer be made up at a later time.[209] One who reads the Shema after this time, is considered merely as one who is reading a paragraph from the Torah [and is thus not obligated to do so, outside of Shacharis].[210] On this sin the Sages[211] applied the verse[212] "Meuvas Lo Yuchal Litaken/A sin that has no fixing." The Divine light that is drawn below through the performance of this Mitzvah is forever lacking and cannot be made up even if the person were to be careful to say the Shema at the right time forever after.[213] The Zohar states that one who does not read Shema on time is put in excommunication.[214] The Baal Shem Tov and his students were very careful to read the Shema on time, and there does not exist any Chassidic tradition to be lenient otherwise, and it is thus forbidden to do so.[215]]

---

[201] Ketzos Hashulchan 14:1
[202] See Rebbe in Toras Menachem 2:134; Toras Menachem 18:282
[203] See Admur 58:1-3; Mishmeres Shalom Kudinov 9; Piskeiy Teshuvos 58:1
[204] Women, however, are exempt from the Mitzvah of Shema. [Admur 70:1]
[205] Admur 58:1; Rebbe Eliezer Brachos 21a
The reason: As the verse states "Ubishachbecha Ubikumacha" [from which we derive that there is an obligation to recite the Shema both by night and day]. [Admur ibid]
[206] Implication of Admur 58:2-3; Admur in Siddur writes it's a Biblical doubt; M"A 58:7 and Taz 58:4 in negation of the opinion of Kesef Mishneh; Peri Chadash 58:1 in length; Rav SZ"A in Halichos Shlomo 11 that so is ruling of all Gedolei Haachronim; See Mishmeres Shalom Kudinov 9; Hisorerus Teshuvah 1:33; Lehoros Nasan 3:4; Piskeiy Teshuvos 58:1
Other opinions: Some Poskim learn that just as Biblically the night Shema may be recited throughout the entire night, so too the day Shema may Biblically be recited throughout the entire daytime, and it is only Rabbinical that it must be recited within the first three hours. [Kesef Mishneh Shema 1, brought in M"A ibid and Taz 58:4; Tomas Yesharim, brought in Peri Chadash 58:1; P"M 60 A"A 1 that implies that so is opinion of Rambam and Semag [See also P"M 58 M"Z 2]; 1st opinion in Mishmeres Shalom Kudinov 9:2; See Mishmeres Shalom Kudinov 9:1 that in his time many people followed this opinion and were not particular to say Shema on time] The Taz and M"A ibid negate this approach of the Kesef Mishneh and explain that the word Beshachbecha implies lying in bed, and hence the entire night is valid for the nighttime Shema, however, the term Ubikumecha implies the act of waking out of bed, which certainly has a time limit. In the words of the Taz ibid "I wonder at how a holy mouth can say such a thing, as certainly the Drasha of Chazal on Ubikumecha is a complete Biblical Drasha just like Ubishachbecha."
[207] Admur 58:3; Michaber 58:1; Rebbe Yehoshua in Mishneh Brachos 9b; It can be said up until <u>the end</u> of the three hours: Admur ibid; Rambam Shema 1:11; Hagahos Maimanis
The reason it may be recited up until three hours: As there are some people who are accustomed to awaken from bed at the end of the third hour of the day, such as the sons of kings and the like. [Admur ibid; Mishneh ibid]
[208] Admur ibid regarding short daylight hours of winter; Siddur Admur regarding early sunrise of summer
[209] See previous footnotes that the timespan is Biblical
[210] See Mishneh Brachos 1:2; Peri Chadash 58; P"M 58 M"Z 2; Mishmeres Shalom 9:2, brought next
Other opinions: Some Poskim rule that one who did not read the Shema on time is to read it after the time with the stipulation that if we rule like the opinion that the Biblical Mitzvah applies throughout the day, then he is intending to fulfill his Biblical command, and if not then his intent is to simply read from the Torah. [Mishmeres Shalom 9:2]
[211] Brachos 26a; Chagiga 9a
[212] Koheles 1:15
[213] Tanya Igeres Hateshuvah Chapter 1
[214] Mishmeres Shalom Kudinov 9:1
[215] Mishmeres Shalom Kudinov 9:1 in name of Kesav Yad of Rav Pinchas of Koretz, and with his own testimony of what he saw by the Baal Shem Tov; Nonetheless, in those times many people were accustomed not to read the Shema on time [i.e. Minhag Haolam] and they would mistakenly say that there is a Chassidic tradition to be allowed to do so. The Mishmeres Shalom ibid completely negates this, although in parentheses learns a Limud Zechus retroactively on what was done.

From when do the three hours begin?[216] The three hours begin from the start of the morning.[217] It is however disputed amongst the Poskim as to when the morning begins in this regard. Some Poskim[218] rule that the day begins from Alos Hashachar/Daybreak [and hence the morning Shema must be recited within three hours from daybreak].[219] [This approach is commonly known, and published, as the time of the Magen Avraham for the morning Shema.] Other Poskim[220] rule that in regard to the three-hour calculation, the day begins from sunrise, and hence the morning Shema may be recited until this time.[221] [This approach is commonly known, and published as the time of the Baal HaTanya and Gr"a.] Practically, much of Jewry is initially stringent to recite the Shema within the earlier timeframe [i.e. Zman Magen Avraham], although make sure to recite it within the later timeframe if that time already passed.[222] Some communities, however, are accustomed even initially to say Shema within the later time frame [i.e. Zman Baal Hatanya/Gr"a].[223] The Chabad custom follows the ruling of Admur in his Siddur, which extends the saying of Shema to the later timeframe, as rules the second opinion.[224] Nonetheless, even those who follow the Poskim who hold of the later time frame are to be careful to recite the Shema at least 45 minutes prior to its end time.[225] [Thus, in conclusion, even according to the Chabad custom to

---

[216] See Mishmeres Shalom Kudinov 9:1; Shiureiy Tziyon p. 75 footnote 16 and Glosses on Siddur of Rav Raskin 30 footnote 123; Piskeiy Teshuvos 58:2-3

[217] Admur 58:3; Siddur Admur and all Poskim in coming footnotes who hold of Alos or Neitz
Other opinions: Some Poskim rule the three hours are calculated from six hours past the Halachic midnight and not from morning. [See Pnei Yehoshua Likkutim on Brachos; Yaavetz in Mur Uketzia 1 and Lechem Shamayim Brachos 1:2; Shulchan Hatahor 58:1 and in Maaseh Oreg Brachos 1:2, and Otzer Hachaim Vaeschanan Mitzvah 421; See Minchas Elazar 1:69; Mishmeres Shalom Kudinov 9:1; Piskeiy Teshuvos 58:2]

[218] Admur 58:3 [unlike his ruling in the Siddur and 443:4; 459:10]; 89:1 regarding Davening; M"A 58:1 that regarding Shema, so applies according to all [See Machatzis Hashekel ibid; Degul Merivava 58; Levushei Serud ibid; Yad Efraim ibid]; Terumas Hadeshen 1; Yad Aaron 58; Elya Raba 58:2; Shalmei Tzibur p. 93; Chaim Sheol 2:38-Ayin; Chesed Lealafim 58:5; Ben Ish Chaiy Vayakhel 4 that so is main opinion; Kitzur SHU"A 17:1; Shesilei Zeisim 58:2; Kaf Hachaim 58:4; Tzemach Tzedek Chidushim 3 brings a proof for this opinion, unlike Admur in Siddur, however, see Igros Kodesh 10:294 that this may not be his actual opinion; M"B 58:4 brings both opinions of M"A and Gr"a without arbitration

[219] The reason: As Biblically one may begin reading the morning Shema from Alos Hashachar [Admur ibid], as some people already begin awakening at that time [Admur 58:2] [and hence the three-hour calculation begins from its start time].

[220] Siddur Admur in the section beginning "Zman Kerias Shema" who counts the three hours from sunrise [unlike his ruling in 58:3 and 89:1; See Shiureiy Tziyon p. 75 footnote 16 and Glosses on Siddur of Rav Raskin 30 footnote 123]; Admur 443:4 and 459:10 regarding the calculation of daytime that it is from sunrise to sunset; Shiltei Giborim on Mordechai Brachos 4:3; Minchas Kohen Mavo Hashemesh 2:6 in name of Rishonim; Levush 233:1 and 266:2; Tosafos Yom Tov Pesachim 3:2; Divrei Chamudos Brachos 4:14; Kneses Hagedola 58:8; Gr"a 459:5; Tzemach Tzedek Chidushim 3 that so is opinion of Admur in Siddur; Aruch Hashulchan 58:14; Igros Kodesh 10:294; Likkutei Sichos 29:378; Igros Moshe 1:24 "The Gr"a and Graz, are the main opinion regarding all matters."; Chazon Ish 13:4; Orchos Rabbeinu 1:52 in name of Chazon Ish; Teshuvos Vehanhagos 1:56 in name of Brisker Rav; See Pear Hador of Machon Yerushalayim Teshuvah 44 who proves this to be the opinion of the Rambam; M"B 58:4 brings both opinions of M"A and Gr"a without arbitration; See Piskeiy Teshuvos ibid footnote 22
The ruling of Admur in his Siddur: In the Siddur ibid, Admur does not explicitly state to count from sunrise [in contrast to his ruling in 58:3], but simply gives a calculation of when Shema must be recited by in the summer in Russia, and based on his calculation, it is understood that he held as a matter of fact that the counting begins from sunrise. He states there that in the sunrise is approximately $3^{1/2}$ hours after midnight, and a ¼ of the daytime at that time is 4 hours and 15 minutes, and thus the end time of Shema is 7:45 am. Now, this calculation that ¼ of the daytime is 4 hours and 15 minutes only makes sense if we count from sunrise to sunset, in which there are 17 hours in the Russian summer. If we were to count from Alos until Tzeis, a ¼ of the daytime would have more hours, and it would not be at 7:45 am. It would either be at 7:09 am [if we measure it based on a set 72 minutes] or would be at 6:00 am if measured based on distance of sun from horizon. [See Glosses on Siddur of Rav Raskin 30 footnote 127-128]

[221] The reason: Some explain that the original widespread calculation from Alos followed the accustomed practice to rule like Rabbeinu Tam regarding sunset. However, now that the practice has become like the Geonim, the above law has also changed to start counting the times from sunrise, as how can one consider after sunset to be part of the day hours if we rule that it is already Bein Hashmashos. [Shiureiy Tziyon p. 75 footnote 16; Yisrael Vehazmanim 1:36 that so agree majority of Poskim who wrote on this issue; Rav Raskin in gloss on Siddur footnote 123; See Divrei Nechemia 15]

[222] Chida in Chaim Sheol 2:38 that so is the widespread custom; M"B 58:4 concludes that Lechatchila there is no practical ramification, as one must say Shema as soon as possible upon awakening; Ben Ish Chaiy Vayakhel 4 that so is custom of Bagdad; Ashel Avraham Butchach 58 that in a time of need one may rely on the later opinion; Maharshag 1:38; Mishmeres Shalom Kudinov 9:1 concludes to suspect for all opinions; Sefer Bein Hashmashos of Rav Y.M. Tukichinsky that so is the custom in all Eretz Yisrael; Yisrael Vihazmanim 1:8 that so is the accepted custom amongst all Israel; Or Letziyon 2:6-1; Halichos Olam Vaeira 1:3 that so is the Sephardi custom for many generations; Orchos Rabbeinu 1:52 in name of Steipler; Halichos Shlomo 7:12

[223] Aruch Hashulchan 58:14 "*So is the main opinion and so is printed in the Luchos*"; Igros Moshe 1:24 "*The custom of most communities in Russia and Lita, as well as the custom of the Bnei Hayeshivos, is like the Gr"a and Graz, and so is the main opinion regarding all matters, and only select individuals were stringent in this.*"; Chazon Ish 13:4 that many follow the Gr"a even initially; Orchos Rabbeinu 1:52 in name of Chazon Ish that one may follow the Gr"a even initially

[224] Igros Kodesh 10:294; Likkutei Sichos 29:378

[225] Siddur Admur "*Therefore one must be careful to finish reading the Shema by 7:00 a.m. during the summer months [in Russia, in which the end time is at 7:45].*"; Directive of Rebbe Rashab to Rav Yaakov Landau even regarding Rabbinical maters, printed in Kovetz Yagdil Torah N.Y. Vol. 52 p. 150

follow the later timeframe [i.e. Zman Baal Hatanya], in actuality, it is to be said close to, and at times even earlier than, the early time frame [i.e. Zman Magen Avraham] in order to say it at least 45 minutes before the end time.]

How many minutes are contained in each hour?[226] The above [three] hours are counted as fluctuating hours [i.e. Zmaniyos] which depend on the amount of day light hours in that day. Every day, whether its daylight hours are long or short, contains 12 "hours" [and hence the definition of three hours is 3/12th of that day's daylight hours]. Accordingly, the end time of reciting the Shema is up until one quarter [1/4] into the daytime hours, whether the daytime hours is long or short.[227] Thus, one must be very careful in the winter days, which contains less daylight hours, to hurry and recite the Shema on time, as the ¼ of daytime hours is short.[228] [Likewise, in areas which experience a very early summer sunrise, such as Russia[229], one must be very careful especially in the summer to say Shema on time.[230]]

Summary:
The morning Kerias Shema must be said within three Zmaniyos hours from sunrise, which is known as the later time of Zman Baal HaTanya/Graz and Gr"a. This is the widespread Chassidic and Ashkenazi custom. Many, however, are stringent to initially recite it within three Zmaniyos hours from Alos Hashachar, which is known as the earlier time of Magen Avraham. This is the Sephardi custom. Even those who follow the former approach, as is the Chabad custom and custom of many, are to endeavor to always recite it at least 45 minutes before its end time, which often falls earlier than the end time of Magen Avraham.

Q&A

If one is asleep, should he be woken up in order to say Shema within the time of Magen Avraham?[231]
There is no obligation to do so unless one knows the person is always particular to say Shema before the time of Magen Avraham, or if there is suspicion that he may also miss the later time of the Baal Hatanya.

For those who follow the earlier approach of saying Shema within three hours from Alos Hashachar, when does Alos Hashachar begin?
There are various calculations and opinions for when the time of Alos Hashachar begins. The opinions

---

The reason: As the clocks are not all accurate, and this matter [of saying Shema on time] is a Biblical doubt [of which one is required to be stringent]. Likewise, it is improper to push oneself to the last minute. [Admur ibid in Siddur]

[226] Admur 58:3; Siddur Admur who writes "1/4 of the day"; Michaber 58:1 "1/4 of the day"; Rama 233:1 regarding Mincha; Rambam Pirush Hamishnayos Brachos 1:4; Teshuvas Harambam Pear Hador 44; Peri Chadash 58:2; Perisha 58:2; Shagas Aryeh 5, brought in Shaareiy Teshuvah 58:1; Chayeh Adam 21:3; Kitzur SHU"A 17:1; Peas Hashulchan that so is the custom amongst all Jewry; Mahariy Chagiz on in his Pirush Eitz Chaim on Mishnayos; Ben Ish Chaiy Vaeira 5; Kaf Hachaim 58:3; Hisorerus Teshuvah 1:34;

Other opinions: Some Poskim rule the three hours are always calculated as 60 minutes during all times of the year and does not fluctuate based on the number of daylight hours in that day. [Pnei Yehoshua Likkutim on Brachos; Yaavetz in Mur Uketzia 1 and Lechem Shamayim Brachos 1:2; Shulchan Hatahor 58:1 and in Maaseh Oreg Brachos 1:2, and Otzer Hachaim Vaeschanan Mitzvah 421; See Minchas Elazar 1:69; Mishmeres Shalom Kudinov 9:1; Kuntrus Alah Letrufa; Eretz Tzvi Likkutim 1:19 in name of the Chozeh Milublin that one may be lenient like this opinion if he is sick; Rav Chaim Zonnenfeld 23; Divrei Yatziv Likkutim 14; Piskeiy Teshuvos 58:2] The calculation is done as follows: There are exactly 12 sixty minute hours between midnight and midday on every day, six of those hours are part of the nighttime, and one thus adds three hours past the six hours, and by the end of that time one is to recite the Shema. Accordingly, the Shema may always be recited up until nine 60-minute hours from midnight. While during the summer months this gives a significant delay to the end time of Shema, in the winter it often ends earlier than the Zmaniyos times. [Piskeiy Teshuvos ibid footnote 20] There is no source, however, based on this opinion to say that the end time of Shema is always at 9:00 am, as not always is the real midnight at 12:00. [Mishmeres Shalom Kudinov 9 mentions 9:00 accoridng to this opinion, However, see Minchas Elazar ibid; Piskeiy Teshuvos ibid] Practically, all the Poskim ibid negate this approach and it may not be relied upon. Nevertheless, in a time of need, such as one already missed the times of M"A and Admur, then he is at the very list to say it within the time held by this opinion. [Piskeiy Teshuvos ibid]

[227] Admur ibid; Siddur Admur; Michaber ibid

[228] Admur ibid; Taz 58:1; Beis Yosef 58 in name of Mahariy Abuhav; Soles Belula 58:1; Ateres Zekeinim 58:1; Elya Raba 58:2; Chesed Lealafim 58:5; Siddur Beis Oved; Kaf Hachaim 58:5

[229] During summer in time in many parts of Russia and surrounding vicinities sunrise is approximately 3.5 hours after midnight, and ¼ of the daylight hours is four hours and 15 minutes. Accordingly, it ends up that the end time of Shema is at 7:45 AM. [Siddur Admur]

[230] Siddur Admur; M"B 58:5

[231] Teshuvos Vehanhagos 2:50; Piskeiy Teshuvos 58:3

fluctuate between a maximum of two fluctuating hours before sunrise to a minimum of 72 fluctuating minutes before sunrise.[232] Practically, one is to be stringent like all opinions.[233] Thus, regarding the end time of Shema, one is to be stringent to calculate Alos Hashachar as 90 fluctuating[234] minutes before sunrise.[235] Nonetheless, the widespread custom in the Diaspora is to calculate it as 72 fluctuating minutes before sunrise.[236]

Which Zmanim calendar should I use? Understanding the Zmanim calendars for the end time of Shema:
Based on all the above, it is evident that many approaches exist regarding the end time of the morning Shema. It is thus imperative that each individual have access to a Zmanim calendar that writes the opinion that he follows. Likewise, being that the times fluctuate based on sunrise or daybreak [depending on opinion] it is imperative that one have a calendar that shows the times of the opinion he follows **for his city**. The standard practice of most calendars is to show both the times of Magen Avraham and Baal Hatanya, however, as discussed above, there are a number of possible end times according to the Magen Avraham, and hence one is to have chart that offers the opinion that one follows.

---

[232] Opinion of Shulchan Aruch and majority of Poskim-72 minutes: Some Poskim rule Alos Hashachar begins **72 minutes** prior to sunrise. [Rashal Pesachim 2a; Minchas Kohen 2/6; M"A 89/2; Levush 261 and 459; Admur in 89/1, 184/3, and 261/5; Derech Hachaim; M"B 89 in Biur Halacha "Veim"; 58 Biur Halacha "Kemo"; and chapters: 92; 163; 235; 261; 459] This is based on the calculation that there are 18 minutes per Mil [as rules Terumos Hadeshen 123; Michaber 459/2; Yoreh Deah 69/6; Rama 261/1; Admur in 89/1, 184/3, and 261/5] and there are 4 Mil between Alos and Neitz [as rules Rebbe Yehuda in Pesachim 93b]
Opinion of some Achronim-90 minutes: Some Poskim rule Alos Hashachar begins **90 minutes** prior to sunrise. [Gr"a 459; Chok Yaakov 459/10; Chasam Sofer in glosses 89] This is based on the calculation that there are 22.5 minutes per Mil [as rules Maharil in Hilchos Pesach] and there are 4 Mil between Alos and Neitz [as rules Rebbe Yehuda in Pesachim 93b]
Rulings of Admur: Admur wrote different calculations regarding Alos Hashachar throughout the Shulchan Aruch, Siddur and Tanya. This created confusion as to Admur's opinion as to the time of Alos Hashachar. From 89:1, 184:3, and 261:5 it is calculated that Alos Hashachar is 72 minutes before sunrise, or possibly 96 minutes. In 249:3, 459:10 and the Siddur [Seder Hachnasas Shabbos] it can be calculated that Alos Hashachar is 96 minutes or 120 minutes before sunrise. From the time of Alos mentioned in the Siddur regarding Sefiras Haomer it is possible to calculate it as 72 or 120 minutes.
Opinion of Admur according to the Gra"ch Naah-Two fluctuating hours: Rav Avraham Chaim Naah ruled that according to Admur, Alos Hashachar begins **two fluctuating** hours prior to sunrise. [Shiureiy Tziyon 37; Yagdil Torah Tzemach Tzedek 23 p. 23] The calculation is as follows: There are 5 Mil between Alos and Neitz [as rules Ula in Pesachim 93b]. Each Mil is 24 minutes [as rules Rambam in Pirush Hamishnayos Pesachim 3/2]. Thus 24 minutes per Mil x 5 Mil between Alos and Neitz equals 120 minutes. [This follows the ruling of Admur in 249/3; 459/10 and Siddur and so rules regarding 24 minutes per Mil: Peri Chadash Y.D. 69/26; Kitzur SHU"A 36/11. However, in 89/1 and 261/5 Admur rules that there is only **4** Mil between Alos and sunrise, hence there is only 96 minutes between Alos and sunrise. As well, although in 459/10 Admur rules that the day begins from sunrise and ends by sunset, in 89/1 he rules that it begins from Alos until nightfall. Nevertheless, the final ruling of Admur follows the ruling of the Siddur in which Admur rules like in 459/10.]
Other opinions amongst Chabad Rabbanim: See article of Rav Raskin in Siddur Miluim 27 for a summary of opinions of Chabad Rabbanim regarding the time of Alos Hashachar according to Admur. The opinions vary between 120 minutes, 72 minutes, 90 minutes and 96 minutes.
[233] Shiureiy Tziyon ibid
[234] Definition of fluctuating minutes: This means that the hours fluctuate in the winter and summer. Some Poskim rule this means it fluctuates in terms of Zmaniyos, meaning that it depends on the number of hours in the day. Thus, in the summer, the hours will be longer [between 120-150 minutes for two hours] while in the winter they will be shorter [between 90-120 minutes for two hours]. [So rules Minchas Cohen 2:6; Rama 233; Peri Chadash 58] However the Alter Rebbe and Gr"a both rule that it follows not the amount of hours in the day but rather the degree of distance of the sun from the horizon. [Admur in Seder Hachnasas Shabbos; Gr"a in 261; See Shut Maharshag 2:34 quoted in Piskeiy Teshuvos 89:2 footnote 59 that this is the way we rule.] Thus, those who hold that Alos is 72 minutes it ends up being in Tishrei and Nissan 16.1 degrees from the horizon and the amount of time it takes the sun to travel to the horizon fluctuates between winter and summer. [See Piskeiy Teshuvos 89:2] According to Admur however who holds of 120 minutes, this would be when the sun is 26 degrees below the horizon.
Other opinions: Some Poskim rule we always measure the hours as set hours and hence there will always be only 120:90:72 minutes between Alos and sunrise at all times. [Admur 89:1; Birkeiy Yosef 261:1; Peri Megadim 261 A"A 9; Derech Hachaim; Siddur Yaavetz; Machatzis Hashekel 235:3]
[235] See Piskeiy Teshuvos 58:3 that the custom in Eretz Yisrael, based on the calendar of Rav Tukichinsky, is to calculate Alos as 90 minutes before sunrise, and Tzeis Hakochavim as 90 minutes after sunset, and then divide those hours by 12 and add three of those hours to the 90 minute Alos. [See Piskeiy Teshuvos ibid footnote 28] On the other hand, a study of the older calendars predating the calendar of Rav Tukichinsky show that they calculated Tzeis Hakochavim as rule the Geonim, which is 13.5 minutes after sunset, and hence their end time of Shema is 18 minutes earlier than the calendars of Rav Tukichinsky. Practically, so is the custom of the Sephardim even today. [See Piskeiy Teshuvos ibid footnote 32]
[236] Piskeiy Teshuvos ibid

------------------Shemoneh Esrei----------------
17. What is one to do if he is in unsure as to which blessing in Shemoneh Esrei he is holding by?[237]

A. Introduction:
In the event that one is unsure as to which blessing in Shemoneh Esrei he is currently holding in, one enters into a difficult Halacha dilemma as to how he should proceed. On the one hand, we have a rule that whenever one is in doubt if he said a blessing, he may not repeat it[238], as Safek Brachos Lihakel, and accordingly, we should rule that he may only continue from a blessing which he knows for certain he has not yet said. On the other hand, one is also required to recite all the blessings of Shemoneh Esrei, and one who skips even one blessing in Shemoneh Esrei is not Yotzei.[239] Thus, if we make him skip the questionable blessings which perhaps he already said, it would render all of his other blessings in vain. Practically, the Poskim debate the proper directive in this issue, as we will now explain.

B. The ruling:
By the first three and last three blessings:[240] If one is unsure as to which blessing in Shemoneh Esrei he is currently up to within the first three blessings or the last three blessings of Shemoneh Esrei, then he is to return to the first blessing of that set and repeat from there. Thus, if he is unsure as to whether he has said the 1st blessing of Magen Avraham, or the 2nd blessing of Michayeh Meisim, or the 3rd blessing of Hakeil Hakadosh, then he is to restart from the beginning of Shemoneh Esrei, from the first blessing of Magen Avraham. If he is unsure as to whether he has said the 17th blessing of Avoda [i.e. Ritzei], or the 18th blessing of Hoda'h, or the 19th blessing of Sim Shalom, then he is to repeat from Ritzei.[241]

By the middle blessings: If one for certain said the first three blessings brought above, but is unsure as to which of the middle blessings in Shemoneh Esrei he is currently up to, then some Poskim[242] rule that he is to skip all the blessings of which he has doubt, and continue Davening only from the blessing that he knows for certain that he did not say.[243] Majority of Poskim[244], however, rule that he must repeat all the blessings of which there is doubt as to whether they were said, and he thus continues Davening from the last blessing that he knows for certain that he said.[245] [Practically, while some Poskim[246] offer various

---

[237] See Piskeiy Teshuvos 119:5; See regarding if one is in doubt if he said Shemoneh Esrei at all, that he should repeat it as a Nedava with a Tnaiy: Admur and Michaber 107:1; Rebbe Yochanon in Brachos 21a

[238] See Michaber 209:3 *"All blessings of which one is in doubt if he said them or not, he is not to recite them"*

[239] See Admur 104:4; 119:4; Michaber 119:2; Rambam Tefila 10:4; Rav Assi in Brachos 34a

[240] Chayeh Adam 24:21; Ben Ish Chaiy Mishpatim 10 regarding first three blessings

[241] The reason: The reason for this is because this doubt is considered a mistake in the blessing, and whenever a mistake is made within the first or last three blessings, we require one to repeat, just as we rule regarding Mashiv Haruach [for Nussach Ashkenaz], Yaaleh Veyavo, Hamelech Hakadosh and so on.

[242] Chayeh Adam ibid, based on Rama 422:1 regarding Yaaleh Veyavo; Ashel Avraham Butchach 119; Tehila Ledavid 108:16; Maharam Arik in Hagahos Minchas Pitim on 119

[243] The reason: One cannot repeat the blessing, as Safek Brachos Lihakel. Likewise, one cannot repeat it as a Nedava, as we do not make a prayer a partial Nedava. [See Admur 107:2; Michaber 107:1; Shmuel in Brachos 21a] A proof for this can be brought from the Rama regarding one who is in doubt if he said Yaaleh Veyavo in Rosh Chodesh, that he does not repeat it and rather continues Shemoneh Esrei. [Rama 422:1; Kol Bo 11] Thus, from this we can deduce that whenever one is in doubt if he said a blessing, the Sages did not require one to repeat it, and the Shemoneh Esrei nevertheless remains valid. [Nishmas Adam on Chayeh Adam ibid] A further proof for this approach can be brought from the Poskim who rule that a skipped blessing only invalidates Shemoneh Esrei if one could have said it. If, however, one does not know all of the blessings, then he is to only say the blessing that he knows. [see Admur ibid; 104:4 in parentheses; M"A 593:2 (implication from Michaber and Braisa); Birchas Habayis 40:29; M"B 593:2] Thus, likewise here, since one is in doubt as if he said the blessing, and he cannot repeat it due to Safek, he may nevertheless continue his prayer. [Ashel Avraham ibid; Tehila Ledavid ibid]

[244] Tzemach Tzedek O.C. 3 letter 9 *"In Shemoneh Esrei, one who is in doubt if he said a certain blessing or did not yet say it, seemingly he may rely on the above opinion and repeat the blessing."*; Implication of Yerushalmi Brachos 5:3 and Tzelach Brachos 29b; Chesed Lealafim 107:1; Ben Ish Chaiy Mishpatim 10; Pischeiy Teshuvah 119; Orchos Chaim Spinka 119:4; Sdei Chemed in Michtav Lichizkiyahu 10:6; Birchas Habayis 40:26; Eretz Tzevi 3 Siach Hasadeh Birchas Hashem 6; Kaf Hachaim 119:20; Kehilas Yaakov Brachos 13 [of Steipler]; Orchos Rabbeinu 3:107 that so ruled Chazon Ish; M"B 188:6 in Biur Halacha "Lachzor" regarding Birchas Hamazon

[245] The reason: As one does not fulfill his obligation of Shemoneh Esrei if he skips a blessing. [Admur 104:4; 119:4; Michaber 119:2; Rambam Tefila 10:4; Rav Assi in Brachos 34a] and hence one is required to repeat from the last blessing that he knows for certain that he said in order not to place his remaining blessings in jeopardy of being in vain. This is not considered a blessing in vain, as some Poskim rule that one may choose to repeat a blessing in order to escape a doubt and one may rely on this ruling in such a case. [Tzemach Tzedek ibid]

[246] Some of the suggested methods of circumventing the dispute: 1) One is to repeat the questionable blessings in his mind. [Ashel Avraham Butchach 582:1; Minchas Yitzchak 5:2 based on Maharam Shick 42, that in a case of need, we rely on the Rambam who rules thought suffices; See also Admur 62:3] 2) Delay continuing Shemoneh Esrei until the Chazan says Chazaras Hashatz and have in mind to be Yotzei with him all the blessings until one reaches the blessing he knows for certain that he did not say. [Piskeiy Teshuvos ibid] 3) To continue until Shomeiah Tefila and repeat all the questionable blessings there without a Chasima. [Me'at Mayim 9, based on Peri Chadash and Biur Halacha 117 "Veim Lo

methods of circumventing the above debate [as stated in the footnote], the final ruling follows the latter opinion, and that one may repeat all the questionable blessings.²⁴⁷ This certainly applies to Chabad Chassidim who follow the rulings of the Tzemach Tzedek, who holds of the latter view.]

The definition of a doubt:²⁴⁸ It is only considered a doubt if upon returning one's concentration to the prayer, he does not remember the words he was saying, or if he remembers the last words but is unsure as to which blessing the words he said belongs to [i.e. he said Baruch Ata Hashem and then realized he does not know what blessing he is up to]. If, however, he knows what words he was saying upon returning his concentration to the prayer, then he is to continue from those words even if he does not have any recollection of saying any of the words or blessings that precede those words.

> **Summary:**
> If one is unsure as to which blessing in Shemoneh Esrei he is currently up to, then if the doubt occurs within the first three blessings, or the last three blessings, of Shemoneh Esrei, then he is to return to the first blessing of that set and repeat from there. If one certainly has said the first three blessings, but is unsure as to which of the middle blessings in Shemoneh Esrei he is currently holding in, then he is to repeat from after the last blessing that he knows for certain that he said.

18. What is one to do if he heard Kaddish, Kedusha, Barchu or Modim in middle of Shemoneh Esrei:²⁴⁹

It is forbidden to answer for Kaddish, Barchu²⁵⁰, or Kedusha²⁵¹ in the midst of Shemoneh Esrei.²⁵² Rather, one is to [stop reciting Shemoneh Esrei and] remain silent [and listen] and concentrate to the words of the Chazan.²⁵³ Doing so is considered as if one is answering the words, as listening is like answering in all

---

Shal"] Practically, it is better not to rely on the above suggestions, as practically the main Halacha is that one does not fulfill his obligation in such a case, and that one is required to repeat the blessings, as rule majority of Poskim.

Repeating the questionable blessings with a Tnaiy Nedava: The Poskim rule regarding if one is in doubt if he said Shemoneh Esrei at all, that he should repeat it as a Nedava with a Tnaiy. [Admur and Michaber 107:1; Rebbe Yochanon in Brachos 21a] This would imply that there exists a simple solution to our above case, which is directed in Shulchan Aruch, that if one is in doubt regarding the blessing that he is holding, he should repeat from that blessing with a stipulation at heart, that if he did not say it, the blessing is being said out of obligation, and if he did say it, then he is repeating it as a Nedava, which is allowed. However, in truth, this solution is incorrect, as the concept of a Nedava only applies by a full Shemoneh Esrei prayer, however within a single prayer, it must either be entirely a Nedava or entirely an obligation, and not a mixture of both, in which some blessings are said as a Nedava and others as an obligation. Accordingly, one this solution does not escape the worry of a blessing in vain, according to the stringent opinion. [See Nishmas Adam 24:21]

²⁴⁷ As so rule the majority of Poskim
²⁴⁸ See Chesed Lealafim 107:1; Yifei Laleiv 118:5; Beis Oveid 159; Kaf Hachaim 119:20; Piskeiy Teshuvos ibid footnote 34; So rule Poskim regarding Shema [See Admur 64:4; Michaber 64:3-4; Brachos 16a]
²⁴⁹ Admur 104:5; Michaber 104:7; Tur 104:7
²⁵⁰ Admur ibid; M"B 104:26; Kitzur SHU"A 18:4; Chesed Lealafim 104:7; Kaf Hachaim 104:37
²⁵¹ This is with exception to the case in which he began Shemoneh Esrei together with the Chazan, as explained in 109:3, or if he did not begin together with the Chazan, although he reached Ata Kadosh just as the Minyan began saying Kedusha, as explained in Admur 109:5
²⁵² Admur ibid; Michaber ibid; Brachos 21b

Other opinions in Talmud: Some opinions rule that while one does not make an interval for Kedusha or Modim, one is to stop to answer Amein Yihei Shmei Raba. [Students of Rebbe Yochanon in Brachos ibid] We do not rule like this opinion. [Brachos ibid]

²⁵³ Admur ibid; Michaber ibid; Tur ibid in name of Rabbeinu Chananel; Tosafos Brachos ibid that so is the custom "Vegadol Haminhag"; Rashi Sukkah 38b; Bahag Brachos ibid; Haeshkol p. 31 in name Rav Haiy Gaon; Ran 19b; Ravayah; Bach 104 in name of Mordechai and that so is custom; Levush 104; Soles Belula 104:2; Chayeh Adam 25:10; Beis Oved 57; Kitzur SHU"A 18:14; Ben Ish Chaiy Mishpatim 5; Kaf Hachaim 104:36

Other opinions: Some Poskim rule one is to continue Davening, as hearing is like answering, and is considered a Hefsek. [2ⁿᵈ opinion in Tur ibid in name of Rabbeinu Tam and Ri; Tosafos Brachos ibid in name of Rabbeinu Tam and Ri and Geonim; Hagahos Maimanis Tefila 10; The Rosh Brachos 18 and Rabbeinu Yona 13b bring both opinions and give no arbitration; See Beis Yosef 104:7] Other Poskim rule that although it is not considered a Hefsek, one is not Yotzei, being that he is not allowed to speak, and hence there is no point of stopping to listen. [Darkei Moshe 104:1 in name of the Iggur that the custom of the Ashkenazi Rabbeim is not to stop and listen; Beis Yosef 25 in name of Rashba and Iggur; Shagas Aryeh 6 in name of Shivlei Haleket; Abudarham, brought in Erech Hashulchan 104:3 and 55:1; See P"M 104 A"A 7] Due to the above opinions, Kaf Hachaim ibid concludes that if stopping to listen will ruin one's concentration of the prayer, or if he anyways cannot hear the Chazan properly, then one may continue his Davening and rely on the other opinions. See Biur Halacha 104 "Keoneh"; Siach Hasadeh; Shaagas Aryeh 6; Mahariy Asad 2:259; Maharash Engel 8:146; Har Tzevi 1:57-59; Piskeiy Teshuvos 104:15

The first blessing: The above ruling applies even if one is in the first blessing of Magen Avraham. [Setimas Kol Haposkim; Halichos Shlomo 8 footnote 57 in name of Rav SZ"A, unlike Teshuvos Vehanhagos 1:76, based on Biur Halacha 101 in name of Rashba]

places [of Halacha].²⁵⁴ [Accordingly, there is no need to participate in another Minyan for the sake of answering Kedusha. Kaddish or Barchu.²⁵⁵ The above law only applies Bedieved, if one already began Shemoneh Esrei. However, initially one may not begin Shemoneh Esrei until after Kedusha and Kaddish are recited, in order so he can verbalize the words, unless one has already recited Goal Yisrael by Shacharis, or Zman Tefila will pass, or one has already heard Kedusha.²⁵⁶]

Until when is one to remain silent by Kaddish:²⁵⁷ When the Chazan [or other individual saying Kaddish] reaches the words Yisbareich and Yishtabach, he may return to his Davening.

Bowing by Modim and Barchu:²⁵⁸ [Although one is prohibited from saying the words of Modim Derabanan in middle of Shemoneh Esrei, nevertheless] he is to bow down when the Chazan reaches Modim, if he is in the middle of a blessing.²⁵⁹ If, however, he is holding in the beginning or end of a blessing, then he is not to bow.²⁶⁰ [Seemingly, there is no need for him to remain silent while the Modim is said, and he may continue Davening. Some Poskim²⁶¹ rule that the above rule likewise applies for Barchu, that if one hears Barchu in the midst of Shemoneh Esrei, then he is to slightly bow if he is in the middle of a blessing.]

Summary:
One who hears Kaddish, Kedusha or Barchu in the midst of Shemoneh Esrei is to remain silent and concentrate on the words of the Chazan. By Kaddish, he may continue Davening upon the Chazzan reaching the words Yisbareich. By Modim, one is to bow if he is in the middle of a blessing, as opposed to the beginning or end.

Q&A

May one answer Kedusha, or Amein Yehei Shmei Raba, in middle of Shema Koleinu?²⁶²
No.²⁶³

Until what part of Kedusha is one to remain silent?²⁶⁴
One is to remain silent and concentrate until the Chazan finishes reciting the last stanza of Yimloch in Kedusha.²⁶⁵ It is not necessary to remain silent until Hakeil Hakadosh.²⁶⁶

---

²⁵⁴ Admur ibid; See Toras Yekusiel 36 in name of Chasam Sofer and Maggid of Mezritch that this is considered as if one actually said the words in light of the saying of the Sages [Kiddushin 40a] that a good thought Hashem considers like action; See Piskeiy Teshuvos 104:15
The reason this is not considered a Hefsek: Nonetheless, this is not considered a Hefsek in Shemoneh Esrei since he is not verbalizing the words with his mouth. [Admur ibid] See, however, other opinions in previous footnote.
Other opinions: See other opinions in previous footnote that one is not Yotzei.
²⁵⁵ Halichos Shlomo 8:37; Piskeiy Teshuvos 104:15
²⁵⁶ See Admur 109:1-3; M"A 109:3 and 9; Michaber and Rama 109:1; Rebbe Yehoshua Ben levi Brachos 21b; Tosafos Sukkah 38b; Semak 11; Hagahos Maimanis Tefila 10; Yerushalmi Brachos 4:6; Terumas Hadeshen 11; Regarding starting Shemoneh Esrei together with the Shemoneh Esrei: See Admur 109:3; Levushei Serud 109; Misgeres Hashulchan 20:4
The reason: As it is a Mitzvah Min Hamuvchar to answer to the Chazan. [See Tosafos ibid; Admur ibid]
²⁵⁷ Admur ibid; M"A 104:7; Bahag ibid; M"B 104:26
Other opinions: Some Poskim rule one is to stop and listen until the end of Demarian Bealma. [Machatzis Hashekel on M"A ibid, in his understanding of M"A; Kaf Hachaim 104:38 that so is to be followed by those who rule like the Arizal and answer Kaddish until Demaran Bealma; Az Nidbaru 3:67; Piskeiy Teshuvos 104:13]
²⁵⁸ Admur 109:2; 127:1 *"Even an individual who is in middle of Shemoneh Esrei is required to bow with the Chazan if he is holding in middle of a blessing"*; Michaber 109:1; Rosh Brachos 3:18; Rabbeinu Tam Tosafos Brachos 21a
²⁵⁹ Admur ibid; Tur 127
The reason: As it is permitted to bow in the middle of any of the blessings of Shemoneh Esrei [Admur 109:2; 113:1; Michaber 113:1; Tosafus Brachos 21b; Rosh Brachos 18] and thus he is required to bow in such a case in order so he does not appear like a heretic, who denies the Being that his friends are bowing to. [Admur 127:1]
²⁶⁰ Admur 109:2; 113:1; 127:1; Michaber 113:1; Brachos 34a; Tosafus Brachos ibid; Taz 113:1
²⁶¹ Toras Chaim Sofer 109:2; Piskeiy Teshuvos ibid; See Biur Halacha 113:3 that so is the custom to slightly bow by Barchu
²⁶² Igros Kodesh 8:339 [printed in Shulchan Menachem 1:]; Imrei Noam Brachos 4b in name of Gr"a; Ashel Avraham Butchach 104; Afikei Maginim 119:2; Einayim Lamishpat Brachos 21b; Dvar Yehoshua 3:68; Tzitz Eliezer 8:10; Yabia Omer 5:13; Tzidkas Tzadik in end in name of Rav Chaim Berlin; Piskeiy Teshuvos 104:13
Other opinions: Some Poskim rule one may recite Amen Yihei Shmei Raba in Shomeia Tefila. [Bnei Levi 6; Toldas Zev Brachos 21b]
²⁶³ The reason: As answering a Davar Shebekedusha is not considered a personal request. [Poskim ibid; Implication of Peri Chadash, Biur Hagr"a and Birkeiy Yosef in 122]
²⁶⁴ Piskeiy Teshuvos 104:13

<u>On Shabbos/Yom Tov:</u>[267] It is not necessary for one to remain silent while the additional parts of Kedusha are said on Shabbos and Yom Tov, and one may continue Davening while it is recited.

Is one who is in the middle of Shemoneh Esrei to lift his feet by Kedusha as is normally done?[268]
Some Poskim[269] rule that one is to lift his feet by the relevant stanzas of Kadosh, Baruch and Yimloch even if he is in middle of Shemoneh Esrei and thus cannot say the words. Other Poskim[270], however, discourage one from doing so.

Is one who is in the middle of Shemoneh Esrei to lift his eyes towards heaven by the stanza of Kadosh?[271]
Seemingly, one may, and should, do so.

What is one to do by Birchas Kohanim [i.e. Nesias Kapayim] if he is in the middle of Shemoneh Esrei?[272]
If the Kohanim are reciting Birchas Kohanim while one is in the midst of Shemoneh Esrei, then he may choose to remain silent and listen to their words in-between the blessings, although if he wishes he may continue his Davening.[273] If he is holding together with the Chazan before Sim Shalom, then some Poskim[274] rule that he is to stop and listen and even answer Amen to the blessings. Nonetheless, if one is in front of the Kohanim, he is not to proceed in front of them.[275]

What is one to do if he is in middle of Shemoneh Esrei, and the congregation began to read Kerias Hatorah?
See Halacha 20!

What is one to do if he hears Kiddush or Havdalah in middle of Shemoneh Esrei?
Initially, he is to continue Davening as usual, and ignore the Kiddush or Havdalah.[276] Nonetheless, if one went ahead and stopped and listened, then if he intended to fulfill his obligation upon hearing it, then some Poskim[277] rule he fulfills his obligation.

---

[265] Aruch Hashulchan 104:13; Chayeh Adam 25:6; Halichos Shlomo 8:37; See Shulchan Shlomo 104:4 and Piskeiy Teshuvos ibid that one is to remain silent for whatever one is allowed to answer during Shema
[266] See Az Nidbaru 2:60; 3:67
[267] Halichos Shlomo ibid; Shevet Hakehasi 4:35; Piskeiy Teshuvos ibid
[268] Piskeiy Teshuvos 104:13
[269] Perisha 109:1; Gloss of Rav Akiva Eiger 109:1; Makor Chaim of Chavos Yair 104:7 and 109:1; Mahariy Asad E.H. 259
[270] Kapos Temarim Sukkah 38b; Kaf Hachaim [Falagi] 15:54; Yabia Omer 6:16; Az Nidbaru 2:10
[271] Piskeiy Teshuvos ibid
[272] See Piskeiy Teshuvos 104:15
[273] Igros Moshe 4:21; 5:20-23; Yabia Omer 7:12; Teshuvos Vehanhagos 1:77; 3:44; Piskeiy Teshuvos 128:50; 104:15
[274] Teshuvah of Avraham son of Rambam, brought in Maaseh Rokeiach; Implication of P"M 128 M"Z 14; Aruch Hashulchan 109:11; Igros Moshe 4:21; Or Letziyon 2:8; Yabia Omer 8:13; Tzitz Eliezer 13:31; Az Nidbaru 1:85; 11:36; 12:28; Teshuvos Vehanhagos 1:77; 3:44; Shevet Halevi 3:15; Piskeiy Teshuvos 128:50; 104:15
[275] Igros Moshe 4:21; Piskeiy Teshuvos 128:50 footnote 235
[276] Har Tzevi 1:57-59; Shevet Hakehasi 3:51; Piskeiy Teshuvos 104:15
[277] Shevet Hakehasi 3:51 based on Shaagas Aryeh 6; Piskeiy Teshuvos ibid footnote 110

------------------Aleinu Leshabeiach----------------

19. Aleinu Leshabeiach-The origin & Purpose of the prayer:

A. The origin of the prayer:[278]

The paragraph of Aleinu:[279] The first paragraph of the prayer of Aleinu was instituted by Yehoshua Ben Nun. Yehoshua instituted this prayer during the conquest of the city of Yericho. Yehoshua left a hint of his name within the prayer, as the first letter of the word Aleinu is an Ayin, the first letter of the words Shelo Sam is a Shin, the first letter of the words Venachnu Korim is a Vav, and the first letter of the words Hu Elokeinu is a Hei, hence spelling out the word Hosheia.

The paragraph of Al Kein:[280] The second paragraph of Aleinu, beginning from Al Kein was instituted by Achan, who was infamously known for having stolen the spoils of war from the city of Yericho after it was conquered. Achan repented for his sin and recited the prayer of Al Kein, expressing his hope that idolatry would be abolished from the lands, and the name of G-d spread to the masses. He left an imprint of his name within the prayer, as the first letters of the first three words "על כן נקוה" spell out the word Achan.

The institution to read it at the end of Davening:[281] Rebbe Yochanan Ben Zakaiy instituted to recite the prayer of Aleinu each day after Davening.

B. The purpose and greatness of the prayer:

Instill belief of G-d in our hearts:[282] The purpose of the prayer of Aleinu Leshabeiach is to instill within our hearts, prior to returning home from Shul, the unity of Hashem and the belief that Hashem will destroy the idols from the land in order to penetrate the belief of G-d into the world. This prayer is recited at the end of Davening, prior to leaving to work, in order so we remember throughout our workday, and dealings with the gentiles, that our success is not the work of a foreign G-d, and in order to protect us from having sinful thoughts.

Protect the G-dliness drawn down during Davening:[283] According to Kabbalah of the Arizal, the purpose of the prayer of Aleinu Leshabeiach is as follows: Through prayer we drew down Divine light into the worlds. This G-dly light is meant to be used for matters of goodness and holiness by the creations of the worlds, although it is possible to be used to fuel and nurture the forces of evil. For this reason, we recite several prayers at the conclusion of Davening in order to thwart any attempt of the side of impurity from receiving nurture from the G-dliness drawn down. The prayer of Pitum Haketores banishes all evil forces from the vicinity of the Divine light while the prayer of Aleinu brings a protective coating of G-dliness [i.e. Or Makif] to this Divine light which prevents the approach of any evil forces. Thus, the prayer of Aleinu Lishabeiach breaks the Kelipos and causes them to be subjugated to holiness.

The Heavenly court listens to the prayer:[284] At the time that the prayer of Aleinu is recited, all the legions in heaven hear the prayer and Hashem stands with His Heavenly court and they recite in unison "Praised is the nation that so is to them."

Segula for Mageifa:[285] The recital of Aleinu Leshabeiach has the power to save one from epidemics.

---

[278] Shaar Hakolel 1:34-35; See Yesod Veshoresh Havoda 5:10;
[279] Kol Bo 16 Laws of Aleinu Leshabeiach; Shelah Hakadosh in Emek Habracha Tefila 40; Shaar Hakolel ibid
[280] Shaar Hakolel ibid
[281] Rav Haiy Gaon; Avodas Hakodesh of Chida 35; Shaar Hakolel ibid; See also Peri Eitz Chaim Shaar Kerias Sefer Torah 6; Shaar Hakavanos
[282] Bach 133
[283] Siddur Yaavetz; Yesod Veshoresh Havoda 5:10; Kaf Hachaim 622:6
[284] M"B 132:8 in name of Mateh Moshe
[285] Shaar Hakolel 1:34

20. Saying Aleinu Leshabeiach together with the congregation:[286]

When the congregation recites Aleinu Leshabeiach, one is to say it together with them.[287] This applies even if one has already Davened, and just happened to walk into Shul at the time the congregation is reciting Aleinu.[288] It likewise applies if he was already in Shul and is in the midst of reciting supplications or verses, in an area that it is permitted for him to stop.[289]

Past Baruch Sheamar:[290] If one is in the midst of Davening, past Baruch Sheamar, he is not to recite Aleinu together with the congregation. [Nevertheless, he is to stand up and bow upon the congregation reciting the words of "Veanachnu Korim", as explained next.]

Bowing together with the congregation:[291] If for whatever reason one is not reciting Aleinu Leshabeiach together with the congregation [such as if he is in an area of Davening in which an interruption may not be made, as stated above] he is nevertheless to [stand up and] bow, upon the congregation reciting the words of "Veanachnu Korim".

Q&A
If one is after Shemoneh Esrei, prior to Aleinu, and the congregation has already reached Aleinu Leshabeiach, is he to stop in middle and recite Aleinu together with the congregation?[292]

> Example: One is in the midst of Uva Letziyon and the congregation is saying Aleinu, must he stop and say Aleinu together with the congregation? This can occur in the event that the Chazan is Davening a quicker pace than oneself, or if one finished Shemoneh Esrei later than the congregation, or one is Davening in a Nussach Ashkenaz Shul which recites Aleinu immediately after Uva Letziyon.

---

[286] Admur 65:2 regarding Shema, Ashreiy and *"the same applies to **any other matter** that the congregation is reciting, one is to read together with the congregation due to Derech Eretz"*; M"A 65:3; Shivlei Haleket 44; Elya Raba 65:2 and 237:4; Soles Belula 65:3; Chesed Lealafim 65:2; Machatzis Hashekel 65:3 "The same applies for Aleinu Leshabeiach"; M"B 65:9 "such as Tehila Ledavid **or Aleinu**"; Ketzos Hashulchan 13:6; Kaf Hachaim 65:4

Background: This concept of saying Aleinu together with the congregation is not explicitly mentioned in earlier Poskim, prior to the Machatzis Hashekel, although is self-understood from the wording of Admur and M"A ibid which state "any other matter". Vetzaruch Iyun if this would include other paragraphs that the congregation states aloud throughout Davening. Seemingly however it does not include parts of Davening which the congregation recites silently, as otherwise the entire Davening would be included in this precept. Likewise, if it is recited quietly, there is no noticeable lack of Derech Eretz if one recites a different psalm during that time. See Piskeiy Teshuvos 66:3 and the Poskim in footnote 26!

Is this an obligation? Some Poskim explain that the above requirement to say Aleinu and Ashreiy together with the congregation is not an obligation, as is the recital of Shema, and rather is merely a proper act to perform, just as the Michaber 65:3 rules regarding reading the rest of Shema together with the congregation. [Mamar Mordechai 65:6; implication of Elya Raba ibid; Kaf Hachaim ibid]

[287] The reason: As one is required to join the congregation upon them reciting a prayer [in unison] as a sign of Derech Eretz, proper conduct. [Admur ibid]

[288] Admur ibid regarding Shema "One who read Shema and entered into the Shul and found the congregation reciting Shema...and the same applies to **any other matter** that the congregation is reciting."

[289] Admur ibid; Michaber 65:3 regarding Shema

[290] 1st opinion in Admur ibid [and Michaber 65:2] regarding Shema, Ashrei and other matters the congregation is reciting; Ketzos Hashulchan 24:11; Minchas Yitzchak 9:8

Background: Admur ibid states regarding Shema, Ashrei and other matters the congregation is reciting *"If he is in the midst of an area that he is not allowed to stop, such as from Baruch Sheamar and onwards, then he is not to stop..."* Now, although Admur ibid brings two other opinions in this matter, and the final ruling is that one may recite the first sentence of Shema in the midst of Pesukei Dezimra, nevertheless, seemingly this only applies to Shema, as it involves Kabalas Ol Malchus Shamayim. However, other parts of prayer that one says with the congregation, one is to be stringent like the first opinion. [So is implied from the fact Admur records this dispute only regarding the first verse of Shema. See Mamar Mordechai 65:6; Elya Raba ibid; Kaf Hachaim ibid who state that these verses have the same status as the rest Shema and not as the first verse of Shema; So is also implied from Ketzos Hashulchan 24:11 which states *"One who is not reciting Aleinu Leshabeiach, such as he is in the midst of Pesukei Dezimra"*; So explicitly rules Minchas Yitzchak 9:8 that one does not stop at all for Aleinu if he in an area that he is not allowed to interrupt.]

[291] Admur 109:2; Shlah Inyanei Tefila in name of Maharash of Lublin; Elya Raba 51:8; Ketzos Hashulchan 24:11

[292] Piskeiy Teshuvos 132:7

Some[293] write he is not required to stop and recite Aleinu with the congregation, although he is to bow upon the words of Veanachnu Korim being said. Others[294] write he is to say Aleinu together with the congregation, and then repeat it again at the end of his Davening. Practically, the Rebbe's directive follows the latter approach, to stop and say the entire Aleinu with the congregation, and then repeat it again in its entirety at the conclusion of Davening.[295]

After Shemoneh Esrei, before Tachanun:[296] If one has finished Shemoneh Esrei and is holding prior to Tachanun, he is not to stop to recite Aleinu Leshabeiach, and is rather to go straight to Tachanun.[297] [However, he is nevertheless to bow upon the words Veanachnu Korim are being said, as stated above.]

If one is in the midst of learning Torah, must he stop to recite Aleinu Leshabeiach with the congregation?
Some Poskim[298] write he is not required to do so, although nevertheless he is to bow upon the words of Veanachnu Korim being said, as stated above.

21. Spitting by Aleinu:[299]

No doubt, one of the more peculiar customs, attributed to Chabad Chassidim, is the act of spitting that we perform during Aleinu. Many are not aware that this spitting is actually not an original Chabad custom, and is recorded in previous Poskim that lived over a century prior to the start of the Chassidic movement [as brought in the footnotes here]. For some reason, this custom of Jewry has been preserved mainly by Chabad Chassidim. Details associated with this custom include when one is to perform this spitting, and how it may be performed in a Shul. Must one rub the spit during Aleinu and may one rub the spit on Shabbos?

The custom: It is customary[300] to spit prior to saying the words "ואנחנו כורעים".[301] Doing so does not pose any Halachic issues and is considered an act of respect of heaven.[302] [However, some Poskim[303] protest against this spitting.[304] Practically, the Chabad custom is to spit after saying the words " שהם משתחוים להבל וריק"[305] and so is the custom of some Gedolei Yisrael.[306] However, majority of Jewry is no longer accustomed to performing this spitting.]

---

[293] Tefila Kehilchasa 17 footnote 31 in name of Rav Fisher; Vayeishev Hayam 5; Birchos Shamayin 1:27; See also Divreiy Moshe 1:35; See Mamar Mordechai 65:6 and Kaf Hachaim 65:4 that saying Aleinu with the congregation is not an obligation but merely a good act.

[294] Implication Admur ibid *"It likewise applies if he was already in Shul and is in the midst of reciting supplications or verses, in an area that it is permitted for him to stop."*; Letter of Rebbe printed in Shulchan Menachem 1:272 in reply to what to do if one is Davening by a Nussach Ashkenaz Minyan *"Say Aleinu at the end of the prayer, as writes the Arizal, and also join the Minyan and say it when they do. Both times you should say the entire Aleinu."*; See also Igros Kodesh 19:430 that if one is praying in a Shul that says Ledavid after Aleinu he is to say Aleinu with the congregation and then say with them Ledavid; Tefila Kehilchasa 17 footnote 31; See Kaneh Bosem 2:8 which seems to learn one is to stop

[295] See previous footnote

[296] Kaneh Bosem 2:8; Piskeiy Teshuvos 131:2

[297] The reason: As one is not allowed to make a long interval between Shemoneh Esrei and Tachanun. [Admur 131:1]

[298] Piskeiy Teshuvos 132 footnote 30; See Mamar Mordechai 65:6 and Kaf Hachaim 65:4 that saying Aleinu with the congregation is not an obligation but merely a good act.

[299] Taz Yoreh Deah 179:5; Ketzos Hashulchan 24:11; Hayom Yom 9th Teves; Answer of Rebbe printed in Hiskashrus 905 p. 11; See Chikrei Haminhagim [Gurary] 1:36

[300] The Taz ibid does not mention how widespread this custom was in his time, and simply mentions it as the custom. The Shelah Hakadosh [brought below] however mentions that it is customary amongst only "some of the people".

[301] The reason: This is done to show our disgust of the idols of the gentiles and our respect for Heaven. It therefore does not fall under the severe prohibition against spitting prior to saying a verse, which makes one lose his portion in the world to come [See Michaber Yoreh Deah 179:8], as everyone knows that here the spitting is being done as an act of respect towards Hashem. [Taz ibid] Alternatively, the reason behind this spitting is because we do not desire to receive benefit from the saliva that stated the words "And they bow to deities." [Hayom Yom 9th Teves] The reason this spitting is not done in other areas of prayer that mention idolatry is because the prayer of Aleinu was established by Yehoshua Ben Nun and is considered a very significant prayer, and thus it is said at the end of prayer and therefore the spitting is also done at this time as everything follows the conclusion.[Answer of Rebbe printed in Hiskashrus 905 p. 11]

[302] Taz ibid brought in previous footnote

[303] Shelah Hakadosh in Emek Habracha Tefila 40

[304] The reason: As they spit while saying the words "Veanachnu Korim" and doing so is a grave prohibition. Likewise, the form of idolatry that existed in the times of Yehoshua is no longer around today. Furthermore, doing so is a danger for the public and breeds anti-Semitism. [ibid]

[305] Hayom Yom 9th Teves; See letter of Rebbe printed in Hiskashrus 905 p. 11 regarding this

Rubbing the spit into the ground:[307] It is permitted to spit in a Shul, so long as one rubs the spit with his feet in order so the saliva does not remain visible in the Shul. [Thus, when spitting in Shul during Aleinu, one is to rub the spit with his shoe in order so it does not remain visible. If, however, one is Davening outside of a Shul, there is no need to rub the spit during Aleinu, unless one spits into a public area.[308] It is permitted to rub the spit on the tiled floor of a Shul even on Shabbos, as will be explained next.]

Spitting on Shabbos:[309] When spitting on Shabbos during Aleinu, it is permitted to rub the saliva as he usually does during the week, if one is spitting on a tiled floor.[310] [Those who desire to be stringent must at least step on the saliva until it disappears.[311]] It is, however, forbidden to rub the saliva when spitting on an earth floor, and one is rather to simply step on it until it disappears.[312]

Women spitting: It is not customary for women to spit during Aleinu.[313]

Spitting in front of Aron: It is forbidden to spit opposite a Sefer Torah.[314] Seemingly, for this reason many avoid spitting opposite the Aron Kodesh, which holds the Sefer Torah.[315]

Spitting in front of others:[316] Spitting in front of other people is considered a repulsive act, and hence when one spits during Aleinu [or during any other time that one feels necessary], one is to do so discreetly.

------------------Kerias Hatorah------------------

22. Should one stand during Kerias Hatorah?[317]

The congregation is not required to stand during the Torah reading [and so is the widespread custom[318], and so is the ruling according to Kabbala[319]].[320] However, there are some who are stringent[321] to stand

---

Regarding the Nussach of Valarik or Varik: See Kuntrus Hasiddur of Rav A.C. Naah who writes that it should say Varik and not Valarik, as so is written in all the Sephardi Siddurim based on the verse in Yeshaya 30:7 and 45:20, as well as because the word Varik is the numerical value of Oso Ish, as writes the Kol Bo, and as recorded in Ketzos Hashulchan 1:24. Likewise, in Shaar Hakavanos p. 50 the Nussach is Lahevel Varik. However, based on Hayom Yom ibid, the correct Nussach is Valarik, as also recorded in Shaar Hakolel.

[306] See Piskeiy Teshuvos 132:8 footnote 38
[307] Admur 90:14; Michaber 90:13 and 151:7; Brachos 62b
[308] Ketzos Hashulchan 146:63 "*If one spit in the street in an area that people pass by one is obligated to rub on the spit with his foot until the spit disappears, as certainly one who spits in an area that people will pass is included in the above statement of the Gemara, and hence one must be very careful in this matter.*"
[309] Ketzos Hashulchan 146:65; Az Nidbaru 6:24; Piskeiy Teshuvos 316:7; See also 337 Biur Halacha "Veyeish Machmirim"
[310] The reason: Being that today majority of houses are tiled, and thus according to all the decree against tiled floors does not apply. [ibid]
[311] Olas Tamid 151:8; Elya Raba 151:12; P"M 151 A"A 9; Kaf Hachaim 151:49
[312] Michaber 316:11; Shabbos 121b; Olas Tamid 151:8; Elya Raba 151:12; P"M 151 A"A 9; Kaf Hachaim 151:49; However some Poskim rule that if majority of the city houses have tiled floors [as opposed to earth floors], it is permitted to rub saliva on a public earth floor, such as on a dirt road, so long as one does not intend to smoothen the gaps. However, by a dirt floor which one owns it remains forbidden to rub in the saliva according to all. [Ketzos Hashulchan 146 footnote 63-13]
[313] The reason: Seemingly this is due to reasons of modesty and female nature, as Kol Kevuda Bas Melech Penima. Perhaps this also explains why women are not accustomed to bow on the ground during Aleinu Leshabeiach which is said during the High Holidays.
[314] Michaber Yoreh Deah 282:1; Tur in name of Rambam
[315] I have not found any source in the Poskim for forbidding to spit when facing the Aron, and on the contrary, from the fact the Poskim ibid who allow spitting in a Shul do not state that it is forbidden to do so opposite the Aron implies that such a prohibition does not exist. Vetzaruch Iyun.
[316] See Michaber 316:11 "It is permitted being that the saliva is repulsive" However see M"A 316:25 "Today people are no longer particular regarding spit"; Chagiga 5a "*On all the acts Hashem will bring to judgment, on all concealed matters, Shmuel says that this verse refers to one who spits in front of his friend and it became repulsive before him*"; See Ketzos Hashulchan 146:63 "*If one spit in the street in an area that people pass by one is obligated to rub on the spit with his foot until the spit disappears, as certainly one who spits in an area that people will pass is included in the above statement of the Gemara, and hence one must be very careful in this matter.*"
[317] Shulchan Aruch 146:4
[318] Beis Yosef 141:1; Tur 146:4; Peri Chadash 146:4; Mateh Yosef 146:9; Kaf Hachaim 146:20 that so is custom today amongst all Jewry, including Chassidim and Anshei Maaseh
[319] Shaar Hakavanos Derush 1 p. 48 that the Arizal was accustomed to sit throughout the entire Kerias Hatorah, unlike those accustomed to stand; Peri Eitz Chaim 14:1; Mishnas Chassidim Yom Sheiyni 5:8
According to Kabbalah must one sit down or is it optional? Some Poskim understand that accoridng to the custom of the Arizal, one is specifically to remain seated during the reading, and it not simply that he is not required to stand. [Mishnas Chassidim ibid "They are not to stand"; Pesach Hadvir 146:3; Chesed Lealafim 135:14; Ruach Chaim; Shulchan Hatahor 146:4; Kaf Hachaim 146:22] Others, however, negate this understanding and rule that even accoridng to Kabala one may stand if he chooses. [Sdei Chemed Mareches Beis Peas Hasadeh 29]
[320] Michaber 146:4; Beis Yosef 146:4 and 141:1 that so is implication of Rashi Megillah 21a and that so is the custom; Tur 146:4 in name of Sar Shalom [as explained in Bach ibid]; Seder Rav Amram Gaon 2:25 in name of Sar Shalom; Hamanhig Hilchos Shabbos 30 p. 158; Mordechai in Halachos Ketanos 968; Gloss of Rabbeinu Peretz on Tashbeitz 182; Implication of Yerushalmi Megillah 4:1; Implication of Teshuvas Harambam 46 regarding negation of standing by Aseres Hadibros; Perisha 141:1; Biur Hagr"a 146:4; Peri Chadash 146:4; Levush 146:3; Mateh Yosef 146:9; Pesach Hadvir 146:3; Chesed Lealafim 135:14; Ruach Chaim [Falagi]; Shulchan Hatahor 146:4; Shaareiy Efraim 4:9
[321] Stringency or letter of law: Some Poskim learn that even according to those who are stringent, it is not due to that they view this matter as an obligation from the letter of the law, but rather simply as a proper act. [Bach 141:1] However, other Poskim seem to learn that it is required from the letter of the law. [See Taz 146:1; Lechem Chamudos Brachos 36; Rameh 91, brought in Elya Raba 146:4; Kaf Hachaim 146:20;]

[during the actual Torah reading, although even they are allowed to sit between the Aliyos³²²].³²³ [Practically, the Sephardi custom, and custom of many Ashkenazim and Chassidim, is not to stand during the reading, although some Ashkenazim and Chassidim are stringent to stand. This applies also according to the Chabad custom, that one may sit during the reading, although some are stringent to stand.³²⁴ Regarding the Chabad custom in a Shul that does not have a Bima platform-see next.]

*On the Bima and in a Shul without a Bima platform:*³²⁵ The above ruling [that one is not required to stand] applies even to those sitting on the Bima, that if there are benches on the elevated Bima platform on which the Torah is read, nevertheless even those who are sitting on the Bima do not need to stand. Likewise, even if there is no elevated platform in the Shul, known as the Bima, and the Torah is simply read on a table, [or reading table figuratively called a Bima] which is resting on equal floor level as the rest of the congregation, the congregation does not need to stand. [This applies even if the reading table of the Sefer Torah is not 4x4 Tefachim and is not 10 Tefachim high.³²⁶ However, some Poskim³²⁷, rule that if the Sefer Torah rests on a table and not on an elevated Bima platform, then one is required to stand from the letter of the law, and may only sit between the Aliyos. Practically, those who are weak and cannot concentrate properly on the reading, may sit even in such a case.³²⁸]

Standing during the blessings: Some Poskim³²⁹ rule that everyone [even those who sit during the actual reading] is required to stand upon hearing the blessings of the Torah [i.e. Barchu³³⁰, Birchas Hatorah before and after³³¹], as is the rule by every Davar Shebekedusha.³³² Other Poskim³³³, however, rule it is

---

³²² M"A 146:7; Bach 141:1 that between the Aliyos everyone agrees that one may sit; Peri Chadash 146:4; Kneses Hagedola 146; P"M 146 A"A 7; Kaf Hachaim 146:20

³²³ Rama 146:4 and that so was the custom of the Maharam of Rothenburg; Teshuvos Upesakim of Maharam 503; Tashbeitz Katan 182 that so was custom of Maharam; Mordechai Shabbos 422 in name of Maharam and that so is custom of some German and French Jews; Besamim Rosh 290 in name of Maharam; Custom of some recorded [and negated] in Tur ibid in name of Sar Shalom; Taz 146:1 that the opinion of Maharam is correct and so is proper to be followed; Teshuvas Rav Ovadia Seforni 90, brought in Taz ibid, that one must stand; Makor Chaim 146 based on Even Ezra; Peri Chadash 146:4 concludes that one is allowed to be stringent like Maharam; Seder Hayom Kerias Hatorah Shabbos, brought in Kneses Hagedola 146, that he saw some meticulous people standing, and it is a good and proper custom; Lechem Chamudos Brachos 36; Rameh 91 that so is proper custom, brought in Elya Raba 146:4; Derech Chaim 76:1

The reason: As the verse in Nechemia 8:5 states "Ubepischo Amdu Kol Ha'am" which they interpret to mean that when the Sefer Torah is open one is to stand. However, in truth, the Talmud [Sotah 39a] itself states that the intent here of the word "stand" is to be silent and not speak, and hence the above reason is negated. [Hamanhig ibid; Mordechai in Halachos Ketanos ibid; Tur ibid; Beis Yosef ibid; Gr"a ibid] However, the Taz ibid defends this reason, saying the intent of the Talmud is to say that the standing must be done quietly, and it is not coming to exclude standing. Alternatively, the reason is because when we received the Torah on Sinai we stood [Devarim 5:5] and the Zohar states that when the Torah is read it is similar to receiving it on Sinai. Thus, when one hears the Torah reading, he must imagine as if he is standing by Sinai and this is what led some to stand during the reading, as it is fit and proper to stand just like we stood on Sinai. [Bach 141:1]

³²⁴ The Chabad custom: When the Rebbe was addressed the question of whether one is to stand for Kerias Hatorah, he motioned the asker to look at the ruling of the Rebbe Rashab in the Siddur. [Igros Kodesh 24:120; Shulchan Menachem 1:261] There, the Rebbe Rashab records the custom of the Arizal to sit, although then mentions the need to be stringent if there isn't an elevated Bima platform. In Hayom Yom [24ᵗʰ Shvat; 1ˢᵗ Shavuos; 13ᵗʰ Menachem Av] it says to stand by Shiras Hayam and Aseres Hadibros, implying that by other times one may sit. The custom of the Chabad Rabbeim: The Rebbe Rashab was almost always accustomed to stand during Kerias Hatorah. [Reply of Rebbe Rayatz to Rebbe, printed in Reshimos Hayoman p. 184] However, on Rosh Hashana and Yom Kippur, he was accustomed to sit during the Keria. [Reshimos Devarim 1:102] The Rebbe Rayatz even in Rostov was witnessed to sit during Kerias Hatorah of Shacharis and stand for the reading of Mincha. [Rav S.Z. Gurary, recorded in Chikrei Minhagim p. 176] The Rebbe until 1978 was accustomed to stand during the entire reading, including between the Aliyos. However, from Simchas Torah of 1978 and onwards [after the heart attack] the Rebbe began to sit and did so for all years thereafter. [See Yalkut Kerias Hatorah Lefi Minhag Chabad [Printed in Chazak Chumash] p. 1374; Chikrei Haminhagim 1:176-186]

³²⁵ M"A 146:6 that even on the Bima platform itself only the reader must stand; Beis Yosef in name of Rashba; Tosafos Menachos 33; Taz Y.D. 282 [?], brought in Machatzis Hashekel ibid, that a Bima table which is ten Tefach high and four Tefach wide is considered another Reshus; Kaf Hachaim 146:24; See Michaber 79:2, Admur 79:4 and Siddur Admur Hilchos Tefillin regarding praying, learning and wearing Tefillin near excrement that if it is on a table of ten Tefach it is permitted to do so, as it is considered another Reshus

³²⁶ Machatzis Hashekel ibid in explanation of M"A ibid who says the reason they do not need to stand is because the Sefer Torah is in its set place and if he was referring to a case that the table is ten Tefach high, then the Bima is considered another Reshus and the people on the Bima have the same status as those off the Bima who certainly do not need to stand as they are in another Reshus.

³²⁷ Siddur Rav Shabsi; Rebbe Rashab in Siddur Torah Or p. 488 printed in Siddur Im Dach p. 640; The Rebbe in Igros Kodesh 24:120 referenced the asker to look in the gloss of the Rebbe Rashab in response to whether one must stand by Kerias Hatorah.

³²⁸ Rebbe Rashab in Siddur Torah Or p. 488 printed in Siddur Im Dach p. 640

³²⁹ M"A 146:6; Taz 146:1; Masas Binyamin in end of Sefer in Chidushei Dinim Latur O.C. 1, brought in Shiyurei Kneses Hagedola 146:5; Rameh 91; Elya Raba 146:4; Magen Giborim 146:10; Soles Belula 146:7; P"M 146 M.Z. 1; Shaareiy Efraim 4:9; Aruch Hashulchan 146:8; M"B 146:18; **So rule regarding all Devarim Shebekedusha**: 2ⁿᵈ opinion in Admur 56:5; Rama 56:1; Hagahos Minhagim in name of Yerushalmi [Arizal ibid claims it is misprint in Yerushalmi]; Shiltei Giborim on Mordechai Birchas Hashachar 5; Reishis Chochmah Shaar Hayirah 15:59

³³⁰ Taz ibid; Masas Binyamin in end of Sefer O.C. 1; Rameh 91; Elya Raba 146:4; Aruch Hashulchan 146:8; M"B 146:18; Yesod Veshoresh Havoda 5:8

³³¹ Implication of M"A ibid, in name of Masas Binyamin and Rameh; Shaareiy Efraim 4:9 "One is to be stringent to stand throughout all the blessings"

not necessary [for the listeners] to stand during the recital of Birchas Hatorah, or even Barchu. Practically, although in general it is proper to suspect for the stringent opinion and stand during a Davar Shebekedusha[334], the custom by Kerias Hatorah is like the latter opinion, not to stand for even Barchu or Birchas Hatorah.[335] Nonetheless, even according to the lenient opinion, in the event that one was already standing prior to the recital of Barchu or Birchas Hatorah, it is good/proper[336] to remain standing, and not sit down, until after it is completed.[337] [Accordingly, those who are stringent to remain standing during the reading, are to remain standing also during the blessings and are certainly to avoid sitting down prior to the blessings completion.]

Standing during Aseres Hadibros:[338] It is an old custom amongst many communities to stand during the reading of Aseres Hadibros.[339] Some Poskim[340], however, rule one is not allowed to stand during Aseres Hadibros.[341] Practically, the Chabad custom is to stand, facing the Sefer Torah.[342] If the entire congregation is standing then one is obligated to stand together with them, even if in general he is accustomed to sit.[343]

Standing for Shiras Hayam:[344] Some communities are accustomed to stand during the reading of Shiras Hayam. Practically, the Chabad custom is to stand.[345]

Other opinions: Some Poskim rule one is not required to stand for Birchas Hatorah and is only required to stand during Barchu. He may sit after Barchu is answered by the congregation, even before the Olah repeats it. [Taz ibid as understands P"M 146 M.Z. 1; Implication of Masas Binyamin in end of Sefer O.C. 1 and Rameh 91; Elya Raba 146:4; M"B 146:18 and Shaar Hatziyon 146:20; Ishei Yisrael 38 footnote 54 in name of Rav Chaim Kanievsky; Piskeiy Teshuvos 146:6 footnote 21]

[332] The reason: One can learn this as a Kal Vachomer from Eglon. The verse [Shoftim 3:20] states that Eglon, the king of Moav, stood up on his own from his throne, upon hearing the word of Hashem. [Now, if a gentile got up in honor of Hashem then] certainly we, Hashem's nation, [should stand up in His honor]. [Admur ibid; M"A ibid]

[333] So rule regarding even Barchu: Shiyurei Kneses Hagedola 146:5; Ledavid Emes [Chida] 7:4; Kaf Hachaim 146: 20-21 in implication of custom of Arizal and that so is the custom today even amongst Chassidim and Anshei Maaseh; See Teshuvos Vehanhagos 1:142 and 3:64; So rule regarding Birchas Hatorah: Taz ibid as understands P"M 146 M.Z. 1; Implication of Masas Binyamin in end of Sefer O.C. 1 and Rameh 91; Elya Raba 146:4; M"B 146:18; Ishei Yisrael 38 footnote 54 in name of Rav Chaim Kanievsky; Piskeiy Teshuvos 146:6 footnote 21; **So rule regarding all Devarim Shebekedusha**: 1st opinion in Admur ibid, brought also in 53:1; Maharil Tefila 3, brought in Darkei Moshe 56:5; Arizal Shaar Hakavanos Kaddish; Peri Eitz Chaim Shaar Hakaddeishim 6; brought in M"A 56:4 and Taz 53:1 and 56:2;

[334] Admur ibid; M"A ibid "one is not to be lenient"; M"B 56:8; Aruch Hashulchan 56:9 that the custom is stand only for the necessary Kaddeishim that must be said during the prayer

Other opinions: Many Poskim conclude like the ruling of the lenient opinion and custom of Arizal. [Kneses Hagedola 55:1; Yad Aaron; Shalmei Tzibur p. 81; Kesher Gudal 8:14; Siddur Beis Oved; Chesed Lealafim 56:7; Kaf Hachaim [Falagi] 13:7; Yifei Laleiv 56:3; Ben Ish Chaiy Vayechi 8; Kaf Hachaim 56:20 that so is custom]

[335] Shiyurei Kneses Hagedola 146:5; Ledavid Emes 7:4; Kaf Hachaim 146: 20-21; Piskeiy Teshuvos 146:6

[336] Admur ibid; M"A ibid does not mention that it is merely "proper" to do so, but simply states that so was the custom of the Maharil; Many of the other Poskim ibid write that one must remain standing and the Kaf Hachaim 56:22 writes it is Mitzvah to remind one who is coming to sit down in middle of Kaddish that he may not sit.

[337] Admur ibid; M"A ibid; Darkei Moshe 56 that so was custom of Maharil; Shaar Hakavanos ibid that so was custom of Arizal; Chesed Lealafim ibid; Ben Ish Chaiy ibid; Many Achronim brought in footnote under lenient opinion

[338] See Kaf Hachaim 146:23; Piskeiy Teshuvos 146:6; Beit Maran [Rav Yitzchak Yosef]; Bayit Neman [Rav Meir Mazuz] No. 14; 51; 65; 100; 113

[339] Ledavid Emes 7:5; Tov Ayin 11; Shaar Efraim 7:37; Kaf Hachaim 146:23; Ketzos Hashulchan 84 footnote 22 that so is custom of world; Igros Moshe 4:22; Shemesh Umagen 57; Mishneh Halachos 11:118

[340] Teshuvas Rambam 46; Maharikash in Ohalei Yaakov 33; Machazik Bracha 146:8 based on Arizal, brought in Kaf Hachaim 146:23; Opinion in Ledavid Emes 7:5 [He originally writes that it is improper for the entire congregation to stand, and then brings from his Sefer Machazik Bracha that even individuals should not stand, and then concludes that in some communities everyone stands, and ends up defending the practice]; Yechaveh Daas 6:8 rules not to stand and that the custom to stand is to be abolished; Toldos Hair Kavna p. 229 that so ruled the Raavad, Rav Leib Shapiro, to abolish the custom; See Beir Moshe 8:60

[341] The reason: As it is forbidden to single out a section of Torah, such as the Aseres Hadibros, due to it leading people to believe that only it is the true part of the Torah. [Poskim ibid; See Admur Basra 1:9, Kama 1:10; Rama 1:5; Brachos 12a; Rashba 1:184] However, others negate this worry by stating that the worry is no longer applicable today and does not apply here as one anyways stands for more than just the ten commandments. [See Ulidavid Emes ibid; Shaareiy Rachamim on Shaar Efraim ibid based on Levush 494 and Machatzis Hashekel 429]

[342] Hayom Yom 24th Shevat; 1st day Chag Hashavuos; 13th Menachem Av; Sefer Haminhagim [English] p. 61; See Shulchan Menachem 1:262 footnote 11 and Chikrei Haminhagim 1:62

[343] Tov Ayin 11; Shaareiy Efraim ibid; Kaf Hachaim 146:23; Ketzos Hashulchan 84 footnote 22; See Kneses Hagedola E.H. 62; Ikarei Hadaat, and other Poskim brought in Kaf Hachaim ibid; Yechaveh Daas ibid concludes that in such a case he is to stand already from the beginning of the reading; Piskeiy Teshuvos ibid [see there that the same applies vice versa, that if the entire congregation is accustomed to sit then one is not to stand, however, see Ledavid Emes and Kaf Hachaim ibid who write that individuals may stand and see Q&A below!];

[344] Ketzos Hashulchan 84 footnote 22 that so is the custom [he writes to stand from Vayoshe Hashem]; Piskeiy Teshuvos 146:6; To note from the custom o stand for Az Yashir in Pesukei Dezimra, recorded in Derech Hachaim

[345] Hayom Yom 17th Shevat regarding Shabbos Shira; 21st Nissan, regarding 7th day of Pesach; Sefer Haminhagim [English] p. 61; See Shulchan Menachem 1:262 footnote 11 that the Rebbe Rashab would likewise face the Sefer Torah by the Shira. This, however, was omitted from hayom Yom. See Chikrei Haminhagim 1:62

Standing during the Haftorah-Haftorah of Shavuos:[346] Throughout all the Haftorahs of the year, the person reading the Haftorah aloud must initially stand when doing so out of honor for the congregation [however, the congregation itself is not required to stand]. However, [on the 1st day of Shavuos] some have the custom for all those who read the Haftorah of Merkavah Yechezkel along quietly with the reader, to stand during its reading.[347] [However, those who do not read along quietly with the reader, there is no custom for them to stand even by the Haftorah of Shavuos. Practically, the Chabad custom is to always read a Haftorah quietly along with the reader[348], although it is not necessarily our custom to stand even for the Haftorah of Shavuos. Each community is to follow the directive of their Rav regarding this matter.]

Summary:
The congregation is not required to stand during the reading, although some are stringent to stand. Some Poskim learn that if the Sefer Torah rests on a table and not on a Bima, then one is to stand during the reading, and may only sit between the Aliyos. However, those who are weak and cannot concentrate properly on the reading, may sit. From the letter of the law, it is best for the congregation to stand when the blessings before and after the Torah reading are recited, although the custom is to remain seated also during this time. Whatever the case, one who is accustomed to stand for Kerias Hatorah is not to sit down when the blessings are recited.

Q&A

May one be stringent to stand if the entire congregations is accustomed to sit?
Some Poskim[349] rule that if the entire congregation sits during the reading one may not be stringent to stand. Other Poskim[350], however, rule that one may stand even in such a case, and so is the custom of those who are stringent.

May one who is lenient to sit do so even if the entire congregation is accustomed to stand?
Some Poskim[351] rule it is permitted to do so. However, from other Poskim[352] it is implied that he must stand.

May one sit opposite the Olah or Baal Korei?[353]
One is not to sit, or even stand, opposite the Olah.

---

23. What is one to do if he is in middle of Shemoneh Esrei, and the congregation began to read Kerias Hatorah?

It is debated amongst the Rishonim and Poskim as to whether one is to stop and listen to a Davar Shebekedusha in the midst of Shemoneh Esrei, as explained in Halacha 18, and practically we rule that one is to stop and listen silently.[354] However, some Poskim[355] write that this ruling does not apply to

---

[346] Admur 494:6; Elya Zuta 494; Chok Yaakov 494:5; Brought in Luach Kolel Chabad
[347] The reason: This is done out of honor for the Haftorah of Merkava Yechezkel. [ibid]
[348] See Admur 284:11
[349] Kol Eliyahu 5; Ikarei Hadaat 6:15; Pischeiy Teshuvah 146:2; Orchos Chaim 146:2
[350] Pesach Hadvir 140:3; Kaf Hachaim 146:22; Imrei Bina 13:4; Dvar Yehoshua 2:15; Betzel Hachochma 5:1; Az Nidbaru 6:43; Piskeiy Teshuvah 146:6
[351] Betzel Hachochma 5:1; Piskeiy Teshuvah 146:6
[352] See regarding Aseres Hadibros: Tov Ayin 11; Shaareiy Efraim ibid; Kaf Hachaim 146:23; Ketzos Hashulchan 84 footnote 22; See Kneses Hagedola E.H. 62; Ikarei Hadaat, and other Poskim brought in Kaf Hachaim ibid
[353] Rebbe Rashab in Siddur Torah Or p. 488 printed in Siddur Im Dach p. 640
[354] Admur 104:5; Michaber 104:7; Tur 104:7 in name of Rabbeinu Chananel; Tosafos Brachos ibid that so is the custom; Rashi Sukkah 38b; Bahag Brachos ibid; Haeshkol p. 31 in name Rav Haiy Gaon; Ran 19b; Ravayah; Bach 104 in name of Mordechai and that so is custom; Levush 104; Soles Belula 104:2; Chayeh Adam 25:10; Beis Oved 57; Kitzur SHU"A 18:14; Ben Ish Chaiy Mishpatim 5; Kaf Hachaim 104:36
Other opinions: Some Poskim rule one is to continue Davening, as hearing is like answering, and is considered a Hefsek. [2nd opinion in Tur ibid in name of Rabbeinu Tam and Ri; Tosafos Brachos ibid in name of Rabbeinu Tam and Ri and Geonim; Hagahos Maimanis Tefila 10; The Rosh Brachos 18 and Rabbeinu Yona 13b bring both opinions and give no arbitration; See Beis Yosef 104:7] Other Poskim rule that although it is not

Kerias Hatorah, and it is thus better to continue with the Davening then to stop and listen to the Keria in middle of Shemoneh Esrei.[356] This applies even if one will not be able to hear Kerias Hatorah again that day.[357] However, other Poskim[358] rule that one may [and should] stop and listen to the Keria.[359] [Practically, it is best to avoid this situation and not begin Shemoneh Esrei at a time that it will conflict with Kerias Hatorah. However, Bedieved if one did so, or must do so due to the passing of Zman Tefila, then those who stop and listen have upon whom to rely. This especially applies if one cannot properly concentrate on his Shemoneh Esrei in the midst of Kerias Hatorah.[360]]

Women: According to most Poskim[361], and the final ruling[362], women are not obligated to hear Kerias Hatorah and hence they may continue Shemoneh Esrei rather than to stop and listen to Keiras Hatorah. Nonetheless, if a woman cannot properly concentrate on her Shemoneh Esrei in the midst of Kerias Hatorah then she may stop and listen, as stated above.

------------------Beis Hakeneses----------------

24. Bringing small children to Shul:

[It is a Mitzvah and obligation upon a parent to educate his child to go to Shul and participate in a Minyan, once they have reached the age of Chinuch.[363]] One is to teach his young[364] children and educate them to answer Amen. From the moment that a child answers Amen he has a portion in the World to Come.[365] One is to educate his children to stand [i.e. behave in Shul] with awe and fear.[366] However, children who run around in Shul for fun, [and make noise and] disturb their parents [and others] in their Davening are not to be brought to Shul at all.[367] [Bringing such children to Shul, asides for it disturbing the prayers and it being a desecration of the holy place, also educates them to treat a Shul improperly, and makes them continue their ways even when they become older.[368] Accordingly, children who are below the age of Chinuch and are unable to sit still in Shul without disrupting, are not to be brought to Shul at all. However, those children who are above the age of Chinuch are to be brought to Shul and educated to properly participate in the Minyan and act with the appropriate respect.[369]]

---

considered a Hefsek, one is not Yotzei being that he is not allowed to speak, and hence there is no point of stopping to listen. [Darkei Moshe 104:1 in name of the Iggur that the custom of the Ashkenazi Rabbeim is not to stop and listen; Beis Yosef 25 in name of Rashba and Iggur; Shagas Aryeh 6 in name of Shivlei Haleket; Abudarham, brought in Erech Hashulchan 104:3 and 55:1; See P"M 104 A"A 7] Due to the above opinions. Kaf Hachaim ibid concludes that if stopping to listen will ruin one's concentration of the prayer, or if he anyways cannot hear the Chazan properly, then one may continue his Davening and rely on the other opinions.

[355] Koveitz Mibeis Levi 12; Teshuvos Vehanhagos 2:70; Piskeiy Teshuvos 104:15 and 135 footnote 13; See Orchos Rabbeinu 3:215 in name of Chazon Ish that if one went ahead and did so he is nevertheless Yotzei; See also Michaber 146:2 for the five opinions regarding learning Torah during the reading.

[356] The reason: As the above matter of stopping for a Davar Shebekedusha is debated amongst the Poskim and we are only lenient due to the custom. Now, regarding Kerias Hatorah, it was not mentioned in the above Poskim who say to stop and listen, and there was never a Minhag to stop and listen. Therefore, it is better to abstain and not stop to listen to suspect for the Poskim who rule it is an interval. [Piskeiy Teshuvos 104:15] Furthermore, most Poskim rule there is no obligation for every individual to hear Kerias Hatorah, and it is rather an obligation on the congregation. [See Poskim in Piskeiy Teshuvos 135:2 footnote 12]

[357] Piskeiy Teshuvos ibid

[358] Az Nidbaru 14:29

[359] The reason: As we rule that one should stop and listen for a Davar Shebekedusha, and if we rule this way regarding a matter that requires answering, certainly we should rule this way regarding a matter that does not require answering. [Az Nidbaru ibid] Furthermore, some Poskim rule it is an obligation upon every individual to hear every word of Kerias Hatorah [See Poskim in Piskeiy Teshuvos 135:2 footnote 12], in contrast to Kaddish and Kedusha which is not an actual obligation for everyone to hear, and only if one is with a Minyan is he required to answer.

[360] See Admur 98:1 *"If he gets a foreign thought during Davening [Shemoneh Esrei] he is to be quiet until the thought leaves him."*; Shaareiy Teshuva 104; Ketzos Hashulchan 20:20 regarding a child crying

[361] Maharsham 1:158 that so is explicitly ruled in Ran Megillah 4; Hisorerus Teshuvah 1:5; Beir Moshe 8:86; Piskeiy Teshuvos 135:2
Other opinions: Some Poskim rule women are obligated in Kerias Hatorah. [M"A 282:6, brought in M"B 282:12]

[362] M"B 282:12 that so is the custom

[363] M"B 98:3; See Admur 98:1 124:10; Admur 343:2 *"It is a Rabbinical command for a father to educate his son and daughter in both negative and positive commands"*

[364] Seemingly this includes even children who are below the age of Chinuch. [See Piskeiy Teshuvos 215 footnote 9]

[365] Admur 124:10; Rama 124:7 in name of Kol Bo

[366] Admur 124:10; M"A 124:11; Shlah p. 256

[367] Admur 98:1 *"Children who disturb their parents, are not to be brought to Shul at all"* and 124:10 *"Children who run around in shul for fun it is better not to bring them to Shul at all"*; M"A 98:1; Elya Raba 98:2; Shlah p. 256 in name of Derech Chaim; M"B 98:3; Kaf Hachaim 98:13

[368] Shlah ibid; M"B 98:3

[369] Machatzis Hashekel 98:1; M"B 98:3; Kaf Hachaim 98:13; See also Shlah ibid *"Bottom line, one is not to bring very small children to Shul"*

> **Summary:**
> Children who are above the age of Chinuch are to be brought to Shul and educated to answer Amen and participate in the prayer. However, children who are below the age of Chinuch and run around or disturb the congregation, are not to be brought to Shul at all, and doing so is detrimental to their education.

> **The words of the Shlah:[370]**
> *In today's times, there are children who come to Shul who cause those who bring them to get punished, as they come to desecrate the holiness of the Shul and play in it like they play in the streets. One kid laughs with another, another kid hits another, another sings, another cries, another shouts, another runs around and chases a friend. Some children even do their needs in Shul and are required to be cleaned and removed. At times, the father gives his child a Sefer and the child throws it on the floor or tears it. To summarize, in conclusion these children disturb the worshipers and desecrate the name of Hashem. One who brings such children to Shul should not aspire to receive reward and is rather to worry of the punishment that is befitting him. This is like a master who brings his retarded slave with him to speak with the king, and the slave mocks and disturbs the entire conversation. Surely the king will release his wrath not on the imbecile slave, but on the master, who brought him along. Furthermore, at times the parent begins playing with the child during his own prayer. The greatest evil of all this is that the child will grow up accustomed to his ill treatment of Davening and a Shul and continue to do so when older. Accordingly, one is not to bring very small children to Shul as he only loses out by doing so.*

------------------Netilas Yadayim-----------------

25. May one wash hands for bread with a Band-Aid/bandage?[371]

One who has an injury on his hand and a bandage that is covering it, may wash his hands [with a blessing] without removing the bandage[372], if he is unable to remove it due to the pain of the injury.[373] [This applies even if the bandage is covering majority of his hand.[374]] It suffices for him to wash the remainder of the hand that is not covered by the bandage. (If, however, he is able to remove it [without it causing pain] then he must do so prior to washing, as otherwise it is considered a Chatzitza.[375]) Thus, if one has a bandage covering a minor discomfort of the skin and not an actual injury, and is able to remove it whenever he desires [without any real pain] then he must do so prior to washing.[376]

---

[370] Shlah p. 256
[371] Admur 161:2; 162:15; Michaber 162:10; Tur; Rosh Chulin 8:18; Ketzos Hashulchan 33:3
[372] Admur ibid; Michaber and Rosh ibid; However, see Michaber 161:1 who states it must be removed due to Chatzitza; see next footnote for Admur's distinction and that of other Poskim
[373] Admur ibid; Rosh, brought in Bach and M"A 162:18; Taz 161:2; This answers the contradiction in the opinion of the Michaber ibid
The reason: This washing is not considered "Netila Lechatzain/half washing" being that he is unable to wash the "second part of the hand" [i.e. the area under the bandage] and is thus similar to one who lost a finger in which case he is to wash the remainder of the hand. [Admur 162:15; Tur and Beis Yosef in name of Rosh; P"M 161 M"Z 2 in explanation of Bach in M"A 162:18] It is thus not considered a Chatzitza at all at this time, although on the other hand is not nullified to the hand and hence requires one to be careful that water not touch the bandage, as will be explained. [Admur ibid]
Other opinions/reasons: Some Poskim rule the reason it is not a Chatzitza is because one is not Makpid on it and if one were Makpid on it then it would be a Chatzitza. [M"A 162:18 in name of Lechem Chamudos in answer to contradiction in Michaber ibid; Admur explicitly negates this explanation in the continuation of 162:15] Other Poskim rule it is not a Chatzitza since one will not remove it during the meal due to the pain involved, and hence the impure area will not touch the bread. If, however, he has a mere skin discomfort that is close to painless, and there is thus worry that he might remove the bandage during the meal, then he must remove it, as it is a Chatzitza. [M"A ibid in name of Bach, and that so is main opinion; Taz 161:2; Olas Tamid 161:3; Elya Raba 161:4; Mamar Mordechai 161:4; Chesed Lealafim 161:1; M"B 161:5; Kaf Hachaim 161:6; See P"M ibid and Rav Akiva Eiger 162:18]
[374] P"M 161 M"Z 2; Kaf Hachaim 161:6; Nishmas Avraham 4:161
[375] Admur 162:15; Taz 161:2
[376] Admur 161:2; M"A 162:18 in name of Bach; Taz 161:2; Olas Tamid 161:3; Elya Raba 161:4; Mamar Mordechai 161:4; Chesed Lealafim 161:1; M"B 161:5 and 162:68; Kaf Hachaim 161:6

How to wash with a bandage:[377] In the event that one is Halachically allowed to wash with a bandage on his hand, care must be taken that water does not touch the bandage.[378] He is to thus wash until the area of the bandage, and make sure that water does not fall onto the bandage. Being however that it is difficult to beware of this, therefore, he is to pour an entire Revius [i.e. 86 milliliters[379]] simultaneously on the entire hand, and thus avoid the need to prevent the water from touching the bandage.[380] [However, according to Admur in the Siddur, one is to beware that water does not touch the bandage even when pouring a Revius of water on the hand.[381] If, however, it is not possible to do so, the washing is valid if he pours a Revius at a time.[382]]

Summary:
One who has a bandage covering part of his hand due to a wound or injury, may wash his hands, with a blessing, without removing the bandage, if he is unable to remove it due to the pain of the injury. If, however, he is able to remove it without it causing pain, then he must remove it prior to washing. In the event that one is allowed to wash with a bandage on his hand, one is to pour an entire Revius [86 milliliters] simultaneously on the entire hand, and in addition one is to beware that water does not touch the bandage. If, however, it is not possible to prevent the bandage from getting wet, the washing is valid if he pours a Revius at a time.

Q&A
What is the law if the band-aid/bandage became removed during the meal?
In the event that one washed his hand while wearing the bandage [in a permitted scenario] and the bandage later fell off during the meal, some Poskim[383] rule he is not required to re-wash his hands and may continue eating as usual.[384] Other Poskim[385], however, rule he is required to rewash that entire hand prior to continuing eating bread.[386] It is implied from Admur like the latter, stringent, opinion.[387] Some Poskim[388] rule that even according to the stringent opinion, in the event that one will return the bandage onto the wound prior to continuing eating, then he is not required to re-wash.

---

[377] Admur 162:15; Michaber ibid; Rosh ibid

[378] The reason: As if the water drops onto the bandage then if it drops back onto the hand it impurifies the hand. A second washing does not help purify this water that is on the bandage. Although the bandage is not considered a Chatzitza at all being that he is unable to remove it now, nevertheless, it is not nullified to the hand to the point that its water can be purified with a second washing, as one does plan to eventually remove it. If, however, in truth he does not care to ever remove it, then it is nullified to the hand and does not require one to beware that water does not touch it. [Admur ibid; Michaber ibid]

[379] Rav Avraham Chaim Naa"h in Shiureiy Torah 3:6
Other opinions: Some Poskim rule a Revius is equivalent to 150 milliliters. [Chazon Ish in Kuntrus Hashiurim]

[380] Admur ibid; Rashal, brought in Taz 162:8; Michaber ibid gives this suggestion as well, although does not advise to follow specifically this suggestion
The reason: As a Revius does not contract impurity and hence avoids this entire issue. [Admur ibid]

[381] See Seder Netilas Yadayim 2 that one who desires to fulfill his obligation according to all is to suspect that even a Revius contracts impurity. Accordingly, it would not help to pour a Revius over the entire hand and allow the water to touch the bandage, and hence even when pouring a Revius one must beware that the water does not touch the bandage. [Ketzos Hashulchan 33 footnote 12]

[382] Ketzos Hashulchan ibid; See Piskeiy Teshuvos 162 footnote 87
The reason: As in such a case one may rely on the ruling of the Admur in his Shulchan Aruch ibid that a Revius does not contract impurity. Furthermore, even from the Siddur it is evident that one may rely on this opinion in a time of need, as Admur in the Siddur rules regarding the morning washing that if one has only a small amount of water he is to pour a Revius over the hands simultaneously. [Ketzos Hashulchan ibid]

[383] Halachos Ketanos 2:132, brought in Hagahos Hatur;

[384] The reason: As since one washed his hands according to Halacha, the entire hand is pure and there is no impurity that resides under the bandage. [ibid]

[385] Mahariy Malko 145, brought in Birkeiy Yosef 161:4; Shaareiy Teshuvah 161:2; Zechor Leavraham 161:50; Ben Ish Chaiy Shemini 14; M"B 162:71; Kaf Hachaim 161:7; Chazon Ish 24:25

[386] The reason: As one may not wash his hands in halves, and the impurity was simply covered over by the bandage, and now that it was removed, the impurity of that area must also be washed off. [ibid]
Is a blessing recited? See Piskeiy Teshuvos 162 footnote 92 that if one desires to eat another Kibeitza of bread and the bandage was over the fingers, then he is to re-wash with a blessing.

[387] As the reason offered by Admur for why the bandage is valid is due to that it is technically not possible to wash it, and not because it is not a Chatzitza due to not being Makpid and being nullified to the hand.

[388] Shaar Hatziyon 162:58
Other opinions: Some Poskim rule that even in such a case one must rewash the hand prior to replacing the bandage. [Chazon Ish 24:25]

If the bandage contains two coverings, must one remove the outer covering?[389]
If the outer covering covers a section of the hand that is not covered by the lower one, then if one can remove it pain-free, it is to be removed prior to washing.

Washing hands in the morning upon awakening?[390]
In a case that one cannot wash one of his hands due to a cast or injury, then he is to wash the one available hand [three times] and is to then say the blessing of Al Netilas Yadayim.[391]

---------------Birchas Hanehnin-General-----------------

26. What is one to do if he began chewing on a food, or drinking a liquid, and then remembered that he did not say a blessing?

Foods:[392] It is forbidden to say a blessing while eating food.[393] Accordingly, one who forgot and entered food into his mouth without saying a blessing [and remembered in the midst of chewing the food], then he must spit it out and say the blessing, if it is a type of food which will not become repulsive to the person after it is spat out [and he will thus return and eat it]. If, however, the food will become repulsive after it is spat out [and will thus no longer be eaten due to its repulsiveness], then one is not required to spit it out and is rather to place the food into one of the sides of his mouth and say the blessing.[394] [Thus, for example, if he began eating gum or a candy[395] without a blessing, he is to spit it out and then say the blessing. If, however he began chewing bread, or a grape[396] and then remembered that he forgot to say a blessing, he is to move it to the side of his mouth and say the blessing. In all cases, if he did not yet begin chewing the food, then he is to remove it and then say the blessing. In the event that one entered so much food into his mouth that he cannot move it to the side and say a blessing, then its law follows the same law as liquids, as explained next.]

Liquids:[397] One who forgot and entered a drink into his mouth without saying a blessing [and then remembered prior to swallowing it] some Poskim[398] rule he is to swallow the liquid [and is not required to spit it out].[399] Amongst these Poskim, some rule that he is not to say the before blessing at all over the

---

[389] See Shaar Hatziyon 162:27

[390] Kaf Hachaim 4:7 in name of Zivcheiy Tzedek 2:13; Rav Poalim 1:8; Ketzos Hashulchan 2 footnote 11; Biur Halacha 4 "Yidakdek" in name of Artzos Hachaim; Minchas Ahron 1:19; See also 161:2 and 162:15 regarding washing for bread that if one has an injury on his hand, and due to it that hand cannot be washed, he is to wash one hand with a blessing.

[391] Kaf Hachaim ibid states explicitly that a blessing is said and so adds the Ketzos Hashulchan in the supplements p. 83 based on M"A 170 regarding washing for a meal. So also rules Biur Halacha 4 "Yidakdek" in name of Artzos Hachaim.
The reason: As even washing one hand is able to remove some of the impure spirit to the point that it can no longer damage and hence since one is unable to wash the other hand he may say a blessing, as he did the most that he can to sanctify himself for service of Hashem. [Ketzos Hashulchan ibid based on Siddur that washing three times on each hand is only to completely remove the impurity and hence a blessing may be said after washing only once if no other water is available.]

[392] Michaber 172:2; Tur 172:2; Brachos 50b; Yerushalmi Brachos 6:1 [44b]; Ketzos Hashulchan 55:8

[393] Brachos 51a; Yerushalmi Brachos 6:1 [44b]; Michaber 172:2 regarding one who forgot and began eating a food without a blessing; M"A 172:4; Taz 172:2; Ketzos Hashulchan 5:10 "It is forbidden to say a blessing with food in one's mouth"; Beir Heiytiv 173:3; M"B 173:7
The reason: As the verse states "Yimalei Pi Tihilasecha" which means that one's entire mouth must be involved in praising Hashem. [See Brachos ibid; M"A 172:4; Taz 172:2; Beir Heiytiv ibid; M"B ibid; Ketzos Hashulchan ibid; Kaf Hachaim 172:4]

[394] The reason: This is due to the prohibition against destroying food.
Does this apply according to all opinions: Some Poskim rule that according to the ruling of the Raavad regarding liquid, that one is to spit it out if he has more liquid available, then the same applies here as well. [Toras Chaim Sofer 172] Other Poskim, however, rule that even the Ravaad agrees in this case that one is not to spit out the food and cause it to go to waste as the concept of Yimalei Pi Tehilasecha is not as severe as eating without a blessing. [Maharam Benet on Mordechai Brachos 7:53; Magen Giborim 172; See Piskeiy Teshuvos 172:4]

[395] See P"M 172 M"Z 2 in name of Rambam and M"B 172:6 "Such as beans and the like which are hard."; Ketzos Hashulchan ibid

[396] M"B 172:8 "strawberries or grapes"

[397] Tur and Michaber 172:1; Brachos 50b

[398] Michaber ibid; Rama ibid; Tur ibid; Brachos ibid "By liquids one is to swallow it"; Rabbeinu Chananel, brought in Tur ibid and Rosh Brachos 33; Rosh Brachos 33; Rashba Brachos ibid in name of Raavad, brought in Beis Yosef 172; Leaning way of learning Rambam Brachos 8:12

[399] The reason: As it is not possible to place the liquid on the side of his mouth to allow a blessing to be said, and if he spits it out it will become repulsive. [See Brachos ibid] Alternatively, as once liquid is placed in the mouth it loses its food status as it is no longer fit for drinking. Accordingly, one is not to be particular to recite a blessing even if he could. [M"A 172:1; Rabbeinu Chananel ibid, brought in Rosh ibid; Kaf Hachaim 172:1]

liquid, even after swallowing.⁴⁰⁰ Other Poskim⁴⁰¹, however, rule that after he swallows the liquid he is to say the blessing.⁴⁰² Practically, the Poskim⁴⁰³ conclude that in order to avoid the disputes, if one has more liquid available, he is to spit it out and say a blessing on the new liquid.⁴⁰⁴ [If he does not have more liquid available, then if he needs the drink and does not want to spit it out, he is to think the blessing in his mind, swallow it, and not recite a before blessing.⁴⁰⁵ Other Poskim⁴⁰⁶, however, suggest that in all cases one is to think the blessing in his mind and then swallow the liquid.⁴⁰⁷ Practically, one is to follow the former conclusion.⁴⁰⁸] In all cases, even if a before blessing was not said⁴⁰⁹, an after blessing is to be recited [if one drank a Revius].⁴¹⁰

Summary:

Food: One who forgot and entered food into his mouth without a blessing, then if it is a type of food that will not become repulsive to the person after it is spat out, then he must spit it out and say the blessing, If, however, the food will become repulsive after it is spat out, then one is not required to spit it out and is rather to place the food in the sides of his mouth and say the blessing.

Liquid: One who forgot and entered a drink into his mouth without saying a blessing, is to spit it out. If, however, he does not have anything more to drink, and desires to drink it, he is to think the blessing in his mind and then swallow it.

Other Opinions: The Yerushalmi Brachos 6:1 rules that the liquid is to be spat out and not drunk without a blessing. Many Poskim and Mefarshim explain that in truth there is no dispute between the Bavli and Yerushalmi, and while the Bavli refers to a case that one has no more liquid available, the Yerushalmi refers to a case that there are more liquids available. [Raavad, brought in Rashba ibid and Beis Yosef ibid; Maareh Hapanim on Yerushalmi ibid; Amudei Yerushalmi ibid; Bach 172; M"A 172:1; Elya Raba 172:1]

⁴⁰⁰ Michaber ibid; 1ˢᵗ opinion in Tur ibid; Rabbeinu Chananel, brought in Tur ibid and Rosh Brachos 33, in his interpretation of Brachos ibid; Possible way of learning Rambam Brachos 8:12 [See Beis Yosef 172; Kaf Hachaim 172:3]

The reason: As we never say a before blessing after a food has been eaten. [Taz 172:1, as explained in 167:8] Alternatively, once the liquid is in one's mouth it is no longer drinkable by most people and hence does not deserve a blessing. [M"A 172:1; Rabbeinu Chananel ibid, brought in Rosh ibid]

⁴⁰¹ Rama ibid "And so is the main opinion"; Darkei Moshe 172:1; 2ⁿᵈ opinion in Tur ibid; Rosh Brachos 33; Rashba Brachos ibid in name of Raavad, brought in Beis Yosef 172; Leaning way of learning Rambam Brachos 8:12 [So learns Darkei Moshe ibid; See Beis Yosef 172]

⁴⁰² The reason: Although we do not say a blessing after a food has already been eaten, since in this case one remembered prior to the swallowing, it is similar to saying the blessing beforehand, even though it is only said after the swallowing, as he has no choice. [Taz 172:1; M"A 172:3; Rosh ibid; See Beis Yosef ibid]

⁴⁰³ M"A 172:2 and 3; Bach 172; Elya Raba 172:1; Raavad, brought in Rashba ibid and Beis Yosef ibid, in explanation of Yerushalmi Brachos 6:1 "Liquids are to be spat out"; Ohel Moed 1:12; Maareh Hapanim on Yerushalmi ibid; Amudei Yerushalmi ibid; P"M 172 M"Z 2 regarding wine; M"B 172:2 "And so should be done" however in Biur Halacha 172 :1 "Vieino" he writes "One who is lenient in this is not to be protested"; Ketzos Hashulchan 55:9

⁴⁰⁴ The reason: This is done to avoid a) the dispute between the Michaber/Rama regarding if a before blessing must be said afterwards, and b) to avoid the dispute between the Bavli and Yerushalmi of whether one must spit it out and c) to avoid the dispute of whether an after blessing may be said after the before blessing, if one follows the Rama ibid. [M"A ibid and ibid as explained in Machatzis Hashekel; See Poskim ibid] See Rebbe Akiva Eiger on M"A ibid who questions as to what dispute one will enter if he has more liquid in front of him and he thus must spit it out, as he can simply swallow it as agree all Poskim and then say a blessing and drink from the more liquid. This avoids the dispute according to all, and hence it is not understood why the M"A ibid directs one to spit it out. In truth, however, one can say that this is done in order to suspect for the opinion of the Yerushalmi and Raavad as explains Machatzis Hashekel ibid and as is understood from M"A ibid. Vetzaruch Iyun! Perhaps, however, one can say that by spitting it out one transgresses the ruling of the Bavli who says to swallow it and not cause the liquid to go to waste, and thus whether one spits or swallows, it will always be under debate. Accordingly, Rav Akiva Eiger questions how spitting out the liquid solves the problem and avoids the dispute.

⁴⁰⁵ Derech Hachaim; Ketzos Hashulchan ibid based on Admur 185:1; See Maareh HaPanim on Yerushalmi ibid that most Poskim, Geonim and Rishonim argue on Rama, and Safek Brachos Lihakel, and hence one is to swallow it without saying any blessing. The Poskim in previous footnote rule that even if one does not have more liquid available, one should only swallow the liquid if he is in need of it. Otherwise, it is best to spit it out in order to avoid the dispute and not benefit from the world without a blessing. [Kaf Hachaim 172:1 and 3]

⁴⁰⁶ P"M 172 M"Z 2; Derech Hachaim; Shulchan Hatahor 172:1; Kaf Hachaim 172:1;

⁴⁰⁷ The reason: As since whatever one does will be under a dispute, it is better in this case to rely on the Rambam Brachos 1:7 who rules one is Yotzei even if he thinks a blessing in his mind. [Poskim ibid]

⁴⁰⁸ See Piskeiy Teshuvos 172 footnote 18 who questions the above ruling of thinking the blessing, as by doing so one enters into a new dispute as to whether he may say a blessing on the remaining liquid. [See P"M 62 A"A 1; Chayeh Adam 5:16]

⁴⁰⁹ The law if a before blessing was said, as rules the Rama: If, however, one followed the Rama ibid and recited a before blessing after swallowing the liquid, then it is questionable if one should recite also an after blessing, as we do not find a before and after blessing said in approximation of each other. Practically, if one drank wine or grape juice, which is from the 7 Minim, then an after blessing is to also be said as some Poskim rule that this blessing is Biblical. However, if one drank water and other beverages then this matter remains in question. [M"A 172:3]

⁴¹⁰ M"A 172:2; Beis Yosef 172; Nanar Mordechai 172:1; P"M 172 A"A 1; Kaf Hachaim 172:2

27. Saying a blessing or Davening with food, or other item, in one's mouth:[411]

It is forbidden to say a blessing [or Daven[412]] while food [or another item] is in one's mouth.[413] [Accordingly, one who is chewing gum, or sucking on a candy, must remove the gum or candy from his mouth prior to reciting a blessing or Davening. Likewise, if one is in the middle of eating a food and desires to say a blessing over a liquid, he is to first swallow the food and then say the blessing. Some are even particular regarding crumbs, to make sure their mouth is free from the crumbs of a food prior to saying a blessing.[414] Certainly, one is not to hold an item with his mouth while saying the blessing, such as some women are accustomed to do upon washing hands, to hold their ring in-between their teeth. If saliva accumulates in one's mouth to the point that it interferes with one's speech, then he is to swallow it or spit it out prior to saying a blessing.[415]]

Bedieved:[416] Bedieved, if one said a blessing, or Davened, while a food or other item was in his mouth, he nevertheless fulfills his obligation.

Summary:
It is forbidden to say a blessing while food, or any item, is in one's mouth and it must hence be removed. Nonetheless, Bedieved one fulfills the blessing even if he said it with a food in his mouth.

Q&A

May one answer Amen or to Kaddish with a food in his mouth?
Yes.[417] [However, if one just said a blessing over the food, he must swallow the food before answering Amen.[418]]

May one learn Torah or recite Tehillim with a food in his mouth?
It is permitted to learn Torah while chewing on food, such as gum. Likewise, from the letter of the law, one may recite Tehillim with food, such as gum, in his mouth. Nonetheless, it is proper to be stringent in this matter.[419]

May one who wears dentures recite a blessing while they are in his mouth?[420]
Yes.[421] [Nonetheless, if they impair with one's speech, it is proper to remove them before saying a blessing.[422]]

May one wear braces while saying a blessing?
Permanent braces, which obviously cannot be removed, are even initially allowed to be placed in one's mouth despite the above issue.[423] However, by removeable braces, it is proper for them to be removed from one's mouth upon saying a blessing, or prayer.

---

[411] Brachos 51a; Yerushalmi Brachos 6:1 [44b]; Michaber 172:2 regarding one who forgot and began eating a food without a blessing; M"A 172:4; Taz 172:2; Ketzos Hashulchan 5:10 "It is forbidden to say a blessing with food in one's mouth"; Beir Heiytiv 173:3; M"B 173:7
[412] Ashel Avraham Butchach Tinyana 172
[413] The reason: As the verse states "Yimalei Pi Tihilasecha" which means that one's entire mouth must be involved in praising Hashem. [See Brachos ibid; Beir Heiytiv ibid; M"B ibid; Ketzos Hashulchan ibid]
[414] See Piskeiy Teshuvos 172:5 footnote 28 in name of Divrei Chana Hashaleim 2:81 and Orach Neman 184:25
[415] Ashel Avraham Butchach Tinyana 172
[416] Bach 172; P"M 172 M"Z 2; Evident from ruling of Michaber 172:2 and Brachos 51a; Aruch Hashulchan 172:1
[417] Ashel Avraham Butchach Tinyana 172
[418] Admur 167:9; Seder 9:1; Luach 6:1; M"A 167:16; Shelah Shaar Haosiyos Kuf p. 81; Olas Tamid 167:11; Kaf Hachaim [Falagi] 23:7; Ben Ish Chaiy Emor 14; Kaf Hachaim 167:45; Ketzos Hashulchan 37:7
[419] See Ashel Avraham Butchach Tinyana 172 regarding Amen
[420] Rivivos Efraim 2:69; Piskeiy Teshuvos 172:5
[421] As a) The dentures actually help one verbalize the words better. [Rivivos Efraim ibid; Vetzaruch Iyun as many people have speech impairment upon wearing dentures.] B) As the dentures have become part of one's mouth and hence there is no need to remove them.
[422] See Piskeiy Teshuvos ibid footnote 31 that some would not use dentures due to this issue.
[423] One can suggest that a) They are part of one's mouth and hence do not form an issue of "Yimalei Pi Tehilasecha", and b) it is similar to one who said a blessing with food in his mouth in which case if he cannot spit it out, we allow him to say the blessing.

---------------Bracha Rishona----------------
28. Which blessing should one precede-Hadama or Haeitz?[424]

> For example: One plans to eat a snack of a date and potato chips, which are both sitting on the table in front of him. Which blessing should one precede; the Haeitz on the fruit, or the Hadama on the potatoes?

Chaviv-If one desires one food more than another:[425] If one is planning to eat two foods which are in his presence[426], and one of the foods receives the blessing of Haeitz while the second food receives the blessing of Hadama [i.e. he has an apple and potato chips in front of him], then if one food is more desirable than another [i.e. Chaviv], then the blessing of the more desirable food must be preceded [even if the more desirable food is only a half a piece while the other food is whole/Shaleim[427]]. Thus, if one desires the Hadama [i.e. potato chips] more than the Haeitz [i.e. the apple], then he must first say the blessing of Hadama [even though the apple is whole]. [If, however, he desires the apple more than the potato chips, then he must precede the blessing over the apple.] This applies even if the Haeitz is from the seven Minim [i.e. an olive, grape, etc.], nevertheless, a more desirable Hadama is to be preceded.[428]

If one desires both foods equally:[429] If both foods are equally desirable, then although there is no complete obligation to precede the Haeitz over the Hadama, nevertheless, it is preferable [i.e. Tov] to precede the blessing of Borei Peri Haeitz [even if the other food is Shaleim[430]].[431] This applies even if the Haeitz is from the seven Minim [i.e. an olive, grape, etc.], nevertheless, it is not an obligation to precede the Haeitz, but is preferable to do so.[432]

Definition of Chaviv:[433] There are two definitions of Chaviv, a more desirable food. 1) A food that the person currently has more desire for, even if he does not generally desire it more.[434] 2) A food that the person usually has more desire for, even if currently he does not desire it more.[435] In a mixture in which the more desirable food is given precedence and one has in front of him two foods, one which is currently

---

[424] Seder 10:7 and 8; Luach 3:7
Background: Regarding the laws of precedence in a mixture of Haeitz and Hadama, there exist three opinions amongst the Poskim: 1) Always precede Haeitz. [Behag; 2nd opinion in Michaber 211:3] 2) Always precede the Chaviv. [2nd opinion in Michaber 211:1; Rambam 8, brought in Michaber 211:2; Tosafos Brachos 41a; Rabbeinu Yona 28b; Rashba Brachos 41a; Semak 151] 3) No precedence at all. [Stam opinion in Michaber 211:1; Rosh; Rashi; Rif; Rav Haiy] Admur ibid, based on the rulings of the Taz and M"A arbitrates between the various opinions.

[425] Seder 10:7; Luach 3:7; 2nd opinion in Michaber 211:1; Opinion of Rambam 8, brought in Michaber 211:2; Taz 211:2; M"A 211:4 and 13; M"B 211:9; Tosafos Brachos 41a; Rabbeinu Yona 28b; Rashba Brachos 41a; Semak 151
Other opinions: 1) Some Poskim rule that one is [always] obligated to precede the blessing of Haeitz [even if the Hadama is more Chaviv]. [2nd opinion in Michaber 211:3; Bahag, brought in Rosh 6:25; Elya Raba 211:2; Kaf Hachaim 211:6 and 14 that so is custom of world; See Taz 211:1, Orchos Chaim p. 38, Kol Bo ibid, Mamar Mordechai 211:5 and Kaf Hachaim 211:13 that according to Bahag this applies even if the Hadama is more Chaviv] 2) Other Poskim rule one can precede whichever fruit one desires, even if one is more Chaviv than another. [Stam opinion in Michaber 211:1; Tur 211; Rosh; Rashi; Rif; Rav Haiy Gaon] 3) Some Poskim rule that according to the Michaber it is best to always precede the Haeitz, and so is the custom, as the main ruling of the Michaber follows that there is never precedence, and thus one should always suspect that Haeitz comes first. In addition, according to Kabala, one is to always precede Haeitz to Hadama, as Haeitz is Tiferes while Hadama is Malchus. Likewise, since Hadama exempts Haeitz Bedieved, it is better to say Haeitz first. [Kaf Hachaim ibid]

[426] Seder 10:2 and 16; If, however, one only wants to eat one of the foods that are present, or one wants to eat both foods but only one of the foods are currently in front of him, then the laws of precedence do not apply.

[427] See Q&A!

[428] Seder 10:8 "Yeish Lo Lehakdimo" [Vetzaruch Iyun from contrast of wording in Seder 10:7 "Tzarich Lehakdimo"]; Luach ibid; 2nd opinion in Michaber 211:1; Tosafos ibid; Rabbeinu Yona ibid; Rashba ibid;
Other opinions: See other opinions in footnotes above. See Biur Halacha 211 "Veyeish Omrim"

[429] Seder 10:7 and 8; Luach ibid; This ruling of Admur is a merge of the following opinions: Stam opinion in Michaber 211:1 and 3 that there is no precedence; Taz 211:2 that always precede Haeitz if equally Chaviv; M"A 211:13 "precede Haeitz"; Kol Bo 24; Tosafos ibid; Semak ibid
Other opinions: Some Poskim rule that one is [always] obligated to precede the blessing of Haeitz [even if the Hadama is more Chaviv]. [2nd opinion in Michaber ibid; Behag, brought in Rosh 6:25; See Taz ibid who rules this way if they are both equally Chaviv; M"A ibid] Other Poskim rule one can precede whichever fruit one desires. [Stam opinion in Michaber 211:3; Rosh; Rashi; Rif; Rav Haiy Gaon]

[430] See Q&A!

[431] The reason: This ruling accepts the Poskim [see above] who rule that from the letter of the law, a mixture of Haeitz and Hadama never has a status of precedence. On the other hand, it suspects for the opinion [Bahag-see above] who rules that Haeitz always receives precedence, and hence Admur ibid concludes that it is best to say Haeitz. [See also Taz ibid who makes a similar arbitration] The reason Haeitz is given precedence over Hadama is because the blessing of Haeitz is a higher quality blessing. [See Admur 202 Kuntrus Achron 1]

[432] Seder 10:8; 1st opinion in Michaber 211:1; Tosafos ibid
Other opinions: Some Poskim rule that one is obligated to precede the blessing of Shiva Minim if both foods are equally Chaviv. [Opinion of Rambam 8, brought in Michaber 211:2; Elya Raba 211:2]

[433] Seder 10:15; Luach 3:15; 212:9

[434] 2nd approach in Admur ibid; Michaber 311:2; Rambam Brachos 8:13

[435] 1st approach in Admur ibid; Luach 3:15; Michaber 211:1; Rosh Brachos 6:25; Rabbeinu Yona Brachos 28b

more desirable and one which is usually more desirable, he may precede whichever food he chooses [although it is best to precede the Haeitz, as stated above[436]].[437]

> **Summary:**
> If one is planning to eat both a Haeitz and Hadama food which are in front of him, then one gives precedence to whichever food is more desirable, and if both foods are equally desirable, then it is preferable to precede the blessing of Haeitz.
>
> **Q&A**
> **If one of the Hadama or Haeitz foods is whole [Shaleim] while the other is not whole, do the above laws of precedence change?**
> ➤ For example: One plans to eat a snack of a date and tomato, which are both sitting on the table in front of him. The date is more desirable, although is cut in half, while the tomato is whole. Which blessing should one precede; the Haeitz on the half a date, or the Hadama on the whole tomato?
>
> Some Poskim[438] rule one always precedes the whole food over the non-whole food, even if the non-whole food is more desirable, and is a higher blessing. Other Poskim[439], however, leave this matter in question. Practically, the implication of Admur and other Poskim, is that the aspect of Shaleim does not affect the laws of precedence when one has a Hadama and Haeitz together.[440]

29. The blessing on Matzah:[441]

During Pesach:[442] Throughout Pesach, the blessing on Matzah is Hamotzi according to all opinions.[443]

Throughout the year: Most Poskim[444] rule the blessing on Matzah remains Hamotzi throughout the year[445], and so appears to be the ruling of Admur.[446] Some Poskim[447], however, rule that throughout the year, Matzah has the same status as Mezonos bread and thus remains Mezonos unless one establishes a meal on the Matzah, as defined in Halacha.[448] Some Poskim[449] conclude due to the above debate, that a G-d fearing Jew is to always eat Matzah within a meal of bread, or establish a meal on it, thus making it Hamotzi according to all. Practically, the custom of Ashkenazi Jewry is like the former opinion to recite Hamotzi and Birchas Hamazon on Matzah throughout the year.[450] However, the custom of Sephardi

---

[436] See Biur Halacha 211 "Viyeish Omrim"; Piskeiy Teshuvos 211:3
[437] Admur Seder ibid; Luach ibid; Admur 212:9; Taz 211:1
[438] Derech Hachaim, brought in Shaar Hatziyon 211:5; See Seder Birchas Hanehnin of Rav Prus p. 218
[439] Shaar Hatziyon ibid; See Piskeiy Teshuvos 211:3 and footnote 68
[440] So is implied from the fact that Admur ibid, and the Poskim ibid, completely omit this aspect, even though Admur brings it in Seder 10:6; So also learns Rav Elyashvili in his glosses on Seder footnote 38
[441] See Yechaveh Daas 3:12; Piskeiy Teshuvos 168:13; Halacha Berurah 168:25
[442] Ginas Veradim [Halevi] Gan Melech 64; Chida in Machazik Bracha 158:5; Maharam
[443] The reason: As a) On Pesach, Matzah is the main food that we eat and b) Due to the Mitzvah it receives greater importance. [Chida ibid]
[444] Kneses Hagedola 158:1 and Teshuvah 344 in name of his teachers; Beis Dovid 70 and 83; Yad Aaron 158; Karban Isha 4; Chida in Machazik Bracha 158:5 concludes like Beis David; Chesed Leavraham 15; Ohel Yitzchak 4; Chukas Hapesach 482:1; Magen Giborim 168:5; Ashel Avraham Butchach 168; Kaf Hachaim 158:43 [negates ruling of Mezonos, although concludes to eat in meal]; Avnei Shoham 1:17; Rav Shlomo Yosef Zevin in Sofrim Usefarim 319; Chelkas Yaakov 48; Minchas Yitzchak 1:71 "There is no person with a scent of Torah who would eat it without washing, saying Hamotzi and Birchas Hamazon."; Shevet Halevi 1:205; Tzitz Eliezer 11:19; Teshuvos Vehanhagos 3:73
[445] The reason: As Matzah is not similar to regular crackers, as a) It is made for the sake of eating a meal and not simply for snacking and b) It is thicker than the regular crackers referred to in 168:7. It is thus not similar to the law of crackers which receive the blessing of Mezonos. [Poskim ibid; See Admur 168:12; M"B 168:36]
[446] As aside for the reasoning brought in the Poskim ibid, Admur in the Seder 2:7-8 and Luach omits the opinion who states that crackers are Mezonos, hence implying that all flour and water crackers always remain Hamotzi. [See Ketzos Hashulchan 48 footnote 11]
[447] See Machazik Bracha ibid for his questions on the ruling of Beis David ibid [although concludes like him]; Olas Shmuel 3; Beis Menucha Dinei Netilas Yadayim 4; Tzror Hamur Chayeh Sarah p. 25b; Pekudas Elazar 168; Minchas Shmuel 3; Sdei Chemed Brachos 1:10 defends ruling of Beis Menucha; Poskim in Yechaveh Daas 3:12; Or Letziyon 2:13-3; Ish Matzliach 2 3:5; Rav Mordechai Eliyahu famously ruled it only becomes Mezonos after Pesach Sheiyni.
[448] The reason: As Matzah is similar to the crackers discussed in Michaber 168:7.
[449] Chida ibid; Chesed Lealafim 168:9; Kaf Hachaim 158:43; Yechaveh Daas ibid; Rav Yaakov Yosef za"l that so is the initial ruling for Sephardim; Minchas Yitzchak ibid; Shevet Halevi ibid; Piskeiy Teshuvos ibid; Halacha Berura ibid
[450] Sdei Chemed Brachos 1:10; Yechaveh Daas ibid; Piskeiy Teshuvos ibid; Halacha Berura ibid; Piskeiy Teshuvos ibid

Jewry is like the latter opinion to recite Mezonos on Matzah throughout the year, unless they establish a meal over it.[451] Those who are meticulous, are to only eat the Matzah within a meal, or establish a meal over it as defined in Halacha.[452] This applies to both Sephardim and Ashkenazim.

Egg Matzah: Throughout the year, egg Matzah is considered Mezonos unless one establishes a meal on the Matzah, as defined in Halacha.

30. The blessing over onions:[453]

Raw:[454] The blessing over raw onions is Hadama.[455] This applies even if one is eating it plain [without a dip].[456] This applies even in areas that people abstain from eating raw onions plain, and only eat it together with other foods, such as bread or in a salad, nevertheless the blessing of Hadama is recited upon eating it plain. [However, whenever the onion is eaten with another food, then the regular rules of Ikkur and Tafel apply, and only one blessing is recited on the Ikkur. The above ruling follows the opinion of

---

[451] Chida ibid that so is the custom of the masses [although he concludes to say Hamotzi]; Sdei Chemed Brachos 1:10 that many Sephardim are accustomed to say Mezonos unlike Ashkenazim and they have upon whom to rely; Yechaveh Daas ibid; Or Letziyon 2:13-3; Piskeiy Teshuvos ibid; Halacha Berura ibid
When after Pesach do they begin reciting Mezonos: On Motzei Pesach, one still recites Hamotzi. Starting the next day, one recites Mezonos. [Or Letziyon ibid] Some Rabbanim, however, rule that one recites Hamotzi until Pesach Sheiyni. [Rav Mordechai Eliyahu za"l]

[452] Yechaveh Daas ibid; Minchas Yitzchak ibid; Shevet Halevi ibid; Piskeiy Teshuvos ibid; Halacha Berura ibid

[453] Seder 6:12; Luach 9:11-12; Admur 205:1-2; Ketzos Hashulchan 51:3; Luach Rav Elyashvili; Luach in end of Seder Birchas Hanehnin in English; Luach of Rav Prus; See Piskeiy Teshuvos 202:35; Article of Rav Chaim Rapaport, printed in Koveitz Hearos Ubiurim Oholei Torah
Other opinions: Some Poskim rule that today, being people no longer eat raw onions without bread, the blessing over raw onions is Shehakol, and they likewise rule that cooked onions are Shehakol [See Poskim below] Nonetheless, even accoridng to their opinion, Bedieved one who says Hadama is Yotzei. [See Rav Akiva Eiger 475 on M"A 475:10 that one is Yotzei Bedieved if he said a Hadama on a vegetable that is Shehakol when eaten raw.]

[454] Admur Seder ibid, Luach 9:11, and 205:1 [in parentheses], *"Even vegetables of which majority of people are not accustomed to eat raw, but rather with bread or another food, such as onions and the like, one recites a blessing of Borei Peri Hadama upon eating them when they are raw."*; Chok Yaakov 475:16 regarding horseradish and the same would apply to onions; Ketzos Hashulchan ibid; Michaber 205:1 regarding raw garlic; Luach Rav Elyashvili; Luach in end of Seder Birchas Hanehnin in English; Luach of Rav Prus; Hearos of Rav Mordechai Eliyahu in Sefer Vezos Habracha p. 361 "a raw onion that is not sharp is Hadama"; So is understood from all the following Poskim who mention using onions for Karpas, which must be a Hadama vegetable: Aruch Hashulchan 473:10 in 1st option; Misgeres Hashulchan 118:1; Yesod Veshoresh Havoda 9:4; Chayeh Adam 130:5 [unlike Binas Adam 51:1]; Implication of Elya Raba 473:27 who only negates onions due to bad breath [However, see Chok Yaakov 475:16 and Ritva Seder Haggadah that even raw Shehakol vegetables used for Karpas get elevated to Hadama]
Very sharp onions: Garlic and onions which are very old and are thereby not fit to be eaten without bread due to their great sharpness, receive the blessing of Shehakol. [Admur 205:1; Luach 9:11; Taz 205:2] Omitted from Admur in Seder ibid, Vetzaruch Iyun as to the reason; See Seder ibid of Rav Elyashvili footnote 74 that perhaps here Admur holds that even very sharp onions are Hadama when eaten with another food; However, see Kaf Hachaim 205:9 that if they are very sharp they do not receive a blessing
Other opinions: Some Poskim rule that today, being people no longer eat raw onions without bread, the blessing over raw onions is Shehakol. [Shaareiy Teshuvah 205:3 concludes like Bach 205 to say Shehakol on raw onions; Binas Adam 51:1; M"B 205:5 based on Shaareiy Teshuvah and Binas Adam, and conclusion of Shaar Hatziyon 205:7 based on implication of M"A 475:10; Kaf Hachaim 205:9; Igros Moshe O.C. 1:64 "The directive is to say Shehakol on raw garlic and onions"; However, see Igros Moshe 1:62 regarding radishes that he suspects for the opinion of Admur and says it is best to eat it only with bread; Rav Wozner in Koveitz Mibeis Levi 17:51; Piskeiy Teshuvos 202:35; 205:2] Furthermore, some Poskim rule that the blessing of raw onions is Shehakol at all times [even when people would eat them raw]. [Implication of Bach 205, brought in M"A 205:3, regarding garlic; Tur 205 in name of Geonim regarding garlic] Nonetheless, even according to their opinion, Bedieved one who says Hadamah on raw onions is Yotzei. [See Rav Akiva Eiger 475 on M"A 475:10 that one is Yotzei Bedieved if he said a Hadamah on a vegetable that is Shehakol when eaten raw.]
Breslov tradition: To note, that in Breslov they have a tradition from the Baal Shem Tov to never eat raw onions whether plain or with other foods. [See Sichos Rebbe Nachman MiBreslov 265]

[455] The reason: Although all foods that are of better taste and quality when cooked rather than raw, receive the blessing of Hadama/Haeitz upon being cooked and the blessing of Shehakol upon being eaten raw, nevertheless, this only applies if majority of people are not accustomed to eating the food raw due to this reason. [Admur Seder 6:11; Luach 10:22; Admur 202:16; 205:1; Michaber 202:12; Tosafos Brachos 38b] If, however, the majority of people eat also the food when raw, such as species of vegetables and legumes, then even though the food is of better quality/taste when cooked, nevertheless one recites the proper blessing of Hadama/Haeitz whether it is eaten raw or cooked. [Admur Seder 6:12; Luach 9:10; 10:22; Admur 202:16; 205:1; M"A 205:3; however M"A 473:4 brings a dispute on this matter; Rashi Brachos 38b; Rabbeinu Yona Brachos 27a; P"M 205 A"A 3; Kaf Hachaim 202:88; 205:5] Now, this applies even if majority of people do not commonly eat the food alone in its raw state, but rather together with bread or another food [i.e. in salad], such as onions and the like [i.e. garlic], nonetheless one recites the blessing of Hadama over them. [Admur Seder ibid; Luach 9:11; 205:1 in parentheses; Chok Yaakov 475:16 regarding why horseradish is Hadama, as it is eaten with a dip, and the same would apply here regarding onions, as writes M"B in Shaar Hatziyon 205:7; See also M"B 203:14; See Shevet Halevi 10:125] However, this only applies if the food is still somewhat edible in its raw state and hence some people do eat the vegetable plain. However, if the food is completely inedible in its raw state, such as horseradish and the like, then no blessing is said over it even if it can be eaten together with other foods. [See Admur 475:23 and M"A 475:10 who says not to say a blessing on horseradish for this reason, and Chok Yaakov 475:16 who argues that one says Hadamah on raw horseradish being that it is eaten with other dips. Thus, in order to avoid a contradiction, we must conclude as above that according to Admur, there is a difference between a food that is edible in a time of need, and a food that is not edible at all; See article of Rav Chaim Rappaport]

[456] Admur 205:1 in parentheses; Luach ibid

Admur, however many are accustomed to reciting the blessing of Shehakol on raw onions, as rule other Poskim.[457] Nonetheless, even according to their opinion, one who said Hadama on raw onions is Yotzei.[458]]

Cooked:[459] The blessing over cooked onions is Shehakol.[460] [However, fried onions are Hadama when eaten plain.[461]]

Summary:
Per the rulings of Admur, raw [and fried] onions are Hadama. Cooked onions are Shehakol. Other Poskim, however, rule that even raw onions are Shehakol, although Bedieved one fulfills his obligation if Hadama was said.

---------------*Bracha Achrona*----------------

31. Sitting during the recital of an after blessing:

Birchas Hamazon:[462] One is required to sit while reciting Birchas Hamazon.[463] He may not stand or lay down.[464] This applies irrelevant of the position in which one ate, whether he was walking in his home when he ate, or he ate standing or laying down, nonetheless, when it comes time to Recite Birchas Hamazon, he must recite it while sitting. In the event that one did not sit during Birchas Hamazon, then he fulfills his obligation, even if he recited Birchas Hamazon while walking.[465]

Meiyn Shalosh:[466] Only Birchas Hamazon is required to be recited in a sitting position, while other [after] blessings are not required to be said sitting.[467] However, some Poskim[468] rule one is required to recite

---

[457] See other opinions in previous footnotes!

[458] Rav Akiva Eiger 475 on M"A 475:10 that one is Yotzei Bedieved if he said a Hadama on a vegetable that is Shehakol when eaten raw, as it is nevertheless a food that grows from the ground

[459] Admur Seder ibid *"However, over cooked onions one recites the blessing of Shehakol Nihyah Bidvaro."*; Luach 9:14; Admur 205:2; Michaber and Rama 205:1 regarding garlic; Brachos 38b regarding garlic; Tur 205; Rosh 6:15; Rabbeinu Yona Brachos 37a; Tosafos Brachos ibid; Bach 205; Shaareiy Teshuvah 205:3; M"B 205:5; Ketzos Hashulchan ibid; Igros Moshe 1:64; Rav Wozner in Koveitz Mibeis Levi 17:51; Az Nidbaru 13:36; Piskeiy Teshuvos 205:2; Luach Rav Elyashvili; Luach in end of Seder Birchas Hanehnin in English; Luach of Rav Prus;

Very sharp onions: Garlic and onions which are very old and are thereby not fit to be eaten without bread due to their great sharpness, receive the blessing of Hadama after they are cooked, even if they are cooked on their own. [Admur 205:1; Luach 9:12; Taz 205:2] Omitted from Admur in Seder ibid, Vetzaruch Iyun as to the reason; See Seder ibid of Rav Elyashvili footnote 75 that perhaps here Admur holds that even very sharp onions are Shehakol when cooked

Other opinions: Some Poskim rule that cooked onions are Hadama. [Kaf Hachaim 205:9; See Piskeiy Teshuvos 205:2 footnote 5 that perhaps they should be Hadama and hence concludes that one should eat a Shehakol and Hadama food to exempt it]

[460] The reason: As onions which are cooked independently become ruined [as their taste is no longer as good as it was when they were raw- Admur 205:2] [and they hence lose their advantageous Bracha]. [Furthermore, even if the onions are cooked with meat and hence become enhanced in taste and quality, nevertheless their blessing is demoted to Shehakol, as the meat or dish which enhanced them is the main food of the mixture, as their entire reason for the onions being cooked with the meat or dish is for the onions to give taste to the meat and dish, and not on the contrary for the meat and dish to give taste to the onions. [Admur Seder ibid; Luach ibid; Admur 205:2 "Their enhancement is not intrinsic...and the meat is the Ikkur"; Rama 205:1; Tur 205; Rosh 6:15; Rabbeinu Yona Brachos 37a; Tosafos Brachos ibid; M"A 205:5; Elya Raba 205:4]

[461] M"B 205:7; Piskeiy Teshuvos 205:2; See Admur 205:2 regarding nuts fried in honey that they are Haeitz being that the main intent is the nut and not the honey

The reason: As the onions become enhanced in their quality and taste when they are fried, and they become the main intent of the food. [M"B ibid] Vetzaruch Iyun regarding if one fried it for the sake of adding to another food, and not for the sake of eating plain.

[462] Admur 183:12; Michaber 183:9; Rambam Hilchos Brachos 4:1; Brachos 51b

[463] The reason: As one is able to concentrate more while sitting. [Admur ibid; Michaber ibid] This is hinted to in the verse "Vesavata Uveirachta", as Vesavata can be read as Vesheiv Eis, that one should sit and then Bentch. [Tosafus ibid in name of Rebbe Moshe Albert]

[464] The reason: One is not to recite Birchas Hamazon in a laying position, as doing so is an act of arrogance, and rather he is to sit in awe. [Admur ibid]

[465] Admur ibid; Rama ibid; Mordechai Brachos 184; Rambam ibid

[466] Admur 183:13

[467] Stam opinion in Admur ibid; Tosafos Brachos 51b; See Biur Hagr"a who implies that all Rishonim who hold one is not required to recite Meiyn Shalosh in the original place of eating agree here as well that one is not required to sit while reciting it; Kaf Hachaim 184:50

The reason: As the Sages were only stringent regarding Birchas Hamazon, being it is a Biblical after blessing. [Admur ibid]

[468] 2nd opinion in Admur ibid; Opinion in Michaber 183:10; Mordechai Brachos 184; Rambam Hilchos Brachos 4:1; See Biur Hagr"a who implies that all Rishonim who hold one is t required to recite Meiyn Shalosh in the original place of eating, agree here as well that one is required to sit while reciting it.

Meiyn Gimel [i.e. Al Hamichya/Peiros/Gefen] in a sitting position, just as Birchas Hamazon.[469] Practically, one is to suspect for the latter opinion, and recite Meiyn Shalosh in a sitting position.[470]

Borei Nefashos:[471] One is not required to recite Borei Nefashos in a sitting position. [However, some Poskim[472] conclude that it is proper to recite all blessings in a sitting position.]

Summary:
One is initially required to recite Birchas Hamazon in a sitting position and should be stringent to also recite Meiyn Shalosh in a sitting position. If one recited the blessing in a standing position, he nevertheless fulfills his obligation. One is not required even initially to recite Borei Nefashos in a sitting position, [although some say it is proper to do so].

Q&A

Until what part of Birchas Hamazon must one remain sitting?
Some Poskim[473] rule one is required to sit for the entire duration of Birchas Hamazon, including the fourth blessing of Hatov Vehameitiv. One is to remain sitting even during the Harachamons, until after Oseh Shalom.[474]

------------------*Birchas Hamazon*----------------

32. Kavana in Birchas Hamazon-Understanding the words of Birchas Hamazon & The preferred language it is be said in:[475]

Understanding the meaning of the words: If one does not know the meaning of the words that he is saying in Birchas Hamazon, such as due to his lack of understanding of the language, then he does not fulfill his obligation.[476] Some Poskim[477] rule that this applies even if one reads Birchas Hamazon in Lashon Hakodesh. This applies even if one knows [generally] that he is blessing Hashem through these words and he intends to do so while reciting them, nevertheless it is invalid.[478] However, some Poskim[479] rule that if one recites Birchas Hamazon in Lashon Hakodesh, in contrast to other languages, then he fulfills his

---

[469] The reason: Although Meiyn Shalosh is only a Rabbinical requirement, nonetheless, since it is similar to the three Biblical blessings, therefore it should be said in the same sitting position. [Admur ibid]

[470] Admur ibid; Chesed Lealafim 183:10; Ben Ish Chaiy Chukas 4; Kaf Hachaim 183:51

[471] Admur 183:13

[472] Chesed Lealafim 183:10; Ben Ish Chaiy Chukas 4; Kaf Hachaim 183:51; See P"M Pesicha Koleles Brachos; 432 M"Z 1

[473] M"B 183:31; See Shaar Hatziyon ibid for explanation; See Halacha Berura [Yosef] ibid

[474] Ruach Chaim 191:2; Kaf Hachaim 191:5

[475] 185:1

[476] Admur 185:1; brought also in Admur 62:2; Tosafos Brachos 45b; Rabbeinu Yona Brachos ibid; Rosh Brachos 7:6; Mordechai Remez 158; Michaber 193:1 regarding hearing Birchas Hamazon from another; Implication of Tur 690; Beis Yosef 690 in name of Maggid Mishneh Megillah 2:4; Ramban Megillah 171; Rashba Megillah ibid
The reason: As the verse states, "And he shall bless Hashem your G-d" and if one does not understand the words of the blessing that he is verbalizing then he is not considered to be blessing Hashem. [Admur 185:1]
Other opinions: Some Poskim rule that one who reads Birchas Hamazon fulfills his obligation even if he does not know the meaning of the words, and only when hearing it from another is it required to understand the meaning of the words. [Levush 193:1; Olas Tamid 193:2; M"A 193:2; Soles Belula 193:1; Shaar Efraim 13; Kaf Hachaim 193:4; Aruch Hashulchan 185:7] This seemingly applies to all languages. [Kaf Hachaim ibid] However some Poskim rule that this only applies to Lashon Hakodesh while other languages everyone agrees that one must understand the language. [P"M 193 A"A 2, brought in Kaf Hachaim ibid] Admur ibid negates this entire ruling and in the gloss on this Halacha [possibly written by Admur or the Maharil] he argues that based on Megillah 18a it is not possible to accept this differentiation between the verbalizer and listener and so is clearly written in Rosh ibid and Rabbeinu Yona ibid that one must always understand the language, even in Lashon Hakodesh. [See however Kaf Hachaim ibid that their intent is only Lechatchila]

[477] Admur 185:1; brought also in Admur 62:2; Tosafos Brachos 45b; Rabbeinu Yona Brachos ibid; Rosh Brachos 7:6; Mordechai Remez 158; Michaber 193:1 regarding hearing Birchas Hamazon from another; Implication of Tur 690; Beis Yosef 690 in name of Maggid Mishneh Megillah 2:4; Ramban Megillah 171; Rashba Megillah ibid

[478] The reason: Regarding Bittul Chametz we find in the M"A 434:6 and Admur 434:8 that one fulfills his obligation even if he does not know the meaning of the words so long as he understands the intent of what he is saying; that he is nullifying the Chametz. Nevertheless, this is because by Bittul Chametz, the main aspect of the Mitzvah is not the verbalization, but the intent of the heart to nullify it, as brought in Chok Yaakov 434:1. However, Birchas Hamazon must be verbalized in order to fulfill the Mitzvah, and hence one must understand the words that he is verbalizing. [Admur ibid in parentheses]

[479] 2nd opinion in Admur 185:1; Rashi brought in Taz 193:2, M"A 193:2, Beis Yosef 193, Rosh and Mordechai ibid; Tosafos and Rabbeinu Yona in name of Yeish Omrim

obligation even if he does not understand the language. Practically, the custom is like this latter opinion to fulfill Birchas Hamazon in Lashon Hakodesh even if one does not understand the language[480], even though it is proper to be stringent like the first opinion.[481] [Thus, initially, one must be very careful to study the language of the words of Birchas Hamazon.[482] However, Bedieved, if one recited Birchas Hamazon in Lashon Hakodesh, he fulfills his obligation even if he does not understand the words of the blessing.[483] However, if one recited it in another language which he does not understand, he must repeat Birchas Hamazon according to all opinions.[484]]

Paying attention: Even if one understands the language of the words of Birchas Hamazon, such as he understands Lashon Hakodesh, if his mind wanders and he thinks of other matters while reciting the blessing, he does not fulfill his obligation.[485] However, some Poskim[486] rule that if one recites Birchas Hamazon in Lashon Hakodesh, in contrast to other languages, then he fulfills his obligation even if he did not pay attention to the words. Practically, initially one must be very careful to pay attention to the words of Birchas Hamazon [even in Lashon Hakodesh].[487] However, Bedieved, if one recited Birchas Hamazon in Lashon Hakodesh, he fulfills his obligation even if he did not pay attention to the words of the blessing.[488] [However, if one recited it in another language and did not pay attention to the words, he must repeat Birchas Hamazon according to all opinions.[489]]

The main words that require concentration:[490] The main words of Birchas Hamazon that require understanding and concentration are the words "Baruch Ata Hashem" and the conclusion of the sentence which states what one is blessing Hashem for. This applies for both the opening and closing blessing of a long blessing [such as the first blessing in Birchas Hamazon which has an opening and closing blessing, however the 2nd-3rd blessing of Birchas Hamazon only has a closing blessing while the 4th blessing only has an opening blessing]. However, the remaining words that are said in the middle of a long blessing, one fulfills his obligation by reciting them even if he does not know the meaning of the words or did not pay attention to them. This applies even towards words that invalidate the Birchas Hamazon if they are

---

[480] Admur ibid; Rama 199:7; Darkei Moshe 193:1"So is the custom and I have never seen anyone protest it"; Bach 193; Taz 193:2; M"A 193:2; Elya Raba 193:2; Kneses Hagedola 293:2; Olas Tamid 193:2; Kaf Hachaim 193:2

[481] Admur 185:1; See Taz ibid that we rule like the first opinion and only when its either this or nothing that we say one should follow Rashi even initially,

[482] Admur 185:2 regarding paying attention to the words and the same would apply regarding learning the meaning of the words; Birchas Habayis 41:43; See Tehila Ledavid 193:1 that questions the Admur as to why in 185:1 he concludes that it is only "proper to be stringent like the first opinion" and here in 185:2 he concludes "one Must be very careful." One can simply say that in 186:1 were discussing a case that one right now has a choice to Bentch either in English or Lashon Hakodesh which he does not understand, and on this Admur states the initial law and custom. However, here in 185:2 Admur is discussing mainly paying attention to the words of the language that he already understands, and thus concludes one must be very careful, especially in Birchas Hamazon, even in Lashon Hakodesh, as some say he does not fulfill his obligation even initially. Accordingly, one is certainly to be "very careful" to make time to learn the words of Birchas Hamazon when saying in Lashon Hakodesh. See Admur 101:5!

[483] Admur 185:1 and 2; Ketzos Hashulchan 44:4

[484] As the entire dispute in Admur 185:1 is only regarding Lashon Hakodesh; P"M 193 A"A 2 that so applies even according to M"A ibid; See however conclusion of Admur 185:2 and Tehila Ledavid 193:1 from which one can learn differently, however simply speaking Admur 185:2 is referring to Lashon Hakodesh; See also Kaf Hachaim 193:4

[485] Admur ibid; This follows all opinions brought in "understanding the language" who hold of the former opinion brought in Admur

[486] 2nd opinion in Admur 185:1; Rashi brought in Taz 193:2, M"A 193:2, Beis Yosef 193, Rosh and Mordechai ibid; Tosafos and Rabbeinu Yona in name of Yeish Omrim

[487] Admur 185:2; Seder 9:3; Ketzos Hashulchan 44:4

The reason: As according to some opinion one does not fulfill his obligation even Bedieved. [Admur 185:2] See Tehila Ledavid 193:1 that questions the Admur as to why in 185:1 he concludes that it is only "proper to be stringent like the first opinion" and here in 185:2 he concludes "one must be very careful." One can simply say that in 185:1 were discussing a case that one right now has a choice to Bentch either in English or Lashon Hakodesh which he does not understand, and on this Admur states the initial law and custom. However here in 185:2 Admur is discussing mainly paying attention to the words of the language that he already understands, and thus concludes one must be very careful, especially in Birchas Hamazon, even in Lashon Hakodesh, as some say he does not fulfill his obligation even initially. Accordingly, one is certainly to be "very careful" to take time to learn the words of Birchas Hamazon when saying it in Lashon Hakodesh. See Admur 101:5!

[488] Admur 185:1 that the custom is like the second opinion and 185:2 that Bedieved one is Yotzei, as Safek Brachos Lihakel; Ketzos Hashulchan 44:4

[489] As the entire dispute in Admur 185:1 is only regarding Lashon Hakodesh; P"M 193 A"A 2 that so applies even according to M"A ibid; See however conclusion of Admur 185:2 and Tehila Ledavid 193:1 from which one can learn differently, however simply speaking Admur 185:2 is referring to Lashon Hakodesh; See also Kaf Hachaim 193:4

[490] Admur 185:2 in parentheses

not recited, such as Bris, and Torah, and Birchas Haaretz, and Malchus Beis David that is recited in Boneh Yerushalayim, as only their lack of recital invalidates and not their lack of understanding.[491]

Summary:
One must be very careful to understand the words of Birchas Hamazon and pay attention to the words while reciting it. If one did not do so, then if he recited Birchas Hamazon in Lashon Hakodesh, it is disputed if he fulfills his obligation, and Safek Brachos Lihakel. However, if he said it in a different language that he does not understand, or did not pay attention to, he must repeat Birchas Hamazon. This applies specifically if he did not understand or pay attention to the sentences of the blessing that begin with Baruch Ata Hashem, however the other words of the blessing do not invalidate the blessing if one recited it without understanding or paying attention.

Segulah to prevent Divine punishment and for Parnasa:[492]
The letter "end Pei" is the only letter in the Alphabet that is omitted from Birchas Hamazon. This is because it stands for "Charon Af", wrath and anger, and whoever recites Birchas Hamazon with Kavana does not receive any wrath. Likewise, his food is found before him in plenty and with honor for his entire life.

Saying Birchas Hamazon within a Siddur:[493]
One is to recite Birchas Hamazon specifically within a Siddur and is not to say it by heart.

Story in Sefer Chassidim:[494]
Sefer Chassidim relates a story of a man who passed away and came in a dream to one of his relatives and related to him that every day he is judged on the fact that he did not have proper concentration in Birchas Hamazon.

33. Are women to perform Mayim Achronim?

Letter of law: The Sages instituted the washing of hands at the end of a meal of bread in order so one recites Birchas Hamazon in purity and cleanses his hands from the leftover food.[495] There is no difference mentioned in Halacha between men and women regarding this obligation, and just as men are obligated to perform Mayim Achronim, so too women.[496]

Custom: Nevertheless, the widespread custom today amongst women is to no longer be particular in performing Mayim Achronim.[497] Some Poskim[498] justify this custom.[499] Other Poskim[500], however, negate

---

[491] The reason: As these words are not considered a blessing to which one can claim that if one does not understand the meaning he is not considered to be blessing Hashem. [Admur ibid]

[492] Beir Heiytiv 185:1; Ateres Zekeinim 185; Bach 185 [regarding the letter Pei]; Mateh Moshe 304, brought in Kaf Hachaim 180:15; Rokeiach 336; Tashbatz 315 or 366; Sefer Hachinuch Parshas Eikev [regarding Parnasa]; Kaf Hachaim 185:2; Ketzos Hashulchan 44:4

[493] Bach 185, brought in Beir Heiytiv ibid

[494] Sefer Chassidim 46, brought in Bach ibid; Beir Heiytiv ibid; Ateres Zekeinim ibid; Kaf Hachaim ibid

[495] The Mitzvah of Mayim Achronim is a Mitzvah of holiness, to sanctify oneself to bless Hashem over the food he ate. The reason this sanctity is needed is because prior to the washing the hands are dirty with the filth of the foods that were eaten, and they are hence invalid for saying the blessing. [Admur 181:1; Rabbeinu Yona 40a; Maadanei Yom Tov on Rosh ibid Taf; Brachos 53b] In additional reason behind the obligation of washing hands is due to the Sodomite salt that rests on the hands after a meal, and the sodomite salt can blind a person if it touches his eyes. The Sages thus obligated that one wash his hands after a meal. [Admur ibid; Rabbeinu Yona ibid; Chulin 105:1;]

[496] Toras Chaim Sofer 181:1; Salmei Chaim [Rav Chaim Zonenfeld] 119 "Without doubt [women are obligated]"; Rav SZ"A, brought in Vezos Habracha 14 and Halichos Bas Yisrael 3; Halichos Olam 2 Parshas Shelach; Halacha Berura 181; Sheivet Haleivi 4:23 that from the letter of the law there is no difference; See Mor Uketzia 181; Aruch Hashulchan 181:5 "One is to warn all his household to perform Mayim Achronim"; See Rashi Yuma 83b that a certain man's wife was killed as a result of him not doing Mayim Achronim

The reason: There is also no logic to differentiate between the genders, as the reasons behind the institution of Mayim Achronim apply equally to men and women, so they have clean and pure hands upon reciting Birchas Hamazon. [Salmas Chaim ibid]

[497] So testifies: Mor Uketzia ibid that our women are not particular to do so as they eat with a fork and do not touch food during the meal; Hagahos Taharas Hashulchan 181 questions why women do not do so

the custom and rule woman are to be careful in this matter just like men. [Practically, each family and community are to follow their custom, and each have upon whom to rely. Regarding the Chabad custom, while there is no known written testimony from the Rabbeim on this matter, the widespread custom amongst women of Anash is not to wash Mayim Achronim.[501]]

34. Covering the knife during Benching:[502]

It is customary to cover the knife during the recital of Birchas Hamazon.[503] It is not necessary to remove the knives from the table, so long as the knife is covered.[504] [One may however choose to remove the knife rather than cover it.[505]]

Shabbos and Yom Tov:[506] On Shabbos and Yom Tov, the custom of many communities is not to cover the knives.[507] The custom of the Jewish people is Torah [and one is thus to specifically leave the knives revealed[508]].

---

[498] Mor Uketzia ibid; Shevet Halevi 4:23; Piskeiy Teshuvos 181:1

[499] The reason: The reason for this is because we find that even by men, many are no longer accustomed to performing Mayim Achronim, as one of its main reasons of performance is to cleanse the hands of the Sodomite salt, and this salt is no longer common today. Likewise, we are no longer particular to wash hands after touching foods, and hence the hands are no longer considered dirty. [Admur 181:9; M"A 181:8; Michaber 181:10; Darkei Moshe 181 that so is Minhag Ashkenaz; Tosafos Brachos 53b, Chulin 105a; Rosh Brachos 8; Mordechai Remez 207] Accordingly, although the widespread custom amongst men is to be stringent despite the above justifications, most women never accepted this stringency upon themselves and hence are not accustomed to perform Mayim Achronim. [Sheivet Halevi ibid] Alternatively, the reason is because women eat with forks and do not get their hands dirty during the meal. [Mur Uketzia ibid] Alternatively, women are constantly in the kitchen during the meal, and end up washing hands regardless. [Heard from Rav Groner]

[500] All Poskim in previous footnotes regarding the letter of the law

[501] Related to me by Rabbi Leibal Groner that they are not accustomed to wash, and there is no need to do so.

[502] Admur 180:6; Michaber 180:5; Shibulei Haleket 155; Rokeiach 332; Abudarham; Ketzos Hashulchan 44:5

Other customs: Some are not accustomed to cover or remove the knives during Birchas Hamazon. [Aruch Hashulchan 1870:6; Darkei Chaim Veshalom 302]

[503] The reason: The reason for this is because a table is similar to a Mizbeiach, and regarding the Mizbeiach the verse states "Don't wave iron over them", as iron shortens the days of man, while the Mizbeiach lengthens the days of man, and it is improper that one wave the "shortening of life" over the "prolonging of life". The same applies to one's table which also lengthens the days of man and atones for his sins upon him hosting guests, as how great is the power of dining [together with others] that it causes the Shechina to rest [upon one's home]. [Admur ibid; M"A 180:4; 1st reason in Beis Yosef and Taz 180:3 and M"B 180:11 in name of Rokeiach ibid]

Other reasons mentioned in Poskim: 1) Rabbeinu Simcha states that the reason why we remove the knives during Birchas Hamazon is due to a certain tragedy that occurred after the destruction: A certain man was reciting Birchas Hamazon and upon reaching the blessing of Boneh Yerushalayim and remembering the destruction he took a knife from the table and stabbed himself. [2nd reason in Beis Yosef and Taz 180:3 and M"B 180:11] 2) Alternatively, the reason is because the blessing of Eisav is to live by the sword, and in Birchas Hamazon we mention the blessing of Yaakov of Tal Hashamayim and Shamneiy Haaretz. We therefore cover the knife of Eisav while reciting the blessings of Yaakov. [Mateh Moshe 304, brought in Kaf Hachaim 180:15] 3) Alternatively, the reason is because the letter end Pei is the only letter in the Alphabet that is omitted from Birchas Hamazon. This is because it stands for "Charon Af", wrath and anger, and whoever recites Birchas Hamazon with Kavana does not receive any wrath, and his food is found before him in plenty and with honor for his entire life. We therefore cover the knife which represents wrath. [Mateh Moshe ibid; Rokeiach 336; Tashbatz 315 or 366; See Beir Heiytiv 185:1] 4) Alternatively, the reason is because in Birchas Hamazon we request that Moshiach arrive, and in the future the sword will no longer be used, and we hence cover the knife to hint to this prediction. [Kaf Hachaim ibid] 5) The Arizal writes that one who is from the root of Kayin must remove the knife from the table. [Ruach Hakodesh p. 10, brought in Kaf Hachaim 180:15]

Ramifications between reasons: The practical ramifications between the reasons mentioned is regarding a) Must one remove the knife, or does covering it suffice. b) Does it apply to all knives, or only iron; c) Does it apply on Shabbos and Yom Tov, or only during the week.

[504] Admur ibid; Michaber ibid; Chesed Lealafim 180:5 "One is to cover the knife or remove it"

Other opinions: According to the reason of Rabbeinu Simcha, it does not suffice to cover the knives, but the knives must be actually removed from the table. [So writes Rabbeinu Simcha brought in sources ibid "to remove the knives" and so concludes Shulchan Hatahor 180:4; Piskeiy Teshuvos 180:5] The Arizal writes that one who is from the root of Kayin must remove the knife from the table, and it does not suffice to simply cover it. [Ruach Hakodesh p. 10, brought in Kaf Hachaim 180:15] Based on this, everyone today is to remove the knife from the table and not suffice with covering it, as the sparks have become mixed and we no longer know if we are from Kayin or Hevel. [Kaf Hachaim ibid]

[505] Chesed Lealafim ibid

[506] Admur ibid; Michaber ibid; Birkeiy Yosef in name of Ramak and Rav Avraham Azulaiy, brought in Shaareiy Teshuvah 180:4

Other opinions: Some are accustomed to cover the knife even on Shabbos and Yom Tov. [Levush, brought in M"A 180:4] According to the reason of Rabbeinu Simcha, there is no difference between Shabbos and the weekday, and the knife is to be removed by all times. [Beis Yosef ibid brought in Taz ibid] Others however rule that even according to the reason of Rabbeinu Simcha, there is no need to remove the knife on Shabbos, as on Shabbos a person is not so distressed. [Taz ibid] According to the reason brought in the Arizal ibid, one is to remove the knives from the table even on Shabbos and Yom Tov, as the souls root in Kayin does not change on Shabbos. [Kaf Hachaim 180:15]

[507] The reason: As only during the week is a knife required to be covered due to it being the weapon of Eisav. However, on Shabbos and Yom Tov there is no Satan and damaging forces. [Admur ibid; Toldas Yaakov brought in Elya Raba 180:7] As Shabbos hints to the world to come, in which all the severities are sweetened, and death will be abolished. [Birkeiy Yosef in name of Rav Avraham Azulaiy, brought in Shaareiy Teshuvah 180:4]

Other reasons mentioned in Poskim: As on Shabbos we do not build the Mizbeiach, and the table thus does not have any hint to the Mizbeiach. [M"A 180:4] The prohibition of waving iron on the Mizbeiach is only while it is being built, and hence since it cannot be built on Shabbos, it is

Q&A

Must one cover knives that are not made of iron, but from other metals, such as gold or silver?
Some Poskim[509] rule one is only required to cover a knife which is made of iron, and not of other material, such as gold, silver, copper or plastic. Other Poskim[510], however, rule that all forms of metal knives are to be covered.[511] Practically, the custom is to cover all metal knives.
Plastic knives: Plastic knives do not need to be covered.[512]

Must one cover the entire knife, or does it suffice to cover just the blade?
Some[513] write the entire knife is to be covered, and not just the metal blade.

Must one cover all the knives on the table, and what is one to if there are other people still using their knives?
Some[514] write one is not required to cover all the knives of the table, but simply the knives that are within his reach. Certainly, one is not required to cover the knives that other people are still using.

Must one cover the knife when reciting Meiyn Shalosh, or Borei Nefashos?[515]
No.

35. How many people must eat together to be able to make a Zimun of ten with Elokeinu?[516]

In order to be obligated/allowed to make a Zimun of ten people with the saying of Elokeinu, one needs to have at least **seven** people who have eaten [a Kezayis of] bread, and another **three** people who have eaten a Kezayis of other vegetables [or any other food], or have drank a Revius of a liquid, including even water.[517] However, if only six people have eaten [a Kezayis of] bread, another four people who did not eat bread cannot join for the making of a Zimun with Elokeinu, even if they ate a Kezayis, or Revius, of other foods and drinks.[518] In all cases, the three non-bread eaters are only valid to join the Zimun of ten if they have not yet recited an after blessing of Al Hamichya or Borei Nefashos.[519]

---

therefore not relevant to require it to be covered. [Machatzis Hashekel ibid] Others however rule that even according to this reason, the knife is to be removed on Shabbos, as even on Shabbos the concept of the Mizbeiach which was built during the week is in existence. [Taz 180:3; Machatzis Hashekel 180:4]

[508] Shulchan Hatahor 180:4; Darkei Chaim Veshalom 302

[509] M"A 180:4 in name of Shulchan Araba [omitted in Admur ibid]; Daas Torah 180; Tehila Ledavid 180

[510] P"M 180 A"A 4; Beis Avi 3:1145; Shevet Halevi 1:205; Az Nidbaru 7:2; Piskeiy Teshuvos 180:5

[511] The reason: As it is not possible to hew the stones of the Mizbeiach using metal knives, as the stones must be smooth. [ibid]

[512] Pashut, as they are not made of metal, and cannot kill, and therefore are not included in any of the reasons mentioned above for why we cover or remove the knife. [See Az Nidbaru 7:2; Piskeiy Teshuvos 180:5]

[513] Piskeiy Teshuvos 180:5

[514] Vayaan David 1:28; Piskeiy Teshuvos 180:5

[515] Ashel Avraham Butchach 180; See Salmas Chaim 187

[516] Admur 197:2; Michaber 197:2; Brachos 48b; Tur 197; Levush 197; Bach 197; Chayeh Adam 48:13; Derech Hachaim 5; Kitzur SHU"A 45:14; Beis Menucha 197:2; Chesed Lealafim 197:9; Ben Ish Chaiy Korach 5; Kaf Hachaim 197:17; Ketzos Hashulchan 45:3
Other opinions: Some Poskim rule four people who ate a Kezayis of foods other than bread can join six people who ate bread for the saying of Elokeinu. [Iggur in name of Or Zarua, brought in Beis Yosef 197; Erech Hashulchan 197:1 in name of Razah; Yerushalmi; Bereishis Raba 91; See Kaf Hachaim 197:17]

[517] Regarding the need for seven bread eaters: Poskim ibid; Regarding that even a Revius of water suffices: Admur ibid; M"A 197:6; Elya Raba 197:5; Chayeh Adam 48:13; Ketzos Hashulchan ibid
Other opinions: Some Poskim rule that it does not suffice to drink water in order to join a Zimun of three or ten. [Michaber 197:2; Levush 197; Beis Menucha 197:4; Bigdei Yesha 197; Magen Giborim; Chesed Lealafim 197:1; Ben Ish Chaiy Korach 5; Aruch Hashulchan 197:5; Shaar Hatziyon 197:10; Kaf Hachaim 197:15 that so is custom; Piskeiy Teshuvos 197:2] Rather, one must drink a significant beverage such as tea or coffee or pure juice. [Aruch Hashulchan 197:5; Piskeiy Teshuvos 197:2]
What should the three participants initially be given to eat? Some Poskim rule that initially, they are to be given bread to eat, as it is a Mitzvah Min Hamuvchar to have ten bread eaters even for Zimun of Elokeinu. [Ginas Veradim 1:10] However, from the Setimas Haposkim it is implied that this Hiddur is only applicable by a Zimun of three and not by a Zimun of ten. [See Admur 197:2; Michaber 197:2] Thus, one may even initially give the three participants other foods to eat. [Piskeiy Teshuvos 197 footnote 8]

[518] The reason: The reason three non-bread eaters can only join seven bread eaters is because seven is a recognizable majority [Rov Hanikur] which has eaten bread. However, six is not a recognizable majority, and hence is not valid to have another four people join. [Admur ibid; Michaber ibid; Brachos ibid]

Orach Chaim

----------------Miscellaneous blessings----------------

36. Which blessing is said first over a new fruit-Shehechiyanu or the blessing over the fruit?[520]

One who eats a new fruit which requires the recital of Shehechiyanu, is to first say the blessing of Shehechiyanu and only afterwards recite the blessing of Borei Peri Haeitz or Hadama.[521] [However, if one forgot and first said the blessing of Haeitz or Hadama, then he may recite Shehechiyanu afterword's, prior to eating the fruit.[522] The above ruling is only regarding the blessing of Shehechiyanu said prior to eating a new fruit, however, when saying Shehechiyanu over a Mitzvah, one first says the blessing over the Mitzvah [i.e. Asher Kidishanu], and only then says the blessing of Shehechiyanu.[523] The above follows the ruling of Admur and other Poskim, although the widespread custom of many is to always recite the blessing over the fruit and only afterwards to say Shehechiyanu.[524]]

37. Rainbow: Saying a blessing upon seeing a rainbow:[525]

One who sees a rainbow is to say the blessing of "Baruch Ata Hashem Elokeinu Melech Haolam Zocher Habris Neman Bevriso Vikayam Bimamaro."[526] [Some Poskim[527], however, rule that the rainbow

---

If one of the four ate Mezonos? It is questionable according to the Tur [who rules that Mezonos is valid like bread for a third person to join a Zimun of two bread eaters], whether a Mezonos eater is considered like a bread eater in this regard as well, and hence if six ate bread and four ate Mezonos, or even one ate Mezonos and three ate or drank other foods and liquids, then they join for Elokeinu. Practically this matter requires further analysis. [Ketzos Hashulchan 45 footnote 9]

[519] Admur 194:1; 197:4; M"A 197:4; Aguda Brachos 187; M"B 197:9

The law if one of the bread eaters already recited Birchas Hamazon: If one of the bread eaters already recited Birchas Hamazon, see Admur 194:1 that he can still join for a Zimun of three, and the same applies regarding a Zimun for ten, so long as there are still seven people remaining who ate bread and did not yet recite Birchas Hamazon. [Biur Halacha 194:1 "Echad Meihem"; Piskeiy Teshuvos 194:2] However, if four of the bread eaters already recited Birchas Hamazon, then they do not join. [Kochav Miyaakov 109; Piskeiy Teshuvos 194:2] Likewise, if three people did not eat bread, then if even one person recites Birchas Hamazon, he no longer joins for the seven bread eaters to recite Elokeinu, as there must remain seven bread eaters who did not recite Birchas Hamazon. [Piskeiy Teshuvos 194:3 based on Biur Halacha ibid in name of Elya Raba regarding Zimun of three]

[520] Seder Birchas Hanehnin 11:12; Yosef Ometz [Minhagim] 422; P"M 225 A"A 7; Conclusion of Mamar Mordechai 225:1; Kesones Yosef 225:18; Ashel Avraham Butchach 225; Chayeh Adam 62:8; Shulchan Hatahor 225:6; Aruch Hashulchan 225:5; Custom of Rav Nasan Adler and Chasam Sofer, brought in gloss on 225; Kesav Sofer 25; Daas Sofer 1:26; Kitzur SHU"A 59:14; M"B 225:11 in name of P"M ibid; Ketzos Hashulchan 63:1; See also regarding saying Shehechiyanu on a Tallis Gadol, that it is said prior to the blessing of Asher Kidishanu: Admur 22:1; Olas Tamid 22:2; Beir Heiytiv 22:2; See Piskeiy Teshuvos 225:12 for different customs and Poskim regarding this matter.

Other Poskim: Some Poskim rule one is to first say Haeitz and then Shehechiyanu and so is the custom of many. [Halachos Ketanos 1:236; Beir Heiytiv 225:6 in name of Halachos Ketanos; Glosses on Tur 225; Mamar Mordechai ibid that so is custom, although he himself concludes differently; Chida in Yosef Ometz 56; Machazik Bracha 22:3; Peri Hadama 1 Brachos 10; Yifei Laleiv 225:4; Maaseh Rav 21; Siddur Derech Hachaim; Ashel Avraham Butchach 600; Gloss of Chasam Sofer 225, even though he was accustomed differently; Avnei Nezer 450; Sdei Chemed Brachos 2:5; Aruch Hashulchan ibid that so is custom, although he concludes differently; Birchas Habayis 24:4; Kaf Hachaim 225:24 that so is the custom; Yechaveh Daas 3:15] See also regarding saying Shehechiyanu on a Tallis Gadol, that it is said after the blessing of Asher Kidishanu: Birkeiy Yosef 22:2 based on Elya Raba and Michaber; Machazik Bracha 22:3; Siddur Beis Oved 23; Shaareiy Teshuvah 22:2; Chesed Lealafim; Kitzur SHU"a 59:8; Kaf Hachaim [Falagi] 10:8; Ben Ish Chaiy Bereishis 7; Ashel Avraham Butchach 225; M"B 22:3; Kaf Hachaim 22:7; See Kaf Hachaim ibid that argues on the Beir Heiytiv who claims the Bach held of the opinion of the Olas Tamid. The reason behind this opinion is because they view Shehechiyanu as an obligatory blessing [see Yosef Ometz ibid] and thus we apply the rule of Tadir and Eino Tadir, Tadir Kodem.

Sephardi Custom: The Sephardi custom is to first recite the blessing of the fruit and only then Shehechiyanu. [See Sephardi Poskim ibid who make this statement]

[521] The reason: Some say the reason one is to precede the blessing of Shehechiyanu is because the blessing of Shehechiyanu is ideally said over the joy of seeing the fruit, and it just happens to be that the custom today is to approximate the blessing to the eating. Thus, one is to first say Shehechiyanu and only then the blessing over the fruit. [P"M ibid] Others, however, explain that the blessing of Shehechiyanu and Hatov Vehameitiv was established over the joy of having the fruit, while the blessing of Haeitz/Hadama was established to be said only when one actually eats the fruit. Thus, one is to first say Shehechiyanu on the joy and only then the blessing over the fruit. Accordingly, if one says the blessing of Shehechiyanu after the blessing of Haeitz/Hadama, but before the eating, it would constitute a Hefsek between the blessing and the eating. [Glosses on Seder by Rav Alyashvili] Alternatively, since the blessing of Shehechiyanu is voluntary, and is hence not appropriate to be said between the main blessing and eating. [Shaar Hatziyon 225]

[522] P"M 225 A"A 7; M"B 225:11; Ketzos Hashulchan 63 footnote 5; Likkutei Maharich

[523] Admur 643:1

The reason: As the blessing of Shehechiyanu over a Mitzvah was established to be recited only at the time of the Mitzvah.

[524] See other opinions in previous footnote who testify that so is the custom of the world, even though some of these Poskim conclude differently.

[525] Michaber 229:1; Brachos 59b

Ruling of Admur: Admur omitted the law of a rainbow from Seder and Luach Birchas Hanehnin. The Rebbe suggests that perhaps the reason is because it was uncommon to see rainbows in Russia [Igros Kodesh 16:328; Likkutei Sichos 10:200; Sichas Bechukosaiy 5741 3:468; printed in Shulchan Menachem 1:131]

[526] Background of Nussach and not to say the sentence of Neman prior to the blessing: In Brachos ibid it states that one is to state the blessing of Baruch Zocheir Habris, and then brings a Braisa which states that one is to say Neman Bevriso. Rav Papa concludes that one is to say both. Based on this Gemara, it became a widespread custom for people to say the sentence of Zocher Habris prior to the blessing of Neman Bevriso, and not

77

referenced to in this law is not necessarily the rainbow that we see today and hence one is to recite the blessing without Hashem's name. Practically, the Poskim[528] negate this opinion and rule the blessing is to be said with Hashem's name upon seeing a rainbow.[529] Nonetheless, one who avoids saying Hashem's name and simply thinks it in his mind is not to be protested.[530] The Chabad custom is to recite the blessing with Hashem's name.[531]]

Not to stare excessively at a rainbow:[532] It is forbidden for one to stare excessively at a rainbow. [However, it is permitted to gaze at it without an intense stare or prolonged contemplation.[533] The rainbow corresponds to the Shechina, and hence one who looks at it is considered to be looking at the Shechina.[534] The Talmud states that one who looks at it excessively is considered to not care for the honor of His Maker, and it is thus befitting for him to not have come into the world.[535] Likewise, one who does so causes his eyesight to weaken.[536] The Zohar[537] states that there are Kelipos which surround the rainbow and try to darken its light, thus explaining another reason for why it should not be looked it.]

Not to tell others of the rainbow:[538] One who sees a rainbow is not to inform others of it, as doing so is considered slander. [If one was informed of its presence, he has no obligation to go see it in order to recite the blessing.[539]]

The blessing

"ברוך אתה ה, אלוקינו מלך העולם, זוכר הברית ונאמן בבריתו וקים במאמרו"

Q&A on the blessing
How much of the rainbow must one see in order to say the blessing?
Some Poskim[540] question whether one is required to see the entire bow of the rainbow, which is half of a circle, or seeing even part of it suffices. [Practically, one may say the blessing even if he does not see the entire bow of the rainbow.[541] However, some Poskim[542] conclude that it is not to be said.]

---

included within it as part of the blessing. This in truth is a mistake, as one must include it in the blessing as writes Michaber ibid. [Taz 229:1; M"A 229:1; Kneses Hagedola 229; Kitzur Shlah p. 27; Machatzis Hashekel ibid; Kaf Hachaim 229:3]

Nussach of Vineman: Some write the Nussach of Neman with a Vav and read Vineman. [Brachos ibid; Tur 229; Rambam; Kneses Hagedola 229; M"B 229:3; Birchas Habayis 29:19; Kaf Hachaim 229:3; Piskeiy Teshuvos 229:1 footnote 1] Others rule it is to be said without a Vav. [Nussach in Michaber ibid; Biur Hgr"a 229; Levush 229] Practically, the Nussach in many Siddurim is printed with a Vav. [See Siddur Tehilas Hashem]

[527] Rav Yonason Eibashitz in Yearos Devash 1 Derush 12 that there are two types of rainbows, one being the natural rainbow and the second being the rainbow which Hashem placed as a sign for the covenant, and therefore [since we do not know which is which] one is to recite the blessing without Shem Umalchus

[528] Ben Ish Chaiy Eikev 17; Kaf Hachaim 229:4; Piskeiy Teshuvos 229:2; Many Mefarshim explain how the sign of Hashem and His covenant is apparent even within the natural phenomenon of the rainbow we see today, hence removing the basis for the ruling of the Yearos Devash. [See Ramban Noach; Shlah Hakadosh Parshas Noach that he heard from the Rama that Hashem could make it rain only by night and hence cause a rainbow to never be seen]

[529] The reason: As all the Poskim record the ruling that a blessing is to be said and do not differentiate in this matter, and so is the custom of all Israel, and hence we cannot uproot this custom simply due to words said in the form of Derush. [Ben Ish Chaiy ibid]

[530] Ben Ish Chaiy ibid; Kaf Hachaim ibid

[531] Hayom Yom 29th Tishreiy; Igros Kodesh 16:328, printed in Shulchan Menachem 1:352, that so was the directive of the Rebbe Rayatz; See Likkutei Sichos 10:200; Sichas Bechukosaiy 5741 3:468; printed in Shulchan Menachem 1:352

[532] Michaber ibid; Chagiga 16a as explains Rosh and Tur

[533] Beis Yosef 229 in name of Rosh *"The prohibition is only to stare as one who stares focuses on all the details in a much greater fashion than one who simply looks"*; Biur Hagr"a *"One must see it in order to say the blessing and Lashon Histalkus means with great contemplation"*; Machatzis Hashekel 229:1; Olas Tamid 229:1; Kaf Hachaim 229:5

[534] Zohar Beshalach 66b

[535] Rebbe Aba in Chagigah ibid; Machatzis Hashekel ibid

[536] M"A 229:2; Chagigah 16a [see Machatzis Hashekel ibid and P"M 229 A"A 2 who replace the word Shlah in M"A ibid]; Olas Tamid 229:1; M"B 229:5; Kaf Hachaim 229:5

[537] Tikkunei Zohar Tikkun 18 p. 36b

[538] Chayeh Adam 63; Pischeiy Teshuvah; M"B 229:1; Kaf Hachaim 229:1

[539] Makor Chaim Kitzur Halachos 229; Piskeiy Teshuvos 229:3

[540] Biur Halacha 229:1; "Haroeh"

[541] Implication of Setimas Haposkim who do not mention such a requirement

[542] Teshuvos Vehanhagos 3:76; Piskeiy Teshuvos 229:1

Is one to stand upon saying the blessing?[543]

There is no requirement to stand upon saying the blessing, although many are accustomed to do so, as with any blessing of praise to Hashem.

If one did not say the blessing right away upon seeing the rainbow, may it still be said?[544]

The blessing may be recited so long as the rainbow is still visible, even if one did not say it at the first glance.

How often is the blessing over a rainbow to be recited?[545]

The blessing is to be repeated each time one sees a rainbow, even within thirty days from a previous sighting, similar to the law which requires one to repeat a blessing for a second lightning or thunder [of another storm]. [However, in a single rainfall, or storm clouds, which creates the reflection of a rainbow, one does not repeat the blessing upon seeing multiple rainbows, unless the clouds cleared up and a new rain/clouds arrived, just as we rule regarding thunder and lightning.[546] Nonetheless, the blessing is to be repeated upon seeing another rainbow the next day even if it is from the same clouds/rain, just as we rule regarding thunder and lightning.[547]]

What is the law if one sees a rainbow in the midst of Davening?[548]

This follows the same law as one who sees lightning or hears thunder, of which we rule that the blessing is to be said so long as one is prior to Shemoneh Esrei.

Q&A on the staring

May one take a picture of a rainbow?

Seemingly, one is to avoid taking a picture of a rainbow, as it is equal to staring at it for the sake of study, which is forbidden to be done. Vetzaruch Iyun.

Is one to avoid staring at the reflection of a rainbow seen within water?[549]

Some write that one is to avoid doing so.

---

[543] Piskeiy Teshuvos 229:1; 218:1; See Siddur Yaavetz that one is to say all the morning blessings in a standing position due to it being a blessing of praise, and so is the custom amongst Ashkenazi Jewry; See however Kaf Hachaim [Falagi] 9:7 and Yechaveh Daas 5:4 who write that Sephardic Jewry is accustomed to sit while reciting the blessings in order to increase concentration.
Background: From the letter of the law, one is only required to stand when saying blessings which involve commands, such as when saying the blessing over Tzitzis, and Tefillin. [Admur 8:3] However, blessings of praise do not require standing. [P"M Pesicha Brachos 18; However, see 432 M"Z 1 who leaves this matter in question] However, the Yaavetz ibid writes that all blessings of praise of Hashem are to be said standing. See Piskeiy Teshuvos 218:1

[544] Piskeiy Teshuvos 229:1

[545] Machazik Bracha 229:1; Shaareiy Teshuvah 229:1; M"B 229:2; Kaf Hachaim 229:2; See regarding thunder and lightning: Seder 13:16; Luach 12:25; Michaber 227:2; Piskeiy Teshuvos 227:7; Halacha Berura [Yosef] 227
Other opinions: Some Poskim rule that the blessing over the rainbow is to only be said one time in 30 days. [Opinion brought, and negated, in Machazik Bracha ibid]

[546] Birchas Habayis 29:19; Piskeiy Teshuvos 229:1; See regarding thunder and lightning: Admur and Poskim ibid
Other opinions: Some Poskim imply from the Shaareiy Teshuvah ibid that the blessing is to be repeated each time one sees a new rainbow, even during the same storm. [Ketzos Hashulchan 66 footnote 26] Vetzaruch Iyun Gadol, as the Shaareiy Teshuvah clearly states in his words "That have ended" which refers to the dispersing of the clouds.

[547] Birchas Habayis 29:19; Piskeiy Teshuvos 229:1; See regarding thunder and lightning: Mamar Mordechai 227:3; Birchas Habayis 30:5; M"B 227:8 based on Yerushalmi; Kaf Hachaim 227:12; Ketzos Hashulchan 66 footnote 23; Piskeiy Teshuvos ibid; Halacha Berurah ibid
Other opinions: From some Poskim it is implied that there is no difference between that day and the next day, and also the next day a second blessing may not be said if the clouds of the previous day's storm have not yet dispersed. [See regarding thunder and lightning: Implication of Setimas Haposkim of Admur ibid; Michaber ibid; Tur 227 who all record the ruling of the Yerushalmi but omit its ruling that the next day a blessing may be recited; brought in Ketzos Hashulchan 66 footnote 23; Gedulas Elisha 227:13]

[548] Piskeiy Teshuvos 229:1; See regarding thunder and lightning: Admur 66:4 [even in midst of a Perek]; M"A 66:5 [like Admur]; Kitzur SHU"A 16:3; M"B 66:19 [brings dispute]; Kaf Hachaim 66:16; Ketzos Hashulchan 19:1; Piskeiy Teshuvos 227:5 [bets to only say between Perakim]

[549] Yalkut Hagershoni 229:2; Ruach Chaim 229; Piskeiy Teshuvos 229:2

> **The message of the rainbow:**[550]
> The purpose of the rainbow is to arouse Divine mercy upon the world and grant it protection. The Zohar[551] states that when the rainbow is seen, it is a sign that the Reshaim have reached the point of needing destruction, and the forefathers Daven on their behalf to save them.
>
> **How can the rainbow serve as a message from G-d if it is part of a natural phenomenon?**
> Several answers have been offered by the Mefarshim:
> 1. There are two types of rainbows, one being the natural rainbow and the second being the rainbow which Hashem placed as a sign for the covenant.[552]
> 2. Hashem could arrange for it to rain only at night, hence causing the rainbow to never be seen.[553]
> 3. To begin with Hashem planted the rainbow within nature because he was aware of the covenant that he would make.[554]

38. The blessing over an earthquake:[555]

Upon [feeling[556]] an earthquake one is required to recite a blessing. [This applies to an earthquake of any magnitude, so long as it is felt.[557] The reason the Sages established a blessing is because earthquakes are frightening events which convey a powerful message to the worlds inhabitants regarding G-d's power and control of earth.[558] Hashem created these events to shake people up from their current state of affairs and begin to fear Him.[559] The Talmud[560] accords various causes to earthquakes, including: 1) Hashem drops two tears into the sea when he sees the pain of his children in exile and the sound causes the earth to shake.; 2) Hashem claps His hands to relieve his anger and the sound causes the earth to shake. 3) Hashem lets out a groan of anger and the sound causes the earth to shake. 4) Hashem kicks the heavens to wake up the inhabitants. 5) Hashem presses His feet under the Kisei Hakavod, and this causes the earth to shake.]

The Nussach of the blessing:[561] One is required to recite the following blessing: *"Baruch Ata Hashem Elokeinu Melech Haolam Oseh Maaseh Bereishis."*[562] Alternatively, if one chooses, he may recite the blessing of *"Baruch Ata Hashem Elokeinu Melech Haolam Shekocho Ugvuraso Malei Olam."*[563]

Within how much time of the earthquake must the blessing be recited?[564] The blessing over the earthquake must be said while it is taking place, or within Kdei Dibbur of feeling it [which is the amount of time it

---

[550] See Piskeiy Teshuvos 229:2 footnote 9
[551] 1:1
[552] Rav Yonason Eibashitz in Yearos Devash 1 Derush 12
[553] Shlah Parshas Noach in name of Rama
[554] Shlah Parshas Noach
[555] Seder 13:15 "On the Zevaos which is a Reidat Adama/earthquake"; Luach 12:24; Michaber 227:1; Haeshkol 1:23; Tosafos Rid and Riaz; Rokeiach 227; Mishneh Brachos 54a "Zevaos" and Gemara Brachos 59a "Goa" and Rashi ibid "It means an Earthquake" [See Halacha Berurah 227 Birur Halacha 6 for all the opinions on this matter]; Yerushalmi Brachos 9:2; See Piskeiy Teshuvos 227:2; Halacha Berura 227:5
[556] One must actually feel the earthquake. Simply hearing about it does not suffice.
[557] Shevet Hakehasi 5:46; Piskeiy Teshuvos ibid; Halacha Berura ibid in name of his father in Chazon Ovadia
The statistics: Of the close to 1,000,000 earthquakes that occur each year throughout the world, only a small percentage can be felt [about 30,000, above 2.5 magnitude on the Richter scale], and an even smaller fraction causes damage [about 500, above 5.5 magnitude on the Richter scale]. See here for statistical details: http://www.geo.mtu.edu/UPSeis/magnitude.html
[558] Rabbeinu Manoach Brachos 10:14
[559] Abudarham Brachos Shaar Shemini; Elya Raba 227:4; Halachos Ketanos 1:38
[560] Brachos 59a
[561] Admur Seder ibid; Luach ibid; Michaber ibid; Rif Brachos 43; Rambam Brachos 10:14; Rava Brachos 59a as explains Tosafos
[562] Rava Brachos 59a as explains Tosafos that one may choose which blessing to recite; Kitzur SHU"A 60:2 only records this blessing; The Mefarshim explain the reason this blessing is to be said is because earthquakes are felt throughout the world, a great distance from the epicenter. [Rashi Brachos ibid; Sefer Hamichtam 58b]
[563] Mishneh Brachos 54a writes that one is to recite this blessing
[564] Seder 13:17 regarding thunder and lightning; Birchas Habayis 30:1 regarding earthquakes; Piskeiy Teshuvos 227:2

takes to say the three words of "Shalom Alecha Rebbe"[565], which is a mere 2-3 seconds]. If the earthquake has already ended and one did not say the blessing within that time, then he is not to say a blessing on the past event.[566] However, other Poskim[567] argue [and rule the blessing may be said even later on]. Practically, one is to say the blessing without saying Hashem's name [i.e. Baruch Shekocho Ugvuraso Malei Olam[568]].[569] Accordingly, if one was unable to say the blessing immediately after feeling the earthquake, such as he was using the bathroom upon hearing/seeing it, then he is to recite the blessing later on without Hashem's name.[570]

Summary:
Immediately upon feeling an earthquake, one is to say the blessing of *"Baruch Ata Hashem Elokeinu Melech Haolam Oseh Maaseh Bereishis" or "Shekocho Ugvuraso Malei Olam."* If the blessing was not said within 2-3 seconds of the conclusion of the earthquake, then it is to be said without Hashem's name, as follows: *Baruch Shekocho Ugvuraso Malei Olam.*

Q&A

How often is the blessing over an earthquake to be said?[571]
Often, earthquakes come with before and aftershocks, thus causing a series of earthquakes within the span of a day or a number of days.[572] Each time a new earthquake occurs, a new blessing is to be recited, [even on the very same day[573]] if one removed his mind from the previous earthquake. Meaning, if an earthquake occurred that day and a blessing was recited and after some time passed another earthquake occurred, a new blessing is to be said if one removed his mind from the previous earthquake event. If, however, one's mind was still thinking about it [such as would occur if the earthquake caused personal damage, or widescale devastation], then a new blessing is not recited.

A Segula to stop earthquakes:[574]
There is a great secret that can be learned from the prophet Yeshaya who prior to describing the shaking [of the doorposts of the Heichal], stated the verse "Vekara Zeh El Zeh Veamar."[575] This is coming to teach us that whenever one feels an earthquake he is to recite the following verse **three** times "Vekara Zeh El Zeh Veamar Kadosh Kadosh Kadosh Hashem Tzevaos Malei Kol Haaretz Kevodo." By doing so, the earthquake will cease!

Jerusalem earthquakes:[576]
There exists a tradition recorded in Sefarim and Poskim that Jerusalem residents will never be harmed of an earthquake. In the year 5687/1927 on the 11th of Tammuz a great earthquake occurred in

---

[565] Admur 206:3; Kneses Hagedola 206; Olas Tamid 206:3; M"A 206:4; Elya Raba 206:5; Chesed Lealafim 206:3; Ben Ish Chaiy Balak 3; Kaf Hachaim 206:15; 582:9
Other Opinions: Some Poskim rule that it contains four words "Shalom Aleichem Rebbe **Mori**". [Beis Yosef in name of Shivlei Haleket; Levush; Taz 206:3; P"M 487]
[566] 1st opinion in Seder ibid; Luach ibid; Implication of Michaber 227:3; Ran Pesachim 4a based on Yerushalmi Brachos 9:2; Olas Tamid 227:2; Birchas Avraham 4:191; Elya Raba 227:6 in end that so is implication of Poskim; Nehar Shalom 227:4; Mamar Mordechai 227:5; Machatzis Hashekel 227:2; Chayeh Adam 63:9; M"B 227:12
[567] 2nd opinion in Seder ibid; Luach ibid; Taz 227:2; Opinion of Elya Raba 227:6; See Admur 46:3 regarding Birchas Hashachar,
[568] So is the custom upon saying a blessing without Sheim Umalchus
[569] Admur in Seder and Luach ibid
The reason: As Safek Brachos Lihakel. [Admur Seder ibid]
[570] Admur ibid
[571] Maharam Chaviv 34; Yad Ahron on Tur 227:4; Birkeiy Yosef 227:6; Shaareiy Teshuvah 227:1; Chesed Lealafim 227:24; Kaf Hachaim 227:3; Piskeiy Teshuvos ibid; Halacha Berurah ibid; Halachos Ketanos 1:38 that it follows the same law as thunder; See regarding thunder and lightning: Seder 13:16; Luach 12:25; Michaber 227:2; Rosh Brachos 9:13; Rabbeinu Yona Brachos; Rif Brachos 43b; Yerushalmi Brachos 9:2; Ketzos Hashulchan 66:13; Piskeiy Teshuvos 227:7; Halacha Berura [Yosef] 227
[572] See Gemara Brachos 59a "Goha Avid"; https://en.wikipedia.org/wiki/Foreshock
[573] Implication of Shaareiy Teshuvah ibid; Piskeiy Teshuvos ibid
[574] Mor Uketzia 227 in name of Sefer Yuchsin; Piskeiy Teshuvos ibid
[575] Yeshayahu 6:3-4
[576] Peri Hadama 4:6; Kaf Hachaim 576:26; Avos Derebbe Nasan

Jerusalem and its surrounding areas. There were many miracles and wonders that occurred. While walls and buildings collapsed, no one in Yerushalayim was injured. However, the surrounding gentile villages did not share the same fate, as they suffered from many casualties. Everyone saw the great miracle Hashem made for the Jewish people, and it caused many to believe in G-d and Divine providence.[577]

Tzefas Earthquake:
Famously, the city of Tzefas suffered from a deadly earthquake on January 1st 1837, in which the city was completely destroyed and devastated. It was estimated that the earthquake was approximately 6.8 on the Richter scale. The earthquake killed approximately four thousand Jews r"l in Tzefas, and another 700 in Tiberius. The Chasam Sofer in his Sefer Toras Moshe[578] attributed the earthquake to the fact the Jews at the time shunned living in Jerusalem, the holiest city of G-d, and chose rather to live in Tzefas. Certainly, today however, the great development of the city of Jerusalem and the tremendous amounts of Torah and Chesed that exist in both cities will stand to protect both cities from any such events reoccurring, Heaven Forefend.

Learn the science behind earthquakes:
A fun children's video, good for adults as well: https://613tube.com/watch/?v=dJplU1rSOFY

------------------Bedtime----------------
39. Making an interval [i.e. eating; drinking; talking] after saying Kerias Shema Sheal Hamita/Hamapil:[579]

One may not eat, drink, or speak after reciting Kerias Shema Sheal Hamita [even if he did not yet say the blessing of Hamapil[580], and certainly if it was already recited]. Rather, he is to go to sleep immediately after its recital.[581] [Some Poskim[582] rule that if one speaks between Hamapil and falling asleep, then the blessing is considered to have been said in vain. Due to this, some communities, and individuals, are accustomed not to recite the blessing of Hamapil with Hashem's name, lest they speak in between.[583] Other Poskim[584], however, rule it is not considered a blessing in vain, and one is thus not to abstain from

---

[577] Kaf Hachaim ibid
[578] Toras Moshe Hesped p. 59
[579] Rama 239:1; Beis Yosef 239; Kol Bo 29 "All Israel is accustomed…"; Rokeiach 327; Rabbeinu Yerucham Nesiv 3:2; Orchos Chaim Kerias Shema in name of Rabbeinu Asher; Sefer Haminhagos of Rabbeinu Asher p. 17; Rabbeinu Manoach Tefila 7:2; Leket Yosher p. 45

Letter of law: The Poskim imply that from the letter of the law, it is permitted to speak and make an interval after Hamapil, as it is no different than speaking after the blessing of Hanosen Lasechvi Bina, prior to hearing the roosters crow, and it is only due to custom that an interval is not made after Hamapil. [See Leket Yosher p. 45; Implication of Rishonim ibid who write it as a mere custom, or custom of some; All Poskim in future footnotes; Tehilas Chaim 2:41 in name of Kuntrus Alei Terufa that this prohibition is not mentioned in the Rishonim, and the Rama brought it as a custom, and it is better to speak many times after saying it than to not say it at all; Orchos Chaim Spinka 239:3 in name of Meorei Or that the custom is to drink and speak when necessary]

[580] M"B 239:4
[581] The reason: As the verse states "Yomru Bilivavchem Al Mishkavam Vedomeh Sela." [Rama ibid; Kol Bo ibid]
[582] Implication of Seder Hayom ibid who rules it is a blessing in vain if the blessing is said prior to drifting off to sleep; Siddur Beis Oveid; Ben Ish Chaiy Pekudei 12 "My custom, and the custom of my forefathers, as well as many of Israel, is not to say the blessing of Hamapil with Hashem's name, lest we speak in between, and some Poskim rule that if one speaks it is a blessing in vain."; Implication of M"B 239:4 and Biur Halacha 239 "Samuch"; Possible way of learning Admur 6:8 and M"A 6:8 who rule regarding one who slept, awoke and then went back to sleep that Hamapil is to be recited without a blessing. This is based on the Seder Hayom who rules that Hamapil is similar to Birchas Hanehnin, and we thus see that Admur ibid does suspect for an interval; See Shevet Hakehasi 1:101; Teshuvos Vehanhagos 2:131; Piskeiy Teshuvos 239:3
[583] Siddur Beis Oveid; Ben Ish Chaiy ibid that so is his custom, and the custom of Jerusalem Jewry; See Shevet Hakehasi 1:101; Teshuvos Vehanhagos 2:131; Piskeiy Teshuvos 239:3 footnote 16
[584] Implication of Rishonim ibid; Kneses Hagedola 239 and Elya Raba 239:3, that Hamapil is said "Al Minhag Haolam", brought in Machatzis Hashekel 239:3 and P"M 239 A"A 3; Chayeh Adam 35:4; Makor Chaim of Chavos Yair Kitzur Halachos [permits saying Maariv after Hamapil]; Siddur Yaavetz permits talking in a time of great need; Biur Hagr"a 432 [that even if one does not fall asleep, it is not a blessing in vain]; Ashel Avraham Butchach Tinyana 239; Maharitz Chayos Brachos 11b; Bireich Es Avraham p. 102 that so is the custom; Yifei Laleiv 239:2; Tehilas Chaim 2:41 in name of Kuntrus Alei Terufa [brought in previous footnotes]; Orchos Chaim Spinka 239:3 in name of Meorei Or [permits even initially to talk]; Aruch Hashulchan 239:6 "Certainly it is not similar to the laws of Hefsek after other blessings"; Birchas Habayis 31:2; Peri Hasadeh 1:93; Hisorerus Teshuvah 1:114; Kaf Hachaim 239:7; Halichos Shlomo 13:15; Beir Moshe 1:63; Tzitz Eliezer 7:27; Yechaveh Daas 4:21; Rivivos Efraim 6:123; 8:81; Piskeiy Teshuvos 239:3

saying the blessing due to worry that one may have to speak afterwards.[585] The final ruling follows the latter opinion.[586]]

A silent Hefsek: Some Poskim[587] say that due to the need to avoid making an interval, one may not recite Kerias Shema [i.e. the blessing of Hamapil] until he feels himself drifting asleep. Other Poskim[588], however, rule that there is no need to wait until this point, and one is rather to read it immediately [upon resting in bed], lest one fall asleep prior to saying it.[589] Practically, the final ruling follows the latter opinion.[590]

Summary:
One may not initially make an interval of talking, or eating/drinking, after the recital of Kerias Shema, even if he did not yet say Hamapil, and certainly if Hamapil was already said. Nonetheless, if an interval was made after Hamapil, the majority of Poskim rule that it is not considered a blessing in vain.

Q&A

May one eat, drink or talk after Kerias Shema/Hamapil, in a time of need?
If one recited Kerias Shema but did not yet recite Hamapil, then it is permitted to speak or drink in a case of need. However, he is to repeat the paragraph of Shema afterwards.[591] If however, he already recited Hamapil, then it is subject to the above-mentioned dispute regarding if doing so is considered a blessing in vain. Accordingly, some Poskim[592] rule he may no longer drink or speak even in a case of great need, due to it being an interval. Other Poskim[593], however, rule that one may eat, drink or talk when necessary, even after saying the blessing of Hamapil. Practically, the final ruling follows the latter opinion, however one should only do so in a time of great need.[594]

Based on the above, the following may be recited after Hamapil, if one forgot say it beforehand:[595]
1. Maariv.
2. Sefiras Haomer.
3. Asher Yatzar after using the bathroom.
4. Kiddush Levana.

---

[585] The reason: As the blessing of Hamapil was instituted to be said on the general benefit of sleeping received by people, and not on one's personal sleep. It is no different than speaking after the blessing of Hanosen Lasechvi Bina, prior to hearing the roosters crow. [Kneses Hagedola ibid; Elya Raba 239:3; Machatzis Hashekel 239:3; P"M 239 A"A 3; Chayeh Adam 35:4; Maharitz Chayos ibid; Orchois Chaim Spinka; Bireich Es Avraham p. 102 that so is the custom; Yifei Laleiv 239:2; Kaf Hachaim ibid] Alternatively, it is because the blessing was established to be recited upon one preparing himself to sleep. [Ashel Avraham Butchach ibid]

[586] As so rule majority of Poskim, brought in previous footnote, and so would apply according to all Poskim in coming footnotes, who permit eating or talking after Hamapil

[587] Seder Hayom, brought in M"A 239:3; Birchas Habayis 31:2;

[588] Kneses Hagedola 239, brought in M"A ibid; Elya Raba 239:3; Machatzis Hashekel 239:3 and P"M 239 A"A 3; Chayeh Adam 35:4; Ashel Avraham Butchach Tinyana 239; Maharitz Chayos Brachos 11b; Bireich Es Avraham p. 102 that so is the custom; Yifei Laleiv 239:2; Tehilas Chaim 2:41 in name of Kuntrus Alei Terufa [brought in previous footnotes]; Orchos Chaim Spinka 239:3 in name of Meorei Or [permits even initially to talk]; Birchas Habayis 31:2; Kaf Hachaim 239:7

[589] Sitting idly on the bed until one falls asleep is not considered an interval. [M"A ibid]

[590] As so rule majority of Poskim, brought in previous footnote, and so would apply according to all Poskim in coming footnotes, who permit eating or talking after Hamapil

[591] Implication of Rama 239:1; Siddur Yaavetz; M"B 239:4

[592] M"B 239:4; Ben Ish Chaiy Pekudei 12 "My custom, and the custom of my forefathers, as well as many of Israel, is not to say the blessing of Hamapil with Hashem's name, lest we speak in between, and some Poskim rule that if one speaks it is a blessing in vain."; Possible way of learning Admur 6:8 and M"A 6:8 who rule regarding one who slept, awoke and then went back to sleep that Hamapil is to be recited without a blessing: This is based on the Seder Hayom who rules that Hamapil is similar to Birchas Hanehnin, and we thus see that Admur ibid does suspect for an interval

[593] Makor Chaim ibid; Siddur Yaavetz; Tehilas Chaim 2:41 in name of Kuntrus Alei Terufa [brought in previous footnotes]; Orchos Chaim Spinka 239:3 in name of Meorei Or [permits even initially to talk]; Birchas Habayis 31:2; Piskeiy Teshuvos 239:3

[594] As so rule majority of Poskim, that it is not considered an interval, and so is the testified custom, to which the rule of Safek Brachos Lihakel does not apply. [See Kaf Hachaim ibid] Nonetheless, from the fact Admur ibid records the opinion of the Seder Hayom regarding repeating Hamapil, it seems that one should only rely on this in a case of great need.

[595] Makor Chaim of Chavos Yair 239; Piskeiy Teshuvos 239:3

5. Heard thunder or lightning.

If one made a long interval after saying Hamapil, is the blessing to be repeated?[596]
If one made a long interval after saying Hamapil, he is to repeat the paragraph without saying the concluding sentence which includes Hashem's name. One is to also repeat the saying of Shema.[597]

If one fell asleep after saying Hamapil, and then woke up, may he eat or drink even initially?
Some[598] write that if one went to sleep with intent to sleep a set sleep, then even if he woke up after a few minutes, he may even initially eat or drink. Certainly, if one slept a set sleep [i.e. at least 30 minutes], he may even initially eat and drink upon awakening.[599] Upon returning to sleep, he is to repeat the paragraph of Shema and Hamapil, without saying the concluding sentence, as stated above.

May one read a book, or learn Torah, after reciting Kerias Shema/Hamapil?
One may read a book, or learn Torah in his thought.[600] One however is not to verbalize the words. If the words are verses of Torah that contain powers of protection, similar to the verses in Kerias Shema Sheal Hamita, then it may be recited.[601]

Should a mother abstain from saying Hamapil if she has a nursing child who may prevent her from falling asleep?
Hamapil is to be said even in such a case, as stated above, that the main ruling follows that one is not to abstain from reciting Hamapil due to worry that he may need to make an interval.

---

[596] So rule regarding if one slept, awoke and then went back to sleep that Hamapil is to be recited without a blessing: Admur 6:8 based on M"A ibid, based on Seder Hayom; Beir Heiytiv 6:7; Machatzis Hashekel ibid; Derech Chaim 227; Ketzos Hashulchan 5:5 footnote 10
Other opinions: Some Poskim rule the blessing is to be repeated. [Siddur Yaavetz] From other Poskim it is evident that the blessing does not need to be repeated at all. [So is evident from all Poskim ibid who rule an interval does not invalidate the blessing; Piskeiy Teshuvos 239:3 footnote 4 and 19]
[597] Implication of Rama 239:1; Siddur Yaavetz; M"B 239:4
[598] Tefila Kehilchasa 20:18; Piskeiy Teshuvos 239:3
[599] See Admur 6:8 and M"A 6:8
[600] Divrei Shalom 6:35; Piskeiy Teshuvos 239 footnote 21
[601] See Rama ibid; Admur 61:9

------------------Shabbos-General----------------

40. May one invite a non-religious guest for Shabbos if he will desecrate Shabbos in order to come to you?[602]

Some Poskim[603] rule it is forbidden to invite guests to one's home for the Shabbos meal if this will cause him to desecrate Shabbos, such as to drive, in order to arrive there.[604] If, however, the home is close by and it is possible that the guest will choose to walk over rather than drive, it is permitted to invite him even though one does not know for certain whether he will arrive by foot or will drive.[605] Other Poskim[606] however rule it is permitted to invite the guest even if one knows that he will drive.[607] Practically, those who are lenient are to abide by the following three conditions:

1. Invite him for the entire Shabbos, beginning with Mincha of Erev Shabbos so a) He can arrive before Shabbos and b) He can stay until after Shabbos.[608] A good advice is to make the mealtime earlier, before Shabbos, so he can arrive beforehand.[609] [One does not have to wait for the guest to verify this invitation, but simply must let him know. He is certainly not to tell the guest that he may drive if he chooses and is not to affirm such a question.]
2. Let the person know that it is forbidden to drive on Shabbos.[610]
3. Some Poskim[611] do not require the above conditions, although rule that one must ask them not to park near your house if they do decide to come by car.

------------------Shabbos-Melacha----------------

41. Making and filtering Turkish/ground coffee on Shabbos:

Ground coffee is made through roasting and then grinding the coffee bean. It does not dissolve like instant coffee and has never been cooked in water. This is in contrast to instant coffee which is made from dehydrated water that had ground coffee cooked in it, and thus dissolves when it reaches contact with liquid. The fact that ground coffee has never been cooked, and does not dissolve, raises the Halachic question of whether one may make this coffee beverage on Shabbos using hot water, and whether one may filter the water from the undissolved ground coffee. Making the beverage using hot water touches upon the cooking and dyeing prohibition, while filtering the water from the coffee touches upon the Borer prohibition. In this article, we will now analyze all these aspects:

---

[602] See Ratz Katzevi 8:28 for a through discussion on this matter; See Hearos Ubiurim 1037:137 and 1039 p. 81; See Hiskashrus 929:15 that when the Rebbe was addressed this question by Shluchim he forwarded the person to Rav Dworkin

[603] Igros Moshe 1:99 regarding prohibition to invite to Shul; Mishneh Halachos 16:31 regarding inviting to house; Shevet Halevi 8:165-6; 8:256-2 [regarding inviting to Simcha]; Chishukei Chemed of Rav Zilberstram, in name of Rav Elyashiv; Rav A.L. Cohen, Rav of Beitar, in response to the authors question

[604] The reason: This is forbidden due to Lifnei Iver, or due to the prohibition of helping another do a sin [Misayeia], or due to the prohibition of Meisis. [Igros Moshe ibid; Shevet Halevi ibid; See Ratz Katzevi 28 chapter 1-2] Or due to it being a Chilul Hashem. [Shevet Halevi ibid]

[605] See Admur 347:4; M"A 347:4; Igros Moshe ibid

[606] Rav SZ"A in Minchas Shlomo 2:4-10; Teshuvos Vehanhagos 1:358; Rav Weiss in Ratz Katzevi ibid; See response of Rav Dworkin, brought ion Hiskashrus ibid

[607] The reason: **a)** As Lifnei Iver only applies when the person would not be able to transgress without the help of the other person, and thus here, since the Jew would drive his car even without the invitation, it is therefore not forbidden due to Lifnei Iver. [Rav Asher Weiss based on Avoda Zara 6b; See Ratz Katzevi 28 chapter 1; See Admur 347:2-3] **b)** It likewise does not involve the Rabbinical prohibition of helping others due a sin, as this prohibition does not apply to a Mumar [See Shach 151:6; Rav Weiss in Ratz Katzevi 28:3] or because it only applies when one gives assistance to the actual prohibition. [Maharsham; See Rav SZ"A in Minchas Shlomo 2:90 for a similar ruling regarding renting houses to Michalilei Shabbos] or because it does not apply when done to save the person from a prohibition. [Rav Akiva Eiger Y.D. 181:6] In other words, when done for Kiruv purposes, he is not helping him do an Aveira but rather a Mitzvah. [Minchas Shlomo 1:35 regarding giving food to a non-religious person even though he may not wash or say a blessing; Teshuvos Vehanhagos ibid; Ratz Katzevi 28:4-5] **c)** It is permitted to desecrate Shabbos for the sake of saving a Jew from heresy. [See Admur 306:29; See Ratz Katzevi 28 chapter 4; See Shevet Halevi 6:36 that in certain cases we say "sin in order to benefit your friend"; This response was given regarding a person traveling for Shabbos for Kiruv purposes to a Yishuv that may not have a Minyan, and hence the questioner asked whether he should miss a Minyan for Kiruv purposes, and on this the Shevet Halevi answered that we learn from Admur 306:29 that one may desecrate Shabbos to help save a soul from Shemad. Thus, perhaps here too, although here one is causing his friend to stumble and transgress Shabbos, which transgresses Lifnei Iver, nevertheless this is all being done for the sake of being Mikareiv him. However, see Shevet Halevi 8:165-6; 8:256-2 who in conclusion rules stringently regarding this question.]

[608] Rav SZ"A, brought in Rat Katzevi 28:5 in length; Directive of Rav Dworkin, brought in Hiskashrus 929:15

[609] Rav Zalman Nechemia Goldberg in letter printed in Ratz Katzevi p. 516

[610] See Igros Kodesh 14 p. 98 regarding inviting people to Hakafos if they will drive on Shabbos or Yom Tov.

[611] Teshuvos Vehanhagos ibid

A. The cooking prohibition-Mixing it with hot water:

Ground coffee which has never before been cooked in water is subject to the debate in Poskim[612] regarding whether a prebaked or pre-roasted food may be cooked in a liquid on Shabbos, of which the final ruling is to be initially stringent like the opinion who rules that it contains a cooking prohibition.[613] Thus, initially one may not place it into a Keli Rishon[614] or pour onto it from a Keli Rishon[615], or place it into a very hot Keli Sheiyni[616], as it has ability to cook.

Not very hot Keli Sheiyni-Keli Shelishi: Regarding a not very hot Keli Sheiyni that is above Yad Soledes, this matter is disputed in Poskim: Some Poskim[617] rule that ground coffee is defined as a spice[618] and may hence be entered into a not very hot Keli Sheiyni [and so is the custom of many Sephardim[619]]. Other Poskim[620] rule that ground coffee is not defined as a spice and hence may not be placed into any Keli Sheiyni that is Yad Soledes[621], and it is to only be made with Iruiy Keli Sheiyni[622] or Keli Shelishi.[623]

---

[612] See Admur 318:12; Michaber 318:5; The dispute: Some Poskim rule there is [a prohibition to] cook [a food] that has been previously baked or roasted, and [thus according to them] if one places baked or roasted [food] even while still burning hot into a Keli Rishon that is Yad Soledes, he is liable. [1st opinion in Michaber and Admur ibid; Yireim 274] However, other Poskim rule it is permitted to place a baked and roasted food, even if cold, even into a burning hot Keli Rishon, being that [according to them] there is no [prohibition to] cook [a food that has been] already baked or roasted. [2nd opinion in Michaber and Admur ibid; Rama 318:5; Ravayah 197]

[613] Admur ibid *"It is the custom to initially be careful like the first opinion to not place bread even into a Keli Sheiyni so long as it is Yad Soledes."*; Rama 318:5

Ruling of Michaber and Sephardim: Some Poskim rule that according to the Michaber it is forbidden to cook a baked or roasted product, and thus coffee may not be entered even into a Keli Sheiyni. [Ginas Veradim 3:2-9, brought in Kaf Hachaim 318:65 even regarding Keli Sheiyni; Shemesh Umagen; Nishmas Hashabbos 21 in name of Sefer Hazichronos] Other Poskim, however, learn that according to the Michaber it is permitted to cook a prebaked or roasted food, and hence coffee may be entered even into a Keli Rishon. [Kneses Hagedola 318; Maharam Ben Chaviv and Mahara Yitzchaki, brought in Kaf Hachaim ibid, regarding Keli Sheiyni; See Kevod Chachamim Ateres 7 p. 363] Other Poskim conclude that according to the Michaber, the main opinion follows the lenient approach, although he is initially stringent. [Or Letziyon 2:30-4] Some Sephardi Poskim rule that it is forbidden to enter the food into a Keli Rishon, although it is permitted to enter it into a Keli Sheiyni. [Minchas Kohen 2:4; Ginas Veradim 3:9 that so is custom] See Kaf Hachaim 318:65; Shabbos Kehalacha 3:18 p. 168 footnote 39 who concludes like this latter opinion for the Sephardim

[614] Admur 318:11 regarding Keli Rishon's cooking status, 318:12 regarding a pre-roasted food; Michaber 318:4

Definition of a Keli Rishon: A Keli Rishon is the original pot of food that was taken off the fire, or off any other heating surface [even if its content is no longer Yad Soledes].

[615] Admur 318:19 regarding Iruiy Keli Rishon's cooking status, 318:12 regarding a pre-roasted food; Michaber 318:10; See Shach Y.D. 105:5

Definition: The pouring of the content of a Keli Rishon that is Yad Soledes onto a food or liquid. [Admur ibid]

[616] Implication of Admur 318:20; Tur 318; M"A 318:34; Levushei Serud ibid; Tzemach Tzedek Mishnayos 3:5; as explained in Ketzos Hashulchan 124 footnote 31; M"B 318:76; and 48; Chayeh Adam Shaar Mitzvas Haaretz 2:9; Rosh Yosef; See Shabbos Kehalacha 1:38 and 2:4

Other opinions: Some Poskim learn that the bathtub case is an exception and was only made forbidden due to a decree that one may come to heat up also in a Keli Rishon. Hence, according to them a very hot Keli Sheiyni would have the status of a Keli Sheiyni. [Machatzis Hashekel 318:35, based on Rashi 42a; Toras Shabbos 318:27; See P"M 318 M"Z 18]

What is the definition of a very hot Keli Sheiyni which has the status of a Keli Rishon? If the Keli Sheiyni is much hotter than Yad Soledes Bo it retains the status of a Keli Rishon. [Ketzos Hashulchan 124 footnote 25] Some Poskim write it is the amount of heat that a person would scold his finger if he entered it into the water even for a moment. [Yad Nichvas Bo] [M"B 318:48 in name of Chayeh Adam; See Shevet Halevi 7:42]

[617] Igros Moshe 4:74-18 writes that coffee has the status of spices and he wonders at those who are stringent. Nevertheless, he concludes that one should not be lenient to place it in a Keli Sheiyni; The following Sephardi Poskim rule that ground coffee may be entered into a Keli Sheiyni, irrelevant of whether it is defined as a spice, due to them holding that there is no cooking after roasting by a Keli Sheiyni: Rav Yaakov Pragi, Mahram Ben Chaviv, Mahara Yitzchaki, Rav Moshe Chiyon, brought in Ginas Veradim ibid; Mateh Yehuda 318:2; Implication of Rav Poalim 3:11; Kaf Hachaim 318:65

[618] See the following Poskim that spices may be entered into a Keli Sheiyni: Admur 318:11-12; 19; M"B 318:65 and 34; Mishneh 42a; See Michaber 318:9-10 that only prohibits a Keli Rishon

[619] See previous footnotes for list of Sephardim Poskim and Kaf Hachaim ibid that so is the ruling, however see Or Letziyon brought next who is stringent.

[620] Ginas Veradim 3:2-9 [that even according to the Michaber it is forbidden due to a cooking prohibition and due to dyeing prohibition similar to that of the dyes that were cooked in the Mishkan], brought in Beir Heiytiv 318:12, Shaareiy Teshuvah 318:14, Kaf Hachaim 318:65; Chasam Sofer 74; Or Letziyon 2:30; Shabbos Kehalacha Vol. 1 p. 54

[621] Admur 318:12 *"Accordingly, even regarding [placing these foods] into a Keli Sheiyni one needs to be stringent Rabbinically. One therefore needs to be careful not to place baked bread even into a plate [of food] that is a Keli Sheiyni so long as it is Yad Soledes."* M"A 318:18; M"B 318:42; Some of these foods carry a Biblical cooking prohibition, while others are Rabbinically forbidden due to it appearing like cooking. [see Admur ibid]

[622] Admur 318:11; Michaber 318:4

[623] Peri Megadim 447 A"A 9 [See however Shabbos Kehalacha ibid in Biurim for other areas that the P"M is stringent]; M"B 318:47 based on P"M ibid ; Ketzos Hashulchan 124 footnote 52; Nimukei Orach Chayim 318 regarding salt; Igros Moshe 4:74; Sheivet Haleivi 7:42; and many other Poskim; See Shabbos Kehalacha Vol. 1 p. 80-82

Other opinions: Some Poskim rule a Keli Shelishi is considered like a Keli Sheiyni itself, and hence all foods that are forbidden to be placed in a Keli Sheiyni would likewise be forbidden in a Keli Shelishi. [Yereim p. 134; Shevisas Shabbos Mevashel 23 based on Chasam Sofer; Chazon Ish 51:17] Practically, the custom is like the lenient opinions which hold that it is allowed to place into it all foods which are allowed to be poured on from a Keli Sheiyni. However, since there are opinions which are stringent by a Keli Shelishi, therefore when applicable one should rather pour

Other Poskim[624] rule that ground coffee is similar to tea and is defined as Kalei Habishul and thus may not be made with any hot water that is Yad Soledes, even in a Keli Shelishi or Revi'i. Practically, the mainstream approach follows the second opinion[625] and hence Turkish/ground coffee may be made on Shabbos using hot water by putting the coffee into a 3rd cup of boiling water [i.e. Keli Shelishi], or pouring the hot water into it from the 2nd cup [i.e. Iruiy Keli Sheiyni].

> **Summary:**
> It is permitted to make a hot beverage of ground/Turkish coffee on Shabbos through using a Keli Shelishi or Iruiy Keli Sheiyni. Many Sephardim are lenient even regarding a Keli Sheiyni.

B. The dyeing prohibition:

It is permitted to dye water on Shabbos for purposes of drinking.[626] Thus, there is no dyeing prohibition involved in placing ground coffee into water and thus causing the water to blacken. However some Poskim[627] rule the dyeing prohibition applies to liquids and one is hence not to place coffee into liquids on Shabbos.[628] Some Poskim[629] conclude that one may add the water to the coffee but not the coffee to the water.[630] Practically, according to the Shulchan Aruch and Alter Rebbe, it is permitted to do it either way

---

onto the foods from a Keli Sheiyni than to place them into a Keli Shelishi, being that the pouring of a Keli Sheiyni is explicitly permitted by all. [Shabbos Kehalacha ibid]

[624] Piskeiy Teshuvos 318:36 that since today people no longer eat the ground coffee, it has the same status as tea of which many Poskim rule that it may not be made at all on Shabbos using hot water. [See M"B 318:39; Aruch Hashulchan 318:28; Bris Olam Ofeh 23; Az Nidbaru 3:23-24; Piskeiy Teshuvos 318:36] Vetzaruch Iyun, as coffee is prebaked and is a dispute if it has a cooking prohibition even in a Keli Rishon, and thus even those who are stringent by tea have room to be lenient by ground coffee.

Opinion of Chabad Rabbanim: Rav Gerelitzky from Tel Aviv testifies that he witnessed that Rav Ashkenazi of Kefar Chabad would prepare coffee on Shabbos by first mixing the milk with the coffee and then add the hot water from a Keli Sheiyni. When asked as to why he did so, Rav Ashkenazi responded that we hold of Bishul even by a Keli Shelishi, and hence one should do it in this order as Tatah Gavar, and the milk cools off the hot water prior to it getting a chance to cook the coffee. According to Rav Ashkenazi, so was the custom of the Chabad Shul in Tel Aviv, and the Tomchei Temimim Yeshiva of Lud. Rav Yaakov Katz a"h also testified as such that they would pour in the cold water to prevent any cooking. [Sefer Harav Ashkenazi p. 469] My personal response to this: The custom of the world is to make coffee in a Keli Shelishi, or Iruiy Keli Sheiyni as evident from Admur in his Siddur regarding sugar and salt and as written in all Hilchos Shabbos Sefarim [mine included] that I have seen. Furthermore, the above ruling and its authenticity is puzzling for the following reasons:

1) We in Chabad are very lenient in the definition of Kalei Habishul, as rules the Tzemach tzedek and Ketzos Hashuclahn regarding tea.
2) Instant coffee is precooked and is subject to a dispute between Admur in his Shulchan Aruch and Siddur if it contains Bishul, and even according to Admur in the Siddur, we find no source for ever being stringent in a Keli Shelishi, as he implies that sugar may be placed in a Keli Sheiyni [although it is a spice] and salt in Iruiy Keli Sheiyni, and hence why would coffee be more strict?! If they referred to Turkish coffee, it would still be puzzling, as Admur rules even regarding prebaked Kalei Habishul, such as bread, that one is only to be stringent by a Keli Sheiyni.
3) Pouring hot liquid into cold is permitted by Admur in the Siddur but prohibited by the Tzemach Tzedek, and hence even if one were to hold that coffee is Kalei Habishul, and we are stringent even if its precooked, it would still be forbidden to do it in the way suggested in the article.
4) Rav Meir Ashkenazi, the current Rav of Kfar Chabad, and son of Rav Mordechai Ashkenazi says he never heard this before from his father, and that in their home they made coffee regularly in a Keli Shelishi like everyone else!
5) Rav Eli Landau, the Rosh Yeshivah of Kfar Chabad, and son of Rav Yaakov Landau, stated to me that he has never heard of this chumra before, and when he learned in the Lud Yeshiva, this was not kept, and that in actuality we do make tea in a Keli Shelishi without issue.

[625] This especially applies for those who allow making tea on Shabbos and do not suspect for it to be Kalei Habishul. [See Peri Megadim 318 A"A 35; Implication of Tzemach Tzedek Mishnayos 41, as explained in Shabbos Kehalacha Vol. 1 p. 51-52; Implication of Maharam Shick 132, Rav Lavut in Haaros to 318:12; Ketzos Hashulchan 124 footnote 21; Minchas Baruch 12; Igros Moshe 4:74-15 [Keli Shelishi]; Or Letziyon 2:30-3; Divrei Shlomo 2:153 ;'Nishmas Hashabbos 2:29; Menuchas Ahava 2:10-39; Shabbos Kehalacha Vol. 1 p. 80-82]

[626] Michaber 320:19 and Admur 320:26 regarding adding Turmeric into a liquid dish; Darkei Moshe 320:2 in name of Yireim; Tal Oros 48; Chacham Tzevi 92; P"M 320 A"A 25 and 321 A"A 24 M"B 320:56; Aruch Hashulchan 320:7; Ketzos Hashulchan 146 footnote 16-12; Sheivet Halevi 9:71; SSH"K 11 footnote 158; Yabia Omer 2:20; Piskeiy Teshuvos 320:24

[627] Avraham of Mintz, brought in Darkei Moshe ibid; Ginas Veradim 3:9 [brought in Rav Poalim 2:3 and Shaareiy Teshuvah 318:4]; Minchas Shabbos 80:152; Chesed Lealafim 320:6; Ben Ish Chaiy Pekudei 2:3; Rav Poalim 3:11; Lev Chaim 3:78; Halef Lecha Shlomo 136; Kaf Hachaim 320:113 and 116; Beir Moshe 8:24-17

[628] The reason: As it is Biblically forbidden to create dye on Shabbos and entering a dyed food into liquid is similar to making a dye. [Rav Poalim ibid; Ben Ish Chaiy ibid]

[629] Chesed Lealafim 320:6; Ben Ish Chaiy Pekudei 3; Rav Poalim 2:3; Kaf Hachaim 320:117; Mishneh Berurah in Shaar HaTziyon 318:65; Beir Moshe ibid; This allows their interpretation of the stringent opinion ibid brought in Ginas Veradim and Darkei Moshe; However see Ketzos Hashulchan 146 footnote 16-12 that according to the Poskim ibid it is forbidden even in this fashion.

[630] The reason: As when adding the dye to the water it is evident to all the color change of the water in the glass, when however, adding water to the dye this is not evident at all. [Rav Poalim ibid; See Ketzos Hashulchan ibid who negates this understanding]

and add water to the coffee or coffee to the water.[631]

C. Filtering the coffee liquid from the ground powder:

The general rule: The Borer prohibition of filtering liquids only applies towards liquids that contain solids which people are not accustomed to eating. However, if the solid material that is found in the liquid is consumable by majority[632] of people together with the liquid, then the liquid may be filtered.[633] This, however, only applies to one who is not always particular to filter the liquid from the solid. If, however, one is always particular to avoid drinking the liquid with this solid, then it is forbidden for him to filter it on Shabbos even if it is drinkable by majority of people.[634] Practically, many people [especially in the army] drink their coffee drink together with the ground coffee [i.e. cowboy coffee, mud, Turkish coffee] and are not particular to filter it. Other's however are particular to always filter their ground coffee, and it is unclear as to which group is in the majority. Using this information, we will now analyze the different forms of filtration available and their practical law:

Pouring the coffee liquid into another cup, having the ground coffee remain on bottom of the original cup: It is permitted to pour the coffee liquid out from the cup without any restriction so long as one leaves some amount of liquid remaining above the ground coffee that remains on bottom.[635] To pour coffee past this point, and completely separate all the coffee liquid from the ground coffee is permitted according to most Poskim[636] if done to drink right away. However, according to Admur in his Siddur, this matter is under several grounds of debate even if one intends to drink the coffee right away and is hence better to be avoided.[637] However, those who are lenient have upon whom to rely especially if they will be drinking the coffee right away and are not always particular to filter it.[638]

Pouring the coffee using a French press strainer and the like:[639] It is permitted to pour the coffee liquid out from the French press without any restriction, so long as one leaves some amount of liquid remaining above the strainer that rests on bottom.[640] To pour coffee past this point, and completely separate all the coffee liquid from the ground coffee which is below the strainer, is debated amongst the Poskim. Some

---

[631] Ketzos Hashulchan ibid; Sheivet Halevi 9:71; SSH"K 11 footnote 158; Yabia Omer 2:20; Piskeiy Teshuvos 320:24
Ruling of M"B: The M"B 320:56 rules one may pour red wine into white wine. However, in Shaar Hatziyon ibid he writes it is best to pour in the opposite way. See Piskeiy Teshuvos 320 footnote 271!
[632] Admur 319:13; Ran; Rashba; Beis Yosef; first opinion in M"B 319:34; Tzemach Tzedek Yoreh Deah 45; Shabbos Kehalacha 2 p. 346
Other opinions: Some Poskim rule it must be fit for drinking to all people. [Bach brought in M"B 319:10; See Tzemach Tzedek ibid]
[633] See Admur 319:13 *"Water or wine which are clear are permitted to be filtered through a filter in order so they become even more clear, or even in order [to remove] the sediment that floats on top of the wine or [to filter out] small twigs that have fallen into it. This is not considered like separating being that [the wine and water] are still drinkable to majority of people even without this filtration"*; Rama 319:10 *"because it is fit to drink regardless of the twigs"*; Michaber 319:9; Shabbos 139b
Other opinions: Some Poskim rule one may never use a filter on Shabbos even if the liquid is clear and fit to be drunk by majority of people. [Rambam 8, brought in Michaber 319:10] Practically, we do not rule like this opinion. [M"B 319:41; Admur omitted this opinion]
[634] See Peri Megadim 319 M"Z 6, brought in Ketzos Hashulchan 125 footnote 28 and Biur Halacha 319 "Hoil"; Maharam Shick 134; Shabbos Kehalacha Vol. 2 p. 347 and 361 footnote 52; Piskeiy Teshuvos 319:33
[635] Admur 319:18; *"It is permitted to gently pour [food or liquid] from one vessel into another in order so the residue and dregs remain on the bottom of the vessel [being poured from]. However, one must be careful once the stream [being poured] has stopped and small trickles begin to drip out from the last remainder [of food that is] amongst the waste, then one must stop [pouring] and leave [that remainder of food] together with the waste. The reason for this is because if one were to not do so, then these last drops prove [to all] that [his true intentions in this pouring] were to separate [the food from the waste]. However, during the initial pouring when the waste is not yet recognizable, then he has done no separation."*; Michaber 319:14; Kaf Hachaim 319:113 regarding tea and all mixtures
[636] Admur 319:18; M"A 319:15; M"B 319:55; Kaf Hachaim 319:113
[637] The reason: As a) perhaps coffee is not considered drunk by majority of people with its ground powder and hence contains the Borer restrictions. [Chayeh Adam 16, brought in Ketzos Hashulchan 125 footnote 21] b) According to many Poskim, Admur in his Siddur rules that when one pours liquid from a cup it is considered that one is removing the solid which remains in the cup from the liquid, and is forbidden due to the Borer restriction against removing bad from good. [see next footnote]
[638] Arguments to permit: 1) Perhaps coffee is considered edible by majority of people together with its ground powder, and hence has no filtering/Borer prohibition. [Ketzos Hashulchan 125 footnote 21] 2) If he pours to drink the coffee right away, many Poskim rule it is considered like taking the food from the waste which is permitted for right away use. [Admur 319:18; M"A 319:15; M"B 319:55; Kaf Hachaim 319:113] Now, although Admur in the Siddur seemingly retracted from this view [Divreiy Nechemia 21; Ketzos Hashulchan 125:9 and footnote 21; Iglei Tal Borer 5; Chayeh Adam 16:9, brought in Shaar Hatziyon 319:44; Or LeTziyon 2:31-10.], those who are lenient, especially in light of the first argument, have upon whom to rely. [See Shabbos Kehalacha Vol 2 pages 113-122]
[639] See Shabbos Kehalacha Vol. 2 p. 368; Piskeiy Teshuvos 319:37
[640] See sources previous footnotes

Poskim[641] rule it is forbidden to do so, as coffee powder is not edible by majority of people, and it is forbidden to separate using a strainer. Other Poskim[642], however, justify the custom to be lenient to allow filtering the coffee liquid even from the bottom area of the strainer, under several grounds.[643] Practically, it is best to avoid pouring out all the liquid and one should rather stop pouring as soon as one reaches the area of liquid that is above the strainer/coffee powder, in which case it is permitted according to all. This especially applies to one who is always particular to filter his ground coffee, in which case he is certainly to avoid pouring out all the coffee liquid.[644]

Pouring hot water into a coffee strainer which contains ground coffee:[645] It is permitted to place ground coffee into a strainer and then pour water [from a Keli Sheiyni or onwards] onto it, thus having the water pass through the ground coffee and strainer. [This applies even if the water will take some time to pass through the strainer.[646] However, one may not pour coffee liquid that is already mixed with the ground coffee through a strainer in order to strain the ground coffee.[647] This especially applies if one is always particular to strain it, in which case it is certainly forbidden to do so, as stated above. Likewise, even when pouring the water onto the ground coffee which is in the strainer, one is to beware of the following: a) Not to do any action to help the water strain faster or better, such as not to shake it, mix it using a finger or a vessel.[648] b) If the strainer is sitting inside the liquid, one is to remove it using a spoon and the like to avoid any drops from falling into the coffee after it is removed.[649]]

Summary:
It is permitted to make a hot beverage of ground/Turkish coffee on Shabbos through using a Keli Shelishi or Iruiy Keli Sheiyni.
Pouring from a cup and French press: One may likewise filter the coffee liquid from the ground coffee powder through pouring the liquid into another cup, although making sure to stop pouring as soon as one reaches the area in which the liquid is mixed with the coffee powder. This allowance applies even if one is using a French press. However, it is best not to pour the coffee liquid out once it reaches the

---

[641] Chayeh Adam 16, brought in Ketzos Hashulchan 125 footnote 21; Beis Menucha 48; Ben Ish Chaiy Beshalach 2:18; Kaf Hachaim 319:113; Shevet Halevy 1:84; Bris Olam Borer 40; Az Nidbaru 1:23; See Piskeiy Teshuvos 319:37

[642] Shevisas Hashabbos Borer footnote 29 and 49 regarding tea questions the allowance but then concludes that so is the custom; Ketzos Hashulchan 125 footnote 21 regarding also coffee; Chazon Ish 53; Rav SZ"A in SSH"K 3 footnote 125; See Minchas Yitzchak 7:23; Or Letziyon 1:27; Yechaveh Daas 2:51; Piskeiy Teshuvos 319:37

[643] The reason: As a) As [most] people are not particular against consuming some of the ground coffee together with the liquid and it is thus permitted to strain the liquid from it. [Shevisas Hashabbos ibid; Ketzos Hashulchan ibid] b) In any even the coffee powder goes to the bottom and is hence not considered to be strained. [Ketzos Hashulchan ibid] c) One does not intend to separate the coffee liquid from the coffee powder but rather just to drink the coffee. [Ketzos Hashulchan ibid; Chazon Ish ibid] d) A vessel which is designated to separate for only right away use, as is a kettle, is not included in the separating restrictions. [Rav SZ"A in SSH"K ibid].

[644] See Peri Megadim 319 M"Z 6; brought in Ketzos Hashulchan 125 footnote 28; Shabbos Kehalacha Vol. 2 p. 347 and 361 footnote 52

[645] See Admur 319:12, Michaber 319:9 and Mishneh Shabbos 139b *"If one had placed dregs in the strainer from before Shabbos then it is permitted to pour water over it in order so the water become more [clean and] clear."*; Shabbos Kehalacha 14:36 and Biurim 8; SSH"K 3:64; Piskeiy Teshuvos 319:32 that from here we can learn the allowance to pour water onto coffee that is in a strainer; Minchas Yitzchak 4:99-2 and Shabbos Kehalacha Vol. 2 p. 370

Must the coffee be placed in the strainer before Shabbos? No. [Piskeiy Teshuvos ibid footnote 274] Now, although Admur in 319:12 discusses a case in which the dregs were placed in the strainer from before Shabbos, this is only because dregs are naturally mixed with wine, and it is forbidden to filter dregs on Shabbos. However, placing dry coffee powder onto a strainer causes no filtering to take place and is hence permitted even on Shabbos. [See Admur 315:14 and 319:12]

Is there a prohibition of Ohel in covering the vessel with the strainer: No. [See Admur 315:19-20; Piskeiy Teshuvos ibid footnote 274] Now, although Admur 315:14 and Michaber 315:9 rules it is forbidden to set up a strainer on Shabbos due to the Ohel prohibition, this only applies to a strainer that contains wine dregs inside of it, being that it is forbidden to strain it on Shabbos, and hence one who sets it up on Shabbos is doing a mundane act and belittling Shabbos. However, if the strainer does not contain wine dregs, then it is permitted to set it up on Shabbos [Admur 315:14; M"A 319:18] even over a vessel, so long as it is not the size of a barrel. [Admur 315:19]. See however Taz 315:9 "It is forbidden due to the vessel under it." who implies the prohibition would apply to ever placing it over a vessel due to Ohel. Vetzaruch Iyun

[646] Pashut. The Poskim do not differentiate in this matter, and this is in fact the Yesod for allowing using tea bags on Shabbos. [See Shabbos Kehalacha ibid in Biurim]

[647] This case is even more severe than the case of a French press, as the only logic of allowance that remains in this case is that coffee powder is edible to majority of people, which is under debate.

[648] Minchas Yitzchak 4:99; Shevet Halevi 8:58; Piskeiy Teshuvos ibid; See however See Shabbos Kehalacha 2 p. 370

[649] Minchas Yitzchak 4:99-2; Sheivet Halevy 8:58; SSH"K 3 footnote 171 in name of Rav SZ"A; See however Shabbos Kehalacha Vol. 2 p. 371 based on SSH"K 3 footnote 125

> level area of the ground coffee/strainer, even if one plans to drink it right away.
>
> Pouring through a strainer: Certainly, one should not pour the coffee liquid directly through a strainer in order to filter the ground coffee. One may however pour hot Keli Sheiyni/Shelishi water into a strainer that contains ground coffee and have the liquid drip into one's cup. One, however, should beware not to shake the strainer and is to remove it from the liquid using a spoon.

42. How to remove dirt [i.e. dust, hair lash, insect] from your food on Shabbos:

➢ An eye lash fell into my tahini dip. How do I remove it?

Background: It is Biblically forbidden to separate waste from the food on Shabbos.[650] This prohibition is called Borer. This prohibition applies even if the waste is the minority of the food.[651] Any item which one does not desire to eat right away and is of a different substance than the remaining food is defined as waste in this regard.[652] Accordingly, the question is asked as to how one is to separate dirt from ones food on Shabbos without transgressing the Borer prohibition.

The law: It is Biblically forbidden to remove the dirt from the food, as explained above.[653] However, some Poskim[654] rule that this only applies if one removes the dirt by itself, without removing any of the food together with it. However, if one removes the waste together with some of the food, such as [using a spoon to] remove a fly from a cup together with some of the liquid, then it is permitted to be done.[655] However, other Poskim[656] negate this allowance and rule that it is Biblically forbidden to remove the waste even together with some of the food, and the Biblical Borer prohibition applies even in such a case. Practically, although many are accustomed to being lenient[657], one is to be stringent like the latter opinion[658], and so is the ruling followed by Chabad Chassidim.[659] Accordingly, the only remaining option for removing the dirt from one's food on Shabbos is to eat around the area of waste, and leave the waste positioned in its place. Once one has concluded eating around the waste, and it is no longer considered mixed with other foods, he may wipe it entirely off the plate. If the dirt is floating in a liquid, such as on a

---

[650] Admur 319:1; Michaber 319:4

The reason: The reason for why removing the waste is forbidden is because the removing of the waste [from the food] is not [considered done in] the normal framework of eating [which is permitted to be done as will be explained below] but is rather [considered] preparing the food so it be fit to eat which is a complete [Biblically prohibited] act. [Admur ibid]

[651] Admur ibid; Rama 319:4; Beis Yosef 319 based on Rambam

Other opinions: This is opposed to the ruling of the Tur 319 which holds that in such a case one is allowed to remove the waste rather than the food as doing so is the way of eating. Admur and others however limit this ruling only to Yom Tov and not on Shabbos. [See Shabbos Kehalacha Vol. 2 p. 141]

Opinion of Michaber: The Michaber agrees with the ruling of the Rama ibid, as is implied from the fact that he did not mention any allowance in his rulings regarding majority food. [Biur Halacha 319:1 "Haborer"]

[652] Admur 319:5; Michaber 319:3

[653] Admur 319:24 "If a fly fell into a cup one may not remove only the fly from the cup being that doing so is equivalent to separating waste from food which is forbidden to be done even in order to eat right away."; Taz 319:13; All Poskim in next footnote

[654] Admur 319:24 [unlike his ruling in the Siddur]; Taz 319:13 and 506:3; Beir Heiytiv 319:19; Ben Ish Chaiy Beshalach 12; Chayeh Adam 16:2; M"B 319:61; Kaf Hachaim 319:42; Even Yisrael 9:25

[655] The reason: Being that then it does not appear like one is separating at all. [Admur ibid] Seemingly, the reason is because when one removes the bad together with the good, it is not recognizable that one has selected bad from good, and it is thus permitted.

[656] Admur in Siddur [unlike his ruling in 319:24] "One may not rely on the customary permission granted that if there is waste in one's food then one removes it together with some of the food etc., as doing so is questionable of containing a sin offering liability and a prohibition of Sekilah G-d forbid."; Peri Megadim 319 M"Z 13 implies that this Heter to remove the bad with the good only applies in certain scenarios, as explained below; Kaf Hachaim ibid concludes it is best to be stringent like Admur in Siddur; Chazon Ish 53 questions ruling of Taz ibid; See Piskeiy Teshuvos 319:44

Opinion of Peri Megadim: Peri Megadim 319 M"Z 13 implies that only if one separates only some of the bad together with good, and will thus still leave some of the bad with the mixture, is one not liable for Borer, however if one separates the entire bad, then he is liable for Borer even if he removes some of the good. Furthermore, he implies that even if one leaves some of the bad with the good, and removes the bad with some of the good, it is only permitted in a case that if one were to remove the entire bad from the good he would not be Biblically liable, otherwise, it remains Rabbinically forbidden."

[657] As testified by Admur in Siddur ibid

[658] As concludes Kaf Hachaim ibid

[659] Shaar Hakolel 1:1; Likkutei Sichos 11 p. 246; Introduction of the Rebbe to the Shulchan Aruch Harav; See Divrei Nechemia 21; Kaf Hachaim and Piskeiy Teshuvos ibid conclude it is best to be stringent

The reason: Whenever there is a difference in ruling between the Siddur and the Shulchan Aruch one is to follow the rulings of the Siddur. The reason for this is because the Siddur was written later than the Shulchan Aruch and hence represents the final ruling of Admur in the given subject. [ibid]

drink or soup, then another available option is to blow the waste to the side of the cup and then pour out the dirt together with some of the liquid.[660]

> **Summary:**
> If dirt fell into one's food, the only option for removing the dirt from one's food on Shabbos is to eat around the area of dirt, and leave the dirt positioned in its place. Once one has concluded eating around the dirt, and it is no longer considered mixed with other foods, he may wipe it entirely off the plate. If the dirt is floating in a liquid, such as on a drink or soup, then another available option is to blow the waste to the side of the cup and then pour out the dirt together with some of the liquid.

---

[660] Admur in Siddur ibid *"One may not rely on the customary permission granted that if a fly or other waste falls into ones cup or plate then one removes it together with a spoon and takes out with it some liquid etc., as doing so is questionable of containing a sin offering liability and a prohibition of Sekilah G-d forbid.* ***Thus, the only solution that remains is to pour out from the cup until the waste comes out from it.*** *One may not blow on [the waste] with his mouth until it is blown out, although he may blow it to bring it nearer to the wall of the cup and then tilt it and pour from it until the waste comes out."*

The reason that tilting it out is allowed: As since the removal of the waste is being done through him holding the cup of liquid in his hand and tilting it with his hand this is considered separating food from waste which is permitted to be done in order to drink it immediately. [Admur in Siddur ibid]

43. Cutting items on Shabbos, such as a tablecloth, garbage bag, paper towel, piece of tinfoil, and toilet paper?

It is Biblically forbidden to perform an action on Shabbos which prepares an item for a use. The principal Melacha of this prohibition is called "Makeh Bepatish," while its offshoot is known as Tikkun Keli.[661] Accordingly, it is forbidden to cut or tear an item on Shabbos for the sake of making a use out of the cut piece. If one cuts the item with a vessel, such as a scissor or knife, it is Biblically forbidden. If one tears it with his hands, it is Rabbinically forbidden.[662] In addition to the above prohibition of Tikkun Keli, cutting or tearing an item on Shabbos [even not for a use] may also transgress other Biblical or Rabbinical prohibitions, including: Koreiah/Tearing[663]; Michateich[664]; Tochein[665]; Soseir/destroying; Erasing letters.

Based on the above prohibition of Tikkun Keli, it is forbidden to cut or tear the following items on Shabbos, and they are all to be prepared, and pre-cut, before Shabbos:[666]

- Tablecloth: It is forbidden to cut a tablecloth roll for the sake of using the cut piece to cover one's table [or other usage]. This applies irrelevant of whether one cuts the tablecloth on the pre-serrated lines. It is forbidden to do so even with one's hands, and certainly with a knife.
- Garbage bags: It is forbidden to cut a garbage bag from a garbage bag roll on Shabbos.
- Plastic sandwich bags: A pack of sandwich bags in which each bag is slightly attached to the bag under it, and needs to be torn off, is forbidden to be torn on Shabbos. This applies irrelevant of whether one cuts the bags on the pre-serrated lines.
- Tinfoil: It is forbidden to cut a piece of tinfoil from a roll, on Shabbos, whether with one's hands or using a knife.
- Paper towel: It is forbidden to cut a piece of paper towel from a roll, on Shabbos, whether with one's hands or using a knife. This applies irrelevant of whether one cuts the paper towel on the pre-serrated lines.
- Toilet paper: It is forbidden to cut a piece of toilet paper from a roll, on Shabbos, whether with one's hands or using a knife. This applies irrelevant of whether one cuts the toilet paper on the pre-serrated lines.

---

[661] Admur 302:5 *"It is the common way for craftsmen who make a metal vessel to strike the vessel with a hammer after it is completed, in order to smooth out any bumps through this striking. This striking is the final work done to this vessel and is a principal form of labor which existed with the vessels[661] of the Tabernacle. [Thus] anyone who does an action which is the finishing work of the vessel and of its fixing, this completion is considered a Melacha and is an offshoot of [the principal prohibition of] "Hitting with a hammer" which existed in the Tabernacle.* **Similarly, anyone who does any fixing to a vessel, this fixing is considered a [Biblically forbidden form of] work, and one is [thus] liable [for a sin offering].**; Mishneh Shabbos 73a and Rashi there; Mishneh 102b; Rambam 23:4; Smak 280; Taz 302:1; M"B 302:9

[662] Admur 340:17; 308:54; 82; 314:12; 508:2; See Michaber 340:13; M"B 322:13

[663] See Admur 302:4; 278:1-3; 317:7; 340:17; Mishneh Berurah 340 Biur Halacha "Eiyn Shovrin"; Piskeiy Teshuvos 340:34

[664] See Admur 314:16; Aruch Hashulchan 321:40; Az Nidbaru 1:79

[665] Admur 314:16; M"A 314:14; M"B 314:41

[666] Piskeiy Teshuvos 340:34

Does the Koreiah prohibition apply in the cases listed below? The Koreiah prohibition only applies if the item is made of several fabrics or pieces which are being torn apart. Accordingly, the Koreiah prohibition would not apply in the cases listed below in which the item is a single solid material. [See Admur 340:17] However, Tzaruch Iyun, as perhaps the beads of plastic which are melted to form the plastic sheet would be considered "several fabrics" which would transgress the Koreia prohibition. Likewise, paper which is made from ground wood may also be defined as "several fabrics" and transgress the prohibition. [See Piskeiy Teshuvos]

Does the Biblical Tikkun Keli prohibition apply in the cases below? As stated above, if one cuts the item with a scissor or knife, it is a Biblical prohibition, while if he tears it with his hand, it is a Rabbinical prohibition. This is unlike Piskeiy Teshuvos 340:34 footnote 308 who writes that according to Admur there is no Biblical prohibition, as in truth, while there is no Biblical prohibition of Koreia according to Admur, there is a Biblical prohibition of Tikkun Keli if cut with a vessel. However, see there based on Maor Hashannos 4 that the Biblical prohibition of Tikkun Keli does not apply being that the vessel is able to be used in a time of need even without cutting and thus the simple act of cutting is not considered a complete fixing. However, in the case of the garbage bags or plastic bags, since the cutting turns it into a useable bag, then it is a Biblical prohibition of Tikkun Keli [if done with a vessel]. The practical ramification is regarding Amira Lenachri and if we can consider it Shevus Deshvus to cut it even with a knife.

Does the Michateich prohibition apply in the cases below? For the most part, the Michateich prohibition does not apply in the below mentioned cases even if one cuts it by the dotted lines as one has no intent to truly cut it to a specific measurement. [See Admur 314:16; Piskeiy Teshuvos 340:34 footnote 308] However, see Aruch Hashulchan 321:40 and Az Nidbaru 1:79 who rules that one who tears paper for a use transgresses Michateich. Vetzaruch Iyun.

- Tissues: A pack of tissues in which each tissue is slightly attached to the tissue below it, and needs to be torn off, is forbidden to be used on Shabbos. This applies irrelevant of whether one cuts the tissues on the pre-serrated lines.

Q&A

Are the above items Muktzah on Shabbos?[667]
All the above items that may not be cut on Shabbos receive the status of Keli Shemilachto Li'issur, of which the ruling is that it may not be moved to save from damage, but may be moved for the sake of using it, or to free up its space.[668] If practically the item is not useable due to one's inability to cut it, then it may be judged under the higher status of Muktzah called Muktzah Machmas Chisaron Kis, or Muktzah Machamas Gufo, of which the ruling is that it may not be moved for any purpose.[669] If, however, one would not abstain from using the item without cutting it [i.e. placing the entire garbage roll in the garbage can and opening the one on top, or placing the plastic tablecloth on the table and resting the roll on a chair at the edge] then seemingly its status would be of Keli Shemilachto Li'issur.

In the above cases, does it help to cut the above items to a larger quantity than necessary to avoid the above prohibition of Tikkun Keli?[670]
The prohibition applies even in such a case, as any cutting which further assists one in achieving his use of the vessel is forbidden due to Tikkun Keli.

In the above cases, does it make a difference if one cuts the item with one's hands versus a knife?
The prohibition applies whether it is cut with a knife or torn with one's hands, although the level of prohibition, and whether it is Biblical or Rabbinical does change if it was cut with one's hands versus a knife and the like, as explained above.

Does it make a difference if one cuts the above items on the serrated lines, or elsewhere?[671]
No. The prohibition of Tikkun Keli applies wherever one cuts it. Likewise, cutting it by the dotted lines does not necessarily transgress the additional Michateich prohibition[672], and hence there is no Halachic difference regarding where one intends to cut it.

May one ask a gentile to cut the above items on Shabbos?
No, as is always the rule regarding Amira Lenachri. However, in a case of great need, or for the sake of a Mitzvah, one may ask the gentile to cut it for him using his hands, without mentioning the use of a scissor or knife.[673]

---

[667] See Piskeiy Teshuvos 340:34 footnote 309
[668] See Admur 308:2, 12; M"A 308:5; M"B 308:10
[669] See regarding blank paper that it becomes both MMCK and MMG: Admur 308:6; M"A 308:10 in name of Shiltei Giborim 8; M"B 308:3
[670] See Admur 308:54 regarding shortening the length of a vine" due to it being too long for him"; However, see Tzitz Eliezer 13:45 that when one does not care of the size of the cut then it is not Tikkun Keli
[671] Piskeiy Teshuvos 340:34
[672] See footnotes above where this matter was explained
[673] See Admur 307:12, 16; Piskeiy Teshuvos 340:34 footnote 310

44. May one open or close a folding table or folding chair on Shabbos?

A. Introduction:

It is forbidden on Shabbos to create a roofing or hovering due to the Ohel prohibition.[674] Nevertheless, this prohibition is only in a case that the intent of the hovering is to protect a person from a certain matter, such as to protect from rain or from the sun and light, and the like.[675] If, however, the intent of the hovering is not to give protection for people under it, then it may be made on Shabbos under certain conditions, such as if it was pre-attached to its legs/walls before Shabbos[676], or does not have any walls under it, or is made with an irregularity.[677]

B. The law:

Practically, due to the above reasons, it is permitted on Shabbos to open and close a folding chair and folding table without restriction, and doing so does not pose a prohibition of Ohel, or any other prohibition.[678] This applies to all forms of folding tables and chairs, even if they form a wall [i.e. box] under them.[679] This applies even if one intends to use the space under the table or chair for some purpose, such as to store boxes, or shoes under it.[680] It is, however, forbidden to do so for the sake of human protection, such as in order to sleep under the table and have it block the light in the room.[681]

<u>If the table/chair surface is not attached to its legs</u>:[682] In the event that the table surface is not attached to the leg frame, and one needs to open the legs and then rest the table on it, then the following is the law: It is permitted to be done on Shabbos without restriction so long as the legs do not form into walls, and one does not actually attach the table surface to the frame using sockets and the like, but simply rests it upon the frame.[683] The same applies if the cushion area of a chair came off, it is nevertheless permitted to rest it

---

[674] Admur 315:1; Michaber 315:1; Shabbos 125b

[675] Admur ibid *"It is forbidden to make a tent, which refers to [any] roofing which hovers over a person **in order to guard him from a given matter**, such as [to protect him] from the sun or from the rain or from another given matter."*

[676] Admur 315:9 *"A temporary roof which one does not intend in making it for it to be a tent to hover over what is underneath it, but rather only in order to use [this roof] for a certain use, such as for example placing the board of a table on its legs, then even though in doing so one makes a temporary roof this does not pose a problem being that one has no intent to make a tent. Nevertheless, if one also places temporary walls under this roof, then this is similar to a tent and is forbidden to be done in its normal form which is [starting] from below to above, and rather [must be done from] above to below [which is] an irregular form."*; Michaber 315:3 as explained in M"A 315:7; M"B 315:17-19

[677] Admur 315:1 *"It is forbidden to make a tent, which refers to [any] roofing which hovers over a person **in order to guard him from a given matter**, such as [to protect him] from the sun or from the rain or from another given matter."* And Admur 315:9 *"A temporary roof which one does not intend in making it for it to be a tent to hover over what is underneath it, but rather only in order to use [this roof] for a certain use, such as for example placing the board of a table on its legs, then even though in doing so one makes a temporary roof this does not pose a problem being that one has no intent to make a tent. Nevertheless, if one also places temporary walls under this roof, then this is similar to a tent and is forbidden to be done in its normal form which is [starting] from below to above, and rather [must be done from] above to below [which is] an irregular form."*; Michaber 315:3 as explained in M"A 315:7; M"B 315:17-19

[678] Admur 315:13 *"Any temporary tent which one has no intention into making into a tent [the Sages] only prohibited spreading over walls which one [had already] set up under it on Shabbos if the roofing had not been attached on its walls from before Shabbos. However, if [the roofing] had already been attached to them from before Shabbos but it was placed there folded, then it is permitted to spread it out and set it up on Shabbos. **For example a chair made from individual parts and when one wants to sit on it one opens it and spreads and stretches the leather [seating] and when one removes [the seat] he closes it up and has the leather fold, then it is permitted to initially open it on Shabbos even if it has walls under it.**"*; Michaber 315:5; Tur 315; Shabbos 138a as explains Tosafos; Piskeiy Teshuvos 315:7 [old] 11 [new]; Biur Halacha 315:5 "Kisei" regarding a folding bed

<u>The reason</u>: The reason for this is because it is not similar to making a tent, as one is not doing anything, as the roofing was already set up and prepared together with the walls from before Shabbos and it's just that one unfolds it on Shabbos and sits on it. [Admur ibid; M"A 315:8] Furthermore, typical folding chairs and tables do not contain actual walls under their roofing and hence are permitted to be set up on Shabbos, even if they are not pre-attached

[679] See Admur ibid in previous footnote

[680] So is clearly evident from Admur 315:9 and 13 [regarding a canopy] and Michaber 315:3; Piskeiy Teshuvos 315:11

<u>Other opinions</u>: Some Poskim rule one may never open a folding chair or table, even without walls under it, if his intent is to use the space that is under it for some purpose. [See Biur Halacha 315:3 "Mitos" in name of Rashba; Menoras Hamaor 315:14 leaves this matter with a Tzaruch Iyun; See Noda Beyehuda Tinyana 30; Piskeiy Teshuvos 315 footnote 129]

[681] Implication of Admur 315:13; Noda Beyehuda Tinyana 30; Menorah Hatehorah 315:14; Shoel Umeishiv Gimel 2:43; Tiferes Yisrael Kalkeles Shabbos Boneh 3; Aruch Hashulchan 315:10 and 12; Daas Torah 315; Tehila Ledavid 315:8; Kaf Hachaim 315:44

<u>Other opinions</u>: Some Poskim understand the M"A ibid to rule that one may open a Chuppah even for protection purposes if it was attached before Shabbos [P"M 315 A"A 8; Tosefes Shabbos 315:14; Beis Meir 315:1; Chasam Sofer 72; Machaneh Mayim 3:23; Shevilei David 315; Shaar Hatziyon 315:35; Chazon Ish 52:6]

[682] See Admur 315:9 brought in previous footnotes that if there are no walls under the table, there is no Ohel prohibition to place the table surface onto it; Piskeiy Teshuvos 315:11

[683] This is due to the prohibition of Tikkun Keli.

onto the leg frame so long as one does not fasten it to the frame.[684] In all these cases, one may likewise remove the table and cushion from the leg frame so long as it is not firmly attached.

> **Summary:**
> It is permitted on Shabbos to open and close folding chairs and folding tables without restriction, so long as one's intent is not to do so for human protection. It is also permitted to rest a seat cushion or table surface onto its leg frame so long as one does not fasten it to the frame.

---------------Shabbos-Muktzah----------------

45. Are flowers in a vase Muktzah on Shabbos?[685]

A. Background:

All items that do not contain a use are considered Muktzah Machmas Gufo on Shabbos and may not be moved for any purpose in a regular fashion, neither for its space, use or to save from damage.[686] Thus, ground products such as plants, flowers, grass, branches and twigs that are laying on the ground are Muktzah on Shabbos, whether they are attached or detached from the ground.[687] However, if one takes any of the above products before Shabbos and designates it for a use, it is no longer considered Muktzah and may be moved on Shabbos like any other non-Muktzah item.[688]

B. The law:

Although flowers that are lying on the ground are Muktzah on Shabbos, flowers that have been gathered and prepared from before Shabbos to be used for decoration of one's home, are not Muktzah.[689] Accordingly, it is permitted without restriction to move a bouquet, or vase, of flowers on Shabbos. Likewise, on Shavuos, it is permitted to move the various flowers and plants [that are not in pots with earth] that have been placed around the house or Shul for decorative purposes.[690] For this reason, it is also permitted to lift and move a good scenting branch or leaf [i.e. myrtle, rosemary, mint, etc.] that has been designated before Shabbos for smelling, and there is no Muktzah prohibition involved.

Plants in pots with earth: Plants or trees that grow within pots that contain earth do have Muktzah restrictions applicable to them, as will be discussed in a further Halacha!

Entering and removing the flower to and from the water vase: It is permitted to remove flowers from the water vase on Shabbos, however, certain restrictions apply regarding placing the flowers into the water vase, as will be explained in a future Halacha.

> **Summary:**
> Flowers in a vase are not Muktzah and may be moved without restriction.

---

[684] Piskeiy Teshuvos 315:11
[685] See Admur 336:18; 494:14; Rama 336:11; M"A 336:13; 494:5
[686] Admur 308:8; Michaber and Rama 308:7
[687] Admur 312:9; 336:4; M"A 312:6; See Peri Megadim 312 A"A 6
Other opinions: Some Poskim rule that all grass which is attached to the ground is not Muktzah. [Elya Raba and Tosefes Shabbos brought in Machatzis Hashekel 312:6; so rules also M"B 312:17; Shaar Hatziyon 336:42] According to this opinion, Muktzah only applies to those things attached to the ground which had a decree of Shimush Gidulei Karka attached to it, such as fruits of a tree. However, grass and the like are not forbidden due to Gidulei Karka, as explained in 336, and it is therefore also not Muktzah. However, once the grass is detached it becomes Muktzah.
[688] Admur 308:50
[689] See Admur 336:18; 494:14; M"A 336:13; 494:5; Piskeiy Teshuvos 336:22
The reason: As they have been designated for a use from before Shabbos and thus have the status of a vessel. [Admur ibid]
[690] Admur 494:14; M"A 494:5

46. Are pets [dogs, cats, birds, fish] Muktzah on Shabbos?

All living creatures, other than humans, are Muktzah on Shabbos and hence are forbidden to be moved [in their normal method[691]].[692] This applies even if the animal is fit for entertaining children.[693] It is forbidden to even pet the animal.[694] In addition, independent of the Muktzah prohibition, it is forbidden to make use of animals on Shabbos, [even in an irregular method] such as to lean on it, play with it, and the like.[695] If, however, one designates the animal/creature for a specific purpose, such as to have as a pet for the sake of pleasure in seeing and interacting with the animal, then some Poskim[696] rule the pet [bird, fish, dog, cat, turtle, etc.] is not Muktzah and may be moved on Shabbos.[697] Other Poskim[698], however, rule that the animal remains Muktzah, and thus remains forbidden to be moved on Shabbos.[699] Practically, one is to be stringent in this matter, and not move even a pet animal on Shabbos.[700] Furthermore, even according to the lenient opinion who permits moving the pet on Shabbos, it remains forbidden to make a use of the pet

---

[691] However, they may be moved with an irregularity, as is the law by all Muktzah. [Admur 308:15; 311:15; 276:9-10; 266:19; 301:39 KU"A 10; So also rules: Mishneh Shabbos 141a; Rosh 3:19 in name of Rabbeinu Yonah; Michaber 311:8; Michaber 308:43; Rama 308:3 regarding blowing; M"A 308:7 regarding kicking Muktzah and 308:41 regarding his question on Michaber regarding sitting on Muktzah; M"B 276:31; 308:13 and 81 and 88; 311:30; 1st opinion in Chayeh Adam; Derech Hachayim; 1st opinion in Aruch Hashulchan 311:20; Kaf Hachaim 311:68, although brings strict opinion in 69.]

[692] Admur 308:78 [See also 308:8]; Michaber 308:39; Shabbos 43a and 128a
The reason: As they have no use on Shabbos when they are alive. [Admur ibid; Levush 308:39; Maggid Mishneh 25:25]

[693] Admur 308:78; Tosafos Shabbos 45a
The reason: This can be understood in one of two ways: 1) It is Muktzah because it was not designated for this purpose before Shabbos, and hence is similar to deciding on Shabbos to use a stone for a certain purpose. Or 2) It is Muktzah because it usually has no use on Shabbos, and hence the Sages did not create any ability of designation from before Shabbos, similar to figs and raisins that are in the drying process, which can never be designated. [See Admur 310:2 and 9] The practical ramification of the two reasons is in a case that one did designate the animal before Shabbos, as will be explained.

[694] See Admur 308:78; Taz 308:23; M"A 308:68; M"B 308:151 that it is forbidden to move any part of Muktzah; Admur 305:23 "Even to rub a child on its back to entertain him is forbidden"; The following Poskim rule it is forbidden to move even the hair both due to Muktzah and due to the prohibition of making use of an animal on Shabbos: Tosefes Shabbos 302:34, brought in Biur Halacha 305:18 "Mikaneach"; Toras Shabbos 302:21; Shevisas Hashabbos Kotzer 137; Kaf Hachaim 302:89; Keren Ledavid 92; Piskeiy Teshuvos 305:5 footnote 34 and 308:54 footnote 446
Other opinions: Some Poskim question that perhaps it is permitted to move the hairs of an animal, and the Sages only forbade against moving their bodies. [Biur Halacha 305:18 "Mikaneach" based on Michaber 302:11 who permits cleaning mud off using the tail of a horse]
Ruling of Poskim permitting cleaning mud with the tail of an animal: The Poskim rule that it is permitted for one to use the tail of a horse or cow to clean mud off one's hands. [Admur 302:22; Michaber 302:11; Rambam 22:19; Tosefta 17:5] This seems to imply that one may use and move the hairs of an animal on Shabbos, and the Sages did not decree against it. [Biur Halacha ibid] Other Poskim however suggest that this ruling refers to a detached tail from a horse and cow, or to a case of Geraf Shel Reiy, which permits moving Muktzah. However, in truth, it is forbidden to move the tail of an animal both due to Muktzah and due to the prohibition against making use of an animal. [Tosefes Shabbos 302; Toras Shabbos 302:21; Shevisas Hashabbos Kotzer 137; Kaf Hachaim 302:89; Keren Ledavid 92; Piskeiy Teshuvos 305 footnote 34]

[695] Admur 305:23; Michaber 305:18; Mishneh Beitza 36b

[696] Halachos Ketanos 1:45, brought in in Minchas Shabbos 88:10; Nezer Yisrael 10:3 in Likkutei Rima 11 in name of Maharach Or Zarua 81 [Or Zarua later retracts his ruling in 82]; Tosafos Shabbos 45b in name of Rav Yosef [Tosafus ibid later rejects this approach]; Minchas Shabbos 88:10 in name of Pachad Yitzchak; Igros Moshe 5:22-21 [contradicts himself in 4:16]; See Betzel Hachochma 5:33-34; Az Nidbaru 8:36; 9:27

[697] The reason: As any Muktzah item which has been designated for a permitted use on Shabbos seizes to be Muktzah [see Admur 308:50-53] and there is no reason to not apply the same rule for animals, and hence if the animal has been designated for a permitted use, such as for a decorative purpose or for entertainment, then it is not considered Muktzah.

[698] Hagahos Rav Akiva Eiger 308:17; Tosafos Shabbos 45b "They are Muktzah like dates and figs" and dates and figs can never be designated; Rosh, brought in Or Zarua 82 "My Heart does not allow me to permit moving the chirping birds, as animals have a different law than vessels [Rules animals are Muktzah even if one was Miyached them, such as to serve as chirping birds]; Conclusion of Maharach Or Zarua 82 like the Rosh, as he was a known Posek; Conclusion of Minchas Shabbos 88:10; Orchos Chaim 308:24; Daas Torah 308; Kaf Hachaim 308:235; Igros Moshe 4:16 [contradicts himself in 5:22]; Yabia Omer 5:26; SSH"K 27 footnote 96 in name of Rav SZ"A; See Ketzos Hashulchan 121 footnote 4 regarding fish; See Betzeil Hachachmah 5:33;
Opinion of Admur: Admur 308:78 rules that one may not move a bird even to entertain a child. This ruling is based on Tosafos ibid who rules that animals are like figs and raisings in the drying process which are Muktzah even if designated. This would seem to imply that according to Admur one cannot designate animals for a use on Shabbos. Furthermore, from the fact Admur omits writing the ability of designating an animal, also seems to reveal his intent in the above words, that it comes to refer even to a case that the animal is designated. On the other hand, however, one can infer from the words "since they have no use on Shabbos" that if they are designated for a use, then they are not Muktzah. Furthermore, the words "even if they are fit to entertain a child" can be inferred that it refers to a case that they were not designated. Furthermore, the logic used by Admur 310:9 to explain why figs and raisins in the drying process always remain Muktzah does not fit with the case of animals, as figs and grapes in the drying process have absolutely no use and therefore cannot be designated for anything, while animals have the use of a pet. [See Az Nidbaru ibid who in truth learns this case is different, as the bird has been designated specifically for this purpose, while perhaps in the case of Admur it has not been designated, and hence according to all remains Muktzah.] Vetzaruch Iyun!

[699] The reason: As a) They are unable to be designated for a permitted use, just like dried figs and grapes may not be designated while in the drying process. [See Tosafos ibid; Rosh ibid] b) As it is forbidden to make use of an animal on Shabbos, and the Sages did not differentiate in their decree. [Rosh brought in Or Zarua ibid; See Admur 305:23]

[700] Minchas Shabbos 308:80; Az Nidbaru 8:36; 9:27; Beir Moshe 2:28; Yabia Omer 5:26; Piskeiy Teshuvos 305:5 and 308:54

on Shabbos, such as to ride on it, or cuddle with it for one's benefit.[701] Hence, one may not pet an animal on Shabbos.[702]

To prevent Tzaar Baalei Chaim:[703] The Sages allowed encouraging the movement of an animal in certain ways in order to prevent Tzaar Baalei Chaim. [Some Poskim[704] rule that pets, which are under the dispute mentioned above, may be moved in any way in order to prevent Tzaar Baalei Chaim.] This matter will be discussed in greater length in a future lesson.

Summary:
According to all, it is forbidden to make use of a living creature on Shabbos [leaning, riding, cuddling], including pets. However, to move a pet not for the sake of making a use of it, is disputed amongst Poskim if it is forbidden due to Muktzah. Practically, one is to be stringent not to move or even pet an animal on Shabbos.

------------------Hadlakas Neiros-----------------

47. Extinguishing the match after lighting candles, before saying the blessing:[705]

The dispute in Poskim regarding if Shabbos is accepted once the candles are lit: Some Poskim[706] rule that Shabbos is accepted as soon as one lights the candles, and it is hence forbidden to perform Melacha and extinguish the match/candle once the Shabbos candles have been lit, unless one made a stipulation upon the lighting not to accept Shabbos.[707] Other Poskim[708], however, rule that Shabbos is not considered accepted with the lighting of the Shabbos candles as one is not dependent on the other at all, and hence it is permitted to extinguish the match after the lighting. Practically, although the main opinion follows the latter and lenient approach, the women are accustomed like the first opinion to accept Shabbos with the lighting.[709]

The practical law for women:[710] Due to the above custom to follow the stringent opinion and accept Shabbos upon the lighting, the women are accustomed that after they say the blessing and light the candles, they throw the match that was used to light the candles, and is still in their hand, onto the ground [or another surface, and let it extinguish on its own], and do not extinguish it [directly]. [Some Poskim[711],

---

[701] Minchas Shabbos 88:10 in name of Pachad Yitzchak; Az Nidbaru ibid
[702] See Admur 305:23 and Poskim ibid that petting is included in the prohibition of making use of animals
[703] See Admur 308:79; Michaber 308:40; Shabbos 128
[704] Betzeil Hachachmah ibid; SSH"K 27:28; Yabia Omer ibid
[705] See Admur 263:7; Michaber 263:10; Piskeiy Teshuvos 263:31; Ner Tamid
[706] 1st opinion in Admur ibid; 1st opinion in Michaber 263:10 and Tur 263; Bahag Hilchos Chanukah; Mordechai Remez 293; Ran Shabbos 23b
[707] 1st opinion in Admur ibid and Michaber ibid; Maharam in Tashbatz 8; Hagahos Maimanis Shabbos 8; Mordechai ibid
Other opinions: Some Poskim rule that according to the Bahag it is invalid to make a stipulation, and in all cases, one accepts Shabbos with the lighting. [2nd opinion in Admur ibid and Michaber ibid; Tashbatz ibid in name of Rabbeinu Yehuda; Kol Bo in name of Rabbeinu Peretz]
[708] 2nd opinion in Admur ibid, Michaber ibid, Tur ibid; Hagahos Maimanis Shabbos 5 in name of Tosafos; Rosh end of Shabbos Bameh Madlikin; Rambam as explains Maggid Mishneh Chanukah 4:13; Ramban Shabbos 23b; Rashba Shabbos 23b and Shut 1:1070; Rabbeinu Yerucham Nesiv 12:1-2;
[709] Admur ibid *"The custom is like the first opinion that the women who lights candles accepts Shabbos with this lighting"*; Rama 263:10
[710] Admur ibid; Michaber ibid *"**Some** women"*; Shibulei Haleket 59
The Sephardi custom: The Sephardi custom regarding several of the points relevant to our discussion is under heavy debate and controversy amongst the leading Sephardi Rabbanim and Poskim of the past and current generation, and hence practically, whether they may extinguish the candle after the lighting is debated amongst the Sephardi Poskim. Some of the Sephardi Poskim of today rule that according to the Michaber, we do not suspect for the ruling of the Bahag and hence a) women are to first say the blessing and then light candles [Rav Ovadia Yosef, as brought in Yabia Omer 2:16; 9:24, Yalkut Yosef, Ner Tamid and defended in length by his sons] and b) they may therefore also extinguish the candle after it is lit. [Rav Dovid Yosef in Ner Tamid 86] Many of the Sephardi Poskim, however, rule that Sephardi women are stringent like the Bahag and hence they too delay the blessing until after the lighting and also do not extinguish the candle. [Kaf Hachaim 263:62 and 45; Ben Ish Chaiy Noach 2:8; All Sephardi Poskim recorded in coming footnotes in stringent opinion; See lengthy article of Rav Yaakov Sofer who proves like this opinion for Sephardim; See Piskeiy Teshuvos 263 footnote166]
[711] Possible understanding of Admur 263:7 and 11 that only if one says the blessing and then lights is the custom to be stringent, however between the lighting and blessing Melacha may be done; Implication of M"A 263:11 that before Chuppah a woman may light and then delay blessing; Beis Yosef 263 in name of Kol Bo that the main acceptance is dependent on the blessing and not the actual lighting; See Ketzos Hashulchan 74:14; Aruch Hashulchan 263:14 *"Women who say the blessing after the lighting may extinguish the match as it is obvious that they do not accept Shabbos until the blessing is said, and I believe that so is the custom, and there is no Halachic question on this"*; Shulchan Hatahor 263:5; Orchos Chaim Spinka 263:6 in name of Meorei Or; SSH"K 43 footnote 179 in name of Rav SZ"A; Mishneh Halachos 8:31

however, rule that this custom only applies to those women who first say the blessing and then light, however, today that the widespread custom is to first light and then say the blessing[712], it is permitted to extinguish the candles after the lighting, prior to saying the blessing.[713] Other Poskim[714], however, rule that this law and custom applies even today that we say the blessing after the lighting, and hence a woman is not to extinguish the match or candle after the lighting, even before saying the blessing.[715] Practically, so is the seeming implication of Admur[716] and so is the final ruling and custom, not to extinguish the match even before the blessing.[717] Nonetheless, those who are lenient have upon whom to rely, especially in the event of a possible fire hazard.[718]]

The law for men:[719] There is no custom at all for men to be stringent like the first opinion and accept Shabbos with candle lighting, and hence we establish the law according to the main ruling [i.e. the 2nd opinion brought above] that accepting Shabbos is not dependent on candle lighting. [Accordingly, men who light Shabbos candles may extinguish the match after the lighting, even after saying the blessing.] Nonetheless, it is initially proper even for men to stipulate before the lighting that they do not intend to accept Shabbos.

Summary:
It is permitted for men to extinguish the match or candle after lighting, however it is best for them to stipulate prior to doing so. Women, however, are not to extinguish the match or candle used for lighting and are rather to put it down and let it extinguish on its own. Nonetheless, those women who are accustomed to extinguish the match after the lighting, before saying the blessing, have upon whom to rely. This especially applies in the event of a fire hazard. Regarding Sephardim, there are different rulings and customs, and each is to follow their Minhag and Rav.

Q&A
May a woman carry the match box to put away after lighting candles, before saying the blessing?[720]
She is not to do so being that she has already accepted Shabbos and the matches are Muktzah. As well,

---

[712] See Admur 263:8; Rama 263:5; Mahariy Viyal 29

[713] The reason: As even according to the Bahag and the custom of women to follow his approach, Shabbos is only accepted after the blessing is said. [Beis Yosef 263 in name of Kol Bo; Aruch Hashulchan ibid; See Admur 263:8 that the custom is to treat the blessing as the acceptance of Shabbos, and hence we delay the blessing until after all the candles are lit. Accordingly, it is possible to understand from Admur that it is not yet considered Shabbos until the blessing is recited after the lighting]

[714] Implication of Admur 263:7-8 and all Poskim brought in next footnote that the main acceptance is dependent on the lighting and not the blessing; Chesed Lealafim 263:6; Ben Ish Chaiy Noach 2:8; Toras Shabbos; Kaf Hachaim 263:62 "Immediately after lighting throw the match on the floor and then say the blessing"; Ketzos Hashulchan 74:14 footnote 14; Beir Moshe 8:63; Kinyan Torah 2:49; Bris Olam 20; Kitzur Dinei Hadlakas Neiros 4:5; Koveitz Mibeis Halevi 11:36 in name of Rav Wozner

[715] The reason: As according to the Bahag the main acceptance of Shabbos is dependent on the candle lighting, and it is just that the women are accustomed to suspect that even the blessing alone can be considered acceptance of Shabbos and hence they delay the blessing until after the lighting. However, this does not come to negate the main opinion of the Bahag, of which the women follow, that Shabbos is dependent on the actual lighting of the candles and not the blessing. Accordingly, the women are even more stringent then Bahag and consider Shabbos accepted either through the lighting or through the blessing. Based on this, there is no room to be lenient against Bahag and extinguish the match after the lighting even though the blessing was not said. [See Biur Hagra 263:13l; Gloss of Rav Akiva Eiger "Kabalas Shabbos is upon completing the lighting"; Ketzos Hashulchan ibid; Piskeiy Teshuvos ibid]

[716] See previous footnotes for the different implications that can be made from Admur, however, it seems clear from the wording Admur uses in 263:8 ["As they think that if they say the blessing first then they accept Shabbos"] that accepting Shabbos with the blessing is a personal added Chumra to the main opinion of Bahag, and since the women are accustomed like Bahag, they may no longer do Melacha after the lighting. Now, although Admur 263:11 rules that technically she may light candles and then go to the Chuppah and later on at night say the blessing, seemingly there it is a different case as she has no intent to accept Shabbos at all with the lighting and it is as if that she is lighting any random candle in her house. Seemingly, even a Tnaiy is not needed in such a case, as the candles are not yet considered Neiros Shabbos. However, in a normal situation when a woman plans to say the blessing immediately after the lighting, certainly the candles have the status of Neiros Shabbos of which she plans to begin Shabbos, and this matter is not dependent at all on the blessing.

[717] Rav Wozner ibid that so is custom; Piskeiy Teshuvos ibid that so is widespread custom; Kitzur Dinei Shabbos 263 footnote 45 that so is custom

[718] Piskeiy Teshuvos ibid

[719] Admur ibid; M"A 263:18; Bach 263; Elya Raba 679:2; M"B 679:1; Kaf Hachaim 263:64 and 679:3

Other opinions: Some Poskim rule that even men are to accept Shabbos upon lighting the candles and hence may not do Melacha afterwards. [Taz 679:1]

[720] Piskeiy Teshuvos 263 footnote 296

> she is not to make an interval between the lighting and the blessing. Rather, she should ask her husband, or male child, to take the matches to their destination.

48. Davening Mincha after candle lighting on Erev Shabbos:[721]

A woman who lights Shabbos candles, and thus accepts Shabbos with her lighting, is to Daven Mincha beforehand.[722] [If she did not do so, and has already lit her candles, then she may not daven Mincha afterwards, and is to rather Daven Maariv twice.[723] However, some Poskim[724] are lenient and rule that Bedieved she may still Daven Mincha after lighting candles and accepting Shabbos, especially if she had in mind to do so before the lighting.[725] Practically, initially, if she sees that she will not have time to Daven Mincha before lighting candles, she is to stipulate that she does not plan to accept Shabbos with her lighting.[726] In such a case, she may light the candles, and then Daven Mincha, and then accept Shabbos, although the accepting of Shabbos must be done within ten minutes from the lighting.[727] If she did not make this stipulation and already lit candles, she is to daven Maariv twice, although those who nevertheless Daven Mincha have upon whom to rely. If a man is lighting candles, he may always delay accepting Shabbos and daven Mincha after the lighting[728], so long as he [Davens Mincha and] accepts Shabbos within ten minutes from the lighting.[729] However, some are accustomed to Daven Mincha before lighting even regarding men.[730]]

49. May one eat or drink after candle lighting?

Some Poskim[731] rule it is permitted to eat or drink after candle lighting until Tzeis Hakochavim. Other Poskim[732] rule it is forbidden to eat or drink anything after candle lighting. Nonetheless, if one is very thirsty, and is afraid to delay lighting candles until after she drinks, she may stipulate upon lighting the candles that she will not accept Shabbos with the lighting. In such a case, she may drink after lighting candles and is to then accept Shabbos within ten minutes from the lighting. If she did not make the above

---

[721] Admur 263:7; M"A 263:19 in name of Masas Binyamin; Elya Raba 263:17; Machatzis Hashekel ibid, P"M 263 A"A 19; Mishneh Berurah 263:43; Ketzos Hashulchan 74:5; See Piskeiy Teshuvos 263:41; Kitzur Dinei Hadlakas Neiros 2:15

[722] The reason: As once a woman lights candles, she accepts Shabbos with that lighting, and one cannot Daven Mincha of Friday once one has just accepted that it is no longer Friday, but Shabbos. [Machatzis Hashekel on M"A ibid, based on Michaber 263:15; P"M 263 A"A 19; Mishneh Berurah 263:43;] The reason for this is because when a woman lights candles she accepts the essence of Shabbos [Itzumo Shel Yom], as opposed to Tosefes Shabbos. If, however, one did not light candles, and did not accept the essence of Shabbos, then even if he accepted Tosefes Shabbos, he may still Daven Mincha. [Ketzos Hashulchan 76 footnote 1; See Admur Seder Hachnasas Shabbos who allows Davening Mincha even after sunset; Mishmeres Shalom 26:23; See Admur 393:2 regarding the difference between accepting Tosefes Shabbos and Itzumo Shel Yom]

[723] Machatzis Hashekel 263 ibid as rules Michaber 263:15 regarding one who said Barchu; M"B 263:43; Kaf Hachaim 263:65; Ketzos Hashulchan 74:5

[724] Ashel Avraham Butchach 263 says to make Tnaiy regarding Mincha alone [and may accept Shabbos]; Orchos Chaim 261:1; 263:12; Lev Chaim 3:57; Eretz Tzevi 1:60 [permits even without Tnaiy]; Minchas Yitzchak 9:20 [permits without Tnaiy as rules Eretz Tzevi]; See Divrei Yatziv 1:121; Beir Moshe 1:15; Az Nidbaru 2:2; Rivivos Efraim 4:69; Piskeiy Teshuvos 253:41 concludes that those who are lenient have upon whom to rely

[725] The reason: As the ruling of the M"A ibid was only regarding Lechatchila and not Bedieved. [Eretz Tzevi ibid; Minchas Yitzchak ibid] Likewise, perhaps, lighting candles is not considered as if one is accepting Itzumo Shel Yom, but rather Tosefes Shabbos. [So rules Chasam Sofer 65] Some suggest that perhaps the acceptance of Shabbos opposes Mincha only when done with the public, such as when answering Borchu and the like, and not by a private acceptance.

[726] Ashel Avraham Butchach 263 says to make Tnaiy regarding Mincha alone [and may accept Shabbos]; Ben Ish Chaiy Noach 9; Kaf Hachaim 263:35; Beir Moshe 1:15; 8:64; Even Yisrael 8:21; Minchas Shlomo 2:35; SSH"K 43 footnote 128; Kinyan Torah 2; Teshuvos Vehanhagos 4:62; Piskeiy Teshuvos 263:41; Admur ibid permits making a stipulation in a time of need
Other opinions: Some Poskim imply that she is not to make a stipulation but is rather to Daven Maariv twice. [See M"B ibid; Piskeiy Teshuvos 263 footnote 387]

[727] See Admur 263:6, 7, 11 that she must accept Shabbos immediately after the lighting, and Kuntrus Achron 263:2 that this is within much less than 14 minutes; Ketzos Hashulchan 74 footnote 17 that this is within 10 minutes; Piskeiy Teshuvos 263:15 and 32 writes ten minutes
Other opinions: Some Poskim rule it is not necessary to accept Shabbos immediately after candle lighting, after the time of Plag Haminjcha. [Rav Akiva Eiger 263; M"B 263:20; Biur Halacha 263:4 "Mibiod Yom"; Eretz Tzevi 113]

[728] See Tehila Ledavid 263:8; See Admur 263:7 that a man does not accept Itzumo Shel Yom with his lighting; Piskeiy Teshuvos 263:41; There were times that the Rebbe lit Chanukah candles, and then Shabbos candles and only then Davened Mincha with the Minyan. [Hiskashrus 908 footnote 77]

[729] See Poskim in previous footnotes

[730] Mishmeres Shalom Kudinov 26:23; See Tehila Ledavid ibid

[731] Minchas Elazar 1:33; 2:11

[732] Peri Yitzchak 2:9; Ketzos Hashulchan 75 footnote 17 and 79 footnote 3 [leaves in question]; Beir Moshe 8:64

stipulation, some Poskim[733] rule that in a time of need [such as a pregnant, or nursing, or ill, or old person] she may nevertheless drink after candle lighting, up until sunset.[734] Nonetheless, if possible, it is better for one to make Kiddush after candle lighting and then eat and drink to one's content according to all opinions, rather than rely on the above ruling.[735]

---------------Kiddush----------------

50. Must one cover Mezonos foods that are on the table during Kiddush?[736]

A. Background:

One is required to cover the bread upon making Kiddush on Shabbos night and day.[737] There are several reasons recorded behind this law and custom, and understanding these reasons is the key to determining whether one is also to cover Mezonos foods upon reciting Kiddush both by the Shabbos night and day meal. The following are the reasons recorded:

1) Honor of Shabbos:[738] One is required to cover the bread upon making Kiddush in order to show that the food was brought to the table for the sake of honoring Shabbos, as when the food is covered during Kiddush and then uncovered at the completion of Kiddush, it is considered as if it was now brought to the table in honor of Shabbos which was mentioned in the Kiddush.

2) Commemoration of Mun:[739] One is required to cover the bread upon making Kiddush in order so the Challahs rest in between two cloths, in commemoration of the Mun which was covered with dew both on top and on bottom.

3) Cover shame of bread:[740] One is required to cover the bread upon making Kiddush in order to "cover" the shame of the bread, as the blessing over bread receives Halachic precedence over the blessing over wine, and hence although one must precede the blessing over wine in this case, the bread should be covered.

The ramifications: According to the 1st reason, possibly the requirement to cover the bread would apply likewise to Mezonos foods, and perhaps even other foods, in order to show that the food was brought to the table for the honor of Shabbos.[741] On the other hand, perhaps this concept only applies to bread.[742] According to the second reason, it would seemingly not apply to Mezonos. However, according to the 3rd reason it would appear that one is required to cover the Mezonos foods, as the blessing of Mezonos foods precede that of Hagafen[743], and hence its shame is to be covered just as by bread. Practically, this matter is debated amongst the Poskim, as explained next:

---

[733] Peri Yitzchak ibid [permits drinking all liquids and even to eat a little]; Daas Torah 271; Pischeiy Teshuvah 271 in name of Binyan Olam 7; Minchas Shabbos 77:2 [permits only water]; Ketzos Hashulchan 79 footnote 3; Beir Moshe 8:64; Mishneh Halachos 7:37; Piskeiy Teshuvos 271:13 [May drink any liquid and eat less than a Kebeitza of Mezonos]

[734] The reason: As perhaps the prohibition of eating or drinking before Kiddush does not begin to apply until sunset, as well as the Rambam always permits drinking water before Kiddush.

[735] Ketzos Hashulchan 79 footnote 3 in name of Minchas Shabbos ibid

[736] See Piskeiy Teshuvos 271:18-19

[737] Admur 271:10 and 17; 289:1 regarding Shabbos day; 299:14 regarding if bread is on the table by Havdalah; 473:44 regarding night of Seder that when cup is raised the Matzos should be covered so they do not see their shame; Rav Yehuda in name of Shmuel in Pesachim 100a

[738] Admur 271:10 and 17; M"A 271:7; M"B 271:15; Sheilasos of Rav Achaiy Yisro 54; Hagahos Maimanis 29 Kuf; Tur 271; Tosafos Pesachim 100b; Rashbam Pesachim ibid

[739] Admur 271:17; Taz 271:12; M"B 271:41; Tur 271; Sefer Hateruma 246; Hagahos Maimanis 29 Kuf; Tosafos Pesachim 100b;

[740] Admur 299:14 regarding if bread is on the table by Havdalah; 473:44 regarding night of Seder that when cup is raised the Matzos should be covered so they do not see their shame; [Omitted from Admur 271:10 and 17; 289:1 regarding Kiddush]; Rama 473:7; M"A 299:12; 473:30; Aruch Hashulchan 299:14 that so is main reason; M"B 271:41; 299:31; Tur 271 in name of Yerushalmi; Igur 798; Haggadah Shel Pesach of Rebbe "Ulichasos Hapas"

[741] See Peri Megadim 271 A"A 7 that one of the reasons behind covering the bread is to show that the food was brought to the table for the sake of Shabbos [i.e. Yikra Deshabbasa] and that initially the custom was not to bring the food at all to the table prior to Kiddush due to this [see Admur 271:17; Tur 271; Tosafos Pesachim 100b; Sheilasos Yisro 54; Rashbam Pesachim ibid], and now that we bring it to the table, at the very least one must cover it, and there is no difference between the Challah and the other foods. [P"M ibid]

[742] So is clear from the concluding wording of Admur ibid that "*The custom is to bring it initially before Kiddush and cover the bread until after Kiddush*"; See Hearos Ubiurim Tzemach Tzedek 7/257

The reason: Perhaps the reason for this is because the main aspect of the meal is the bread, and only by it is applicable the concept of Yikra Deshabbasa. Alternatively, perhaps it is a Tircha to cover all the foods and hence it is not done.

[743] See Admur in Seder Birchas Hanehnin 10:13-14 that if one has wine or grape juice and Mezonos products in front of him, then if the Mezonos is made of wheat or barley it precedes the blessing of Hagafen in all circumstances, even if the Hagafen is more desirable. [However, if the Mezonos is of spelt, rye, or oats, then the Hagafen receives precedence.]

B. The ruling:

Some Poskim[744] rule that the Mezonos foods on the table are to be covered.[745] This especially applies if one plans to fulfill his Mitzvah of Makom Seuda with the eating of this Mezonos product.[746] Other Poskim[747], however, rule that there is no need to cover foods other than the Challahs, even if one plans to eat Mezonos after Kiddush.[748] [Practically, if there are Challahs on the table, then only the bread needs to be covered and there is no need to cover any of the other foods, including the Mezonos foods that are on the table.[749] If, however, there are no Challahs on the table, and one plans to eat Mezonos after Kiddush, then one is to be stringent to cover it as rules the first opinion.[750] This, however, only applies if the Mezonos is made of wheat or barley, in which case it precedes the blessing of Hagafen. If, however it is made of spelt, rye or oats, then it does not need to be covered, as it does not precede the blessing of Hagafen.[751]]

Summary:
If there are Challahs on the table, there is no need to cover any of the other foods, including the Mezonos foods that are on the table. If, however, there are no Challahs on the table, and one plans to eat Mezonos after Kiddush, then one is to be stringent to cover the Mezonos foods if made of wheat or barley.

Q&A

Does it suffice for the Mezonos to be covered by a plastic see-through bag?[752]
Yes. Thus, if the Mezonos is still in its package it does not require a second covering, even if the Mezonos can be seen through the package.

The custom of the Rebbe:
Rabbi Label Groner related through a written correspondence that the Mezonos was always covered on the table when the Rebbe made Kiddush by Farbrengens, however, he is unaware of what the Rebbe did in private, when he would make Kiddush in his room prior to going downstairs.

---

[744] Peri Megadim 271 A"A 7; Kitzur SHU"A 55:5; Levushei Mordechai 1:46; Shvilei David 271; Orchos Rabbeinu See Piskeiy Teshuvos 271 footnote 184; 194

[745] The reason: As the blessing of Mezonos foods precede that of Hagafen [See Admur in Seder Birchas Hanehnin 10:13-14], and hence its shame is to be covered just as by bread. [Levushei Mordechai ibid based on 3rd reason recorded in Admur and Poskim ibid] Likewise, as one of the reasons behind covering the bread is to show that the food was brought to the table for the sake of Shabbos [i.e. Yikra Deshabbasa]. Now, initially the custom was not to bring the food at all to the table prior to Kiddush due to this [see Admur 271/17; Tur 271; Tosafos Pesachim 100b; Sheilasos Yisro 54; Rashbam Pesachim ibid], and now that we bring it to the table, at the very least one must cover it, and there is no difference between the Challah and the other foods. [P"M ibid] Practically, this later reason seems to be negated by Admur, as in his conclusion he writes "The custom is to bring it initially before Kiddush and cover the bread until after Kiddush";

[746] See wording in Kitzur SHU"A ibid; See Piskeiy Teshuvos 271:19

[747] Birchas Habayis 46:50; Shut Rav Akiva Yosef Schlesinger 95; Taamei Haminhagim Kuntrus Achron 365; See Ashel Avraham 271

[748] The reason: As the concept of shame only really applies to bread, which is the head of the meal, and not to Mezonos, even though technically its blessing precedes. [Poskim ibid]

[749] Implication of Admur 271:17 that "The custom is to bring it initially before Kiddush and cover the bread until after Kiddush"; See Hearos Ubiurim Tzemach Tzedek 7/257; See Tehila Ledavid 74; Ashel Avraham 282; Az Nidbaru 2:8; Piskeiy Teshuvos ibid

[750] Simple implication of wording of Admur in 299:14 regarding if bread is on the table by Havdalah

[751] Implication of Admur in Seder Birchas Hanehnin 10:13-14; Peri Megadim A"A 211:7-8 on M"A 211:7; Birchas Habayis 13:9
Implication of Admur: So is implied from Admur 10:13-14 which only mentions barley and wheat by Mezonos that has precedence over wine, and so is also implied from the next Halacha in which Admur emphasizes that Hamotzi **of all 5 grains** has precedence to wine. Now, if it was already established in the previous Halacha that even Mezonos of the 5 grains has precedence to wine, then certainly Hamotzi would have precedence to wine and thus what would be the novelty of this ruling. Hence, one must conclude that wine has precedence to all grains which are not mentioned explicitly in the verse, which include spelt, rye and oats.
Other opinions: Some Poskim rule that the Mezonos of all 5 grains have precedence to wine. [Rama 211:4, as explained in Mishneh Berurah 211:24]

[752] See SSH"K 47 footnote 116 in name of Rav SZ"A; Piskeiy Teshuvos 271 footnote 187 and 194

---------------Havdalah---------------

51. May one drink water before Havdalah?[753]

It is a Rabbinical prohibition to eat, drink, or even taste, any amount of food or liquid [other than water, as will be explained] prior to saying, or hearing, Havdalah over wine, or other valid beverages [if one did not begin a meal of bread prior to sunset[754]].[755] This prohibition applies even if one recited Havdalah within Maariv Shemoneh Esrei.[756] This, however, is with exception to water, which is allowed to be drunk prior to Havdalah [if it is after nightfall/Tzeis Hakochavim[757]].[758] [However, some Poskim[759] argue and rule that even water is forbidden to be drunk prior to Havdalah, and thus the prohibition of drinking prior to Havdalah extends to all liquids without exception. Practically, the Chabad custom is to avoid drinking even water prior to Havdalah, starting from sunset.[760] If, however, one is in the midst of a meal of bread, then he may drink water during the meal, just like any other food or drink, with exception to drawn water during Bein Hashmashos, as explained next.]

Drinking water after sunset, before nightfall:[761] The above discussion of allowance of drinking water before Havdalah, only applies after nightfall. However, prior to nightfall, during the period of Bein Hashmashos, it is forbidden to drink water that was drawn at that time, even if one is in the midst of a meal, due to Sakana. This matter will be elaborated on in a future Halacha IY"H.

Summary:
From the letter of the law, it is permitted to drink water prior to Havdalah, however some are stringent and so is the Chabad custom. Even those who are lenient, are not to drink drawn water between sunset and nightfall, even if they are in the midst of a meal.

Q&A

From the letter of the law, may one drink water based soft drinks before Havdalah?[762]
It is questionable whether soft drinks that are water based are permitted to be drunk before Havdalah just as is the law regarding water itself. [Practically the custom is to avoid drinking even water prior to

---

[753] Admur 299:1 *"The Sages prohibited one from eating anything, or drinking any liquid other than water, on Motzei Shabbos until Havdalah is done over the cup, even if he said Havdalah during the Shemoneh Esrei, and even to taste a small amount is forbidden, due to the reason explained in 271:1."* Michaber 299:1; Pesachim 105a

Severity of eating prior to Havdalah: Anyone who tastes anything before Havdalah is liable for death through the illness of Askara. [Rebbe Akiva in Pesachim 105a] Askara is a form a strangulation in which the person cannot breathe [similar to an asthma attack]. The reason for this punishment is Midah Kineged Midah, as just as he satiated his throat in a prohibited way, so too his throat will strangle. [Tosafos Pesachim ibid "Lo Kadi Amaya"; See Maggid Meisharim Vayeishev that the reason for this severity is because the Kelipos attach to the food at this time.

[754] If one began eating a meal [that consists of bread-Ketzos Hashulchan 94 footnote 3; Aruch Hashulchan 299:5] prior to sunset, he may continue to eat and drink without limit even after nightfall. [Admur 299:2; Pesachim ibid]

[755] The reason: The reason for this prohibition is because one is to say Havdalah as soon as Shabbos takes leave, without delay. Thus, although in general the Sages only forbade a meal from being eaten prior to fulfilling a Mitzvah while snacking prior to the Mitzvah was allowed, nevertheless, here even merely snacking or tasting food was forbidden, as Havdalah is to be said close to the leave of Shabbos and thus even snacking will cause one to delay saying it within this time. [Admur 271:9; Kuntrus Achron 299:2; See also Admur 431:6 regarding Bedikas Chametz that it must be done immediately after nightfall]

[756] Admur ibid and 299:16; M"A 299:13; Ran Pesachim 21a

[757] See below!

[758] Admur ibid; Michaber 299:1; Rav Amram in name of Rav and Rabanan Divei Rav Ashi in Pesachim ibid; Rashi Pesachim ibid "And so is the Halacha"

The reason: As water is not considered a significant beverage to need to prohibit. However, prior to Kiddush it is forbidden to drink even water, due to the honor of Shabbos. [See Rashi Pesachim ibid; Aruch Hashulchan 299:1]

[759] Rav Huna in Pesachim ibid *"I saw a man who drank water prior to Havdalah and I told him do you not fear from the death of Askara"* and so rule: Geonim in Shaareiy Teshuvah in end of Sefer Neharos Damesek 80 p. 6; Midrash Talpiyos "Havdalah" 4 p. 118 *"It is forbidden to drink water before Havdalah and one who does so is liable for death"*; Arizal in Peri Eitz Chaim Shaar 18:24 *"My master severely warned me not to drink water before Havdalah as one who drinks water by Bein Hashmashos of Motzei Shabbos can die of Askara"*; Yalkut Reuveini; Likkutei Maharich; Kaf Hachaim 291:16 and 299:6; Ketzos Hashulchan 94 footnote 1

[760] Hayom Yom 3rd Iyar; Sefer Haminhagim p. 68; Ketzos Hashulchan 94 footnote 1 based on Arizal.

[761] Drinking water on Shabbos after sunset, prior to nightfall: Prior to nightfall, during the period of Bein Hashmashos, it is forbidden to drink drawn water due to Sakana, even if one is in the midst of a meal. [See Admur 291:2; Opinion in Rama 291:2; See Kaf Hachaim 291:16-17; Piskeiy Teshuvos 291:3] See Rama ibid for a number of opinions on this matter; See Admur ibid that we are stringent although that this prohibition only applies to drawn water; See Admur ibid and Kaf Hachaim and Piskeiy Teshuvos ibid that it only applies by Bein Hashmashos and not after nightfall.

[762] See Piskeiy Teshuvos 299:1 footnote 6

> Havdalah, and thus certainly water based soft drinks are to be avoided.]

52. Saying a blessing of Besamim upon smelling a tea bag:[763]

Plain teas [non-herbal; black tea, green tea, etc.]:[764] One may not recite a blessing upon smelling generic teas which are manufactured from the Camellia sinensis plant.[765] [These include all the following teas: White tea, yellow tea, green tea, oolong, dark tea, Pu-erh tea, and black tea.] This applies even if one enjoys the smell.[766] Nonetheless, if one enjoys the smell, then he is to avoid smelling it for the sake of benefit, [or is to only smell it after reciting a blessing on another valid scent].[767]

Scented or flavored teas [herbal and non-herbal]:[768] One may not recite a blessing upon smelling scented or flavored teas, being that the scent is not intrinsic to the leaves but is an additive imparted onto the leaves through various methods.[769] This applies even if the added flavor and scent derives from natural herbs, and certainly applies if the flavors themselves are adulterated and chemically produced. This applies to both herbal and non-herbal teas.[770] Although a blessing is not recited, nonetheless, initially one is to avoid smelling it for the sake of benefit, [or is to only smell it after reciting a blessing on another valid scent].[771]

Herbal teas [made from leaves other than Camellia sinensis without flavorings or additives]:[772] Natural unflavored and unscented herbal teas which have an intrinsic good scent are to have a blessing recited over them prior to smelling the leaf. This, however, only applies if the following conditions are fulfilled:

---

[763] The question of smelling tea bags touches upon many of the laws discussed in the laws of "Smelling spices". See Seder Birchas Hanehnin chapter 11; Shulchan Aruch Michaber 216; Ketzos Hashulchan 62-63; Piskeiy Teshuvos 216

[764] Background on how plain tea is manufactured: Tea is made through curing leaves of the Camellia sinensis plant. Camellia sinensis is a species of evergreen shrub or small tree whose leaves and leaf buds are used to produce tea. White tea, yellow tea, green tea, oolong, dark tea (which includes pure tea) and black tea are all harvested from the Camellia sinensis, but are processed differently to attain varying levels of oxidation. Kukicha (twig tea) is also harvested from Camellia sinensis, but uses twigs and stems rather than leaves.

[765] The reason: The plant does not usually have a good smell and hence does not deserve a blessing. Furthermore, even if it were to have a good smell, since it is manufactured for eating/brewing and not for smelling, it is therefore subject to the debate recorded in the next footnote of which we rule that a blessing is not to be recited.

[766] See Admur Seder 11:9; Shach 108 Yoreh Deah in Nekudos Hakesef; M"A 297:1

The reason: As the herb is mainly manufactured for food and tea brewing and not for its smell, and one may not say a blessing on spices which are not commonly used by people for smelling and is rather used for spicing food. [1st opinion in Admur Seder 11:9 and so is final ruling; Shach 108 Yoreh Deah in Nekudos Hakesef; M"A 297:1]

Other opinions: Some Poskim rule that one may say a blessing over all spices that one benefits from their smell even if they are not commonly smelled. [2nd opinion in Admur ibid; Taz 297:5; Yoreh Deah 108:10] Practically, Admur ibid suspects for both opinions and rules that one is to refrain from smelling them.

[767] Admur Seder ibid *"It is proper to abstain from smelling them in order to avoid [the dispute brought in previous footnote and avoid] a Safek Bracha"*; M"A ibid

[768] Background on how flavored and scented tea is manufactured: Flavored Teas are created by adding fruits, flowers and flavors to black, oolong or green teas. Genuine scented teas, such as Jasmine or Rose Congou, are made by forcing hot air over Jasmine or Rose blossoms that have been layered on top of the Camellia sinensis tea leaves. This imparts the scent of the flowers to the Camellia sinensis leaves used in plain tea and influences the taste. Other teas of this type are Magnolia and Orchid. One of the most famous scented teas is Earl Grey. True Earl Grey employs bergamot oil sprayed onto the finished tea to achieve its unique flavor. Bergamot is a pear-shaped citrus fruit grown in southern Europe. Flavored teas, both regular and herbal, are processed in the same way. After placing the leaves in a rotating drum, the liquid flavor is sprayed directly onto the product.

[769] See Admur Seder 11:11; Michaber 217:3; Rambam Brachos 9:8

The reason: As if the source of the good smell has been removed, such as by scented clothing, then some opinions rule one cannot recite a blessing on this smell, as it does not have a source. [Michaber ibid; Rambam ibid] Practically one should suspect for their opinion and avoid smelling such items. [Admur Seder ibid]

Other opinions: Some Poskim rule that one may say a blessing over all spices that one benefits from their smell even if their source has been removed. [Tur 217; See Taz 217:2]

[770] As it is difficult to determine what is the natural smell of the leaf versus the imported scent of the flavoring, and hence a blessing cannot be recited.

[771] Admur Seder 11:11 in suspicion of the opinion of Tur ibid

[772] What is herbal tea: The term herbal tea refers to teas not made from Camellia sinensis but is rather made from infusions of fruit, leaves, or other parts of the plant, such as steeps of rosehip, chamomile, or rooibos. These are sometimes called tisanes or herbal infusions to prevent confusion with tea made from the tea plant. Herbal teas should not be confused with true teas (e.g., black, green, white, yellow, oolong), which are prepared from the cured leaves of the tea plant, Camellia sinensis), nor with decaffeinated tea, in which the caffeine has been removed.

List of common herbal teas: Anise tea; Chamomile, Cinnamon, Citrus peel, including bergamot, lemon and orange peel, Dried lime tea, made from dried limes, is popular in western Asia, Ginger root, Ginseng, popular tea in China and Korea, Hibiscus, Honey bush, Labrador tea, Lemon Balm, Lemon and ginger tea, Lemon grass, Mint, especially peppermint (also mixed with green tea to make mint tea), Red raspberry leaf, Rooibos (Red Bush), In the US it is sometimes called red tea, Rosemary, Sagebrush, Sage, St. John's Wort, Turmeric tea.

1) The herb is commonly smelled for its good scent also outside of the tea bag.[773] [This would exclude all herbal teas of which their herbs are primarily used for food or tea brewing, and are not commonly smelled by people. An example of natural and unscented herbal teas which are smelled outside of their tea use and therefore would deserve a blessing prior to smelling their leaf is: Mint, including peppermint, spear mint, and other mint teas; cinnamon tea.] **2)** One picked up the teabag for the purpose of smelling it.[774] [This would exclude one who lifted the tea bag for the sake of making tea, in which case a blessing may not be recited unless he raises it to his nose for the sake of smelling it.[775]]

<u>*What blessing is to be recited upon smelling the herbal teas?*</u> The blessing that is to be recited upon smelling the above herbal teas depends on the form of growth of the leaf and whether it is defined as the leaf of a grass or the leaf of a tree. If the leaf grows as a grass, or on a soft stalk, then one says the blessing of Borei Isvei Besamim. If it grows on hard stalk, and certainly if grows on a tree, its blessing is Atzei Besamim.[776] This applies whether the tea contains whole leaves or ground leaves, as found in a tea bag.[777] [Thus, natural herbal mint tea made of peppermint, or spearmint leaves, is to have the blessing of Isvei Besamim recited.[778]] Practically, if one does not know how the leaf grows or if its form of growth is Atzei or Isvei, then one is to say the blessing of "Boirei Minei Besamim".[779]

Summary:
One is to avoid smelling tea bags for the sake of their good scent, and is not to say a blessing over them in the event that they are smelled, unless all the following conditions are fulfilled:
1. The herb/leaf that is in the tea bag contains a natural and intrinsic good scent [as opposed to flavored or scented additives].
2. The herb/leaf is commonly smelled by people outside of its tea use.
3. One picked up the teabag for the purpose of smelling it.

Practically, the above conditions exclude smelling/blessing all plain and flavored teas, and only herbal teas which contain a natural good scent and are commonly smelled outside of their tea use may be smelled and blessed upon when lifting for the purpose of smelling. The blessing of Atzei or Isvei Besamim is to recited depending on its source. [Thus, natural herbal mint tea made of peppermint, or spearmint leaves, may be smelled, and the blessing of Isvei Besamim is to be recited.] If the source or form of growth is unknown, then the blessing of Borei Minei Besamim is to be recited.

---

[773] See Admur Seder 11:9; See opinions brought in previous footnotes regarding plain tea
[774] Seder 11:3; Michaber 216:2; Tosafos Brachos 43b
[775] See Admur in Seder ibid; P"M 217 M"Z 1; Piskeiy Teshuvos 216:3 footnote 27
[776] Seder Birchas Hanehnin 11:1-2; Michaber 216:2; Brachos 43b
[777] See Admur Seder 11:7 that only if a mixture of Atzei and Isvei leaves have been ground together do we say Minei Besamim, otherwise the correct blessing of Atzei or Isvei is recited even though it is ground. This is unlike the law by foods which become Shehakol upon being ground.
[778] Birkeiy Yosef 216:2; Kaf Hachaim 216:13 that so is custom; See Beir Heiytiv 216:7; Piskeiy Teshuvos 216:2-6
[779] Admur Seder 11:3 [in end]; Michaber 216:2; Rambam Brachos 9:5

---------------Rosh Chodesh----------------
53. Sof Zman Kiddush Levana-Until what day of the month may Kiddush Levana be said?[780]

The opinions: Kiddush Levana may only be recited within the first half of the month. A lunar month consists of 29 days, 12 hours and 793 Chalakim.[781] Thus, it may only be said up to 14 days 18 hours and 396.5 chalakim [i.e. 22 minutes] past the Molad.[782] [This time is known as Zman Rama. However, there are opinions[783] who allow it to be said until 15 complete days past the Molad. This time is known as Zman Michaber. Other opinions[784] allow in a time of need to say Kiddush Levana with a blessing up until the night of the 16th of the month, including the night of the 16th. Others[785] rule it may even initially be said in a time of need up until 15 days 12 hours and 22 minutes from the Molad, which is 18 hours past the time of the first opinion.[786] This time is known as Zman Chasam Sofer. Others[787] suggest it may be

---

[780] See Sanhedrin 41b; Michaber/Rama 426:3; Yabia Omer 8:42 for a thorough analysis of all opinions
Background and other opinions:
The Talmudic ruling "until the 16th day" The Gemara in Sanhedrin 41b state that *"Rebbe Yochanon says the month may be sanctified until the moons lacking is complete."* The Gemara offers two opinions as to when this time is reached. Rav Yehuda says it is reached by the 7th and Nehardaiy says it is reached by the 16th [i.e. full moon]. The Rishonim rule like the latter opinion of Nehardaiy. [Haeshkol Rosh Chodesh 2:4; Sefer Hameoros Brachos; Tur 426]
Interpreting and calculating "until the 16th day": The intent of "until the 16th" is up until the start of the 16th day, but not including the 16th day [i.e. a full 15 days]. [Tur ibid; Sefer Hameoros ibid; Rambam 10:17 as learns Rabbeinu Manoach and Kesef Mishneh ibid; Michaber 426:3; Peri Chadash 426] **Furthermore**, these days are measured from the Molad, and not from the start of the month. [Tur ibid; Michaber ibid] Likewise, these days are calculated as 24-hour days and not by weekdays. [M"A 426:12; M"B 426:17] **Furthermore**, some Poskim rule that it is measured as half of the true days of the lunar orbit, which is half of 29 days, 12 hours and 793 Chalakim which equals 14 days 18 hours and 396.5 chalakim past the Molad. [Beis Yosef 426 in name of Teshuvah Ashkenazis; Maharil 19; 155; Maryu 159; Mateh Moshe 533; Rama 426:3; Bach 426; Shlah; Chayeh Adam 118:14; Noheg Katzon Yosef p. 144; Nishal David 3:10; Noda Beyehuda Kama O.C. 41; Sefer Yehoshua 14; Rav Poalim 2:38; Taharas Hamayim Beis 29; Kitzur SHU"A 97:10; Kaf Hachaim 426:53] **Other Poskim**, however, argue that it is literally 15 days. [Beis Yosef 426; Michaber 426:3; Halacha Berurah 426:7; Shvus Yaakov 3:31; Siddur Yaavetz; Yeshuos Yaakov 426; Rosh Mashbir 14; Biur Halacha 426:3; Atzei Berushim 63; Yagel Yaakov 60; Shnos Chaim 14:21] Furthermore, **some Poskim** argue and rule that it is slightly half way into the 16th day, which is 15 days, 12 hours, and 22 minutes. [Chasam Sofer 102] Furthermore, **some Poskim** argue and rule that the 16th day mentioned in the Gemara includes the entire 16th, and thus one may say Kiddush Levana until the night of the 16th, including that entire night. [Kneses Hagedola 426 in name of Rabbeinu Peretz; Meiri; Elya Raba 426:8; Heishiv Moshe 14; Tzeror Chesed; Shoel Umeishiv Kama 3:151; Yagel Yaakov 60; Beis Yisrael 80 that so did Apter Rav, and Yismach Moshe] Furthermore, **some learn** that all the above times are calculated from the start of the month and not from the Molad and hence one may say it always until the night of the 16th of that month, throughout that entire night. [See Beis Yisrael 80]
Summary ruling of Michaber and Sephardi custom: The Michaber ibid rules that Kiddush Levana may be said up to 15 full days past the Molad. Once the 16th day past the Molad has begun, it may no longer be said. [Michaber 426:3; Beis Yosef 426] Thus according to the Michaber one has 6 more hours past the time of the Rama to say Kiddush Levana. Regarding the Sephardi ruling: Many Sephardi Poskim rule that one is to follow the opinion of the Rama in these matters, as Safek Brachos Lehakeil, even against the Michaber. [Rav Poalim 2:38; Kaf Hachaim 426:53; Rav Yaakov Yosef] However, some rule that Sephardim may be lenient like the Michaber, although not like any of the other opinions. [Yabia Omer 8:42]
Summary ruling of Rama and Ashkenazi custom: The Rama rules it may be said until 14 days 18 hours and 396.5 chalakim past the Molad. [Rama 426:3] Some Ashkenazi Poskim conclude like this opinion [Chayeh Adam 118:14; Kitzur SHU"A 97:10; Poskim ibid] However, others rule one may be lenient like the Michaber [Biur Halacha "Velo Tes Zayin Bechlal"; Poskim ibid] or even like the Chasam Sofer and latest approach. [see Poskim ibid]
Chabad custom: The Rebbe in 1961 15th Sivan said Kiddush Levana 1.5 hours past the time. The Rebbe stated he relies on the Chasam Sofer ibid; Rabbi Mordechai Perlow states that he remembers that a number of times they said Kiddush Levana in Lubavitch on the night of the 16th from a Gemara Sanhedrin; The Rebbe Rashab once said Kiddush Levana 17 days past the Molad [Memoirs of Rav Yaakov Landau, brought in Shemuos Vesipurim p. 184] Rav Avraham Chaim Naa'h in Shnos Chaim 14:21 rules it may be said until 15 full days from the Molad
[781] There are 1080 Chalakim in an hour. [Tur 427]
[782] Rama 426:3; Beis Yosef 426 in name of Teshuvah Ashkenazis; Maharil 19; 155; Maryu 159; Mateh Moshe 533; Rama 426:3; Bach 426; Shlah; Chayeh Adam 118:14; Noheg Katzon Yosef p. 144; Nishal David 3:10; Noda Beyehuda Kama O.C. 41; Sefer Yehoshua 14; Rav Poalim 2:38; Taharas Hamayim Beis 29; Kitzur SHU"A 97:10; Kaf Hachaim 426:53
Calculating from Molad: The month begins at the time of the Molad of that month. Hence, one can say Kiddush Levana until the above time passes from the Molad and he is not to calculate it from Rosh Chodesh. [See Michaber and Rama ibid and Poskim in background]
Other Opinions: Some write one counts the above time not from the Molad but from Rosh Chodesh. [Taamei Haminhagim p. 200; See M"A 426:12; Beis Yisrael 80]
[783] Michaber 426:3; Beis Yosef 426; Halacha Berurah 426:7; Shvus Yaakov 3:31; Siddur Yaavetz; Yeshuos Yaakov 426; Rosh Mashbir 14; Biur Halacha 426:3 "Velo Tes Zayin Bechlal"; Atzei Berushim 63; Yagel Yaakov 60; Shnos Chaim [Rav Avraham Chaim Naah] 14:21
[784] Kneses Hagedola 426 in name of Rabbeinu Peretz; Meiri; Elya Raba 426:8; Heishiv Moshe 14; Tzeror Chesed; Shoel Umeishiv Kama 3:151; Yagel Yaakov 60; Beis Yisrael 80 that so did Apter Rav, and Yismach Moshe [These opinions are recorded in: Shvus Yaakov 3:31; Chasam Sofer 102; Alef Lamagen 581:22; Biur Halacha 426:3; Yabia Omer ibid]; Shvus Yaakov 3:31 and Biur Halacha 426:3 conclude to say without a blessing like this opinion; Rabbi Mordechai Perlow states that he remembers that a number of times they said Kiddush Levana in Lubavitch on the night of the 16th from a Gemara Sanhedrin
[785] Chasam Sofer ibid that it may even initially be said up until 18 hours past the time of the Rama; The Rebbe in 1961 15th Sivan said Kiddush Levana 1.5 hours past the time. The Rebbe stated he relies on the Chasam Sofer ibid
[786] The reason: As it takes 18 hours for the effects of the moon to be seen on earth. Thus, the diminishing of the moon is not visible to earth until this time. [Chasam Sofer ibid; See also Shvus Yaakov ibid; Yabia Omer ibid]

said even past this time [up until the end of the month].[788] Others[789] allow saying it past the above times [up until the end of the month] if one says it from the Tur or Gemara.[790]

The final practice: **Practically,** initially one is to be very careful to recite Kiddush Levana prior to the end time of the first/earliest opinion [i.e. Zman Rama]. This applies to both Ashkenazim and Sephardim.[791] However, in the event that one already missed the time of the first/earliest opinion, then many Ashkenazim rely on the second opinion above, to recite it until 15 full days past the Molad [i.e. Zman Michaber].[792] Likewise, some Sephardim rely on this opinion, although many recite it without Hashem's name once it is past the Zeman Rama.[793] Amongst Chabad Chassidim, many rely on the third opinion to recite it up until 15 days, 12 hrs. and 22 minutes from the Molad [i.e. Zeman Chasam Sofer].[794] Practically, one is to contact a Rav for direction as whether he may rely on one of the later approaches and whether he may rely to read the blessing from the Tur or Gemara.[795]]

Summary:
One is to beware to recite Kiddush Levana prior to 14 days 18 hours and 396.5 chalakim past the Molad. If it is past the first half of the month, some allow saying it even past the time.

Example of opinions:
Molad of Adar was on Monday evening, the 30th of Shevat, at 12:00 AM [Jerusalem time]:
This is a theoretical example-for the actual accurate calculation see the next step!

1. First opinion-Zman Rama [14 days and 18 hours and 22 minutes]: Kiddush Levana may be said until Tuesday evening, the 15th of Adar 1, until 6:22 p.m. [in Jerusalem]. [In the Diaspora, it can only be said until this time arrives **in Jerusalem**.]
2. Second opinion-Zman Michaber [15 days]: Kiddush Levana may be said until Tuesday evening, the 15th of Adar 1, until 12:00 a.m. [in Jerusalem]. [In the Diaspora, it can be said until this time arrives in Jerusalem.

---

[787] Suggestion in Chasam Sofer 102 [Nevertheless, he does not permit it unequivocally as is understood there from the Teshuvah]; Directive of Rebbe Maharash and Rebbe Rashab in Shemuos Vesipurim p. 184 [From the testimony of Reb Yaakov Landau recorded there it is evident that the Rebbe Maharash and Rebbe Rashab allowed saying Kiddush Levana even past the 16th of the month, and even without using a Gemara. The Rebbe Rashab once said Kiddush Levana 17 days past the molad. It was said with a blessing and not from a Gemara. [Memoirs of Rav Yaakov Landau, brought in Shemuos Vesipurim p. 184 see below]

[788] The reason: The Chasam Sofer 102 defends saying Kiddush Levana with a blessing even within the second half of the month if one receives much joy from this, such as when the moon had not been seen the entire month and one looks forward to seeing it as a good omen. [See Teshuvah there for the exact case of allowance of Chasam Sofer] His reasoning is because it is a blessing of praise to Hashem for the joy and benefit of the moonlight.

[789] Divrei Torah 4:107; Darkei Chaim Veshalom 495; Yeshuos Yaakov ibid in name of Tzadik [although he negates it]; Mor Vohalos Posek in name of Tzadik [although he negates it]; Mishmeres Shalom Kudinav 31:7 in name Bnei Yissachar in name of the Chozeh Milublin; See also Avnei Nezer 383; Taamei Haminhagim p. 199 brings from Derech Pekudecha in name of the Chozeh Melublin that after the time has passed one may nevertheless read the blessing from the Gemara. Alef Lamagen 581:22 concludes from Derech Pekudecha that so is the custom of the world to say it from a Gemara with a blessing after the correct time; Mentioned in words of Rebbe Rashab in Shemuos Vesipurim p. 184; See Sheilas Yaavetz 81 that one may mention Hashem's name when reading a blessing in the Talmud

Other opinions: Many Poskim forbid reading a blessing with Hashem's name from a Gemara or Tur. [See M"A 215:5; Birkeiy Yosef 215 that so is custom of elderly Rabbis; Machazik Bracha in name of Tashbatz Katan 419 in name of Maharam, brought in Shaareiy Teshuvah 215:4; P"M 215 A"A 5; M"B 215:14; Yabia Omer 8:42]

[790] Gemara Sanhedrin 42a

[791] Rav Poalim 2:38 and Kaf Hachaim 426:53 that so applies even for Sephardim that they should suspect for the opinion of Rama ibid

[792] As so concludes the M"B in Biur Halacha ibid that one may be lenient like Michaber ibid

[793] Rav Poalim and Kaf Hachaim ibid rule to say without Hashem's name; Yabia Omer ibid rules to say with Hashem's name

[794] Hiskashrus 961 writes [Vetzaruch Iyun as to his source] that one may say Kiddush Levana up to 18 hours past the time of the Rama [15 days 12 hours and 22 minutes from the Molad] as rules the Chasam Sofer, however he may not say it anymore once 18 hours have passed. In correspondence with Rav Ginzberg he wrote to me that this was the ruling of Rav Yaakov Landau, as was told to him by his son Rav Eliyahu Landau, that after 18 hours of the time of the Rama one may not be lenient to say it. This is despite the fact that the story mentioned above took place with Rav Yaakov Landau and he received a directive from the Rebbe Rashab to say Kiddush Levana on the night of the 20th. This story had been authenticated by the Rebbe Rayatz and was passed over his holy eyes prior to its publishing. Nevertheless, in actuality we are not lenient to rule this way. In an earlier volume of Hiskashrus [409] as well as in the glosses of Rav Raskin on the Siddur they wrote one may rely on the above story and recite Kiddush Levana even past the above time.

[795] See glosses of Rav Raskin on Siddur who writes he recalls a directive of the Rebbe to say it from the Gemara when it is being said past the time.

3. <u>Third opinion-Zman Chasam Sofer [15 days 12 hrs. 22 min]</u>: Kiddush Levana may be said until Wednesday 12:22 p.m., the 15th of Adar 1, until 12:00 p.m. [in Jerusalem]. [In the Diaspora, it can be said until this time arrives in Jerusalem.]

How to practically calculate the end time for Kiddush Levana:
1. **Step 1**-<u>Molad time</u>: Look up the exact time that the Molad occurred in Jerusalem [See https://www.torahcalc.com/molad/ to look up what time the Molad of the current month took place in Jerusalem].
2. **Step 2**-<u>Detract solar versus watch time difference</u>:[796] Detract 21 minutes from that time to supplement for the difference between the current watch time in Jerusalem versus the real solar time [Jerusalem is 21 minutes later than its real solar time.]
    a. To note that there are three other approaches regarding the amount of time one must calculate as the difference between the solar and watch time. See Luach Itim Lebina for all four opinions. Above we have chosen the most commonly accepted approach.
3. **Step 3**-<u>Calculate to your local time zone</u>: Calculate the exact time it was in your time zone when the Molad occurred in the above calculated time in Jerusalem.
4. **Step 4**-<u>Add end time of Kiddush Levana</u>: Add the end time of Kiddush Levana in accordance to whatever opinion you follow [i.e. Zeman Rama; Zeman Michaber; Zeman Chasam Sofer].

Example for one in New York:
1. Molad in Jerusalem occurred at 11:57 p.m. on a Monday night, the 30th of Shevat
2. Minus 21 minutes = 11:36 p.m.
3. Seven hours back for New York time zone = 4:36 p.m., Monday afternoon, 29th of Shevat.

Add opinion of end time for Kiddush Levana, calculating it from 4:36 p.m. Thus, for example, according to the Zeman Rama, add 14 days 18 hrs. and 22 min, to the above time achieved in step 3. This would calculate the end time of Kiddush Levana in Jerusalem to be on Tuesday the 14th Adar 5:58 p.m. and in New York on Tuesday the 14th of Adar 10:58 a.m. According to the Zeman Michaber, it would be Tuesday the 14th Adar [night of 15th] 11:36 p.m. and in New York on Tuesday the 14th of Adar 4:36 p.m. According to the Zeman Chasam Sofer, it would be Wednesday the 15th Adar 11:58 p.m. and in New York on Wednesday the 15th of Adar 4:58 a.m.

---

[796] See here https://www.e-education.psu.edu/eme810/node/530 and here https://susdesign.com/sunangle/ ; https://fate.windada.com/cgi-bin/SolarTime_en

<u>Background</u>: There are two important ways of describing time. "Clock time" is the artificial time that we use in everyday life to standardize our time measurements. It allows people in different locations to use the same time or to easily convert time from one location to another. "Local solar time" (or simply "solar time") is the time according to the position of the sun in the sky relative to one specific location on the ground. In solar time, the sun is always due south (or north) at exactly noon. This means that someone a few miles east or west of you will realize a slightly different solar time than you, although your clock time is probably the same. For the purpose of calculating local solar time, clock time must modified to compensate for three things: (1) the relationship between the local time zone and the local longitude, (2) daylight savings time, and (3) the earth's slightly-irregular motion around the sun (corrected for using the equation of time). Local solar time (LSoT) is calculated as follows: LSoT = LST + 4 minutes * (LL - LSTM) + ET Where: LST (local standard time) = Clock time, adjusted for daylight savings time if necessary. LL = The local longitude; positive = East, and negative = West. LSTM = The local standard time meridian, measured in degrees, which runs through the center of each time zone. It can be calculated by multiplying the differences in hours from Greenwich Mean Time by 15 degrees per hour. Positive = East, and negative = West. ET = The equation of time adjustment in minutes.

---------------Pesach----------------

54. Must one check books/Sefarim for crumbs of Chametz?

A. Background:

One must search for even an insignificant crumb of Chametz, and destroy it.[797] This applies even if one has already nullified his Chametz, or plans to nullify it before Pesach.[798] If, however, the Chametz is slightly dirty to the point that it is not fit for eating, and one has already nullified his Chametz, or plans to do so before the 6th hour, then if the Chametz is less than the size of a Kezayis, one is not required to search for this Chametz or destroy it.[799] Based on this information, we will now analyze the law regarding checking for Chametz in Sefarim.

---

[797] Admur 433:13 "Perhaps any crumb of Chametz fell from it"; 442:28 and 446:3 [regarding less than Kezayis]; 444:9 "The thin crumbs.." [however, possibly there it refers to more than a Kezayis]; 432:11 "Perhaps a **small crumb** will fall from it….and he will need to search for it as he might find something."; 433:17 "Maybe they hid a little bit of Chametz there"; 433:18 "Perhaps it fell and a little bit of Chametz rolled under"; 433:25 "Small crumbs do not have to be picked up if they are in an area that people step on them and they get destroyed"; 433:39 "Perhaps there is in there a small amount of Chametz"; 434:1 "One must guard it so no Chametz piece break away from it"; 434:6 "The crumbs of Chametz that he did not find in his Bedika are nullified on their own"; Chayeh Adam 119:10; Poskim in M"B 442:33

Background: In the end of 433:13 Admur says that one needs to check for even "Shum Pirur Chametz" and in 442:28 that Rabbinically one may not own even less than a Kezayis. In 444:9 Admur rules that one needs to destroy the small leftover crumbs when Erev Pesach falls on Shabbos, and in 446:3 that on Pesach one must destroy even less than a Kezayis of Chametz which one has done Bittul to.

Other opinions of Admur: In Kuntrus Achron 442:18 Admur rules that all insignificant crumbs which are less than a Kezayis, not a Geluska Yafa, and is not dough, are automatically nullified and considered destroyed, thus implying that one is not required to search for, or destroy, insignificant crumbs of Chametz. This directly contradicts all the sources above. Perhaps in truth this Kuntrus Achron represents a retracting of Admur's position from that which he held in his Shulchan Aruch. Vetzaruch Iyun!

The reason: As the Sages decreed against owning even less than a Kezayis of Chametz, lest one come to own a Kezayis. [Admur 442:28] This decree only applies in a case that one did not nullify his Chametz before Pesach, or does not plan to do so. In such a case, one transgresses a Rabbinical prohibition of Baal Yiraeh over such Chametz, even though it is less than a Kezayis. If, however, one nullified the Chametz, then it follows the law and reason explained next. [Admur Kuntrus Achron 446:1]

Other opinions: Some Poskim rule one is not required to search for a crumb of Chametz which is less than a Kezayis. [Opinion brought in Admur 446:3 regarding nullified Chametz and Kuntrus Achron 442:18 regarding even unnullified Chametz; Admur KU"A 442:18 in understanding of Rosh Pesachim 3:2 and other Poskim that all crumbs are nullified and don't need to be destroyed; M"A 442:12 and Admur 446:3 in their understanding of all the following Poskim to refer to nullified Chametz although in KU"A 442:18 Admur understands them to refer to even unnullified Chametz: Abayey in Pesachim 45a; Riy in Tosafos ibid; Rosh 3:2; Tur 442 in name of Rosh; Peri Chadash 442:7; See many Poskim in Nitei Gavriel 3 Teshuvas 1 and Chazon Ovadia Haggadah who hold that crumbs which are less than a Kezayis do not need to be destroyed.]

[798] Admur 442:28; 446:3; KU"A 438:2 and 446:1

The reason: One must search for even less than a Kezayis crumb of Chametz which is anyways nullified because one may come to forget and inadvertently eat it on Pesach. [Admur 442:28; Kuntrus Achron 446:1; See Kuntrus Achron 438:2] It, however, is not prohibited due to a Rabbinical Baal Yiraeh prohibition [as if it was already nullified it would be a double Derabanan, which is a decree upon a decree]. [Kuntrus Acharon 446:1] Due to this, one does not say a blessing of Bedikas Chametz if one only has suspicion that less than a Kezayis of Chametz has remained to be checked for. [Admur 432:5] Likewise, when burning less than a Kezayis of nullified Chametz on Pesach, a blessing may never be said. [Admur 446:3; Kuntrus Acharon 446:1]

Other opinions: Many Poskim rule it is permitted even Rabbinically to own less than a Kezayis of Chametz which has been nullified before Pesach. [See previous footnote!]

[799] Admur 442:28; KU"A 442:16 gloss 1 and 442:18 gloss 3; M"A 442:10; Yireim 301; Hagahos Maimanis 2:15 Taf

The reason: As less than a Kezayis of nullified Chametz is not prohibited due to a Rabbinical owning prohibition of Baal Yiraeh, but rather simply due to worry that one may come to eat it. Now, since when the Chametz is dirty there is no need to suspect that one will come to eat it, therefore, there is no need to get rid of it. [See Admur Kuntrus Achron 446:1]

Other opinions: Some Poskim rule that even nullified Chametz that is less than a Kezayis is forbidden Rabbinically due to the prohibition of Baal Yiraeh/Tashbisu, and thus must be destroyed even if dirty. [Opinion inferred from Admur 446:3 and KU"A 1; Shiltei Giborim Pesachim 3:2-2, brought in Admur KU"A 442:18 in first gloss; Ran Pesachim 3a as understands Peri Chadash 466, brought and negated in Admur KU"A ibid]

What is the definition of dirty? Seemingly it does not suffice for the crumb to be in a dirty area, but it must also visibly contain physical dirt on it and thus no matter where this crumb will reach people will avoid eating it. [So is implied from 1) Admur 442:28 who writes that it must be slightly dirty to the point that it is not fit for eating; 2) Many Halachos in Admur ibid in which one must search for a crumb even though it is in cracks around the house, or in the mouth of a rat, or is a crumb which people would anyways not eat, as brought in Admur 434:6, and certainly people will not come to eat it. Thus, we must conclude that the actual Chametz must be dirty [However, perhaps one can say that in those areas of Admur it refers to a more than Kezayis crumb, or that back then people were more prone to eat these things, as opposed to today.] 3) See Admur Kuntrus Achron 433:4 Gloss 2 that "Whenever there is suspicion that it can come to being eaten, even though many suspicions, the Sages suspected." And hence if the actual crumb does not contain physical dirt, it is not considered dirty and must be destroyed. Vetzaruch Iyun as the above refers to the Rabbinical Baal Yiraeh, and not to the general worry of "perhaps he may eat"]

May one dirty a less than Kezayis nullified piece instead of destroying it? Tzaruch iyun if one finds a less than a Kezayis piece of Chametz which was nullified, if it sufficed for one to dirty it to the point that people will not come to eat it, or to simply throw it out of one's house on Pesach. See, however Admur 444:9 and 460:6 from which it is implied that it does not suffice to throw less than a Kezayis of nullified crumbs onto the ground [to dirty them] and rather one must destroy them. However, perhaps it refers to more than a Kezayis. Vetzaruch Iyun!

Must one actively nullify a less than Kezayis piece? All insignificant size crumbs of baked Chametz which are less than a Kezayis is considered automatically nullified, and thus it is not necessary to actively nullify it before Pesach. However, a significant size crumb of baked Chametz even if less than a Kezayis is not considered automatically nullified, and thus must be actively nullified before Pesach. [See Admur 434:6; 460:5] A piece of dough is considered significant and must be actively nullified before Pesach. [Admur ibid]

B. The Law:

The debate: Some Poskim[800] rule that Sefarim/books do not need to be checked for Chametz at all. This applies even if one was not careful to avoid eating Chametz while studying from them and there is thus possibility that crumbs may have fallen inside.[801] Other Poskim[802], however, rule that all books which one was not careful to avoid using while eating, and there is thus possibility that a crumb of Chametz has fallen inside, are required to be checked for Chametz.[803] The way such books are to be checked is through opening each page individually and looking in the area of the binding to make sure that it is clean.[804] If necessary, a knife is to be used to remove any crumbs stuck in the area. It does not suffice to simply shake the book, bang it, or flip the pages in the air.[805] All Sefarim that one does not desire to check are to be included in Mechiras Chametz and be put away in the area designated for the gentile.[806]

Final ruling and custom: There is no clear arbitration from Admur on the above debate.[807] Practically, the widespread custom of the world, including Chabad, is like the first opinion, to be lenient and not require checking of books for Chametz.[808] These books are nevertheless used over Pesach and are not segregated to an area designated as sold to the gentile. Nevertheless, some are stringent throughout the year to not eat Chametz while learning from their Sefarim in order to avoid the above debate and possible necessity to check them for Chametz.[809] This especially applies starting from thirty days before Pesach, from Purim and onwards.[810] Likewise, some are stringent regarding Sefarim used on a constant basis throughout the year during meal/snack times, to either clean them thoroughly in the above-mentioned method, or to include them in the sale to the gentile.[811] The above is a proper stringency to abide by.[812] Others are

---

[800] All Poskim who rule that insignificant crumbs, or less than a Kezayis, do not need to be checked, as brought in other opinions above; Possible way of learning Admur 442:28 that these crumbs are considered dirty and don't need checking; Possible way of learning Admur's final conclusion based on Kuntrus Achron 442:18 that insignificant crumbs are considered nullified and destroyed; Or Letziyon 1:32 that he did not see this accustomed; Haggadah Chazon Ovadia; Rav Shlomo Zalman Auerbach; Madrich Eida Hachareidis; Nitei Gavriel footnote 9 and in Teshuvos 1 that from the letter of the it does not need to be checked; Rav Eli Landau related to me that in his father's home, they were very particular during the year not to place Sefarim near Chametz or on a table with Chametz. They thus did not clean out the Sefarim before Pesach.
The Rebbe's custom: Rabbi Groner related to me regarding the Sefarim in the Rebbe's office that "We did not check the Sefarim in the room, and neither did the Rebbe" However, the Mashbak Chesed Halberstam related to me that he had the job in the Rebbe's home to clean all the books that the Rebbe learned from while there was Chametz on the table. "I would take the books to the porch on the third floor and open the books into the air, one page at a time. Each page was cleaned."

[801] The reason: **1)** As the crumbs of Chametz found in between the binding of a book is certainly less than a Kezayis and it is dirty, and thus it may be owned if one does Bittul. [See Admur 442:28, brought in Introduction] **2)** Possibly we rule like Admur in Kuntrus Achron 442:18 that crumbs are considered destroyed on their own and don't need checking or destruction. **3)** Possibly the crumbs found in a closed book are crushed and thus considered destroyed, similar to those which are on the ground in areas where people walk. **4)** Today we sell all our Chametz to the gentile, and include even our worthless crumbs in the sale, thus, there is no need to search for it as it is the gentiles Chametz, and there is no worry that one may accidentally come to eat it, as people are disgusted by such crumbs, and would not eat it even during the year.

[802] Possible way of learning Admur 433:13 that all crumbs must be checked even if insignificant, and it's not considered dirty unless there is physical dirt on it that can be seen; Maaseh Rav of Gra 178; Aruch Hashulchan end of 447 that from Purim and onwards one is to be careful that crumbs do not fall inside; Yeshuos Chochma on Kitzur SHU"A [use a knife to edge out the Chametz from between the pages]; Chazon Ish 116:18; Orchos Rabbeinu Pesach 21; Mishneh Halachos 7:64; Piskeiy Teshuvos 431:4; Sefarim brought in Nitei Gavriel footnote 9; Tzanzer Rebbe that so is Minhag of Klal Yisrael of many generations, brought in Nitei Gavriel ibid; Nitei Gavriel concludes in his Teshuvos that the custom is to do so, and hence one is not to be lenient

[803] The reason: As **1)** Admur rules that even a mere crumb must be destroyed if it is not dirty to the point of inedibility, and in truth the crumbs in Sefarim are not dirty to the point of inedibility. **2)** As we suspect for the Poskim who rule that even a dirty crumb needs to be destroyed. [See Admur 446:3 and Kuntrus Achron 442:18] **3)** As Yisrael Kedoshim Heim and destroy Chametz even when not obligated. [See Admur 442:30]

[804] See Yeshuos Chochma ibid; Based on the rulings of Bedikas Chametz [one is to check the Sefarim specifically at night, as initially one may not perform Bedikas Chametz during daytime even in the face of sunlight. Performing Bedikas Chametz by daytime is invalid even Bedieved if it was not done outside, or opposite a window. [Admur 433:5-6] See however Shevet Halevi 1:136 regarding checking the pockets of clothing

[805] Pashut as **a)** Doing so does not remove crumbs which are stuck deep in the area of the binding of the page and **b)** the Mitzvah of Bedikas Chametz requires physically seeing the area, and thus to fulfill the stringent opinion one must look in between each page. See previous footnote!

[806] Madrich Eida Hachareidis for Machmirim

[807] See footnotes above that it is possible to learn either way into Admur's opinion!

[808] Madrich of Eida Hachareidis that so is custom; So is evident from all Shul's and Batei Midrashim throughout the world, including Chabad, that they are not particular to check all the Sefarim of their library for Chametz, even though people often eat Chametz while learning from them throughout the year, and nevertheless they go ahead and still use it over Pesach for learning. Likewise, Rabbi Groner related to me regarding the Sefarim in the Rebbe's office that "We did not check the Sefarim in the room, and neither did the Rebbe." Now, although some are particular to shake or flip through the Sefarim, as stated above, this is worthless and does not accomplish a true Bedika according to Halacha, as required by the second opinion. However, see Nitei Gavriel ibid and in his Teshuvos that the custom of Jewry is to clean the Sefarim, and seemingly different areas follow different customs

[809] So I was told by Rav Eli Landa Shlita

[810] Aruch Hashulchan ibid

[811] So I was told by Rav Eli Landa Shlita; Madrich Eida Hachareidis

completely stringent like the second opinion above, and hence perform Bedikas Chametz [as described above] to all books that have possibility of containing a crumb of Chametz, if they wish to have them accessible on Pesach [and not be segregated with the Chametz sold to the gentile].[813]

Bookcase: All the above discussion is only regarding checking the actual books through opening them and flipping through their pages, however, the bookcase itself must be checked for Chametz according to all. Thus, one must at the very least remove the Sefarim from all shelves that have a Halachic suspicion of containing Chametz, and do a Bedika on these shelves.

Summary:
It is debated amongst Poskim as to whether books need to be cleaned/checked for Chametz. Practically, the widespread custom is not to require checking of books for Chametz. Nevertheless, some are stringent throughout the year to not eat Chametz while learning from their Sefarim in order to avoid the above issue, while others are stringent to perform Bedikas Chametz [in the way described above] to all books that they wish to have accessible on Pesach, and have possibility of containing a crumb of Chametz. The remainder of the books are included in the sale to the gentile and not used throughout Pesach. This is a proper stringency to abide by.

Q&A

Are the pages of your book/Sefer produced with Chametz starch?[814]
In the paper production industry today, starch is used to bind the saw dust into paper sheets. Starch today is produced from either corn, potato, **or wheat**. Thus, there is great chance that one's Sefarim/books contains starch in the actual paper, and possibly even Chametz starch. Accordingly, even if one was stringent and cleaned his books for Pesach, or bought new books just for Pesach [i.e. a Haggadah!], there is room to abide by some of the following matters to be explained.[815] [To check if your paper contains starch, perform the iodine test explained in "The Laws of Pesach" Chapter 6 Halacha 4.]

Matters that one is advised to beware when using books/Sefarim due to worry of Chametz:[816]
Irrelevant of the debate of whether books must be checked for Chametz, being that it is possible that there are crumbs of Chametz in the books, either due not having checked them, or due to having missed an area, or due to a Chametz starch being used in their production, therefore it is strongly advised to abide by the following precautions in order to avoid the possibility of accidentally consuming a crumb of Chametz:

1. Do not bring Sefarim to the table that you eat on [even if they were cleaned for Chametz] [However, if the Sefer is was never used near Chametz and one simply suspects for starch, then there is no issue, as the starch is attached to the paper and cannot accidently fall onto your food.[817]]

---

[812] *The reason*: As a) Perhaps the crumbs found in Sefarim are not truly defined as dirty or inedible, and thus must be destroyed. b) Even if we were to hold like the first opinion, Yisrael Kedoshim Heim and are Machmir to destroy Chametz even when not required.
[813] Madrich Eida Hachareidis
[814] See here: https://www.sciencedirect.com/science/article/pii/B9780127462752000185 "*The papermaking process consists of several major steps: stock preparation, sheet forming, pressing, drying, and surface finishing.* **Starch is an important component of many paper grades.** *Starch consumption by weight in papermaking and paper conversion processes ranks third after cellulose fiber and mineral pigments.* **Starch is used as a flocculant and retention aid, as a bonding agent,** *as a surface size, as a binder for coatings, and as an adhesive in corrugated board, laminated grades, and other products.* **The major starch sources are corn, potato, waxy maize, wheat, and tapioca.** *Refined starches are supplied in powder form or as slightly aggregated pearl starch. Unmodified (native) starch is rarely used in the paper industry, except as a binder for laminates and in the corrugating process. Most starches for use in papermaking are specialty products that have been modified by controlled hydrolysis, oxidation, or derivatization. This chapter also covers various topics such as: application requirements for starch, dispersion of starch, environmental aspects of starch, starch analysis in paper, and use of starch in papermaking furnish, for surface sizing of paper, as a coating binder, as adhesive in paper conversion, and in newer specialty papers.*"
[815] However, technically one can argue that even if the starch is Chametz based, it's paper mixture is nullified from edibility to a dog, and hence since one never has any intent to eat it, therefore there is no need to worry of having it on the table and or eating from food that fell on it. [See Admur 442:34] Furthermore, perhaps the starch is well ironed into the paper that there is no chance of any of it flicking of and entering one's food.
[816] See Madrich Eida Hachareidis; Heard from Harav Eli Landa Shlita

2. Wash hands after using the Sefer, prior to eating or touching foods.
3. Do not lick your finger to turn a page in the Sefer.
4. If food falls onto your Sefer, don't eat the food. [However, if the Sefer was never used near Chametz and one simply suspects for starch, then seemingly one may eat dry foods that fall on it, as the starch is attached to the paper and cannot become attached onto your food. However, if the food is wet it is proper not to eat it.[818]]

---------Sefiras Haomer---------

55. Why we celebrate Lag BaOmer/Did Rashbi pass away on Lag BaOmer?

The discussion in Poskim for why we rejoice on Lag BaOmer: It is accustomed to increase slightly in joy on Lag BaOmer.[819] For this reason, all Jewry omit Tachanun[820], and Ashkenazim even rescind the mourning customs on this day.[821] The reason for this joy, however, remained a mystery and was the subject of discussion for many generations of Poskim. In search for an explanation behind this mysterious holiday, the Poskim offered various alternatives of events that happened on this day thus explaining why it is a day of celebration.[822] Some Poskim[823], however, simply gave up their quest, stating that there is no satisfactory reason to defend the exorbitant joy expressed on Lag BaOmer, and thus in their eyes, the celebration of Lag BaOmer remains a mystery. The following is a list of the classical reasons offered by the Poskim:

1. The classical reason recorded in Poskim[824] is that on this day, Lag BaOmer, the last of the 24,000 students died. This explanation, however, is not agreed upon by all opinions. Some Poskim[825] hold that in truth the students of Rebbe Akiva did not stop dying on Lag BaOmer and hence the increase in joy is due to some other unknown reason.[826]
2. Others[827] write the reason is because on this day Rebbe Akiva gave Semicha to Rashbi and his other four remaining students.[828]
3. Some[829] write the reason for celebration is because on this day the Mun began to fall for the Jewish people in the desert.[830]
4. Others[831] write it is because on this day we have reached the Sefira of Hod Shebehod, which contains mystical significance.

All the above however, even if accepted as true, only explains why we omit Tachanun on this

---

[817] Heard from Harav Eliyahu Landa Shlita
[818] Heard from Harav Eliyahu Landa Shlita
[819] Admur 493:5; Rama 493:2; Maharil 157
[820] Admur 493:5; Siddur Admur; Rama 493:2
[821] Admur 493:5 [according to all opinions mentioned there]; Rama 493:2

Other opinions-Custom of Sephardim: The above ruling is only in accordance to the ruling of the Rama ibid that the last of the students stopped dying on the 33rd day of the Omer. However according to the Michaber 493:2 the mourning custom fully apply up until the morning of the 34th day of the Omer as in his opinion the last of the students died on the 34th day of the Omer. This is the custom of the Sephardim, and they hence do not get married or cut hair, or cease any of the mourning customs until the morning of the 34th day of the Omer. [Michaber 493:2; Peri Chadash 493:1; Mamar Mordechai 493:3; Kaf Hachaim 493:25; Yabia Omer 3:26; Minchas Yitzchak 4:84 that so is the Sephardi custom]

[822] See sources listed in coming footnotes, and Maaras Ayin of Chida in Likkutim; Shem Aryeh 14; Sdei Chemed Asifas Dinim 6
[823] P"M 493 M"Z 1; Peri Chadash 493:2; Chasam Sofer ibid
[824] Rama 493:2; Admur 493:5; Biur Halacha 493 "Yeish"
[825] Michaber 493:2 as explained in M"B 493:7; Tosafos brought in M"A 493:5; P"M 493 M"Z 1
[826] P"M 493 M"Z 1
[827] Implication of Shaar Hakavanos Shaar Sefiras Haomer p.87a, as explained in Kaf Hachaim 493:26; Chida in Maaras Ayin Likkutim 7:8, brought in Sdei Chemed and Kaf Hachaim ibid; See also Peri Chadash 493, brought in Kaf Hachaim 493:26
[828] These were Rebbe Yehuda, Rebbe Elazar Ben Shamua, Rebbe Meir and Rebbe Nechemia. On this day there was a special spiritual revelation which allowed these students to receive Semicha. [Shaar Hakavanos ibid, brought in Kaf Hachaim ibid]
[829] Chasam Sofer Y.D. 233; However, see also Chasam Sofer O.C. 163
[830] This follows the opinion of the Midrash, however according to the Gemara Shabbos 87b the Mun began falling on Shabbos the 15th of Iyar, and according to Tosafus there it began falling on Sunday the 9th of Iyar, which is before the 18th of Iyar. So is also apparent from Kiddushin 38a that the Mun lasted for 40 years minus 30 days, and the Mun ceased on the 16th of Nissan, hence proving it began falling before the 18th of Iyar. See Igros Kodesh 29:157
[831] Siddur Yaavetz, recorded in Chasam Sofer Y.D. 233

day, it however does not explain the exorbitant joy expressed on Lag BaOmer, with the various customs associated with it, hence turning Lag BaOmer to a day almost equal to other Holidays.[832]

The Kabalistic reason-Celebrating the day of Rashbi: Often in Jewish literature, when a sufficient explanation for a certain law or custom has not been uncovered, we turn to the works of Kabbalah to try to uncover the mystery, and here is no different. The classical Sefarim of Kabbalah, which include the Shaar Hakavanos, Peri Eitz Chaim and Mishnas Chassidim state that on Lag BaOmer one is to rejoice the joy of Rashbi. The Shaar Hakavanos[833] and Peri Eitz Chaim[834], a work of Rav Chaim Vital based on the teachings of his famed master the Arizal, writes that people go to the grave of Rashbi on Lag BaOmer to celebrate, and that so was the custom of the Arizal. Rav Chaim Vital continues and adds that in fact the Arizal conveyed a message to one of his students from the Rashbi himself. What did Rashbi tell the Arizal to convey? He told him to ask his student *"Why he said Nacheim on the **day of his joy**, and as a result of doing so he will soon enter into mourning."* Thus, we see that Lag BaOmer is a day celebrating the joy of Rashbi, as quoted from Rashbi himself, and that everyone is meant to celebrate on this day and it is dangerous to ignore it.[835] An additional source for this is also found in the Mishnas Chassidim[836], which is a major work of Kabbalah written faithful to the teachings of the Arizal. There he states that on Lag BaOmer *"**It is a Mitzvah to celebrate the Simcha of Rashbi.**"* This reason which is sourced in Kabbalah found its way into the classical works of the famed Posek, the Chida, who writes *"And it is known that his desire is for us to celebrate on this day, as was revealed regarding the story with Rav Avraham Halevi."*[837] It is likewise recorded in many later Achronim in their Halachic works as the reason for celebrating Lag BaOmer.[838] Thus, in conclusion, that which was clouded in mystery to the Poskim of earlier generations has become revealed to the later generations through the teachings of Kabala, that on Lag BaOmer we celebrate because Rashbi himself instructed us to do so. The only question that remains is what is this joy all about? What happened to Rashbi on this day that he has instructed us to rejoice with him? This is what leads to our next discussion of did Rashbi pass away on Lag BaOmer.

Why Rashbi told us to celebrate: While the teachings of Kabbalah uncovered for us the mystery behind the celebration on Lag BaOmer, it has opened for us a new mystery regarding why Rashbi instructed us to celebrate. The Shaar Hakavanos and Mishnas Chassidim ibid write the reason one is to celebrate is because the Rashbi was one of the remaining students of Rebbe Akiva who was responsible for the continuity of the oral tradition of the Torah.[839] The Shaar Hakavanos ibid explains based on Kabbalah why this celebration of the continuity of Rebbe Akiva and his teachings is connected specifically to Lag BaOmer. Some[840] suggest, as stated above, that Rashbi actually received Semicha on this day, and thus instructed us to celebrate. The most common explanation, however, is that this is the day that Rashbi passed away and he instructed us to celebrate on his Yom Hilula, the day of his passing. The only problem is, what is the source for this statement? The Shaar Hakavnos and Mishnas Chassidim, which are quite

---

[832] So questions Peri Chadash 493:2; Chasam Sofer ibid
[833] Shaar Hakavanos Shaar Sefiras Haomer p.87a
[834] Peri Eitz Chaim Sefiras Haomer 7
[835] See Ateres Zekeinim 493 that after bringing the story of Reb Avraham Halevi and the Arizal [recorded above] he concludes "We thus see one is not to say Tachanun on this day"
[836] Mishnas Chassidim Iyar 1:6
[837] Birkeiy Yosef 493:2 and Morah Bietzba 8:123
[838] Bnei Yissachar Mamar Lag BaOmer 3:3; Sdei Chemed Eretz Yisrael 6; Minchas Elazar 1:60; Divrei Nechemia 34-7; Chayeh Adam 131:11; Aruch Hashulchan 493:5; Kaf Hachaim 493:27
[839] See also Peri Chadash 493, brought in Kaf Hachaim 493:26
[840] Chida in Maaras Ayin Likkutim 7:8 and Kaf Hachaim 493:26 in their understanding of Shaar Hakavanos Shaar Sefiras Haomer p.87a

reputable sources, make no mention of it. So, in truth the answer lies in the Peri Eitz Chaim itself. Rav Chaim Vital in Peri Eitz Chaim ibid, writes in his conclusion of the above discussion [of Rashbi's instruction to celebrate this day] *"The reason **that Rashbi died on Lag BaOmer** is because he was from the [24000] known students of Rebbe Akiva who died on Lag BaOmer."* Thus, a clear source from Rav Chaim Vital himself that this is the day of Rashbi's passing. The only problem, however, is that this statement is blatantly inaccurate. It is clear from the Talmud[841] and other sources that Rashbi was not part of the 24000 students who died in the plague and Rashbi passed away many years later.[842] Thus, some Poskim[843] conclude that this entire statement in the Peri Eitz Chaim must be a misprint, and so falls our source. Nonetheless, despite the above question on wording of the Peri Eitz Chaim, many Poskim[844] record this tradition and write that Lag BaOmer is the day of the passing of Rebbe Shimon. The earliest undisputed source is from the Alter Rebbe who writes in several Chassidic discourses of the passing of Rashbi on Lag BaOmer, and discusses its celebration within his discourse.[845] The Rebbe also concludes in his letters that this is the true reason for the celebration of Lag BaOmer, as on this day Rebbe Shimon passed away.[846] Furthermore, even the Diver Nechemia[847] who is one of the Poskim who questioned and invalidated the Nusach of the Peri Eitz Chaim concludes *"Despite the invalidation of the source in Peri Eitz Chaim, certainly the concept is true that Rashbi passed away on Lag BaOmer, as has already been publicized **in the entire world for many generations the Hilula of the Rashbi** on Lag BaOmer."* Last, but not least, in truth the wording of the Peri Eitz Chaim has been recently discovered to be authentic, although with a slight change of wording. A careful study of the original manuscripts of the Peri Eitz Chaim found in multiple famed libraries [i.e. Oxford] show that although he did not write the above quoted wording which was questioned and invalidated by Poskim, he did write *"The reason **for Rashbi's Simcha on Lag BaOmer** is because he was from the students of Rebbe Akiva, **who is the one who died on Lag BaOmer**."*[848] Thus, the last of the mysteries has been solved. Rashbi instructed us to celebrate on Lag BaOmer because this is the day of his passing, as corroborated by the true manuscripts of Rav Chaim Vital, many Poskim, and the tradition of world Jewry.

<u>Why the day of the Rashbi's passing is a reason for celebration</u>: A final and last step in the mysterious puzzle of the Lag BaOmer celebration is understanding why the established reason of Rashbi passing away should be a source of joy or celebration. In fact, some Poskim who accept the tradition that this is the day of his passing, still question as why this should be a source of joy. The Rebbe[849] suggests that since Rebbe Shimon requested that the day of his death be

---

[841] Yevamos 62b
[842] See Divrei Nechemia 34-7
[843] Divrei Nechemia ibid; Chida in Maras Ayin Likkutim 7, recorded in Sdei Chemed ibid, however Cleary contradicting his earlier statement from Moreh Baetzba ibid
[844] Chida in Birkeiy Yosef 493:2 and Morah Bietzba 8:123 *"Lag BaOmer is the **Yom Hilula of Rashbi**, and it is known that his desire is for us to celebrate on this day, as was revealed regarding the story with Rav Avraham Halevi"*; Chasam Sofer 233 *"Lag BaOmer Yoma Hilula Derashbi"*; Bnei Yissachar Mamar Lag BaOmer 3:3; Sdei Chemed Eretz Yisrael 6; Minchas Elazar 1:60; Divrei Nechemia 34-7 *"Despite the invalidation of the source in Peri Eitz Chaim, certainly the concept is true that Rahsbi passed away on Lag BaOmer, as has already been publicized **in the entire world for many generations the Hillula of the Rashbi** on Lag BaOmer."*; Chayeh Adam 131:11; Aruch Hashulchan 493:7 *"It is customarily called Hilula Derashbi, and they say he passed away on this day and left the cave on this day"*; Kaf Hachaim 493:27 accepts the version of Peri Eitz Chaim and says that both concepts are true
[845] Admur in Siddur Im Dach; Igros Kodesh Admur Hazaken p. 117 *"The 18th of Iyar the **Yom Hillula of the Rashbi"***; Sefer Hamamarim 5564 p. 101 *"To understand the Hillula of Rashbi"*
[846] Igros Kodesh 4:275: *"Many reasons have been recorded regarding the festival of Lag BaOmer. We only have the reason written in the Kisvei Arizal and brought in Dach that this day is **the day of passing of Rashbi**-the Yom Hilula of Rashbi"*
[847] Divrei Nechemia 34-7
[848] See here for an analysis of the original manuscripts and the above stated conclusion http://www.shturem.net/index.php?section=news&id=62737
[849] Likkutei Sichos 3:1002; 32:256

celebrated, it is thus a Mitzvah to fulfill the request of the deceased and celebrate on this day.[850] Another reason brought down is that in truth the day of a Tzaddik's passing is a great day of celebration above, as all the Tzaddik's Torah and Avoda of his lifetime receives revelation on that day.[851] This was stated by the Rashbi himself who coined the day of his Yahrzeit as a Yom Hilula.[852] Alternatively, the day of the Rashbi's passing a great treasure of the inner dimensions of Torah became revealed and thus we celebrate our access to his teachings in these later generations.[853] Due to all the above, as writes the Alter Rebbe, *"One is to rejoice with all his heart and soul and make a day of feasting and joy on the 18th of Iyar, and sing praise to Hashem from the book of Tehillim, however he is not to enter into drunkenness and frivolity, Heaven forbid."*[854]

Summary:
One is to celebrate and rejoice on Lag BaOmer due to the various reasons mentioned above, of which the main reason is that on this day the Rashbi passed away and he instructed for us to celebrate on this day, to the effect that lack of celebration can bring negative consequences. The fact that Rashbi instructed us to celebrate on this day is undisputable, and a careful research of the original manuscripts of the Peri Eitz Chaim show that the reason for this is due to the passing of Rashbi on this day, and so is accepted in the Poskim, amongst the Chabad Rabbeim, as well as the tradition of world Jewry.

Old manuscripts of Peri Eitz Chaim read as follows:

Manuscript from 1641
"וטעם שמח/ רשב"י ביום ל"ג לעומר כי הוא מתלמידי רבי עקיבא שהוא שמת ל"ג לעומר."

Oxford 1760

"וטעם שמחת רשב"י ביו/ ל"ג בעומר כי הוא הי/ מתלמידי ר"ע והו/ שמת בל"ג בעומר."

Oxford 1700
"וטעם שמ/ רשב"י ביום ל"ג לעומר כי הוא מתלמידי ר"ע שהוא שמ/ ל"ג לעומר"

---

[850] See Shach Y.D. 344:9 in name of Rav Yaakov Viyal [Mahariv]
[851] See Tanya Igeres Hakodesh 28
[852] See Zohar Vayechi p. 218a; Haazinu end of Idra Zuta p. 286; Divrei Nechemia ibid; Kaf Hachaim ibid
[853] See Divrei Nechemia ibid
[854] Igros Kodesh Admur Hazaken p. 117;

------------------Shavuos------------------

56. Eating dairy on Shavuos & the reason we wait six hours after meat but not after milk

Why we wait six hours after meat but not after milk & Its connection to eating dairy on Shavuos-A fascinating explanation of the Alter Rebbe:

Eating a Dairy and Meat meal on Shavuos:[855] It is customary amongst all Jewry in all places[856] to eat dairy products on the first[857] day of Shavuos. This custom is Halachically binding, "Minhag Yisrael Torah Hi", as many reasons have been said behind this custom. Nevertheless, since it is a Mitzvah to eat meat on Yom Tov[858], therefore, one is to also have a have a meat meal.[859] One is to eat both meals in a way that avoids any prohibitions of eating meat and milk, following all the laws written in Yoreh Deah 88-89 regarding having a separation between the two meals.[860]

Waiting six hours after meat and not milk: The Halacha is that while one is required to make a separation between his meat and dairy meals[861], and wait six hours[862], one is not required to make a separation between his dairy and meat meal[863] and wait six hours[864], with exception to certain hard cheeses in which Ashkenazim are accustomed to wait six hours.[865] The Halachic reason behind this is because meat gets stuck between the teeth and regurgitates its fat odor for up to six hours, as opposed to [most] cheese.[866] The Alter Rebbe, in a tradition recorded in the Sefer Pardes Haaretz[867] [written by Rav Yeshaya Horowitz, a Lubavitcher Rav in Tzefas in the early 1900's] sheds deeper light onto the reason behind this distinction and explains that this distinction served as the fundamental principal to allow us to receive the Torah. This explanation is based on the following Midrash:

The Midrash:[868] The Midrash[869] famously states that the supernal angels attempted to litigate against the giving of the Torah to the Jewish people for various reasons. The final rebuttal, or comeback, which closed all litigation and allowed the Torah to be given, involved the Mitzvah of not eating meat and milk together. The argument was as follows:[870] After the angels told Hashem that they desired to keep the Torah for themselves, Hashem answered the angels that it states in the Torah "Thou shall not eat a kid in its mother's milk." Now, you angels surely remember the meal you ate in the home of Avraham Avinu? You ate meat and milk together during that meal as the verse[871] states "Vayikach Chema Vechalav," so how can you now ask to receive the Torah? This, states the Midrash, was the final comeback which refuted any claims from the angels, and allowed the Torah to be given. Accordingly, we eat dairy and

---

[855] Admur 494:16; Rama 494:3 *"In certain places it is customary to eat dairy on the first day of Shavuos"*; Kol Bo 52

[856] Admur ibid, in contrast to wording in Rama ibid

[857] Admur ibid; Rama ibid; See Q&A regarding the second day

[858] Admur 529:3

[859] Admur ibid; Rama ibid "the custom is to eat a dairy meal and then a meat meal"

[860] Admur 494:16; Shlah; Peri Megadim brought in M"B 494:17; Aruch Hashulchan 494:5; Toras Menachem 5743 3:1579 [brought in Shulchan Menachem 3:41]

Other opinions: Some Poskim rule one may be lenient in the laws of separation between milk and meat on Shavuos, and not wait 6 hours between eating them. [Kol Bo brought in Beir Heiytiv 494:8; Noam Elimelech Mishpatim "Lo Sivashel"; Piskeiy Teshuvah 285; See Darkei Teshuvah 89:19] Other Poskim however decried against this leniency. [Shlah; Peri Megadim brought in M"B 494:17; Aruch Hashulchan 494:5] The Rebbe ibid stressed against being lenient as one of the entire reasons of eating milk is to commemorate our strict observance of the Kashrus laws which merited us to receive the Torah over the angles, so how can one now be lenient in these laws. It is also clear from Admur ibid that he is against being lenient in any laws of meat and milk.

[861] Rav Chisda in Chulin 105a

[862] Michaber 89:1; Rambam Machalos Assuros 9:28; Ran Chulin 37b that so is opinion of Rif; Rabbeinu Chananel; Baal Haitur 2:13; Tur O.C. 173 in name of Rosh; Tur Y.D. 89; Rosh Chulin 5 that so is custom; Shut Min Hashamayim 55 that so is opinion of majority of Poskim, and in Heaven there is no dispute in this, as everyone now agrees its forbidden; Taz 89:2 in name of Shaareiy Dura that custom is like Rambam and not like Tosafos; Rashal Kol Habasar 70 wonders why Ashkenazi Jewry became accustomed to be lenient against the Rambam and Rif; Rama ibid that those who are meticulous are to wait six hours; Shach 89:8; P"M 89 S.D. 5 and 8; Chochmas Adam 40:13; Aruch Hashulchan 89:7; Kaf Hachaim 89:20

[863] Michaber Y.D. 89:2

[864] Some, however, wait one hour, and so is the Chabad custom. See Shach 89:16; Beis Yosef 173; Toras Chatas of Rama; Shlah Tractate Shavuos p. 30; Levush 173; P"M 89 S.D. 6; Darkei Teshuvah 89:19; Rebbe in Igros Kodesh 20 p. 289

[865] See Rama Y.D. 89:2

[866] See Tur 89; Taz 89:1 and Shach 89:2

[867] Sefer Pardes Haaretz [Horowitz] Vol. 3 p. 548 in footnote

[868] See Beir Heiytiv 494:8 [towards end]; Toras Menachem 5743 3:1579 [brought in Shulchan Menachem 3:41]

[869] Midrash Raba Yisro 28

[870] Midrash Tehillim 8; Daas Zekeinim on Vayeira ibid

[871] Vayeira 18:8

then meat on Shavuos to emphasize the reason why we received the Torah over the angels, as they did not keep the dietary laws of separating between meat and milk.[872]

The Alter Rebbe's explanation: An even deeper approach is stated in the name of the Alter Rebbe:[873] The law is that while one may not eat dairy after meat, one may eat meat after dairy.[874] The above Midrash is hence puzzling, as the verse explicitly states that it offered first dairy and then meat to the guests, and they therefore performed no transgression. The explanation is as follows: The reason for the prohibition against eating meat and milk together is because milk is from Chesed and meat is from Gevurah, and their combination can be catastrophic. However, this only applies if the Gevurah overpowers the Chesed, while if the Chesed overpowers the Gevurah then it is actually a positive matter. Now, we have a general rule of Tatah Gavar, the bottom overrules, and hence if one first eats dairy, he may eat meat afterwards, as the bottom which is dairy/Chesed, overrules the meat/Gevurah. However, if one eats meat first, then the Gevurah overpowers the Chesed. This system however only applies in this world, in which we hold that the lower realms are of greater importance than the higher realms, and hence the lower item overpowers. However, in the Heavens, they believe that the higher realm is greater than the lower realms, and therefore the rule of Tatah Gavar does not apply. Accordingly, Hashem told the angels that if the Torah is given to them, and thus the higher realms prevail, it would end up that they ate meat and milk together, hence transgressing the Torah. Furthermore, by the mere fact that by Avraham they agreed to eat first dairy and then meat shows that they too agree that the lower realms overpower, and hence they have no claim to receive the Torah. [Accordingly, we can explain the custom of eating a dairy meal on Shavuos, and then eating a meat meal, as this commemorates the victorious rebuttal which gave us the Torah to begin with. It also emphasizes that the purpose of the Torah is for the lower realms.]

------------------Yom Tov------------------

57. May one remove food from the freezer on the first day of Yom Tov on behalf of the second night meal?

A. The general law:[875]

It is forbidden to do anything on the 1st day of Yom Tov on behalf of the next day, including on behalf of the 2nd day in the Diaspora.[876] This applies even for the two days of Rosh Hashanah which is considered like one long day.[877] [This applies even in a year that Shabbos falls after Yom Tov and one performed Eruv Tavshilin before Yom Tov.[878]] This prohibition applies even against doing acts of preparation that

---

[872] Beir Heiytiv 494:8 [towards end] *"I heard that we eat dairy and then meat, unlike what the angels did by Avraham in which they ate meat and milk, as due to this the Torah was given to the Jewish people"*; Toras Menachem 5743 3:1579 [brought in Shulchan Menachem 3:41]

[873] Brought in Sefer Pardes Haaretz [Horowitz] Vol. 3 p. 548 in footnote

[874] See Michaber Y.D. Chapter 89

[875] Admur 503:1-3; Michaber 503:1 regarding Melacha; Rama 667:1 regarding Hachana

[876] Admur 503:1-2 regarding Melacha from Yom Tov to weekday or Shabbos, and 503:3 regarding Hachana from Yom Tov Rishon to Yom Tov Sheiyni Shel Galiyos; Michaber ibid regarding Melacha

Is the prohibition Biblical or Rabbinical? All the Melachos of Ochel Nefesh were only permitted to be performed on Yom Tov for the sake of benefiting from it on Yom Tov. It is however forbidden to bake, slaughter, and cook on Yom Tov for the sake of eating it after Yom Tov. One who does so, transgresses a Biblical prohibition and is liable for lashes. [Admur 495:2 "For the sake of eating on Yom Tov"; 503:1-2; 527:8; M"A 518:1 "One who cooks on Yom Tov for the weekday gets lashes"; M"B 527:3; Rambam Yom Tov 1:9; Beitza 17a; Pesachim 46b; See Aruch Hashulchan 527:3; Piskeiy Teshuvos 527:3 for other opinions in this matter] This however only applies if the Melacha was done on Yom Tov near evening in a way that one cannot benefit from it at all on Yom Tov itself [do to there not being enough time to receive the benefit]. If, however, it is possible for one to benefit from the food on Yom Tov itself, then he is exempt from a Biblical transgression even if he does not plan to benefit from it on Yom Tov and intended to do the Melacha for the sake of eating the food the next day. Nevertheless, the Sages prohibited this to be done, and one who does so is liable for Rabbinical lashes. Even if the Melacha is not needed at all for Yom Tov, being that one already ate all his meals in entirety, it is nevertheless only Rabbinically forbidden. [Admur 503:2; M"A 527:1; Razah Pesachim 14b; Ran ibid] The reason it is only Rabbinical, is because if he were to receive guests that did not yet eat that day, then this Melacha would be considered a need for the guests, and would have been permitted to be performed by him. Therefore, this Melacha is called Mileches Ochel Nefesh, and even though he does not have guests, its performance does not contain a Biblical prohibition. [Admur 503:2; M"A 527:1; Tosafos Pesachim ibid]

[877] Admur 503:3; Michaber 503:1; Drashos Maharil Hilchos Rosh Hashanah; Hagahos Maimanis in name of Semak

The reason: Although the two days of Rosh Hashanah is one holiness, and is considered long day, nevertheless, this only applies for purposes of stringency and not to leniency. The reason for this is because as we are expert in the date of the month, and we know that the first day is holy from a Biblical perspective, while the 2nd day is completely mundane according to the Biblical perspective, and it is thus found that one is preparing on Yom Tov for a weekday. [Admur ibid; M"A 503:1; Taz 503:1; Beis Yosef; Levush; Kneses Hagedola 503:1; Drashos Maharil Hilchos Rosh Hashanah; Hagahos Maimanis in name of Semak; Shulchan Gavoa 503:2; Kaf Hachaim 503:10]

[878] Pashut, as Eiruv Tavshilin only permits doing Melacha from Friday to Shabbos. [Admur 527:23]

do not contain any forbidden Melacha at all.[879] [Rather, all the preparations for the 2nd night are to be done after Tzeis Hakochavim/nightfall of the first day.[880] However, some Poskim[881] rule that in a time of need, such as to prevent loss, and for the sake of a Mitzvah, one may be lenient to prepare on the first day of Yom Tov on behalf of the 2nd day, if one completes the preparation with much time left in the day[882], and the preparation does not involve any Melacha normally forbidden to be done on Yom Tov.[883]]

Examples: One must beware not to bring wine on the first day of Yom Tov on behalf of Kiddush of the second night.[884] Likewise, one is not to search in a Sefer Torah on the first day of Yom Tov for the reading of the second day, or for Shabbos, even if one performed Eruv Tavshilin.[885] Likewise, one may not wash dishes on the first day on behalf of the second day [until after Tzeis Hakochavim].[886] [Likewise, one may not make the beds [or tidy the home] on the first day of Yom Tov on behalf of the next day, unless it is also done for the sake of having a clean home on the first day of Yom Tov.[887] Likewise, one may not set the table or prepare the candles until after Tzeis Hakochavim.]

Summary:
It is forbidden to do anything on the 1st day of Yom Tov on behalf of the 2nd day, or on behalf of Shabbos, even if the action does not involve any forbidden Melacha, and even if one performed Eruv Tavshilin. This applies until after Tzeis Hakochavim of the first day.

B. May one remove food from the freezer on the first day of Yom Tov on behalf of the second night meal?

Some Poskim[888] rule it is permitted to remove foods from the freezer on the first day of Yom Tov on behalf of the meal of the second night of Yom Tov.[889] Other Poskim[890], however, rule that it is forbidden

---

[879] Admur 503:3; 254:10; 494:14; Rama 667:1; M"A 503:1 based on Michaber 416:2; Hagahos Maimanis; Maharil; M"B 503:1; 667:5
[880] P"M 503 M"Z 1; Kaf Hachaim 503:4
The reason: As we never allow one to initially be lenient by a Safek Derabanon. [P"M ibid]
[881] Chayeh Adam 153:6; M"B 667:5 regarding wine for the 2nd night of Yom Tov; Kaf Hachaim 503:2; Maharshag 1:61; Piskeiy Teshuvos 302:17; 503:1; Nitei Gavriel "Erev Pesach Shechal Beshabbos" in Teshuvah 4
The reason: As in a time of need the Sages did not make their decree. [See Chayeh Adam ibid] This especially applies for the sake of a Mitzvah. [M"B ibid] Alternatively, the entire prohibition of Hachanah is only when the action is being done to save time, while if it is being done to save an item from a loss, Hachana is permitted. [Maharshag ibid]
Opinion of Admur: There exist many different rulings in Admur regarding if one may prepare for after Shabbos/Yom Tov for the sake of loss prevention. [See Admur 254:10 and M"A 254: 23 that it is forbidden to remove bread from the oven for the next day, and seemingly, this is despite the fact that it will cause a loss to the bread, as explains, and questions the Elya Raba 254:18; In 319:18 regarding saving a food from spoilage Admur only permits preparing to prevent **through a gentile**. In 321:6 regarding watering vegetables to prevent shriveling, Admur only permits doing so being that it is for the sake of preventing loss and is not noticeable to others that it is for the next day, such as that perhaps he will eat it that day, and he thus does not extend the allowance to soaking three-day meat. However, in 500:20 Admur permits soaking meat of three days in water to prevent its prohibition in cooking being that soaking is less of an effort than washing dishes. This seemingly contradicts the ruling of Admur in 321:6, brought earlier, however, in truth the difference is that in 321:6 it discusses Shabbos when the raw meat cannot be cooked and is hence not edible, while in 500:20 it is discussing Yom Tov, when the meat is edible and hence does not appear to others like a preparation.] The final summary of his opinion seems to be as follows: It is forbidden to prepare for after Shabbos/Yom Tov even in a time of need, to prevent loss to the item, unless the following conditions are met. 1) One does so through a gentile. Or 2) It does not involve much effort [i.e. soaking] and it is not apparent to others that it is being done for after Shabbos/Yom Tov. No mention is made in Admur regarding if a case that involves a Mitzvah should receive greater leniency than above. Now, although in 503:3 Admur prohibits bringing wine on the first day of Yom Tov for Kiddush of the second day, which implies that no extra leniency is given even for the sake of a Mitzvah, nevertheless, perhaps if it's both for the sake of a Mitzvah and a time of need or loss prevention, Admur would be more lenient. Vetzaruch Iyun!
[882] See M"B ibid "*With much time left in the day as then it is not apparent to others that it is being done for the sake of the next day*"; See also Admur 321:7 "*being that they are fit today to be eaten by any person and it is thus not at all evident that one is [doing an action that entails] effort on Shabbos for the [need of a] weekday being that he may eat these [vegetables] today.*"
[883] As if it involves Melacha, it is forbidden not just due to Hachana or Tircha from one day to the next, but also in its own right, as the Torah only permitted Melacha to be done on Yom Tov for the sake of Yom Tov.
[884] Admur 503:3; M"A 667:3; Chayeh Adam 99:1; 153:6; M"B 667:5; Kaf Hachaim 503:2
[885] Admur 503:3; M"A 667:3; Maharil Hilchos Tefilas Yom Tov
[886] Admur 503:3; Elya Raba 503:1; Drashos Maharil Hilchos Yom Tov p. 180; Minhagei Maharash 394
[887] M"B 667:5; Admur 302:10 regarding Shabbos
[888] Shevet Hakehasi 1:158; Piskeiy Teshuvos 302:17 footnote 146; 503:1; Nitei Gavriel Yom Tov 26:9; and in "Erev Pesach Shechal Beshabbos" in Teshuvah 4 [Based on ruling of Chayeh Adam 153:6; M"B 667:5; Kaf Hachaim 503:2; Maharshag 1:61]
[889] The reason: As in a time of need, for the sake of a Mitzvah, one may prepare on the first day on behalf of the second day if the action does not involve a Melacha [Chayeh Adam 153:6; M"B 667:5-although stipulates to do with much time left in day; Kaf Hachaim 503:2] and this case is

to remove the food even in such a case.[891] [See footnote for opinion of Admur in this matter.[892] Practically, it is best to avoid removing the food from the freezer until after Tzeis Hakochavim. This especially applies in light of the fact that the food can be defrosted after nightfall on top of a source of heat and be ready for the night meal. Nonetheless, if these options are not viable and delaying the removal until Tzeis Hakochavim will cause a real delay to the meal, then one may be lenient to remove the foods from the freezer with much time left in the day of Yom Tov, so it does not appear to others that it is being done for the night.[893]]

C. May one place drinks in the fridge or freezer on the first day of Yom Tov on behalf of the second day?[894]
This follows the same dispute as above. Practically, it is best to avoid doing so unless one plans to taste the cold drinks while it is still the first day of Yom Tov, in which case it is permitted according to all.

------------------Chol Hamoed-----------------
58. May children, or adults, draw pictures and make paintings on Chol Hamoed?
A. Background:
It is forbidden to write [or draw pictures or designs[895]] on Chol Hamoed.[896] Some Poskim[897] rule that it is only forbidden to write in a professional script, known as Maaseh Uman, which is the scribal lettering used for writing a Sefer Torah, Mezuzah and Tefillin [i.e. Ksav Ashuris]. It is however, permitted to write in a commonly known script [i.e. Maaseh Hedyot] on Chol Hamoed [so long as it has a need for the Moed[898]]. However, other Poskim[899] imply that even amateur writing is forbidden to be done during the Moed, as all script was considered by the Sages to be professional. Practically, we rule like the former opinion.[900] From the letter of the law, this script may be written even without an irregularity/Shinuiy, however, the widespread custom is to write it with a Shinuiy.[901]

---

considered a time of need and prevention of loss, as if he would have to wait until Tzeis Hakochavim to defrost the food, he would begin the meal very late, and his kids may fall asleep, and Simchas Yom Tov will be nullified. [Nitei Gavriel ibid] Alternatively, the entire prohibition of Hachanah is only when the action is being done to save time, while if it is being done to save an item from a loss, Hachana is permitted. [Maharshag ibid]

[890] SSH"K 10:10

[891] The reason: As it is forbidden to prepare for the next day of Yom Tov even if it will cause one to need to delay his meal later on.

[892] Opinion of Admur: See previous footnotes above in A for an analysis on the opinion of Admur! All in all, if we view the concept of delaying the meal for many hours in wait for the food to defrost as equivalent to a loss, then Admur would permit defrosting it on the first day of Yom Tov with much time left in the day on the basis that one is not really doing any action other than removing it from the freezer. It is hence similar to the law regarding three-day meat.

[893] Implication of Admur ibid, as explained in previous footnote! M"B ibid who qualifies his allowance to only if it is done with much time left in the day

[894] See Piskeiy Teshuvos 302 footnote 146 who permits doing so on the same basis as removing from the freezer.

[895] See Admur 340:10 *"One who makes marks and designs on a document and the like, in the way that the artists design, is liable to an offshoot of the writing prohibition. The same applies for one who erases it."* See also Admur 519:6; M"A 340:6; Rambam Shabbos 11:17; Degul Merivava 340; Tehila Ledavid 340:3

[896] Michaber 545:1; Rambam 7:13; Mishneh Moed Katan 18b; Smag Lavin 75:28

The reason: As this is considered a Melacha which does not have a need for the Moed. [Rambam ibid; Smag ibid; Beis Yosef 545]

[897] Beis Yosef 545:5 based on Rif, Rambam, Rosh, Ravad, and Ramban who all permit writing letters and Cheshbonos *"Practically, the Halacha is...that one may write letters [in regular writing" even without an irregularity"*; Bach 545 *"It is obvious that the Sages only prohibited the Ashuris scribal writing during the Moed and not any other form of writing that we do today"*; Rabbeinu Tam; Agudah; Rabbeinu Yerucham Toldos Adam Vechavah Nesiv Daled 5 in name of Rabbeinu Tam; Orchos Chaim Chol Hamoed 7; Taz; Kneses Hagedola 545:1; Olas Shabbos 545:1; Elya Raba 545:5; M"B 545:35; See Michaber 545:5 regarding Sheilas Shalom and Prakmatya; M"B 545:4 and 30; See M"B 545:4; Rama ibid regarding writing for a public need that is not for the need of the Moed writes "The custom is to be lenient regarding our script of writing which is not Maaseh Uman"

[898] Implication of Bach ibid that only if it is for the need of the public may it be written for after the Moed; M"B 545:30; Chol Hamoed Kehilchasa 6:8 footnote 19; Piskeiy Teshuvos 545:1

[899] Implication of Terumos Hadeshen 85, brought in Bach ibid and Beis Yosef 545, who forbids writing even for the sake of the public, even in a regular script; See Kaf Hachaim 545:11

[900] M"B 545:30; Chol Hamoed Kehilchasa 6:8 footnote 19; Piskeiy Teshuvos 545:1

[901] Bach 545; Kneses Hagedola 545:1; Olas Shabbos 545:1; Elya Raba 545:5; Rama ibid regarding writing for a public need that is not for the need of the Moed; See Kaf Hachaim ibid

A place without a custom: In all areas without a set custom, those who are lenient to write regular script without any irregularity, have not lost out. [Darkei Moshe 545:4; Elya Raba ibid; Kaf Hachaim ibid]

B. The law:[902]

It is permitted for children or adults to draw amateur pictures, drawings, and paintings on Chol Hamoed as a fun activity for recreational and entertainment purposes.[903] However, a professional picture or painting may not be done.

59. May one go fishing on Chol Hamoed?[904]

Commercial fishing and fishing for food purposes: It is permitted to go fishing during Chol Hamoed if one's intent in doing so is to eat the fish during the Moed.[905] There is no limit as to how many fish one may catch, and one may thus catch as many fish as possible.[906] It is permitted to fish even in public.[907] [Some Poskim[908] rule that this applies even if one is a professional or occupational fisher. Other Poskim[909] rule that an occupational fisher may not fish in public.[910] This applies especially in today's times that occupational fishers freeze fish for storage.[911]] Those who were accustomed not to fish during the Moed may break their custom, and are encouraged to do so.[912]

Recreational/sport fishing:[913] Some Poskim[914] rule it is permitted to go recreational/sport fishing on Chol Hamoed, even if one does not intend to eat the caught fish.[915] Other Poskim[916] rule it is forbidden to go recreational/sport fishing on Chol Hamoed, even if one plans to eat a caught Kosher fish.[917]

---

[902] Chol Hamoed Kehilchaso 6:84 "Children who draw and color, there is no prohibition involved at all" and Footnote 197 "This is obvious"; Shemiras Hamoed Kehilchaso 8:12; Piskeiy Teshuvos 545:12

[903] The reason: As since they enjoy this activity it is considered for the need of the Moed [See Michaber 536:1], and it is permitted to write amateur script for the sake of the Moed. [See Poskim ibid in background]

[904] Michaber 533:4; See Chol Hamoed Kehilchaso 7:21-24

[905] Michaber 533:4; 541:1 "It is permitted to make an amateur fishing net"; M"A 541:1 "If it is done for the need of the Moed"; Rambam Yom Tov 7; Moed Katan 11b

[906] Michaber 533:4

The reason: As it is possible that he will eat the fish during the Moed. [Michaber ibid] Now, although it may not be physically possible to consume all the fish over Yom Tov, nevertheless since there are different levels of quality of fish and by every catch there is possibility of a greater quality fish which will be chosen to be eaten during the Moed, therefore it is allowed without limit. [M"A 533:7; M"B 533:18; Kaf Hachaim 533:26]

[907] Rama ibid; Mordechai

The reason: As everyone knows that one is catching the fish for the need of the Moed. [Rama ibid]

[908] Implication of Rama 533:4-5; Kaf Hachaim 533:29; See Biur Halacha 533:5 "Shel Chayos"

[909] M"A 533:10 based on Rambam and Michaber; Elya Raba 533:5; Biur Hagr"a; Poskim in Shaar Hatziyon 533:33 and conclusion of Biur Halacha 533:5 "Shel Chayos" that so is the correct Girsa in the Gemara that even fish may not be trapped in public; See Chol Hamoed Kehilchaso 7:22

[910] The reason: As people who see an occupational fisherman out fishing will think he is running his business as usual, and is not fishing for the sake of the Moed. [Biur Halacha ibid]

[911] Chol Hamoed Kehilchaso 7 footnote 65

[912] M"A 533:8; Kaf Hachaim 533:30

The reason: As they diminish in Simchas Yom Tov. [ibid]

[913] Background: Ideally, it is forbidden to perform even food related Melacha during the Moed, such as catching fish, if one's intent in doing so is not for the purpose of eating the fish, but rather as a sport or recreation. Nonetheless, being that there is a certain pleasure/Taanug derived from fishing, the mere act itself, irrelevant of whether one eats the fish, can possibly be considered "for the need of the Moed", the same way it is permitted to ride an animal for leisure purposes. [See Michaber 536:1] This matter is under debate amongst today's Poskim.

[914] Rav Moshe Feinstein in Sefer Hilchos Chol Hamoed 13, although concludes it is best to eat the Kosher fish that is caught; Shemiras Hamoed Kehilchaso 3:7 and footnote 16 in name of Rav Elyashiv

[915] The reason: As receiving pleasure from an action during the Moed is considered a type of Tzoreich Hamoed which allows doing Maaseh Hedyot. [Poskim ibid based on Michaber 536:1]

[916] Rivivos Efraim 1:356; Rav Moshe Shtern in Hilchos Chol Hamoed in English regarding public fishing [forbids even if possible that he will eat fish]; Chol Hamoed Kehilchaso [Farkash] 9:24 in name of Rav SZ"A, Rav Wozner, Rav Bransdofer; Piskeiy Teshuvos 534:4 [see however footnote 11 there that if one plans to place the fish in an aquarium in one's home and will not have an opportunity to fish after the Moed, then it is permitted to do so.]

[917] The reason: As one's main intent is for the sport and not for eating purposes, and this is recognizable to all when done in public. Now, pleasure alone is not considered a tangible enough "Tzoreich Hamoed" definition to justify the performance of Melacha. [Poskim ibid]

----------------Bein Hametzarim----------------

60. Music therapy-May one listen to music during the three weeks for emotional and mental health purposes?

In general, one may not play or listen[918] to music during the three weeks.[919] [It is forbidden to listen to music, whether live or recorded.[920] This applies likewise to Chassidic Niggunim, whether a slow or fast Niggun.[921] Thus one may not listen to music on a tape, CD, Ipod, MP3 and the like.] However, this only applies if one is doing so for purposes of pleasure.[922] One may, however, listen to music for therapeutic purposes, such as to remove depression, anxiety and other mental or emotional turmoil's that one may be experiencing. This applies especially towards women.[923] [However, if one is able to accomplish the same music therapy without listing to actual musical instruments, such as through listening to A Cappella music, or through listening to various nature sounds, then one is to do so.]

61. May one continue wearing Shabbos clothing on Motzei Shabbos which is Tisha Beav? Are they to be switched after nightfall before Maariv?

In general, it is forbidden to wear Shabbos clothing during the nine days [with exception to Shabbos], and certainly on Tisha Beav this prohibition applies.[924] Accordingly, some Poskim[925] rule that one is to remove his Shabbos clothing immediately after the conclusion of Shabbos [after reciting Baruch Hamavdil], prior to Maariv. According to this approach, it is proper for Shul's to schedule for people to go home between Mincha and Maariv, change clothing after Shabbos, and then come to Shul sometime after Shabbos for Maariv and Eicha.[926] However, other Poskim[927] negate the above and rule that one may remain wearing his Shabbos clothing even after Havdalah on Motzei Shabbos.[928] Practically, the widespread custom in many communities on Motzei Shabbos which is Tisha Beav is like the former opinion, although some follow the latter approach.[929] The Chabad custom is like the latter opinion, to continue wearing the Shabbos clothes until after Eicha and Kinos, and so was the custom of the Rebbe.[930] The Rebbe spoke quite negatively of the custom to change one's Shabbos clothing.[931] Those who follow

---

[918] Aruch Hashulchan 493:2 regarding Sefira
[919] P"M 551 A"A 10; Kitzur SH"A 122:1
[920] Shevet Halevi 2:57; 127; Igros Moshe 1:166; 3:87; Minchas Yitzchak 1:111; Kinyan Torah 2:99; Yechaveh Daas 3:30; Mishneh Halachos 8:128; Az Nidbaru 10:23; Piskeiy Teshuvos 551:13; 493:4
[921] See Moed Lekol Chaiy 10:19, brought in Kaf Hachaim 551:41 that even by singing of the mouth it is better not to sing even slow Niggunim which break the heart; Piskeiy Teshuvos 551:13; There is no reason to differentiate, as all music has a power of Simcha, and singing a soulful Niggun also gives one Simcha. Admur in various areas of Chassidus writes that some people enjoy fast music while others enjoy slow, depressing music, and each one has a different pleasure. So I received from various Morei Horaahs. However, some are lenient in this matter. Each person is to contact his Rav.
[922] So is understood from all Poskim who rule a musician may play for gentiles due to that for him it is not for pleasure. [See P"M 551 A"A 10; Kitzur SH"A 122:1; Ben Ish Chaiy Devarim 5; Biur Halacha 551 "Mematin"; Kaf Hachaim 551:39; Igros Moshe 3:87; Kinyan Torah 2:99] So is also understood from M"A 560:9; and Sota 49a regarding the allowance to sing during laborious work in order to hasten their work ability.
[923] See Shevet Halevi 8:127 "Especially the women who do so to remove their depression, and it is permitted" [however it is unclear if he refers to during the year or even during Bein Hametzarim, although, in truth the reason of the Heter should apply during all times]; See Piskeiy Teshuvos 493 footnote 36; Chelkas Yaakov 1:61 and 3:98 regarding Shabbos; See Sefer "Eileh Heim Moadaiy" 3:63-65 for a discussion from Poskeiy Zemaneinu on this matter
The reason: As the music is not being listened to for purposes of joy and dancing but for therapeutic purposes, and in such a case the custom was never accepted to prohibit the music.
[924] Rama 551:1 "By a Mila the custom is for the Baal Bris to wear Shabbos clothing, **although otherwise it is forbidden.**"
[925] Maharil, brought in M"A 559:10 "After the Mila they remove the clothing"; Piskeiy Teshuvos 553:1; Nitei Gavriel 94:5
[926] Nitei Gavriel ibid
[927] Ashel Avraham Butchach Mahadurah Tinyana 551
[928] The reason: As the accustomed prohibition of wearing Shabbos clothing is only the initial wearing, while if he already wore it under allowance, such as on Shabbos or for a Mila, then there is no prohibition to continue wearing it. [Ashel Avraham ibid]
[929] Nitei Gavriel ibid; Minhagei Mahariv Sulitza [Rav Yaakov Yisrael Rubin 1900's] 507 that he remained wearing his Shtreimal for Maariv and removed it before Eicha; Yechidei Segula in Yerushalayim would remove the Shtreimal after Eicha
[930] Yoman of Rav Groner that the Rebbe stated that so was the custom of Jewry in Russia, and of Lubavitch Chassidim; Rav Eli Landa confirmed with his brother Rav Y.L. Landa that the custom is to remain wearing Shabbos clothing until after Maariv/Eicha
[931] The diary of Rav Leibal Groner documents the Rebbe's reaction after being told by Rabbi Groner of the custom of some to change their Shabbos clothing "The Rebbe was very surprised at this and asked me to show him where it states such a thing. I showed him in the Sefer Tishe Beav Shechal Beshabbos who brings that a number of Chassidic communities are accustomed to do so. The Rebbe responded that in Yakaterinoslav no one did this and I do not understand this and why to delay Maariv for such a thing. Later the Rebbe said on Motzei Tisha Beav that this custom of delaying Maariv to go home and change Shabbos clothing is a wild custom that was the custom of Hungarian Jewry but not in

this custom are to wear their Shabbos clothing [i.e. hat, shtreimal, Kapata] before the conclusion of Shabbos, and continue wearing it after Shabbos.[932] According to all, one may not change his Shabbos clothing before the conclusion of Shabbos. According to all, leather shoes must be removed immediately after Shabbos, and the above discussion is limited to other Shabbos garments.

-----------------Fast Day-----------------
62. When does the fast begin-Which Also is one to follow?
A fast day, such as 17th of Tammuz, 10th of Teves, Tzom Gedalia, and Taanis Esther, begins by Alos Hashachar.[933] There is general dispute amongst the Poskim as to the definition of Alos/daybreak according to Halacha. Some Poskim[934], and calendars, rule Alos Hashachar begins **72 minutes** prior to sunrise. Other Poskim[935], and calendars, rule Alos Hashachar begins **90 minutes** prior to sunrise. Other Poskim[936], and calendars, rule Alos Hashachar begins **two fluctuating**[937] **hours** prior to sunrise, and so is

---

Russia. The Rebbe added that the Rabbanim, and you included, were never in Russia. Practically, the Rebbe would remain in his room until after Shabbos was over, would remove his shoes, but not his Shabbos clothing."

[932] May one even initially put on the Shabbos clothing after Tzeis if he was not wearing it beforehand? If one removed his Shabbos clothing, such as he removed his Kapata, and it is now after Tzeis, it is questionable as to whether he may even initially put on his Shabbos clothing for Maariv and Eicha, as the entire Heter of the Ashel Avraham ibid was based on the fact one remains in his Shabbos clothing into Shabbos, however to initially put on, who says is allowed? Accordingly, ideally one is to wear the clothing before Tzeis. Nevertheless, even if one took it off and is now going to Shul for Maariv, there is room to learn that he may wear it. This is similar to the Heter written in Shulchan Aruch for a Baal Simcha to wear [put on] Shabbos clothing on Tisha B'av itself [See Rama 559:8; Bigdei Yesha, brought in Kaf Hachaim 559:65], and the reason is because it is only a Minhag not to wear Shabbos clothing on Tisha B'av and not forbidden for the letter of the law. This is why we wear Shabbos clothing on Shabbos even though the same Rama writes its forbidden. The same way the custom allows wearing it on Shabbos Lekavod Shabbos, it allows wearing it even initially on Motzei Shabbos Lekavod Motzei Shabbos. Vetzaruch Iyun!

[933] See Michaber 550:2 *"One is not required to start fasting Mibiod Yom"*

[934] Rashal Pesachim 2a; Minchas Kohen 2:6; M"A 89:2; Levush 261 and 459; Admur in 89:1, 184:3, and 261:5; Derech Hachaim; M"B 89 in Biur Halacha "Veim"; 58 Biur Halacha "Kemo"; and chapters: 92; 163; 235; 261; 459; This opinion is based on the calculation that there are 18 minutes per Mil [as rules Terumos Hadeshen 123; Michaber 459:2; Yoreh Deah 69:6; Rama 261:1; Admur in 89:1, 184:3, and 261:5] and there are 4 Mil between Alos and Neitz [as rules Rebbe Yehuda in Pesachim 94a] Accordingly there are 72 minutes before Alos, as 18 x 4=72.

[935] Gr"a 459; Chok Yaakov 459:10; Chasam Sofer in glosses 89] This opinion is based on the calculation that there are 22.5 minutes per Mil [as rules Maharil in Hilchos Pesach] and there are 4 Mil between Alos and Neitz [as rules Rebbe Yehuda in Pesachim 94a] Accordingly there are 90 minutes before Alos, as 22.5 x 4=72.

[936] Ruling of Admur in accordance to Harav Hagaon Avraham Chaim Naah printed in Shiureiy Mikveh 37; Yagdil Torah Tzemach Tzedek 23 p. 23 [see there for a full organized summary on the subject]; See Shiureiy Tziyon 37; Yagdil Torah Tzemach Tzedek 23 p. 23; Siddur Raskin p. 625 and Miluim 27 [summary of opinions according to Admur]; Rav Sangwai in Habracha 5:162 [defends and proofs the opinion of Gra"ch Naah in Admur and that so learned the Rebbe to be the opinion of Admur]; Piskeiy Teshuvos 89:2

Rulings of Admur: Admur wrote different calculations regarding Alos Hashachar throughout the Shulchan Aruch, Siddur and Tanya. This created confusion as to Admur's opinion as to the time of Alos Hashachar. From 89:1, 184:3, and 261:5 it is understood that Alos Hashachar is calculated as 72 minutes before sunrise, or possibly 96 minutes. From 249:3, 459:10 and the Siddur [Seder Hachnasas Shabbos] it is understood that it can be calculated that Alos Hashachar is 96 minutes or 120 minutes before sunrise. From the time of Alos mentioned in the Siddur regarding Sefiras Haomer it is possible to calculate it as 72 or 120 minutes. In Igeres Hateshuva 3 Admur extends the time of starting a fast to three hours before sunrise. The following are the opinions of Chabad Rabbanim in this matter:

Opinion of Admur according to the Gra"ch Naah-Two fluctuating hours: Rav Avraham Chaim Naah ruled that according to Admur, Alos Hashachar begins **two fluctuating** hours prior to sunrise. [Shiureiy Tziyon 37; Yagdil Torah Tzemach Tzedek 23 p. 23] The calculation is as follows: There are 5 Mil between Alos and Neitz [as rules Ula in Pesachim 93b]. Each Mil is 24 minutes [as rules Rambam in Pirush Hamishnayos Pesachim 3:2]. Thus 24 minutes per Mil x 5 Mil between Alos and Neitz equals 120 minutes. [This follows the ruling of Admur in 249:3; 459:10 and Siddur and so rules regarding 24 minutes per Mil: Peri Chadash Y.D. 69:26; Kitzur SHU"A 36:11. However, in 89:1 and 261:5 Admur rules that there is only **4** Mil between Alos and sunrise, hence there is only 96 minutes between Alos and sunrise. As well, although in 459:10 Admur rules that the day begins from sunrise and ends by sunset, in 89:1 he rules that it begins from Alos until nightfall. Nevertheless, the final ruling of Admur follows the ruling of the Siddur in which Admur rules like in 459:10.]

Other opinions amongst Chabad Rabbanim: See article of Rav Raskin in Siddur Miluim 27, and Rav Sangwai in Habracha, for a summary of opinions of Chabad Rabbanim regarding the time of Alos Hashachar according to Admur. The opinions vary between 120 minutes, 72 minutes, 90 minutes and 96 minutes.

Opinion of three hours before sunrise: In Tanya, Igeres Hateshuva 3, Admur writes that one may eat up to three hours before sunrise, of a penitential fast. This implies that by a fast day one is to begin fasting even before Alos, when 1:3rd of the night has entered. [See Igros Kodesh 18:557] It requires further analysis however if this applies to all fasts, or just a penitential fast. [Sefer Haminhagim p. 45] However, from Admur in Siddur by Sefiras Haomer, it is implied that one may eat on a fast day up until Alos. [Hiskashrus 424:18 footnote 113] Likewise, Rav Groner states that he heard clearly from the Rebbe that the three hours is only applicable by a penitential fast. [Hiskashrus] However in Sichos Kodesh 2:494 the Rebbe mentioned a scrupulousness to begin the fast some time before Alos Hashachar. Vetzaruch Iyun.

[937] Definition of fluctuating hours: Fluctuating hours means that the hours fluctuate in the winter and summer. Some Poskim rule this means it fluctuates in terms of Zmaniyos, meaning that it depends on the number of hours in the day. Thus, in the summer, the hours will be longer [between 120-150 minutes for two hours] while in the winter they will be shorter [between 90-120 minutes for two hours]. [So rules Minchas Cohen 2:6; Rama 233; Peri Chadash 58] However the Alter Rebbe and Gr"a both rule that it follows not the amount of hours in the day but rather the degree of distance of the sun from the horizon. [Admur in Seder Hachnasas Shabbos; Gr"a in 261; See Shut Mahrshag 2:34 quoted in Piskeiy

understood by many to be the opinion of Admur. This latter opinion means to say that the fast begins when the sun is 26 degrees below the horizon, and it does not refer to 120 Zmaniyos minutes.[938] [Practically, those who follow the rulings of Admur, are to be stringent like all opinions[939], and so is the widespread Chabad custom in Eretz Yisrael. Thus, regarding a fast day, one is to be stringent to consider Alos Hashachar to begin approximately two fluctuating hours prior to sunrise. Accordingly, even if one was awake the entire night, or went to sleep on condition to wake up before Alos to eat/drink, he must stop eating and drinking two fluctuating hours before sunrise. Being that different calendars follow different opinions regarding the definition of Alos, it is imperative that by a fast day, one look at a calendar which shows the time of Alos in accordance to the ruling of Admur, which is 2 fluctuating hours before Alos. [The correct time according to Admur can be found in Luach Kolel Chabad, Hiskashrus, Chabad Dvar Malchus, Luach of Rav Sangwai[940] and **certain** Chabad websites. The time of Alos for a fast day found on Chabad.org does not follow the above understanding of Admur and should not be relied upon for those who follow the stringent understanding, as is accepted in Eretz Hakodesh. However, the Hebrew Chabad.org.il contains the accurate times.]

63. The secret fast day of the 9th of Teves and its uncovering of the origin of Christianity:[941]

The Shulchan Aruch lists a number of days in which it is customary to fast due to tragedies that occurred on that day. Amongst the list of days in which tragedies occurred, and is hence proper to fast on, is the 9th of Teves. [Practically, it is no longer customary to fast on these days, and thus we no longer fast on the 9th of Teves.[942] Nonetheless, below we will explore the background behind this fast and its meaning.]

What happened on this day? We do not know what tragedy occurred on this day.[943] [Some Poskim[944], however, write that in truth Ezra Hasofer passed away on this day, as written in the Selichos[945] of Asara B'Teves. In addition, some say that also Nechemia Ben Chakilia passed away on this day.[946] They thus

---

Teshuvos 89:2 footnote 59 that this is the way we rule.] Thus, those who hold that Alos is 72 minutes it ends up being in Tishrei and Nissan 16.1 degrees from the horizon and the amount of time it takes the sun to travel to the horizon fluctuates between winter and summer. [See Piskeiy Teshuvos 89:2] According to Admur however who holds of 120 minutes, this would be when the sun is 26 degrees below the horizon.
Other opinions: Some Poskim rule we always measure the hours as set hours and hence there will always be only 120:90:72 minutes between Alos and sunrise at all times. [Admur 89:1; Birkeiy Yosef 261:1; Peri Megadim 261 A"A 9; Derech Hachaim; Siddur Yaavetz; Machatzis Hashekel 235:3]
[938] See the previous footnote
[939] Shiureiy Tziyon ibid; It is important to note that there are Chabad Rabbanim who take a different approach in their understanding of the opinion of Admur, and each person is to follow his Rav. [See opinions of other Chabad Rabbanim in previous footnotes.] Those, who do not necessarily follow the rulings of Admur, should speak to his Rav for a final ruling regarding this matter, and which time, and calendar he should follow.
[940] https://sites.google.com/site/zmanimadmorhazaken.israel
[941] Michaber 580:1-2; Tur 580; Kol Bo 63; Bahag [900's; times of Geonim] Hilchos Tishe Beav Vetaanis 39; M"A 580:1 in name of the Tanya, in name of the Geonim, and Shibulei Haleket; Megillas Taanis [written by the Tanaaim], brought in M"A ibid and Gr"a; Shlah p. 201, brought in Kaf Hachaim 580:2
Who established these fasts? See M"A 580:1 in name of the Tanya, in name of the Geonim, and Shibulei Haleket that we do not know who established these fast days and so writes Beis Yosef 580. However, the M"A ibid concludes that he found them written in Megillas Taanis, hence proving that it was established in the times of the Tanaaim
[942] Beis Yosef 580 "I have never seen anyone fast on these days and I have also not heard of anyone doing so"
Background and other opinions: The Bahag and Tur ibid write these fasts are Biblical, however the Beis Yosef 580:1 explains that this is not to be taken literally, and rather it means to say that it is Rabbinical but should be treated as if it were Biblical. The Beis Yosef concludes that *"I have never seen anyone fast on these days and I have also not heard of anyone doing so. In truth these fasts are a great wonderment, and I wonder at who established them, as some were established even on Rosh Chodesh"*; The Michaber 580:1 simply records that it is proper to fast on this day and does not write it as an obligation; The M"A 580:1 writes in name of the Tanya, in name of the Geonim, and Shibulei Haleket that we do not know who established these fast days. Nonetheless, the M"A concludes that since he has read the lists of these fasts in Megillas Taanis, and also the Bahag [of whose words are all Divrei Kabbalah], therefore it must have been written in the times of the Tanaaim and every Baal Nefesh is to be stringent to fast on these days if he is able. Practically, we no longer fast on these days
[943] Michaber 580:2 "On the 9th of Teves we do not know what Tzara happened"; Tur 580 and Bahag ibid "The Sages did not write what happened"; Orchos Chaim "On the 9th the Sages did not write what happened, and it remains a secret."; Birkeiy Yosef
[944] Taz 580:1; M"A 580:6; Perisha 580:6; Beir Hagoleh 580 and Elya Raba 580:5 in name of Kol Bo; Bahag ibid, brought in P"M 580 M"Z 1; Orchos Chaim
Passing of Rav Yosef Hanaggid: In the Sefer Kabbalah of the Raavad, it is written that on the 9th of Teves Rav Yosef Halevi Hanaggid, the son of Rav Shmuel Hanaggid, was killed. Together with him the entire congregation of Graneda and many other Jews were killed. [See Hagahos Baruch Frankel 580]
[945] So is written in the first Piyut of Selichos of Asara Beteves " זועמתי בתשעה בו [בחודש טבת] בכלמה וחפר, חשך מעלי מעיל הוד וצפר טרוף טורף בו הנותן אמרי שפר, הוא עזרא הסופר"
[946] Bahag ibid, brought in P"M ibid; Orchos Chaim

question the above assertion that the tragedy of the day is unknown.[947] The Poskim[948], however, explain that although Ezra Hasofer did pass away on the 9th of Teves, an additional tragedy also occurred on this day for which the fast was established, and it is this tragedy that is left unknown. We will now explore what secret tragedy could the Sages have been referring to.]

What secret tragedy occurred? While the above asserted tragedy was kept hidden, as stated above, we do find some revelation amongst Sefarim as to what occurred, and the reason it was kept secret is blatantly obvious, to shield the Jewish people from the wrath of the Christians, as we will now see. Some Poskim[949] write that the secret tragedy that happened on this day is that on this day Oso Ish [Yoshka] was born. Other Poskim[950] write that on this day Shimon Kippa passed away. Shimon Kippa, also known as Shimon Hakalfus, was none other than Peter, who was the first Bishop/Pope of Rome of which all the other popes are considered his heirs. This Shimon Kippa who became the founder of Christian theology after the passing of Yoshka, was in truth a hidden Tzadik, who helped sway Christianity away from Judaism and make it unattractive to Jews. He also helped save the Jewish people from persecution from the Christians, and hence the Sages established this day, which is the day of his death, as a fast day for the scrupulous, in commemoration of his passing.[951]

---------Rosh Hashanah---------

64. From what age may a boy/Bochur blow Shofar for others on Rosh Hashanah?

A. Background:

[Biblically[952]], one can only be Motzi another in a Mitzvah if he is of equal, or greater, level obligation as the person who is being Yotzei with him. Thus, in order for one who is Biblically obligated in a Mitzvah to be Yotzei with another person's performance of the Mitzvah, that other person must likewise be Biblically obligated in the general Mitzvah [whether that person is currently obligated or not[953]].[954] This applies likewise to the Mitzvah of Shofar, (as although the main Mitzvah of hearing[955] Shofar is merely to hear the sound, nevertheless[956]) if the blower is exempt from the Mitzvah then he cannot fulfill the obligation on behalf of others through blowing for them.[957] Based on this, it is clear that a child who is not yet of age of Mitzvos cannot be Motzi an adult for a Mitzvah, as the child is only obligated in it due to

---

[947] Taz ibid concludes "Vetzaruch Iyun Rav"

[948] Birkeiy Yosef 580 based on Rishonim brought next; See Kol Bo and Bahag ibid who writes *"The Sages did not tell us what happened, and [in addition it happens to be that] on that day died Ezra Hakohen and Nechemia Ben Chakilia"*; See also Orchos Chaim *"On the 9th the Sages did not write what happened, and it remains a secret, and on this day died Ezra Hakohen and Nechemia Ben Chakilia"* The wording of all these Rishonim imply that the death of Ezra and Nechemia is in addition to the main reason of establishment, and the Sages did not write what actually happened and it is left a mystery.

[949] Hagahos of Tosafos Yisheinim in name of Gadol Echad, brought in the Hosafos of some editions of the Shulchan Aruch on chapter 580 [Machon Yerushalayim-Friedman edition] removed from regular editions due to censorship of the church

[950] Hagahos Baruch Frankel on 580 *"I found in a manuscript that on the 9th of Teves Shimon Hakalfus, who helped save the Jewish people from a great tragedy in the times of the Peritzim, died and the Sages established it as a day of fasting in Jerusalem"*; See Sefer Toldos Yeshu *"Shimon Hakalfus passed away and the Jewish people mourned his passing and they established his day of death as an annual fast day. **This day was the 9th of Teves**"*; Accordingly, the words of Toldos Yeshu and Baruch Frankel reveal the secret that on this day Shimon Hakalfus died.

[951] See Sefer Chassidim 191 [Mosad Rav Kook-censored from some versions] *"Even a Tzaddik who they make into a deity it is a Mitzvah to call a derogatory name, for example Shimon Kipah should be called Peter Chamur"*; See Rashi Avoda Zara 10a which was censored and brought in Dikdukei Sofrim Avoda Zara p. 12 footnote 9 *"The Gemara states that all the writings and language of the nations is not from them. This means as follows: All of their books of heresy Yochanon Paulus [Paul] and Petrus which were Jews wrote. They purposely infected their culture in order to sway the Christian faith away from Judaism. They themselves were not heretics and did so for the benefit of the Jewish people, as written in the book Teliya Yeshu"* Seemingly this refers to the book Toldos Yeshu, which brings the history of Yeshu from a Jewish perspective and writes how Peter infiltrated the ranks of Yeshu and turned away Christianity from being a threat to Judaism. Peter was appointed by the Sages to do so. For the full story in all details see: Sefer Toldos Yeshu [dating back to at least times of Rashi]; Beis Hamidrash vol. 5:60 and vol. 6 [1860; Likkut of old Midrashim] Midrash brought in Otzer Hamidrashim p. 557 [1920, by Rav Y.D. Eizanshtein]

[952] Sdei Chemed Mareches Rosh Hashanah in name of Beis Menucha, brought in gloss on Alef Hamagen 589:7

[953] Meaning, that if one is ideally Biblically obligated, then even if he already fulfilled his obligation, or is not ready to fulfill it yet, he may still be Motzi another. Thus, a man may blow Shofar for another man even if he was already Yotzei, or plans to do so later on. [Admur 591:1; Michaber 591:1; M"B 594:1; Kaf Hachaim 589:1]

[954] Admur 588:6 regarding Shofar; 37:3; 39:1 regarding Tefillin; 55:6; 128:49; 199:9 regarding Birchas Hamazon; 271:7; M"A 271:2; M"B 271:3; Rav Poalim 1:10; Kaf Hachaim 271:9

The reason: Since Hashem does not desire this person himself to perform the command, how can he fulfill the command on behalf of others. [Levush 589; Kaf Hachaim 589:2]

[955] The Kuntrus Hashulchan states that in truth this word should read "blowing Shofar".

[956] Parentheses is in original.

[957] Admur 588:6; Michaber 589:1

Chinuch, while the adult is fully obligated in it either Biblically or Rabbinically.[958] Now, when does a child reach the age of Mitzvos and become Biblically obligated in the commands to be able to be Motzi other adults? Only if the child is above Bar/Bas Mitzvah and has reached puberty through the growth of two pubic hairs.[959] Now, what does one do if he knows the child is Bar Mitzvah but does not know if the child has indeed reached this stage of development? Can he be Yotzei with him anyways or not? So if the boy has already grown a nice amount of facial hair, or is above age 18, it is assumed that he is fully developed, and he may therefore be Motzi others in all Mitzvos just as any other adult.[960] If, however he is below age 18, and has not yet grown facial hair to this extent, then he maintains a questionable status of which the ruling is that he may be Motzi others for a Rabbinical command, but cannot be Motzi others for a Biblical command.[961] With that said, we will now analyze the law regarding if such a boy may blow Shofar for others on Rosh Hashanah.

B. The law:
The law on the first day of Rosh Hashanah: Men are **Biblically** obligated to hear Shofar on the first day of Rosh Hashanah.[962] Accordingly, on the first day of Rosh Hashanah a man cannot be Yotzei the blowing of Shofar with the blowing of another man unless that man is verified to have developed the signs of puberty [i.e. above age 18, or has grown a nice amount of facial hair, or one knows that he has grown two pubic hairs].[963] [If he already did so, he must rehear the Shofar blowing, without a blessing.[964]]
The law on the second day of Rosh Hashanah: Men are **Rabbinically** obligated to hear Shofar on the second day of Rosh Hashanah.[965] Accordingly, on the second day of Rosh Hashanah a man may be Yotzei the blowing of Shofar with the blowing of a boy above Bar Mitzvah even if the boy is under age 18 and has not begun to grow facial hair.[966] Nonetheless, initially, it is proper to be Yotzei the Shofar of even the second day through a man that is above age 18 or has grown facial hair.[967]
Blowing for women: Although some Poskim[968] rule that a child may not blow Shofar for a woman even if he has reached the age of Chinuch, nevertheless, seemingly, if he is above the age of Bar Mitzvah, he may do so even on the first day of Rosh Hashanah, even if he is under 18 and has not grown facial hair.[969] Practically, this should only be done if a man above 18 or with facial hair is unable to blow for her.

> **Summary:**
> On the first day of Rosh Hashanah, a man cannot be Yotzei the blowing of Shofar with the blowing of another man unless that man is above age 18 or has grown a nice amount of facial hair. On the second day of Rosh Hashanah, a man may be Yotzei the blowing of Shofar with the blowing of a boy above

---

[958] See regarding if both are Chad Derabanon and if the child is potentially Chad Derabanon: Admur 186:3; Degul Merivava 271; Rav Akiva Eiger Teshuvah 7; Derech Hachaim ibid; M"B 271:2; Chayeh Adam 5:23, brought in Shaar Hatziyon 271:2; Shaar Hatziyon 271:2 and 4; Kaf Hachaim 271:9
[959] All Poskim ibid; See Michaber E.H. 155:15 regarding Miun and 169:10 regarding Chalitza
[960] Facial hair: M"A 271:2; Admur 199:9; Michaber E.H. 169:9 regarding Chalitza; C.M. 35; M"B 271:3; Shaar Hatziyon 271:5
Age 18: Admur 39:1; M"A 39:1; See Miasef Lekol Hamachanos 39:7; Chikrei Halachos 5:62; Yagdil Torah N.Y. 8:44
[961] See Admur 55:6 regarding Minyan [Rabbinical]; 199:9 regarding Zimun [Rabbinical]; 271:7 regarding Kiddush [Biblical]; 37:3 and 39:1 regarding Tefillin [Biblical]; Rama 55:5; Maharik 49
The reason: As by a Biblical command, one of questionable obligation cannot be Motzi one of certain Biblical obligation. [Admur 271:7] However, by a Rabbinical obligation, we rely on the Chazaka of Rava [Nida 46a] that a child above Bar/Bas Mitzvah has grown two pubic hairs, even if this has yet to be verified. [Admur 55:6 and Poskim ibid] Some Poskim rule that the above invalidation for Biblical Mitzvos is only Rabbinical, however, Biblically, we apply Chazaka Derava even by Biblical commands. [Heard from Rav Yaakov Yosef z"l]
[962] Admur 585:6; 588:6; 592:3-4, 7; 595:1-2
[963] Mateh Efraim 589:7; Shoel Umeishiv 3:177; M"B 589:2; Sdei Chemed Mareches Rosh Hashanah 2:5; Nitei Gavriel 48:16; Rav Yaakov Yosef
[964] A blessing should not be repeated as perhaps the boy has indeed reached the age of development unbeknownst to him. Vetzaruch Iyun.
[965] Admur 585:6
[966] See Poskim ibid in introduction; Shoel Umeishiv ibid regarding Tekios Meumad; Mateh Efraim 589:7 regarding if not possible to get another adult
[967] Mateh Efraim ibid; Poskim in Nitei Gavriel ibid
[968] Tiferes Yisrael R"H 3:8
[969] The reason: As women are not Biblically or even Rabbinically obligated to hear Shofar, and do so simply due to the custom. Vetzaruch Iyun, as perhaps the custom to accept the Mitzvah on the first day is to fulfill it under Biblical standards, and a Neder has the status of a Biblical command.

Bar Mitzvah even if the boy is under age 18 and has not begun to grow facial hair. Nonetheless, initially, it is proper to be Yotzei the Shofar of even the second day through a man who is above age 18 or has grown facial hair.

Directives for appointing a Baal Tokeia:
Based on the above, a community or Shul may not appoint as a Baal Tokeia a boy who is below age 18 and has yet to grow a substantial amount of facial hair. Preferably, this applies for even the second day of Rosh Hashanah.

Directives for Mivtzaim:
When performing Mivtzah Shofar on Rosh Hashanah, precedence should always be given to a Bochur above age 18 or with facial hair, to perform the blowing. This applies on both days of Rosh Hashanah, but especially applies on the first day when blowing for men. Thus, it is proper for those below age 18 or without facial hair to partner up with one above 18 or with facial hair, who can blow the Shofar. If this is not possible, then so long as one is over Bar Mitzvah, he may blow Shofar on the second day of Rosh Hashanah, and blow Shofar for woman on the first day of Rosh Hashanah. Furthermore, if the boy in truth knows that he has developed the growth of two pubic hairs, he may blow Shofar for men on even the first day of Rosh Hashanah, if there is no other choice available and they would not hear Shofar otherwise.[970] He should not be discouraged from doing so, and meriting other Jews with this great Mitzvah.

65. May one eat garlic on Rosh Hashanah?

Background: Customarily, just as certain foods are eaten on Rosh Hashanah to serve as a good omen for the coming year[971], so too certain foods are avoided due to them containing a negative component. Thus, it is customary not to eat nuts[972], or sour [or bitter[973]] foods on Rosh Hashanah.[974] Now, the question is asked whether garlic contains any negative component for which it should be avoided on Rosh Hashanah. The following is the ruling:

The law: Some are accustomed not to eat garlic on Rosh Hashanah.[975] Others[976] however are not particular in this matter. Each person and community are to follow their custom.

---

[970] The reason: As seemingly, the entire law of verifying the growth of two hairs by a Biblical command is for the person to initially be Yotzei, if however, in truth the boy has two hairs, then even if this was unbeknownst to the person, he is Yotzei Bedieved, in the eyes of Heaven, as in truth the boy is an adult! Now, although it's possible to learn that until testimony is given regarding his development, he is considered a child even in the eyes of heaven regarding another person, since it is customary for all Jewry to immerse in a Mikveh on Erev Rosh Hashanah, certainly testimony exists, and hence the man is Yotzei with him Bedieved. Accordingly, in Mivtzaim when dealing with an unobservant crowd who would not hear Shofar otherwise, one below age 18 who does not have facial hair should not be discouraged from blowing for other Jews, if they would not hear Shofar otherwise!

[971] Admur 583:1-5; Michaber 583:1; The Talmudic source of the Simanim is found in Gemara Horiyos 12a. The Gemara mentions the following Simanim: Kara Rubya; Karty; Silka; Tamri. It does not mention the apple, ram, or fish.

[972] Admur 583:6; Rama 583:2 "*Some do not to eat Egozim as it is the Gematria of sin and causes saliva*"; Darkei Moshe 589:3 in name of Maharil
Other opinions: There were some Poskim who did not avoid eating nuts, as well as other foods that increase seed. [Darkei Moshe 583:1 in name of Kol Bo; Kaf Hachaim 583:26]

[973] M"E 583:3; Kaf Hachaim ibid; Piskeiy Teshuvos 583:5

[974] Admur 583:2; Teshuvos Hageonim 114 brought in Kaf Hachaim 583:18

[975] Implication of Tashbatz 118 and Kol Bo 64 [29a] and Darkei Moshe 583:1 that some were accustomed to avoiding garlic just as they avoid nuts; Ketzei Hamateh 583:17; Piskeiy Teshuvos 583:8
The reason: As garlic increase one's seed and since relations are abstained on Rosh Hashanah therefore these foods are to be avoided. [Implication of Elya Raba 583; See Admur 608:8 regarding Erev Yom Kippur]

[976] Tashbatz 118 and Kol Bo 64 [29a] in name of Maharam, brought in Darkei Moshe 583:1; Kaf Hachaim 583:26

------------------- *Yom Kippur* -------------------

66. May one use Maaser money for Kaparos on Erev Yom Kippur?

Background: It is disputed in Poskim[977] as to whether one may use Maaser money for the sake of a Mitzvah, or if it must be given as charity to paupers. Practically, it is permitted to use Maaser money for the sake of a Mitzvah under certain conditions.[978] These conditions are as follows: a) The Mitzvah is not an obligation for one to fulfill, and rather is voluntary[979]; b) One is unable to afford the voluntary Mitzvah and hence would abstain from doing so unless he uses his Maaser funds.[980] Now, although Kaparos is merely a custom rather than a Biblical or Rabbinical institution, nonetheless, this custom receives an obligatory status. Thus, ideally Maaser money cannot be used for the fulfillment of this custom of Kaparos. However, it is disputed amongst the Poskim as to whether one must to take a single chicken per family member, or if a single male chicken suffices for all the male family members, and a single female chicken for all female family members.[981] The final ruling follows that one is to take one chicken per family member[982], although if one is unable to afford to do so, then one male chicken may be used for all the male members of one's household and one female chicken may be used for all the female members of one's household.[983] Based on this, the following is the final ruling regarding using Maaser money to purchase Kaparos:

The law: One may not use Maaser money to perform the Mitzvah of Kaparos.[984] If, however, one cannot afford to buy one chicken per family member, then he may use Maaser money to do so. However, even in such a case, at least one male and female chicken is not to come from the Maaser funds.[985]

67. May one take medicine on Yom Kippur?[986]

One who is currently sick: On Yom Kippur, if one is bedridden, or feels ill/weak in his entire body, then he may swallow **a tasteless or bitter** pill [without water, as will be explained].[987] If the pill has a non-bitter taste, then he is to wrap it in a precut tissue [as one may not cut it on Shabbos or Yom Kippur] and

---

[977] Stringent opinion-Must give to pauper: Rama Y.D. 249:1 "One is not to use his Maaser money for a Mitzvah, such as to donate candles to a Shul or other Devar Mitzvah, and rather the money is to be given to paupers"; Maharil Rosh Hashanah and Teshuvah 56; See Beir Goleh ibid who explains that the Rama refers to a Mitzvah that one already obligated himself to pay, and on this he can't use Maaser money, however in general he agrees with the Maharam that Maaser may be used for a Mitzvah, and hence there is no dispute. [Pischeiy Teshuvah 249:2] So can also be implied from Taz 249:1 that there is no dispute. [See Tzedakah Umishpat 6 footnote 7] However, see Chasam Sofer 231[brought in Pischeiy Teshuva ibid and Ahavas Chesed 18:2] who negates this explanation and states that according to Rama:Maharil it is always forbidden to sue it for a Mitzvah, and so explains Rebbe in Toras Menachem 34:272.
Lenient opinion-May use for Mitzvah: Shach 249:3; Taz 249:1; Maharshal; Derisha 249:1; Maharam Menachem 459; Admur Hilchos Talmud Torah 1:7 regarding using Maaser to pay tuition of Talmud Torah; Admur Seder Birchas Hanehnin 12:9 "The Maaser of the son may be used for other Mitzvos"

[978] Admur Hilchos Talmud Torah 1:7 regarding using Maaser to pay tuition of Talmud Torah; Admur Seder Birchas Hanehnin 12:9 "The Maaser of the son may be used for other Mitzvos"; Likkutei Sichos 9:346; Toras Menachem 34:272 [brought in Shulchan Menachem 5:110]

[979] Beir Hagoleh ibid [in explanation of opinion of Rama ibid]; Chasam Sofer 231, Pischeiy Teshuvah 249:2

[980] Shach 249:3; Taz 249:1; Maharshal; Derisha 249:1; Maharam Menachem 459; Admur Hilchos Talmud Torah 1:7 regarding using Maaser to pay tuition; Toras Menachem 34:272 [brought in Shulchan Menachem 5:110]

[981] In the Shulchan Aruch 605:3 Admur records a difference in custom and rules as follows: Some [Levush brought in M"A 605:2] are accustomed to take a single male chicken on behalf of all the male members of the family and a single female chicken on behalf of all the female members of the family. Others [Poskim ibid] however are accustomed to take a Kapara chicken for each individual family member.

[982] Siddur Admur; Second custom in Admur 605:3; Custom of the Arizal brought in Shaar Hakavanos and Peri Eitz Chaim Shaar Yom Kippurim; M"A 605:2; Shelah Yuma 235; Elya Zuta 605:4; Tashbatz 125; Bach in name of Mordechai Katan; Mateh Efraim 605:2; see Piskeiy Teshuvos 605:1

[983] Mateh Efraim 605:2; M"B 605:3

[984] Elya Raba 605:6 in name of Shlah; Mateh Efraim 605:10; M"B 605:6 that one should not use Maaser money to redeem the chickens

[985] Piskeiy Teshuvos 605 footnote 4; See regarding Matanos Laevyonim: M"A 694:1 from Shlah 260b; Maharil 56; Elya Raba 686:4; M"B 694:3; Aruch Hashulchan 694:2

[986] See Sdei Chemed Yom Kippur 3:8; Yeshuos Yaakov 612; Kesav Sofer 111; Pischeiy Teshuvah Y.D. 155:6; Shoel Umeishiv Mahdura Daled 1:55; Orchos Chaim 618:1; Eretz Tzevi 88; Kaf Hachaim 554:34 in name of in name of Kesonos Yosef 4, Ikarei Hadaat 29:36, Pischei Olam 554:6 regarding regular fast days; Igros Moshe 3:91; Tzitz Eliezer 10:25; SSH"K 39:8; Nishmas Avraham 612:7; Piskeiy Teshuvos 612:2; Nitei Gavriel 37:23; 39:12-15

[987] Poskim ibid

The reason: One who is bedridden, or weak in his entire body has the Halachic definition of a Choleh Sheiyn Bo Sakana, of which we rule that the Rabbinical prohibitions against taking medicine on Shabbos, and against eating Rabbinical prohibited foods, is lifted. Thus, being that swallowing a bitter pill is only Rabbinically forbidden on Yom Kippur, as it is not a food, and is not being eaten in the normal method, it therefore may be swallowed by an ill person. [ibid]

swallow it with the tissue.[988] This allowance applies even if the illness does not involve danger. If, however one is not bedridden, and does not feel ill in his entire body, then he may not take medication, even if he is in pain, such as he is suffering from a headache and the like.[989]

One who is not currently sick but suffers from a medical condition: Those who are not sick but suffer from a medical condition which requires a daily dose of medication, are to verify with their doctor if they can fast, and skip the dose on Yom Kippur, without any health risks involved. In the event that the doctor states that skipping the medicine can lead to medical complications that can lead to a life-threatening situation, then he must take the pill even on Yom Kippur.[990] If swallowing the pill in one of the above-mentioned methods is not possible, one may swallow it with water.[991]

How to take the pill: One who is permitted to take a pill on Yom Kippur, as stated above, must swallow the pill plain, without water, and if the pill has a non-bitter taste, he is to swallow it in a precut piece of tissue. He may not swallow the pill with water, unless the illness poses a danger of life and he cannot manage to swallow it without the water.[992] Alternatively, some Poskim[993] suggest that before Yom Kippur, one can crush the **bitter** pill into powder, add it to the water, and then drink the **bitter** mixture. This applies even if one's illness does not pose any danger of life.

------------------Sukkos-----------------

68. Entering pots into a Sukkah:[994]

[It is permitted to enter pots and pans of food into a Sukkah for the sake of serving the foods.[995]] Nonetheless, once the meal has been completed, one is to remove the pots, pans, and plates from the Sukkah, being that after their use they are considered repulsive [and it is belittling to the Sukkah to have them remain]. [According to some opinions[996], leaving dirty pots and plates in a Sukkah can invalidate the Sukkah, and it is hence to be removed immediately after the meal is completed.[997] The above allowance to initially bring pots of food into a Sukkah is from the letter of the law, however, many Poskim[998] record that the custom is not to enter pots and pans of food into a Sukkah at all even for the purpose of serving the food, and rather the food is to be brought in a serving dish a tray.[999] However, if there are no plates available, and one needs to eat directly from the pot, then one may enter it into the Sukkah.[1000]]

---

[988] Rav SZ"A in SSH"K ibid; Nishmas Avraham ibid; Piskeiy Teshuvos ibid

[989] Piskeiy Teshuvos ibid; Nitei Gavriel ibid

The reason: This is due to two prohibitions 1) The prohibition against eating, which Rabbinically includes even bitter and inedible foods. 2) The prohibition against taking medication on Shabbos and Yom Kippur.

[990] Igros Moshe ibid based on ruling of Rav Akiva Eiger

The reason: As we view a potential life-threatening illness that can come as a result of not eating, or not taking medicine, as a life-threatening situation, for which one can break his fast on Yom Kippur. [ibid]

[991] Igros Moshe ibid

[992] Igros Moshe ibid; SSH"K ibid; Nishmas Avraham ibid; Piskeiy Teshuvos ibid

[993] See Kaf Hachaim 554:34 in name of Poskim regarding Tisha B'av; Heard from Rav Yaakov Yosef that the same applies on Yom Kippur, and so seems Pashut; SSH"K ibid; Piskeiy Teshuvos ibid; Nitei Gavriel ibid

[994] Admur 639:2; Michaber 639:1; Rambam 6:5; Sukkah 29a; See also Michaber 666:1

[995] Implication of Admur ibid; Michaber ibid, as brought in M"A 639:3; Machatzis Hashekel 639:3; P"M 639 A"A 3

Other opinions: Some Poskim rule one may not enter pots into a Sukkah even for the purpose of serving food. [Opinion in Beis Yosef 639 in name of Mordechai, brought in Machatzis Hashekel 639; Birkeiy Yosef 639:2 in name of Rabbanei Izmor, brought in Shaareiy Teshuvah 639:3 and Kaf Hachaim 639:18; Merkeves Hamishneh Sukkah 6]

[996] Raavad Tamim Deim 241 in understanding of Rif; Ritva Sukkah ibid; Erech Hashulchan 639:2; Chayeh Adam 147:2 that the Sukkah is Rabbinically invalid so long as the dirty vessels remain, and one may not say a blessing of Leisheiv Basukkah; Kaf Hachaim 639:16; See Michaber 666:1 that one is to enter dirty pots into the Sukkah to show that it is Pasul. However, see Kaf Hachaim 666:12 who implies from the Michaber ibid that on the contrary it's just a Heker and does not actually invalidate it.

Other opinions: Some Poskim completely negate the above opinion that states dirty plates can invalidate a Sukkah. [Bach 639; Ran and Ramban on Rif end of Sukkah, brought in Kaf Hachaim 666:12]

[997] Kaf Hachaim 639:16

[998] M"A 639:3; Machatzis Hashekel ibid; Chayeh Adam 147:2; Derech Hachaim 1; Aruch Hashulchan 639:2; M"B 639:5; Kaf Hachaim 639:17

Other opinions: Some Poskim rule one may enter pots into a Sukkah for the purpose of serving food, and negate the ruling of the Poskim ibid. [Machatzis Hashekel 639; implication of Admur who omitted the ruling of the M"A ibid] Others suggest that the above ruling only applies to those who throughout the year never bring pots to the dining room table and only serve the food on plates. [P"M 639 A"A 3]

[999] The reason: As doing so is considered belittling to the Sukkah. [P"M ibid] Alternatively, it is because one is to live in the Sukkah as he does at home, and in one's home, the pots are not brought to the table. [Machatzis Hashekel ibid]

[1000] Chayeh Adam 147:2; M"B 639:5; Kaf Hachaim 639:17

> **Summary:**
> It is permitted from the letter of the law to enter pots of food into one's Sukkah for the sake of serving the food, although the custom is to avoid doing so. In all cases in which one is lenient, one is to be careful to remove the pots right away, as soon as the meal concludes.

69. Aravos-The Kashrus status of an Arava with missing leaves:[1001]

Bedieved-Letter of law: If majority of the leaves of an Arava branch have fallen off, then the Arava is Pasul/invalid.[1002] One must be very careful regarding this matter, as it occurs that upon inserting the Aravos into the [binding of the] Lulav, and likewise upon shaking the Lulav, that leaves fall off.[1003] [It is thus advisable to check the Aravos daily to verify they still contain majority leaves. Likewise, it is advised to purchase a number of sets of Aravos on Erev Sukkos, which can be used in a case of need throughout Sukkos. When replacing the Aravos, one is not to stick the new Aravos into the knot of the Lulav, which can cause its leaves to fall out, and rather one is to undo the knots and then place the new Aravos inside.[1004]] If only minority of the leaves fell off, the Arava is valid.[1005]

Lechatchila-Mitzvah Min Hamuvchar:[1006] It is a Mitzvah Min Hamuvchar to take an Arava branch which contains all its leaves. Thus, although a majority leaved Arava is valid, as explained above, nevertheless, Lechatchila one is not to take such an Arava if finding a fully leaved Arava of which none of its leaves fell off, is easily attainable.

> **Summary:**
> It is a Mitzvah Min Hamuvchar to use a fully leaved Arava branch of which none of its leaves have fallen off. However, from the letter of the law, the Arava branch remains Kosher so long as majority of its leaves remain intact.
>
> **Q&A**
>
> **Must majority of the Shiur [i.e. 24 cm] of the Arava contain leaves, or majority of the entire branch?**[1007]
>
> ➢ Example: If the Arava is seven Tefachim long and is majority/fully leaved within its Shiur of three Tefachim, but is not leaved for the remaining four Tefachim, what is the law?
>
> We follow majority of the Shiur of 24 centimeters and not majority of the branch, and hence in the above case the Arava remains Kosher.
>
> **If the Arava was originally Kosher, and the leaves fell off as a result of the shaking, does the Arava become invalid?**
> The Arava is invalid if majority of its leaves fell off as a result of the shaking.[1008] However, some Poskim[1009] suggest that the invalidation of an Arava due to the falling of its leaves is only in the event that one did not yet fulfill the Mitzvah with it. If, however, one already fulfilled the Mitzvah of Daled

---

[1001] Admur 647:5
[1002] Admur ibid; Michaber 647:2; Tur 647; Mishneh Sukkah 33b as understands Rosh Sukkah 3:13
The reason: As it is no longer considered Hadar. [ibid]
[1003] Admur ibid; M"A 647:1; Elya Raba 651:6
[1004] Bikureiy Yaakov 654:4; M"B 654:4
[1005] Admur ibid; Michaber 647:3; Mishneh ibid
[1006] Admur ibid; M"A 647:3 in implication of Michaber 647:2 that Lechatchila one should not use such an Arava; Machatzis Hashekel ibid; Kaf Hachaim 647:19; Alef Hamagen 647:13; Nitei Gavriel 22:2
Other opinions: Some Poskim rule the Arava is Kosher even initially if it is only missing minority of leaves. [Elya Raba 647:6, brought in Machatzis Hashekel ibid; Bikureiy Yaakov 647:9; Chaim Ubracha 223; See Nitei Gavriel 22:2]
[1007] Zechor Leavraham 6 Lulav; Mishnas Yaakov 647; Nitei Gavriel 22:4; See Admur 646:3 regarding the Hadas that the majority Meshulash leaves are only required within their Shiur of 24 cm!
[1008] Admur ibid and M"A ibid "And likewise through the shaking"; Setimas Kol Haposkim; See also Admur 649:18 and Michaber 649:5
[1009] Hisorerus Teshuvah 3

> Minim with this Arava, such as on the 1st day of Sukkos, then it remains Kosher throughout Chol Hamoed even if the leaves fall off due to the shaking.[1010] Based on this suggestion, we can justify the custom of many to not bother to inspect the validity of the Aravos and its state of intact leaves throughout Chol Hamoed. Practically, one is to not rely on this approach, and is to perform a daily inspection of his Arava prior to doing the Mitzvah in order to verify its Kashrus state and that majority of its leaves have not fallen off.[1011]
>
> **Directives for Mivtzaim:**
> Those fulfilling the great and holy Mitzvah, and directive of the Rebbe, to merit other Jews with the shaking of Daled Minim, must be very careful to periodically verify throughout the day that their Aravos remain intact with majority of leaves. This especially applies when people shake the Lulav very forcefully. A number of sets of Aravos should be brought with the person so he can change the branches as deemed necessary.

---------------Chanukah----------------

70. May one make/use a Menorah of seven branches?[1012]

It is [Biblically[1013]] forbidden to make a Menorah which resembles the Menorah in the Temple, [and is valid for use in the Temple[1014]]. Accordingly, one may not make a Menorah of seven branches, but rather of 5, or 6, or 8 branches.[1015] This prohibition to make a seven branch Menorah applies even if the Menorah is made of non-gold metals, and even if it does not contain [the features of the Biblical Menorah such as] the goblets, buttons and flowers, and even if it is not 18 Tefachim [1.4 meters] high.[1016] [The prohibition applies even if one makes the Menorah into a different shape than that of the Temple, such as with half circle branches, or triangle shaped branches and the like.[1017] Those Shuls which make/own a seven-branched metal Menorah are to be protested and forced to remove a branch or add an eight branch.[1018]

A non-metal Menorah of seven branches:[1019] It is permitted to make a non-metal Menorah which contains seven branches.[1020] Thus one may make a seven-branched wood, earthenware, [glass or plastic] Menorah.

[1010] The reason: As it is considered "Shiyurei Mitzvah" or Mitzvah leftovers. Now, although we find no precedence in the Poskim regarding such a concept regarding the Hadas or Arava, we do find it regarding Tzitzis, that if it later tore to below the Shiur, it nonetheless remains valid under certain conditions. [Hisorerus Teshuvah ibid]

[1011] So is clearly implied from Admur ibid who warns one to be very careful with the shaking that a) It is invalid for the rest of Sukkos if it falls off and we do not apply the rule of Shiyurei Mitzvah; b) One has an obligation to verify this matter, hence the warning of "One must be very careful"

[1012] Michaber Y.D. 141:8; Rambam Beis Habechira 7:10; Avoda Zara 43a; Likkutei Sichos 20:169 [printed in Shulchan Menachem 3:275]

[1013] Maharik 75; Birkeiy Yosef 141

[1014] See Shach 141:35-36; Chidushei Rav Akiva Eiger ibid; Pischeiy Teshuvah 141:14

[1015] Seven branched Menorah with eight candles: Some Poskim rule that one may make a seven branched Menorah which will hold eight candles. [Chacham Tzevi 60, brought in Yad Efraim 141]

[1016] Michaber ibid; Maharik Shoresh 75 in name of Rabbeinu Yitzchak of Krubel

The reason: As a metal Menorah remains valid for use in the Temple even though it is not made of gold. [Shach 141:35] Likewise, the Menorah remains valid for use even if it does not contain the goblets, flowers, and buttons, and even if it is not 18 Tefach high. [Shach 141:36]

A gold Menorah which does not have the flowers etc.: Some Poskim suggest that one may make a gold Menorah of seven branches so long as it does not contain the goblets and buttons, being that a gold material Menorah is invalid if it does not contain these features. [Implication of Shach ibid, brought in Bechor Shur on R"H 24, Rav Akiva Eiger 141, Pischeiy Teshuvah 141:15] However, other Poskim clearly rule that it is forbidden to make a seven-branched gold Menorah even without these features. [Bechor Shur on R"H 24, brought in Rav Akiva Eiger ibid; Pischeiy Teshuvah 141:15] Practically, one is to be stringent regarding a questionable Biblical prohibition. [See Maharik ibid; Birkeiy Yosef 141; Pischeiy Teshuvah 141:14]

[1017] Tevuos Shur on R"H 24, brought in Pischeiy Teshuvah 141:14

Other opinions: Some Poskim lean to permit making a seven branched Menorah which contains circle shaped branches. [Mishnas Chachamim on Avodas Kochavim p. 64, brought in Pischeiy Teshuvah 141:14]

[1018] Birkeiy Yosef 141; See Maharik ibid; Devar Moshe 1:122

[1019] Shach 141:35; Implication of Michaber and Tur ibid; Rambam Beis Habechira 7:10

[1020] The reason: As only a metal material Menorah is valid for use in the Temple. [Menachos 28a; Rambam Beis Habechira 1:18 and 7:10] Thus, all other materials may be made into a Menorah of the same shape as the Temple. [Shach ibid] However, see Tevuos Shur on R"H 24, brought in Pischeiy Teshuvah 141:14 and Rav Akiva Eiger ibid that even in invalid Menorah may not be made to replicate the Temple Menorah

---------------Purim----------------

71. Must the two foods of Mishloach Manos be of two different blessing?

It is disputed amongst Poskim[1021] whether the two gifts given for Mishloach Manos should be made up of **two different foods**. Seemingly, this debate has led to the misconception that the two foods must be made up of **two different blessings**. In truth, the identity of the blessing of the two foods has no relevance to the validity of the Mishloach Manos gifts, as evident from the omission of this criteria from all the Poskim, in addition to the fact that there is no logic to connect the two matters to each other. There is hence no need for the two foods to consist of two different blessings. One may thus send a bottle of juice[1022] and a bar of chocolate as Mishloach Manos, even though both have the blessing of Shehakol, and there is no reason or source to being careful that the foods retain two different blessings.

> **Summary:**
> There is no requirement, or even Hiddur, for the two gifts of Mishloach Manos to be of two different blessings, and this idea is a common misconception.

72. May a woman write a Megillah?[1023]

Some Poskim[1024] rule a woman is valid to write a Megillah, and one may thus even initially read and fulfill the Mitzvah from a Megillah written by a woman.[1025] Other Poskim[1026], however, rule a woman is invalid to write a Megillah, and thus one who reads from it does not fulfil the Mitzvah even Bedieved.[1027] [Practically, the widespread custom is like the latter opinion for women not to write Megillahs for reading purposes and even if such a Megillah was written, one is not to initially use the Megillah to fulfill the Mitzvah of Megillah reading. However, in a time of need such as when there is no other Megillah is available, one may read from it without a blessing.[1028] Even in such a case, if another Megillah written by a man later becomes available, one is to read from it again without a blessing.[1029]]

[1021] Some Poskim rule that the gifts must be made up of two different foods in order to be Yotzei the Mitzvah. [Aruch Hashulchan 695:14; Ashel Avraham Butchach 695 leans to be stringent; Shem Mishimon 31 based on Arizal; The Aruch Hashulchan ibid interprets the statement of the Rambam and Michaber 695:3 of two pieces of meat to refer to different tasting pieces of meat, and so is also implied from the wording of the Rambam "or two types of food"; See Nitei Gavriel 58:1 footnote 2] Other Poskim, however, rule that there is no need to have two different foods, and one even fulfills his obligation if he gives two serving portions of the same food, even if they were not cut to two pieces. [Possible implication of wording of Rambam and Michaber ibid "such as two portions of meat" implying that one may give two portions of the same food; Implication of Karban Mincha 385 [of Rav Yaakov Chagiz]; Rosh Yosef Megillah 7a [of P"M] leans to rule it is allowed; Afrakasta Deanya 25; Orchos Chaim 695:12 in name of Devar Beito; Meiy Yehuda 86; Sheiris Yehuda 93; Tzitz Eliezer 14:65; See Nitei Gavriel 58:1 footnote 1]

[1022] Shlah; M"A 695:11; Elya Raba 695:9; Peri Chadash; M"B 695:20

Other Opinions: Some Poskim rule one must send two foods while drinks are invalid. [Afrakasta Deanya 25] See Teshuvos Eliezer [brought in Yagdil Torah Yerushalayim 13:113] that perhaps one should not send Mashkeh as it is not considered a Mana [important item] however if it is within an enclosed bottle then perhaps it is considered important.

[1023] See Shaareiy Teshuvah 691:1; Kol Yaakov 691:6; See Admur 39:1 regarding Tefillin; Sdei Chemed Asifas Dinim Purim 12; Nitei Gavriel 30:1

[1024] Birkeiy Yosef 691:6 based on Peri Chadash 691:3 and Mateh Yehuda 691:2 who validate writing with left hand, brought in Shaareiy Teshuvah and Kaf Hachaim ibid; Machazik Bracha 691:2; Beis Oveid 6, p. 169b; P"M 691 M"Z 2; Nishal David 12

[1025] The reason: As women are obligated in the Mitzvah of Kerias Megillah and there is thus no reason to invalidate them from writing it. [Chida ibid; Beis Oved ibid; P"M ibid] Furthermore, the Megillah itself states that Esther wrote it, from which various Halachos are derived as explained in Megillah 19a!

[1026] Maaseh Rokeiach on Rambam Megillah 1; Mileches Shamayim Hilchos Stam 24:3; Rav Akiva Eiger 691:2 "It seems that if a woman wrote the Megillah then it is invalid, just as we rule regarding Tefillin and Mezuzah"; Avnei Nezer O.C. 516:19 "If only all our Torah would be as clear as the ruling here that women are invalid to write a Megillah"; Mikraeiy Kodesh 33

[1027] The reason: As women are invalid to write any Stam [scribal writing], even if they are obligated in the Mitzvah, as ruled regarding Mezuzah and Sefer Torah. [Rebbe Akiva Eiger ibid; See Michaber Y.D. 281:3]

[1028] See Shaareiy Teshuvah and Kol Yaakov ibid

[1029] Shaareiy Teshuvah and Kol Yaakov ibid

73. May a woman read the Megillah on Purim on behalf of herself or others?[1030]

The subject of whether a woman is valid to read the Megillah is subject to the following debate: On the one hand she is obligated in the Mitzvah, and hence should be able to read it on behalf of others as is always the rule regarding Mitzvos that one is obligated in. On the other hand, perhaps women are not commanded in the Mitzvah of reading the Megillah, but simply of hearing it read. Now, just as we have conflicting arguments to validate or invalidate the reading of women, so too we find conflicting sources in the Talmud regarding their status.[1031] Practically, there is a four-way debate in the Poskim on this matter, with some Poskim[1032] invalidating women all together, and other Poskim[1033] validating women in all cases. Other Poskim[1034] differentiate between a woman reading on behalf of men versus on behalf of women, while others[1035] differentiate between reading for a group of people versus reading in private. No matter what the outcome, in all cases, all agree that a woman can only be valid to read the Megillah if she has a Kosher Megillah available **and knows how the to read the words with the proper pronunciation.**[1036]

A. Reading on behalf of men:[1037]

In general, we rule that whoever is obligated in a Mitzvah can be Motzi others in that Mitzvah.[1038] However, there are Poskim[1039] who rule that although women are obligated to hear the Megillah reading just like men, nevertheless, they cannot read the Megillah on behalf of men.[1040] [Practically this is the final ruling, and thus women are initially invalid to read Megillah on behalf of men.[1041] This applies even when a woman is reading for a single man and not in a public forum.[1042] In the event that a woman read the Megillah for a man, or group of men, then the men are to hear it a second time without a blessing.[1043]

[1030] See 689:2; Nitei Gavriel 34:1-2; 9-10

[1031] See Megillah 19b and Erechin 2b which imply she is a valid reader, versus Tosefta Megillah 2:4 which implies she is an invalid reader

[1032] See Lechatchila opinion brought in B.

[1033] See other opinions brought in footnotes in A.

[1034] See Poskim brought in A and B

[1035] See Poskim brought in B

[1036] See Michaber 690:14

[1037] Michaber 689:2

[1038] See Michaber ibid; 271:2; Admur 271:6 regarding Kiddush; See Q&A regarding if a woman may read for others after she already fulfilled her obligation

[1039] Yeish Omrim in Michaber ibid; Yeish Omrim in Rama 689:2-3 [as explained in M"A 689:7 and 9]; Tosefta Megillah 2:4 "Women are exempt from reading the Megillah" [brought in Biur Hagr"a 689:3 and P"M 689 A"A 2 and Machatzis Hashekel 689]; Tosafos Sukkah 38a [brought in M"A 271:2]; Smag and Reiam [brought in M"A 689:5]; Bahag Hilchos Megillah [brought in Tosafos ibid and P"M 689 A"A 2]; Mordechai 779 in name of Ravaya 529; Opinion in Rosh Megillah 1:4 and so is his implied ruling as writes Beis Yosef 689

Other Opinions: Some Poskim that it is valid for women to read the Megillah on behalf of men and to be Motzi them. [Implication of first and Stam opinion brought in the Michaber ibid that whoever is Chayav is Motzi; Implication of Megillah 19b and Erechin 2b "Everyone is Kosher to read"; Rashi Erechin ibid "Women are obligated in reading Megillah and they may read for even men and be Motzi them"; Implication of Rambam, as explains Maggid Mishneh Megillah 1:2 and Biur Hagra 689; Opinion in Rosh Megillah 1:4; Opinion in M"A 689:7, 8 and 9; Biur Hagra ibid that so rules 1st opinion in Michaber ibid and so rules Rambam who omitted the law of Androganus, and Kol Bo, and Tosafos Megillah 4a; Rashi, brought in Machatzis Hashekel 689 and P"M 689 A"A 2; M"B in Shaar Hatziyon 689:16 that the main opinion is like the first opinion; Kaf Hachaim 689:12; Michaber 271:2 and Admur 271:6 regarding Kiddush that a woman is Motzi a man]

[1040] The reason: The reason for this is because: 1) The reading the Megillah is similar to Kerias Hatorah of which women are invalid to read due to Kavod Hatzibur. [M"A 689:5 in name of Smag and Reim; M"B 689:7; Kaf Hachaim 689:13] Alternatively, they are invalid to read for the public because "Zeilu Behu Milsa," that doing so is belittling to the Mitzvah. [Tosafus ibid, brought in M"A 271:2; See Admur 271:6 regarding Kiddush] 2) Alternatively the reason is because women were never obligated in reading the Megillah but simply in hearing it, and thus she is not considered obligated in the Mitzvah of reading, and can't be Motzi a man who is of higher obligation status than she. [Taz 271:2 based on Rama ibid that for this reason they say Lishmoa Megillah; Bahag ibid "They are not Motzi men being that they are not obligated to read"; Biur HaGr"a ibid; Rosh Yosef Megillah 4a; Machatzis Hashekel 689:7; Nesiv Chaim 271; M"B ibid; Kaf Hachaim ibid;] 3) Alternatively the reason is because a woman's voice is considered an Erva, and is hence forbidden for men to hear. [Kol Bo 45; Orchos Chaim brought in Kaf Hachaim ibid; Omitted from Taz and M"A ibid; See Maharash Engel 3:45; Chavalim Beni'imim 36]

[1041] Poskim ibid; Taz 271:2 that so rules Michaber ibid and so should be initially followed; Bach 271; Rashal, brought in Taz ibid; Levush 689; Peri Chadash 689; Elya Raba 689:2; P"M 689 A"A 4; Teshuvos Bad 408; Derech Hachaim 3; Kaf Hachaim 689:14; See Admur 271:6 that even by Kiddush "Ein Morin Kein"

[1042] M"A 689:5 in name of Reiam

The reason: As although the main reason of invalidation is because of Kavod Hatzibur, nevertheless once their reading was invalidated the Sages did not differentiate in their decree and hence invalidated it in all scenarios. [M"A ibid] Certainly, according to the second and third reason recorded above by the Poskim, they are invalid to read for even a single man.

[1043] Ben Ish Chaiy Tetzaveh 2; Kaf Hachaim 689:14; See P"M 689 A"A 6; However, see Taz ibid who implies that Bedieved one is Yotzei

If the only person who knows how to read Hebrew[1044] is a woman, then she may read it without a blessing on behalf of men.[1045] If however a male reader later becomes available, the listener must re-hear the Megillah without a blessing.[1046]]

B. Reading on behalf of other women or on behalf of oneself:

From the letter of the law, a woman may read the Megillah on behalf of herself and on behalf of another woman.[1047] [See Q&A regarding if she may read even if she was already Yotzei.] However, some Poskim[1048] rule that she may not read the Megillah on behalf of a group of women, as she cannot be Motzi a group of people. Practically, initially women are not to read the Megillah at all, not even on behalf of themselves, and are rather to hear the reading from a man.[1049] However, if men are not available to read the Megillah on behalf of a woman, or group of women, then a woman may read it with a blessing on behalf of herself, and on behalf of another woman [and even on behalf of a group of women[1050]], making sure to read it from a Kosher Megillah, and with proper pronunciation.[1051] If, however, a male reader later becomes available, she should re-hear the Megillah.[1052]

The blessing: When a woman reads the Megillah she is to recite the first blessing using the words "Lishmoa Megillah". See our Sefer "The Laws of Purim" Chapter 7 Halacha 8 for the full details on this subject! The blessing may only to be said if she will be able to read the Megillah with proper pronunciation.

Summary:
Initially, a woman is to hear the Megillah from a man and is not to read it on behalf of herself, or on behalf of others. If, however, there are no men available to read the Megillah, then she is to read the

---

[1044] However, if there is a man present who is able to read Hebrew, then it is better for him to read it and have the woman correct his pronunciation than for him to be Yotzei from her, even though she knows how to read the Megillah fluently. [So seems Pashut from Poskim]

[1045] Implication of Taz ibid *"Therefore it is certainly **initially** improper for a woman to read for men"* thus implying that Bedieved or in a time of need she may read; Beis Oved 689:4; Kaf Hachaim 689:16; M"B in Shaar Hatziyon 689:16 that the main opinion is like the first opinion

The reason: On the one hand, we suspect for the Poskim who rule a woman may be Motzi a man and hence we rule that she should read for him. Nonetheless, a blessing may not be said due to Safek Brachos, as we suspect for the Yeish Omrim who rule it is an invalid reading.

Opinion of Admur: See Admur ibid that even by Kiddush we rule that one should not direct women to say Kiddush on behalf of men, even though she is for certain Motzi him, and this would imply that certainly in this case where her ability to be Motzi is under question, we should rule that we should not tell her to read for a man. Nonetheless, seemingly the ruling there of Admur is only initially, however, if in truth there is no one else available to read for him, then certainly she may do so.

Reading for a group of men: Some Poskim rule that a woman can never be Motzi a group of people, whether men or women. [See list of Poskim brought in B] Accordingly, Piskeiy Teshuvos 689 footnote 7 concludes that she should never read the Megillah on behalf of a group of men. Vetzaruch Iyun, as since there are opinions who rule a woman can read the Megillah for a group of men, why then should one not suspect for this opinion! Perhaps, however, this is due to the suspicion of Kol Isha. Vetzaruch Iyun, as majority of Poskim negate this worry.

[1046] Beis Oved 689:4; Kaf Hachaim 689:16

[1047] Implication of Michaber ibid, M"A ibid and Taz ibid that their entire invalidation is only towards men; Rama ibid who rules for women to say the blessing of Lishmoa Megillah; Bahag Hilchos Megillah "They are Motzi women but not men" [brought in P"M 689 A"A 2]; Mordechai 779 in explanation of Erechin 3a; Ateres Zekeinim 689 "They are Motzi other women"; Chayeh Adam; M"B 689:7 and Shaar Hatziyon 689:16 based on Rosh in beginning of Megillah, Gr"a, Peri Megadim and that the main opinion follows the first opinion in Michaber ibid and even according to the second opinion, she can be Motzi herself

The reason: Although she can't be Motzi a man due to not being included in the Mitzvah of reading, she can be Motzi a woman, as they are of the same level obligation. [Bahag ibid; P"M ibid]

[1048] M"B in Shaar Hatziyon 689:15; Karban Nesanel Megillah 1:4; Possible implication of Tosefta ibid and Tosafos Sukkah 38a and so rule Karban Nesanel ibid and Nesiv Chaim 271 in their understanding of Tosafos Sukkah 38a [however, to note that he quotes the Bahag, who explicitly permits reading for women]; See Kaf Hachaim 689:17; See Piskeiy Teshuvos 689 footnote 7 that this applies even in a time of need that no other men are available.

Other opinions: Some Poskim rule there is no issue with a woman reading on behalf of even a group of other women. [Implication of Michaber, M"A and Taz ibid; Bahag ibid, P"M ibid, Ateres Zekeinim ibid; Machatzis Hashekel 689:7; See M"A 271:2; Admur 271:6; Nitei Gavriel 34:9 footnote 14]

[1049] M"A 689:6 in name of Midrash Hanelam; Elya Raba 689:3; Biur Hagr"a in name of Zohar Rus; Machazik Bracha 689:3 that so is custom; Ben Ish Chaiy Tetzaveh 1; See Shaar Hatziyon 689:16

[1050] Pashut from all Poskim brought in the other opinions in previous footnotes; Implication of Taz 271:2; Beis Oved 689:4; Kaf Hachaim 689:16; Nitei Gavriel ibid based on M"A and Admur ibid; However, see Piskeiy Teshuvos 689 footnote 7 that she may not read for a group of women even in a time of need that no other men are available. Vetzaruch Iyun as there are opinions who rule a woman can read the Megillah for a group of women and hence why should one not suspect for this opinion!

[1051] Chayeh Adam 155:11; M"B 689:8; Kaf Hachaim 689:18

[1052] Peri Megadim 689 A"A 6 as explained in Kaf Hachaim 689:18

Megillah with a blessing on behalf of herself. In such a case, she may be Motzi another woman, or even a group of women, with her reading. In a time of need that the men present do not know to read Hebrew, she may read the Megillah even on behalf of other men, although without a blessing. In all the above cases, if a man later becomes available to read the Megillah, those who were Yotzei from a woman's reading should re-hear the Megillah reading from a man, without a blessing.

Q&A

May a woman read the Megillah on behalf of male children?[1053]

No.

May a woman who already heard Megillah read it again on behalf of another?[1054]

It is best for a woman who already heard the Megillah not to read the Megillah on behalf of another woman who was not yet Yotzei.[1055] However, if there is no one else available, then a woman who was already Yotzei may read it for her with a blessing.[1056]

[1053] Elya Raba 689:8 in name of Amrakel unlike the simple implication from Olas Shabbos 689:3 [Kaf Hachaim 689:23]

[1054] See the following Poskim regarding a debate if women are included in the Mitzvah of Areivus, and can hence be Motzi others if they were already Yotzei: Rosh and Rabbeinu Yona Brachos 20b [no Areivus]; Ritva Brachos 5:2 and Mordechai Megillah 797 [There is Areivus]; Admur 186:2; 263 KU"A 5; 271:3; 296:19; 608:4-5 [All these sources implies there is Areivus and she can be Motzi]; P"M 271 A"A 2; 689 A"A 4 [questionable]; Degul Merivava 271 and Tzlach Brachos 20b [No Areivus]; Rav Akiva Eiger 271 and Shut Rav Akiva Eiger 7 [There is Areivus]; M"B 271:5; 273:20; 675:9; 692:10-11 [All these sources implies there is Areivus and she can be Motzi]; Biur Halacha 689 "Venashim"; Kaf Hachaim 675:20 [Permitted]; The following Poskim all rule she is considered within Areivus: Chasam Sofer 271; Rosh Yosef Brachos ibid; Avnei Nezer 439; Shaar Hatziyon 271:9; Minchas Yitzchak 3:54; Har Tzvi 2:122; See Piskeiy Teshuvos 271:8 footnote 89 and 92 for the full list of Poskim on each side of the debate

[1055] P"M 689 A"A 4; Biur Halacha 689 "Venashim"
The reason: Due to the debate of whether a woman is included in Areivus, it is best for one who was not yet Yotzei to read to herself than to have another woman who was already Yotzei read on her behalf.

[1056] As so is the main ruling of Admur, M"B and Poskim ibid, that a woman can be Yotzei others even if she was already Yotzei

Yoreh Deah

------------------Kashrus-General-----------------

1. May one enter a non-Kosher restaurant?[1]

In general, it is forbidden to enter into a non-Kosher restaurant due to Maras Ayin even if there are no Jews in the vicinity, and one does not intend to order any food.[2] However, in a time of great need [such as one is very thirsty and would like to order a Kosher drink, or needs the bathroom] and there is no active Maras Ayin involved in one's entering the restaurant [such as there are no Jews in the vicinity who will see him there], then it is permitted to enter the restaurant, preferably in a secluded area, and he may even order a food or beverage that is clean from any Kashrus concerns [i.e. fruits, coffee].[3] If, however, there are Jews around who will see him in the restaurant, then it is forbidden to do so even in a time of great need, unless he informs them of the situation.

2. Does fish oil require a Hashgacha:[4]

The oil of a non-Kosher fish is likewise Biblically non-Kosher.[5] Accordingly, all fish oil products require a Hashgacha to verify that the oil is derived from a Kosher fish. Fish oil is added in many foods such as Vitamins, medicines. The following will discuss the various non-food products that contain fish oil and their Hashgacha status.

Dental Floss:[6] Many types of Dental floss are waxed with fish oil. Nevertheless, dental floss does not require a Hashgacha being that one is not eating the oil and has no intent to swallow it.

Fish oil medicine for one who is sick:[7] It is permitted for one who is sick to the point of being bedridden [Choleh Sheiyn Bo Sakana] to drink fish oil for treatment of his illness, even if his illness does not involve danger, and even if the fish is certainly not Kosher.[8] Nonetheless, it is best to enter the oil into a capsule and only then swallow it.[9] Likewise, if there is Kosher fish oil available, then one must buy it even if it is very expensive.[10] Practically, today there are various companies of Kosher fish oil available on the market and hence it is forbidden to use a fish oil that does not contain a Hashgacha.

Omega 3 fish oil capsules: Based on the above Poskim, it is understood that there is no allowance for one who is currently healthy to drink fish oil that does not contain a proper Hashgacha. Nonetheless, some Poskim[11] rule that one may swallow **fish oil capsules** without a Hashgacha even if he is currently healthy. This is permitted even if one knows the fish oil derives from non-kosher fish. However, if there is Kosher

---

[1] Igros Moshe O.C. 2:40; See Toras Chatas 17:4, brought in Taz 91:2, that in a time of need one may eat Kosher foods in the home of a gentile using his non-Kosher vessels, however, perhaps there he refers to a private home and it is hence not relevant to the discussion of a public restaurant.

Background and other approaches: The Poskim [prior to Igros Moshe] do not make any mention of a prohibition of Maras Ayin involved in eating in a non-Kosher restaurant. The Rama in Toras Chatas ibid who discusses eating in a gentile's home also does make any mention of it [although perhaps he refers to a private home and not a public hotel or restaurant]. Now, whether or not we are allowed to create new decrees of Maras Ayin that are not recorded in the Talmud, it is evident from various rulings that one may do so [see Rama 87:3-4 and Shach 87:6 based on Rashba; Peri Toar 87:9]. However, some Poskim rule that one may not create new decrees of Maras Ayin that are not based on the Talmud or Rishonim, as if we it were allowed to be done, there would be no end to the suspicions. [Peri Chadash 87:7; See Yechaveh Daas 4:50] Vetzaruch Iyun on Igros Moshe ibid who makes no mention of any of these matters.

[2] The reason and source: It is forbidden to enter a non-Kosher restaurant to do both Maras Ayin [that people will think it is permitted to eat there] and Chashad [that people will suspect that one is eating non-Kosher]. [Igros Moshe ibid based on Avoda Zara 11a and Michaber Y.D. 149 regarding the prohibition to travel on a road that leads to a city of idolatry due to Chashad that people will think one is coming to serve idolatry, and the same applies whenever one enters an area of prohibition, such as a non-Kosher restaurant; This follows the Poskim ibid who rule that one may make new decrees of Maras Ayin that are not recorded in Poskim] The prohibition of Maras Ayin by a Biblical Issur applies even in private. [See Admur 301:56; 305:14; M"A 301:56; Taz 301:28; Rosh 23:8; Tosafos Kesubos 60a; M"B 301:165]

[3] The reason: As in a case of loss and pain the sages did not make their decree of Maras Ayin. [Igros Moshe ibid, based on Kesubos 60a that the Sages allowed one who is in pain to suckle milk from a cow's udder on Shabbos and did not suspect for Maras Ayin]

[4] Hakashrus 11:21-22

[5] Rama Y.D. 83:5, in contrast to Tzir of the fish which is only Rabbinically forbidden, as ruled in Michaber 83:5

[6] Hakashrus 11:21 in name of Rav Elyashiv

[7] See Yabia Omer 2:12

[8] Dvar Moshe 1:8, brought in Darkei Teshuvah 155:25; Halef Lecha Shlomo Y.D. 22; Divrei Chaim 2:52; Salmas Chaim 2:20; Yabia Omer 2:12
The reason: As it is permitted for a sick person to benefit from non-Kosher food in an irregular way, and it is irregular to drink oil. [ibid; see Y.D. 155:3]

[9] Rama 155:3; Mahariy Halevi 1:62; Yabia Omer ibid

[10] Dvar Moshe 1:8, brought in Darkei Teshuvah 155:25

[11] Yabia Omer 2:12 based on the fact that swallowing a capsule is not Derech Hanaah, and the Shach 155:13 who rules that when it's not Derech Hanaah, then a non-Kosher food that is permitted in benefit is permitted even for a healthy person.

fish oil available, then one must buy it even if it is very expensive.[12] Practically, today there are various companies of Kosher fish oil capsules on the market and hence it is forbidden to take fish oil capsules that does not contain a Hashgacha.

3. The Arlah fruits of a gentile and matters to beware when purchasing fruits even in the Diaspora:

Do the laws of Arlah apply to the fruits of a gentile owned tree/May a Jew eat the fruits of the first three years from a gentile owned tree?[13] The fruits of all trees contain the Biblical Arlah prohibition, whether the tree is owned by a Jew or a gentile, and whether it is in Eretz Yisrael or in the Diaspora. [Even the Arlah fruits of a gentile in the Diaspora is Biblically forbidden.[14] Some Poskim[15] however rule that the Arla fruits of a gentile in the Diaspora is merely Rabbinically forbidden. Due to the above prohibition, if one witnessed one's gentile neighbor planting a fruit tree, then it is forbidden for one to benefit from the fruits of that tree until he calculates that the Arla years have passed. If the gentile offers him the fruit, he is to kindly decline acceptance.]

The law if one is unsure as to the status of the fruit of the gentile?[16] The above prohibition against eating Arla fruit in the Diaspora only applies if one knows for certain that the fruit is Arla, however in any case that one does not know for certain that the food is Arla, then in the Diaspora it is permitted to be eaten. [Thus, in the Diaspora, it is permitted for one to purchase fruits indiscriminately from gentile owned stores even though they do not carry a Hashgacha, and it is possible that the fruits derive from the Arla years. There is no need for one to investigate this.] The above, however, only applies in the Diaspora, while in Eretz Yisrael fruits may be prohibited if they have not been verified to be clear of Arla suspicions. This matter will IY"H be explained in greater depth in a future Halacha.

If a gentile who is selling fruit states that the fruit is from the first 3/4 years of planting, is he believed?[17] If a gentile who is selling fruits claims that the fruits are from Arlah or Neta Rivai [within the first 3-4 years of the tree], he is not believed [and one may thus eat the fruit].[18] This applies even if he mentions who he purchased the fruits from.[19] [Nonetheless, the above only applies if there is reason to suspect that the gentile may lie about his fruits, to increase their quality in the eyes of the buyer. If, however, this suspicion is not applicable, and the gentile is making the statement out of mere casualness, then one should suspect for his words and avoid eating the fruit.[20] Accordingly, if one heard the gentile state casually on the phone that a certain fruit is from the first year of harvest, or if there is a sign which testifies as such, then one may not purchase those grapes.]

---

[12] Dvar Moshe 1:8, brought in Darkei Teshuvah 155:25
[13] Michaber 294:8; Tur 294:8; Tosafos Kiddushin 36b; Rosh 62; Ran 15a; Mordechai 501; Semag Lavin 146; Rabbeinu Shimshon Arlah 3/9; Rashba 1734; Rambam Maaser Sheyni 10:5; Radbaz 580; Birkeiy Yosef 294/6
Other opinions: Some Poskim rule that the Arlah fruit of a gentile is not prohibited for a Jew. [Pirush Hamishnayos of Rambam Arlah 1:3; See Beis Yosef 294 and Birkeiy Yosef ibid; The Rambam in Mishneh Torah ibid retracted from this opinion]
[14] Aruch Hashulchan 294:11
[15] Chasam Sofer 286, brought in Pischeiy Teshuvah 294/7
[16] Michaber 294:9
[17] Michaber 294:28; Braisa Yevamos 122a
[18] The reason: As he may be lying for the sake of making his merchandise sound of greater quality, as a younger tree produces better fruit than an older tree. [Taz 294:29; Yevamos ibid]
[19] Michaber ibid; Rabbeinu Yerucham
[20] Taz Y.D. 122:4; Shach 127:20; Aruch Hashulchan 295:45

------Kashrus-Blood------

4. The law of blood found in an egg:[21]

The Torah prohibits one to eat blood of a creature. The Talmud and Poskim discuss whether this prohibition likewise applies to blood found in an egg. In other words, is the blood in an egg considered the blood of a creature or not.[22] While the final Halachic ruling follows that all egg blood is at the very least Rabbinically forbidden to be consumed due to Maras Ayin[23], nevertheless, the egg itself is at times permitted to be eaten after discarding the blood. This matter depends on where the blood was found, and whether the egg was fertilized by a male chicken or not.[24]

A. Fertilized egg [Mufaros[25]]:

The status of the blood:[26] Blood [of a fertilized egg[27]] which is found in the area of the start of the formation of a chick [i.e. the Rokeim Haefroach] is Biblically forbidden to be eaten under the penalty [of lashes]. If one is unsure if this blood is from the formation of the chick, it is not Biblically forbidden to be eaten, although the Sages prohibited it.

Must one throw out the entire egg or only the blood:[28] If the blood is found on the yolk of the egg, then the entire egg is forbidden; both the white [Chelbon] and the yellow [i.e. Chelmon].[29] If, however, the blood is found on the white of the egg, then some Poskim[30] rule one is to discard the blood and the remainder of the egg is permitted. However, other Poskim[31] rule that in certain cases, the entire egg is forbidden. Practically, the custom of Ashkenazi Jewry is to forbid the entire egg irrelevant of where blood is found, whether it is found on the Chelmon or the Chelbon.[32]

---

[21] Tur and Shulchan Aruch Y.D. 66; Kerisus 20b; Chulin 64b
[22] See Kerisus 21a
[23] Teshuvos Rashba 1:46; Michaber Y.D. 66:7 and Tur 66:7 even regarding Muzaros; Based on Chulin ibid as explained in Beis Yosef 66:7
Other opinions: Some Poskim rule that certain bloods found in eggs are permitted to be eaten. [Riy, brought in Tur ibid, regarding blood found outside of Kesher]
[24] The difference between fertilized and unfertilized eggs comes down to whether a rooster has been involved in the fertilization process. Hens do not need a rooster to lay an egg; they do so on their own every 24 hours simply according to light patterns. However, if a rooster does mate with a hen, the eggs she produces are fertilized and, under the right incubation conditions, can bear chicks. If a rooster is not involved it means that there is zero possibility of the egg ever becoming anything more than just that.
[25] Mufaros refer to eggs that have received male fertilization and hence can develop into a chick.
[26] Michaber Y.D. 66:2; Tur 66:2; 2nd answer of Tosafos Chulin 64b and Rosh 63; Rashba Chulin 64b; Toras Habayis Aruch 3:5-9; Shut Rashba 1:66
Other opinions: The Mishneh in Kerisus 20b states one is not Biblically liable for eating blood of an egg. Some understand this to apply to all eggs. [1st answer of Tosafos Chulin 64b and Rosh ibid, brought in Beis Yosef 66:2] Accordingly, some Poskim rule that egg blood is only Rabbinically forbidden. [Rambam Machalos Assuros 3:8; Chinuch Mitzvah 148]
[27] Michaber 66:7; Braisa in Kerisus 64
[28] Michaber 66:3; Chulin 64b
[29] Michaber ibid; Tur 66:3 in name of Geonim; Rif; Rambam Machalos Assuros 3
[30] Michaber 66:3; Rif; Rambam Machalos Assuros 3; Tur 66 in name of Geonim; Those countries that are lenient like the ruling of the Michaber regarding blood found on the white are to discard a peels worth of the egg together with the blood. [Rama ibid; Aruch; Semag]
[31] Rama ibid *"Some opinions rule that if blood is found on the white knot that connects the yolk to the white and the blood slightly extends outside this knot, the entire egg is forbidden."* [Rosh; Rashba; Rashi; Tosafos; Tur 66] Furthermore, there are those who are stringent to forbid the entire egg even if the blood did not spread past the knot." [Issur Viheter Haruch 42]; Furthermore, some Poskim rule that blood found on the Chelbon is more severe than blood found on the Chelmon, and if the blood is found on the Chelbon, everything is forbidden. [Rav Avraham Halevi, brought in Shach 66:8; Taz 66:2; Bach 66; Lechem Chamudos p. 38; Rokeiach 447; Rashal; Peri Chadash 66]
[32] Rama ibid
The reason: Due to the above dissenting opinion, the custom in these countries is to forbid the entire egg irrelevant of where blood is found, whether it is found on the Chelmon or the Chelbon. [Rama ibid] The reason for this is because we are no longer expert as to what is considered the Kesher of the egg. [Toras Chatas 62:1, brought in Shach 66:8 and Taz 66:2] Alternatively, the reason is because we suspect for the opinion who holds that blood found on the Chelbon is more severe then blood found on the Chelmon, and hence we forbid the entire egg whether the blood was found on the Chelmon or Chelbon, to suspect for both opinions. [Shach ibid; Taz ibid; Bach 66; Rokeiach 447; Lechem Chamudos p. 38; Rashal]

B. Unfertilized egg [Muzaros]:[33]

[Blood that is found in an unfertilized egg is only Rabbinically forbidden to be eaten due to Maras Ayin.[34] Thus] if blood is found in Muzaros eggs [i.e. unfertilized eggs[35]], it is permitted to throw out the blood and then eat the remaining egg.

C. Status of eggs today:[36]

The vast majority of eggs on the market today[37] are unfertilized and hence do not contain Biblically forbidden blood.[38] Based on this, some Poskim[39] rule that if blood is found in a typical store-bought egg today, the egg is permitted and the blood is to be discarded.[40] Other Poskim[41], however, suspect for a minority of fertilized eggs that make it to the market, and hence forbid the entire egg.[42] Practically, one is to be stringent to discard the entire egg, and so is the widespread custom today, although some are lenient to simply discard the blood.[43]

> **Summary:**
> If one finds a blood spot in a store-bought egg, it is proper to discard the entire egg. Nonetheless, some are lenient to simply discard the blood, and permit eating the remainder of the egg.

---

[33] Michaber Y.D. 66:7; Tur 66:7; Braisa in Kerisus 64b "Eggs which are Muzaros may be eaten by the strong minded"; Rashba Chulin ibid; Toras Habayis Hakatzar 3:5; Yabia Omer 3:2; Yechaveh Daas 3:57; Igros Moshe 36; Minchas Yitzchak 1:106; 4:56

How does blood grow in an unfertilized egg? A blood spot inside an egg does not indicate a fertilized egg. They can be caused by the rupture of a blood vessel on the yolk surface during formation of the egg in a hen's reproductive system or by a similar accident in the wall of the oviduct. They can also be a result of a vitamin A deficiency, genetics, or some random occurrence. Mass candling methods reveal most eggs with blood and those eggs are removed. However, even with mass scanners, it's impossible to catch them all. [Taken from https://www.incredibleegg.org/eggcyclopedia/b/blood-spots/]

Other opinions: Some Rabbanim rule that unfertilized eggs are only permitted if the egg has begun to spoil, otherwise, all eggs with blood are forbidden, whether fertilized or unfertilized. [Rav Mordechai Eliyahu, brought in Sefer Kashrus Kehalacha [Edrey] p. 21]

[34] Rashba Chulin ibid; Toras Habayis Hakatzar 3:5; Beis Yosef Y.D. 66:7

The reason: As egg blood is only Biblically forbidden if it is the start of the development of a chick. Thus, an unfertilized egg which will never develop a chick will never be Biblically forbidden, as such blood can never form into a creature. Nevertheless, the blood itself is Rabbinically forbidden to be eaten and thus must be discarded [due to Maaras Ayin]. [Rashba ibid]

Other opinions: Seemingly according to the Riy, brought in Tur 66:3 the blood is completely permitted to be eaten.

[35] Muzaros are eggs that have not received male fertilization and hence can never develop into a chick. [Shach 66:14; Beir Hagoleh 66; Tur 66:7; Rashi Chulin ibid; Rashba] The actual term Muzaros refers to eggs that have begun to rot and become stringy. [Beis Yosef 66:7] Such eggs are also known as Safna Deara, as they are developed from the heat of the ground. [Tur ibid] Based on this latter definition, some Rabbanim rule that unfertilized eggs are only permitted if the egg has begun to spoil, otherwise, all eggs with blood are forbidden, whether fertilized or unfertilized. [Rav Mordechai Eliyahu, brought in Sefer Kashrus Kehalacha [Edrey] p. 21]

How to determine if an egg is not fertilized: Some Poskim rule one can only consider an egg as unfertilized if the chicken who laid the egg was closed up in a coop [for the entire duration of its development], or if there were no male chickens found for a distance of 60 houses. [Toras Chatas, brought in Chidushei Rav Akiva Eiger 66:7] Other Poskim rule that if there is a river without a bridge that prevents the male chickens from crossing then it is also valid. [Minchas Yaakov ibid] Other Poskim rule the chicken must be closed in its coop for 21 days of its development. [Peir Chadash 66:13, brought in P"M 66 S"D 14, Rav Akiva Eiger ibid]

[36] See Yabia Omer 3:2; Yechaveh Daas 3:57; Igros Moshe Y.D. 1:36; O.C. 3:61; Minchas Yitzchak 1:106; 4:56; Shevet Halevi 2:22; Hakashrus 12:33-35

[37] In Minchas Yitzchak 4:56 it states that 99% of market eggs are not fertilized

[38] Nearly all eggs sold commercially are produced by hens that have not mated [i.e. Muzaros], says Lauren Cobey, media representative for the American Egg Board [AEB]. There are no males kept near the female chickens and the eggs are laid without any fertilization. Nevertheless, there are a minority of eggs that are Mufaros. This at times occurs when the egg farmer also develops eggs for chicks and the excess eggs he sells as eggs.

[39] Yabia Omer Y.D. 3:2; Yechaveh Daas 3:57; Igros Moshe O.C. 3:61 writes that certainly it is permitted from the letter of the law if not found by the Kesher, due to the majority, however, see next footnote for his conclusion

[40] The reason: As although there remains a minority of eggs which are fertilized and sold on the market, nevertheless, certainly one follows the majority in this regard. [Igros Moshe ibid]

[41] Tefila Lemoshe brought in Pischeiy Teshuvah 66 is stringent by Safek egg; Minchas Yitzchak 1:106; 4:56; Shevet Halevi 2:22; Conclusion of Igros Moshe Y.D. 1:36 that initially one is to be stringent to discard the entire egg, as eggs are cheap. This certainly applies if the blood is found on the Kesher of the egg, in which case one is to be stringent from the letter of the law as possibly such blood can only be found on Muzaros egg; Rav Mordechai Eliyahu, brought in Sefer Kashrus Kehalacha [Edrey] p. 21; Mishneh Halachos 4:96; Teshuvos Vehanhagos 2:384

[42] The reason: As since there are a minority of eggs on the market that are fertilized, therefore one must suspect for this minority. The reason for this is because it is much more common for a fertilized egg to contain blood, and hence whenever we find blood in the egg, we suspect it was fertilized. [Tefila Lemoshe brought in Pischeiy Teshuvah 66:2 Minchas Yitzchak ibid]

[43] Hakashrus ibid

> **Q&A**
> **What is the law if one found a blood spot in a mixture of many eggs?**
> Coming up in a future Halacha!

5. May a child check eggs for blood?[44]

Any child who [has reached the age of Chinuch[45] and] knows how to check eggs for blood, may be trusted to check an egg for blood even if they are below the age of Bar/Bas Mitzvah.[46] This applies to both fertilized and unfertilized eggs.[47] This applies whether the child is checking the eggs for himself, or on behalf of others.[48] A child who is not yet old enough to know how to properly check eggs for blood, may not be entrusted to do so.[49]

------------------Basar Bechalav------------------

6. If one is in doubt as to whether a certain vessel is dairy, meat, or Pareve, what is the law?

If one is unsure as to a vessel's dairy or meat status and 12 months have not passed since its last use, then it is required to be Kashered if one desires to use the vessel for dairy or meat meals.[50] If one does not

---

[44] See Admur 432:10 [Child may be trusted with Rabbinical matter even initially and even no Mitzvah Min Hamuvchar to not trust him if does not involve any trouble] and so rules: Chok Yaakov 43:10; Elya Raba 432:6; Maharil Bedikas Chametz 12:43; Michaber 437:4 and Pesachim 4a [If a child checked home is trusted]; Michaber and Rama Y.D. 66:8 [There is no obligation to check eggs for blood, and is just a Minhag]; Michaber Y.D. 66:4-7 [All bloods of Mufaros [unfertilized eggs] are only Rabbinical due to Maaras Ayin, and the vast majority of eggs today are Muzaros]; See Hakashrus 13:26

Background:
May children be entrusted with the Kashrus of an item? Children below the age of Bar/Bas Mitzvah may not be entrusted with any Biblical matter. [Admur 437:10; Michaber 437:4; Y.D. 120:14] Children who have reached an age of understanding and responsibility may be trusted for all Rabbinical matters. [Admur 432:10; Michaber 437:4; Pesachim 4a; Rav Akiva Eiger Y.D. 120] They may be trusted even initially. [Admur 432:10; Chok Yaakov 43:10; Elya Raba 432:6; Maharil Bedikas Chametz 12:43] If the matter does not involve any trouble, and there is no worry that they will be too lazy to do a proper job, there is not even a Mitzvah Min Hamuvchar involved in having an adult do it. [Implication of Admur 432:10] They may be trusted even initially as an emissary, to do the Mitzvah on another's behalf. [Admur and Poskim ibid, unlike Rav Akiva Eiger ibid]

Is the blood found in eggs Biblical or Rabbinical? This depends on the type of egg [fertilized versus unfertilized] and the area of the egg in which the blood was found. [See Michaber Y.D. 66:4-7] Unfertilized eggs, which is the majority of eggs on the market today, do not contain Biblically forbidden blood. [Michaber Y.D. 66:7; See Yabia Omer 3:2; Yechaveh Daas 3:57; Igros Moshe 36; Minchas Yitzchak 4:56]

Is one obligated to check eggs for blood? From the letter of the law, one is not required to check eggs for blood as we follow the majority of eggs which do not contain blood. [Michaber and Rama Y.D. 66:8; Hagahos Maimanis; Aruch] Nevertheless, the custom is to check all eggs that are placed into foods during the day, to see if they have blood. [Rama ibid]

[45] M"B 437:19

[46] The reason: As children may be trusted with all Rabbinical matters, and the blood found in today's eggs which are unfertilized is only Rabbinically forbidden due to Maaras Ayin. This in addition to the fact that from the letter of the law there is no need to check even fertilized eggs for blood, and it is a mere custom.

[47] The reason: As even by fertilized eggs which may contain Biblical blood, from the letter of the law there is no need to check the eggs for blood, as majority of eggs do not have blood. [Michaber and Rama Y.D. 66:8]

[48] Admur 432:10; Chok Yaakov 43:10; Elya Raba 432:6; Maharil Bedikas Chametz 12:43
Other opinions: Some Poskim rule a child may not initially be entrusted to fulfill a Rabbinical command on behalf of another. [See Rebbe Akiva Eiger Y.D. 120]

[49] Admur 432:10; Michaber 437:4

[50] So is evident from Chaim Shaul 2:38-86 regarding one who is unsure if a new vessel bought from a gentile was previously used for non-Kosher, that we do not consider this a Rabbinical Safek of Eino Ben Yomo, and we are stringent to require Kashering unless other leniencies apply, as will be explained; See also Admur 451:5 that one is not to purchase vessels from a gentile for Pesach use if one is unsure of its Chametz status; See also Rama 122:9 and Taz 122:8 regarding a vessel left by a gentile that we only permit it after 24 hours due to Sfek Sfeika, and in this case it is more severe as a) Perhaps there is no Sfek Sfeika, as explained next in the reason; b) Perhaps we only apply Sfek Sfeika to be lenient in the above case where the vessels had a Chezkas Kashrus, Viein Machzikin Issura [See Aruch Hashulchan 122:20], as opposed to here where such a Chazaka or rule does not exist. [So is clearly evident from Chaim Sheol ibid who makes no mention of the Sfek Sfeika leniency of Rama ibid, thus proving that we do not apply it in this case. Furthermore, the above case of the Rama serves as a precedent to be stringent in this case even though it is a doubt after 24 hours, as the cases are not the same.]

The reason: As it is a case of doubt in which we rule stringently. Now, although if the pot is no longer Ben Yomo it is a case of Rabbinical doubt, nevertheless, since this doubt is due to ignorance, perhaps it is not considered a doubt at all and one cannot apply the rule of Safek Derabanan Lihakel. [See Michaber Y.D. 98:3, Shach 98:9 and Taz 98:6 regarding Daas Shotim that it is not considered a Safek even by a Rabbinical case, although in truth one can say that forgetting the status of an item is not considered Daas Shotim, as there is no one else in the world who can answer the doubt. If this were to be true then at least according to the Rama 122:9 there is possibility to apply the Sfek Sfeika to be lenient, however, as stated above, the Rama's case contains a Chezkas Kashrus and the rule of Ein Machzikin Issura to its benefit, as opposed to here. Whatever the case, it is clear from the Chaim Sheol ibid that we do not apply the Rama's leniency in this case] Furthermore, one may come to use

desire to Kasher the vessel, or it is unable to be Kashered, it may only be used for Pareve foods. If Pareve food is cooked in this vessel [i.e. a pot] then if it does not contain a Davar Charif, the food may be eaten together with dairy or meat in the same meal. If it contains a Davar Charif, it may not be eaten within a meat or dairy meal.[51]

If 12 months have passed: Some Poskim[52] rule that after 12 months of non-use of a vessel, the taste absorbed in the walls of the vessel becomes nullified and is considered Halachically irrelevant. Accordingly, if one is in doubt as to the status of the vessel which has not been used for the past 12 months, then there is room to permit designating it for meat or milk.[53] Nonetheless, it is best to Kasher the utensils beforehand, [especially if it is made of Kasherable material], and avoid the need to resort to this leniency. If the vessel is made of non-Kasherable material [i.e. porcelain], then it should be immersed three times in the Hagalah waters.[54]

Glass vessels: If one is unsure as to a glass vessel's dairy or meat status, one may designate it for whatever food one desires, whether meat or dairy.[55] Nonetheless, if the vessel is a Pyrex pot or baking pan, it is proper to have Hagalah performed to it three times prior to use.[56]

7. Am I Fleishig-If one tasted a meat food must he wait 6 hours prior to eating dairy?

Chewed but did not swallow: One who chews meat is required to wait 6 hours prior to eating dairy even if he did not swallow the meat.[57] The same applies towards any food cooked with meat, that if one chewed that food, even if he did not swallow it and did not chew actual meat, he must wait six hours prior to eating dairy.[58] [Thus, if one chewed a potato that was cooked in a chicken soup or Chulent, he must wait six hours even if he did not swallow it and immediately spat it out.]

---

the pot with a Davar Charif and the opposite dish, which according to many Poskim makes it Biblically considered like the taste of the pot even when not Ben Yomo. [See Panim Meiros 1:64; P"M 96 M"Z 1 based on Rashba 496; Shivas Tziyon 32; Rav Akiva Eiger, brought in Pischeiy Teshuvah 95:4]

[51] Rama 95:2; Implication of Aruch 24; Rashba 449; Admur 447:45; See also Michaber 103:6; Pischeiy Teshuvah 96:4

Other opinions-Ruling of Michaber: Some Poskim rule that according to the Michaber [mentioned in 96:1 regarding a knife which cut a Davar Charif that if it was not Ben Yomo it remains Pareve according to the first opinion then] if the pot was clean and not Ben Yomo, Bedieved if it was cooked with the opposite food it does not require nullification. [Hakashrus 10:113; See Kaf Hachaim 96:11] Other Poskim argue on the Rama's conclusion based on Rashba and Aruch ibid and suggest that even according to the Rashba and Aruch who rule regarding a knife that Charif turns non-Ben Yomo into Ben Yomo, by a pot the rule is different and Charif does not make non-Ben Yomo into Ben Yomo. The reason is because the concept of Nat Bar Nat still applies even by Charif, and hence only when there are two Nats, such as by a knife, do we say the taste is Beiyn, however when there are three Nats, such as the case in the case of a pot, then it is permitted. Practically, this opinion concludes that by definite Charif one is to be stringent like the Rama while by questionable Charif one may be lenient. [Makom Shmuel 89, brought in Pischeiy Teshuvah 95:4]

[52] Chacham Tzevi 75, 76 and 80 [regarding Bedieved even with Charif, based on Michaber Y.D. 135 that 12 months suffice for Yayin Nesech vessel, although, Lechatchila is Machmir], brought in Pischeiy Teshuvah Yoreh Deah 122:3 and Shaareiy Teshuvah Orach Chayim 451:1; Maharitz 75; Chaim Sheol 2:38-86 that so agreed Rav Naftali Hakohen, to ruling of Chacham Tzevi; See Sefer Hakashrus p. 176

Other opinions: Some Poskim rule a vessel remains forbidden forever due to its absorbed taste, even after 12 months. [Rashba 1:575, brought and explained in Chaim Sheol ibid, "Waiting 12 months only applies by Yayin Nesech"; Implication of Radbaz 739 *"The ability to delay 12 months for the vessel was only applied to Yayin Nesech and not other Issurim"* [However, see Chaim Shaul 2:38 for alternative explanation that the Radbaz refers to Lechatchila, while he agrees that Bedieved it becomes Kosher after 12 months]; Panim Meiros 1:31; Teshuvas Rav Akiva Eiger 43; Sew Pischeiy Teshuvah ibid; P"M 103]

[53] Conclusion of Chaim Shaul 2:38 regarding a porcelain vessel bought from a gentile and one is unsure if it was used for non-Kosher that possibly one may be lenient after 12 months due to a Sfek Sfeika, although he concludes with a Tzaruch Iyun.

[54] Conclusion of Pischeiy Teshuvah and Shaareiy Teshuvah ibid

[55] See the supplement in the end of our Semicha Aid "Basar Bechalav" Sefer regarding the status of glass, and that the main opinion follows as rule the Sephardim that is does not absorb. Hence, in a case of doubt certainly even Ashkenazim may be lenient, as writes Chaim Sheol ibid

[56] See the above Halacha regarding glass, that glass cookware is more stringent than regular glass, and hence it would be proper for Ashkenazim to Kasher it if they are unsure of its status.

[57] Michaber Y.D. 89:1; Tur 89:1; Following reason of Rambam Machalos Assuros 9:28, brought in Tur ibid, Taz 89:1 and Shach 89:2; Levush 89 and Issur Viheter 40:7 that so applies even according to Rashi; P"M 89 S.D. 2; Kitzur SHU"A 9

The reason: As some Poskim rule that the entire reason for waiting six hours is due to the meat stuck between the teeth, and hence it makes no difference regarding this matter whether one goes ahead and swallow it afterwards. [Taz 89:1 and Shach 89:2 in understanding of Rambam, ibid]

Other opinions: Some Poskim rule that one is not required to wait six hours after simply chewing the meat if one did not swallow it, as the main reason for the wait is not due to the meaty getting stuck between one's teeth but rather due to that after meat is swallowed it has the ability to give off a fatty taste for up to six hours after consumption. [First reason and opinion in Tur ibid, Taz ibid and Shach ibid, which follows the opinion of Rashi in his reasoning behind waiting six hours; However the Levush 89 and Issur Viheter 40:7 rule that even according to Rashi one must wait six hours after chewing, although the Shach ibid negates this approach] We follow the stringent opinion in this matter. [Tur ibid; Poskim ibid]

[58] Rama 89:3 that the custom is to wait six hours after Tavshil Shel Basar just like after meat itself; P"M 89 M"Z 1 that this applies even if one only chewed the food; Pischeiy Teshuvah 89:1 in name of Peri Megadim; Levush 89 and Issur Viheter 40:7 in their understanding of Rashi that even chewing releases fat

Swallowed but did not chew: If one swallowed meat, he is required to wait 6 hours prior to eating dairy even if he did not chew the meat.[59] The same applies towards any food cooked with meat, that if one swallowed that food, even if he did not eat or chew actual meat, he must wait six hours prior to eating dairy.[60] [Thus, one who swallows some chicken soup for the sake of tasting it, must wait six hours.]

Did not chew or swallow:[61] If one licked a meat food, or entered a meat food or dish into his mouth and immediately spat it out without even chewing or swallowing it, then he does not need to wait 6 hours prior to eating milk.[62] [He is however to rinse his mouth beforehand.[63] Hence, one may taste a meat soup or chicken soup, or lick a piece of meat, to see if it needs spices, and spit out the liquid and then rinse his mouth, and he may then eat dairy.]

Blessing: A blessing must be recited prior to eating and swallowing any amount of a food even if he is eating it for mere taste, to see if it needs spices. If, however, one plans to spit out the food, a blessing is not recited unless he chews/tastes a Kezayis/Revius or more of the food. See Topics in Practical Halacha Volume 1 Halacha 33 for the full details of this matter.

Summary:
One who chews or swallows a meat food or dish is required to wait six hours before eating dairy. If one did not chew or swallow the food, and simply licked it, or entered it into his mouth and spat it out prior to chewing, then he is not required to wait.

---

8. Onion problems-The law if a Davar Charif was used with meat and milk utensils:

A. If one cut an onion [or any other Charif] with a meat knife and then cut the same onion with a dairy knife, what is the status of the onion and dairy knife?

Background:[64] Sharp foods, such as onions and garlic[65], have ability to absorb the taste that is absorbed in a knife. Thus, if an onion was cut with a meat knife [that has been used to cut hot meat[66], or is washed with meat dishes in hot water], the entire[67] onion absorbs the meat taste and becomes meaty. This applies

---

The reason: Although in such a case that one did not chew actual meat and did not swallow it, neither the reason of Rashi or the Rambam behind the waiting of six hours is applicable, and hence one should not need to wait, nevertheless, one is to be stringent to wait six hours. This is due to a "Lo Pelug" [a non-negotiable status] and due to that so is the custom of the Jewish people who are holy and therefore one is to be stringent and not be Poretz Geder. [P"M ibid; Shaareiy Teshuvah ibid]

Other opinions: Some Poskim rule that one who ate a "Tavshil Shel Basar is not required to wait 6 hours prior to eating dairy, even if he chewed and swallowed it. [Michaber 89:3; Rav Nachman in Chulin 105] Practically, the custom today of even Sephardic Jewry is to be stringent like the Rama to wait 6 hours. [Beis Yosef 173; Peri Chadash 89:18; Zivcheiy Tzedek 89:31; Birkeiy Yosef 89:30; Lechem Hapanim 89:33; Kaf Hachaim 89:50 and 55] See however Peri Chadash 89:18 and Aruch Hashulchan 89:14 that tasting a Tavshil Shel Basar does not require waiting, and he does not differentiate between chewing and not chewing, Vetzaruch Iyun

[59] Following reason of Rashi, brought in Tur 89:1; Taz 89:1, Shach 89:2, that if one ate [i.e. swallowed] the meat, he must wait.
Other opinions: Some Poskim rule that one is not required to wait six hours after swallowing the meat without chewing it, as the main reason for the wait is not due to its ability to give off a fatty taste for up to six hours after consumption but rather due to that the meat gets stuck between one's teeth. [So is implied from the reason of Rambam, brought in Tur ibid, Taz 89:1 and Shach 89:2] We follow the stringent opinion in this matter. [Tur ibid; Poskim ibid]

[60] Rama 89:3 regarding Tavshil Shel Basar that so is the custom; Aruch; Beis Yosef 173; Opinion of Rashi, Vetzaruch Iyun why the Poskim ibid [Shach, Taz, P"M 89 M"Z 1,] omit this ramification between the reason of Rashi and the Rambam
Other opinions: See previous footnotes.

[61] Hagahos Maharshak on P"M 89 M"Z 1; Ben Ish Chaiy Shelach 9; Zivcheiy Tzedek 89:5; Darkei Teshuvah 89:22; Aruch Hashulchan 89:14; Kaf Hachaim 89:4; Kapei Aaron 30

[62] The reason: As in such a case that one did not chew anything and did not swallow it, neither the reason of Rashi or the Rambam behind the waiting of six hours is applicable, and hence one does not need to wait. Now, although we ruled that one is to be stringent to wait six hours even if he simply chews a Tavshil Shel Basar. This is due to a "Lo Pelug" [a non-negotiable status] and due to that so is the custom of the Jewish people who are holy and therefore one is to be stringent and not be Poretz Geder. However, in this case that one did not even chew it, the Lo Plug and custom does not apply.

[63] Michaber 89:2 regarding eating meat after cheese and the same would apply here; Darkei Teshuvah 89:31 and Hakashrus 10:48 regarding one who drank milk that only Hadacha is required; Aruch Hashulchan in name of Peri Chadash 89:18 that both Kinuach and Hadacha is required, however seemingly the case there is referring to one who chewed the food.

[64] Michaber and Rama 96:1-2
[65] Michaber 96:2; Admur 447:40
[66] Beis Yosef 96 in explanation of Rambam; Beis David Y.D. 38; 39; Zivcheiy Tzedek 96:34; Kaf Hachaim 96:48
[67] Rama 96:1; Peri Toar 96; Rashba Toras Habayis Hearuch 4:1, brought in Tur ibid; Ran Chulin 41a

even if the knife was clean and was not Ben Yomo at its time of use.[68] We will now analyze the law regarding if both a meat and dairy knife were used for the same onion:

The status of the onion: If the onion that was cut with a meat knife was then cut with a dairy knife [that have been used in the past to cut hot meat/dairy] then the onion is forbidden, as it has absorbed from both meat and dairy. This applies even if both knives were clean and not Ben Yomo.[69] [However, if the meat or dairy knife have never been used to cut hot meat/cheese, and have not been washed with hot meat or cheese, then the onion remains Kosher, and requires a mere rinsing.[70]]

The status of the dairy knife: If the meat knife has been used in the past for cutting hot meat, or being washed with hot meat, then the following is the law regarding the dairy knife: Some Poskim[71] rule the dairy knife is forbidden and must be Koshered.[72] Other Poskim[73], however, rule the knife remains Kosher.[74] [Seemingly, one may be lenient if the original knife was not Ben Yomo, or if the Charif was cut on its other side, beyond the Netila area of the original cut, to permit the knife without Koshering.[75] Nonetheless, it is best to Kosher it being that doing so is so easily attainable. One can simply place the blade of the knife over a flame, and have it Koshered through Libun Kal.]

Summary:
If an onion was cut with both a meat and dairy knife [that have been used in the past to cut hot meat/dairy] then the onion is forbidden. Regarding the knife: It is disputed in Poskim if it remains Kosher, and hence is best to be Koshered.

B. What is the law if one cut onions with a dairy knife and fried them in a meat pot?
If a Pareve Charif/sharp food was cooked in a meat pot then even if the pot was clean and not Ben Yomo, the food becomes meaty and is forbidden to be eaten with milk.[76] Likewise, if a Charif [i.e. sharp] food,

---

Opinions in Rishonim who hold only Netila is required: The following Rishonim explicitly rule that one is only required to remove a Netila's worth: Raavad Avoda Zara 76a, brought in Rashba ibid; Semag Lavin 140; Reah in Bedek Habayis 4:1, brought in Ran Chulin 41a [See Beis Yosef 96:1]

[68] Shach 96:6 and 19 "*So is the custom, and so rule all the Achronim.*"; Admur 447:40 and 55 and 59; Daas Torah 96

Other opinions: Some Poskim rule that if the knife was not Ben Yomo and is clean then one may use the spicy food for the opposite food. [Stam opinion in Michaber 96:1; 3; 103:6; 114:8; Maharam Teshuvos Upesakim 22, brought in Tur 96:2 and Rosh Avoda Zara 38]

Custom of Sephardim: The Michaber ibid does not arbitrate between the two opinions that he records. According to the Kelalim of ruling of the Shulchan Aruch, whenever the Michaber writes like one opinion and then brings a second stringent opinion, his intent is to rule that one is initially to be stringent like the second opinion, although one may be lenient in a case of great loss. Hence, if the Charif was cut with a clean non-Ben Yomo knife, a Netila worth must be removed and 60x is required, although in a time of great need or loss one may permit the food even if it does not contain 60x. The reason the Michaber omitted this stringency from other areas [see 103:6; 114:8] is because he relied on the fact that he already recorded their opinion here. [Kaf Hachaim 96:10, 11, 50; See Shach 96:19; Taz 96:10] However, other Poskim learn that the Michaber in truth is lenient. [P"M 10 S.D. "Gimel Middos Besakin"]

[69] If the onion was cut from opposite sides: If the onion was cut from opposite sides, two Netila's distances [4 cm] from each other, then seemingly, Bedieved the onion remains Kosher, and each half [Netila area by each side] becomes dairy or meaty. Furthermore, even if one cut the onion on the Netila side, seemingly past the Netila area remains Kosher as we rule Bedieved like the opinion who rules that Charif does not absorb more than Kdei Netila. [See Rama 96:1] This certainly applies according to the Sephardim who never prohibit more than a Netila. Vetzaruch Iyun.

[70] Beis Yosef 96 in explanation of Rambam; Beis David Y.D. 38; 39; Zivcheiy Tzedek 96:34; Kaf Hachaim 96:48

[71] Magen Avraham 451:31; Chochmas Adam 49:10; Implication of Admur 451:54 that Charif transfers taste to the knife; See also Even Haezer 96:3

[72] The reason: As the Charif has power to absorb the meat taste into the dairy knife.

[73] P"M 447 M.Z. 13; Daas Torah 96 p. 258

[74] The reason: As a knife which cut a Charif only has ability to transfer taste to the Charif and does not have ability to extract its absorbed taste into itself. [P"M ibid]

[75] The reason: As this is a case of Sfek Sfeika, as some Poskim rule non-Ben Yomo knives do not prohibit a Charif, and other Poskim rule that knives do not absorb from the Charif. Certainly, if one cut the onion from opposite ends, in which case we rule that Bedieved the onion did not absorb past its Netila worth, then the knife does not need to be Koshered.

[76] Rama 95:2; Implication of Aruch 24; Rashba 449; Admur 447:45; See also Michaber 103:6; Pischeiy Teshuvah 96:4

Other opinions-Ruling of Michaber: Some Poskim rule that according to the Michaber [mentioned in 96:1 regarding a knife which cut a Davar Charif that if it was not Ben Yomo it remains Pareve according to the first opinion then] if the pot was clean and not Ben Yomo, Bedieved if it was cooked with the opposite food it does not require nullification. [Hakashrus 10:113; See Kaf Hachaim 96:11] Other Poskim argue on the Rama's conclusion based on Rashba and Aruch ibid and suggest that even according to the Rashba and Aruch who rule regarding a knife that Charif turns non-Ben Yomo into Ben Yomo, by a pot the rule is different and Charif does not make non-Ben Yomo into Ben Yomo. The reason is

such as onions and garlic[77], was cut with a meat or dairy knife [that has been used in the past to cut hot meat/cheese[78]], then the entire[79] food becomes meaty/dairy and is forbidden from being eaten/cooked with the opposite food.[80] This applies even if the knife was clean and was not Ben Yomo [i.e. had not cut hot meat or cheese within the past 24 hours] at its time of use.[81] Accordingly, if an onion was cut with a dairy knife that has been used in the past to cut hot dairy, the entire onion absorbs the dairy taste and becomes dairy. If one later fries this onion in a meat pot, then the onions extract and absorb the meat taste in the pot, thus making it forbidden due to a mixture of meat and milk. This causes that everything becomes forbidden, including the onions, pot and any utensils used for mixing the food.

C. What is the law if one cut onions with a dairy knife and cooked them in a meat pot together with water or other foods?

If one cut onions with a dairy knife [that has been used in the past to cut hot cheese[82]] and then cooked the onion in a meat pot, then if one did not fry the onion first, but initially cooked the onions together with other foods in the meat pot [i.e. in a soup or Chulent], then if that food contains 60x versus the onion[83], or

---

because the concept of Nat Bar Nat still applies even by Charif, and hence only when there are two Nats, such as by a knife, do we say the taste is Beiyn, however when there are three Nats, such as the case in the case of a pot, then it is permitted. Practically, this opinion concludes that by definite Charif one is to be stringent like the Rama while by questionable Charif one may be lenient. [Makom Shmuel 89, brought in Pischeiy Teshuvah 95:4]

Is the concept of a Davar Charif a Biblical or Rabbinical concept? See "The Practical laws of Basar Bechalav" Chapter 5 Halacha 3!

The reason: As the sharp food enriches the meaty taste of the pot and effects that its taste be considered Beiyn [direct taste from meat] and is thus no longer considered Nat Bar Nat. [Shach 95:7; Admur ibid that it becomes Tam Rishon]

[77] Michaber 96:2; Admur 447:40 [Rav Yaakov Yosef ruled on one occasion that the onions of today are no longer considered Charif and one may hence be lenient. I have not found this opinion in other Poskim.]

[78] Beis Yosef 96 in name of Rambam; Beis David Y.D. 38; 39; Zivcheiy Tzedek 96:34; Kaf Hachaim 96:48; See Q&A!

[79] Rama 96:1 in final ruling that so is the Lechatchila custom; Peri Toar 96; Rashba Toras Habayis Hearuch 4:1, brought in Tur ibid; Ran Chulin 41a

The reason: The reason behind this opinion is because they hold that all spicy foods have the same status as a Kurt Shel Chalatis for all matters and hence they absorb the taste of the knife throughout their entire mass. [Taz 96:7; Lechem Hapanim 96:11; Beis Lechem Yehuda 96:9; Kaf Hachaim 96:25]

Other opinions who hold only Netila is required: Some Poskim rule that one is only required to remove a Netila's worth from the Charif and the remainder is Pareve. [Michaber ibid; Raavad Avoda Zara 76a, brought in Rashba ibid; Semag Lavin 140; Reah in Bedek Habayis 4:1, brought in Ran Chulin 41a; See Beis Yosef 96:1]

The Sephardic custom: The Sephardim follow the ruling of Michaber that a Davar Charif only absorbs a Netila worth even when used with a dirty Ben Yomo knife. [Erech Hashulchan 96:2 that so rule majority of Poskim; Zivcheiy Tzedek 96:4 and 21; Kaf Hachaim 96:4 and 27] However, the Peri Toar rules to be stringent like the Rama to forbid the entire Charif.

[80] The reason even a clean knife transfers taste: As the sharpness of the food and the pressure of the knife together causes the Ben Yomo taste that is absorbed within the knife to get extracted and absorbed within the food to the point of a thumbs width. This absorption is of such good quality that it is considered as if it became directly absorbed from the actual meat and is hence not defined as Nat Bar Nat. [Shach 96:2; Kreisi 96:1; Peri Toar 96:1; P"M 96 S.D.2; Chavas Daas 96:1; Chochmas Adam 49:1; Beis Yitzchak 96:2; Aruch Hashulchan 96:5; Zivcheiy Tzedek 96:1; Kaf Hachaim 96:1] Now, if the knife is not Ben Yomo but is dirty with fat, then the fat becomes absorbed into the food due to its sharpness and pressure of the knife. [Taz 96:1]

[81] 2nd opinion in Michaber 96:1 regarding forbidding Netila [omitted from 96:3, 103:6, 114:8]; Sefer Hateruma 60, brought in Tur 96:1; Shach 96:6 and 19 "So is the custom, and so rule all the Achronim"; Admur 447:40 and 55 and 59; Daas Torah 96

The reason: The reason behind this opinion is because they hold that all spicy foods have the same status as a Kurt Shel Chalatis and hence have the ability to extract and enhance the spoiled non-Ben Yomo taste absorbed within a knife. This absorption of such good quality that it is considered as if it became directly absorbed from the actual meat and is hence not defined as Nat Bar Nat. The reason that the quality of taste absorbed is so great is because a) knives commonly have fat residue on them and b) The sharpness of the Charif and pressure of the knife cause a greater quality of taste to be absorbed. [Taz 96:3; Shach 96:6; Admur 447:59; Kaf Hachaim 96:9]

Other opinions: Some Poskim rule that if the knife was not Ben Yomo, and is clean, then one may use the spicy food for the opposite food. [Stam opinion in Michaber 96:1; 3; 103:6; 114:8; Maharam Teshuvos Upesakim 22, brought in Tur 96:2 and Rosh Avoda Zara 38] The reason behind this opinion is because they hold that only a Kurt Shel Chalatis is a true Charif, as it can puncture the intestines of a cow which eats it, and hence even when cut with a clean and non-Ben Yomo knife, it has ability to extract and enhance the taste. However, other sharp foods, are not sharp enough to extract and enhance non-Ben Yomo taste. [Taz 96:1]

Custom of Sephardim: The Michaber ibid does not arbitrate between the two opinions that he records. According to the Kelalim of ruling of the Shulchan Aruch, whenever the Michaber writes like one opinion and then brings a second stringent opinion, his intent is to rule that one is initially to be stringent like the second opinion, although one may be lenient in a case of great loss. Hence, if the Charif was cut with a clean non-Ben Yomo knife, a Netila worth must be removed and 60x is required, although in a time of great need or loss one may permit the food even if it does not contain 60x. The reason the Michaber omitted this stringency from other areas [see 103:6; 114:8] is because he relied on the fact that he already recorded their opinion here. [Kaf Hachaim 96:10, 11, 50; See Shach 96:19; Taz 96:10] However, other Poskim learn that the Michaber in truth is lenient. [P"M 10 S.D. "Gimmel Middos Besakin"]

[82] Beis Yosef 96 in name of Rambam; Beis David Y.D. 38; 39; Zivcheiy Tzedek 96:34; Kaf Hachaim 96:48; See Q&A!

[83] When measuring versus the onion, does one measure versus the entire onion or only a Netila worth of the onion? If the Charif food was sliced in half then one only requires 60x versus the Netila/finger area of the Charif food [i.e. 2 cm of each side of the slice], or 60x versus the blade of

60x versus the blade of the dairy knife[84], then everything is permitted, including the onion.[85] This applies even if one cooked the onion in chicken soup, or a meat cholent.[86] If, however, the food does not contain 60x the onion, or the blade of the knife, then if the pot or spatula was Ben Yomo of meat use, or there were meat ingredients in the pot together with the onion, then everything is forbidden [i.e. the pot, soup, and spatula]. If, however, there were only Pareve ingredients cooking in soup, and the pot and spatula was not Ben Yomo, then if the onion is a minority ingredient of the mixture[87], then the food remains permitted [and becomes dairy], although the pot is forbidden and must be Koshered.[88] If the onion is the majority ingredient in the food, then everything is forbidden, even if the pot was not Ben Yomo.[89] If one first fried the onion in a meat pot and then mixed it with other foods [whether Pareve or meaty/dairy], then in all cases, the other foods must have 60x versus all the onions[90], otherwise everything is forbidden.

Summary:
Fried: If one **fried** onions that were cut with a dairy knife [that was used in the past to cut hot dairy] in a meat pot, everything is forbidden [the pot, onions and spatula].
Cooked with other foods: If one **cooked** onions that were cut with a dairy knife [that was used in the past to cut hot dairy] in a meat pot together with other foods, everything is forbidden [the pot, onions and spatula], unless the food contains 60x versus the blade of the knife [or onions, whatever is less], or the food is Pareve, and the pot is not Ben Yomo, and the onions are a minority ingredient, in which case only the pot is forbidden while the food remains Kosher.

A word of advice regarding Charif:
Due to the complex Halachic issues that a Charif vegetable poses if it is cut with a meat or dairy knife [and then gets used with the opposite food or vessel], it is highly recommended that every kitchen

---

the knife, whichever is less. [Michaber 96:1; Rama ibid that Bedieved we are lenient like Michaber; Peri Toar 96; Raavad Avoda Zara 76a, brought in Rashba ibid; Semag Lavin 140; Reah in Bedek Habayis 4:1, brought in Ran Chulin 41a; See Beis Yosef 96:1] If, however, the spicy food was cut into small pieces [less than a Netila worth-2 cm-each] then according to all opinions if one went ahead and cooked it with the opposite food, one requires 60x versus the entire spicy food or 60x versus the blade of the knife, if it is of smaller size. [Rama ibid; Shach 96:9; Kneses Hagedola 96:34; Peri Chadash 96:8; Kreisi 96:6; Lechem Hapanim 96:10; Beis Lechem Yehuda 96:8; Chochmas Adam 49:3; Kaf Hachaim 96:22]

[84] Does one measure against the blade or the onion? If one cut a sharp food with a meat knife and cooked it together with milk, one needs to measure 60x in the dairy food versus the Netila area of the food, or versus the knife which he used to cut with. One can choose to measure against whichever amount is less; if the area of the blade is less than the Netila area, he may measure versus the blade; if the Netila area of the food is less than the blade one may measure versus the Netila. [Michaber 96:1; This applies even according to the Rama as the food has absorbed Heter and not become Chanan.; Taz 96:6; Shach 96:9; Lechem Hapanim 96:9; Beis Lechem Yehuda 96:7; Chavas Daas 96:5 Biurim 1; P"M 96 M.Z. 6; Kaf Hachaim 96:21]

How much of the blade is one to measure against? If one is unsure how much of the blade was used to cut with, one is to measure 60x against the entire blade. [Shach 96:8 Taz 96:4; Rashal Gid Hanashe 42; Kol Habasar 62; Kneses Hagedola 96:33; Minchas Yaakov 61:7; Lechem Hapanim 96:7; Beis Lechem Yehuda 96:5; Chavas Daas 96:4; Chochmas Adam 49:2; Kaf Hachaim 96:17]

Measuring versus the amount of dairy the knife absorbed: In all cases that one is aware of the amount of hot dairy that the knife was used for cutting since its purchase, then one may measure versus the meat if it is a smaller amount than the blade or food. [Bach 96; Zivcheiy Tzedek 96:19; Kaf Hachaim 96:124]

[85] Taz 96:5; Shach 94:23; Maharam Melublin 28; Admur 447:60; M"A 447:38; Kneses Hagedola 96:2; Peri Chadash 94:21; Minchas Yaakov 61:6; Beis David Y.D. p. 16; Lechem Hapanim 96:7; Beis Lechem Yehuda 96:5; Chavas Daas 96:5 Biurim 1; Erech Hashulchan 96:5; Kaf Hachaim 94:60; 96:19

[86] See sources in previous footnote!

[87] See Rama 95:2; Taz 103:9 that if the Charif is a minority ingredient, then the mixture is not considered Charif. See next footnote

[88] As we consider it that the pot has absorbed the dairy taste carried in the onion, and it is hence similar to one who cooked dairy in a Non-Ben Yomo meat pot in which case we rule that the pot is nevertheless forbidden. [See Michaber 93:1; Shach 93:3 based on Rama in 94:5; Beis Lechem Yehuda 93:4; Chavas Daas 93:3; Kaf Hachaim 93:16; 94:54] Now, although the onion here is in minority, it is only its Charifus, and ability to extract non-Ben Yomo meat taste from the pot, which is negated, and not its ability to transfer taste into the pot. It is also similar to the case that a potato from a meat cholent was cooked in a dairy pot with other foods, in which case we rule that if there isn't 60x versus the potato, the pot is forbidden even if it is not Ben Yomo. [See Rama 94:5 as explained in Shach 94:18; Taz 94:8; Toras Chatas 57:14; Chavas Daas 94:16; P"M 94 S.D. 18; M.Z. 7; Biur Hagr"a 94:18; Kaf Hachaim 94:52; See the following Poskim that by food we do not say Nat Bar Nat: Shaareiy Dura 60:3; Kneses Hagedola 95:26; P"M 93 S.D. 4; 94 M.Z. 1; 95 M.Z. 1; Chavas Daas 95:2; Kehilas Yehuda 95:1; Zivcheiy Tzedek 95:8; Kaf Hachaim 95:10; All the more so does this apply in this case, where we view the Charif as Beiyn of dairy.]

[89] See Rama 95:2; Taz 103:9 that if the Charif is a majority ingredient, then the mixture is considered Charif and hence extracts the meat taste from the pot, thus making everything forbidden.

[90] In such a case the onions become Chanan and it does not suffice to measure 60x versus the blade of the knife, or versus a Netila's worth of the onion.

> establishes a rule that all Charif vegetables be cut with a Pareve knife and Pareve cutting board. Experience has shown that leaving a meat or dairy cut Charif vegetable around the fridge is bound to create problems, as people forget its status and can come to use it for the opposite food.

---------------Machalei Akum----------------

9. The bread and cooked food of a non-religious Jew?

Some Poskim[91] rule that a Jew which is a Mumar or desecrates Shabbos in public[92] has the status of a gentile with regards to all matters, and hence all foods that are forbidden to be eaten if baked by a gentile are forbidden to be eaten if baked by this Jew.[93] Other Poskim[94] however rule that the prohibition of Bishul/Afiyas Akum applies only to a gentile and does not apply at all to a Jew, even if he is not religious.[95] Practically, one is initially to be stringent in this matter.[96] However, Bedieved, one may be lenient to eat the food.[97] It is customary amongst the Mehadrin Hashgachas to be stringent in this matter, to only have an observant Jew turn on the flames for the cooking of the food.

> **Q&A**
> **May one have a non-religious family member cook food for the family in one's home?**
> Initially, one is not to have him to do so unless a religious Jew turns on the flame. In a time of need, one is to contact his Rav.

10. May one drink Kosher coffee brewed by a gentile? Is coffee considered Bishul Akum?[98]

Kashrus of the coffee powder, and pot: Drinking coffee made by a gentile poses several Kashrus concerns such as a) Is the coffee powder Kosher? b) Was non-Kosher milk added to the coffee pot within the past 24 hours? c) Is the coffee pot washed in hot water together with non-Kosher ingredients and has it been washed within 24 hours of the current use? d) Bishul Akum; e) Drinking in a party of gentiles. Below we will address only the concern of Bishul Akum. [In general, all non-flavored coffee is considered Kosher, and hence if one knows that the coffee pot is used only for plain coffee [no milk] and is washed alone without other utensils, then the only remaining concern is Bishul Akum. Some say that coffee pots on planes fulfill the above conditions, and hence its only remaining issue is of Bishul Akum, which will be

---

[91] Admur O.C. 39:1 "He is like a gentile for all matters"; Michaber Yoreh Deah 2:5 "He is like a gentile"; Admur Y.D. 2:10 "He is a like a gentile regarding Shechita **and for the entire Torah**, except for Kiddushin"; Rashba 7:53; Tiferes Lemoshe 113:9 [brought in Pischeiy Teshuvah 113:1] regarding Bishul Akum [however not Pas Akum]; Erech Hashulchan 112:2; Kaf Hachaim 112:11; Ketzos Hashulchan 101:5 and Kitzur Shulchan Aruch 72: "Anyone who publicly desecrates Shabbos is considered like an idle worshiper and [thus] if he touches wine he forbids it, and the bread which he bakes is like Pas Akum, as well as the food which he cooks is like Bishul Akum."

[92] Regarding who is defined as one who "desecrates Shabbos in public" in this regard-see next Q&A!

[93] The reason: As there is an additional reason mentioned in the Beis Yosef against Pas/Bishul Akum which is so one does not come to eat non-kosher foods, and this worry is applicable also by a non-religious Jew. [Kaf Hachaim 113:1 in name of Tiferes Lemoshe] Alternatively, this is due to a fine enacted by the Sages.

[94] Pischeiy Teshuvah 112:1 in name of Tiferes Lemoshe 113:9 regarding Pas Akum and even regarding Bishul Akum, according to the main reason mentioned, it is not applicable

[95] Pischeiy Teshuvah ibid
The reason: As the main reason behind the prohibition is because one may come to marry the daughter of the cook, which is a worry that is only applicable if the daughter is a non-Jew.

[96] Kaf Hachaim 112:11; 113:1; Sefer Hakashrus 19:18; Teshuvos Vehanhagos [of Harav **Shternbuch**] 1:470, 2:386 rules that at times of need one may be lenient so long as the Jew is not reform. Harav Asher Lemel Cohen ruled to me that it is allowed if the person does not desecrate "Lehachis". [Vetzaruch Iyun from ruling of Admur/Shach brought in 2:10 which does not differentiate between the two.] Rav Avraham Osdaba however ruled to me that it is not allowed due to a question of Bishul Akum, and even if the person will get offended, he must be told that he may not turn the fire on when he cooks. Practically, in a time of need one is to

[97] Kaf Hachaim 113:1
The reason: As in a Rabbinical dispute we rule leniently. [ibid] In addition, there are various conditions that need to be fulfilled for a Jew to be defined as a public desecrater of Shabbos, as explained in the next Q&A, and hence since most [if not all] non-observant Jews do not fulfill all these conditions, it is therefore a further reason to be lenient, even according to the stringent opinion.

[98] See Birkeiy Yosef 113 Shiyurei Bracha 3; Pischeiy Teshuvah 114:1; Kaf Hachaim 113:21

addressed below.⁹⁹ However, others have testified of Kashrus concerns with the coffee pots.¹⁰⁰]

Bishul Akum: Some Poskim[101] rule it is permitted to drink coffee that is brewed by a gentile, and it does not contain the prohibition of Bishul Akum.[102] Other Poskim[103] rule it is forbidden to drink coffee that was brewed by a gentile due to the prohibition of Bishul Akum.[104] Furthermore, some Poskim[105] rule a Torah scholar is not to drink coffee cooked by a gentile, even if it is not prohibited due to Bishul Akum.[106] Other Poskim[107] however argue that if coffee is free of the issue of Bishul Akum, as rules the former opinion, then it is not necessary today for a Torah scholar to be stringent in this matter. Practically, one who desires to be stringent, should be stringent upon himself, while one who desires to be lenient is not to be protested.[108]

Practical suggestion for airplane coffee:[109] In order to avoid any Kashrus issues, it is suggested that one use a disposable, or glass cup for one's coffee, and likewise get hot water from the main tank, rather than drinking from the coffee served in the coffee pot.

11. Bishul Yisrael by candies and cereals:
A. The general law:

All foods that are cooked are subject to the laws of Bishul Akum, with exception to Mezonos products that are baked, which are subject to the laws of Pas Akum.[110] The prohibition of Bishul Akum only applies to foods that cannot be eaten raw, and are of importance to be served at a kings table. All foods that are edible raw, or are of unimportance and hence not served at a kings table, are not subject to the laws of Bishul Akum, and may hence be cooked by a gentile.[111] If, however, the food is eaten on a kings table and is not eaten raw, then it is prohibited due to Bishul Akum even if the food is not eaten together with bread, but rather as a desert or appetizer.[112] [However, some Poskim[113] are lenient and rule that only foods that are eaten with bread are prohibited due to Bishul Akum, and thus even if the food is eaten on a kings table and is not eaten raw, if it is not eaten with bread it is exempt from the prohibition of Bishul Akum. Aside for the above discussion, it is questionable as to what is the exact definition of an "important food which is served at a kings table?" Some[114] suggest it refers to any food that is not normally served at a wedding meal or at a White House dinner, and so is the approach followed by the

---

[99] Rav Heinman of Chof Kei and Rav Belski of OU allows drinking plane coffee.

[100] In one case the flight attendant admitted to heating bacon in the pot and then washing it out for use for the coffee; In another case they said they randomly switch off pots used with milk.

[101] Radbaz 637; Peri Chadash 112:17; 114:6; Yaavetz 2:142; Beis Yehuda 91; Yad Efraim 114; Beir Oshek 105, brought in Gilyon Maharsha 113; Teshuvos Bach 155 is stringent upon self, but does not protest others; Mahrikash 114; Bnei Chayeh 145; Darkei Teshuvah 113:2; Zivchei Tzedek 113:15 that so is custom of Bagdad; Ben Ish Chaiy Chukas 16; Chochmas Adam 66:14; Aruch Hashulchan 113:22-23; Shearim Hametzuyanim Behalacha in name of Chasam Sofer; Yechaveh Daas 4:42

[102] The reason: As coffee is mainly made of water, and water can be drunk plain, and is hence exempt from Bishul Akum. [Peri Chadash ibid]

[103] Kneses Hagedola 113:17; Arizal in Nagid Mitzvah, brought in Kneses Hagedola, Kaf Hachaim ibid [Kneses Hagedola and Kaf Hachaim ibid learns that according to Arizal it is forbidden, however other Poskim learn the Arizal was only stringent upon himself]; Panim Meiros 2:62, brought in Pischeiy Teshuvah 114:1; See Shevet Halevi 2:44; 5:93

[104] The reason: As coffee is not viewed as plain water, and it is fit to be brought to a kings table. Therefore, it shares all the prohibitions of Bishul Akum. Thus, a Baal Nefesh should be stringent not to drink any coffee or tea made by a gentile. [Panim Meiros ibid]

[105] Shach 152:2; Shabbos 51a; Arizal Shaar Hamitzvos Vayeilech regarding Turmisin, even though they are not Oleh Al Shulchan Melachim; Divrei Yosef 45; Maharikash 113; Rashbatz 1:89; Chida in Birkeiy Yosef 113 Shiyurei Bracha 4; Mizmor Ledavid 113; Kaf Hachaim 113:12; Shevet Halevi 6:108-3

[106] The reason: As when people see him being lenient, they will come to be even more lenient than him. [Rashi ibid]

[107] Kneses Hagedola 113:14; Peri Chadash 113:3; Lechem Hapanim 113:2; Peri Toar 114:9; Erech Hashulchan 113:3; Bach, based on omission of Rof and Rambam, brought in Shach ibid; Minchas Yaakov 75:30; Degul Merivava 113:1; Aruch Hashulchan 113:11; Zivcheiy Tzedek 113:10; Yeshuos Yaakov 113:1

[108] Zivchei Tzedek ibid; Ben Ish Chaiy Chukas 16; Kaf Hachaim 113:21; Panim Meiros ibid *"A Baal Nefesh should be stringent not to drink any coffee or tea made by a gentile."*

[109] Sefer Hakashrus Lehalacha p. 395

[110] See Michaber 112:1; Taz 112:6; Shach 112:18; Toras Chatas 75:12; Beis Yosef 12 in name of Rav Yechiel; Peri Chadash 112:17; Beis Lechem Yehuda 112:11; Kaf Hachaim 112:35; See Hakashrus 19:2

[111] Michaber 113:1; Avoda Zara 38a

[112] Implication of Michaber 113:1 "Or to eat as a Parperes" as writes the Peri Chadash 113:3 and so conclude the following Poskim: Chochmas Adam 66:1; Aruch Hashulchan 113:7; Kaf Hachaim 113:7

[113] Peri Chadash 113:3

[114] Many Rabbanim and Kashrus organizations including: Rav Yisrael Belsky of the OU; Rav Heinman of the Star K; See Kashrus Halacha Lemaaseh p. 373

OU and Star K. Others[115] suggest it includes any food that will be put out in front of guests to eat, such as on Shabbos, even during breakfast, but not foods that are only eaten as a mere snack. Others[116] ascertain that due to the complexity of defining this matter, all cooked foods should be treated today as important foods that can be eaten at a kings table, and so is the approach of some Mehadrin Hashgachas in Eretz Yisrael, such as the Eida Hachareidis and others.[117] Regarding the definition of "cooked by a gentile" there is discussion in Poskim[118] as to whether electric machinery which is used in food plants to cook their products is considered cooked by a gentile or not. Practically, the Poskim conclude stringently in this regard.[119] In addition to all the above, some Poskim[120] rule a Torah scholar is not to eat any food cooked by a gentile, even if it is not prohibited due to Bishul Akum.[121] Other Poskim[122] however argue that it is not necessary today for a Torah scholar to be stringent in this matter. Practically, one who desires to be stringent, should be stringent upon himself, while one who desires to be lenient is not to be protested.[123]

B. Must non-Mezonos cereals, such as cornflakes, be Bishul Yisrael and what is the status of Kellogg's?

Cereals are made of ingredients that cannot be eaten raw and are usually first cooked and then puffed or baked. If they are a Mezonos product, then they are subject to the laws of Pas Akum, while if they are a non-Mezonos product then they are subject to the laws of Bishul Akum. Below we will discuss the laws of non-Mezonos cereals and whether they are subject to the laws of Bishul Akum: Some Rabbanim[124] and Hashgacha companies[125], hold that cereals are not considered food that is fit to be served on a king's table, and thus do not need to be Bishul Akum.[126] However, other Rabbanim[127] and Hashgacha companies[128] hold that cereal is defined as fit to be served on a king's table and thus must be Bishul Yisrael in order to be considered Kosher.[129] Practically, one is to follow the directive of his Rav regarding this matter. Even according to the lenient approach, there is room to be stringent in this matter if one desires.[130]

---

[115] Beis Vaad Lachachamim p. 303 and onwards; See Kashrus Halacha Lemaaseh p. 373

[116] See Beis Vaad Lachachamim p. 303 and footnote 39 in name of some Rabbanim and Mehadrin Hashgacha's; Opinion of Rav Moshe Yosef, the Rav Hamachshir of Badatz Beit Yosef; See Igros Moshe Y.D. 4:48 regarding potato chips; See Aruch Hashulchan 113:18 that foods that are only eaten by the poor are defined as Eino Oleh; See Kashrus Halacha Lemaaseh p. 373

[117] So I was told by a representative of the Vaad Hakashrus of the Eida Hachareidis that they ae initially careful that the boiler for the candy production be turned on by a Jew.

[118] See Kashrus Halacha Lemaaseh p. 380-384

[119] See Shevet Halevi 6:108-6; Minchas Yitzchak 3:26; Yabia Omer 5:9; Igros Moshe Y.D. 4:48 rules stringently although says the world is accustomed to be lenient and are not to be protested

[120] Shach 152:2; Shabbos 51a; Arizal Shaar Hamitzvos Vayeilech regarding Turmisin, even though they are not Oleh Al Shulchan Melachim; Divrei Yosef 45; Maharikash 113; Rashbatz 1:89; Chida in Birkeiy Yosef 113 Shiyurei Bracha 4; Mizmor Ledavid 113; Kaf Hachaim 113:12; Shevet Halevi 6:108-3

[121] The reason: As when people see him being lenient, they will come to be even more lenient than him. [Rashi ibid]

[122] Kneses Hagedola 113:14; Peri Chadash 113:3; Lechem Hapanim 113:2; Peri Toar 114:9; Erech Hashulchan 113:3; Bach, based on omission of Rof and Rambam, brought in Shach ibid; Minchas Yaakov 75:30; Degul Merivava 113:1; Aruch Hashulchan 113:11; Zivcheiy Tzedek 113:10; Yeshuos Yaakov 113:1

[123] Zivchei Tzedek ibid; Ben Ish Chaiy Chukas 16; Kaf Hachaim 113:21; Panim Meiros ibid "A Baal Nefesh should be stringent not to drink any coffee or tea made by a gentile."

[124] Rav Mordechai Eliyahu; Rav Yisrael Belsky of the OU; Rav Heinman of the Star K; See Kashrus Halacha Lemaaseh p. 373; Rav Padvah of England told me that he personally holds it does not need to be Bishul Yisrael

[125] Such as the OU; I received a similar reply from the OK.

[126] The reason: As, they hold that a king's food refers to a food that is served at a wedding and the like. Other reasons which helps exempt non-Mezonos cereals from the prohibition of Bishul Akum: 1) Cereal is not eaten together with bread, and thus according to some Poskim is exempt from Bishul Akum, even if it were eaten at a kings table. 2) The batter is not directly cooked by a gentile but rather through automatic machinery that is turned on by a gentile.

[127] See Beis Vaad Lachachamim p. 303 and footnote 39 in name of some Rabbanim and Mehadrin Hashgacha's; Opinion of Rav Moshe Yosef, the Rav Hamachshir of Badatz Beit Yosef; See Igros Moshe Y.D. 4:48 regarding potato chips; See Aruch Hashulchan 113:18 that foods that are only eaten by the poor are defined as Eino Oleh; See Kashrus Halacha Lemaaseh p. 373

[128] So is the initial policy of the Eida Hachareidis in Eretz Yisrael, to require cereals to be Bishul Yisrael.

[129] The reason: As cereals are served in fancy hotels for breakfast, and hence can be considered fit to be served at a kings table, which would require it to be Bishul Yisrael.

[130] Besides for the unclarity in the exact definition of Eino Oleh Al Shulchan Melachim, it is also a Hiddur for a Talmid Chacham not to eat food cooked by a gentile even if not forbidden due to Bishul Akum.

Practically, how do I know if my cereal is Bishul Yisrael? Those who follow the stringent approach and require cereals to be Bishul Yisrael, must pay attention to the Hashgacha on the cereal and whether or not it states Bishul Yisrael on the box or package. Some Hashgacha's, such as the Eida Hachareidis, have a policy of Bishul Yisrael on all their cereals, even though it is not explicitly stated on the package.[131] Other Hashgacha companies, including companies who consider themselves to be Mehadrin, give a Mehadrin Hashgacha even though the cereal is not Bishul Yisrael, as they hold that cereals is not fit for a kings table. One is to contact the certifying Hashgacha company for clarity in this matter regarding the specific cereal in question, and as to whether it is Bishul Yisrael even according to the stringent approach.

Kellogg's cornflakes: The famous cereal "Kellogg's cornflakes" is under the Hashgacha of the Manchester Beis Din [i.e. MK] and is marketed as a Mehadrin product, with "Kosher Lemehadrin" printed on the boxes. However, after verification from the MK, it was discovered that Kellogg's cornflakes is in truth not cooked by Jews, and is thus not Bishul Yisrael. Accordingly, those who rule like the stringent approach which requires cereals to be Bishul Yisrael, may not eat this product. [After correspondence, the MK stated they would remove the Mehadrin label from the product, due to it being misleading to consumers who generally understand Mehadrin to mean that it is valid accoridng to all opinions.]

C. Must Twizzlers and other candies be Bishul Yisrael?

The recipe: The Twizzler candy produced by Hershey corporation contains as main ingredients: Corn syrup, wheat flour [25%], sugar, and cornstarch. These ingredients are cooked together for several hours and then cooled to form the Twizzler candy.

The law by Twizzlers and other candies: Twizzlers are cooked and are made of ingredients that cannot be eaten raw, therefore making it applicable to the subject of Bishul Akum rather than Pas Akum. The same applies to all candies made through cooking. Nonetheless, there exist several joint reasons to exempt the Twizzler and other candies from the prohibition of Bishul Akum. 1) According to most approaches in A, Twizzlers and candies are not an important food that is fit to be served at a kings table, and the flour is a secondary ingredient, and hence is not viewed on its own regarding this matter to form an issue of Pas Akum. 2) The Twizzler is not eaten together with bread, and thus according to some Poskim is exempt from Bishul Akum, even if it were eaten at a kings table. 3) The batter is not directly cooked by a gentile but rather through automatic machinery that is turned on by a gentile. Practically, based on all this, it is permitted to eat Twizzlers and other candies cooked by a gentile, and so is the widespread custom of Jewry as well as majority of all Hashgacha agencies [including Mehadrin Hashgacha's].[132] Nonetheless, there is room to be stringent in this matter if one desires, and so is the initial policy of some Mehadrin Hashgacha's in Eretz Yisrael, to require initially that even candies be Bishul Yisrael.[133]

Summary:
Twizzlers and other candies are not required to be Bishul Yisrael, and so is the widespread custom and ruling. Nonetheless, there is room for those who desire to be meticulous in this matter.

---

[131] So I verified with a Vaad Hakashrus representative
[132] So I was told by Rav Padvah, a known Kashrus Authority.
[133] Besides for the unclarity in the exact definition of Eino Oleh Al Shulchan Melachim, it is also a Hiddur for a Talmid Chacham not to eat food cooked by a gentile even if not forbidden due to Bishul Akum.

-----------------Machalei Sakana----------------

12. May one cook fish in a clean meat pot?[134]

It is even initially permitted to cook fish in a clean meat pot. This applies even if the pot is Ben Yomo.[135] However some Poskim[136] are stringent to initially forbid cooking fish in meat pots and hence they require having separate pots for meat and fish.[137] Practically, the widespread custom is to be lenient.[138] However, some are meticulous and designate separate pots for fish and do not to use the meat pots for fish products.[139] [The widespread custom of Chabad Chassidim in Russia was to be very stringent on this matter and so is the custom of many Chabad Chassidim today.[140] Accordingly, the Hashgacha of Rav Landau in Bnei Brak has separate utensils for fish and meat, including pots, pans, knives, cutlery, grinders, microwaves, and mittens.] Nevertheless, even according to those who are accustomed to being stringent, Bedieved if they cooked fish in a meat pot, the fish remains permitted even if the meat pot was Ben Yomo.[141]

If the pot is dirty:[142] It is forbidden due to Sakana to cook fish in a meat pot that contains residue of meat. If one did so, the fish is forbidden. If the fish contains 60x the meat residue, then some Poskim[143] rule the fish is permitted while other Poskim[144] rule it is forbidden. Practically, we rule like the former opinion that the fish is permitted if the meat residue is nullified in 60x.[145]

Summary:
It is permitted to cook fish in a clean meat pot, and so is the widespread custom, although some are meticulous not to do so, and so was the original widespread Chabad custom.

---

[134] See Michaber 95:1; Taz Y.D. 95:3; Darkei Teshuvah 116:27; Halacha Berurah 173:9

[135] Implication of Michaber 95:1 and Chulin 111a "One who roasts fish in a meat pot may eat it"; Taz 95:3 "One can learn from here that there is no danger in eating fish that contains the taste of meat through being cooked in a Ben Yomo pot of meat"; Issur Viheter 39:26 "All secretion of taste of meat that is absorbed in a vessel into fish is not Bedieved forbidden due to danger"; Rashal Kol Habasar 9; Kneses Hagedola 116:18; Minchas Yaakov 57:1 concludes "The custom is to be lenient [even initially-Kaf Hachaim 116:20] if the pot is clean"; Peri Megadim 95 M.Z. 3 defends the ruling of the Taz ibid; Lechem Hapanim 116:3; Beis Lechem Yehuda 116:4; Chochmas Adam 68:1; Eidos Biyihosef 2:46; Divrei Hillel 2:32; Daltei Teshuvah 95:5; Ikareiy Hadat Y.D. 14:10; Zechor Leavraham 3:186; Darkei Teshuvah 116:27; Kaf Hachaim 116:20; Sheivet Halevi 6:111 writes it is the custom of the world to be lenient.

The reason: As the danger of eating fish with meat only applies if it contains substance of the meat, and does not apply towards the indirect taste transferred through a pot. [Taz ibid; Issur Viheter ibid]

The proof: As the Gemara Chulin ibid discusses the law of fish that was cooked in a meat pot and whether it may be eaten with dairy, thus proving that regarding Sakana there is no issue. [Issur Viheter ibid, brought in Taz ibid]

[136] Tur 116:2 "Some are stringent to designate vessels for fish" [brought in Chochmas Adam 68:1, Omitted from Michaber 116:2]; Rashal Chulin 7:15, as understood by Minchas Yaakov 57:1, that it is forbidden to eat it [brought in Derisha 116:5; Taz ibid; P"M ibid; However, see P"M ibid who vehemently negates this understanding of Rashal concluding "I wonder at this great Rav, as seemingly he did not look at the words of the Rashal"]; See Issur Viheter ibid who implies that it is only permitted Bedieved

[137] The reason: As the danger of meat and fish applies even by mere taste that is transferred through a pot. Now, although the Gemara and Michaber ibid write that it is permitted to eat fish cooked in a meat pot, that is referring to the laws of meat and milk, as in truth due to Sakana, it is forbidden. [See Rashal ibid; Taz ibid in his initial explanation]

[138] Minchas Yaakov ibid; Chut Hashani 67; Sheivet Haleivi ibid "The custom of the world is to do so"; Halacha Berurah ibid

[139] Sheivet Halevi ibid

[140] So I was told by Rav Eli Landa Shlita that Chassidim were very careful in this matter, and it was common knowledge amongst all that we do not use meat pots for fish. Seemingly, after the war, this tradition became lost amongst some of the new generation of Chabad. The Tzemach Tzedek stated that indeed the above-mentioned danger of meat and fish is not a physical one, but a spiritual one that can cause the Ruach Ra'ah to come upon the person, and prevent him from wanting to Daven and learn for three days. Chassidim in Russia were so particular in this matter, that it once occurred that Rav Itche Der Masmid was hosted in the home of Rav Yaakov Landa in Latvia, and he told him that although he does not eat fish at anyone else's home due to worry that the onions that were cooked with the fish were cut with a meat knife, he does not have this worry in this home of Rav Yaakov Landa. [Heard from Rav Eli Landa]

[141] See Tur ibid; Minchas Yaakov ibid

[142] Taz 95:3; Michaber 116:2; Yad Avraham 95

Ruling of Michaber: The Michaber 95:1 rules that one may eat fish that was cooked with meat residue even if it does not contain 60x the residue, and if it does, then it may be eaten even with dairy. The Taz ibid explains that this is referring to the letter of the law regarding Kashrus and Nat Bar Nat, however, due to Sakana, in truth even the Michaber agrees that it is forbidden.

[143] Shach 116 in Nekudos Hakesef; Taz 116:2 in name of Mordechai and Or Zarua; Kneses Hagedola 116:21; Peri Chadash 116:4; Beis Lechem Yehuda 116:3; Shvus Yaakov 2:104; Erech Hashulchan 116:3; Chochmas Adam 68:1; Aruch Hashulchan 116:10; Kaf Hachaim 116:12

[144] Taz 116:2 in understanding of Darkei Moshe and Rashal; See Yad Avraham ibid

[145] Kaf Hachaim ibid as rule majority of Poskim

> **Q&A**
>
> **May one cook fish in a meat pot if it contains a Davar Charif?**
> Some Poskim[146] rule that one may not cook fish in a meat pot together with sharp foods, such as onions.[147] However, the widespread custom of the world is to be lenient to do so.[148] As stated above, the original Chabad custom was to be stringent in this matter.
>
> **May one cook and eat onions that are cut with a meat knife together with fish?**
> Some Poskim[149] rule that Lechatchila one is to be stringent not to cut onions with a meat knife and cook them together with fish.[150] However, the widespread custom of the world is to be lenient to do so.[151] As stated above, the original Chabad custom was to be stringent in this matter.

13. Peeled eggs, onions and garlic left overnight:[152]
One may not eat peeled garlic or a peeled onion or a peeled egg which stayed overnight.[153] [One who eats this food enters himself into danger.[154]]

If the food was in a bag or container:[155] The above prohibition applies even if the peeled garlic/onion/egg are wrapped in a cloth [or container] and sealed shut.

Leaving some of the peel or root and mixing with other foods:[156] If one left the root on the peeled garlic/onion, which is defined as the hair [or stub[157]] at the head of the garlic and onion, then it is permitted to be eaten. Likewise, if one left some of the peel [or shell] on the garlic/onion [or egg], it may be eaten. [In addition, mixing the garlic/onion/eggs with other foods also evades the issue, as explained in Q&A!]

---

[146] Daltei Teshuvah 95:5 and other Poskim brought in Darkei Teshuvah 116:27; Hakashrus page 425

[147] The reason: As a Davar Charif that is cooked in a meat pan carries the actual taste of the meat, and the meat is considered Beiyn.

[148] Conclusion of Darkei Teshuvah ibid "Pashut there is no need to be stringent in this"; Sheivet Halevi ibid; Darkei Teshuvah ibid in name of Megadim Chadashim that from the letter of the law one may be lenient like the opinion who does not consider onions Charif
The reason: As only the actual taste from a piece of meat is a Sakana to eat with fish, however, the taste of meat that is carried in a Davar Charif, even though its Beiyn, is not problematic regarding Sakana. [ibid]

[149] Darkei Teshuvah 116:27 in name of Megadim Chadashim 116:3 to initially be stringent; See Poskim in Darkei Teshuvah ibid regarding cooking a Davar Charif in a meat pot with fish; Hakashrus 10:111 [page 425]; See story with Rav Itche Der Masmid, recorded above in footnotes.

[150] The reason: As a Davar Charif that is cut with a knife carries the actual taste of the meat, and the meat is considered Beiyn.

[151] Sheivet Halevi ibid; Darkei Teshuvah ibid in name of Megadim Chadashim that from the letter of the law one may be lenient like the opinion who does not consider onions Charif
The reason: As only the actual taste from a piece of meat is a Sakana to eat with fish, however, the taste of meat that is carried in a Davar Charif, even though its Beiyn, is not problematic regarding Sakana. [ibid]

[152] Admur Hilchos Shemiras Haguf Vihanefesh Halacha 7; Rashbi Niddah 17a and Rashi there; Derech Eretz Raba 11; Kol Bo 118; Semak 171; Tosafos Shabbos 141a; Peri Chadash 116:9; Zivcheiy Tzedek 116:61; Ben Ish Chay Pinchas 2:14; Kaf Hachaim 116:92; Chofetz Chaim in Likkutei Halachos Niddah ibid; Divrei Yatziv 2:16; See Hakashrus 18:11-14
Other opinions: The majority of Poskim omit the above ruling from their Halachic works, hence implying that it is no longer relevant. [This ruling is omitted from the Michaber/Rama/Tur/Rambam; See Peri Hasadeh 3:61; Kav Hazahav 12; Igros Moshe Y.D. 3:20; Shevet Halevi 6:111] Some Poskim explicitly rule that in truth all the dangers of Ruach Raah written in the Talmud are no longer relevant today and it is not necessary to avoid eating such foods. [Rashal in Perek Kol Habasar 12, brought in Zivcheiy Tzedek 116:61 and Kaf Hachaim 116:92-93 as possible explanation for why people are not particular in this anymore today; Yabia Omer 2:7 that so also rules Hagahos Mordechai that it no longer applies; Shevet Halevi ibid that Min Hadin is permitted as rules Rashal] Some Poskim rule one may be lenient for the sake of a Seudas Mitzvah, such as Seudas Shabbos and the like. [Yaskil Avdi 8:4]

[153] The reason: As an evil spirit resides on them. [Admur ibid; Rashbi ibid] This evil spirit can cause one danger. [Rashbi ibid]

[154] Rashbi ibid "He is liable for his life and his blood is on his own head"

[155] Admur ibid; Niddah ibid; See Rivivaos Efraim 3:495 and 4:51

[156] Admur ibid; Niddah ibid; See Hagahos Yaavetz, Aruch Laner and Likkutei Halachos of Chofetz Chaim on Niddah ibid

[157] Heard from Rav Eli Landa Shlita that by garlic in which hairs do not grow, the stub is in place of the hair in this regard

Summary:
One may not eat an onion, garlic or egg that was left overnight completely unpeeled, and without its root, even if it was in a closed container.

Other exceptions

Mixing the peeled egg/onion/garlic with other foods:
Some Poskim[158] rule that the above prohibition only applies if the peeled egg/onion/garlic stayed overnight without being mixed with other foods. If, however it was mixed with other foods then it is permitted. Thus, if one adds oil or salt to the egg/onion/garlic, or mixes it into a salad or dish, it may remain overnight in its peeled state.[159] Practically, the custom follows this opinion[160], and so is accepted by all the Mehadrin Hashgacha's.[161]

If an onion, garlic or egg stayed overnight, may it be eaten if cooked?
Some Poskim[162] suggest that perhaps the prohibition only applies if one eats the food raw. If, however the onion/garlic/egg is cooked or pickled afterwards, then the prohibition does not apply. [Practically, the custom is to be stringent.]

Does it help to wash the egg/onion/garlic three times if it stayed overnight?
Some Poskim[163] rule one may do so and then eat the onion/garlic/egg. However, majority of Poskim[164] negate this opinion.

Does the prohibition apply if one needs to peel a large amount many days in advance?
Some Poskim[165] rule the prohibition only applies when it is common to peel the item for right away use, however if one is peeling for mass production over the course of many days, then the prohibition does not apply. Practically, the custom is not like this approach.

May one eat an onion/garlic/egg that was left unpeeled overnight on the 15th of Nissan?[166]
Some write that on the night of Pesach one may even initially eat unpeeled foods that stayed overnight, as it is Leil Shimurim, and the evil spirit does not have permission to reside on the food.

Q&A on definition of egg/garlic/onion

To which species of garlic/onion does the prohibition apply?
Some Poskim[167] suggest that perhaps the prohibition does not apply to any species of onion/garlic which is so bitter that it is inedible on its own.
Chives/green onions:[168] The above prohibition does not apply to chives and green onions.

Does the above hazard of garlic/onions apply to both cooked and raw onions/garlic?
The prohibition only applies if the garlic/onion was left overnight while raw. If, however the onion/garlic is cooked, or pickled, then the prohibition does not apply.[169]

---

[158] Semak 171; Zivcheiy Tzedek 116:61; Ben Ish Chay Pinchas 2:14; Kaf Hachaim 116:92 and O.C. 505:1; Chazon Ish, brought in Hakashrus 18 footnote 53
[159] Hakashrus 18:12
[160] Ben Ish Chaiy ibid
[161] Badatz Eida Hachareidis and Landa give a Hashgacha to pre-broken eggs in cartons, used by bakeries, and instruct the factory to add sugar or salt to the eggs when they are broken and entered into their carton. [Teshuvos Vehanhagos 3:256 writes this is based on a directive of the Minchas Yitzchak] Likewise, the custom of Mehadrin Hashgacha's is to add oil or salt to crushed garlic containers.
[162] Kaf Hachaim 116:93; See also Taamei Haminhagim Likkutim Tosefes Chaim that mixing it with spices help after the fact.
[163] Yad Meir 19
[164] See Hakashrus 18 footnote 57
[165] Igros Moshe Y.D. 3:20
[166] See Vayaged Moshe 3:10; Piskeiy Teshuvos 473:12; Hakashrus 18:26 footnote 109
[167] Kaf Hachaim 116:93
[168] Hakashrus 18 footnote 50
[169] See Kaf Hachaim 116:93; and previous Q&A regarding if the garlic/onion was mixed with other foods.

Does the above hazard regarding eggs apply to both cooked and raw eggs?[170]
Some Poskim[171] rule the above hazard only applies to raw eggs. Other Poskim[172] however rule it applies to both cooked and raw eggs, and so is the practical custom. [This refers to a plain hardboiled egg. If, however, the egg was fried with oil, or mixed into a salad, then the prohibition does not apply.[173]]

Does the above prohibition apply to crushed onions/garlic/eggs?[174]
Yes. Thus, the custom is to add oil or salt to the mixture, and this is the practice of Mehadrin Hashgacha's who sell crushed garlic containers.

Does the prohibition apply to egg powder and garlic/onion powder?
Some Poskim[175] rule that the above prohibition does not apply to powdered egg/garlic/onion.[176] Practically, so is the custom.

Q&A on "Overnight"
Must the garlic/egg/onion stay peeled over the <u>entire</u> night for it to be forbidden? What if it remained peeled for only part of the night?[177]
Some Poskim[178] rule that the peeled onion/garlic/egg is only forbidden if it passed the <u>entire</u> night, from Tzeis until Alos, in this state. Other Poskim[179] suggest that it is forbidden even if it only passed through part of the night, such as if it was peeled at the end of the night.

Q&A on "leaving peel"
How much of the peel must be left on the garlic/onion/egg?[180]
Any amount suffices.

If the garlic/onion/egg was completely peeled/shelled, does it help to place some of its peel/shell back on it?[181]
Some Poskim[182] rule that it is valid. Other Poskim[183] rule that it is not valid.

---

[170] See Hakashrus 18 footnote 50
[171] Beis Shlomo Y.D. 1:159
[172] See Darkei Teshuvah Y.D. 116:74; Shevet Halevi 6:111; Hakashrus ibid
[173] Yaskil Avdi 7:44; Shevet Halevi ibid; Hakashrus ibid based on previous Q&A!
[174] Tosafos Shabbos 141a
[175] Beis Shlomo 1:159; Degel Efraim 28; Sheivet Halevi 6:111-5-7; Yabia Omer 2:7 based on Har Tzvi Y.D. 74; See also Kaf Hachaim 116:93
[176] <u>The reason</u>: As the food is no longer edible in its current state.
[177] Hakashrus p 428
[178] Divrei Yatziv 2:16
[179] Shevet Hakehasi 2, brought in Hakashrus ibid
[180] Admur ibid "Some of its peel"; Hakashrus 18:11 footnote 52
[181] See Hakashrus 18 footnote 52
[182] Shemiras Haguf Vihanefesh p. 21 in name of Shevet Hamussar
[183] Olelos Moshe 28 in name of Maharsham

----------------Tevilas Keilim----------------

14. May a child be trusted to immerse a vessel?[184]

The general rule: A child [who is below Bar/Bas Mitzvah] may not be trusted to immerse a vessel [alone] in the Mikveh.[185] However, if the child immerses the vessel in the presence [and under the supervision] of an adult [male or female above Bar/Bas Mitzvah] who watches him immerse it, then the immersion is valid.[186] This applies even if the child has not been educated in the purpose or meaning behind the immersion, and simply performs the act of entering the vessel into the Mikveh.[187] [In such a case that a child immersed the vessel under supervision, the adult supervisor must inform the person for whom the vessel was immersed, that the child immersed the vessel properly. Whenever a child immerses under adult supervision, the child is to recite a blessing over the immersion.[188]]

Glass vessels, and all vessels which require Rabbinical immersion: Some Poskim[189] rule that the above invalidation of a child immersing a vessel without supervision, only applies if the vessel requires Biblical immersion, such as if it is made of metal. However, if the vessel only requires Rabbinical immersion, such as if it is made of glass[190] [or plastic] then a child who has reached an age of mental understanding[191] may be trusted to immerse it even without adult supervision. Other Poskim[192], however, rule that a child may never be trusted without supervision even if the vessel is made of glass.[193]

---

[184] Yoreh Deah 120:14

[185] Michaber ibid; Terumos Hadeshen 257; Kitzur SHU"A 37:12

The reason: As the Mitzvah of immersion is a Biblical obligation, and by all Biblical obligations, a child may never be trusted. [Taz 120:16; Terumos Hadeshen ibid; Beir Hagoleh ibid; Admur 432:10; 437:6 regarding trusting a child to perform a Biblical Bedikas Chametz and Admur Y.D. 1:42 regarding trusting a child to slaughter] The following Poskim rule that Tevilas Keilim is a Biblical obligation: Stam opinion in Admur 159:21; 2nd opinion in Admur 323:8 and final ruling there; Implication of Michaber 320:9 and 14 and 17 who rules a Katan is not believed; Taz 120:16; Peri Chadash 120:1 [see there in length]; Rashba in Teshuvah; Raavad; Ramban; Rashi Avoda Zara 75b; Tosafos Avoda Zara ibid; Rabbeinu Tam Yuma 78; Semak 199; Issur Viheter 58:91; Aruch Hashulchan 120:4 that so agree majority of Poskim

Other opinions: Some Poskim rule the Mitzvah of immersing vessels is a Rabbinical obligation. [1st opinion in Admur 323:8; Rambam Machalos Assuros 17:5, as understood by Rashba in Toras Habayis p. 155 and Peri Chadash ibid [however see Rashba in Teshuvah ibid and Aruch Hashulchan 120:1-3 for alternative understanding in Rambam]; Ran; Ritva; Or Zarua 1:359; Radbaz 34 that so rule majority of Poskim; Yeshuos Yaakov O.C. 509:4] Accordingly, a child who has reached the age of Chinuch, may be trusted to immerse the vessel. [Implication of Taz ibid; Terumos Hadeshen ibid; Admur 432:10; 437:6 regarding trusting a child to perform a Rabbinical Bedikas Chametz]]

[186] Rama ibid; Terumos Hadeshen 257; Misgeres Hashulchan 37:9

[187] Implication of Michaber and Rama 120:15 who validate the immersion of a gentile; Shach 120:28 and Taz ibid that so is implied to be the final ruling of Rama who does not make this condition, and so is their final ruling; Levush, brought in Shach ibid; 2nd answer in Terumos Hadeshen ibid and so is his conclusion

The reason: As Tevila from impurity to purity does not require intent at all. [Poskim ibid; Teshuvas HaRashba and Ramban 151, brought in Bach 120]

Other opinions: Some Poskim rule that one is to educate the child in the purpose of the immersion, that it is done to purify the vessel, otherwise, the immersion is invalid even under supervision. [Bach 120, brought in Shach 120:28; 1st answer in Terumos Hadeshen ibid; Biur Hagra 120 based on Rama 198]

[188] Darkei Teshuvah 120:105

[189] Implication of Admur 432:10, as explained below; 1st approach in gloss of Rav Akiva Eiger 120:14 and that so holds Shagas Aryeh; Panim Meiros 2:96; Aruch Hashulchan 121:13; Chochmas Adam permits to be lenient for the sake of Shabbos, brought in Misgeres Hashulchan 37:9; Implication of Shach 127:31 in name of Rivash that a child is trusted even if there is Chezkas Issur if it is Beyado; Implication of Erech Hashulchan 115 in name of Radbaz Implication of Admur 432:10 in parentheses and M"A 437:8 regarding trusting a child to perform a Rabbinical Bedikas Chametz even though it is Ischazeik Issur and concludes *"And anything which a child can do, he is believed to say he did it as explained in Yoreh Deah 120 see there"*, however see Admur Y.D. 1:42 that a child is only believed by matters that have no Biblical root.

Opinion of Admur: Admur 432:10 in parentheses rules that we always believe a child by a Rabbinical matter that is within his hands to perform, even if there is a Chezkas Issur. This would imply that Admur rules like the Poskim ibid that a child can be trusted to immerse a glass vessel. However, Admur Y.D. 1:42 states that this only applies if the obligation does not have a root in the Biblical law. Hence, a child would not be trusted to immerse a glass vessel, as the concept of Tevilas Keilim is Biblical. Vetzaruch Iyun, as according to this a child should not be trusted by even Rabbinical Bedikas Chametz, unlike the ruling of Admur 432:10!

[190] Peri Chadash 120:3 and 26; Gloss of Rav Akiva Eiger 120:14; Shagas Aryeh; Panim Meiros 2:96; Chochmas Adam 73:19, brought in Pischeiy Teshuvah 120:3; Aruch Hashulchan 120:24; Rashi, brought in Aruch Hashulchan 120:1 "Specifically metal"; See Taz 120:1 "It is only common to use for a meal vessel made of metal."

[191] See Admur ibid and Michaber 437:4 that we only trust a Katan "Sheyeish Bo Daas"

[192] Implication of Admur Y.D. 1:42, as explained above; Peri Megadim 451 M.Z. 7, brought in Pischeiy Teshuvah 120:14; 2nd approach in gloss of Rav Akiva Eiger 120:14; Ben Ish Chaiy Matos 2:9; See Rama Y.D. 127:3 that we only believe a child by Bedikas Chametz because there is no Chezkas Issur.

[193] The reason: As a vessel contains a Chezkas Issur, and a child is never believed to testify by a Chezkas Issur, even if it is Rabbinical. [P"M ibid; See Rama ibid] Alternatively, as even by Rabbinical matters, a child is only believed by actions that he has responsibility to do for himself, such as to immerse a vessel that he owns, as opposed to matters which he performs as a Shliach, on behalf of others. [Rav Akiva Eiger ibid based on Tosafos Eiruvin 31b] These two reasonings are negated by Admur and M"A ibid regarding Bedikas Chametz, as they hold that whenever one has ability to fix it himself, a child is believed even by Chezkas Issur. However, an additional reason for stringency added by Admur Y.D. 1:42 is that since the Mitzvah of Tevilas Keilim has a Biblical root, therefore a child is not trusted even for its Rabbinical immersions.

Sending the vessel with a child to give to an adult to immerse:[194] Although a child cannot be trusted to personally immerse the vessel without **verified** adult supervision, as stated above, nevertheless, he can be trusted to bring the vessel to the Mikveh and have an adult immerse it on his behalf. There is no need in such a case to receive verification from the adult, and one may trust the word of the child that he had an adult immerse it for him.[195] Nonetheless, this only applies to a trustworthy child, who is not known to lie or perform deceptive activities, otherwise he cannot be trusted even regarding having an adult immerse it for him, without independent verification from the adult.[196]

Summary:
One may not send a child below the age of Bar/Bas Mitzvah to immerse one's vessels. It is best to abstain from doing so even with vessels of non-metal materials, such as glass. It is, however, permitted for the child to immerse the vessel under adult supervision, and have the child say the blessing. Thus, one may take his child with him to the Mikveh Keilim and have him immerse the vessels in the Mikveh while one is watching. Likewise, one may send the child to immerse the vessels if he prearranges for an adult to supervise him and report that the immersion was done correctly.

Q&A

May a child who is Bar/Bas Mitzvah be trusted to immerse a vessel, if one does not know if he has grown the signs of puberty?[197]
Some Poskim[198] rule a child who is above Bar/Bas Mitzvah may be trusted even if one does not know whether they have grown signs of adulthood [i.e. two pubic hairs].[199] Other Poskim[200], however, rule that the child may only be trusted to immerse Rabbinical vessels, such as glass, but cannot be trusted to immerse metal vessels.

May one trust a child to give the vessel to an adult and have the adult immerse it?
Yes. As stated above, a trustworthy child may be entrusted to do so if he returns and testifies that he did as asked, and an adult immersed the vessel.

---

[194] Admur Y.D. 1:42 regarding sending a chicken or cow with a child to bring to the Shochet to slaughter, that "Nonetheless, the custom is to send a child to give the animal to a Shochet to slaughter, and we do not suspect that he will do so himself." Thus, we see that the child can be trusted to do so, and we do not suspect that he may have a gentile slaughter it, or may slaughter it himself; Likewise, it is accustomed to trust a child to purchase Kosher meat from the butcher and we do not suspect that perhaps he bought it from a gentile; Likewise, we trust a child to bring a Shaalah to a Rav and return with his answer, as we assume the child fears to lie about the answer. See Rashba in Mishmeres Habayis 1:1; Simla Chadasha 1:35; Tevuos Shur 1:62; Beis Hillel 120:2; Chanoch Lanaar 30 footnote 2, brought in Hakashrus 4 footnote 39

[195] The reason: As a) there is a Chazaka that a child will not do things to stumble others, and will not do destructive actions. Thus, it is not that we believe the child to have done what he claims, but that simply we have a Chazaka to assume that he did not do otherwise. b) He fears telling a lie, as one may ask him as to which adult immersed it for him. [See Admur ibid]

[196] Admur ibid; Simla Chadasha ibid; Tevuos Shur ibid

[197] Pischeiy Teshuvah 120:14; This is known as Chazaka Derava. A child is not Halachically considered obligated in Mitzvos until they have grown two pubic hairs. Rava held that by Rabbinical matters one may assume that they have grown it, and they may thus be trusted to be Bar/Bas Mitzvah, however, by Biblical matters they are not trusted. See Rava Nida 46a; Admur 39:1; 53:9; 55:6; 128:49; 199:9; 271:7

[198] Pischeiy Teshuvah 120:14; Rav Yitzchak Elchonon in Zecher Simcha; Teshuvos Vehanhagos 3:405; See Hakashrus 4 footnote 108

[199] The reason: As since using a vessel prior to immersion does not prohibit the food, therefore, it is given a lesser severity than a regular Biblical obligation, and one may adapt the Chazaka of Rava. [Poskim ibid]

[200] P"M 451 M"Z 6, brought in Pischeiy Teshuvah ibid

15. May one use a new vessel one time without immersion?[201]

It is a [Biblical[202]] obligation to immerse a food vessel that was purchased from a gentile prior to using it for food products.[203] One must immerse the vessel prior to using it for food even if he only plans to use it for food on a temporary basis prior to immersion.[204] [Accordingly, one must immerse the vessel even prior to using it for the first time[205]]. [Hence, unlike the common misconception that a new vessel may be used one time prior to Tevila, there is in truth no allowance to use a new vessel even a single time before immersing it, and this prohibition has consensus amongst the Poskim, and they have vehemently protested the mistaken custom.[206] This applies to all sects of Jewry, whether Ashkenazi, Sephardi, or Chassidic.] Nonetheless, if one transgressed, and used the vessel prior to immersion, the food nevertheless remains permitted to be eaten.[207] [This applies even if one used it several times prior to immersion.] The above, however, only applies to a permanent vessel, however a disposable vessel, which is manufactured for a single use, does not need to be immersed in a Mikveh prior to use.[208] [Seemingly, this ruling is the cause of the misconception above which erroneously allows using a vessel one time prior to immersion.]

Summary:
It is forbidden to use a vessel even one time prior to immersion, unlike the common misconception which has no basis in Poskim.

---

[201] See Sefer Ohel Yaakov Dinei Tevilas Keilim p. 319; Minchas Shlomo 2:66-14; Hakashrus 4:5; Or Yitzchak 2:17-9; Chayeh Halevi 4:57-9

[202] Stam opinion in Admur 159:21; 2nd opinion in Admur 323:8 and conclusion of Admur there "The main opinion follows that Tevilas Keilim is Biblical, as explained in Yoreh Deah ibid"; Implication of Michaber 320:9 and 14 and 17 who rules a Katan is not believed; Taz 120:16; Peri Chadash 120:1 [see there in length]; Rashba in Teshuvah; Raavad; First option in Ramban on Avoda Zara 75b; Ritva on Avoda Zara ibid in name of Ramban that it is Biblical; Rashi Avoda Zara 75b; Tosafos Avoda Zara ibid; Rabbeinu Tam Yuma 78Semak 199; Issur Viheter 58:91; Aruch Hashulchan 120:4 that so agree majority of Poskim

Other opinions: Some Poskim rule the Mitzvah of immersing vessels is a Rabbinical obligation. [1st opinion in Admur 323:8; Rambam Machalos Assuros 17:5, as understood by Rashba in Toras Habayis p. 155 and Peri Chadash ibid [however see Rashba in Teshuvah ibid and Aruch Hashulchan 120:1-3 for alternative understanding in Rambam]; Leaning explanation of Ramban Al Hatorah Matos and second option in Ramban on Avoda Zara 75b; However see Ritva on Avoda Zara ibid in name of Ramban that it is Biblical; Ran; Ritva; Or Zarua 1:359; Radbaz 34 that so rule majority of Poskim; Yeshuos Yaakov O.C. 509:4]

[203] Michaber Y.D. 120:1; Mishneh Avoda Zara 75

[204] Rama Y.D. 120:8 "*The first person is prohibited from using the vessel for the need of a meal even temporarily without immersion.*"; See Aruch Hashulchan and Minchas Shlomo in next footnote

[205] Rav SZ"A in Minchas Shlomo 2:66-14; Hakashrus 4:5; Or Yitzchak 2:17-9; Chayeh Halevi 4:57-9; Ohel Yaakov ibid; Pashut as the Poskim make no mention of such an allowance. It is not mentioned in any of the discussions of what should be done if a Mikveh is not available, or if it is Shabbos and one cannot immerse the vessel [see Michaber Y.D. 120:16 and Admur 323:8 regarding Shabbos; Rama 120:16 regarding during the week in an area without a Mikveh; Mordechai Beitza Reemes 677] It is also not mentioned amongst the reasons of why we rule disposable vessels do not require immersion. [Maharil Diskin Kuntrus Achron 136 [regarding if food is already in vessel]; Chelkas Yaakov 2:47; Minchas Yitzchak 5:32; Igros Moshe 2:40; Rav SZ"A in SSH"K 9 footnote 41; Rav Yaakov Yosef Za"l; See Hakashrus 1:34 and 4:23] Chazon Ovadia Shabbos 2 p. 38] and there is also no logical reason to allow a first-time use; so is also proven from the Rama Y.D. 120:8 who goes even further and rules "However, the first person is prohibited from using the vessel for the need of a meal even temporarily without immersion." Thus, showing that not only is a first-time use forbidden but it is even forbidden if one only plans to use the vessel one time and then sell it to another! Now, although the Aruch Hashulchan 120:41 explains that even accoridng to the Rama ibid, it is permitted to use it a on occasion, this refers to the case of the Rama ibid where the vessel was not purchased for purposes of food, however, if the vessel was purchased for food purposes, no one holds that it can be used even one time prior to immersing. [Minchas Shlomo ibid]

[206] See Ohel Yaakov ibid; Or Yitzchak ibid

[207] Rama 120:16

[208] Maharil Diskin Kuntrus Achron 136 [regarding if food is already in vessel]; Chelkas Yaakov 2:47; Minchas Yitzchak 5:32; Igros Moshe 2:40; Rav SZ"A in SSH"K 9 footnote 41; Rav Yaakov Yosef Za"l; See Hakashrus 1:34 and 4:23

The reason: As by wine and coffee, the food is already in the vessel, and the laws of immersion do not require one to remove the food. [Maharil Diskin ibid] Furthermore, only permanent vessels require immersion as according to some Poskim [Shev Yaakov 31, brought in Yad Efraim 120] the obligation of immersing vessels is dependent on if the vessel is Mikabel Tuma, and a temporary vessel that one plans to discard is not Mikabel Tuma. [Chelkas Yaakov ibid and Minchas Yitzchak ibid, based on Rambam Keilim 5:7] In addition, even according to those Poskim [Mahariy Asad 216; Gidulei Taharah 17] who rule that immersion of vessels is not dependent on their status of Kabalas Tuma, the Sages only established the Mitzvah of immersion to meal vessels, and a vessel that does not have a continued use is not considered a meal vessel. [Minchas Yitzchak ibid, based on Gidulei Taharah ibid]

Other opinions: Some Poskim rule that aluminum baking pans and the like need to be immersed prior to use, and hence should preferably only be purchased from a Jewish owned company. [Chazon Ovadia Shabbos 2 p. 38]

----------------Kashrus-Kashering----------------
16. Koshering a Microwave & May the same microwave be used for meat, milk and Pesach:[209]

Some Rabbanim[210] say that a microwave does not need to be Kashered at all prior to use for meat/milk/Pesach, and simply needs to be wiped clean between uses.[211] Accordingly, it may be used intermittently for meat and then dairy and Pesach, after cleaning it. The majority of Poskim[212], however, rule that a microwave requires Kashering and hence cannot be used intermittently for both meat/dairy/Pesach in its un-Kashered state.[213] This applies even if the microwave is cleaned, and has not been used for 24 hours[214], unless the food is hermetically sealed and the microwave is Koshered, as explained below. Practically, one must abide by the latter opinion, as the former opinion does not take all factors into account, and is evidently a mistaken ruling.[215] Thus, microwaves are to be designated as either meaty, dairy, or Pareve, and not be used for the opposite foods unless on occasion, as per the guidelines to be explained. According to all, a combination microwave oven, which is both an oven and a microwave, requires Kashering. We will now discuss if and how a microwave can be Kashered:

How to Kasher the microwave: Some Poskim[216] rule that it is not possible to Kasher a microwave.[217] Other Poskim[218] rule it can be Koshered through steaming water inside it.[219] This is accomplished through the following steps: The microwave is to be cleaned, not used for 24 hours[220], and have water with bleach/soap placed in it and heated for about 10-20 minutes[221], until it steams out.[222] Practically, one is to purchase a new microwave for Pesach and is to try to have separate microwaves for meat and milk in order to avoid Kashrus issues from arising.[223] If this is not possible, and one is in need to use the microwave, then one is to use a hermetically sealed container to cook the food, as stated next.

---

[209] See Piskeiy Teshuvos 451:22; Sefer Hakashrus [Fuchs] 1:47-50 [pp. 48-49]; Nitei Gavriel 80:16; See also Hadarom Choveret 6 Nissan 5722; Kovetz Beis Ahron Yisrael 4:3

How does a microwave cook? A microwave is a rapid cooking element, which can warm and cook food much quicker than traditional cooking methods. Now, how does the microwave achieve its rapid cooking? The microwave does not use the heat of a fire or electricity to cook but rather cooks the food using radiation, or radio electromagnetic waves, which is projected from a vacuum tube and bounced off the metal lined walls of the microwave which penetrate the food from all sides. These waves hasten the movement of the water molecules in the food to atomic levels hence generating heat. [Heat is generated from movement and friction.] This form of cooking cooks the food much quicker than fire or electricity, as the radioactive waves hits the food equally in all areas and furthermore, penetrates the inside of the food molecules hence making the entire mass of the food an equal recipient of the heat. This is unlike fire or electric cooking which heats the external part of the food, and that heat then must travel to the inner part of the food in order to cook it. Likewise, this form of cooking only heats the actual food, as it does not actually send heat to the food but causes the food to heat itself up. Accordingly, all other areas and items of the microwave might remain cold, including the walls and certain plastic or glass containers which cover the food. The only way these items will become hot is if they are in contact with the food itself. The radio waves harmlessly pass through these containers into the food and do not cause any heating within them being they do not contain water molecules or other polar charge component. [See Hakashrus ibid footnote 100; See here for an educational video on how a microwave works. https://www.youtube.com/watch?v=kp33ZprO0Ck]

[210] Rav Yitzchak Yosef, as he related in his weekly Shiur, published in Beit Maran

[211] The reason: As the actual walls of the microwave do not heat up at all, and only the food itself heats up.

[212] See all Gedolei HaPoskim mentioned in Hakashrus ibid and Piskeiy Teshuvos ibid, which include Rav Wozner, Rav Elyashiv, Rav Sheinberg, Rav Halbershtam; Nitei Gavriel ibid footnote 26 in name of Rav Neiman of Montreal;

[213] The reason: a) Although the walls of the microwave do not give heat, nevertheless the steam and spills of the food inside make the walls absorb the food and hence it must be Koshered. [Piskeiy Teshuvos ibid; See Admur 451:41, Michaber 451:14, and M"B 451:81 that a vessel which absorbed the steam of an Issur requires Hagala] b) As there is a vent duct in the microwave that contains actual steam of food, and that area is not Kosherable. [Rav Neiman ibid]

[214] As due to the steam it is similar to baking dairy in a modern-day meat oven, which is similar to cooking dairy food in a non-Ben Yomo meat pot, which prohibits the vessel, and is initially forbidden to be done even though the food remains permitted.

[215] As although the walls don't heat up the microwave receives steam from the foods and hence must be Koshered.

[216] See Piskeiy Teshuvos ibid; Siddur Pesach Kehilchaso page 8:3 that it can only be Kashered through Iruiy Keli Rishon and Even Meluban

[217] The reason: a) Although the walls of the microwave do not heat, nevertheless the steam and spills of the food inside make the walls absorb the food and hence it must be Kashered. Now, it is not possible to Kasher the microwave as one cannot blow torch it, place it in boiling water, and many Poskim rule an item cannot be Kashered through steaming water inside it. [See Shoel Umeishiv Telisa 3:125; Sdei Chemed Mareches Hei 24; Chametz Umatzah 17:12 that it is not possible to Kasher through vapor] It therefore has no viable path for Kashering. A second reason is b) As there is a vent duct in the microwave that contains actual steam of food, and that area is not cleanable or Kasherable. [Rav Neiman ibid]

[218] Teshuvos Vehanhagos 2:212; Yalkut Yosef Pesach p. 360; Piskeiy Teshuvos ibid regarding Shaas Hadechak

[219] The reason: As we rule that it is possible to Kasher an item through steam, and just like the microwave absorbed the food through steam, so too it can be Kashered through steam. [See Peri Chadash 121; P"M Y.D. 94 M"Z 1; Tevuos Hasadeh 3:3]

[220] See Hakashrus ibis footnote 105 that so ruled Rav Wozner, Rav Shternbuch and Rav Mordechai Eliyahu

[221] Piskeiy Teshuvos ibid writes to leave it on for one hour; Sefer Hakashrus ibid writes [based on Mitbach Kehalacha p. 58 and Techumin 8:21] to enter a half a liter of water and leave the microwave on until it steams out; Rav Yitzchak Yosef says to leave it on for six minutes

[222] Teshuvos Vehanhagos 2:212; Koveitz Mibeis Levi 3:22; 7:25; Yalkut Yosef Pesach p. 360; Piskeiy Teshuvos ibid; Hakashrus ibid

[223] Piskeiy Teshuvos ibid; Hakashrus ibid footnote 105; Nitei Gavriel ibid concludes that due to the many opinions, one is not to use it for Pesach without directive from a Rav

Cooking in a hermetically sealed container:[224] In all cases, it is permitted to cook in a microwave food [meat/dairy/Pesach] that is contained within a hermetically sealed container which does not allow any vapor to escape or enter. This applies even if the microwave has not been Koshered, and certainly if it has been Koshered in the method mentioned above.[225] Some Poskim[226] however discourage using the microwave in this method as it occurs that the hermetic sealing tears or opens during the cooking, which would then pose a Kashrus issue. It is therefore best to only use the microwave in this method after first Koshering it.

Bedieved, if used meat microwave for uncovered dairy: If one heated a dairy food in a meat microwave, or vice versa, and the food was uncovered, then if the microwave has been used for meat within the past 24 hours, or if it was dirty with meat residue, the food is forbidden. If the microwave was clean and was not used for 24 hours with uncovered meat, then the food remains permitted, although the microwave must be Koshered through the method explained above. See our Sefer "The Practical Laws of Basar Bechalav" Chapter 7 in the section regarding "Ovens" for the sources and full details of this matter!

---------------- **Sakana & Superstitions** ----------------

17. Not to blow out candles with one's mouth:[227]

The Sages state that one is not to blow out a candle with his mouth, and one who does so is held liable for self-affliction.[228] [Thus, one is to be careful to not blow out a candle with one's mouth but rather with the wave of one's hand, and the like.[229] Accordingly, when blowing out candles on a birthday cake, one is not to use his mouth to blow it out. Nonetheless, those who are not careful in the above, seemingly do not have to be protested, and on them we would apply the statement of "Shomer Pesaim Hashem" that Hashem guards the fools.[230]]

For the sake of a Mitzvah:[231] Those women who blow out the Shabbos candle using their mouth[232], may continue to do so, as one who guards a Mitzvah knows no evil.

18. The mystical danger of stepping on eggshells:[233]

One who steps on eggshells endangers himself to receive Tzaraas/leprosy. [Although many of the Talmudic, and even codified warnings of mystical dangers are no longer followed today[234], practically,

---

[224] See Admur 447:10; Rama 92:8; Michaber 108:1; Hakashrus ibid; Nitei Gavriel ibid in name of Rav Neiman
[225] Pischeiy Halacha Kashrus p. 28; Piskeiy Teshuvos ibid footnote 106
[226] See Kovetz Mibeis Levi 3:22-9; Hadarom ibid; Beis Ahron Veyisrael ibid
[227] Kol Bo 118 [in Din Maaseh Torah which were said by Rabbeinu Hakadosh-Rebbe Yehuda Hanassi] "There are four things that if one does them his "blood is on his head"...3) One who extinguishes a candle with his mouth' "; Reishis Chochmah Chupas Eliyahu 3:7 "There are three things that if one does them his "blood is on his head"...2) One who extinguishes a candle with his mouth"; Pirkei Derabbeinu Hakadosh p. 27 [Shenbloom]; Ksav Yad Ashkenazit [early 15'00's]; Otzer Hamidrashim Eizanshtat p. 162; Lechem Hapanim Y.D. 116:5 in name of Kol Bo ibid; Zivcheiy Tzedek 116:74; Ben Ish Chaiy Pinchas 18 in name of Arizal in Shaar Ruach Hakodesh; Kaf Hachaim 116:115; See Yabia Omer 9:95-14; Halichos Olam 7 p. 248; Shemiras haguf Vihanefesh 2:267-8;
[228] Literally "His blood is on his head"
The reason: As this causes the Nichfeh illness. [Kol Bo ibid; Reishis Chochma ibid; Nichfe or Kifyon, is a neurological illness similar to seizures- See here https://www.yeshiva.org.il/wiki/index.php?title=%D7%9B%D7%A4%D7%99%D7%95%D7%9F#cite_note-18] To note that a candle is the soul of a person "Ner Havayah Nishmas Adam" and one's soul is found in his breath.
[229] Seemingly, on this law we do not apply the rule of "Shomer Pesaim Hashem" to allow people to even initially disregard its warning, as many people still abide by this until today. [See Yabia Omer ibid; See Shabbos 129b and Tzemach Tzedek E.H. 11 that when the public becomes accustomed to perform a danger Chazal state "Shomer Pesaim Hashem; See Igros Kodesh 2:144 that when the danger is associated with matters of Segula [unnatural] then only when people beware from doing it does the Segula danger apply, while if people are no longer careful then the danger subsides completely; See Rashal Yam Shel Shlomo Kol Habasar 12 that today the Ruach Raah no longer resides and only applies in Talmudic times, just as we rule regarding Zugos.]
[230] As this warning is not recorded in the Talmud, Tur, or Shulchan Aruch, and hence gives room for leniency. See Yabia Omer ibid; Vetzaruch Iyun
[231] Lechem Hapanim Y.D. 116:5; Zivcheiy Tzedek 116:74; Kaf Hachaim 116:115
[232] Seemingly this refers to those women who followed the custom of lighting the wick and then extinguishing it before lighting, in order so it light well at the time of the blessing. [See Admur 264:14; Tur 264; Rosh Shabbos 2:18] However, possibly, it also refers to those women who followed the custom of not accepting Shabbos with the lighting. [see Michaber 263:10]
[233] Admur Hilchos Shemiras Haguf Vihanefesh 9; Abayey in Pesachim 112b; Shemiras Hanefesh Os 76; Omitted from Michaber/Rama and Nosei Keilim in Y.D. 116, including Kaf Hachaim 116; Vetzaruch Iyun
[234] See Shabbos 129b and Tzemach Tzedek E.H. 11 that when the public becomes accustomed to perform a danger Chazal state "Shomer Pesaim Hashem; See Igros Kodesh 2:144 that when the danger is associated with matters of Segula [unnatural] then only when people beware from doing

many people are accustomed to abstaining from stepping on eggshells even today. Thus, eggshells are not to be thrown in areas that people walk. There is a story recorded regarding the Rebbe Maharash, that he once admonished someone to be careful in this matter.[235]]

19. May one sleep with his feet or head towards the door of the room?

It is permitted to sleep facing the door of a room in any direction that one chooses, whether his head is facing the door, or his feet are facing the door. There is no known source in Judaism, neither in Halacha nor in Kabbala, that restricts the sleeping directions of a person who is sleeping facing the door of a room. Furthermore, the Poskim[236] omit writing any restriction in this matter within the Halachic topic of bed directions, hence solidifying the fact that no such prohibition exists. Nonetheless, it is customary amongst many people to avoid sleeping with one's feet facing the door due to it being similar to a corpse who faces the opening of the room.[237] [Practically, one who has not received this custom as a family tradition is not required to start keeping it.[238] However one who has traditionally guarded this custom is to continue doing so.[239]]

------------------ *Avoda Zara*------------------

20. Is Christianity considered Avoda Zara?

Christianity is considered Avoda Zara for a Jew, and carries all Avoda Zara related prohibitions.[240] However, some Poskim[241] rule that for gentiles, Christianity is considered Shituf and is not prohibited due to Avoda Zara.[242] Other Poskim[243] however rule that Christianity is considered like idolatry even for gentiles.

---

it does the Segula danger apply, while if people are no longer careful then the danger subsides completely; See Rashal Yam Shel Shlomo Kol Habasar 12 that today the Ruach Raah no longer resides and only applies in Talmudic times, just as we rule regarding Zugos.

[235] Shemuos Usipurim 1:173 tells over that the Rebbe Maharash once passed the inn of Yitzchak Shaul in Lubavitch and noticed eggshells laying in front of the inn. The Rebbe went on to warn Yitzchak Shaul that in the future he is not to throw eggshells in areas that people walk, as it is forbidden to walk over them.

[236] See Kama 3/9-10. Michaber 3/6; Omitted in Basra

[237] Custom of many; Heard from Harav Eliyahu Landa; Harav A.L. Kohen; See Tzavas Rav Yehuda Hachassid 6, recorded in many Poskim, that the body of the deceased is to be positioned facing the opening of the room, and

[238] This is the traditional ruling regarding all matters that are not Halachically based, that one cannot enforce their practice upon others.

[239] Rav Eliyahu Landa and Rav Kohen ibid

The reason: As even customs that have no written source are customarily respected, such as the custom of pregnant woman not to enter a cemetery [see Minchas Yitzchak 10/42; Nitei Gavriel Aveilus 2/84-4; Our Sefer on Rosh Hashanah Supplement "Visiting a cemetery" Halacha 22]; or the custom not to step over a child, or not to allow a child to look in the mirror until he grows teeth. [see Beir Moshe 36]; or the custom not to have two people dress a child or not to place a candle on the floor. [Rav Eliyahu Landa]

[240] Rambam Machalos Assuros 11:7; Avoda Zara 9:4; Pirush Hamishnayos Avoda Zara 1:3; Teshuvas Harambam 448; Rama Y.D. 148:12 [in uncensored editions] lists Xmas and New Years as Holidays of idolatry; Likkutei Sichos 37 p. 198; Rebbe in handwritten editing remarks to a letter "Christianity is Avoda Zara, is in contrast to the seven Noahide laws, as opposed to Islam. However, the Christians of today are simply "Maaseh Avoseihem Beyadeihem".

The reason: As they believe that Yoshka is one of the three parts of Hashem and they worship him. [In truth however, there are different sects of Christianity with different belief systems. See Haemuna Vehadeios of Rasag 2:7 that there are four groups of Christians and not all are idol worshipers; See here https://www.thoughtco.com/faith-groups-that-reject-trinity-doctrine-700367]

[241] Rama O.C. 156:1 [Omitted in Admur 156]; Darkei Moshe O.C. 156; Y.D. 151; Shach Y.D 151:7; Tosafos Sanhedrin 63b and Bechoros 2b; Ran Sanhedrin 63b, end of first Perek in Avoda Zara; Meiri Bava Kama 113b; Rabbeinu Yerucham Nesiv 17:5; Beir Hagoleh C. M. 425 Shin; Aruch Hashulchan 156:4; Reb Yeshaya Berlin, brought in Mishnas Chachomim Yesodei Hatorah Lav Alef and Pischeiy Teshuvah 147:2; See Sefer Hamamarim Rebbe Maharash 5637 "Mi Kamocha"; Melukat 1 p. 323 Mamar Mayim Rabim 5717; Melukat 3 Nissan p. 128 Mamar "Beyom Ashtei Asar" 5731; Toras Menachem 5743 3 p. 1386; See Pischeiy Teshuvah Y.D. 157:2 that so is clearly implied from Rama ibid; See Sdei Chemed Peas Hasadeh Kelalim 3:6

[242] The reason: The definition of Noahide idolatry according to this opinion: According to this opinion, the form of idolatry prohibited for Noahites is the belief that Hashem has completely left the earth, and plays no role in it. That it has been left completely to the authority of a deity to whom they pray and worship. In other words, they believe in G-d's existence, but simply call him "Eloka Dielokaya/The G-d of G-d's/." This is prohibited for even a gentile to believe, and he must believe that G-d has direct influence on the world. It goes without saying that denial of G-d's existence at all, and believe in a foreign deity, is defined as idolatry. However, Shituf, which is permitted for a gentile according to this opinion, believes Hashem interacts with the world, although has given authority to other deities or powers to also have some control in the world, and He is thus not the sole ruler. While Jews are prohibited from believing this due to idolatry, gentiles are not. [See Sefer Hamamarim Melukat 1:323, Mamar Mayim Rabim 5717 Melukat 3 ibid footnote 20]

[243] Noda Beyehuda Tinyana Y.D. 148 [Says that Shituf is Avoda Zara even for gentiles, and the Rama and Ran never intended to say that Shituf is permitted for them, and thus the common statement of people that based on the Rama there is no Issur of Shituf for gentiles, is incorrect; However, see Pischeiy Teshuvah ibid that in truth one must say the Rama holds Shituf is permitted for gentiles, as the Rama Y.D. 151:1 permits selling them items, as explains Shach 151:7]; Mahara Sasson; Vishev Hakohen 38; Meil Tzedakah 22; Shaar Efraim 24; P"M 156; Y.D. 65 S"D end of chapter that is nevertheless Rabbinically prohibited; Binyan Tziyon 1:16; Mishnas Chachomim Yesodei Hatorah Lav Alef; Pischeiy Teshuvah Y.D. 147:2 [concludes that Shituf is forbidden also for gentiles]; Rebbe in handwritten editing remarks to a letter "Christianity is

21. May one greet a gentile on the day of his holiday?[244]

It is forbidden to enter the home of an idolater on the day of his Holiday and wish him Shalom/peace.[245] If one found the gentile outside of his home, he may greet him with a low voice and melancholy demeanor. [Some Poskim[246] rule the above prohibition only refers to using the word "Shalom" being that it is the name of Hashem, however, one may greet him using other terms. Practically, although one is to initially avoid greeting an idol worshiper on the day of their holiday, if one knows the gentile, or not doing so can cause enmity, then one may greet the gentile with a greeting other than Shalom, and even Shalom may be recited in a low voice if he meets him, as stated above.[247]]

Q&A on greetings on Christian Holidays

*Christianity is considered idol worship according to Halacha, and thus the following questions relating to the above law are relevant:

May one wish a merry Chris-mas, or happy holidays, to a gentile acquaintance or neighbor?
Merry chris-mass:[248] The term Chris-mas is forbidden to be mentioned, due to the prohibition against mentioning the name of idols.
Other greetings: If the gentile does not believe in the religious connotations behind the holiday, then there is no prohibition to mention to him "Happy Holidays."[249] If, however, the gentile believes in the idolatry related content behind Christmas, seemingly, one may only do so in a pressing situation, to avoid enmity.[250] Certainly one should not go out of one's way to greet him and send him Holiday wishes, such as through social media, unless lack of doing so will cause enmity. In all cases that one meets a gentile acquaintance outside who is a practicing Christian, he is to greet him with a low voice, as stated above.

Avoda Zara, is in contrast to the seven Noahide laws, as opposed to Islam. However, the Christians of today are simply "Maaseh Avoseihem Beyadeihem."

[244] Michaber 148:9; Gittin 62b

[245] The reason: As we suspect that this level of closeness of going to the home and greeting him can bring unwanted closeness between him and the gentile's idolatry. [Bach 148:10]

[246] Bedek Habayis 148 in name of Orchos Chaim Avoda Zara 21 in name of Maharam, brought in Shach 148:7 and Nekudos Hakesef on Taz 148:6; [The Shach however leaves this matter in question]; See also Taz 148:6 in name of Semak 133 regarding the prohibition to repeat Shalom that it only applies to the word Shalom; Practically, see Birkeiy Yosef 148 in name of Maharikash regarding repeating Shalom that the custom is to repeat a blessing that does not have the name Shalom and seemingly the same would apply here that one may enter the home of a gentile and greet him with other words, or that he may greet him outside in a normal tone if he does not say the word Shalom. [To note however that although the Shach ibid records this ruling of the Bedek Habayis regarding this Halacha discussing greetings on the day of the Holiday, in truth it was said regarding repeating the word Shalom, and perhaps it is limited to that case, and not to the case under our discussion which prohibits entering the home on the day of his holiday and greeting him.] Vetzaruch Iyun.

[247] See Rama 149:12 and Terumos Hadeshen 195 regarding presents and seemingly the same should apply here regarding greetings

[248] See Michaber 147:2; Mordechai in name of Ravayah; Hagahos Maimanis; Rabbeinu Yerucham that it is not permitted to refer to their festivals in a manner of eminence as do the worshipers, and certainly if its name connotes a deity; See Teshuvos Rav Ezriel Hildsheimer 180 and Mishneh Halachos 9:169 regarding the word Christ that one is not to use this term as it connotes a Messiah and savior, and according to some even a deity, and so is the custom of all Jewry to not say this term. Seemingly, the same would apply to avoiding the word Christmas which is rooted in the word Christ and so is the custom. One is rather to use an epithet [i.e. nickname] such as Kratzmacht; Nittel, and the like. Seemingly however the term X-mass is not to be used, as the X is short for Ch***, and is used also by Christians as a formal name of the holiday. [See here http://www.thefreedictionary.com/Xmass]

[249] See Michaber 148:5 and Avoda Zara 65a regarding presents and seemingly the same would apply here; This is in addition to the Heter brought in Rama in next footnote

[250] See Rama 149:12 and Terumos Hadeshen 195 regarding presents and the same would apply here

> **May one wish others a happy New Years on the 1st of January?**[251]
> There is no prohibition involved in wishing a happy New Years to a gentile who does not affiliate the day with any Christian connotations, or worship of a deity.[252] One is to avoid wishing a happy New Years to a practicing Christian [particularly Catholics, and Lutherans] who believes in the Christian doctrine behind the New Year's Holiday.[253] However, even in such a case, one may do so in a pressing situation, in order to avoid causing enmity and anti-Semitism.[254] Certainly one should not go out of one's way to greet him and send him Holiday wishes, such as through social media, unless lack of doing so will cause enmity. In all cases that one meets a gentile acquaintance outside who is a practicing Christian and believes in the holiday of New Years, he is to greet him with a low voice, as stated above. [In general, it is not customary of Jews to wish other Jews a Happy new year on the first of January.[255] However, it is related, that Rebbe Levi Yitzchak of Berditchev would wish others a Happy new year on the 1st of January. Likewise, the Rebbe once wished a Chassid a happy new years on the morning of January first, in continuation of the tradition from Rebbe Levi Yitzchak.[256] This is based on the verse in psalms 87:6 "Hashem Yispor Bichsov Amim.."]

---------------- **Haircuts & Shaving**----------------

22. Men shaving armpit and pubic hair:[257]

It is forbidden for a man to remove his armpit hair or his pubic hair.[258] This applies even against using scissors to shave the hair to a razor like cut [i.e. Keiyn Taar].[259] [One who transgresses the above has transgressed a Rabbinical command.[260]] In previous times, one who shaved the above areas would have been liable for receiving Rabbinical lashes [i.e. Makas Mardus].

---

[251] Historical background on New Years: The history of New Year's celebrations date back to the Julian calendar [pre-Christendom], in which it was celebrated as a day of worship of the Greek deity called Janus, hence its name "January", according to some historians. Later on, in the Gregorian calendar [Christendom], it was celebrated in Europe, and all Christian countries, as a Christian Holiday, commemorating the circumcision and naming of Yoshka. It was customary for the gentiles to receive gifts on this day as a good omen for the coming year. [Rama 149:12 [in non-censored editions]; Darkei Moshe Haaruch 148:5; Terumos Hadeshen 195] Until this very day, Catholic churches throughout the world hold a New Years mass, which is considered a day of obligation for Catholics. Protestants, however, do not necessarily view it as a day of obligation, do not hold mass, although many hold services on New Years. Practically, today, many gentiles do not affiliate New Year's with any religious observance, and in fact are not even aware of the above history. It is simply a day to celebrate the start of the new year on the calendar, and make new year resolutions. Nonetheless, being that this holiday of New Years was affiliated with Christianity, which is defined as idolatry, the Poskim [Rama 149:12 [in non-censored editions]; Darkei Moshe Haaruch 148:5; Terumos Hadeshen 195; recorded in Likkutei Sichos 15/554; Shulchan Menachem 3/292] therefore discuss how Jews are to intermingle with gentiles on this day.

[252] Michaber 148:5 regarding presents, that they may be given to a gentile on his holiday if he does not worship idolatry; Avoda Zara 65a

[253] See Michaber 148:9 that one may not greet an idolater on the day of his Holiday unless he sees him outside, in which case he may greet him in a melancholy voice; See Shach 148:7 regarding if this applies only to the word Shalom, or any greetings; However, certainly saying the words "Happy Holiday" is more severe than simply saying good morning, as it gives credence to their idolatry, and hence should only be done for the sake of preventing enmity, as ruled regarding presents in Rama 149:12; Terumos Hadeshen 195

[254] Rama 149:12; Terumos Hadeshen 195 regarding presents

[255] The reason: As a) New Years is considered a Christian Holiday. And b) It denies the true New Year which is on Rosh Hashanah. Hence, we do not want to give credence to the Gentile new year. From the letter of the law however, seemingly there is no prohibition in doing so.

[256] Rabbi Sholom Hecht of Hecht's bookstore on Coney Island in Flatbush, NY, merited to enter the Lubavitcher Rebbe's inner chamber for "Yechidus." One time Rabbi Hecht had a Yechidus with the Rebbe on the morning of January 1st. At some point during the Yechidus the Rebbe told him "Happy New Year". Rabbi Hecht was very surprised. The Rebbe then told him that Rabbi Levi Yitzchok of Berdichev used to tell his congregants "Happy New Year", and it's based on Kapitel 87 verse 6 in Tehillim where it says "Hashem Yispor Bichsov Amim.." "Hashem will count in the register of people…" [Translation courtesy of Tehillim Ohel Yosef Yitzchok with English translation, by Kehot] The Rebbe is also recorded to have wished his secretary, Rabbi Nissan Mindel, a happy new Years on the 1st of January. So is also recorded of the Apter Rav, author of Ohev Yisrael, that he would wish a happy new year and bless the Jewish people on this day. The author of Baal Hayeshuos [Zlotchiv] would also bless the Jews with a good year, and would say with a smile that when Hashem sees how the gentile celebrate the new years, and compares it to the Jews, He tears their evil decrees.

[257] Michaber 182:1; See Tzemach Tzedek Y.D. 93

[258] The reason: This is forbidden due to the prohibition against Lo Yilbash, that a man may not dress like a woman. The Sages expounded that this verse includes not only a prohibition against wearing actual clothing of a woman but towards doing any action done to the body by women for beauty purposes.

[259] Michaber ibid; Bahag; Tosafos Nazir 59b; Rosh; Rif

Other opinions: Some Poskim rule it is permitted to use a scissor to shave the armpit and pubic hair to even a razor like shave. [Rabbeinu Tam, brought in Tzemach Tzedek ibid]

[260] Taz 182:6

Areas that men also shave:[261] The above prohibition only applies in an area that only women shave their armpits and pubic area. However, in an area which is common also for men to shave the above places of the body, then one who shaves it does not receive Rabbinical lashes.[262] Furthermore, in such communities a man may even initially shave these areas of the body.[263] Nevertheless, the scrupulous Jews [i.e. Chaveirim] avoid shaving these areas of the body even in such communities.[264] [Likewise, according to Kabbalah, one is to abstain from doing so.[265]]

Areas that women do not shave:[266] If a man shaved his pubic hair in a community that even women do not shave their pubic hair, then he is not liable for lashes [although a Rabbinical prohibition remains].

Full body shave:[267] One who shaves his entire body, from head [under the Peiyos and beard[268]] to toe, some Poskim[269] rule it is permitted for him to shave also his armpit and pubic hairs.[270]

Itching the armpit and pubic area:[271] It is forbidden to itch with one's hands the hair of one's armpit and pubic area with intent to remove the hair. It is however permitted to itch it through his clothing.

Shaving for medical purposes:[272] [It is permitted to shave the armpit and pubic hair for medical purposes.[273] Thus] one who has a painful skin ailment in his armpit or pubic area, and the pain is being aggravated due to the hair, may shave off the hair.[274]

Summary:
It is forbidden for a man to remove his armpit hair or his pubic hair even with a scissor. [It is forbidden to trim the armpit and pubic hairs at all, even a very small amount-see Q&A!] The above prohibition only applies in an area that only women shave their armpits and pubic area. However, the scrupulous Jews avoid shaving these areas of the body even in such communities. It is forbidden to itch with one's hands the hair of one's armpit and pubic area with intent to remove the hair. It is however permitted to itch it through his clothing. It is permitted to shave the armpit and pubic hair for medical purposes.

The reason: Removing the hair of the body does not contain a Biblical transgression of Lo Silbash being that the Biblical transgression only applies to actions that visibly make the person appear like the opposite gender, and thus since removal of hair in private areas is not visible to others, it does not fall under the Biblical prohibition. [Taz ibid]
Other opinions: Some Poskim rule it is a Biblical prohibition to shave the armpit and pubic hair using a razor. [Rav in Nazir 58b as explained in Tzemach Tzedek ibid; Semak 33; Conclusion of Tzemach Tzedek 93:4]

[261] Michaber ibid; Tur; Rambam
[262] Michaber ibid
The reason: As the entire reason for the prohibition is so one does not make his body appear similar to that of a woman. [Michaber ibid]
[263] Rama ibid; Ran Avoda Zara
[264] Rama ibid; Ran ibid; Nimukei Yosef
[265] Torah Leshma 215 based on Arizal in Shaar Hamitzvos Parshas Kedoshim
The reason: As just as the upper worlds contain a higher beard with the 13 Tikkunei Dikna, the same applies below by the lower beard. [Arizal ibid]
[266] Taz 182:5
[267] Michaber 182:2
[268] Shach 182:4; Perisha 182; Tzemach Tzedek Y.D. 93-1
[269] Tur in name of Geonim; Tosafos and Rosh Yevamos
[270] The reason: As it is clearly evident that such a shave is not done for beauty purposes. Furthermore, even if the man intends to do so for beauty purposes, since in truth it does not beautify him but rather makes a mockery of him, therefore we ignore his intents. [Shach 182:5]
[271] Michaber 182:3; Nazir 59a
[272] Michaber 182:4; Rashba
[273] Shach 182:5
[274] The reason: As the prohibition of Lo Yilbash is specifically when done for the sake of beauty to mimic a woman. [See Shach 186:1, 5 and 7; Ketzos Hashulchan 143 footnote 3]

> **Q&A**
>
> **May a man trim armpit and pubic hair?**
> Some Poskim[275] rule it is permitted to trim down armpit and pubic hair, so long as the final result is not a razor like shave. Other Poskim[276] rule it is forbidden to trim the armpit and pubic hairs at all, even a very small amount. The Chabad ruling follows the latter opinions.
>
> **In judging the common practice of men in an area vis a vis shaving pubic hair, does one follow the gentile or Jewish custom of men?[277]**
> It is possible to learn that this refers even to gentiles, that if the male gentiles commonly shave these areas then it is permitted for Jewish males to do so as well. On the other hand, it is possible to learn that it refers to the Jewish male population, that when this is the common practice then they are not to be protested. The Rebbe leans to rule like the former approach.[278]
>
> **May one pluck out pubic hair with his finger?[279]**
> No. However, in areas that it is common for men to shave the pubic hair, then even a scrupulous person may do so.

> **Women growing pubic hair:**
> It used to be in Temple times that Jewish girls did not grow pubic hair, neither under the arm pit or pubic area. This was an advantage of beauty held by Jewish girls over the daughters of the other nations as the verse states *"Vayeitzei Lach Sheim Bagoyim Beyafyeich."*[280] Some[281] explain this to mean that they did not grow any hair at all, while others[282] interpret it to mean that they grew very short hairs. After the destruction of the Temple, the girls advantage of beauty was removed and they began to grow hair.[283] Nonetheless, since ideally, they are not meant to have hair in these areas, therefore there is no reason to abstain from shaving it even according to Kabala.[284] Practically, it is customary amongst women of Sephardi origin to be particular to shave their pubic hair prior to immersion in a Mikveh.

23. Men trimming/shaving their legs, arms, chest:[285]

Trimming with scissor:[286] From the letter of the law, it is permitted for men to remove with a scissor the hair of the legs, arm, and chest. [Doing so does not transgress the prohibition of Beged Isha, or any other prohibition. However, removing hair from the Peiyos, beard, pubic hair and armpit, is subject to various restrictions and Biblical or Rabbinical prohibitions, as discussed elsewhere.]

Razor and razor like scissor shave: One may shave the above limbs [arm, leg, chest, not including armpit or pubic hair] using a scissor, to even a razor like shave.[287] It is, however, forbidden for a man to shave any area of his body using an actual razor.[288] [The above prohibition only applies in an area that only

---

[275] Michaber 182:1 that only a razor like shave is forbidden and not a trim; Beis Yosef 182; Kitzur SHU"A 171:2; Torah Leshma [of Ben Ish Chaiy] 215 [However perhaps he refers only to an area that also men shave]

[276] Rashba 1:106; Tzemach Tzedek Y.D. 93 *"If the Beis Yosef would have seen the ruling of the Rashba ibid certainly he would have ruled this way"*; Semak 33 writes a Baal Nefesh is to be stringent

[277] Perisha 182, brought in Rav Akiva Eiger 182

[278] Igros Kodesh 6:268, [printed in Shulchan Menachem 4:133]

[279] Torah Leshma [of Ben Ish Chaiy] 215

[280] Sanhedrin 21a

[281] 2nd explanation in Ran ibid; Torah Leshma [of Ben Ish Chaiy] 215

[282] 1st explanation in Ran ibid; Maharshal

[283] Rashi ibid

[284] See Torah Leshma ibid

[285] Michaber Y.D. 182:1

[286] Michaber ibid; Tur 182:1; Rav in Nazir 58b

[287] Shach 182:3; Taz 182:2; Beir Hagoleh 182; Misgeres Hashulchan 171:1; See Tzemach Tzedek Y.D. 93

[288] Shach 182:3; Taz 181:4 and 182:1; Beis Yosef 181 in name of Rabbeinu Yona in Igeres Hateshuvah 2:36

women shave their arms and legs. However, in an area where it is common also for men to shave with a razor the above places of the body, then a man may even initially shave these areas of the body.[289]]

Summary:
From the letter of the law, it is permitted for men to trim body hair that grows on the legs, arms, or chest, [with exception to the hair of the Peiyos, beard, pubic hair and armpit, which is subject to its own restrictions]. It is forbidden to shave even the above areas using a razor, unless it is common for men to do so in one's country.

Q&A

If one suffers from an overabundance of hair growth on his leg/arm/chest, may he have it removed using a laser?[290]
It is permitted to be done in those areas where it is common for also men to shave these areas.

May a runner or swimmer remove the hair from his arms, legs for the sake of the sport?
As stated above, it is permitted to trim the hair using a scissor although not a razor, unless it is common for men to do so in one's country.

---------------- Chukos Hagoyim----------------

24. Wearing red colored clothing:

Red colored clothing is forbidden to be worn [by either men or women], as they are worn by gentiles for purposes of promiscuity, [and one who wears it transgresses the prohibition of "Thou shall not go in their statutes"[291]].[292] It is likewise not befitting for modest people to wear red colored clothing. [This especially applies to women, as red is a seductive color which attracts the eye of the male and leads to sin.[293]] Furthermore, there is a tradition from our ancestors to avoid wearing red colored clothing.[294] [However, some Poskim[295] are lenient today to permit men to wear red colored clothing, as it is no longer a color that is worn by gentiles, and thus is no longer included in the prohibition of "Thou shall not go in their statutes." Practically, one is to be stringent in this matter.[296] This especially applies towards women, due to reasons of Tznius, and so was the custom in all Frum Jewish homes, to avoid wearing any red colored clothing.[297]]

The reason: As this makes the man appear like a woman, even if it involves only the arms. [Taz 181:4; Beis Yosef ibid in name of Rabbeinu Yona]

Other opinions: Some Poskim rule it is permitted for a man to shave the limbs of his body even using a razor. [Tur, brought in Taz 182:1 and Hagahos Hataz]

[289] Rama ibid regarding pubic hair; Ran Avoda Zara; See however Rama ibid: Nevertheless, the scrupulous Jews [i.e. Chaveirim] avoid shaving the pubic hair even in such communities, and perhaps the same would apply to these hairs as well.

[290] Rav Elyashiv, brought in Kovetz Tel Talpiyos Tishreiy 5773; Ohel Yaakov p. 275

[291] See Michaber Y.D. 178:1; Maharik Shoresh 88; Igros Moshe Y.D. 1:81; Dibros Eliyahu 34

[292] Rama Y.D. 178:1; Beis Yosef 178; Maharik Shoresh 88; Aruch on Brachos 20a

[293] Aruch ibid; Rashi on the verse [Bereishis 49:11] "Ubidam Anavim Susa" that "Clothing which are colored with the blood of grape are worn by women to seduce the male, and is therefore called Susa by the verse"; Dibros Eliyahu 34

[294] Shach 178:3; Maharik ibid; See Drashos Chasam Sofer 2:244

The reason: See below for the discussion of "What is wrong with the color red"

[295] Darkei Teshuvah 178:16 in name of Rav Yitzchak Elchonan of Kovna; Orchos Rabbeinu that so ruled Rav Kanievsky even regarding women; Dibros Eliyahu 34 regarding men; See Igros Moshe Y.D. 1:81 based on Maharik ibid that red clothing is considered "Nidnud Peritzus" and hence may not be worn due to Chukos Hagoyim so long as Jews avoid wearing it. Thus, we see its dependent not on whether the gentiles actually wear it, but on whether Jews avoid wearing it or not.

[296] See Shach ibid that aside from Chukos Hagoyim, we have a tradition not to wear it, and hence why should the tradition stop simply because Chukos Hagoyim is no longer applicable; See Igros Moshe ibid; So rules Rav Eliezer Melamed and Poskim brought in next footnote [although most only discuss women and not men]

[297] Shevet Halevi 6:24-2; Beir Moshe 4:147 *"Such clothing, such as a red skirt or blouse, are an abomination, and such clothing cannot be found amongst G-d fearing Jews."*; The Chasam Sofer did not allow any red clothing into his home; See Drashos Chasam Sofer 2:244; Rav SZ"A, and Rav Chaim Kanievsky, brought in Malbushei Kavod ibid; Halichos Bas Yisrael 7 footnote 7 in name of Rav Elyashiv; Teshuvos Vehanhagos 1:136; Dibros Eliyahu 34

Summary:
Men and women are to avoid wearing red colored clothing. This especially applies to women, due to reasons of modesty.

Q&A

May one wear clothing which are not entirely red but contain red parts?
Some[298] write that the above avoidance of wearing red colored clothing is only when the majority of the clothing is red.

May one wear a small article of clothing which is red, such as socks, a head band or hair clip, a watch, or shoelaces?[299]
One is to avoid wearing anything that is red, even if it is a small item, such as socks, a headband and the like.

May a woman wear red lipstick?
Based on the above, and due to reasons of Tznius, possibly a woman is to avoid wearing bright red colored lipstick.[300] Nonetheless, other shades of red, such as maroon, or pink, are certainly valid.

May one wear undergarments that are red, and may one wear red clothing in the privacy of one's home?
Some[301] write that one is to avoid doing so.[302] Others[303] however rule it is permitted.

May children wear red colored clothing?
Some Poskim[304] rule that children who are below the age of Chinuch may wear red colored clothing, while children who are above the age of Chinuch are to be educated not to do so. [However, based on the tradition recorded next, seemingly, even young children should not wear such clothing.]

May one wear pink or maroon colored clothing?
The above prohibition and tradition is only associated with the color red, and not to any other shade of color, such as pink or marron.[305] However, some[306] argue that all colors associated with red are included in the avoidance, such as pink and marron. Practically, any color which shouts attention to the male eye is not to be worn by G-d fearing women.[307]

---

[298] Halichos Bas Yisrael 7 footnote 7 in name of Rav Elyashiv; Dibros Eliyahu 34
[299] Beir Moshe 4:147-13
[300] I have not found this matter discussed in the Poskim, and have not found any mention of avoidance of red colored makeup in the Poskim. Nonetheless, due to reasons of Tznius, it is improper for a woman to wear makeup in a way that attracts undue attention from bystanders, and hence a bright red lipstick which highlights the lips very extravagantly should be avoided.
[301] Malbushei Kavod 1:25 in name of Rav Chaim Kanievsky
[302] The reason: As it may involve Bechukoseihem Lo Seileichu, and certainly goes against the tradition and bad effect that red clothing brings onto a Jew.
[303] Rav SZ"A, brought in Malbushei Kavod ibid; See Dibros Eliyahu 34
[304] Shevet Halevi 6:24
[305] Halichos Bas Yisrael 7 footnote 7 in name of Rav Elyashiv
[306] Hatzenius Vehayeshua 12 of the Admur of Zutchka; See Shevet Halevi 6:24 that any color which is immodest is included in the prohibition
[307] See Shevet Halevi 6:24 that any color which is immodest is included in the prohibition

> **What is wrong with the color red?**
> Despite what we may think, colors effect our feelings and attraction. Red is a color associated with blood, and is therefore the color of Eisav and Edom, of whom the verse states "By your sword you shall live." A Jew who wears this color is spiritually affected by it.[308] Furthermore, red represents love, romance and promiscuity, and naturally draws the attention of the male eye.[309] This is referred to as the red dress effect. Studies and social experiments performed by universities and journalists have proven that the color red attracts the eye of a man more than other colors, and can be viewed as promiscuous even by women. In one study, it was found that the vast majority of wives would not allow their husbands to chat with a woman wearing a red dress, as opposed to if the same woman was wearing another color. In another study, it was found that men who dated women who wore red felt a more promiscuous atmosphere by the date, as opposed to if the same woman wore another color. The color red shouts for attention from the onlooker, and is thus avoided by the Jewish people who are traditionally modest and avoid wearing things that seek attention of others.

---------------- *Niddah*----------------

25. Bedikos-The amount of Bedikos needed to be done during Shiva Nekiyim and the law if one missed a Bedika?[310]

A woman is obligated to be clean of sightings of blood for seven days after menstruation, or any invalidating sighting of blood, in order to be able to immerse in a Mikveh and be intimate with her husband. To properly ascertain that she indeed is cleared of any sightings of blood, she is required to perform internal examinations with a Bedika cloth during this seven-day period.[311] An absence of these examinations can potentially invalidate her seven clean day period, due to it not having been properly verified. This Halacha will discuss the ideal number of examinations required during the seven day period, the minimal requirement of examinations in a case that the proper number of examinations was not done, and the cases of leniency in which we even initially allow a woman to perform the minimum number of examinations. This Halacha will not deal with laws pertaining to women who suffer from vaginal injuries which release non-uterine blood, and how she is to fulfill her Bedika requirements to permit her to immerse in a Mikveh. This latter case will G-d willing feature in a future publication.

A. Lechatchila- The amount of Bedikos that are initially required to be done [312]

On each one of the seven clean days a woman must initially examine herself [in all the internal vaginal crevices] **twice**[313] every day, once in the morning and once near twilight.[314] [The cloth/Eid should then be checked to be certain it is free of any stain.]

---

[308] See Drashos Chasam Sofer 2:244 in name of Rabbeinu Bechayeh that red draws down the power of Maadim, which is detrimental for a Jew

[309] Aruch ibid; Rashi on the verse [Bereishis 49:11] "Ubidam Anavim Susa" that "Clothing which are colored with the blood of grape are worn by women to seduce the male, and is therefore called Susa by the verse"; For a secular study on this matter-see here http://www.sciencemag.org/news/2012/02/red-dress-effect [This site was viewed by us with a filter which prevents potential immodest pictures, which may or may not be on this page. You can avoid immodest pictures from showing up by attaching a filter to your internet, and/or disabling your browser from showing pics. In general, every G-d fearing Jew must have some filtering system and/or picture blocking method installed onto his internet, to allow for Kosher internet access.]

[310] Michaber 196:4; See Nitei Gavriel 56

[311] See Q&A regarding if this examination requirement is Biblically mandated, or is of Rabbinical institution

[312] Michaber 196:4; Rosh; Tosafos; based on Mishneh Niddah 68b; Semag; Semak; Mordechai
Other opinions: Some Poskim rule that even initially she is not required to check herself daily. [Razah in Hasagos of Baalei Hanefesh of Raavad] Other Poskim rule she is only required to check herself only one time daily. [See next footnote]

[313] Michaber ibid; Semag ibid
Other opinions: Some Poskim rule she is only required to check herself one time daily. [Ramban, Rosh, Hagahos Maimanis, brought in Beis Yosef 196; Haeshkol 44]

[314] Some women have the custom to actually say: *"Today is the such and such day of my count."* Some say it after the evening examination and others after the morning examination. [Kitzur Dinei Taharah 4:14]

B. Bedieved-The law if a Bedika was not done on a certain day:[315]

Skipped Hefsek Taharah:[316] If she skipped the Hefsek Taharah, then the first Bedika she does within her Shiva Nekiyim serves as the Hefsek Taharah, and her Shiva Nekiyim begins only from the evening after that Bedika.

Skipped 1st or 7th: If she did not examine herself twice on each day of the Shiva Nekiyim, then some Poskim[317] rule that so long as she checked herself one time throughout any one of the days of the Shiva Nekiyim, whether the first day, the seventh day, or one of the middle days, then it is valid. Other Poskim[318] however rule that she must examine herself once[319] on the 1st day and once on the 7th day of Shiva Nekiyim for it to be valid.[320] [Some Poskim[321] rule that even according to this opinion, it suffices to check one time in any one of the middle days and one time on the seventh day. Furthermore, some Poskim[322] rule that even one time on any two days between 1-7 suffices. Other Poskim[323] however negate this understanding and rule she must check herself specifically on the 1st and 7th day.] Practically, one is not to be lenient [and the examination is invalid if she did not check herself on both the first[324] and seventh day of Nekiyim].[325] [Even if she already immersed, she is required to wait until she has done a Bedika on the 1st and 7th day and then re-immerse.[326] However, if she already slept with her husband[327], we do not require her to recount and re-immerse so long as she checked herself on the 1st or 7th day.[328] If she only checked herself in one of the middle days, then even if she already had intercourse, some Poskim[329] rule she must wait four days and then recount the Shiva Nekiyim from after four days. Another case of leniency is in a scenario where she cannot perform clean Bedikos due to an injury, in which case we only require her to achieve a clean Bedika on the 1st or 7th day, and perhaps even only on one of the middle days.[330]] According to all Poskim, the above Bedikos is in addition to the Hefsek Taharah.[331]

---

[315] Michaber 196:4; Taharah Kehalacha 196:7-11; Kitzur Dinei Taharah 4:12; Nitei Gavriel 56

[316] Shach 196:8; Degul Merivava 196

[317] 1st and Stam opinion in Michaber ibid; Rav in Niddah 69a that she must check on either 1st or 7th; Rambam Issurei Biyah 6:21; Raavad in Baalei Hanefesh Shaar Sefira Vehabedika [any day, including middle]; Rosh Niddah 10:5 [any day, including middle]; Razah Sela Hamachlokes 36 and Reih in Bedek Habayis [only 1st or 7th]; Ramban Niddah 2:3 [any day, including middle]; Rashba in Toras Habayis Bayis Shevi Shaar Chamishis Tur 10:196 [requires Bedika on 1st or 7th]; Rashbatz "1st or 7th", brought in Lechem Vesimla 196:8

[318] 2nd opinion in Michaber ibid; Rebbe Eliezer in Mishneh Niddah 68b that 1st and 7th suffices; Rebbe Chanina in Niddah 69a that she must check on both 1st and 7th; Hagahos Maimanis on Rambam ibid in name of Raavan; Rabbeinu Simcha; Sefer Haterumah; Semag Lavin 111; Mordechai Niddah 737

[319] So writes Sidrei Taharah 196; Piskei Dinim 196:5; Lechem Vesimla 196

[320] It might happen that she gave up counting in the middle of the seven days. [For example: her husband planned to travel to another city for a long duration, and she therefore stopped counting. He then changed his mind and did not travel.] Although she may have missed counting, the count is still valid and need not be repeated, provided she examined herself once on the 1st day (besides the hefsek taharah) and once on the 7th. [Kitzur Dinei Taharah 4:13]

[321] Degul Merivava, brought in Pischeiy Teshuvah 196:6, that this applies even according to Semag; Teshuvah Meahava 3:44; Ayaleh Shlucha 19

[322] Shoel Umeishiv in Sheol Yosef Daas Y.D. p. 97 that two Bedikos on any two days during the seven suffices; Aruch Hashulchan 196:25

[323] Noda Beyehuda Tinyana Y.D. 128, as understood by Pischeiy Teshuvah 196:6 [unlike his ruling in Degul Merivava, however see Ayaleh Shlucha 19]; Lechem Vesimla 196:24 and 9 based on Raavad in Baal Hanefesh regarding Zava; Chesed Leavraham Kama Y.D. 62; See Chasam Sofer 178; Beis Shlomo 2:41; Taharas Habayis 2:320; Shiureiy Shevet Halevi 196:9; Taharah Kehalacha 17 footnote 33 that so is the ruling of Morei Horas, unless it's a time of great need, such as for pregnancy.

[324] If she checked herself on one of the middle days and the 7th, Taharah Kehalacha 17:13 concludes that in a case of great need, such as if she has a chance to become pregnant depending on the validation of this Bedika, one is to ask a Rav as perhaps there is room to be lenient like Degul Merivava and others.

[325] Michaber ibid

The reason: As this is case of Safek Issur Kareis. [Beis Yosef 196]

[326] Chasam Sofer Y.D. 178, brought in Pischeiy Teshuvah 196:7; Yabia Omer 5:16

[327] Chasam Sofer ibid "If she slept/Lansa with her husband." Some Poskim suggest that perhaps this does not mean actual intercourse but rather that she spent the night with her husband, even without intercourse, and now it's already the next day, then we do not require her to re-Tovel. The same would apply if the Mikveh is now closed and it is not possible for her to re-Tovel. [Badei Hashulchan Tziyunim 158; Taharah Kehalacha 17 footnote 25 and Biurim 17:2; Based on Shach 198:25 in name of Maharam Melublin, and brought in Sidrei Taharah 196:42, regarding other cases of Bedieved that to require her to re-immerse the next day is Mechuar, and therefore we rely on the Bedieved opinion.]

[328] Chasam Sofer Y.D. 178, brought in Pischeiy Teshuvah 196:7; Yabia Omer 5:16; Taharah Kehalacha 196:9; Shiureiy Shevet Halevi 196

The reason: As majority of the Rishonim rule that a single Bedika on the 1st or 7th day suffices. [Chasam Sofer ibid]

[329] Chasam Sofer ibid; Yabia Omer 5:16 however is lenient in such a case even if she only did a Bedika in one of the middle days; Taharah Kehalacha 196:9 rules that if she only checked in the middle, she must wait four days and then recount, although see there footnote 24 in which he gives room to be lenient based on those Poskim who suffice with a middle day Bedika for one with an injury; Shiureiy Shevet Halevi 196 rules like Chasam Sofer that she must re-immerse

[330] Chavas Daas 196:3, brought in Pischeiy Teshuvah 196:5; Noda Beyehuda Tinyana 134 in end; Tzemach Tzedek Y.D. 123 regarding a woman with injury *"It suffices for such a woman to do a Hefsek Taharah and the first day of the Shiva Nekiyim, and the other six days she is not to check"*; Chochmas Adam 117:12 regarding Chashash Iggun; Aruch Hashulchan 196:25 *"Those women who suffer from injury in the womb are*

How to recount if she skipped the first or seventh day: See Q&A!

Skipped days 2,3,4,5,6:[332] If she checked herself once on the 1st and 7th day, the Shiva Nekiyim is valid according to all, even if she missed all the days in-between.

Skipped all seven days:[333] According to all, if she did not do a Bedika throughout any of the seven days, but did on the 8th day, she must wait a full seven clean days beginning from the 8th day. [Furthermore, even if she did a Bedika on the first day she must wait a full seven clean days beginning from the 8th day, if she did not do any Bedikas in the intermediate days.[334] When restarting the Shiva Nekiyim from the 8th day, some Poskim[335] question that perhaps according to all she must check herself for each of the next six days, and if she does not do so, she may not immerse on Motzei the 14th day. Other Poskim[336] however are lenient even in such a case to suffice with the same rules as the rules followed during the regular Shiva Nekiyim.]

	Lechtachila	*Bedieved*	
Bedika 1st through 7th	Lechatchila must do Bedikas daily		*Bedika 1st through 7th*
Did Bedika only on 1st and 7th		Valid according to all	*Did Bedika only on 1st and 7th*
Did Bedika only on middle day and 7th		Dispute if valid-Contact Rav	*Did Bedika only on middle day and 7th*
Did Bedika only in two of the middle days and not on 1st or 7th		Dispute if valid-Contact Rav	*Did Bedika only in two of the middle days and not on 1st or 7th*
Did Bedika only on 1st or 7th		Dispute if valid. Final ruling: Invalid	*Did Bedika only on 1st or 7th*

Summary:
Lechatchila, a woman must examine herself twice each day throughout all seven days of Shiva Nekiyim. Bedieved, if she missed a Bedika, then so long as she checked herself one time on the 1st day and one time on the 7th day, it is valid. If she missed the 1st or 7th day, it is invalid, and she must continue checking until her 1st and 7th day were checked. Nonetheless, in a case of great need, if two, or even one Bedika, was performed during the seven days, she is to contact a Rav for guidance.[337]

---

told to do a clean Bedika for the Hefsek Taharah and one clean Bedika on any day of the Shiva Nekiyim, and so is how Rabbanim Pasken."; Beis David 2; Maharash Engel 1:50; Taharas Yisrael 196:29-30 and Beir Yitzchak 98 "This is obvious according to all"; Beis Efraim 48; See also Kinas Sofrim 45; Malbushei Taharah 6-8; Taharah Kehalacha 17:14-17 footnote 39

[331] Shach 196:8; Degul Merivava ibid
[332] See previous part of this Halacha
[333] Michaber ibid
[334] See the next Halacha in Case B where this matter is elaborated on in length!
[335] See Rashbatz end of Niddah, brought in Lechem Vesimla 196:8 that even according to the lenient opinion who requires only one Bedika in the Shiva Nekiyim, this only applies within seven days of the Hefsek Taharah, and thus perhaps everyone would agree that a check on every day between the 8th and 14th is required even Bedieved. The Rashbatz ibid concludes with a Tzaruch Iyun; See Tzemach Tzedek 155:8 *"The Rashbatz leans to be stringent to require a daily Bedika after the 8th day"*
[336] Haeshkol 44; Minchas Pitim; Implication of Noda Beyehuda Tinyana 128 who validates a check on 1,3,9; Taharah Kehalacha 17:10 footnote 28 concludes based on the Eshkol, who is an early Rishon, that Bedieved is valid even if checked only on 8th and 14th, and so rule other Achronim, and so is implied from Tzemach Tzedek; See Sidrei Taharah 196:18
[337] If two Bedikos were performed on two different days, there is room to be lenient like the Degul Merivava and Aruch Hashulchan and Shoel Umeishiv, so also concludes Taharah 17:13; If only one Bedika was performed, then in a case of an injury that prevents her from getting clean Bedikos, there is room to be lenient. See Taharah Kehalacha 17:17

Q&A

Are the Bedikos during Shiva Nekiyim Biblically or Rabbinically required?

Some Poskim[338] rule that the Bedikos during Shiva Nekiyim are a Biblical requirement. Other Poskim[339] rule it is merely a Rabbinical requirement.

In which scenarios may a woman be lenient to skip doing Bedikos during the intermediate days of the Shiva Nekiyim?[340]

In certain scenarios, and under the guidance of a Rav, we direct a woman to skip the Bedikos of the intermediate days and simply perform a single Bedika on the first and seventh day. It is, however, advisable to also perform a Bedika on one of the intermediate days, in order to save the seven day count in the event that the seventh day Bedika is skipped.[341] The following are amongst the scenarios that a Rav may direct a woman to skip the intermediate day Bedikos:

1. <u>Pain in vagina</u>:[342] In the event that a woman is experiencing pain in her vagina [which does not cause spotting], then she may be directed to perform a single Bedika on the first day and seventh day, and does not need to perform them during the intermediate days. However, she is to perform a wipe on her vagina throughout each of the intermediate days.[343] [She must also perform a Hefsek Taharah beforehand, although does not need to perform a Moch Dachuk.[344]]

2. <u>Injury in vagina which releases blood</u>:[345] In the event that a woman contains a blood extracting injury in her vagina [which extracts non-uterine blood, such as a cut in her vaginal cavity], then she is to be directed to only perform a single Bedika on the first day and seventh day. This Halacha will IY"H be discussed in a future volume in its full details.

3. <u>Staining not due to injury</u>:[346] A woman who suffers from blood staining that is not the result of injury but rather the untimely expelling of uterine blood [often triggered by various oral and vaginal contraceptives, such as the IUD], then some Poskim[347] rule that she may not be lenient to skip any of the daily required Bedikos simply to escape discovering an invalidating stain.[348] However, other Poskim[349] argue and rule that she may be directed in such a case to only perform a single Bedika on the first day and seventh day, and not to perform them during the intermediate days. Practically, in all such cases, she is to see a specialist to try to determine the source of the blood, and how it can be stopped, and contact a Rav for final guidance in what should be done regarding the Bedikos.

If a woman has a bleeding injury during Shiva Nekiyim, how is she to perform the Bedikas of Hefsek Taharah and Shiva Nekiyim, and how many clean Bedikas must she achieve to be allowed to go to Mikveh?

See Topics in Practical Halacha Volume 4!

---

[338] Implication of Beis Yosef 196 who says one is to be stringent by Issur Kareis to require a Bedika on the 1st and 7th; Chavas Daas 196:3; Yosef Daas in name of Sefer Haterumos; Sidrei Taharah 196:18 that according to opinion who requires Bedika on 1st and 7th, the Bedikos are Biblical; Meil Tzedakah, brought in Sidrei Taharah ibid, requires a Biblical Shiva Nekiyim even according to Poskim who only require one Bedika

[339] See Sidrei Taharah 196:18 that counting the seven clean days is required but not the actual checking; Chasam Sofer Y.D. 177

[340] See Taharah Kehalacha 17:14-17

[341] Directive of Rav Asher Lemel Hakohen; See next Halacha!

[342] Tzemach Tzedek 113:4; Noda Beyehuda Tinyana 129, brought in Pischeiy Teshuvah 196:8; Chavas Daas 196:3; Rav Akiva Eiger Tinyana 34; Malbushei Taharah 197:7; Nitei Gavriel 56:4

[343] Tzemach Tzedek ibid; Noda Beyehuda ibid

[344] Nitei Gavriel 56:4 footnote 5

[345] See Shiureiy Shevet Halevi 187:5-3 p. 72; Taharah Kehalacha 17:14-18; Nitei Gavriel 56 footnote 26

[346] See Nitei Gavriel 56:6

[347] Shem Aryeh 39; Darkei Teshuvah 196:39; Kaneh Bosem 2:47-2; Taharah Kehalacha 17

[348] <u>The reason</u>: As the entire purpose of the examinations is to negate the discovery of these untimely secretions, and hence on the contrary, she must be even more careful to perform these examinations than a regular woman who is not known to suffer from untimely secretions.

[349] Marcheshes 35; Igros Moshe Y.D. 2:78; See Nitei Gavriel ibid footnote 11

> **If she did not check herself on the 1st day, how is the Shiva Nekiyim calculated?**[350]
> As stated above, the checking on the first day of Shiva Nekiyim is mandatory, and hence if it was skipped, she is required to delay the start and end of the seven clean days, as will now be explained. If she did not check herself on the 1st day, but did check herself during the coming days, then her first day of count begins from the day that the first Bedika was done. For example, if she did not check herself on the 1st or 2nd day but did check herself on the 3rd day and 7th day, then the 3rd day is counted as her first day of Shiva Nekiyim and she must continue to check herself until the 9th day.[351] On Motzei the 9th day, she may immerse in a Mikveh. Nevertheless, in a case of great need she is to contact a Rav to verify if there is room to be lenient to allow her to immerse on Motzei the 7th day even in such a case.
> <u>Skipped 1st but did Moch Dachuk previous night</u>: In the event that she used a Moch Dachuk by her Hefsek Taharah, which was only removed after nightfall, some Poskim[352] rule that Bedieved it suffices to consider it a Bedika for her 1st day, and she may immerse Motzei the 7th, if she did a Bedika on the 7th day. Practically, she is to contact a Rav for guidance.
>
> **If she did not check herself on the 7th day, how is the Shiva Nekiyim calculated?**
> See next Halacha!

26. If she did not check herself on the 7th day, how is the Shiva Nekiyim calculated?

As stated in the previous Halacha, if she did not check herself on the seventh day, she cannot go to Mikveh that night, and is to check herself on the 8th day or whatever day she remembers. This applies even if she checked herself throughout all the other days between 1-6.[353] However, regarding whether she may immerse the evening of her next examination [i.e. Motzei the 8th, which is done to make up for the missed 7th day], is dependent on when was the last time that she checked herself prior to this days examination. In certain cases, if too many days have passed between the current day's examination and the last prior examination, the entire seven-day count becomes invalidated, and the current days examination returns to become her first day of Shiva Nekiyim. The general rule is as follows: If six days have passed without a Bedika then all her previous examinations become invalid and the current days examination is considered her first day of Shiva Nekiyim. The following are the various scenarios and laws:

Case A: Five days passed without a Bedika-Checked herself exactly seven days prior [i.e. 2nd & 8th day]:[354]

If a woman did not check herself on the seventh day, and checked herself on one of the later days to make up for the missed Bedika [i.e. the 8th day], then if she also checked herself exactly seven days prior, then she may immerse that night. For example, if she checked herself on the 2nd day and 8th day then she may immerse on Motzei the 8th. This applies even if she did not check herself prior to the 2nd day and did not check herself in-between the 2nd and 8th day.[355] Thus, the rule is that whenever one is checking herself past the 7th day to make up for the missed Bedika of the 7th day, she is to calculate seven days back and make sure that a Bedika was done that day in order to be able to immerse in a Mikveh that evening. If a Bedika was not done that day, then we enter scenarios B-C!

---
[350] Noda Beyehuda Tinyana Y.D. 128, brought in Pischeiy Teshuvah 196:6 [unlike his ruling in Diggul Merivava]; Lechem Vesimla 196:24 and 9
[351] <u>The reason</u>: As she must check herself on the first and seventh day, and hence her check on the 3rd day serves as her first day of Nekiyim. [ibid]
[352] See Shev Yaakov 36, brought in Lechem Vesimla 196:5; Levanon Neta 196:5; Mahariy Levi 1:241; Giddulei Taharah 72; Taharas Habayis 2:320; Taharah Kehalacha 17 footnote 33 questions whether today the Moch is valid as a Bedika, being it is not fully penetrated inside her.
[353] Noda Beyehuda Tinyana Y.D. 128, brought in Pischeiy Teshuvah 196:6; See Tzemach Tzedek 155; Lechem Vesimla 196:24; Taharah Kehalacha 17:10 [p. 307]; Darkei Taharah 14 [p. 135]; Shiurei Shevet Halevi p. 285
[354] Noda Beyehuda Tinyana Y.D. 128, brought in Pischeiy Teshuvah 196:6
[355] <u>The reason</u>: As the 2nd and 8th day both serve as the 1st and seventh day. [ibid]

Case B: Six days passed without a Bedika [i.e. she checked herself only on the 1st day and 8th day]:[356]

If six days passed without a Bedika, then her Shiva Nekiyim restarts and the Bedika she does on the 8th day, or whatever day she remembers, is considered her first day of Shiva Nekiyim. For example, if she checked herself on the 1st day and 8th day, and did not check herself on any other day in-between, then she must restart her count from the 8th day, and the 8th day now becomes her first day of Shiva Nekiyim. She must subsequently check herself for the next six days[357], or at the very least on the 8th and 14th day, and if she does not do so, she may not immerse on Motzei the 14th day.

Checked herself on 1st-2nd day and on 9th day:[358] If she checked herself on the 1st and 2nd day, and then did not check herself until the 9th day, then since six days have passed without a Bedika she has therefore invalidated her previous Bedikos, and must recount seven clean days from the 9th day and onwards. The same applies if she checked herself on the 1st, 3rd and 10th day, that she must recount the seven clean days from the 10th day.

Checked herself on 1st day and on Bein Hashmashos of between the 7th/8th day: If she checked herself on the 1st day, and then did not check herself until the end of the 7th day by Bein Hashmashos, then some Poskim[359] rule that the examination counts for the 7th day and she may thus immerse that night without requiring to wait another seven days.[360] Practically, it is best if the couple is willing and able, to restart the Shiva Nekiyim and delay the Tevila for another seven days. If, however, there is difficulty in doing so, such as due to causing issues of Shalom Bayis, or Zera Levatala, then she may follow the above ruling and immerse that night.[361]

Case C: Did not check herself seven days prior, but checked herself prior to seven days [i.e. on 1st day] and within seven days, and on 8th day:[362]

If she checked herself on the first day, and on only one of the middle days in-between, then if she checks herself on the 8th day, she may immerse that night.[363] For example, if she checked herself on the 1st day and 3rd day and 8th day then she may immerse on Motzei the 8th day. The same applies if she checked herself on the 1st, 4th, and 9th day, then she may immerse on Motzei the 9th day. If, however she checked herself on the 1st, 3rd and 10th day, then her seven days restart, as explained in Case B.

Summary:
In all cases that a woman did not do a Bedika for the past six days, then her Shiva Nekiyim restarts and her current days Bedika counts as the first day of Shiva Nekiyim. Thus, if she did not check herself on days 2-7, then her 8th day is her first day of Shiva Nekiyim.

---

[356] Lechem Vesimla 196:24; Tzemach Tzedek Y.D. 155 based on Gemara, Tosafos, Ramban, Sefer Hateruma, Ran; Taharah Kehalacha 17:10 [p. 307]; Darkei Taharah 14 [p. 135]; Shiurei Shevet Halevi p. 285; Nitei Gavriel 2 56:9

[357] See previous Halacha in B for a dispute in this matter regarding whether a daily Bedika is required even Bedieved from after the 8th day.

[358] Noda Beyehuda Tinyana Y.D. 128, brought in Pischeiy Teshuvah 196:6; Taharah Kehalacha 17:12

[359] Implication of Shaareiy Tzedek 130; Binyan Olam 42; Shoel Vinishal 7:168; Darkei Teshuvah 196:50; Shaareiy Tohar 15:5; Shiureiy Shevet Halevi 1964:9, p. 285; Taharah Kehalacha 17:8 [p. 305] footnote 23; Nitei Gavriel 56:10; Taharas Habayis p. 315

[360] The reason: This is due to Sfek Sfeika, as perhaps Bein Hashmashos is considered day, and even if not, some Poskim rule that a check on the first day alone suffices, as explained above. [Poskim ibid]

[361] So I received from Harav Yitzchak Yehuda Yaroslavsky Shlita

[362] Noda Beyehuda Tinyana Y.D. 128, brought in Pischeiy Teshuvah 196:6; Shaareiy Tohar; Taharas Yisrael; Tiferes Tzevi; Ayala Shlucha 19; Taharah Kehalacha 17:11; See also Chasam Sofer 178; Beis Shlomo 2:41; Lechem Vesimla 196:9

[363] The reason: Although seven days have passed between the 1st and the 8th, nevertheless the Bedika done in-between connects the 1st and 8th day. [ibid]

---------------- *Hataras Nedarim* ----------------

27. Women performing Hataras Nedarim:

One of the grave and serious offences in the Torah is the breaking of a vow. If one made a vow and desires to break it, he must go through the procedure of annulment, called Hataras Nedarim. The severity of breaking a vow and its process of annulment applies equally to both men and women. The following will discuss detailed laws of how to perform Hataras Nedarim, with an emphasis on the practical way this can be done by a woman who is unable to appear before a formal Beis Din.

A. Severity of vows and its definition:

The severity of vows: One is not to be accustomed to make vows. One who makes a vow, even if he fulfills it, is called a Rasha and a sinner.[364] One who makes a vow is considered like one who built a Bama at a time that building Bamos are forbidden. One who fulfills the vow is considered as if he has brought a sacrifice on a Bama altar, as it is better to revoke the vow through a sage than to fulfill it.[365] One is to avoid swearing even regarding truthful matters. King Yanai caused 1000 of his cities to be destroyed due to making swears even though he fulfilled his word.[366] One who is not careful regarding vows and swears, causes death to his wife and young children.[367] Accordingly, every person is to accustom himself to recite Bli Neder upon giving his word for something. This applies even when pledging charity and the like.[368]

When does a Chumra/custom become a Neder and require Hataras Nedarim?[369] If one performed a Chumra one time with intent to continue doing so forever, it has the status of a vow. If he performed the Chumra or custom three[370] times, it is considered a vow even if he did not have in mind to do so forever.[371] For this reason, whenever accepting a new Hiddur, Chumra, or custom one is to explicitly state that he is not accepting this upon himself as a vow, and he is only doing so one time, or whenever he decides.[372]

When does a Mitzvah pledge become a Neder:[373] If one accepted upon himself to perform a certain Biblical or Rabbinical Mitzvah [and not merely a stringency[374]], such as to distribute charity[375], or learn a certain matter of Torah, or perform another Mitzvah, then it is considered a vow [unless he explicitly stated "Bli Neder"]. One is thus to initially state "Bli Neder" upon taking a new Shiur or learning schedule upon himself.[376]

B. Women performing Hataras Nedarim on Erev Rosh Hashanah:

It is customary to perform Hataras Nedarim on Erev Rosh Hashanah in order to rid oneself of vows, and their potential transgressions, prior to the day of judgment.[377] Ideally, there is no difference between men

---

[364] Yoreh Deah 203:1
[365] Yoreh Deah 203:3
[366] Admur 156:2
[367] Alef Hamagen 581:102
[368] Michaber Y.D. 203:4
[369] See Yoreh Deah 214:1; Admur 249:13; 161:8; 468:17; Alef Hamagen 581:102; Glosses of Rav Raskin on Siddur [Miluim 25]
[370] Admur 249:13; 468:17; Nussach of Hataras Nedarim in Siddur; Shaar Hakolel 41:3 [see there for a lengthy discussion of proofs for this matter]
Ruling of Michaber: The Michaber ibid does not state how many times the following of a Hiddur turns the Hiddur into a vow. The Kitzur SHU"A [in previous prints, brought in Shaar Hakolel ibid; Alef Hamagen ibid] questions this wording of the Nussach of "three times" stating that even one time requires Hatara. The Shaar Hakolel ibid answers his questions.
[371] Michaber ibid; Admur ibid; Alef Hamagen ibid
[372] Michaber ibid; Admur 161:8 [regarding Netilas Yadayim and other Mitzvos]; 249:13; 468:17 [that if one said Bli Neder it is not binding]
[373] Michaber and Rama 213:2 [Michaber regarding learning and Rama regarding all Mitzvos]; Michaber 203:4 and Shach 203:4 regarding charity; M"B 238:5 [regarding all matters of a Mitzvah]
[374] Meaning that upon performing this Mitzvah he fulfills a Biblical or Rabbinical command, even though he is not obligated to do so at the moment, such as pledging to give charity to an institution. Although the giving of this charity fulfills a Biblical Mitzvah of Tzedakah, initially he was never obligated to pledge the charity to this specific institution to begin with. This is opposed to a mere stringency of which its laws were discussed in the previous part of this Halacha.
[375] Regarding a pledge to give a loan: See Ahavas Chesed Halva 1:11
[376] M"B ibid
[377] Siddur Admur; Shla"h [beginning of Miseches Yuma]; Peri Eitz Chaim [Shaar Rosh Hashanah] Shach Al Hatorah Matos; Birkeiy Yosef 581:21; Shaareiy Teshuvah 581:1; Kitzur SH"A 128:16; Chayeh Adam 138:8; Kaf Hachaim 581:19 and 99
Reasons mentioned for this custom: The reason we annul all previous vows is in order to save oneself from retribution during the judgment of Rosh Hashanah, for not keeping a vow. [Chayeh Adam 138:8; Kaf Hachaim 581:99] The custom for stipulating on future vows is based on the

and women in the status of a vow, and the severe prohibition to transgress it, and hence women require annulment of vows just like men. Nonetheless, it is not customary for women to perform Hataras Nedarim in mass on Erev Rosh Hashanah, as is performed by men.[378] This is primarily due to reasons of Tznius.[379] This, however, does not remove a woman from the obligation to annul vows that she has made in order to be allowed to break them. The following will discuss how a woman can annul a vow and if it may be done through a Shliach, such as her father or husband.

C. How to do Hataras Nedarim throughout the year-Men & Women:

Appointing an emissary to annul one's vow: A person must personally appear before the judges in order to have his vow revoked, and he cannot appoint an emissary to do so in his place.[380] The only exception to this rule is regarding one's wife. One's wife may appoint her husband to nullify vows on her behalf, having the husband mention this during the annulment.[381] Nevertheless, in such a case, the husband may not assemble a tribunal specifically for the purpose of annulling his wife's vows and rather only if they are already assembled can he act as an emissary to do so.[382] [Some[383] write based on this law that it is proper on Erev Rosh Hashanah for the husband to annul his wife's vows upon him doing Hataras Nedarim, in order so the wife also benefits from Hataras Nedarim. In such a case, the husband is to tell the tribunal that he is annulling the vows also on behalf of his wife and in return the tribunal is to answer him in plural tense "Hakol Mutarim **Lachem**".[384]] No other woman may appoint a man as an emissary to nullify vows for her before a court, and rather she must do so herself.[385] Thus, a father cannot do Hataras Nedarim on behalf of his daughter.

The tribunal: In order for a vow to be annulled one must present the vow before a tribunal of three observant Jews who are above the age of Bar Mitzvah and have either grown a beard, [or are past 18 years of age[386]].[387] The members of the tribunal who annul the vow may be relatives of each other and may even be a relatives of the person asking for the annulment.[388] Thus a girl/woman may do Hataras Nedarim through presenting the vow to her father and two older brothers, or other relatives, who will

---

Gemara Nedarim 23a that one who wants to annul all his vows of the future year, is to perform Hataras Nedarim on Rosh Hashanah. From this spread the custom to say Kol Nidreiy on Erev Yom Kippur, although Zerizin Makdimim and do so already on Erev Rosh Hashanah. [Shla"h beginning of tractate Yuma].

Other customs: Some have the custom to perform Hataras Nedarim 40 days before Rosh Hashanah and again 40 days before Yom Kippur. The reason for this is because the Zohar states that one who was excommunicated in the heavenly courts remains in this state for a period of forty days, and his prayers are not accepted above. Therefore, they are careful starting from forty days earlier, to revoke any excommunications, so one's prayer is accepted above on Rosh Hashanah and Yom Kippur. The Beis Keil community of Jerusalem is accustomed to reciting Hataras Nedarim every Erev Shabbos throughout the entire year. [Kaf Hachaim 581:12] Some recite Hataras Nedarim on Erev Rosh Chodesh Elul. [Mishmeres Shalom 41:1]

[378] Piskeiy Teshuvos 581:18
[379] In Piskeiy Teshuvos ibid he writes that the women rely on Kol Nidrei to revoke their future vows. To note, however, that not all future vows are revoked with this stipulation, as will be explained later on. Likewise, it does not help to revoke any of her previous vows. In any event those women who rely on Kol Nidrei must make sure that they understand the words they are reading, and must read along with the Chazan. Vetzaruch Iyun regarding reading it loud enough for another three people to hear, if this is valid even with other women.
[380] Michaber Y.D. 228:16
[381] Michaber Y.D. 234:56

The reason: Although the law states that one cannot be an emissary to annul another person's vows [Michaber 228:16], nevertheless by one's wife it is valid, as one's wife is considered like his own body, and hence it is as if she is present in the court room when her husband is present. [Shach 234:70; Taz 234:46]

What vows may the husband be an emissary to annul for on behalf of his wife? A husband may be an emissary to annul any vow of his wife if she appoints him to do so for her. The limitation on the type of vows a husband can revoke is only with regards to Hafara. [234:55 and 59]
[382] Michaber ibid

The reason: Some rule the reason for this is because ideally one must personally appear before the tribunal and it is only due to leniency that they allowed the wife to send her husband. However, to allow her husband to summon the tribunal on her behalf is considered a belittlement of the tribunal. [Taz 234:47] Alternatively, the reason for this is in order to protect the wife's privacy. [Shach 234:71] According to this latter reason, if the wife allows her husband to gather the tribunal on her behalf, it is valid. [Levush, brought in Shach ibid]
[383] Piskeiy Teshuvos ibid; Yabia Omer 2:30
[384] Teshuvos Vehanhagos 1:338; Yabia Omer 2:30 that so is said in the Nussach; Piskeiy Teshuvos ibid
[385] Michaber Y.D. 228:16
[386] Admur 39:1; M"A 39:1; See Miasef Lekol Hamachanos 39:7; Chikrei Halachos 5:62; Yagdil Torah N.Y. 8:44
[387] Pischeiy Teshuvah Yoreh Deah 228:2; Reb Akiva Eiger 73 and in 228:3; Sheivet Haleivi 4:94;

The reason: The reason they are to have a beard is because by Biblical matters, we do not rely on the Chazaka of Rava which assumes they have grown two hairs by this time. Hence, we require a full beard as proof. [Pischeiy Teshuvah ibid; Rav Akiva Eiger ibid]
[388] Michaber Yoreh Deah 228:3; Piskeiy Teshuvos 581:16

serve as members of the tribunal of three. A husband, however, cannot serve as part of the tribunal of judges to annul the vow of his wife.[389]

Mentioning the vow and asking a Rav if the vow is annullable: If one does not remember a particular vow at the time of the annulment, and is simply asking to annul all vows that he has possibly made, or vows that their details were forgotten, then the annulment is valid. However, those vows which one remembers their details, must be verbalized to at least one of the members of the tribunal which is performing the annulment. If one does not mention the vow, despite having knowledge of it, then the tribunal may not annul the vow. In the event that one particularizes a specific vow, the people annulling the vow must know the laws involved in whether such a vow may be annulled and how. Accordingly, one is to contact a Rav who is knowledgeable in this subject and ask if the vow is annullable and as to how the tribunal is to annul it.

How is a vow revoked?[390] There are two ways a vow can be revoked. One is through Charata/regret and a second is through a Pesach/opening. Practically, today we perform both a Pesach and Charata when annulling a vow on one's behalf. The following is how it is done: The person requesting the annulment must regret the vow <u>from the time of its initiation</u>. This means that he regrets ever having made the vow to begin with. This is called Charata. If he does not regret the vows initiation and simply regrets its continued validity, then the annulment is invalid. In such a case the judge is to find a Pesach [i.e. convincing argument] for the asker. This is done by asking him *"If you would have known that this and this would occur would you have still made the vow?"* If he answers "no" then it is a valid Pesach. He is then to also be asked if he regrets making the vow to begin with.[391] Practically, the custom is to be stringent and perform a Pesach even when the asker expresses regret for the vow. Thus, in all cases, after he expresses his regret, the judge is to ask him *"If you would have known that this and this would occur would you have still made the vow"*.[392] It is proper that the judges be told by the asker the reason that he regrets the vow.[393] The person requesting the annulment must truthfully regret having made the vow to begin with. If in truth he does not regret it from its initiation, then even if he tells the judges, upon being asked, that he regrets it from that time, the annulment is invalid, and the vow is still in effect.[394]

The Nussach of the annulment:[395] The annulment is finalized by the tribunal reciting one of the following set of words to the person requesting the annulment: "Mutar Lach" or "Sharuy Lach" or "Machul Lach". The chosen set of words is to be recited three times by the tribunal to the person requesting the annulment.[396] Bedieved, if the set of words was only recited one time it is nevertheless valid.[397] The above set of words may be said in any language.[398] [The custom today, however, is for the tribunal to recite the Nussach written in the Siddur[399] for Hataras Nedarim. This Nussach is recited three times and contains all the above set of words and a particularization of the effect of the annulment.]

Summary:
Although, it is not customary for women to perform Hataras Nedarim in mass on Erev Rosh Hashanah, as is performed by men, nevertheless, this does not remove a woman from the obligation to annul vows that she has made in order to be allowed to break them. Thus, a woman who desires to annul a vow that she made is to either appoint her husband to annul it on her behalf on Erev Rosh Hashanah, upon him

---

[389] Michaber Y.D. 234:57
<u>The reason</u>: As one's wife is considered like the same body as her husband, and he is hence invalid to revoke her vow. [Shach 234:7]
[390] Michaber Y.D. 228:7
[391] This follows the stringent opinion that requires one to do both a Pesach and Charata. [Michaber and Rama ibid]
[392] Rama ibid
[393] Taz 228:11
[394] Michaber 228:7
[395] Michaber Yoreh Deah 228:3
[396] Michaber ibid
<u>The reason</u>: This is done in order to form a Chazaka. [Shach 228:6]
[397] Shach ibid; Beis Yosef; Bach in name of Rambam
[398] Rama ibid
[399] Siddur Admur; Shlah Tractate Yuma

performing Hataras Nedarim, or is to perform the following procedure:

Checklist of how to do Hataras Nedarim throughout the year:
1. Gather three observant Jewish men who are above the age of 13 and have grown an abundance of facial hair or are above age 18. They may even be relatives, such as one's father and brothers, although not one's husband. A wife may send her husband to perform Hataras Nedarim on her behalf, if the three men are anyways gathered there
2. Tell one of the judges [or an independent Rav] the vow that one wishes to revoke and verify that it is revocable.
3. The judge/Rav must determine whether such a vow is able to be revoked according to Halacha.
4. If it can be revoked, the tribunal is to ask the person whether he regrets making the vow <u>from its initiation</u> and what his reason is for the regret.
5. The tribunal is then to perform a Pesach by asking the person *"If you knew that such and such would have come up would you have not made the vow to begin with."*
6. If the person truthfully answers that he would not have made the vow, then the tribunal is to tell him "Machul Lach" three times.
7. After the above procedure the vow is officially annulled.

---------------- *Talmud Torah*----------------

28. Learning Chumash and Tanach and being an expert in its content:[400]

It is a Biblical obligation upon every [male[401]] Jew to study the entirety of scripture, [the 24 books[402] of] Torah Nevi'im and Kesuvim[403], and know its content by heart.[404] This is included in the positive command of Torah learning.[405] This is the first subject that a father is obligated to teach a child[406], as will be explained, and takes precedence over the study of all other subjects of Torah, including Halacha.[407] [It is included in the Mitzvah of Yedias Hatorah, although is not considered part of the main Mitzvah of Yedias Hatorah.[408]] Those who are not accustomed to learning Torah, Nevi'im and Kesuvim, do not have upon whom to rely even if they learn the Talmud daily, as all of Tanach must be studied and reviewed many times until one is an expert in all its content.[409] [In other words, one may not rely on the study of

---

[400] Admur Hilchos Talmud Torah 1:1, 4, 6; 2:1 and 9; O.C. 155:1; Kuntrus Achron 1:1; Michaber Y.D. 245:6; 246:4; Tur 245 and 246; Rambam Talmud Torah 1:7; Kiddushin 30a "Until when must one teach his child...Mikrah which is Torah"; See Likkutei Sichos 36:16 [printed in Shulchan Menachem 4:202]

[401] See Admur 1:14

[402] Michaber Y.D. 246:4 "24 books"

[403] Admur 1:1, 4 and 6; 2:9; See Kuntrus Achron 1:1 "Also includes Nevi'im and Kesuvim....According to this there is no merit to the custom to not learn Nevi'im and Kesuvim"; Michaber Y.D. 245:6 "Entire scripture" and 246:4 "24 books"; Shach 245:5 that so is implied from Michaber ibid; Tur 245 and 246 "Torah, Nevi'im and Kesuvim"; Rambam Talmud Torah 1:7 and 12 "The entire scripture...The words of Kabbalah are included in scripture"; See Bach 245:5 in length; Likkutei Sichos 36:16 footnote 38

<u>Other opinions</u>: Some Poskim rule it is not necessary to teach one's child Nevi'im and Kesuvim. [Rashi on Kiddushin ibid; See Bach ibid in length] Practically, we do not rule like Rashi, as stated in the above Poskim. [See Bach ibid; Kuntrus Achron ibid]

[404] Admur Hilchos Talmud Torah 2:2-3

[405] See Admur and all Poskim ibid that it is part of the Mitzvah of Vishinantam Livanecha and Talmud Torah

[406] Admur 1:1

[407] Admur 2:9 "All this is aside for the reading of Tanach at set times, which has priority over everything."

[408] See Likkutei Sichos 36:16 footnote 38 and 45 that the study of the verses which relate the Mitzvos are included in the main Mitzvah of Yedias Hatorah, while the study of the remaining parts of scripture is similar to the obligation to study Agados, which is included in the Mitzvah of Yedias Hatorah, but is not the main Mitzvah. Accordingly, although its study is required, it does not push off the Mitzvah of getting married. See there in length.

[409] Admur Hilchos Talmud Torah 2:2-3 "According to all, in the start of one's learning one must study scripture every day and repeat it not just one or two or three times, but a great abundance of times, each person in accordance to his memorization capabilities, so he memorize it well."; Admur O.C. 155:1 "At this time one must learn the written Torah"; Admur Kuntrus Achron 1:1 "According to this there is no merit to the custom to not teach Nevi'im and Kesuvim, and what the Shach wrote...is inaccurate"; Bach ibid; Admur in 2:1-3 and O.C. 155:1 completely omits the allowance of Rama/Shach/Tosafus [brought in other opinions] to rely on the study of Talmud for one's knowledge of Tanach and he explicitly negates this opinion in Kuntrus Achron ibid saying in truth that even the Rama and Rabbeinu Tam agree that to begin with one must first study Tanach; See in great length glosses of Rav Ashkenazi on Kuntrus Achron 1 in Vol. 2 p. 890- 899

<u>Other opinions and customs</u>: Some Poskim rule it is not necessary to teach one's child Nevi'im and Kesuvim. [Rashi on Kiddushin ibid; See Bach ibid in length] This is the widespread custom today, to not learn Nevi'im and Kesuvim. [See Bach ibid in length; Shach ibid; Kuntrus Achron ibid] The Bach ibid completely negates this custom. However, some Poskim defend this custom saying that it is a Minhag Yisrael which is Torah

Talmud to gain expertise in Tanach and fulfill the obligation of having knowledge in its content, and rather he must study the entire scripture of Tanach from the original Sefarim in order to fulfill his obligation of Yedias Torah in this subject.]

The required daily learning of Tanach:[410] Although children are first taught Tanach and only then proceed to study Mishneh and Talmud[411], an adult who has yet to learn and know the content of Tanach, is not to schedule his learning time to first learn the entire Tanach and only then proceed to Mishneh and Talmud.[412] Rather, an adult's daily[413] learning schedule is obligated to include three subjects, **Mikrah** [i.e. Tanach[414]], **Mishneh** [i.e. Halacha[415]] and **Talmud** [i.e. the reasons behind the Halachos[416]].[417] This is a Biblical obligation, received from Moses on Sinai.[418] Even one who is unable to study and remember a great amount of Torah, and is hence required to dedicate all his time to the study of practical Halacha, is required to also study Tanach at the set times.[419] [Thus, one's daily learning schedule must include the study of scripture [i.e. Tanach], in addition to the study of Halacha and Talmud.]

---

and relies on the opinion of the Poskim [Rama 246:4; Tosafos Kiddushin 30a; Hagahos Maimanis; Rabbeinu Peretz on Hagahos Hasemak 105; Rabbeinu Yerucham 2] who rule that the Babylonian Talmud includes all parts of the Torah and Tanach, and hence this obligation of learning Tanach is fulfilled through the study of Talmud. [Shach Y.D. 246:5] Practically, Admur rules as follows: While this custom is correct from the aspect that the father does not need to hire a teacher to teach him all of Tanach when he is a child [Admur 1:6, unlike Bach ibid, See Kuntrus Achron 1:1] it is not correct from the perspective that there is no obligation to learn and be an expert in Tanach, and in truth one does not fulfill this obligation through the study of Talmud, unlike the Shach ibid. Admur novelizes and explains that even according to the above Poskim ibid who rule one fulfills his obligation of 1/3 learning of Tanach through studying Talmud, this only applies once he has studied all of Tanach and become an expert in it, memorizing all its content. However, until one has reached this level of knowledge in Tanach, all the above Poskim agree that one may not fulfill his obligation with simply learning Talmud. [Admur Kuntrus Achron ibid] In other words, everyone agrees that to fulfill the Mitzvah of Yedias Hatorah one must learn and become expert in all of Tanach, and it is only once this is accomplished that the Poskim discuss the Mitzvah of Vihagisa Bo Yomam Valyal, in which one can fulfill his 1/3 of Tanach through studying the Talmud. [See glosses of Rav Ashkenazi ibid] While this is the ruling of Admur, the widespread custom today is like the Shach's understanding. See Glosses of Rav Ashkenazi ibid who explains that perhaps according to the Shach ibid there is no obligation of Yedias Hatorah by Tanach and it is rather only an obligation for the sake of understanding Talmud [see also Admur 1:6 for a similar idea], however according to Admur ibid there is a complete obligation of Yedias Hatorah in Tanach in it of itself.

The reason: As the Talmud does not contain all the verses of Tanach and it is not in the correct order. It is hence impossible to fulfill one's Mitzvah of Yedias Hatorah of Tanach through studying Talmud. [See Glosses of Rav Ashkenazi ibid] See other opinions!

[410] Admur Hilchos Talmud Torah 2:1
[411] See next part of this Halacha
[412] Admur 2:1

The reason: As only by children who are not mentally mature or knowledgeable enough to study Mishneh and Talmud do we first teach them the entire scripture for five years. However, an adult who has ability to also study Mishneh and Talmud is not allowed to spend his entire learning schedule first learning all of Tanach, as there is no telling how long he will live [and he has an obligation to study Mikrah, Mishneh and Talmud]. [Admur ibid; See Kiddushin ibid]

[413] Admur Hilchos Talmud Torah 2:1 "Each and every day"; Michaber Y.D. 246:4; Tur 246; Tosafos 30a; Rambam 1:12; Kiddushin 30a "For daily"

Other opinions: Some Poskim rule one is to split the week to three subjects. [Rashi Kiddushin ibid] This means that one is to study two days Mikrah, two days Mishneh, and two days Talmud. [Tosafus ibid in explanation of Rashi ibid]

[414] Admur Hilchos Talmud Torah 2:1 only mentions Tanach as Mikrah; See Kuntrus Achron 1:1 and all that was explained in the previous paragraph that even according to the Rama 246:4 and Rabbeinu Tam in Kiddushin 30a one may not rely on the study of Talmud which includes Mikrah for his Tanach studies; Even in Likkutei Torah Vayikra 5c where Admur offers other alternatives for Mikrah, he concludes that one is first obligated to learn and review the entire Tanach, and only afterwards move forward to studying the other subjects of Mikrah [i.e. Agados, Zohar, Midrash].

Other alternatives of Mikrah: 1) Agados [Likkutei Torah Vayikra 5c]; 2) Reading Zohar and other Sifrei Kabbalah (without proper understanding) [Likkutei Torah Vayikra 5c; However, see Admur Hilchos Talmud Torah 2:1 who states "The wisdom of Kabbalah is included in the 1/3 of Talmud"; See Likkutei Sichos 30:173 who makes the distinction between in depth learning of Kabbalah which is like Talmud, and superficial learning which is like Mikrah; See also Igros Kodesh 11:277]; 3) possibly also Midrash Raba [Likkutei Torah Vayikra 5c and Shir Hashirim 3c; However, Admur in Hilchos Talmud Torah 2:1 writes "The Pirush Hamikraos and Drashos and Hagados are included in the 1/3 of Mishneh." Admur in Shir Hashirim ibid differentiates between Midrash of Halachos which is part of Mishneh, and Midrash of stories which is part of Mikrah.] As stated above, one is first obligated to learn and review the entire Tanach, and only afterwards move forward to studying the other subjects of Mikrah. [Likkutei Torah ibid]

[415] Admur ibid

Other alternatives of Mishneh: Midrash [Admur ibid] of Halacha such as Sifra [Likkutei Torah Shir Hashirim 3c]

[416] Admur ibid

Other alternatives of Talmud: Kabbalah study [Admur ibid] that is in depth. [Likkutei Sichos 30:173]

[417] Admur Hilchos Talmud Torah 2:1; O.C. 155:1; Michaber Y.D. 246:4; Tur 246; Rambam Talmud Torah 1:11; Kiddushin 30a

[418] Kuntrus Achron 3:1 "This obligation is from the Sinai Tradition, as all the detailed laws of the oral Torah, which were received from generation to generation" See Kiddushin ibid that it is learned from the verse "Veshinantum Livanecha" that one should read it Veshilashtem. However, Admur ibid learns that this verse is a mere Asmachta.

[419] Admur Hilchos Talmud Torah 2:9; Vetzaruch Iyun as to the intent of Admur's ruling here regarding if such an individual is required to split his daily learning time to the three subjects of Tanach, Mishneh and Talmud. The following are the possibilities: 1) He is to study every day Tanach, plain Halacha, and the Mefarshim of Halacha until he becomes an expert in Tanach, in which case he spends all day studying practical

How much time must one dedicate daily for learning Tanach:[420] Some Poskim[421] rule one must divide the amount of time he has available each day for Torah learning by three and dedicate exactly 1/3 of that time to the study of Tanach. [Thus, if for example he has nine hours a day available for Torah learning, he is to study three hours Tanach, three hours Mishneh, and three hours Talmud.[422]] Other Poskim[423], however, rule that one is not meant to divide the learning hours to three and give each subject the same amount of time, as Mishneh is more severe than Tanach and requires more learning time, while Talmud is more severe than Mishneh, and require more learning time than it. Rather, one is to schedule his daily Torah learning in a way that he will complete all three subjects of Tanach, Mishneh, and Talmud at the same time. Thus, each day he studies a little bit of Tanach, even more of Mishneh, and even more of Talmud. Practically, it is good to suspect for this latter opinion.[424] [However, in Likkutei Torah[425] Admur implies that in the beginning of one's learning he should dedicate literally 1/3 of his time for learning Tanach, until he is well versed in it.]

Until when must one have a daily study session in Tanach?[426] Even if he has already completed the study of the entire scripture [i.e. Tanach] one time he is required to repeat its study from the beginning several times, and learn it every day as stated above, until all its content is well versed and memorized in his mind.[427] [It is, however, not necessary to memorize the context word for word, as it is forbidden to recite the written Torah by heart.[428]] Once he has reviewed the Tanach enough times to memorize its content, he is no longer required to have a daily session of studying Tanach, and rather he is to only read it on occasion in order to prevent him from losing memory of its content.[429] [He may spend the remainder of his day studying Mishneh and Talmud.[430]]

The learning schedule for children:[431] Children, in the beginning of their study, are first taught Chumash. In previous times it was accustomed to teach them the entire Tanach many times until age ten.[432] However, in today's times, the custom is no longer to teach children the entire Tanach, and rather they are

---

Halacha and on occasion reviews Tanach. [See Admur 2:2] 2) He is to only study Halacha, and once in a while study Tanach. 3) He is to split his daily learning time to three and study Tanach daily, as stated in option 1, but only study those parts of Tanach that relate to the practical Mitzvos, and on occasion also study the other parts of Tanach. [See Admur 1:6] Vetzaruch Iyun!

[420] Admur Hilchos Talmud Torah 2:1-2

[421] 1st opinion in Admur 2:1; Michaber Y.D. 246:4; Rambam Talmud Torah 1:11

[422] Michaber ibid

[423] 2nd opinion in Admur 2:2; Darkei Moshe 246:2; Ran Avoda Zara 5b; See Kuntrus Achron 1:1 that so is also the opinion of Tosafos Kiddushin 30a

[424] Admur ibid; Vetzaruch Iyun as to why this is considered a Chumra to suspect for the opinion of the Ran. [See Glosses of Rav Ashkenazi ibid 2:186]

[425] Likkutei Torah Vayikra 5c; See Glosses of Rav Ashkenazi ibid 2:182-186

[426] Admur Hilchos Talmud Torah 2:2-3

[427] Admur Hilchos Talmud Torah 2:3 "According to all, in the start of one's learning one must study scripture every day and repeat it not just one or two or three times, but a great abundance of times, each person in accordance to his memorization capabilities, so he memorizes it well."

[428] See Admur Hilchos Talmud Torah 2:2 "As the written Torah may not be said by heart"; See Admur 49:1 for a dispute in this matter; Likkutei Torah Vayikra 30d that one should memorize the entire five books of Moshe, and the implication there is to memorize the actual words. See Likkutei Sichos 14:237 that this statement of Admur in Likkutei Torah is referring to memorizing it in one's mind and not verbalizing with one's mouth. See Glosses of Rav Ashkenazi ibid 2:203 who explains that perhaps from the aspect of Talmud Torah it is not required to memorize the actual words, but for the sake of having the Shechina dwell within oneself the words must be memorized. However, from Likkutei Sichos ibid it is implied that the memorization of the actual words is part of the Mitzvah of Talmud Torah. See Hayom Yom 2nd of Nissan that the Rebbe Rashab would recite daily Tanach from memory.

[429] Admur 2:2; Michaber Y.D. 246:4; Rambam Talmud Torah 1:11

Other opinions: See Admur in Kuntrus Achron 1:1 that the intent of the ruling of Tosafos Kiddushin ibid [and the Rama 246:4 who rules like him], is that even after one has already finished learning and memorizing all the content of Tanach he is still obligated to learn Mikrah daily, as the Talmud Kiddushin ibid states that "**Forever** one is to learn the three subjects…" However, at this stage they rule that it suffices to learn the Talmud, as the Talmud includes all three parts of the Torah. Admur 2:2 completely omits this opinion, thus ruling like the Rambam, and learning that even according to the Ran ibid there is no longer a requirement to learn Mikrah/Tanach once one has completed his studies. However, see Admur in Likkutei Torah Vayikra 5c who implies that according to the Ran ibid one is to learn Mikrah every day for his entire life, and so concludes Admur there that after the study of Tanach one is to study the other alternatives of Mikrah daily.

[430] See Admur and Michaber ibid who write the above statement regarding one who finished learning and memorizing all the three subjects of Mikrah, Mishneh and Talmud, however, in truth the same would apply if he finished Mikrah first but did not yet finish Mishneh and Talmud. See Admur 2:3

[431] Admur Hilchos Talmud Torah 1:1

[432] Admur Hilchos Talmud Torah 1:1

only taught Chumash.[433] Nevertheless, they are required to study and repeat the study many times of all the Parshiyos of the Torah which have the Mitzvos written in them that are explained in the Talmud.

> **Summary:**
> It is a Biblical obligation upon every male Jew to have a daily study session in Tanach [i.e. Torah, Nevi'im, and Kesuvim] and review it several times from the beginning until he becomes an expert in its content. One is to split his time of daily Torah study between the subjects of Tanach, Mishneh [i.e. Halacha], and Talmud, dedicating some time to each subject. Nevertheless, one should dedicate more time daily to the study of Mishneh, and certainly to the study of Talmud, than to the study of Tanach. Once one has become an expert in the content of Tanach after studying it several times, he is no longer required to have a daily learning session in Tanach and is to simply review it on occasion to prevent lapse of memory.
>
> **The custom of Chassidim:**
> The Rebbe Rashab would recite Tanach daily.[434] The Chassidim, even of mediocre status, were experts in Tanach. They had a set custom to study a session of Tanach upon folding their Tallis, in a way that they would complete it in its entirety every three months.[435]

---------------- *Tzedakah*----------------

29. Giving Maaser money to relatives?[436]

Tzedakah money and Maaser funds, is not only permitted to be distributed to poor relatives, but one is even required to precede a relative in need over other paupers. This includes one's parents, one's older[437] children, one's brothers, and any other relative. Nevertheless, one who has enough money to support his parents without needing to use his charity money, is not to use charity money to support them. One who does so, a curse will befall his household r"l.[438] [Some Poskim[439] suggest that it is proper for one not to distribute all of his Maaser money to his relatives and is rather to give 50% to other paupers. If, however, one's relative is in a very dire state of need, one may distribute to him all of one's charity money.[440]]

30. Must one take Maaser off the value of a present that he was given or inherited?[441]

> - One received presents in honor of his wedding, or birthday, is Maaser to be deducted from it or its value?
> - One was given a diamond ring as a present from their mother or grandmother, is Maaser to be deducted from its value?
> - One inherited many objects from a deceased parent or relative, is Maaser to be deducted from its value?

Cash presents and gifts and inheritance:[442] The Mitzvah and custom of giving Maaser from one's income applies likewise towards money that one inherited or was given as a present. Even if one was given the

---

[433] Admur Hilchos Talmud Torah 1:6; See Bach 145:5; Shach 246:5; Kuntrus Achron 1:1
The reason: As in previous times the written Tanach was unavailable with vowelization, and hence they had to be taught in school, however today that it is available in print the children are only taught a small amount of Tanach [for about two years-Kuntrus Achron 1:1], as they are expected to learn it on their own when they get older. [Admur ibid]
[434] Hayom Yom 3rd Nissan
[435] Hayom Yom 19th Adar Rishon
[436] Michaber 251:3
[437] See Shach 251:4 that this refers to children above six years old
[438] Rama 240:5; Shach 251:5; Hagahos Mordechai Bava Basra
[439] Avkas Rochel "One is to try to give half to his poor relatives"; Chasam Sofer 231; Pischeiy Teshuvah 249:2; Chochmas Adam 145:5; Maharsham 249 in name of Kneses Hagedola; Igros Moshe Y.D. 1:144 that may give majority to relative, but should give some to other causes; Or Zarua 1:22 rules that if one separated the Maaser with intent to distribute it to paupers, he may only give up to half to his relative, while if he separated it Stam, he may give the entire amount to his relative.
[440] Derech Emuna Matanos Aniyim 7:247
[441] See Mishpat Utzedaka 5:5; Sefer Maaser Kesafim 3:5-6; Pesakim Uteshuvos 249:24

money for a specific purpose, he is to separate Maaser from the money.[443] If, however, the giver explicitly stipulated with the receiver that he may only use the money for that specific purpose, then he may not separate Maaser from it.[444]

Non-Cash presents and gifts, including real estate: Ideally, the Mitzvah of giving 1/10th of one's profits towards charity applies also towards non-cash gifts and presents that one has received, including real estate.[445] The same applies towards items of inheritance. Practically, however, the custom is not to deduct Maaser from non-cash presents that one receives, including real estate, that one was given as a gift or inheritance.[446] Nonetheless, this only applies so long as one keeps the item for his personal use, however, if one sells the item, then he is to distribute Maaser from his earnings.[447]

Summary:
One is to give Maaser from all cash that he inherited or was given as a present. The custom is not to deduct Maaser from non-cash presents that one receives, unless one sells the item, in which case he is to distribute Maaser from his earnings.

31. May one use Maaser money to purchase a seat in a Shul, or to pay for membership?

Background: Under certain conditions, it is permitted to use Maaser money for the sake of fulfilling a Mitzvah.[448] These conditions are as follows: a) The Mitzvah is not an obligation for one to fulfill, and

---

[442] So rule regarding a present:Matana: Implication of Rabbeinu Yonah in Sefer Hayirah 213; Chikreiy Lev Tzedakah 2:102; Mishpat Utzedaka 5:5; Sefer Maaser Kesafim 3:5; Pesakim Uteshuvos ibid
So rule regarding Yerusha: Shlah Miseches Megillah 27 p. 262; Elya Raba 156:2 in end "We give Maaser from an inheritance even from one's father"; Pischeiy Teshuvah 249:1; Shiyurei Bracha 249:3; Ahavas Chesed 2:18-3; See Igros Moshe 1:143; Maaser Kesafim 3:19; p. 35; Pesakim Uteshuvos ibid

[443] See Chikreiy Lev Tzedakah 2:102 and Mishpat Utzedaka 5:5 footnote 26 who depends this on whether the receiver may choose to use the money for something else, and if the giver stipulated that he wants him to use the full amount for the purchase, and concludes that in normal circumstances the giver is not Makpid and hence Maaser should be separated; See also Orchos Rabbeinu 2:138 in name of Chazon Ish writes that if one was given cash, he must separate Maaser even if given for a specific purpose; So also writes Derech Emunah 7:67 in name of Chazon Ish; Pesakim Uteshuvos ibid
Other opinions: Rav Elyashiv is quoted to rule that one is not obligated to separate Maaser from this money. [See Sefer Maaser Kesafim 3:10]

[444] Implication of Chikreiy Lev and Mishpat Utzedaka ibid; Teshuvos Vehanhagos 3:282; Sefer Maaser Kesafim 3:11

[445] Implication of Sefer Hayirah 213 *"Even if he found something or received a present"* [See Mishneh Halachos 12:241; Tinyana 2:249]; Implication of Sefer Chassidim 144 *"Or from a stolen object"* [This means that one found an item that was stolen from him after giving up hope of its retrieval, in which case he is to separate Maaser from its value. See Makor Chesed ibid; Other Mefarshim however write that the word stolen is a misprint and it means to say lost object and thus Sefer Chassidim is saying that one who found a lost item and is allowed to keep it for himself then he is to give Maaser from the value of his findings. See Mefarshim in new print of Sefer Chassidim; Nonetheless, while the implication of Sefer Chassidim is to include also found objects, it is possible to argue that he limits his statement to money]; Ramban on Lech Lecha [Bereishis 14:20] that Avraham gave Maaser from all the spoils of war that he took; Sefer Maaser Kesafim 3:6-8 in name of Rav SZ"A; Yad Halevi 2:44; Pesakim Uteshuvos 249:24 in name of Poskim ibid and Chikrei Lev ibid

[446] Yosef Ometz 2:306 *"Here [in Farnkfurt] I have witnessed that the custom is not to separate Maaser from real estate that one receives as part of the dowry or inheritance"*; Shevet Halevi 5:133 regarding real estate *"The custom is not to give Maaser from inheritance of real estate, and we have never heard that one who was given a home or apartment to live in that he must separate Maaser"*; Orach Tzedakah p. 351 in name of Rav Wozner; Sheiris Simcha 31, brought in Mishpat Utzedaka 5 footnote 27 that only if he sells must he separate; Orchos Rabbeinu 1:296 in name of Chazon Ish; Derech Emunah Matanos Aniyim 7:67 that so ruled Chazon Ish and so rule the Gedolei Haposkim; Chut Hashani 2:331; Emes Liyaakov 249; Pesakim Uteshuvos 249:24 and Sefer Maaser Kesafim 3:6 that so is custom of world
The reason: As Maaser is given due to the Mitzvah of charity, and there is no obligation for one to sell his items for the sake of Tzedakah. [Orchos Rabbeinu ibid]
Other opinions: Some of today's Poskim conclude that one is required to separate Maaser if he has cash available. [Kol Torah 39:87 in name of Rav SZ"A; So also records Sefer Maaser Kesafim 3:6-8 in name of Rav SZ"A that presents are obligated in Maaser although he is only obligated to give it when he has cash available or sells the item. Likewise, he evaluates the worth of the item based on its cheapest available price, and separate 10% from 2:3 of that price; Shaareiy Tezdek 8:3; Even Yisrael 9:92-13; Pesakim Uteshuvos 249:24] Other Poskim suggest that if the person would have bought the object anyways then he is to separate Maaser, otherwise he is not required to separate. [Mishpat Utzedaka 5 footnote 27]

[447] Sheiris Simcha 31, brought in Mishpat Utzedaka 5 footnote 27; Teshuvos Vehanhagos 1:560; Pesakim Uteshuvos 249:24 footnote 221; See Sefer Maaser Kesafim 3 footnote 61

[448] Shach 249:3; Taz 249:1; Maharshal; Derisha 249:1; Maharam Menachem 459; Admur Hilchos Talmud Torah 1:7 regarding using Maaser to pay tuition of Talmud Torah; Admur Seder Birchas Hanehnin 12:9 "The Maaser of the son may be used for other Mitzvos"; Likkutei Sichos 9:346; Toras Menachem 34:272 [brought in Shulchan Menachem 5:110] based on Admur ibid; See Tzedakah Umishpat 6:12
Other opinions: Some Poskim rule it is forbidden to use Maaser money for the sake of a Mitzvah, and rather it must be given as charity to paupers. [Rama Y.D. 249:1; Maharil Rosh Hashanah and Teshuvah 56; Kneses Hagedola 249; Beis Dino Shel Shlomo Y.D. 1; See Beir Goleh

rather is voluntary[449]; b) One is unable to afford the voluntary Mitzvah and hence would abstain from doing so unless he uses his Maaser funds.[450] c) Some Poskim[451] also require that one precondition prior to separating the Maaser money that he will use the money for whatever he chooses. [Practically, however, one may use Maaser money for Mitzvos even if he already separated it without a precondition, and already separated three times to a pauper.[452] Thus, it is permitted to use Maaser money to donate to a Shul. This applies even if the Shul will use the funds for its personal upkeeping and will not distribute it to the poor.[453] This applies even if one will be receiving a benefit from the donation.[454] It is, however, forbidden to do so if the Gabbaim of the Shul are not G-d fearing and cannot be trusted with the money to use it for the Shul's benefit.]

The ruling: One may use Maaser money to pay for seats in a Shul or for Shul membership [if it would be difficult to afford otherwise[455]], as the money is going towards the Mitzvah of upkeeping a Shul, and to give one the ability to properly participate and Daven with the Minyan in a set area.[456] This, however, only applies if one had intent to do so upon making the purchase of the seat or membership. If, however one did not have intent to do so upon purchasing it, then it is forbidden to use Maaser money to pay for it later on.[457]

---

ibid who explains that the Rama refers to a Mitzvah that one already obligated himself to pay, and on this he can't use Maaser money, however in general he agrees with the Maharam that Maaser may be used for a Mitzvah, and hence there is no dispute. [Pischeiy Teshuvah 249:2] So can also be implied from Taz 249:1 that there is no dispute. [See Tzedakah Umishpat 6 footnote 7] However, see Chasam Sofer 231[brought in Pischeiy Teshuva ibid and Ahavas Chesed 18:2] who negates this explanation and states that according to Rama/Maharil it is always forbidden to use it for a Mitzvah, and so explains Rebbe in Toras Menachem 34:272.

[449] Beir Hagoleh ibid [in explanation of opinion of Rama ibid]; Chasam Sofer 231, Pischeiy Teshuvah 249:2

[450] Shach 249:3; Taz 249:1; Maharshal; Derisha 249:1; Maharam Menachem 459; Admur Hilchos Talmud Torah 1:7 regarding using Maaser to pay tuition; Toras Menachem 34:272 [brought in Shulchan Menachem 5:110]

[451] See Chasam Sofer 231, brought in Pischeiy Teshuvah; Toras Menachem 34:272 who mentions such a differentiation even according to the lenient opinion; Hilchos Maaser Kesafim 14:1

[452] Toras Menachem 34:272 based on Admur Hilchos Talmud Torah 1:7 regarding using Maaser to pay tuition who does not differentiate in this matter

Other opinions: Some Poskim are stringent like the former opinion mentioned, and rule one is not to use Maaser money for Mitzvos unless he preconditioned its use prior to beginning separating for the first time in his life, as rules Chasam Sofer 231 that in such a case all Poskim agree. [Kaneh Bosem 3:84]

[453] As stated above, that one may use Maaser money for a Mitzvah

[454] Taz 249:1 regarding paying for a Kibbud purchased in a Shul

The reason: As although one benefits from the Kibbud, nonetheless, this does not invalidate its Tzedakah status, being that all Tzedakah has some benefit. [Taz ibid]

[455] Minchas Yitzchak in next footnote; As stated above in condition b, one should avoid using Maaser money for the purpose of a Mitzvah unless it would be difficult to afford otherwise. If, one can afford only some of the sum, while the remaining sum is above his affordability, then he can use Maaser money for the remaining sum.

[456] Minchas Yitzchak 8:83; Shaareiy Tzedek 10:92 that so ruled Rav Fisher; and Rav Karelitz; Tzitz Eliezer 20:35; Pashut based on all the reasons mentioned below and the background above; Pesakim Uteshuvos 249:35 that so rule many Poskei Zemaneinu

The reason: As a) The money is going for a Mitzvah purpose, to support a Shul; and b) The benefit received is a Mitzvah, so one can Daven properly in a set seat and have a set place in Shul, as recorded in the Gemara in Brachos 6b and Admur 90:18. [Now, although this matter is seemingly an obligation, nonetheless, we do not find anywhere that this obligation is connected with purchasing the area, and one can establish a set place for standing by Shemoneh Esrei anywhere he wants that is available in the Shul, whether he paid or not, and hence buying the area is an extra Hiddur and not an obligation] c) The seat is not really purchased and acquired by the member, and hence it does not have the Halachic status of being inherited. [Shaareiy Tzedek ibid] Certainly, this allowance applies if there are many available unpurchased seats in Shul, or one would in any event have a seat, and one's entire intent is to give a donation and assist with the upkeep of the Shul.

Other opinions: Some Poskim rule that one may never use Maaser money to pay for Shul membership. [Shraga Hameir 8:54; Sefer Maaser Kesafim 17:4; Emes Liyaakov 249] Other Rabbanim limit it only to cases where there are many unpurchased seats anyways available. This is due to several reasons which are independent of each other: a) As one may not use Maaser money for a Mitzvah and it must go to paupers. [See other opinions above; However, in truth we do not rule like those opinions]; b) As one is receiving a seat in the Shul in return and is hence receiving a physical benefit and item with market value. [However, in truth, receiving benefit in return does not invalidate the use of Maaser, as stated in Taz 249:1 regarding an Aliya; See also Taz ibid regarding buying Sefarim, however there the Sefer remains belonging to Maaser, and he must lend it to others if asked] c) As the benefit received [a seat] is not a Mitzvah, as there is no Mitzvah for one to sit in that seat in Shul. [However, in truth Davening with Kavana, and having a set place to Daven is a Halacha in Shulchan Aruch 90 and hence certainly is considered a Mitzvah. Now even if one were to say that the Mitzvah is only by Shemoneh Esrei, where one stands, nonetheless, just as building a Shul is a Mitzvah, certainly participating in the Minyan is a Mitzvah, and thus buying a seat is to facilitate one's participance. Vetzaruch Iyun if having a set place in Shul is defined as an obligation to the point that one cannot purchase a seat for that purpose. See above in reason of Matirim] Some Rabbanim rule the following way to help escape some of the issues mentioned above: The Gabbai and donor stipulate with each other that if Maaser money is being given for the seat, then it is considered like a mere donation, and the seat is being given as a present from the Gabbai with no liability.

[457] The reason: As the money has already become a personal debt, and it is forbidden to use Maaser money to pay for a debt. [Taz ibid]

> **Summary:**
> One may use Maaser money to pay for seats in a Shul, or for Shul membership, if it would be difficult to afford otherwise.

32. May one pay for an Aliyah, or other Kibud, using Maaser money:[458]

It is permitted to use Maaser money to pay for a Kibud [i.e. Aliya, Pesicha, Hagba, etc.] that was purchased in Shul, **if one had intent to do so upon purchasing it**.[459] If, however one did not have intent to do so upon purchasing it, then it is forbidden to use Maaser money to pay for it.[460] [Furthermore, some Poskim[461] rule that if the Mitzvah is being auctioned, one may only give from Maaser the amount of money that surpassed the previous bidder. For example, if he bought an Aliya for $50 and outbid the second closest bidder who said $40, then only $10 may be deducted from Maaser. Other Poskim[462] however negate this opinion, and rule that the entire amount may be given from Maaser.]

---------------- *Sefarim/Genizah*----------------

33. Writing ב"ה or בס"ד on a letterhead:

A. The Custom:[463]

It is an old Jewish custom to write the Hebrew letter abbreviations of Beis Hei [ב"ה] on the letterhead of a letter, article, or document [involving even mundain matters[464]].

The meaning of the abbreviation ב"ה/B"H:[465] The abbreviation of ב"ה/B"H stands for "Biezrat Hashem/With the help of G-d" or "Baruch Hashem/Blessed is Hashem."

Other alternatives: An alternative to writing ב"ה/B"H is to write BEZ"H[466]-Biezrat Hashem [בעז"ה] or BS"D[467]-Besiyata Dishmaya[468] [בס"ד].

---

[458] Taz 249:1; Elya Raba 156:2; So applies according to all Poskim who allow using Maaser money for Mitzvos, which includes: Shach 249:3; Maharshal; Derisha 249:1; Maharam Menachem 459; Admur Hilchos Talmud Torah 1:7 regarding using Maaser to pay tuition of Talmud Torah; Admur Seder Birchas Hanehnin 12:9 "The Maaser of the son may be used for other Mitzvos"; Likkutei Sichos 9:346; Toras Menachem 34:272 [brought in Shulchan Menachem 5:110] based on Admur ibid; See Tzedakah Umishpat 6:12

Other opinions: Some Poskim rule it is forbidden to use Maaser money for the sake of a Mitzvah, such as to donate candles to the Shul, and rather it must be given as charity to paupers. [Rama Y.D. 249:1; Maharil Rosh Hashanah and Teshuvah 56; Kneses Hagedola 249; Beis Dino Shel Shlomo Y.D. 1; See Beir Goleh ibid who explains that the Rama refers to a Mitzvah that one already obligated himself to pay, and on this he can't use Maaser money, however in general he agrees with the Maharam that Maaser may be used for a Mitzvah, and hence there is no dispute. [Pischeiy Teshuvah 249:2] So can also be implied from Taz 249:1 that there is no dispute. [See Tzedakah Umishpat 6 footnote 7] However, see Chasam Sofer 231[brought in Pischeiy Teshuva ibid and Ahavas Chesed 18:2] who negates this explanation and states that according to Rama:Maharil it is always forbidden to use it for a Mitzvah, and so explains Rebbe in Toras Menachem 34:272.] Accordingly, these opinions would rule that it is forbidden to use Maaser money to purchase an Aliya. However, in truth, perhaps one can suggest that money which goes to Shul is considered pure Tzedakah, even though it does not go to a pauper, and only regarding those Mitzvos that remain within one's possession, [such as Sefarim], do we say that the dispute applies. [So is implied from Taz ibid who says regarding purchasing an Aliya "As the money is going to Tzedakah", and only later doe she bring the opinion of the Maharam] However, in truth there is no way to coincide this with the Rama ibid who explicitly states that "even candles of a Shul" cannot be donated from Maaser, and hence we see that only actual paupers may receive Maaser according to the Rama.

If the money is going towards the poor: Whenever the donated money for the Aliya or Kibud will be going towards funding the needs of the poor and not towards the Shul, it is permitted according to all for one to use Maaser money to pay for the Aliya. [Kneses Hagedola 249; Beis Dino Shel Shlomo Y.D. 1; Ahavas Chesed 19:2]

If one can afford to pay for the Aliya without Maaser funds: The Taz ibid does not condition the above ruling that one may only purchase the Aliya with Maaser funds if he does not have other funds available. However, based on the ruling of the Maharam, it would seem that here too one may only use Maaser for an Aliyah, if he cannot afford it otherwise. Vetzaruch Iyun.

[459] The reason: As although one benefits from the Kibbud, nonetheless, this does not invalidate its Tzedakah status, being that all Tzedakah has some benefit. [Taz ibid]

[460] The reason: As the money has already become a personal debt, and it is forbidden to use Maaser money to pay for a debt. [Taz ibid]

[461] Shlah Miseches Megillah p. 262, brought in Elya Raba 156:2; Reb Akiva Eiger 249:1; Hilchos Maaser Kesafim 14:32

[462] Elya Raba ibid negates the opinion of Shlah

[463] Toldos Yitzchak [Uncle of Beis Yosef] Parshas Metzora p. 88 "Therefore the custom is to write in the heading of every letter B"H, as the verse states in all your ways you shall know Him"; Aruch Hashulchan Y.D. 276:28; See Shut Tzafnas Paneiach [Rogatchaver] 196-197; 303; Igros Moshe Y.D. 2:138 that so is custom; Igros Kodesh 21:5 [brought in Shulchan Menachem 5:218]; letter 1384, 7759 [brought in Menachem Meishiv Nafshi 2:650; 817]; Likkutei Sichos 6:190; 24:599; Answer to Rav Tzinner, printed in Tzadik Lemelech 7:230 and Menachem Meishiv Nafshi 2:755 regarding BS"D; Heichal Menachem 1:243 and 3:57; Mishneh Halachos 6:183; Piskeiy Teshuvos 154:18

[464] Likkutei Sichos 6:190

[465] Se Mishneh Halachos 6:183

The reason for the custom:[469] The above abbreviations are written in order to invoke Divine assitance in one's written activity and to show that even ones mundain activities are connected with G-d. The abbreviation is considered like the actual words themselves[470], and hence has the spiritual ability to arouse Divine favor.[471]

The historical background of its inception: It is unclear as to when this custom first began.[472] The custom is hinted to already in the writings of Rav Yehuda Hachassid[473] and its earliest explicit source dates back to the 1500's.[474] Although this custom was not widespread amongst all Jewish communities, and it is not found in the letters of the Rishonim and many Achronim[475], nonetheless, in today's times it has become practically universal.

> ### The words of Rebbe Yehuda Hachassid:[476]
> *The verse[477] states "And on that day they began calling in the name of G-d" and the very next verse states "This is the Sefer." From here we learn that when an author begins [to write a Sefer] he is to Daven to Hashem that he be successful to finish it. There was once a Sage who saw an author write the name of G-d in the top of the Sefer [Torah[478]] and he questioned him as to why he wrote it, and the author replied as stated above. The Sage replied that one is to simply pray to G-d for assitance and not write His name, as other verses speak against doing so. [This refers to a Sefer Torah, however] by other Sefarim the custom has become to write "Bisheim Hashem" which symbolizes that the person is writing Lisheim Shamayim [for the sake of Heaven] and that one who learns from it should do so Lisheim Shamayim. One is not to write on the book [the actual verse of] "And on that day.." [but rather simply Bisheim Hashem][479].*

B. The Halachic debate and practical directive:

Does the abbreviation of ב"ה contain holiness? Some Poskim[480] rule that the abbreviation of ב"ה does not contain holiness, and thus may be discarded regulalry.[481] Other Poskim[482] rule that the letters ב"ה contain

---

[466] Letter of Rebbe to Rogatchaver printed in Igros Kodesh 21:5 [and Menachem Meishiv Nafshi 818 and Shulchan Menachem 5:218]; Igros Moshe ibid

[467] Answer to Rav Tzinner, printed in Tzadik Limelech 7:230 and Menachem Meishiv Nafshi 2:755; Igros Moshe ibid; Teshuvos Vehanhagos 1:640; Mishneh Halachos 6:183; Piskeiy Teshuvos ibid

[468] The term "Shemaya/heavens" is a paronym for G-d.

[469] See Sefer Chassidim 884; Toldos Yitzchak ibid; Likkutei Sichos 6:190

[470] See Tzafnas Paneiach ibid that so is apparent from Rav Haiy Gaon, brought in Maggid Mishneh Shabbos 11:10 that even abbreviations are considered words regarding liability over writing on Shabbos; Igros Moshe ibid that even one letter of Hashem's name contains sanctity

[471] See Igros Kodesh 1384 [brought in Menachem Meishiv Nafshi 2:650] that it should be written by a letterhead especially today when we need Divine assistance

[472] See Igros Moshe ibid that we have not found a precedent for this custom amongst our ancestors; See Igros Kodesh 21:5 [letter 7759, brought in Shulchan Menachem 5:218 and in Menachem Meishiv Nafshi 2:817] that the Rebbe asked the Rogatchaver Gaon as to the source of writing this, and in fact brought Talmudic proofs to discredit it, and that it is, and never was, customarily done in documents such as Kesubos, Gittin and loan documents. See Rav Yosef Kapach in Kesavim 1 p. 124 that this custom originally began in Europe and then spread to some, but not all, Sephardi communities.

[473] See Sefer Chassidim 884, brought in Koveitz Zalman Shimon p. 71 as a source for the custom

[474] See Toldos Yitzchak ibid who lived in the 16th century "Therefore the custom is to write in the heading of every letter B"H"; Such headings can be found on letters dating back to the 16th century.

[475] See Rav Yosef Kapach in Kesavim 1 p. 124 that it is clearly evident from the many letters found in archives that the above heading was not written in previous times. For example, in Yemen there are no letter which bear this heading, as the custom never spread to there. Many letters from the Rambam and his collegues have been found in archives and they also do not contain any such heading.

[476] Sefer Chassidim 884

[477] Bereishis 4:26

[478] Pirush on Sefer Chassidim [Mosod Harav Cook]

[479] Pirush ibid

[480] See Sefer Chassidim 935 that one may erase two Yuds; Aruch Hashulchan Y.D. 276:28 that it has no Kedusha at all although may not be used for a belittling matter; Mishneh Halachos 6:183; See Piskeiy Teshuvos 154 footnote 121 in name of Mahariy Asad Y.D. 304; Maharsham 1:159 in Hashmatos; Melamed Lehoil 113:20; Maharshag 1:3

[481] The reason: As some Poskim rule that even two letters of Hashem's name does not have Kedusha, and certainly this would apply by a single letter even according to those who are stringent. [See Mishneh Halachos ibid]

some level of sanctity, being the Hei is a letter of Hashem's name and is reffering to it. [However, the English abbreviation of B"H does not contain any holiness accoridng to any opinion.] The following is the final arbitration on this matter:

The various customs for and against: Due to the above latter opinion, some Gedolei Yisrael voiced oppossition to the custom of writing ב"ה on letterheads due to worry of its sanctity getting desecrated.[483] However, writing BS"D or בעזהש"י as opposed to ב"ה avoids the issue of desecration, and is hence permitted even according to the previous mentioned Poskim who negate the writing of ב"ה.[484] Accordingly, many today write בס"ד, or another alternative, rather than ב"ה to avoid this issue, even though the original custom was to write ב"ה. Others do not write anything at all, and so was practiced by some Geodlei Yisrael.[485] The accepted practice, however, is to continue with the old custom and write ב"ה [486] and so was the custom of many Gedolei Yisrael[487], and so was the custom of the Baal Shem Tov and the vast majority of his students[488], including the Chabad Rabbeim.[489] However, interestingly, on the heading of Mamarim the Rabbeim would write בעז"ה or בס"ד and not ב"ה, which was reserved only for the heading of letters that they wrote.[490] [According to the accpeted practice, papers that contain the words ב"ה do not contain kedusha, and may be discraded in the garbage.]

Practical directive of the Rebbe:[491] Practically, the Rebbe instructed people to write ב"ה on all forms of letters, although also mentions the alternative of [492]בס"ד or בעז"ה.[493] [The Rebbe's custom was to write ב"ה on the letterhead of all letters, while בס"ד was written on the letterhead of Mamarim.] The Rebbe instructed that this applies even towards a Torah publication [such as a Torah journal, Kuntrus and even Likkutei Sichos pamphlets[494]], that it should nevertheless begin with the above abbreviation of ב"ה.[495]

---

[482] See Rama Y.D. 276:10 that it is only permitted to erase two Yud's for a need; Shach Y.D. 276:14 in name of Terumos Hadeshen and Darkei Moshe that two Yud's may only be erased for a **great need**; Chida in Bris Olam in name of Radbaz 207 regarding two Yuds; Maharsha Sukkah 53; Maharitz Chayos 1; Ruach Chaim [Falagi] Y.D. 276; Tzafnas Paneiach 196 "One is to beware not to erase it"; See Tzafnas Paneiach 303 that so is apparent from Rav Haiy Gaon, brought in Maggid Mishneh Shabbos 11:10 that even abbreviations are considered words regarding liability over writing on Shabbos; Igros Moshe ibid that even one letter of Hashem's name contains sanctity

[483] Tzafnas Paneiach ibid "One is to beware not to write it on letterheads" [See Piskeiy Teshuvah 3:233 for the correspondence letters of the Imrei Emes with the Rogatchaver on this matter; However, see Migdal Oz p. 100 for a letter of the Rogatchaver to the Rebbe Rashab in which Beis Hei was written]; Igros Moshe Y.D. 2:138 [brought below]; Igros Kodesh 21:5 [letter 7759, brought in Shulchan Menachem 5:218 and Menachem Meishiv Nafshi 2:817] that the Rebbe asked the Rogatchaver Gaon as to the source of writing this, and in fact brought Talmudic proofs to discredit it, and that it is, and never was, customarily done in documents such as Kesubos, Gittin and loan documents. Interestingly, the Rebbe in two of his letters to the Rogatchaver indeed omitted the term B"H or any other opening term. However, in this letter he did write it, and so was the Rebbe's final position as evident from other letters and from his custom.

Opinion of Igros Moshe: See Igros Moshe ibid that some avoid doing so being that it is considered part of Hashem's name and it may come to be desecrated. The Igros Moshe negates this opinion being it is not common to reuse papers and they are simply burnt. Nonetheless, he concludes that he does not see any need to be particular to write B"H, being it is not mentioned in previous Poskim. Furthermore, why should Hashem's name be mentioned on a paper that has secular matters, or even forbidden matters written on it, such as Lashon Hara.

[484] Igros Moshe ibid; Teshuvos Vehanhagos 1:640; Mishneh Halachos 6:183; Piskeiy Teshuvos ibid

[485] The following is a list of Gedolei Yisrael who did not write any heading on their letters: Teshuvos Vehanhagos 1:640 that the Gr"a and Rav Chaim Velozhin did not write any heading; Rogatchaver; Chazon Ish, brought in Orchos Rabbeinu p. 247, would not even write BS"D; Igros Moshe; Rav Kapach; Rav Elyashiv; Rav Mashash

[486] Likkutei Sichos 6:190 "It is accustomed amongst all Jewry to write B"H in the beginning of the letter"; Mishneh Halachos ibid; Piskeiy Teshuvos ibid

[487] Letter of Imrei Emes [printed in Piskeiy Teshuvah ibid] in name of many Gedolei Yisrael; Orchos Rabbeinu ibid that so was the custom of the Steipler; So is evident from letters of the Sdei Chemed; Rav Ovadia Yosef; Rav Yoel Teitelbaum; Rav Wozner, and many other Gedolei Yisrael of today as can be readily verified in looking at their Haskamas to Sefarim.

[488] See Sefer Maggid Devarav Leyaakov in the Hosafos of letters in which the heading B"H is written on the letterhead of letters written by the Baal Shem Tov and many of his students, including: The Maggid; Pinchas of Koretz; Leib ben Sara's; Reb Zusha of Anipoli; Shlomo Karlin; Rav Aaron Karlin; Rav Levi Yitzchak of Berditchiv; Rav Chaim Chaika of Amdura;

[489] See Igros Kodesh Admur Hazakein who writes B"H on all of his letters; See All letters of Rebbe Rashab, Rayatz and the Rebbe

[490] So can be readily seen from any Sefer Mamarim of the Rabbeim, including the Alter Rebbe [who writes BEZ"H] Mittler Rebbe [who interchanges between BEZ"H and BS"D], the Rebbe Rashab, Rebbe Rayatz, and Rebbe who would all write BS"D; See Hiskashrus 749 p. 9; Shulchan Menachem 5:220 footnote 4

[491] Igros Kodesh letter 1384 [brought in Menachem Meishiv Nafshi 2:650] *"It is of upmost importance in today's times to begin all relevant matters with the abbreviations of Beis Hei"*; Likkutei Sichos 6:190 *"It is the custom of all Israel, and a custom of Israel is Torah, that upon writing even a mundane letter, they begin to write Beis Hei and the like."*; 7:190; 24:599; Heichal Menachem 1:249; Letter to Rav Tzinner printed in Tzadik Limelech 7:230 and Menachem Meishiv Nafshi 2:755

[492] Letter to Rav Tzinner ibid the Rebbe wrote Beis Samech Daled; Likkutei Sichos ibid and ibid "and the like"

[493] Letter of Rebbe to Rogatchaver printed in Igros Kodesh 21:5

[494] See Maaneh of Rebbe in next footnote

[495] Igros Kodesh letter 1384 ibid *"So too you should write it in the Torah publication, and if only that this would suffice."* Maaneh of Rebbe to a Kuntrus that he was handed *"Thank you. It is a wonder that the abbreviations of Beis Hei and the like were omitted from the Kuntrus. We already*

> **Summary:**
> It is an old age Jewish custom to write the abbreviations of ב"ה on a letterhead, or Sefer. The Rebbe encouraged this to be done on all letters and publications, even if they are of Torah matters. Some write the alternative of בס"ד in order to avoid writing an abbreviation of Hashem's name. Others avoid writing it all together.
>
> **Q&A**
> **Should B"H be written in English instead of ב"ה?**
> Upon writing letters in English, many choose to preface the letter with the English abbreviation of B"H versus the Hebrew abbreviation of ב"ה, while when writing letters in Hebrew, the Hebrew abbreviations are used. The Halachic advantage of writing the English initials is that it does not contain holiness according to any opinion.
>
> **Should one write B"H/ב"ה or בס"ד/BS"D on emails?**
> It is a good custom to do so. This especially applies to long email letter, in which the custom of writing Beis Hei in its top corner is identical to the old age custom of writing it by a handwritten letter.
>
> **Should one write B"H/ב"ה or בס"ד/BS"D in text messages, chats, WhatsApp's?**
> The custom is not to be particular to do so.
>
> **Does a letter which contains the words ב"ה require Genizah?**
> This matter is dependent on the dispute recorded above. Practically, according to the accepted practice to write the words ב"ה, papers that contain the words ב"ה do not contain Kedusha, and may be discraded in the garbage.

---------------- *Mezuzah*----------------

34. May a woman put up a Mezuzah or is only a man to do so?[496]

A. Introduction:
On the one hand we find that women are obligated in the Mitzvah of Mezuzah just like men, which implies that certainly they are valid to put it up.[497] On the other hand, we find that women are invalid to write the Mezuzah, just as they are invalid to write Tefillin.[498] Now, perhaps just as women are invalid to make the Tefillin due to their invalidation to write Tefillin, so too they are invalid to put up the Mezuzah, just like they are invalid to write it. This matter is discussed and debated amongst the Poskim as we will now explain.

B. The law:
Some Poskim[499] rule that it is permitted for a woman to put up a Mezuzah, and it is not required to be done specifically by a man.[500] Other Poskim[501], however, rule that a woman may not put up a Mezuzah

---

have a Pesak Din from Moshe Rabbeinu that even a house filled with books requires a Mezuzah [and thus so too a Torah publication]. Even the Mamarim of the Rabbeim begin with a Beis Samech Daled. Now, the fact that in Likkutei Sichos this is not done, this itself is difficult [i.e. not to my satisfaction]."

[496] See Eretz Tzevi 15; Beir Moshe 2:100; Sefer Kevius Mezuzah Kehilchasa 13:8

[497] Michaber Y.D. 186:1; Mishneh Brachos 20a that "*Women, children, and slaves are obligated in the Mitzvah of Mezuzah.*"; Yuma 11b; Kiddushin 34a

[498] Michaber 281:3; Beis Yosef 281; Gittin 45b; Shach 281:6; Aruch Hashulchan 281:1

[499] Setimas Haposkim who do not write such a Halacha that women are invalid; Possible implication of Admur 14:2 and 39:1 regarding the invalidation of women for Tzitzis and Tefillin that it is because they are not obligated in the Mitzvah, thus implying that if they were obligated, then they may prepare the Mitzvah; Chasam Sofer Y.D. 211 "*They are not included in the Mitzvah of writing but are included in the Mitzvah of setting*"; Implication of Maharshag Y.D. 57 regarding even gentile; Sdei Chemed Mareches Mem 131; Shevet Halevi 2:158-3 "*I saw the opinion of Yeshuos Malko and in my opinion one cannot say this...and there is no doubt in my mind that it is valid.*"; Kevius Mezuzah Kehilchasa ibid in name of Poskei Doreinu

[500] The reason: As women are obligated in the Mitzvah of Mezuzah [Michaber 186:1; Mishneh Brachos 20a that "*Women, children, and slaves are obligated in the Mitzvah of Mezuzah.*"; Yuma 11b; Kiddushin 34a] and therefore they are certainly valid to put it up to fulfill the Mitzvah.

and is rather to have a man do so for her.[502] Practically, if a woman/wife put it up, it remains Kosher and does not need to be replaced.[503] Nevertheless, some conclude that initially it is best for a man, such as the husband, to put up the Mezuzah.[504] Nevertheless, if there is no man/husband at home, the woman is even initially to put up the Mezuzah with a blessing and not delay until a man is available.[505]

> **Summary:**
> Women are obligated in the Mitzvah of Mezuzah and are thus also valid to put the Mezuzah up on their doorpost, and it is not necessary to have it done by a man. Nevertheless, if the husband is at home, it is initially best for him to do so.

------------------ *Medical ethics*------------------

The following segment is an excerpt from a future, broader, article about vaccines and Halacha which will G-d willing be published in a future volume. We are publishing this segment of the article at this point, with the hope to encourage orthodox Jews, who are still sitting on the fence, to vaccinate themselves and their children, and protect themselves and the community from spread of disease which has already unfortunately infiltrated us. This article is particularly pertinent towards Chabad Chassidim, as it analyzes the position of the Lubavitcher Rebbe on this question.

35. The Lubavitcher Rebbe's opinion on vaccinations:[506]

<u>Halacha requires one to listen to the medical community</u>: As is known, a Jew is obligated according to Torah law to guard his health.[507] According to Halacha, the opinion of professional doctors and health care providers are the sole authorities in regard to all health matters.[508] Accordingly, the Rebbe throughout his life encouraged people who turned to him for advice to follow the directives of the doctors and medical community and explained that the Torah gave them the power to heal, and one is Halachically[509] obligated to adhere to their directives due to the principal that guiding ones health is a

---

[Poskim ibid; Implication of Admur ibid; See Shevet Halevi ibid] Furthermore, some Poskim rule that even a gentile who put up a Mezuzah, the Mezuzah is Kosher. [See Maharshag ibid] Furthermore, some Poskim rule that women are even valid to write a Mezuzah! [See Perisha Y.D. 281:1 in implication of Tur 281, Rif and Rosh who all omit the Gemara in Gittin 45b which invalidates a woman; Now, although we do not rule like this opinion, as writes Michaber 281:3; Shach 281:6; Aruch Hashulchan 281:1, nevertheless, there is no precedent to extend the Hekesh of invalidation also for the Tikkun of the Mezuzah, and only the writing is invalid. See Shevet Halevi ibid]

[501] Yeshuos Malko Hilchos Tefillin Umezuzah [on Rambam] 5 rules the Mezuzah is invalid if placed by a woman; Eretz Tzevi ibid debates this issue and leaves this matter in question

[502] <u>The reason</u>: As women are invalid to write the Mezuzah [Michaber 281:3; Beis Yosef 281; Gittin 45b; Shach 281:6; Aruch Hashulchan 281:1] due to a Hekesh of Keshira and Kesiva with Tefillin [see Gittin ibid; Admur 32:10] and just like women are excluded from all matters of Tikkun with the Tefillin due to this, so too they are excluded from all matters of Tikkun of the Mezuzah due to this, which includes putting it on the doorpost. [See Yeshuos Malko ibid and Beir Moshe ibid who offer two slightly different reasons behind their invalidations based on the above reasoning]

[503] Beir Moshe ibid; Shevet Halevi ibid; Kevius Mezuzah Kehilchasa ibid in name of Poskei Doreinu; all Poskim in previous footnotes

[504] Beir Moshe ibid in order to escape the above dispute; Likewise, an additional reason to precede the husband is because he is the owner of the home, and Mitzvah Bo Yoser Mibeshlucho. [See Daas Kedoshim 289:12; Nachalas Tzevi 291 in name of Rav Akiva Eiger]

[505] See Shevet Halevi ibid that there is no doubt in this matter, and they are certainly obligated to do so and thus Pashut that they may not delay the Mitzvah simply due to a Chumra of some Poskim

[506] See Healthy in Body, Mind and Spirit Vol. 2. Chapter 11

[507] See Michaber Y.D. 116, 335:1 and C.M. 427:10; Admur C.M. Hilchos Shemiras Haguf Vehanefesh 4

[508] See Michaber Y.D. 335:1 *"Do not involve yourself in medicine unless you are an expert and there is no one greater than you, otherwise you are a murderer"*; Admur 618:9 *"A doctor who does not have experience with the illness is viewed like any other amateur, of whom their medical opinion has no bearing or weight, neither to be lenient or stringent"*; Admur 328:2 *"Even if there is a definite danger one may only transgress Shabbos for medical treatment that is known to all or is done by a professional [doctor]."*; Tzemach Tzedek Y.D. 81 regarding not to follow an amateurs advice on curing rabies; Aruch Hashulchan 336:2 *"It is forbidden for one to heal unless he is an expert who has received permission from Beis Din, and in today's times, who has received licensing from the government…one who practices medicine without this licensing is spilling blood"*; Igros Kodesh 7:303 See also our Sefer "Topics in practical Halacha Vol. 1 on the Hashkafa of alternative medicine and http://98.131.138.124:articles:ASSIA:ASSIA9:R0091090.asp

[509] See Admur 328:11 *"If [the sick person] refuses to accept the treatment because he does not want Shabbos to be desecrated on his behalf, then he is to be forced [into taking it] as this is a ludicrous form of [supposed] piety."*; This certainly applies during the week, that we force him to take a medicine or listen to doctors' orders even to cut off a limb, even if he does not want to do it due to the pain and ridicule he will have to live with. [Mor Uketzia 328]

Torah command.[510] In a case of medical debate amongst doctors, the Torah instructs that a Jew must follow the majority and most expertise opinion amongst doctors.[511] The case of vaccinations is no different, as will now be explained.

Summary of the Rebbe's position on vaccinations: The Rebbe encouraged people to immunize themselves and their children with the recommended vaccinations that are customarily taken by the masses to prevent the spread of disease, and negated those who argued that it should not be done due to worry of possible side effects, or death. The Rebbe also encouraged that the vaccine used should be produced by the most medically reliable and professional pharmaceutical companies. [This is due to the fact that there exist many formulas of vaccines, and many manufacturing companies throughout the world, who produce vaccines, with some being less reliable than others. In general, the Rebbe's position throughout his letters is that a vaccine formula and company which already has been seen to work on the populace is to be trusted.] While the Rebbe's opinion is not necessarily intended to be universal and all-inclusive for people of all medical background, and for all manufactured vaccines, in all situations, it does give a general perspective that one should not shrug off and ignore the recommendations of vaccinating oneself and his children, and as in all matters that relate to health, one is to speak to his professional health care provider to receive guidance in any cases of doubt or question.

The following is a free translation of excerpts from the letters and talks in which the Rebbe discussed vaccinations. The full text is available in the PDF posted on our website. We have bolded words to emphasize the main points of the letter, although it is not found in the original text.

1. Listen to your Doctor! Vaccines prevent illness-Take them:[512]

*"The Torah obligates that in matters of health **one must consult with a doctor and obey his instructions**. Now, there are two approaches to medicine, one being healing through finding a cure for a current illness, **and the second being preventive medicine. It is clearly understood that preventive medicine is the ideal and most desirable any way you look at it**, including cost, not to mention the fact it prevents illness and suffer r"l. In addition, it prevents needing to resort to more complex medical intervention such as surgery, which is sometimes necessary when dealing with an existing condition. **In order for preventive medicine to be most beneficial, it requires one to commence prevention at the earliest possible age, beginning with vaccinations**, brushing the teeth to prevent cavities, and a balanced diet etc."*

2. Doctors have the Torah right to administer preventive medicine in the form of vaccines:[513]

*"In reply to your query as to whether doctors are [according to Torah] only permitted to heal a current condition or may also administer preventive medicine, such as vaccines. **Preventive medicine has been administered by the most distinguished Gedolei Yisrael on a regular basis.**"*

3. One is to take vaccines and rely on the medical community and its successful administration:[514]

*"The deaths that resulted in America from vaccinations occurred at the early onset of the use of the vaccine, prior to its conclusive ingredient list being established. Now, however, after several months of experience with the vaccine [this is no longer the case]. Thus, after verifying the reliability of [the company who] manufactured the vaccine, there is no worry at all against taking it, **and on the contrary [one is to do so].**"*

---

[510] The Rebbe's directives to visit professional doctors and adhere strictly to their instructions are documented in hundreds of letters and talks printed in the three-volume series Healthy in Body, Mind and Spirit.

[511] See Admur 618:3-5 regarding fasting on Yom Kippur that if one doctor says the patient needs to eat while two doctors say the patient does not need to eat then he is not to be fed. If, however, the doctor who says that he needs to eat is a much greater physician than the other two doctors, then the patient is to be fed.

[512] Letter of Rebbe 15th Tammuz 5746 [1986], printed in Healthy in Body, Mind and Spirit Vol. 1

[513] Igros Kodesh 14:107 printed in Healthy in Body, Mind and Spirit ibid

[514] Igros Kodesh 14:343, printed in Healthy in Body, Mind and Spirit ibid

4. If most people in one's country and city vaccinate; one is not to exclude himself from doing so:[515]

"That which you write regarding vaccinations, in this country it is customary to vaccinate all the children. Nonetheless, prior to doing so, the manufacturer of the vaccine and its ingredients should be verified that it has been tested and successfully administered. Being that you write that many people in your city vaccinate their children, **you should not exclude yourself from doing so**."

5. Urgent! I have already answered many people that since most people do it, you should do so as well:[516]

"Due to the urgent nature of your query regarding vaccinations, I am replying to your question before even the other most pressing letters. It is a wonder that you ask your question [regarding whether you should vaccinate] as many have already asked me this in Eretz Hakodesh **and I have replied in the affirmative**, that since close to all people vaccinate, and successfully [therefore, you too should do so]."

6. Vaccinate your child if it is done to majority of the children in his class:[517]

"In reply to your query regarding my opinion on vaccinations that are currently given to young children, **with regards to these matters the Talmudic dictum of "Al Tifrosh Min Hatzibur/Do not separate from the community" applies**. Therefore, **you should act according to that which is practiced by the majority of children** who are in your children's class."

7. Salk-Polio vaccine-Since close to everyone already does so, it is proper to do so:[518]

"To Nishei Ubenos Chabad. In response to your query regarding the Salk [Polio] vaccine for children [and if the residents of Kfar Chabad should be vaccinated for it], it has already been administered in many countries, and in the USA close to everyone does so, and successfully, and therefore **it is proper to do so**. Regarding the company brand that you should choose for the vaccine, this is dependent on quality and reliability, and one should choose the best one after doing the proper research."

8. No Kashrus issue involved in taking vaccines-but choose a reliable brand:[519]

"That which you ask if one may use vaccines if they contain non-Kosher ingredients, every day people do so even amongst the G-d fearing without any question, as **it is permitted** to benefit from non-kosher foods. Regarding the Polio shot, it is done even by the most G-d fearing and there is no Kashrus worry of doing so, although one should verify that the vaccine comes from a reliable company."

9. The lesson in Avodas Hashem from vaccines:[520]

"Several decades ago, medicine discovered that the body could avoid certain diseases through vaccination. The vaccination works through stimulating the body, through injecting it with a weakened version of those diseases, to create antibodies to guard against them. The lesson in service of G-d that

---

[515] Igros Kodesh 14:426, letter 5203
[516] Igros Kodesh 14:357, printed in Healthy in Body, Mind and Spirit ibid
[517] Igros Kodesh 11:137, Healthy in Body, Mind and Spirit ibid
[518] Igros Kodesh 14 p. 238, printed in Healthy in Body, Mind and Spirit ibid
[519] Igros Kodesh 14 p. 108, printed in Healthy in Body, Mind and Spirit ibid
[520] Igros Kodesh 11 p. 58, printed in Healthy in Body, Mind and Spirit ibid
The following incident was related by the Rebbe in Sicha Parshas Shoftim 1982. "*A Jew visited me recently, and we discussed education. He told me that statistics have shown that a bad education harms only 5 percent of children. I asked him if he vaccinated his children for measles, polio, etc. He replied: "Of course! We are parents!" "Do you know what percentage of children who do not receive the vaccine actually contract the disease?" I asked. He happened to know the statistic—less than 3 or 4 percent. In other words, even for a possibility of 4 percent, and especially in these countries where these diseases are even more rare, it is still worthwhile to vaccinate, with all of the pain, etc., that it causes. Why? "Who cares about those minor inconveniences, as compared to what possibly could happen without vaccinating?" he responded. I said to him: "If for a doubt of 4 percent it is worth causing the child pain, enduring the child's screaming and all the other effects of the vaccination, just to avoid the disease—even though for the most part there is not even a possibility of any life danger, but rather just severe discomfort for some time—how much more so is it worthwhile to ensure the health of the child's soul, where the doubt is 5 percent, and where the vaccine does not cause any pain. All that is required is to sign the child up for studies in a Torah-true educational facility! This action will affect his entire life!*" [Taken from https://www.chabad.org/library/article_cdo/aid/2870103/jewish/What-Does-Jewish-Law-Say-About-Vaccination.htm]

can be learned from this is that minor challenges and difficulties which people face in new endeavors should be viewed as a vaccine against a more severe challenge later on."

The statistics:[521]
In Israel, 97% of children are vaccinated, holding one of the highest rates of vaccinated children in the world. In the USA 92% of children receive the MMR vaccine, while 99.3% of children receive at least some vaccines. The worldwide estimate of vaccinations against measles [MMR] stands at 85%.

An analysis of the Rebbe's opinion:
While it is clear that the Rebbe looked positively upon the administration of vaccines as an integral duty of a Jew in preventive medicine, and thus advised people to do so, in a number of the above letters the Rebbe depends this on whether majority of people have taken the vaccine, and the question is asked as to why this point makes a difference. If according to medical science vaccines are a necessity for disease prevention, and one must heed their words according to Halacha, then why should it make a difference whether majority of people do the right thing or not. The following are several **speculations** on the possible intent of the Rebbe:

1. The Torah follows majority: The successful administration of a vaccine to majority of the population shows that it works and does not have lasting side effects, thus proving its reliability according to Torah law, which follows the majority.
2. Hashem guards the masses-Shomer Pesaim Hashem: When the majority of people and Jewry perform an action which carries certain health risks, they receive Divine assistance and protection against any harm coming as a result of it.[522] Accordingly, there is no need to worry of any possible long-term side effects of a vaccination, as one receives Divine assistance regarding it, and thus the long-term benefits of disease prevention override.
1. Not to separate from the community practice-Halacha: The Torah does not desire one to disengage from the common practice of the community, and it thus instructs one to join their efforts.[523] Doing so may have both Halachic and spiritual ramifications. In Halacha we find that if a certain standard of living is accepted in a neighborhood, then people who live in that neighborhood must adhere to those public standards.[524] In the case of vaccines, one who does not vaccinate his children in a community where this is the standard practice makes that community susceptible to potential outbreaks due to their unimmunized child who walks around the neighborhood and attends in their schools and classes. Thus, Halachically, a parent does not have the right to live in such a community with unvaccinated children and endanger, and go against the wishes of, the majority.
2. Not to separate from the community practice-spiritual:[525] Another reason for why one should not separate from the community practice is spiritual, as doing so can cause undue personal observation and scrutiny of the spiritual attribute of judgment. A community receives certain Divine protection that is not afforded to one who separates himself from them. Accordingly, one who does not vaccinate possibly places himself under the eyes of scrutiny of the attribute of judgment, heaven forefend.[526]

---

[521] See https://www.statista.com/topics/3283/vaccinations-in-the-us/ and http://www.who.int/en/news-room/fact-sheets/detail/immunization-coverage

[522] See various instances where this rule has been used to allow a dangerous activity: Yevamos 12, 72; Kesubos 39; Avoda Zara 30a; Nida 31a; Beis Yosef E.H. 9; Chaim Sheal 59; Terumos Hadeshen 211; Machatzis Hashekel 260; Teshuvah of Tzemach Tzedek, elaborated on in Shaareiy Halacha Uminhag 3:13

[523] Hillel in Pirkeiy Avos 2:4; Bava Metzia 86b *"A person should never swerve from the norm and common practice"*; Tanya Igeres Hakodesh 16 and 23

[524] See Choshen Mishpat 156 and particularly Rama 156:7 for various powers a community has in preventing others who cause a potential financial risk from coming to live in the city, and certainly this would apply to a health risk

[525] The concept of a global protection provided to a community over that of an individual is well document in Torah literature, and is itself the foundation of the ruling of Shomer Pesaim Hashem, that even when a community does foolish activity, Hashem protects them, as opposed to the individual. [See Poskim in previous footnotes]

[526] So we see statistically that the first to become inflicted with a given disease are those who did not receive vaccinations against it. Meaning, the Satan who inflicts the plague focuses on them first and in majority r"l.

Q&A

Does this mean that according to the Rebbe everyone should immunize themselves and their children? What if I know people who had bad side effects, or I or my children had bad side effects? In fact, I even know someone whose child passed away r"l right after an immunization!

As in everything in life, there is no one shoe that fits all, and specific medical conditions and/or family history require special scrutiny by a medical professional regarding the question of whether vaccines are in their best health interest. This concept can be found in the Torah itself. While, the Torah obligates every male child to receive a "spiritual vaccine" called the Bris Milla on the 8th day, it recognizes special cases and situations of illness where this cannot medically be done and thus must be pushed off indefinitely until the child is deemed healthy. Likewise, we find parents with a family history of death caused by circumcision to at least two of their children, are required to push off the great Mitzvah of circumcision and not circumcise their child until, if at all, it is deemed medically safe.[527] From here we can learn a number of Halachic perspectives: a) Don't ignore family history or a medical condition when it comes to taking a normally accepted medication or treatment. b) Don't abstain from taking medication [in our case vaccines] just because you know of a case where it had negative or lethal effects. The Torah speaks to the majority, and for every case of negative consequences due to vaccines you have millions of others who attest to their reliability and health benefits. One cannot sabotage the norm due to the exception, without medical reason to believe that he is part of that exception group. A simple example of the above is with regards to peanuts. About 1.4 percent of children in the U.S. are said to be allergic to peanuts, and between 150-200 people die each year as a result.[528] Now, does this mean that the average and normal child is to avoid peanuts and is Halachically mandated to do so. Absolutely not! Since 99% of children are not allergic, we follow the majority, and only in a case of a medical reaction witnessed in one's child is one required to avoid it. The same applies regarding killing bees on Shabbos, that we do not allow one to kill a bee on Shabbos under the worry that he may be allergic, if there is no evidence to support that he personally contains an allergy to it.[529] Another example; Car crashes: We probably are all aware of someone who became injured in a car crash or perhaps even died r"l. Nonetheless, we do not rule according to Halacha that it is forbidden to drive a car due to the danger, as the danger is so minute in percentage when comparing the ratio of actual crashes versus the amount of road travel, that it falls short of reaching any bar of Halachic significance. In short: It is not enough from a Halachic or even secular perspective, to sabotage or negate a practice done by the public due to exceptional cases of negative reaction that have occurred, unless a significant percentage point of negative reaction has been established. If this applies towards mundane matters, such as driving a car, then certainly it applies towards matters of health which are done to prevent debilitating diseases. Thus, anyone who is absent of a medical condition or family history that has proven negative reaction to vaccines, must vaccinate himself as recommended by the medical community and cannot use the exceptional cases of reaction as a guidance for his own decision. Furthermore, even those with family history or medical conditions are to consult a doctor for a final decision of whether the vaccine should be administered, and if a different company vaccine may be used.

Perhaps the Rebbe's opinion is "outdated" and was correct at the time based on the information known. However, today, many people have shown and proven the potential damaging effects of vaccinations, especially regarding autism, the Rebbe would reverse his opinion?

Without getting into the subject of belief in the words of a Tzadik and the immortality of his teachings, the statement above is factually and Halachically misleading, misguided, and incorrect. As stated in the opening of this discussion, according to Halacha, the opinion of professional doctors and health care providers are the sole authorities regarding all health matters, and it is **forbidden to take an amateur's**

---

[527] See Michaber Y.D. 262:2 and 263:1-3
[528] See https://health.howstuffworks.com/diseases-conditions/allergies/food-allergy/peanut/how-many-people-die-each-year-from-peanut-allergies.htm
[529] See our article published on Shulchanaruchharav.com on this issue.

opinion into account. Halacha does not give credence to conspiracy theorists, or any other amateur opinion, regarding medicine. Accordingly, a Halachically valid medical opinion regarding vaccines must come from a medical professional and not a conspiracy writer, or an individual with a prior agenda, or even from an unbiased medical novice who is analyzing the subject to the best of his ability. Any and all information that the non-medical community provides regarding the danger of vaccines is to be given to the medical community for them to review and establish, or reject. Many people read various articles of propaganda against vaccinations and become convinced with the "facts" and statistics they read. Once, again, the Torah gave the authority of digesting this information, and giving medical advice based on it, solely to professional doctors, and not to the amateur writer irrelevant of how convincing his one-sided arguments may seem. This is aside for the very unfortunate reality where junk pseudoscience science is being portrayed as real science, and manipulated statistic data is being portrayed as real statics and being consumed and propagated by the antiestablishment conspiracy theorists. In addition, any attempt to suggest a change in the Rebbe's position would require the person to provide solidly established evidence **agreed to by the majority of the medical community** which shows a change in vaccine production and ingredients between now and then, and that proves their dangers of now versus then. Plain and simple, this evidence does not exist, and the evidence that has thus far been suggested has been debunked and rejected by almost all the medical community.

With that said, aren't there MD'S and people in the medical community who have voiced the dangers of vaccines, past the Rebbe's times?
Yes. From amongst the over 1,000,000 medical doctors in the United States[530] and between 10,000,000-15,000,000 doctors around the world[531], there do exist some credible doctors from within the professional medical community who have shared different concerns regarding vaccines, with some opposing it in its entirety. There have also been clinical studies performed which claim to show links between vaccines and other medical issues.[532] Nonetheless, this represents but a mere fraction of the medical community, and medical research. The overwhelming majority of research and clinical studies, including reports by the most prestige and professional scientific medical research firms, contradict these findings.[533] Likewise, the overwhelming majority of doctors in the medical community are in agreement that vaccinations are necessary to prevent disease and should be administered.[534] [For example, a letter signed by 500 orthodox pediatricians who serve in Jewish neighborhoods was recently publicized speaking of the absolute need and obligation for members of the community to vaccinate themselves and their children.[535]] It is their opinion that is followed by all nations and governments throughout the world, and the vast majority of people place trust in the medical community and administer vaccines to themselves and their children [see statistics above]. Accordingly, since the Torah instructs that a Jew must follow the majority and most expertise opinion amongst doctors[536], and

---

[530] https://www.statista.com/topics/1244/physicians/ ; https://www.statista.com/statistics/209424/us-number-of-active-physicians-by-specialty-area/
[531] See https://www.cia.gov/library/publications/the-world-factbook/fields/2226.html
[532] One of the more famous MD's who took the public stand to call out vaccines after doing an acclaimed thorough medical research on 12 patients was a British doctor named Dr. Andrew Wakefield and 11 colleagues. His findings were published in 1998 in the highly esteemed medical journal called The Lancet. In his essay he claimed to have found a link between autism and other neurological related disorders and the old MMR vaccinations which used Thimerosal [a now extinct mercury-based ingredient used in the MMR vaccinations of previous decades]. While at the time his findings received much media attention and medical speculation, it was rejected by the medical community as being sloppy, not adhering to medical standards of research, and being logically flawed. As a result, the research paper was retracted and eventually redacted after discovering that the said Dr. had in fact received funding for his research by lawyers who were representing a lawsuit [which they eventually lost] against the pharmaceutical companies who manufacture vaccines. He eventually went on to lose his license to practice medicine after the British Medical Council (GMC) found that he had been dishonest and irresponsible in his research.
[533] See here for links to **52** clinical studies that have been done by top medical researchers and scientists which negate any link between vaccines and other illnesses https://www.healthychildren.org/English/safety-prevention/immunizations/Pages/Vaccine-Studies-Examine-the-Evidence.aspx; see also: https://www.nap.edu/download/10997; http://nationalacademies.org/HMD/Reports/2004/Immunization-Safety-Review-Vaccines-and-Autism.aspx
[534] A letter signed by 500 orthodox pediatricians who serve in Jewish neighborhoods was recently publicized of the absolute need and obligation for members of the community to vaccinate themselves and their children.
[535] See
[536] See Admur 618:3-5 regarding fasting on Yom Kippur that if one doctor says the patient needs to eat while two doctors say the patient does not

the Rebbe instructs not to separate from the community, the Rebbe's directive and the Halachic ruling stands strong likewise today.

A story with the famed Posek Rav Y.S. Elyashiv and Rav S.Z. Auerbach:[537]
It occurred in Jerusalem in the early 90's that a toddler passed away suddenly after receiving a vaccination. He fell sick immediately afterwards and passed away the next day. The police, based on directives of the ministry of health, wanted to perform an autopsy on the child to see what caused the death and if it was related to the immunization. Although in general we forbid autopsies on the deceased, it is permitted under the rationale of saving lives, and hence the above said Rabbanim, Gedolei Torah, were asked by the family whether according to halacha it is allowed for them to have an autopsy performed to see if the vaccination ingredients must be modified. The above Poskim replied that it is forbidden to do an autopsy, as the chances that the vaccination caused the death is so rare, that it does not enter a Halachic justification of saving lives. Indeed, the child was buried without an autopsy against the wishes of the health department.

Conclusion- The antivax controversy and current measles outbreak:
Unfortunately, over the past few years, the number of people who refuse vaccines as a general policy have continued to grow, in part due to the publicization of a marginalized medical opinion, coupled with the spread of fake news, the distribution of junk pseudoscience, the manipulation of statistic data, and the desire to hold an anti-establishment position. This has all led to the marginal, outdated, and debunked beliefs that vaccines are dangerous and cause illness or autism. This position, aside from being contrary to Halacha [which follows the most prestige and majority medical opinion, as explained above] and the ruling of the Rebbe, and the leading Rabbanim of world Jewry from all factions, has caused much heartache, discord and illness through Jewish communities in Israel and abroad. Hundreds of Jewish children and adults have fallen ill with a preventable disease that has been spread due to those who have irresponsibly taken matters into their own hands and decided not to protect themselves or their children. In some cases, people have been left crippled, with long-lasting medical damage. Public events and simchas have turned into pandemonium due to measles outbreak fears set by the unvaccinated attendants. This breach that they have caused in society is causing others, who do care to protect their children, to become exposed to this illness. Certain communities have acted to battle this ongoing trend, and protect the public, by administrating a policy which bans any child who is not up to date with his vaccination charts from attending school, absent of a doctor's permission based on his personal medical record. We will conclude with a sincere request from all the Orthodox antivax population: Please have mercy on our community and the damage that this reckless avoidable spread of disease has caused. Have mercy on yourselves and follow the ruling of G-d in His holy Torah, as transmitted by the Poskim and Rabbanim, who as orthodox Jews you claim to follow. If you consider yourself a Chassid of the Rebbe, fulfill his directive to vaccinate and not separate from the community, without questions or hesitations, and certainly not to alter or manipulate his words so it fit your personal approach. So, if you do not have a personal medical exemption from taking vaccinations, please do the right thing and get your children vaccinated as soon as possible and help protect our communities. On the other hand, as a message to school directors and community leaders, we plead that you take a stronger stance on school policy against acceptance of unvaccinated students and not allow a small minority who hold onto a marginalized belief, which is anti-Halacha, to infect the rest of our communities and children with avoidable disease and panic.

---

need to eat then he is not to be fed. If, however, the doctor who says that he needs to eat is a much greater physician than the other two doctors, then the patient is to be fed.

[537] This episode was heard from Harav Yaakov Yosef z"l, a student of Rav Elyashiv and Rav Auerbach, and the eldest son of Rav Ovadia Yosef

------------------ *Cemeteries*------------------

36. Pregnant wife of Kohen and other pregnant women visiting cemeteries:[538]

Not married to Kohen: From the letter of the law, it is permitted for a pregnant woman to enter a cemetery.[539] However, many women are accustomed not to visit a cemetery when they are pregnant.[540] Those who have received such a custom are to abide by it.[541] However, it is permitted for them to visit the grave of a Tzaddik, or the grave of a loved one, on the day of the Yahrzeit and the like.[542] Many women are lenient in all cases, as is the letter of the law.[543]

Wife of a Kohen: It is permitted for the pregnant wife of a Kohen to enter a cemetery.[544] Nonetheless, some Poskim[545] rule it is proper to be stringent not to do so [even on a Yahrzeit or by Kivrei Tzaddikim]. This especially applies if she knows that the gender of the child is male[546] or she is at the end of her term and is ready for birth.[547] Nevertheless, even in such a case, most Poskim rule it is allowed from the letter of the law.[548]

37. Burying in a Shomer Shabbos burial section:[549]

Shomer Shabbos cemeteries or burial plots refer to a cemetery, or section of a cemetery, that is designated only for burial of those people who were Shabbos observant. While the earlier Poskim do not record such a concept of making a Shomer Shabbos cemetery, or Shomer Shabbos section within a cemetery, nevertheless, it has become widespread in the last hundred years, based on the law[550] that one may not bury a Rasha near a Tzaddik. Although defining who is a Rasha and who is a Tzaddik is not in the parameters of general people, nevertheless, certain basic guidelines have become accepted, thus creating the Shomer Shabbos section in the cemetery. Accordingly, it is forbidden to bury one who is Shomer

---

[538] Minchas Yitzchak 10:42; Nitei Gavriel Aveilus 2:84-4

[539] Pashut as there is no source for forbidding it, and so is proved from the fact the Poskim [below] bring that even the wife of a Kohen that is pregnant may enter a cemetery, and as writes the Kneses Hagedola [brought in Birkeiy Yosef 343:4] that even by the pregnant wife of a Kohen those who are stringent are doing Minhag Borus [custom of ignorance], hence certainly the wife of a Yisrael is allowed.

[540] This custom has no known source. A number of possible reasons are suggested: 1) Perhaps this is due to the fact that it is proper for the pregnant wife of a Kohen to avoid a cemetery, and hence we see that the fetus can receive impurity. Now since we await the rebuilding of the Temple every day the women avoid going to a cemetery, as if the Temple is rebuilt while they are still pregnant, they will be able to give over their pure sons to perform the necessary actions required for the Para Aduma. [Minchas Yitzchak ibid; See Parah Mishneh 3:2] 2) Alternatively, it is because they desire to avoid any impurity during the pregnancy. [Nitei Gavriel ibid; See Sheivet Hamussar 24]

[541] Poskim ibid based on Rashba that we do not differ a tradition received from righteous women even if we have 600,000 proofs against it. [brought in Heishiv Moshe 13]

[542] Nitei Gavriel ibid

[543] Heard from Rav Asher Lemel Hakohen

[544] Shach Y.D. 371:1; Rokeiach 366; M"A 343:2; Radbaz 200; Kneses Hagedola [brought in Birkeiy Yosef 343:4-there he writes it's a Minhag Borus to be stringent] Derech Hachaim; Chochmas Adam 160:1; Kitzur SHU"A 202:15; M"B 343:3; See Pischeiy Teshuvah 371:1; Gilyon Maharsha 371; Darkei Chesed p. 208

The reason: As there is a Safek Sfeika; perhaps the fetus is a female and perhaps it will be a stillborn. [Shach ibid; Rokeiach ibid] Alternatively a fetus cannot receive impurity as it is considered within a Beis Hablia. [M"A ibid; Radbaz 200, brought in Shaareiy Teshuvah 371:1; See there that even the Rokeiach agrees to this.] Others however argue that a fetus is considered part of the mother [Yerech Imo] and hence can contract impurity even during pregnancy. [Birkeiy Yosef 343:1]

[545] Birkeiy Yosef 343:4; Kaf Hachaim 343:4; Minchas Yitzchak 1042

The reason: As if in truth the child is a boy he contracts impurity. [This is proven from fact the Rokeiach only allows it due to Safek Sfeika. See previous footnote for the dispute regarding Beis Hablia] Hence, it is proper to initially avoid doing so. [ibid]

[546] The reason: As then there is no longer a Safek Sfeika according to the Rokeiach [as learns Birkeiy Yosef ibid], although according to many Poskim this would still remain permitted being that the fetus is considered within a Beis Hablia, as brought from M"A ibid and Radbaz ibid and so is evident from other Poskim mentioned in next footnote] See Even Yisrael 8:77 that deals with this question in regards to giving birth in a hospital that is not careful about Tumas Meis. He concludes there that ultrasounds are not 100% accurate, and that it is for the needs of a Yoledes who is in Sakana and hence she may choose to go to whatever hospital she wishes. Nevertheless, she is not initially to take an ultrasound and hence remove the Safek Sfeika. This is all with regards to which hospital to give birth and does not relate to a pregnant woman entering a Beis Hakevaros if she knows the child is male. It is understood that in such a case there are more Poskim who rule stringently.

[547] Sheilas Yaavetz 2:174 forbids in such a case [as the child may be born]; opinion in Darkei Chesed p. 208; Most Poskim however permit even in such a case, as the Safek Sfeika still remains. [M"B 343:3; Radbaz ibid brought in Pischeiy Teshuvah ibid, that this was the original case of allowance written by the Rokeiach; Betzeil Hachochmah 3:105]

[548] See previous footnotes; and so ruled to me Harav Asher Lemel Cohen that practically it is not accustomed to be stringent.

[549] See Darkei Chesed p. 225; Sefer Umikarev Beyemin 22 for a general overview of this subject; Igros Moshe Y.D. 2:152; 3:157; Teshuvos Vehanhagos 1:716; 2:598

[550] Michaber Y.D. 362:5; Mishneh Sanhedrin 46a and Gemara 47a

Shabbos in the non-Shomer Shabbos cemetery, if the surrounding graves are also not Shomer Shabbos.[551] The same applies vice versa, that it is forbidden to bury one who was not Shomer Shabbos in the Shomer Shabbos section, or near one who was Shomer Shabbos. This law created the Shomer Shabbos section of many cemeteries today. However, some Poskim[552] are completely lenient in this regard, and are not particular to bury a Shomer Shabbos Jew near one who was Shomer Shabbos. In the event that the deceased requested to be buried near his family which were not Shomer Shabbos, one may do so.[553]

Gentiles buried in Jewish cemeteries: Another issue to bear in mind when burying in a non-Shomer Shabbos section of the cemetery, is that unfortunately, some Jewish cemeteries are not particular to prevent people who are not Halachically defined as Jewish from being buried there. This is especially pertinent to reform and conservative cemeteries, which accept conservative and reform conversions, and bury children born from non-Jewish mothers in the Jewish cemetery. Thus, burying in a Shomer Shabbos section guarantees that one will not accidently be buried near a gentile.

What to do when burying in a non-Shomer Shabbos section: Despite the above, many cemeteries do not contain a Shomer Shabbos section. In such a case, one is to try to find a plot that is surrounded by graves of those who were Shomer Shabbos. If necessary, one may be buried in the cemetery even if he will be near non-Shomer Shabbos graves, although in such a case there should be a distance of eight Amos between his grave and the surrounding graves.[554] Alternatively, if one cannot make such a distance, a Mechitzah of ten Tefachim [80 cm] that separates his grave from the other graves is to be set up.[555] One can surround the grave with Hadassim that reach such a height, or place a bench or Ohel surrounding it.[556] If one is unable to do the above, he should bury the deceased in a different cemetery, even if he is required to be buried in a different city.[557] However, as stated above, some Poskim are completely lenient in this regard and in a case of doubt one is to ask his Rav.

38. May a body be buried in an over ground structure [i.e. Mausoleums; Kevurat "Komot"; Rama, Sanhedrin cave burials]?[558]

Background: In today's times, various Chevra Kadisha's and municipalities in search of space have introduced alternative burial methods which differ from the accustomed ground burial within a field. These methods include building a platform of several stories, similar to a multi deck parking lot, and burying the dead in these platforms. This allows the ground space to be utilized as much as possible. This form of burial is known as Kevurat Rama. Others build a structure on the ground which includes several decks of shelves which house the bodies. This form of burial is known as mausoleums, or Kevurat Komot, or Sanhedrin. The question that rises regarding the above forms of burial is as to whether they are valid

---

[551] Darkei Chesed p. 225; Teshuvos Vehanhagos ibid; Igros Moshe 2:152 that if the person was well known to be Michalel Shabbos in public then it is forbidden for the Chevra Kadisha to bury him near one who was Shomer Shabbos, or vice versa. If, however, it was not public knowledge that the person was Michalel Shabbos, even though it is known to certain individuals, then it is permitted to bury him near one who was Shomer Shabbos, unless the deceased who was Shomer Shabbos explicitly stated that he does not want to be buried near one who is rumored to have desecrated Shabbos, or transgressed another sin; Rav Yaakov Roza, Chief Rabbi of the Chevra Kadisha in Israel, related to me in a correspondence like the opinion of the Teshuvos Vehanhagos and Igros Moshe ibid

[552] Seridei Eish 2:98; Misgeres Hashulchan p. 179 that today we are no longer particular in this law; See Igros Moshe 3:157 that states one may bury a non-Frum Jew near a Frum Jew as he still has Kedushas Yisrael and wants to be buried in a Jewish cemetery according to Jewish law, and only gentiles, or Jews that rebel against Torah and Mitzvos and do not have a portion in the world to come must be distanced from a Jewish cemetery; However see Igros Moshe 2:152 that clearly states it is forbidden to bury a Michalel Shabbos near one who was Shabbos observant. See Koveitz Techumin 17 for an article by Harav Bakshi Doron that today the Chevra Kadisha is no longer particular in this matter. Vetzaruch Iyun also from the fact that we do not find any special Shomer Shabbos plots in the old cemeteries in Europe and Russia, and thus how were they careful to follow the above law! Rav Eli Landau told me that he is unsure regarding whether the custom is to be particular in this matter, and he did not receive any directive from his father in the issue. Rav Y.S. Ginzberg related likewise that Rav Chaiken mentioned in a correspondence, that while it is praiseworthy to be particular, it is not obligated by the cemeteries and many are accustomed to being lenient.

[553] Igros Moshe 2:152

[554] Sefer Chassidim 707 to distance 8 Amos from a Menuda; Gilyon Maharsha 362:5 regarding a Mumar; Melamed Lehoil 2:115; Igros Moshe 2:152; 3:157 that one is to make a fence of 10 Tefachim around the gentile and distance it 8 Amos; Teshuvos Vehanhagos 1:716 that by a Tinok Shenishba a four Ama distance suffices, however in 2:598 he requires an 8 Ama distance; See 362:3;

Other opinions: Some Poskim rule it suffices to distance him four Amos. [Imrei Yosher 2:3]

[555] Igros Moshe ibid; See Teshuvos Vehanhagos 1:716

[556] So I was told by Harav Y.S. Ginzberg that so is the custom in Russia.

[557] Teshuvos Vehanhagos 2:598

[558] See Kuntrus Komos of Rav Akselrud, Dayan in Haifa

according to Halacha. The question is whether they fulfill the requirement for the body to buried within earth, and not simply be left in a casket. In truth, these new forms of burial do have a precedent. In the times of the Sanhedrin it was customary to bury within caves. Shelves were carved out within the cave and bodies were entered inside of these shelves. This burial form was known as Kuchin. These forms of cave burial dating to the Tananaic period can be seen today in various areas, especially the old cemetery of Tzfat and in the Jerusalem neighborhood of Sanhedria. Thus, seemingly, the newly introduced forms of burial have the precedent of Halacha to be relied upon. However, in truth, a careful analysis shows that despite the good will to compare the modern burials to the alternative burial method used by the Sanhedrin, there is a major difference between the original Komot burial of the Sanhedrin and that which is used today. The Sanhedrin burial was done in an **underground** cave, and hence fully fulfilled the requirement of being buried within the earth of the ground. The new burial structures, however, are built above ground and are then filled with earth, hence attempting to give it the status of underground. Can such a structure which is in truth over ground be considered underground and within the earth just because it is covered with earth? Practically, this matter is debated amongst the Poskim of today as will be explained next.

The ruling:[559] Many Poskim[560] rule that above-ground structures used for burial in some cemeteries and Chevra Kadisha's, is invalid, and it is considered as if the body was never buried.[561] Some Poskim[562], however, defend the use of this form of burial, claiming that it has Halachic basis. Practically, one is required to be stringent and do all in his power that his deceased relative receives a traditional ground burial and not a burial within a built structure.

The position of the Israeli Rabbanut: The position of the Israeli Rabbanut for many years was to invalidate above-ground structure burials. Nonetheless, the current ruling of the Israeli Rabbanut, and its directive to the Chevra Kadisha's, does permit certain forms of over ground burial, under various Halachic arguments that they deem acceptable. This has created a major obstacle for those who desire to follow the majority of Poskim who invalidate such a burial, as the national insurance [Bituach Leumi] does not provide free ground burials in overly urbanized cities [i.e. Tel Aviv, Jerusalem], and paying for a ground burial privately can cost thousands, and up to tens of thousands of dollars. Practically, one is to do all in his power that his deceased relative receives a ground burial and is not to suffice with a burial of

---

[559] See Migdal Tzufim [Akselrod] 6:74

[560] Beis Yitzchak Y.D. 161 [unlike his previous Teshuvah 160] *"Burying in a walled building does not fulfill the Mitzvah of burial"*; Igros Moshe Y.D. 3:142-143 [unlike 3:144 where he permits] *"It is a great prohibition to burry in over ground Kuchim called Mausoleums, as the burial must be within the actual ground and one who does so transgresses the Biblical command of burial...It is thus obvious that one is obligated to publicize this prohibition that no Jew may be buried in these buildings due to transgressing two grave prohibitions of a negative and positive command each and every day, in addition to the grave sin of causing pain to the souls of the dead"*; Minchas Yitzchak 10:122 *"There is no doubt that the burial must be within the ground, and not within material that was removed from the ground and then attached"*; Divrei Yatziv Likkutim 133 p. 153; Rav Mashash and Rav Yisraeli in Chavas Binyamon 1:24 required that the Komot be fully covered with earth from all sides to be considered underground; Rav Elyashiv, printed in Piskeiy Teshuvos Y.D. 64, ruled it is forbidden to change the traditional method of burial; Rav Wozner ruled that the Komot are seemingly contradictory to the simple Halachic requirement; Badatz Eida Hachariedis including the Raavad, Rav Moshe Shturnbuch; Rav Meir Bransdofer ruled it is not considered a burial and one who was buried in such a way is to be exhumed and reburied within the ground; Many Rabbanei America from previous generation, brought in Kuntrus Migdal Tzufim ibid

[561] The reason: As **a)** The burial must take place underground, within the natural earth, and building an over ground structure and covering it with earth does not suffice. Being that this burial is invalid, one who does so transgresses the positive and negative command to bury the body. [Igros Moshe ibid; Minchas Yitzchak ibid; See the Sugya of Tolshu Ulibasof Chibru and if this is considered part of the ground: Bava Basra 66b] **b)** Even if burying within a mound of earth over ground is valid, the grave must be surrounded by earth from all sides; **c)** Even if one were to hold that the burial ground is not required to be surrounded by earth on all sides, in some of the over ground burial structures, there is no earth at all, and it is a cement building. **d)** It delays the decomposition of the body, and thus delays the atonement of the soul. [Igros Moshe ibid] **e)** One should not change from the normal burial method used throughout all generations. [Rav Elyashiv ibid] **f)** Burying with a shelf of a wall is like the ways of the gentiles and transgresses Chukos Hagoyim. [Kol Bo-Greenwald]

[562] Implication of Michaber 364:1 "Kever Shel Binyan"; Implication of Rashi Sanhedrin 47b "It refers to a building used for graves which was built over ground"; Beis Yitzchak Y.D. 160-3 [unlike his next Teshuvah 161] that if one attached the earth to the ground, its valid; Igros Moshe 3:144 [unlike 3:142-143] based on Rashi Sanhedrin 47b *"Since the building is made of stone and cement and is attached to the ground, seemingly it does not transgress the prohibition against delaying burial, although it is not considered a proper burial"*; Rav Moshe Shaul Klein from the Beis Din of Rav Wozner ruled in 5764 in the name of Rav Wozner that the Komot burial is valid [Rav Wozner later retracted from his ruling in 5771]; Rav Yaakov Roza, head of the Chevra Kadisha

The reason: As they bury the body in actual earth or material which has the same Halachic status as earth, such as cement, and this earth is attached to the actual ground, and we rule that Talshu Ulibasof Chibru is viewed as attached.

Komot or Rama. One is to do so even if the cost of the ground burial is exorbitant. There are various cities and villages which sell ground burial plots and the full range of prices and locations are to be weighed.

------------------ *Mourning* ------------------

39. Until when is Kaddish recited?[563]

Ideally, one is to say Kaddish for 12 months, however the custom is to only recite Kaddish for a period of 11 months [from the passing[564]].[565] The Avel is to stop reciting Kaddish on the last day of the 11th month; for example if the Yahrzeit is the 10th of Shevat then Kaddish is recited until the 9th of Teves, including the 9th of Teves.[566] [This applies even in a leap year.[567] One is to be very careful in this matter.[568] This applies even if the deceased was known to be a great Tzaddik.[569] Nevertheless, even during the 12th month, participating in the Minyan and answering Amen to Kaddish helps elevate and effect the Neshamah of the Niftar.[570]]

---

[563] Rama 376:4; Maharil Semachos; Levush 133; Beir Heiytiv 132:5 in name of Kneses Yechezkal; See Taz 340:12 and 376:5; Sefer Haminhagim p. 180 [English]; Igros Kodesh 4:106; Sefer Hasichos 1989 1:175 [printed in Shulchan Menachem 5:290-298] Sichas 9th Shevat 1951; Nitei Gavriel chapter 51

One who knows his father is a Rasha: One who knows his father or mother is a Rasha is obligated to say Kaddish for 12 months. [Chomos Yerushalayim 257, brought in Pischeiy Teshuvah 376:3; See Chasam Sofer E.H. 1:69]

One who committed suicide: If the deceased committed suicide it is permitted to say Kaddish for 12 months on his behalf. [Chasam Sofer E.H. 1:69]

One whose father told him to say Kaddish for 12 months: If one's parent commanded him to say Kaddish for 12 months then he is to do so. [See Beis Yitzchak 2:157; Mishmeres Shalom Tzaddik 26 that so did the son of the Maharshak for his father; Shevet Halevi 2:161 and 165; Igros Kodesh 4:140 regarding Reb Nissan Tloshkin who asked for Kaddish to be recited for 12 months; Poskim in Pnei Baruch 34 footnote 4 and Nitei Gavriel 51:10]

One who does not know the date of his father's passing: See Pnei Baruch 34:6

If another relative passed away within the 11 months, may he say Kaddish in the 12th month of the parent? See Sefarim in Igros Kodesh 12:197; The Rebbe there concludes it may be recited; See also Gesher Hachaim 30:9-13; Chelkas Yaakov 3:157; Pnei Baruch 34:7

Other customs: Some Poskim rule one is to recite Kaddish for 12 months minus one week. Meaning they stop saying Kaddish on the last week of the 12th month. [Birkeiy Yosef 376 based on Arizal that the Kaddish helps even souls that are not in Gehinnom; See Rav Poalim 3:32; Poskim in Pnei Baruch 34 footnote 4; Various opinions brought in Igros Kodesh 4:106 footnote 1]

[564] See Q&A!

[565] The reason: This is done in order not to turn one's father and mother into Reshaim, as the judgment of a Rasha is 12 months. [Rama ibid] The mere ending of the Kaddish after 11 months has the ability to refine the judgment of the deceased and cause him to be elevated above. [Sefer Hasichos 1989 1:175, printed in Shulchan Menachem 5:290]

[566] Beir Heiytiv 132:5; Shvus Yaakov 2:129; Machatzis Hashekel on M"A 132:2; Chayeh Adam 32:18; Kitzur SHU"A 26:17; Sefer Haminhagim p. 180 [English]; Igros Kodesh 4:106; Sefer Hasichos 1989 1:175 [see there for explanation]; Igros Kodesh Rashab Halacha 80; Vol. 2:904; [See Sichas 9th Shevat 1951 that the Rebbe Rashab once added one day to the Kaddish and he was very distressed]; See Pnei Baruch 34 footnote 3 for other Poskim and opinions

If the last day is Friday: Some Poskim rule that if the last day is Friday one is to say Kaddish also on Shabbos. [See Poskim in Pnei Baruch 34:8; See Shevet Halevi 165 that he is not to say Kaddish]

Other customs: Some are accustomed to end the Kaddish 30 days before the 12th month. [P"M, in end of Noam Megadim, and so was the custom of the Rebbe Rayatz, brought in Sefer Hasichos ibid]

[567] Poskim brought in Nitei Gavriel 51:3

[568] Sichas 9th Shevat 1951 that the Rebbe Rashab once added one day to the Kaddish and he was very distressed

[569] Sichas 9th Shevat 1951 that so was the custom of the Rebbe Rashab, and so followed the Rebbe, see there for the explanation; Sefer Hasichos 1989 1:175

[570] See Sefer Hasichos 1989 p. 182

Summary:
One begins reciting Kaddish immediately after receiving knowledge of the passing, and concludes the Kaddish 11 months from the passing, on the last day of the 11th month. For example, if the Yahrzeit is the 10th of Shevat then Kaddish is recited until the 9th of Teves, including the 9th of Teves.

Q&A

How does one calculate the end of the eleven months for Kaddish-from the time of death or the time of burial?[571]

Some Poskim[572] rule that the eleven months of Kaddish is counted from the day of burial. Other Poskim[573] rule it is counted from the day of the death. Practically, one is to follow the day of death.[574]

How does one calculate the end of the eleven months for Kaddish if one was in a different time zone at the time of death?[575]

In the event that the son and the deceased parent were in different time zones at the time of death, the date to end Kaddish follows the time zone of the deceased with regards to starting the count of the eleven months.

If one did not begin saying Kaddish after the burial, for how long is Kaddish to be recited?[576]

It is only recited until 11 months from the day of death, even if he only began saying Kaddish on the last day of the 11th month.

Is one who is not a child of the deceased [such as a hired person] to recite Kaddish for 11 or 12 months?[577]

The custom is to recite it for only 11 months.[578] Nevertheless, some[579] write he may/should recite it for 12 months. Practically, we follow the former opinion.[580]

---

[571] See Igros Kodesh 3:199; 4:107 [published in Shulchan Menachem 5:292-295]; Gesher Hachaim 30:9-10; Nitei Gavriel 51:4 footnote 6-8; Pnei Baruch 34:9

Background: There is known dispute regarding whether the 12 months of Aveilus is counted from the day of death/burial, and whether the Yahrzeit is the day of death or burial, and whether the 12 months in Gehinnom is counted from the day of death or burial. It is possible to learn that regarding Kaddish there is a similar dispute, as depending on when the 12 months of Gehinnom concludes would depend on when to conclude Kaddish [see Kneses Yechezkal 47]; On the other hand perhaps it depends on the start date of the Kaddish, whether one started the day of burial or the day of death [see Daas Torah 376:6].

[572] Implication of Shach 402 in Nekudos Hakesef that Mishpat Reshaim of 12 months begins from day of burial [see Kneses Yechezkal 47]; Levush brought in Elya Raba 132:4; Noam Megadim 1; Kitzur SHU"A 26:17; Neharei Afarsimon 97; Biur Halacha 132; See Daas Kedoshim 377; Levushei Mordechai 223

[573] Implication of Taz 568:4 that Mishpat Reshaim of 12 months begins from day of death; Beir Heiytiv 132:5; Siddur Yaavetz 39 [see Nitei Gavriel ibid footnote 6]; Kneses Yechezkal 47; Mateh Ephraim 4:1; Alef Lamateh Kaddish Yasom 3:5

[574] Igros Kodesh 4:107; Custom of Rebbe Rayatz as brought in Reshimos Hayoman p. 416; However, see Igros Kodesh 3:199 that the Rebbe directed the asker to follow the day of burial and not the day of death! See also Igros Kodesh 13:410 in which the Rebbe implies to follow the day of the burial. Vetzaruch Iyun!

The reason: As Admur 71:1 rules to begin saying Kaddish the day of death and according to some Poskim [see Daas Torah ibid] the dispute is dependent on this matter.

[575] Igros Kodesh 13:410, brought in Shulchan Menachem 5:295

[576] See Taz 568:4; Shach 402 in Nekudos Hakesef; P"M 132 A"A 2; M"A 132:2 in name of Ran; Beir Heiytiv 132:2; Rav Akiva Eiger 376 and Beis Lechem Yehuda 376; Gesher Hachaim 30:9-5; Sefer Haminhagim p. 180 [English]; See Pnei Baruch 34:4-5

[577] See Pnei Baruch 34:11

[578] See Shevet Halevi 165 that if the son hired him then he may not say it in the 12th month; Gesher Hachaim 30:9-4 that so is custom of some; See Pnei Baruch ibid; Nitei Gavriel 50:15; The Rebbe recited Kaddish for only 11 months for the Rebbe Rayatz and the Rebbetzin; See Sichas 9th Shevat 1951 and Sefer Hasichos 1989 of 21 Teves that the Rebbe stopped saying Kaddish after 11 months and explained why. The Rebbe was not a son or daughter!; Rav Y.L. Groner in a written correspondence that the Rebbe told people to say Kaddish for his brother and for the Rashag only for 11 months; Rav Y.S. Ginsberg that so is the custom;

[579] Gesher Hachaim 30:9-4; Meishiv Devarim 213; Nitei Gavriel 50:19

[580] Nitei Gavriel 50:15; See sources in previous footnote that so is the custom and so was the Rebbe's custom

May the Avel recite Kaddish Derabanan in the 12ᵗʰ month?
Some Poskim[581] rule he may recite Kaddish Derabanan even in the 12ᵗʰ month. Other Poskim[582] however rule he is not to recite it.

Lechayim:[583]
Some are accustomed to make Lechayim in Shul on the day they finish reciting Kaddish.

---

[581] Rav Poalim 4:32; Gesher Hachaim 30:9-10; Shevet Halevi 165; See Even Shoham 20, brought in Pischeiy Teshuvah 376:4; See Pnei Baruch 34:10
[582] Maharshag 52; Even Yaakov 49; See Pnei Baruch ibid
[583] Nitei Gavriel 52:4 in name of Rav Poalim 3:62 [I did not find this in the source mentioned in Rav Poalim]

Even Haezer

-----------------Marriage-----------------

1. Marrying a Kohenes:[1]

An Am Haaretz/Ignoramus is not to marry a Kohenes. If he does so, their marriage will not be successful, as either she or he will quickly die, or they will be in constant fight with each other [or they will be poor[2]].[3] However, a Torah scholar who marries a Kohenes, [their marriage] is pleasant and praised, as the Torah and priesthood complement each other [and their marriage is a Segula for wealth[4]].[5] [Some Poskim[6] rule that this type of Am Haaretz no longer exists today, as it refers to one who belittles and scorns at the Mitzvos, and is not measured by scholarliness. Other Poskim[7], however, rule that an Am Haaretz includes anyone who is not Halachically defined as a Talmid Chacham. Nonetheless, today, one may be lenient in the definition of a Talmid Chacham, and so is the custom to marry a Kohenes even if one is not Halachically defined as a Talmid Chacham.[8]]

The directive of the Chabad Rabbeim: The directive of the Tzemach Tzedek was for the Chasan to be well versed in one Misechta, in order to leave the status of an Am Haaretz in this regard.[9] The Chabad Rabbeim instructed that the Chasan is to study by heart one tractate of the Talmud and repeat it from memory each day.[10] Elsewhere, the Tzemach Tzedek directed that the husband gives a small amount of money each day to charity, throughout his life.[11] Thus, one has an alternative to learn daily, or give charity daily. The above is to be done without a Neder.[12] Practically, the Rebbe negated the need for one to follow the above directives and give charity daily, or review the Tractate of Mishnayos daily, and rather suggested as follows:[13] The Rebbe advised that the Chasan add in Torah learning.[14] He is to be well versed in one Misechta before his wedding.[15] One may choose any Tractate in the Talmud, even the small Tractates, such as Miseches Kallah.[16] One is not required to memorize the text, but rather to know its

---

[1] Michaber E.H. 2:8; Admur 444:15; Rambam Issurei Biya 21; Rebbe Yochanan Pesachim 49a; Tzemach Tzedek Even Haezer 11; Otzer Haposkim 1:2-8:44; See Shulchan Menachem E.H. 6:247

[2] Pesachim ibid

[3] The source: This is learned from the verse [Vayikra 22] which states that if a Kohenes marries a Zar, and she becomes a widow, or divorcee, or has no children, from which we learn that a Kohenes is meant to marry a Kohen, and if she marries a Zar, then any of the above may occur. [Rav Chisda in Pesachim ibid]

Case examples: Rebbe Yehoshua married a Kohenes and became weak. He stated that seemingly Ahron is unhappy with him marrying one of his daughters. Rav Kehana blamed his exile and wandering on the fact he married a Kohenes. [Pesachim ibid]

[4] Pesachim ibid *"Rebbe Yochanan said: One who desires wealth is to marry a descendant of Aaron. Rav Sheshes said in the name of Rav Papa that he became wealthy due to marrying a Kohenes."*

[5] Michaber ibid; Pesachim ibid; Rivash 15; Maharam 605; Tzemach Tzedek ibid

Other opinions: See Tzemach Tzedek ibid for a discussion of why the above Amoraim, who were certainly Talmidei Chachamim, nevertheless felt they were punished for marrying a Kohenes. He explains there that these Amoraim held that even a Talmid Chacham cannot marry a Kohenes, thus arguing on the conclusion of the Gemara ibid. See however Maharsha ibid that one can simply say that due to his humility, Rav Kahana did not view himself as a Torah scholar.

[6] Chavos Yair 70, brought in Pischeiy Teshuvah 2:9 and Y.D. 217; Aruch Hashulchan 2:5

[7] Tzemach Tzedek ibid; Maharam Shick 6 *"In today's times an exceptional Bachur who is G-d fearing person may marry"*; Avnei Tzedek 5 that there is a middle level of one who is not a Talmid Chacham but also not an Am Haaretz;

[8] See Poskim ibid

The reason: Although, in truth, having knowledge of one Misechta does not define one as a Talmid Chacham, nevertheless, since the Kohanim today do not have true proof of lineage, and thus cannot eat Biblical Teruma, as well as that many are anyways lenient in this matter, and Shomer Pesaim Hashem, it therefore suffices to study only one tractate. [Tzemach Tzedek ibid; Likkutei Sichos 19:509; Igros Kodesh 11:115; Avnei Tzedek 5]

[9] Tzemach Tzedek Even Haezer 11 *"So long as he knows one Misechta"*, mentioned in various responses of the Rebbe, brought in Igros Kodesh below.

[10] Maaneh of Rebbe Rashab to Rav Klotzkin, printed in Yagdil Torah N.Y. 20 Nissan 5738

[11] Response of Rebbe Rashab that so directed the Tzemach Tzedek, printed in Yagdil Torah N.Y. 20 Nissan 5738, mentioned in Likkutei Sichos 19:509

[12] Response of Rebbe Rashab that so directed the Tzemach Tzedek, printed in Yagdil Torah N.Y. 20 Nissan 5738, mentioned in Likkutei Sichos 19:509

[13] Likkutei Sichos 19:509

The reason: As the custom today has become to be lenient in this matter, and Shomer Pesaim Hashem, and the more careful one is to negate any harm, itself emphasizes the harm. It thus suffices for one to be considered like a Talmid Chacham before the wedding, and he then no longer has to worry about this matter. [Likkutei Sichos 19:509]

[14] Igros Kodesh 5:283; 6:83; 7:154

[15] Likkutei Sichos 19:509; Igros Kodesh 5:283; 11:115; 13:123; 14:383

Marrying the granddaughter of a Kohen: On one exceptional occasion, the Rebbe directed one who married the granddaughter of a Kohen to be an expert in one Tractate. This was a personal directive and is not a directive for the public. [Rishumo Shel Shana 5744, brought in Shulchan Menachem 6:249]

[16] Likkutei Sichos 19:509; Igros Kodesh 6:83; 14:383; Mikadesh Yisrael p. 215, brought in Shulchan Menachem 6:249

content.[17] On one occasion, the Rebbe directed the Chasan to study the entire Shisha Sidrei Mishneh prior to the wedding, or at the very least one or two Sedarim.[18] On another occasion, the Rebbe directed that if possible, one is to be an expert in the laws written in Kitzur Shulchan Aruch.[19]

> **Summary:**
> One who is not a Talmid Chacham is not to marry a Kohenes. The custom in today's times is to be lenient in this matter, although prior to the wedding, the Chasan is to study and be well versed in at least one Tractate of the Talmud. It suffices to be well versed even in a small Misechta, such as Miseches Kallah. In general, the Chasan is to increase in Torah study.

2. Parents of Chasan and Kallah share the same names:

If the parents of the Chasan and Kallah have the same exact name, they should not have their children marry each other.[20] This applies for the names of both the mother and the father.[21] [However, some Poskim[22] rule this only applies if the names of the fathers are identical, and not regarding the names of the mothers. Other Poskim[23] rule the above only applies to small children, while children who are already adults may choose to marry someone even if their parents share names. Other Poskim[24] rule the concern only applies if the parents share the same rare name, however by common names, such as Avraham and Yitzchak, no concern applies.]

A second name: If, one of the parents with the identical name has a second name which is not shared with the other parent, then there is no worry involved.[25] [For example, if one is called Chaim Baruch, while the second is called Chaim, it is not a problem.] Likewise, even if the parents share the same exact name, if a second name is added to one of the parents, it suffices.[26] Accordingly, if the mothers share the same name, then one of the mothers should have a name added.[27]

> **Q&A**
> **If one of the parents has a nickname, or a secular name, are the names considered identical?[28]**
> Seemingly, one may be lenient in this matter if the parent is called by this nickname or secular name.

What is Miseches Kallah and where is it found? Miseches Kallah is part of a number of very small Tractates that are laws without commentary, and do not have on them the commentary of the Talmud. These Misechtos are found in the end of Seder Nezikin, after Tractate Horiyos. This Tractate contains one chapter and should not be confused with Tractate Kallah Rabasi which is a later work.

[17] Igros Kodesh 13:123; 14:383; In one reply, the Rebbe directed the Chasan to learn the Tractate 40 times. [Mikadesh Yisrael p. 215, brought in Shulchan Menachem 6:249]

[18] Igros Kodesh 6:83; See also Shemuos Vesippurim for a similar directive of the Rebbe Rashab to Harav Morozov, who married the daughter of a Kohen, that *"This matter is not to be taken lightly, and he is to be an expert in Seder Kodshim."*

[19] Igros Kodesh 5:283

[20] Tzavas Rebbe Yehuda Hachassid 24; See there that it is questionable whether this directive of Rebbe Yehuda was for everyone or only for his descendants, and hence we are only careful in this due to doubt [See Even Yikara Kama E.H. 15; Makor Chesed footnote 36]

[21] Sdei Chemed Asifas Dinim Mareches Chasan Vekala 10; Igros Kodesh 18:136

[22] Even Yikara Kama E.H. 15; Beis Naftali 12; Ruach Chaim E.H. p. 34; See Poskim in Sdei Chemed Asifas Dinim Mareches Chasan Vekala 10

[23] Avnei Tzedek E.H. 6 and 10

[24] Shem Mishimon E.H. 6

[25] Tzemach Tzedek Even Haezer 1:143; Piskeiy Dinim Y.D. 116; Igros Kodesh 18:136

[26] Igros Kodesh 18:136

[27] Igros Kodesh 18:136

[28] See Michaber E.H. 129 that a nickname or English name is considered a real name and must be written in the Get. See also Igros Kodesh 4:349 and Shulchan Menachem 6:140 that if he uses the similar name only for an Aliya and the like, then it falls under the allowance of the Tzemach Tzedek.

----------------CASTRATION----------------

3. Is a gentile prohibited from castrating a human/animal as part of the Noahide laws?

This matter is disputed in the Talmud[29] and Poskim. Some Poskim[30] rule that gentiles are not prohibited against castrating. Other Poskim[31] rule that gentiles are prohibited against castrating. Practically, one is to be stringent like the latter opinion.[32] [The practical ramification of this matter is a) Can one sell an animal to a gentile if one knows he will castrate it [this matter will be explained in a further volume], and b) What should one instruct gentiles to do, if they desire to keep the seven Noahide laws.]

----------------Shemiras Eiynayim----------------

4. Are women commanded in the laws of Shemiras Eiynayim?[33]

Innocent looking-No pleasure involved: Some Poskim[34] rule that women are to avoid looking at men, just like men are to avoid looking at women. Thus, the women section in a Shul is to be built in a way that the women cannot look at the men. The majority of Poskim[35], however, negate this view and rule there is no prohibition whatsoever for a woman to innocently stare at a man, even though a man is restricted against gazing at a woman, and so is proven from the Talmud[36], and so is the final ruling and custom of all Jewry.[37] This applies even if the man is not modestly dressed, such as he is wearing shorts or does not have a shirt, and the like.[38] This, however, is with exception to the Erva area, as explained next.

A sexually stimulating gaze-Pleasure involved:[39] It is Biblically forbidden for a woman to look at the body of a man for the sake of sexual pleasure or arousal, just as is the law by men.[40] Thus, it is forbidden

---

[29] Rav Chida and Tana Divei Menashe in Sanhedrin 56b and in Bava Metzia 90a rule that one of the seven Noahite laws is not to castrate [they remove the prohibition of Birchas Hashem and replace it with Sirus], and hence gentiles are commanded against castrating, just like they are commanded to follow the other Noahite laws; However, the Tana Kama in Sanhedrin ibid rules that gentiles are not commanded against castrating. [As they list Birchas Hashem as one of the seven Noahite laws, which thus excludes the prohibition of Sirus from being included.]

[30] Implication of Michaber E.H. 5:14 and Stam opinion in Rama ibid, who permits selling to a gentile even if one knows that he will castrate [See Chelkas Mechokeik 5:8]; Rambam; Rosh [brought in Chelkas Mechokeik ibid]; Rashba; Hagahos Maimanis, brought in Beis Shmuel 5:16; Minchas Chinuch Mitzvah 291 in opinion of Rambam and Chinuch. Chelkas Mechokeik 5:8 concludes that we rule like this opinion, as so rule vast majority of Poskim; [The Chelkas Mechokeik ibid explains that the final understanding of the Gemara Bava Metzia ibid is what determines whether we hold like Rav Chidka or not, disputed as, and all those who rule that the prohibition of Amira Lenachri applies to all Issurim, dispute the ruling of Rav Chidka, and since the final ruling in the Shulchan Aruch follows that Amira Lenachri applies in all cases, it is a proof that we do not rule like Rav Chidka, and if so, then the Rama should not have recorded this opinion.] Gra 5:37 "We do not rule like Rav Chidka, as write all the Poskim"; Aruch Hashulchan 5:26 writes that most Poskim rule gentiles are not commanded, and so is the main Halacha, although some are stringent.

[31] 2nd opinion in Rama ibid who forbids selling an animal to a gentile, as explained in Taz 5:10, Chelkas Mechokeik ibid and Terumos Hadeshen 299; Semag; Hagahos Ashri, brought in Beis Shmuel 5:16; Raavad, brought in Rosh, brought in Chelkas Mechokeik ibid

[32] Beis Shmuel 5:16; 18; brought in Aruch Hashulchan ibid

[33] See Ohel Yaakov 21:25; Piskeiy Teshuvos 75:3; Dirshu 75:21

[34] Teshuras Shaiy 1:125 [Seagate], brought in Otzer Haposkim 21 based on Yalkut Shimoni Shmuel Remez 105 brought below

[35] Setimas Kol Haposkim in O.C. chapter 75; Aruch Hashulchan 75:5; Letter of Rav Yoel Teitelbaum of Satmar, brought in Otzer Haposkim ibid and Taharas Yom Tov vol. 6; Shevet Halevi 5:197 *"We have never seen our ancestors and Rabbis suspect for this"*; Chut Hashani p. 262; Ohel Yaakov ibid

[36] Sukkah 51b that by the Simcha Beis Hashoeiva the women were on top [and would look at the men dancing]; Brachos 20a that Rebbe Yochanon would sit by the Mikveh and women would gaze at his beauty.

[37] The reason: As the sexual psyche and stimulation of a woman is very different than that of a man, and we do not suspect that an innocent gaze will lead to forbidden thoughts, in contrast to a man for whom even an innocent gaze can instantaneously turn promiscuous. [See Nida 13a "Nashim do not have Hargasha"; Aruch Hashulchan ibid "By a man there is more worry of Hirhur"; Shevet Halevi ibid]

[38] Setimas Kol Haposkim in O.C. chapter 75 that there is no Hirhur for a woman to Daven in the presence of a man whose body is uncovered, with exception to the Erva area.

[39] Yalkut Shimoni Shmuel Remez 105 *"Rebbe Yehuda stated that the reason Bnos Yisrael spoke in length with Shaul is in order to gaze at his beauty. Rebbe Yossi said, if so you have turned the Jewish girls into Zonos, as just as it is forbidden for a man to gaze for pleasure at a woman who is not his, so too it is forbidden for a woman to gaze for pleasure at a man who is not hers."*; Sefer Chassidim 614 *"A woman should not hear the voice of a man as whatever a man is commanded in so too a woman"*; Shevet Halevi 5:197; Divrei Yatziv 5:35; Chut Hashani p. 262; Rav SZ"A, brought in Ohel Yaakov ibid; See Igros Moshe Even Haezer 1:69

[40] The source and reason: As the verse states "Lo Sasuru Acharei Levavchem Veacharei Eiyneichem" from which we learn that it is forbidden to entertain thoughts promiscuity, and there is no differentiation between a man and woman in this command. Thus, looking at a man in a way that stimulates forbidden thoughts is Biblically forbidden. [Shevet Halevi ibid; Igros Moshe Even Haezer 1:69; See Sefer Chassidim ibid] Likewise, it is also prohibited due to the prohibition of Lo Sikrav, as just as a woman is prohibited from doing all the other matters listed in E.H. 21:2 with a man, so too she is forbidden in looking for the sake of pleasure if she is an Erva. Now, although some rule that women are not Halachically relevant to the prohibition of Zera Levatala [See Mishneh and Gemara Nida 13a "Nashim Lav Bnei Hargasha Ninhu" and Tosafos and Tosafus Rosh on Nida ibid], this prohibition applies irrelevant to if it will lead to Zera Levatala as: **a)** It may lead to sin with that person and **b)** Looking for pleasure is an intrinsic prohibition, even if it will not lead to Zera Levatala, as sexual interaction with a prohibited relation is Biblically forbidden in its own right, irrelevant of what it does or does not lead to. Likewise, it is Biblically forbidden even for women to think forbidden

for women to watch movies and the like that contain sexually stimulating scenes. It goes without saying that looking at pornography is a Biblical prohibition for both men and women.

Davening and learning Torah in view of a man whose body is not properly covered: It is permitted for a woman to learn Torah or Daven in the presence of a man whose body is not properly covered [wearing shorts, or no shirt, and the like].[41] This, however, is with exception to the private area of a man [i.e. the Erva] in which case it is Biblically forbidden to Daven or learn in its presence.[42] The above, however, only applies if seeing the man does not stimulate forbidden thoughts, however, if it does, then it is forbidden for her to learn Torah or Daven in his presence.[43]

5. May one walk in areas in which there are women who are not modestly dressed?[44]

Due to the grave prohibition against staring at the beauty of a woman[45], the question is raised regarding walking in public, in immodest areas, and if or how, it is to be avoided.

If another path is available:[46] It is forbidden for one to walk in areas in which women are not modestly dressed if another path is available that does not contain immodest women. One who nonetheless goes through the immodest path is considered a Rasha. This applies even if one is sure of himself that he will not give into the temptation to look at the women.[47] [The definition of another path available is that there is another viable option to reach one's destination that will not take extra time, or cost more money.[48] If, however, it will take extra time or cost more money, then one is not obligated to go the more modest route, although certainly he is considered a Chassid if he does so. The same would apply if one is traveling to a certain store, that contains immodestly dressed women, that if another modest store is equally available for the same distance and price, then he may not go to the immodest destination.]

If another path is not available: It is permitted for one to walk in areas in which women are not modestly dressed if he is going there for a purpose and there is no other way to get to one's destination. Nonetheless, one who closes, or turns away, his eyes while walking, and avoids seeing a woman as much as he can, is considered a Chassid, and on him it says "Otzeim Eiynav Miros Bera."[49] There is, however, no obligation to do so.[50] [Nonetheless, it always remains forbidden to stare, or take a second glance, and

---

sexual thoughts. [See Igros Moshe ibid] Furthermore, according to the Mekubalim, the prohibition of "Zera Levatala" applies equally to women, and those that do so increase evil spirits and Kelipos. [See Shaar Hakavanos Inyan Drush Layla; Yifei Laleiv 239; Kaf Hachaim 239:3]

[41] Setimas Kol Haposkim in O.C. chapter 75; Aruch Hashulchan 75:5 [questions this matter but concludes that so is implied from the Poskim and Kesubos ibid]; Piskeiy Teshuvos 75:3

The reason: As women do not have the same level of Hirhur as men. [Kesubos 9; Aruch Hashulchan ibid]

[42] See Admur 74:1; See M"B 73:5 that a wife may not say Kerias Shema if she is facing her husband who is unclothed

[43] Makor Chaim [Chavos Yair] 75; Piskeiy Teshuvos ibid

[44] Bava Basra 57b; See also Bava Kama 48a; Piskeiy Teshuvos 75:6; Sefer Histaklus Behalacha 4 footnote 8

[45] Michaber E.H. 21:1; Tur 21:1; Riy, brought in Beis Shmuel 21:2; Orchos Chaim 2:13; Rabbeinu Yona Igeres Hateshuvah 19:20, brought in Beis Yosef 21; Braisa in Avos Derebbe Nasan; See Eiruvin 18b *"One who gives money to a woman in order to look at her, is not saved from judgment of Gehennom"*; Nedarim 20a *"One who stares at women in the end will come to sin."*; Avoda Zara 20a *"One may not stare at a beautiful woman even if she is single, and may not stare at a married woman even if ugly"*; M"B 75:7

The reason the Torah prohibited looking at the beauty of an Erva: 1) Leads to sin with the Erva. 2) Leads to Zera Levatala. 3) It is intrinsically a sin to receive sexual pleasure.

[46] Bava Basra ibid

[47] Rashbam ibid

[48] Piskeiy Teshuvos 75:6 footnote 65

[49] Gemara ibid as explained in Rashbam; See also Brachos 62b that when walking outside, one is to avoid looking in areas where women are found.

[50] Gemara ibid; See regarding the allowance to see a woman in a mere glance [even immodest] so long as one does not stare, or look for pleasure: Admur 75:1 *"Some Poskim permit Davening opposite the uncovered area of a woman if he does not stare at her, even though he sees it at a glance, as the entire prohibition is due to it causing forbidden thoughts, and only staring can cause forbidden thoughts."*; So rule: Rabbeinu Yona Brachos 25; Rambam Shema 3:16; Beis Yosef 75 in name of Rabbeinu Yona; Makor Chesed on Sefer Chassidim 9:2 that "Histaklus" means to stare; Sefer Chassidim 1000 that may look at woman while talking to her; Rosh brought in Sefer Chassidim Tinyana 99 that whenever it says Histaklus means stare, and hence an innocent glance at a woman is permitted; [See however Smeh C.M. 154:14 who says Histaklus means a mere look and not stare, while Reiyah means to stare.]; Rashal Kesubos 2:11; Yosef Ometz 474; P"M 75 M"Z 1 *"If he sees and gets pleasure he transgresses and if not it is permitted"*; M"B 75:7 *"A mere unintentional glance alone without pleasure is permitted"*; Emek Sheila 52:1; Salmas Chaim 438 [685]; Piskeiy Teshuvos 75:6-7; Poskim in Nitei Gavriel Yichud 55:3 footnote 6; Story in Avoda Zara 20a that Tanaim said *"Mah Rabu Maasecha Hashem when saw a beautiful woman"*

The reason: As he is Onus, and in a case of Onus the Torah exempts one from liability. [ibid]

only the basic sight necessary while walking is permitted.[51] Likewise, one is to walk in a way that prevents him from seeing the women as much as possible, as explained next.]

How to walk in public: Every man is obligated as much as possible when walking in the streets, in public, to walk with his head facing in a downward direction, in order so he does not see women, and so he walks in a humble manner.[52] Nonetheless, one should not bend his back forward like a hunchback, or have his head bent too much to the point that he cannot see the people in front of him. Rather he is to walk in an average bent manner so he could see the people walking towards him (without having to lift his eyes too much[53]).]

------------------Tznius-Arayos-----------------

6. Woman visiting a male doctor/Gynecologist:[54]

It is permitted for a woman to visit a male doctor, even if the Doctor will need to touch her body, such as to check her pulse and the like.[55] This applies even if the woman is married, and even if there are other gentile [or female[56]] Doctors available.[57] This applies even if the doctor will need to examine intimate areas such as is done by a gynecological exam.[58] [Nonetheless, if a female doctor of equal expertise is available, it is better for a woman to visit a female doctor.[59] This especially applies by a gynecologist, that a female gynecologist should always be preferred over a male, if available, unless there is a medical issue involved in which the male gynecologist has greater expertise.[60]]

Yichud: When one visits a male doctor, care must be taken not to transgress the laws of Yichud during the visitations. This matter will G-d willing be discussed in a further volume!

7. Talking and flirting with the opposite gender:[61]

A man is required to distance himself from women very, very, much. It is forbidden to do any activity for the sake of sexual pleasure or lust. All the above matters receive Rabbinical lashes [i.e. Makas Mardus] and the above matters are forbidden also due to a negative command.

---

[51] Bach 1 *"When he sees the woman, he is to close his eyes"*; Poskim in previous footnote

[52] Igros Moshe O.C. 1:40 regarding Shemiras Einayim; Piskeiy Teshuvos ibid; See Admur Basra 2:5; Kama 2:7; Michaber 2:6 regarding the general requirement to walk in a humble manner, in a way that he sees the ground near his feet.

[53] These parentheses are in the original

[54] See Darkei Teshuvah 157:8; Nishmas Avraham Y.D. 195:11; Shevet Halevi 3:186; 4:167; Shiureiy Shevet Halevi 195:274; Minchas Yitzchak 7:73; Igros Moshe E.H. 2:14; Taharah Kehalacha 7:1; Halichos Bas Yisrael 7:17; Ohel Yaakov p. 286

Regarding a caretaker/nurse of opposite gender [not a doctor]: See Michaber Y.D. 335:10 and Poskim there!

[55] Shach 195:20 that so is the custom; Sidrei Taharah 195:24; Kreisiy Upleisi 195; Piskeiy Dinim 195:17; Darkei Teshuvah ibid that so is evident from all Poskim, Rishonim and Achronim, who deal with the question of a male doctor checking a woman; Noda Beyehuda Kama Y.D. 66; Tinyana 122; Binyan Tziyon 1:75; All Poskim ibid; Igros Kodesh 14:100 [printed in Shulchan Menachem 5:248] *"I never heard that people were careful in this matter"*

The reason: As the prohibition of Giluiy Arayos only applies when done out of lust and not when done with other intents in mind, such as for medical purposes. [Shach 157:10 and 195:20]

Other opinions: Some Poskim rule even unaffectionate touch with an Erva is Biblically forbidden. [Beis Shmuel E.H. 20:1 that so holds Ramban to be the opinion of Rambam; Beis Yosef 195 in opinion of Rambam that even in a case of Sakana one may not touch even unaffectionate] Other Poskim rule unaffectionate touch with an Erva is Rabbinically forbidden. [Beis Shmuel E.H. 20:1 and Beis Yosef Y.D. 195 in opinion of Ramban; See Ezer Mikodesh 20:1] Some Poskim however rule that even according to the stringent opinions, unaffectionate touch is only forbidden with one's wife who is a Nida while with other woman it is completely permitted [in a case of need]. [Toras Hashelamim 195:15; Igros Moshe E.H. 2:14]

[56] So is evident from Shach ibid

[57] Shach ibid

[58] Darkei Teshuvah ibid that so is evident from all Poskim, Rishonim and Achronim, who deal with the question of a male doctor checking a woman's vaginal area to determine the source of bleeding; Noda Beyehuda Kama Y.D. 66; Binyan Tziyon 1:75; Letter of Rebbe in Shulchan Menachem 5:248; Divrei Yatziv 7:122; Nitei Gavriel 80:25 in name of Satmar Rebbe; See however Michaber Y.D. 335:10 and Shach 335:9 that a man may not be a caretaker for a woman if he will see her intimate areas. Perhaps however there is a difference between a caretaker and a doctor, as by a caretaker the visitations are frequent as opposed to a doctor.

[59] Letter of Rebbe in Shulchan Menachem 5:248; Igros Kodesh 14:100; Minchas Yitzchak 7:73; Shevet Halevi 4:167; Shiureiy Shevet Halevi ibid; Halichos Bas Yisrael 7:17

The reason: Besides for the reasons of Tznius, a woman also naturally feels more comfortable with a female doctor. [Rebbe ibid]

[60] Poskim ibid

[61] Michaber 21:1; Rambam Issurei Biya 21

The Law:[62]

It is permitted for a man to talk to a woman regarding work/business related subjects, as well as all necessary conversations.[63] One is not to talk excessively, more than necessary.[64] A woman who talks to men more than necessary, even if it is not a lightheaded/flirtatious conversation, transgresses Daas Yehudis.[65] Some Poskim[66] rule that one is not to stare directly at the woman while talking with her. [This law applies to men/woman of all ages, whether young or old.[67]]

Flirtation/affection/intimate subjects: It is absolutely forbidden to flirt with a girl/woman or do any lightheaded activity with her.[68] [This is defined as any speech or activity which is done with the other gender for the sake of pleasure, or from which pleasure is derived.[69]] Doing so transgresses a Biblical negative command [of Lo Sikravu].[70] Doing so falls under the prohibition of Giluiy Arayos of which we rule Yaharog Veaal Yavor.[71] It goes without saying that one may not say to her words of affection that can lead towards feelings for one another, even when talking of business related subjects, as even the saying of Shalom to a woman is forbidden for this reason, as explained next. It is certainly forbidden to talk with her regarding intimate subjects that can lead to Erva.[72]

Summary:
It is permitted to talk with the opposite gender regarding necessary subjects. It is forbidden to talk excessively, regarding unnecessary matters. It is Biblically forbidden to flirt with the opposite gender due to a negative command, and doing so is included in Yaharog Veal Yavor.

Q&A

May a man be a woman's therapist?
Being that therapy involves opening up one's inner emotions, thoughts and feelings, it is highly inappropriate for a man to give therapy to a woman, even if the laws of Yichud were to be followed, and the conversation is purely work related. This is certainly included in the words of the Michaber that one is required to distance himself very, very, much from women, and certainly applies regarding therapy in which "Rabim Challalim Hipilu" Practically, each case is to be individually studied to determine whether the therapy required can lead to emotional dependence or closeness, and whether it

---

[62] See Michaber 21:1 and Ohel Yaakov p. 169

[63] Pirkeiy Avos 1:5 *"Do not talk excessively with a woman, certainly not with another man's wife"*; Eiruvin 53; Nedarim 20; See Beis Shmuel 21:4 *"However hearing her voice during speech is permitted"*; There is no prohibition found in Poskim regarding interaction with a woman for business related matters or other everyday activity, and so is the custom even amongst G-d fearing Jews to have work conversations with women when necessary; See Maharsha Bava Metzia 87a that Eily spoke with Chanah and Elisha spoke with the Shunamis.

[64] Beis Shmuel E.H. 115:12; Bach 115; Pirkeiy Avos ibid; Maggid Mishneh Issurei Biyah 21:2 "One who talks excessively receives Makas Mardus"; See also Maharal Nedarim 20a that talking with a woman is the beginning of an intimate connection that can lead to sin; See Shabbos 140b and Rashi there; See Derech Pikudecha Lo Sasei 35-8 that ideally it is forbidden to talk even one word more than necessary, although the custom is to be lenient being that in today's society, men are used to seeing woman and talking to them, and it hence does not lead to forbidden thought. Nonetheless, he concludes, it is best to turn one's head slightly during the conversation.

[65] Beis Shmuel E.H. 115:12; Bach 115; Such a woman can be divorced without a Kesuba. [Michaber 115:4; Kesubos 72]

[66] Derech Pikudecha ibid; Igros Moshe 1:40; Nitei Gavriel Yichud 50:1

[67] Nitei Gavriel 50:5

[68] Beis Shmuel and Bach ibid; Michaber 21:1 *"One is to distance himself from Arayos very much....It is forbidden to have fun with her [i.e. Lischok Ima], to be light headed with her."*; Based on this, Rama Y.D. 195:1 explicitly prohibits flirtatious conversation regarding a wife who is a Nida; Shach Y.D. 157:10, Rambam Yesodei Hatorah 5:9, Sanhedrin 75 "Even to speak with her behind the fence is forbidden, and better he die from his infatuation"; Pirkeiy Avos 1:5 "Do not talk excessively with a woman, certainly not with another man's wife"; Maggid Mishneh ibid that he receives Makas Mardus; Gur Aryeh Vayeira 18:9 "If he intends to hear her voice it is forbidden"; If even asking Shalom to a woman is forbidden [as brought in Topics in Practical Halacha Volume 2] then certainly flirting with her is forbidden, Upashut! Those who state that the Shulchan Aruch does not forbid flirting are walking in darkness and miss the entire spirit of the laws mentioned here by the Michaber, aside for the fact that even saying Shalom was explicitly prohibited. There is no greater gateway action that leads towards promiscuity than flirting with the opposite gender. It is certainly included in the ruling of Michaber 21:1 "One must distance himself very very much from women"; See also Maharal Nedarim 20a that talking with a woman is the beginning of an intimate connection that can lead to sin.

[69] See Gur Aryeh ibid

[70] Michaber ibid *"All the above matters receive Makas Mardus and the above matters are forbidden also due to a negative command"*; Shach ibid *"And he may not even talk to her for pleasure, and doing so is Biblically forbidden under Lo Sikrav"*; Nitei Gavriel 50:2

[71] Shach Y.D. 157:10; Rambam Yesodei Hatorah 5:9; Sanhedrin 75

[72] See Rama Y.D. 195:1

is being done in a group or with an individual, and whether a female therapist of similar quality is available. One is to contact a Rav and make the necessary precautions when giving such therapy. This applies for both the therapist and patient.

May a male/female privately tutor a person of the opposite gender?
Although privately tutoring the opposite gender is work related conversation and is not a forbidden form of interaction, so long as the laws of Yichud are guarded, nevertheless it is not appropriate, and is certainly included in the words of the Michaber that one is required to distance himself very, very, much from women. Tutors should therefore place effort to only teach students of the same gender. Likewise, students in need of tutoring are to choose tutors of the same gender.

May a man teach a group of women?[73]
A married man may teach a group of women, and so is the custom, although some are stringent. This matter will G-d willing be elaborated on in a future Halacha.

8. Educating one's children against predators, pedophiles, and molesters:

Unfortunately, a known and growing epidemic, which has seen greater light in the recent years, is the plague of pedophilia, of which almost no Jewish community has come unscathed. One of the basic principles of Torah Judaism is Kedusha, keeping a holy environment of sexual morality. The Torah is well aware of the challenges people have in containing sexual lusts and hence provided a number of guidelines which are meant to prevent one from falling prey to his instincts and desires, or for that matter, to falling prey to the sexual gratification of another individual.[74] Accordingly, it is the responsibility of every parent and educator to educate his children or students in a clean and Kosher way of the very real dangers of predators and the guidelines they are to keep and matters to beware from, so they do not fall prey to such an individual, and so they stop it before it progresses.[75] Aside for the religious responsibility to prevent sinful activity and moral depravity from occurring, educating one's children in the above is included in the basic responsibilities a parent has in keeping their child safe from physical dangers. Just as a parent must teach his child how to cross the street, and a school must rehearse fire drills, so too, children must be educated in the above for their own physical safety, aside for the religious reasons of morality. The enormous damage that child molestation can potentially cause the innocent soul of a child is indescribable, and the statistics of the potential affects speak for themselves without needing to give this matter any further proof.[76] Accordingly, educating one's children to beware from predators is a Halachic responsibility both due to reasons of morality and safety. The reason for why educating children in this matter is, and has been, avoided is because it is viewed as a taboo subject that is more comfortable to ignore than to discuss, and due to the desire to keep children sheltered from knowledge of such depravities. Unfortunately, the spread of this epidemic and the spiritual and physical destruction that it has caused, and continues to cause, the innocent children who fall victim, do not allow us to remain silent any longer. By lifting the level of awareness to our children regarding this matter, we both stop our own children from falling prey to a predator, as well as put a deterrent against a predator attempting to lure victims. In the following paragraphs we will analyze a Halachic discussion regarding the need to beware from people due to worry of homophile behavior, thus lending the Halachic basis for the above said obligation of education:

---

[73] See Admur Talmud Torah 11:13; Michaber Y.D. 245:20; E.H. 22:20; Mishneh Kiddushin 82a; Sefer Chassidim 313; Devar Halacha 12:7; Teshuras Shaiy Kama 170; Salmas Chaim 648; Beis Avi 3:40; Shulchan Menachem 4:271; 5:50; Article of Rav Yaakov Horowitz, printed in answer to Kuntrus Matzdikei Rabim Kikochavim Koveitz Beis

[74] See Shulchan Aruch Even Haezer chapters 21-24

[75] See Rambam Issurei Biyah 22:5 [brought in A]

[76] Effects of child sexual abuse include shame and self-blame, depression, anxiety, post-traumatic stress disorder, self-esteem issues, sexual dysfunction, chronic pelvic pain, addiction, self-injury, suicidal ideation, borderline personality disorder, and propensity to re-victimization in adulthood. Child sexual abuse is a risk factor for attempting suicide. Much of the harm caused to victims becomes apparent years after the abuse happens. [See https://www.ncbi.nlm.nih.gov/pubmed/19733950 for scholarly articles on the subject]

A. May a man have Yichud with another man?[77]

The Jewish people were not suspected of homophile relations [i.e. Mishkav Zachar], and therefore there is no prohibition [for a man or child] to be in a state of Yichud with another man. [This is in contrast to gentiles, who are suspected of homophile relations, and one is hence prohibited from sending his child to learn under a gentile teacher.[78]] Nonetheless, a man who distances himself from having Yichud even with another Jewish man [including male relatives[79]], is praised. [The above was relevant in previous times, however] in these later generations in which the number of [Jewish] individuals who are sexual deviants have increased, a man is [obligated[80]] to distance himself from having Yichud [even] with a [Jewish] male.[81] [Some Poskim[82], however, rule that this only applies in countries where homophile relations are common, while in countries in which this is an unaccepted and rare occurrence, there is no need even today for a man to distance himself from Yichud with another man, although it remains an act of piety to do so.]

From this Halacha we can derive two points vis a vis the proper attitude towards educating our children to beware from predators, pedophiles, and molesters:
1. One must not only distance himself from situations which ignite him to act on his own lusts, but one must also distance himself from falling prey to the lust of another individual. Accordingly, children must be educated so they do not fall victim.
2. The distances required are all dependent on the level of morality in one's society. Thus, in a depraved society in which a certain immoral behavior has become abundant, one must distance himself in increased measures from this behavior, even though this distance was not necessary in previous generations. Accordingly, the level of pedophilia rampant today obligates one to take increased measures to make sure his children do not fall victim.

B. Matters to beware and educate children in:

Various organizations have blossomed over the recent years which specialize in child education and awareness in the above matter. The following is some of the suggestive actions and guidelines which have been acclimated from leading child psychologists and educational experts. For further information, visit their website.[83] The education of a child in this topic is split to two parts, Prevention and Awareness, sometimes known as P&A:
1. **Prevention**-Teach your child certain guidelines and precautions that prevent him from entering situations that make them vulnerable to a preying predator.
2. **Awareness**- Teach your child to identify an attack and deter it from progressing.

Prevention guidelines:
1. Yichud-Not to be alone: Children must be educated from a young age against Yichud. Halachically, it is forbidden for a three year old girl to remain alone with a man above the age of Bar Mitzvah, and it is forbidden for a boy who is nine years of age or older to be alone with a girl

---

[77] Michaber E.H. 24:1; Tur 24:1; Rosh 4:24; Rambam Issurei Biyah 22:2; Chachamim in Kiddushin 82a

[78] Implication of Michaber ibid; Beis Yosef E.H 24; Tur 24 *"The nations are suspected on everything and hence one may not give them a child to be taught by them, even a male to a male"*; Rambam Issurei Biyah 22:5; Avoda Zara 15b and 36b; Shabbos 17b; However, see Rama Y.D. 153:2 and Tur 153 that the reason is due to that the gentile will teach the child heresy. See Rashi Avoda Zara 15b who mentions both reasons; See Derisha E.H. 24:1, Vetzaruch Iyun!

[79] Tur 24 "Even with one's father"; See Bach 24 who states the novelty here is that even though the person is a Jewish male and one's father, nevertheless, it is praiseworthy to distance oneself from Yichud. The Bach, however, concludes that he is unsure of the source of the Tur's ruling; This ruling of the Tur is omitted in Michaber ibid

Other opinions: Some Poskim rule that it is not necessary to distance oneself from Yichud with his father and the above statement in the Tur is a misprint. [Yad Ahron 1 24:1; Implication of Michaber ibid]

[80] Implication of Michaber ibid and Bach 24, as brought in Chelkas Mechokeik and Beis Shmuel 24:1

[81] Michaber ibid

[82] Bach E.H. 24, as brought in Chelkas Mechokeik and Beis Shmuel 24:1

[83] See http://www.jewishcommunitywatch.org/education-center/ ; https://childmind.org/article/10-ways-to-teach-your-child-the-skills-to-prevent-sexual-abuse/ ; https://ourkidscenter.com/learn/how-to-educate-children-about-abuse/

who is above the age of Bas Mitzvah.[84] Furthermore, in light of the above ruling in A, regarding even a man distancing himself from Yichud with another man, children and adolescents should be educated that it is Halachically proper and necessary to distance themselves from being alone with another person even of the same gender, and even if they are relatives, unless under parental consent. If a man or woman asks or lures a child to a private area without parental consent, the child should be educated to say that it is not allowed for them to be alone, or at the very least to have the intuition to inform his or her parents. Certainly, in light of the above Halacha, teachers or tutors should not be having one on one sessions with a child in a closed or locked room, and the room should always remain accessible to the public. Likewise, parents are to supervise that siblings of opposite genders stop sharing rooms after a certain age, and even when same gender children share rooms, clear modesty guidelines must be given. This especially applies during the pubescent years of a child, in which raging hormones search for outlets that can cause another family member to fall victim. Parents must be cautious and know that statistically a large percentage of abuse actually occurs within the family, and hence they must educate their children and pay attention as to how they act when they are together. While this suggestion of avoiding Yichud is unpopular and may sound exaggerated and unrealistic to some, this is the Torah's suggestion and obligation in how to distance oneself from falling prey to a predator-Avoid Yichud. It is certainly obligatory of a Torah institution to follow the laws in Shulchan Aruch which state that in communities suffering from homophile epidemics, it is an obligation for boys to distance themselves from Yichud with other men, and vice versa. This suggestion and obligation is unique to the Torah world and has yet to enlighten the secular populace [who come up with various other suggestions] of its powerful deterrence,.

2. Mikveh:[85] The Mikveh is by no exaggeration one of the main centers where child molestation occurs in the Jewish community. We tend to think that since it is a public area, and one is never in a state of Yichud with another man while there, that it is therefore a safe haven for our children. Nonetheless, experience shows that the Mikveh is in fact a safe haven not for the children, but for the predators, and they use it as one of their primary bases of opportunity to launch attacks. Accordingly, together with a parent's desire to educate their child in a Chassidishe Hanhaga of purity of soul, in going to Mikveh, they must be realistic and take precautions with their child. Practically, what this means is as follows: **a)** Young children have no business ever going to a Mikveh alone. A young child who is not near the age of Bar Mitzvah has no Chinuch obligation to go to Mikveh, and if he can't go under supervision, it is better that he not go at all. **b)** Even when fathers accompany a child to the Mikveh, they must have four pairs of eyes on the child. One should not be mistaken to think that since he is in the same building as his child that therefore the child is safe, as experience proves otherwise. **c)** Children who are near, or over Bar Mitzvah, and are accustomed to go to Mikveh daily before Davening, must be educated by their parents in how to act in a mikveh and be told of the Awareness guidelines, explained in length below. Following the above steps will help keep a Mikveh that that which it is supposed to be-a place to enhance a person's holiness and purity, and not the opposite.

3. Be aware of known community offenders: The United States Department of Justice contains a list of convicted sex offenders within one's area. Likewise, local organizations [i.e. JCW] and community Rabbi's and leaders periodically release information of suspected or convicted predators. Parents should make themselves aware of who these people are and make sure to keep their children a safe distance from them. On this note, it is every community's obligation to warn the public of the said individuals and to say something if they see something, and not ignore red flags which allow predators to continue their victim list for years on end.

---

[84] Michaber E.H. 22:11
[85] This paragraph follows the directives of Rav Yaakov Yosef z"l, as heard by the author

Awareness guidelines:
1. <u>Your body is only yours</u>: Explain to the child the concept of privacy for his/her body and that their body is only theirs and is not allowed to be touched ,or even seen, by others, unless the person is a doctor, parent or caretaker who needs to do so in the position of their job, and is doing so under other adult supervision. Explain to your child the existence of the private areas of his or her body, and how they must be kept clothed and out of contact of others. Practice this at home, teaching the child modesty and privacy with their body, such as locking the door when they take a shower or use the bathroom [age dependent] and educating them how to act with other siblings. Some suggest teaching the child the traffic light system regarding touch. Label innocent and clean touches as green light [i.e. shaking hands, holding your hand to cross the street, tapping your shoulder]. Touches that make a child feel slightly uncomfortable as yellow light [i.e. a hug, or kiss from an unwanted individual, touches that occur under clothing]. Touches that reach under the bathing suit area is a red light. Yellow and red-light touches must always be informed to the parents or other legal guardian. Emphasis must be made that anyone, including siblings, cousins, friends, and teachers, must be informed on if a yellow or red-light touch has been made. Explain to the child that often body touches may even feel good, although this is not a sign that such touches are ok. An inappropriate touch [i.e. red light] is never ok, no matter how it feels.
2. <u>Another person's body is only theirs</u>: We cannot forget that many children are not the victims, but are themselves the innocent perpetrators who experience with the body of other children. Likewise, often the predators do not touch the child's body, but ask the child to touch their body. Accordingly, children must also be educated that just as their body is private to themselves, so too other peoples, and children's, bodies are not theirs to look at or touch. Furthermore, this applies even if the other person consents or asks them to touch their body, nonetheless, it is an immoral [un-Tznius] thing to do.
3. <u>Saying NO</u>: Often, children are intimidated against telling off another individual, especially if they are an adult figure. Train your child to say NO if an inappropriate touch is made or attempted. Teach them to escape the situation.
4. <u>Not to keep secrets</u>: Teach your child that there is no such thing as keeping a secret from their parents, from Mommy and Tatty. Anyone who tells them not to tell something to their parents, is a sign that they must tell their parents right away. Even if a person tells them that they will get hurt or punished if they tell the parents, the child is to be told that such a person is lying. Parents must ensure their children that they will not get into trouble for telling their parents, and on the contrary will be believed and cherished for sharing it with them.
5. <u>Even very nice and friendly people, relatives, or other children can do bad things</u>: According to the US Department of Justice (nsopw.org) only 10% of perpetrators were strangers to the child and 23% of the perpetrators were children themselves! Accordingly, all the above guidelines of touch and secrets must be clearly spelled out to the child that they apply even to very nice people, people they know, and even very close relatives, friends or siblings, or other parent. They apply even if the person shows much love to them and spends time with them and buys them treats.
6. <u>Occasional review of the guidelines</u>: It is imperative for parents to review these guidelines with their children periodically. One can preschedule on a reminder/calendar to review the guidelines a couple of times per year, such as before the school year begins, and after Pesach vacation and the like.

It is our prayers, that with G-d's help, the implementation of these education guidelines will help prevent and stop this epidemic, and allow our children to live peaceful and un-abused lives.

------------------Covering hair----------------

9. Must a divorcee, or widow cover her hair?

It is forbidden for a woman who was once married, such as a widow or divorcee, to walk in public with uncovered hair, just as is the law regarding a married woman.[86] [Some Poskim[87] rule that this obligation for a widow or divorcee to cover her hair is merely Rabbinical.[88] Accordingly, some Poskim[89] are lenient in certain situations to be explained, to allow a widow or divorcee to uncover her hair in public.[90] This refers to a situation in which if she covers her hair, she will lose her job[91], or if she is in a situation that covering her hair will ruin her prospects of finding a new husband.[92] Most Poskim[93] however reject this ruling and rule that there is no room for leniency even in the above pressing situations, just as is the law regarding any Biblical or Rabbinical obligation, and so is the standard practice amongst G-d fearing Jews.[94] Even according to the lenient approach, she must cover her hair at all times of the day, week and year that the above necessities and worries are inapplicable, and there is thus no unlimited allowance according to any opinion for a once married women to freely walk around with uncovered hair. Practically, the above situations of necessity are rarely applicable, as one can find a job or new husband, regardless of if the hair is covered, and hence the allowance of the lenient opinion is irrelevant. In the rare case however that it relevant, those who would like to follow the lenient approach are to contact their Rav for a final arbitration on this matter.]

------------------Tznius-Clothing----------------

Wearing red colored clothing:
See above in the Yoreh Deah section Halacha 24!

---

[86] Michaber E.H. 21:2 and Rambam Issurei Biya 21:17 "It is forbidden for a married woman, **or single girl**, to walk in public with uncovered hair."; The term single written above refers to a widow or divorcee, and they must cover their hair even when single: Beis Shmuel 21:5; Chelkas Mechokeik 21/2; Bach 21; Beir Heiytiv 21:5; Degul Merivava 21; Based on Yerushalmi Kesubos Halacha 1 who states that once a woman was married, she does not uncover her hair even if she became divorced or widowed prior to having marital relations

The reason: The reason even a widow or divorcee must cover her hair is due to Daas Yehudis, the laws of Tznius that the Jewish people accepted upon themselves. [see next] Perhaps one can also suggest based on Kaballah, that just as a married woman must cover her hair in order to quash the Gevuros and Tzimtzumim which can potentially nurture the Kelipos [see Likkutei Torah Emor 32a], so too regarding a once married woman.

[87] Igros Moshe E.H. 1:57; Yabia Omer E.H. 4:3 based on M"A 75:3 and Shvus Yaakov 103 [Vetzaruch Iyun on his proofs from the M"A and Shvus Yaakov which are all dealing with a Besula and not an Almana or Gerusha!]

[88] The reason: While all agree that a married woman is Biblically required to cover her hair, due to Daas Moshe, a divorcee or widow is only required to cover her hair due to Daas Yehudis, which is a Rabbinical obligation of Tznius. [Igros Moshe ibid]

[89] Igros Moshe E.H. 1:57; 4:32

[90] The reason: As there is a doubt as to whether the Mitzvah of covering the hair for a married woman is a positive Biblical command or a negative command [i.e. prohibition]. [Igros Moshe ibid based on his understanding of Rashi and Ritva] The practical ramification of whether it is a positive or negative command is regarding if one may be lenient in a situation that guarding the command will cause one a loss of 20% of their income. If the matter is a command and not a prohibition, then one may be lenient in such a case. [See Rama 656:1] Accordingly, by a married woman there is no room to be lenient, as Safek Deoraisa Lechumra, and we must suspect for the approach that it is a prohibition. However, by a Rabbinical command we may be lenient, as Safek Derabanon Lekula. [Igros Moshe ibid]

[91] Igros Moshe E.H. 1:57

[92] Igros Moshe E.H. 4:32

The reason: As this is considered a great need, and is no less of a consideration of losing 20% of one's income, in which case one may be lenient.

[93] Yabia Omer E.H. 4:3; Dibros Eliyahu 9:157; Michzei Eliyahu 120; Lev Avraham Weinfeld 107

[94] The reason: As a) In truth covering the hair is a prohibition and is not a positive command. And b) The allowance of giving up a positive command if it costs one more than 20% of his income is only relevant to a command that does not have an action, and that is not connect with a prohibition. [See Yabia Omer ibid]

------------------Yichud----------------
10. May a man and a group of women be alone together?[95]

*Important note: There are several circumstances that can break a Yichud prohibition between a man and women, such as a Shomer, child, wife/husband in area. Pesach Pasuach to public, etc. The following law does not come to negate any of these valid Yichud breakers, and exclusively refers to a case that other Yichud breakers are not in place, and if the fact that many women are present can be a Yichud breaker in its own right.

A. Stringent approach-Sephardim:[96]

It is [Rabbinically[97]] forbidden for a man to be alone with a group of women [irrelevant of number, even 100, and so is the ruling of the Sephardim[98]].[99] [This applies whether the man is a Jew, or gentile, and applies even if there are gentiles amongst the group of women.[100]]

B. Lenient approach-Ashkenazim:

Some Poskim[101] rule it is Rabbinically forbidden for a single man to be alone even with a group of many women, as stated above. However, other Poskim[102] rule that a man be alone with many women, so long as the man is not accustomed to work with women.[103] [Practically, it is best to initially be stringent and apply one of the other Yichud breakers, although in a time of need, one may be lenient.[104]]

How many women is "many"?[105] The definition of "many women" is defined as no less than three women. [Thus, even according to the lenient opinion, it is forbidden for a man to be alone with two women.[106] The above number of three women, suffices during the day while one is in the city, however, at night, or when traveling out of the city, one is to initially require there to be four women present, as explained in the Q&A section.]

Qualifications of the above allowance: As stated above, even according to the lenient opinion, it is only permitted for a man to be alone with a group of women if the man is not accustomed to work with women [as defined in the Q&A]. [Likewise, it only applies if he is not overly acquainted with all the women in the group.[107]] If, however, the man does work with women [or is overly acquainted with all of them], then it is forbidden according to all. [Some Poskim[108] rule that the above leniency applies even if the man, or

---

[95] See Even Haezer 22:5; Dvar Halacha 10:1-2; Nitei Gavriel 21; "The Laws of Yichud" [Dubov] 1:20

[96] Michaber E.H. 22:5; 1st opinion in Tur 22; Rambam Issurei Biyah 22:8; Tosafos Kiddushin 82a; Dvar Halacha ibid in name of following Rishonim and Achronim: Ramban, Ritva, Semak, Aguda, Kol Bo, Mordechai in name of Riy, Rashal, Chida; Taharas Yisrael 22:15; Maharsham 3:152; 1st opinion in the following Poskim: Levush 22, Chochmas Adam 126:20, Kitzur SHU"A 152:3, Aruch Hashulchan 22

[97] See Pischeiy Teshuvah 22:4 in name of Shev Yaakov 19 that Biblical Yichud is only one with one; Nitei Gavriel 21 footnote 14

[98] So is ruling of Michaber ibid, and the Sephardim accepted upon themselves the rulings of Maran; Heard from Harav Yaakov Yosef Z"l; Nitei Gavriel ibid

[99] The reason: As Nashim Daatan Kalos and can come to sin even if there are many women there. [See Rashi Kiddushin 80b]

[100] Noda Beyehuda E.H. Kama 69, brought in Pischeiy Teshuvah 22:4; Shevet Halevi 5:202; See Nitei Gavriel 21:5

Other opinions: Some Poskim rule that if one of the women is a gentile, then it is permitted for the man and group of women to be alone. [Erech Shaiy 22:5; See Shev Yaakov 19, brought in Pischeiy Teshuvah 22:4; Dvar Halacha 10:2]

[101] Poskim ibid in A; There are many Ashkenazi Poskim, Rishonim and Achronim [recorded in previous footnotes], who either rule like this opinion, or record it equally with the second opinion brought next. Hence, this opinion also has weight even for those who follow the rulings of the Rama, brought next.

[102] Opinion in Rama ibid; 2nd opinion in Tur 22 in name of Rashi Kiddushin 82a; Bach 22, brought in Chelkas Mechokeik 22:8; Tosafos Riy Hazakein Kiddushin 80b; Semag Lavin 126; Rashba 1:1175; Meiri Kiddushin ibid; Tosafos Rosh; Ovadia Bartenura; Mahariy Levi 18; Divrei Chaim 2:16; Divrei Malikeil 4:102; 2nd opinion in the following Poskim: Levush 22, Chochmas Adam 126:20, Kitzur SHU"A 152:3, Aruch Hashulchan 22

[103] The reason: As the women are embarrassed to sin in front of the others, as certainly the man will not sin with all the women, and thus there is fear that the matter will become publicized. [See Rosh ibid; Poskim ibid]

[104] Taharas Yisrael 22:15; Maharsham 3:152; Igros Moshe E.H. 4:65-14; Shevet Halevi 3:183; Nitei Gavriel 21:2; "The Laws of Yichud" [Dubov] 1:20

[105] Chelkas Mechokeik 22:8; See also Beis Shmuel 22:8

[106] Mishneh Kiddushin 80b; This applies even if the man if Kosher [Rashba 1:1178; Meiri Kiddushin 80b] and even if the women are modest. [Yad Rameh Kiddushin ibid; Nitei Gavriel 21:1]

[107] Chochmas Adam 126:4 regarding Libo Gas Ba; Dvar Halacha 10:4 that if he is not overly acquainted with even one of the women, even though he is acquainted with the remaining women, then it is permitted.

[108] Dvar Halacha 10:2-3 in name Rashba, Radbaz; See there for other opinions

women, are not modest [i.e. Parutz], and thus it is permitted even with a gentile man, or with women who dress immodestly.]

Summary

Sephardim:
It is forbidden for a Sephardi man to be alone with a group of women, or a group of Sephardi women to be alone with a man, unless one of the valid Yichud breakers are in place.

Ashkenazim:
Yichud of man and two women: It is forbidden for any man to be alone with two women, unless one of the valid Yichud breakers are applicable.
Yichud of man and three women or more: In a time of need, one may be lenient to allow a man who does not work with women for his occupation, to be alone with three women, even if no other Yichud breakers are applicable. However, at night, or on the road outside of the city, it is initially best to have four women present.

Q&A

What is the definition of a man who works with women?
This matter is unclear from the Poskim. Some[109] explain that it applies to anyone who has a job with female clientele, coworkers, or employees, of which he deals with on a constant basis. [Thus, a bus driver or taxi driver, and many other jobs today, would be excluded from the above allowance.] Others[110], however, limit this definition only to a man whose main clientele is specifically women, such as a jeweler, or man who works in a female clothing store. [Accordingly, a bus driver, or taxi driver, is included in the above allowance.] One who is defined as "working with woman" may not be alone with a group of women who he is not acquainted with.[111]

How many women must be present at night, or during travel?
Even according to the lenient opinion, some Poskim[112] rule that it is only permitted to be with three women during the day, and only when in the city. However, at night, or during travel, three women does not suffice. Rather, in such a case, there needs to be four women present.[113] However, some Poskim[114] rule that at night it is forbidden for a man to be alone with any number of women, even according to the lenient opinion above. Other Poskim[115] however suggest that even at night, or on the road, three women suffice. Practically, one may be lenient in a time of need, even if there are only three women present.[116]

May a group of women/girls have a male bus/cab driver?[117]
In any situation in which there aren't other Yichud breakers in place [i.e. husband in city; other men on bus; daytime and there is traffic], then it is forbidden for Sephardi women to be on the bus alone with a

---

[109] See Dvar Halacha 10:7
[110] Nitei Gavriel 22:3
[111] Nitei Gavriel 22:2 footnote 4 in name of Rashba 1178; Chidushim Kadmonim on Kiddushin ibid; Toras Hayichud 3:16; See however Minchas Ish 3:11
[112] See Rama 22:5 regarding a woman being with many men, that at night or during travel, we are more stringent; So rules regarding travel: Pnei Yehoshua Kiddushin 80b; So rules regarding night: Tosefes Chaim E.H. 22; See Igros Moshe E.H. 4:65-20 who leans to permit even three at night, although concludes to be stringent unless it is a time of need; Nitei Gavriel 21:7
[113] Pnei Yehoshua ibid regarding travel [however, not regarding night]; Tosefes Chaim E.H. 22 regarding night; Dvar Halacha 10:6 regarding night; See Nitei Gavriel 21:7 footnote 18
[114] Bach 22 that so applies even according to Rashi ibid; Pnei Yehoshua ibid regarding night; Misgeres Hashulchan 152:8
[115] Divrei Malkiel 4:102; Igros Moshe E.H. 4:65-20; Implication of Beis Yehuda E.H. 13; Dvar Halacha 10:6 regarding on the road that so is implied from Rameh, Rashal, Taz, and Chochmas Adam, however regarding night he is stringent to require 4; See Shevet Halevi 5:202; Nitei Gavriel ibid
[116] Igros Moshe ibid; Nitei Gavriel 21:7 is lenient in a time of need to suffice with three women even at night
[117] Heard from Harav Yaakov Yosef Z"l based on the above rulings; See also Nitei Gavriel 21:3 that if the drivers wife is present, Yichud is broken, and 21:4 that if one of the woman's husband is present, Yichud is broken,

single man, and it is likewise forbidden for a Sephardi man to be alone with women. Likewise, initially, even Ashkenazi women are to be stringent.[118] However, in a time of need, Ashkenazi women may be lenient so long as there are at least four women on the bus at all times, and so is the accustomed practice. Thus, while a group of at least four Ashkenazi women may be lenient to hire a male driver to take them somewhere, Sephardi women, or a Sephardi bus driver, may not do so unless they prearrange another Yichud breaker to take effect. Thus, by organized trips that will be traveling late at night, or early morning, or through deserted areas, it is best for them to arrange that either the driver's wife comes with them [if they are Jewish], or that other men be on the bus.

May a man sleep in a home of only women?
Initially, one is not to do so. However, in a time of need, one may be lenient if there are at least four women present in the home, and the man does not work with women, and is not overly acquainted with all of them.[119]

11. Yichud between a brother and sister:[120]

Some Poskim[121] rule it is permitted for a brother and sister to remain alone together in the same room on a **temporary** basis.[122] [This applies whether to a maternal or paternal sister.[123]] Other Poskim[124] rule it is forbidden for a brother and sister to remain together in Yichud even temporarily. Practically, the main ruling follows the lenient opinion, and so is the custom of all Jewry.[125] Nevertheless, one who is stringent to not have Yichud with a sibling of opposite gender, is blessed.[126] This especially applies in a promiscuous generation [and to children who are going through puberty during their pubescent and prepubescent years[127]].[128] [Some Poskim[129], however, rule that a sibling who is known to be promiscuous may not share even temporary Yichud with a sibling if opposite gender.] According to all opinions, it is Rabbinically[130] forbidden to have Yichud with a sibling of opposite gender on a permanent basis.[131] The

---

[118] As a) we suspect for the first opinion initially; b) Perhaps a bus driver is defined as "Isko Im Nashim" and is hence forbidden even according to the lenient opinion.
[119] See Beis Yehuda E.H. 13
[120] See Nitei Gavriel Yichud 3; The Laws of Yichud [Dubov] p. 9
[121] Rav Assi in Kiddushin 81b "A man may have Yichud with his sister and live with his mother"; Yerushalmi Sotah 1b; Chelkas Mechokei E.H. 20:9, 21:1; Beis Shmuel 22:1 [unlike 20:14]; Rashal in Yam Shel Shomo Kiddushin 27; Perisha 22:3; Kitzur Piskeiy Rosh Kiddushin 24; Semak 99; Ran Kiddushin ibid; Mishneh Limelech Sotah 1; Chochmas Adam 126:12; Chikrei Lev E.H. 6 and 17; Avnei Nezer 2:233; Aruch Hashulchan 22:2; Maharsham Mafteichos 76; Nidchei Yisrael [of Chofetz Chaim] 24:6; Nachalas David 23; Erech Shaiy E.H. 22 based on Zohar; Misgeres Hashulchan 152:1
[122] The reason: Although a sister is an Erva, nonetheless, the Sages [Yuma 69b; Sanhedrin 64] removed the inclination for relatives such as one's sister, and hence permitted temporarily living together. [Tosafus Harosh Kiddushin ibid; Hamakneh, Rashash and Pnei Yehoshua Kiddushin ibid; See Eiyn Yitzchak E.H. 8 and Nitei Gavriel 3 footnote 1 and 2]
[123] Dvar Halacha Hosafos 2; Igros Moshe 4:64-1; Kinyan Torah 5:126; Nitei Gavriel 3:11 footnote 21; See however Toras Hayichud in name of Rav SZ"A
[124] Beis Shmuel E.H. 20:14 "And so too Yichud is forbidden" [unlike 22:1]; Radbaz 7:32; Yosef Ometz 22; Od Yosef Chaiy Shoftim 3 "Although there are Poskim who permit Yichud with a sister, the main opinion follows that it is forbidden, especially in this promiscuous generation."; Shmuel in Kiddushin 81b [regarding all Arayos, including mother]; Implication of Rambam, Tur and Michaber who all omit the allowance of Yichud with a sister even though they mention the allowance of a mother [so leans to understand Beis Shmuel ibid; See Eiyn Yitzchak E.H. 8 and Nitei Gavriel 3 footnote 1 for an analysis on their opinion]; Implication of Kitzur SHU"A 152:1 who omits a sister
[125] The vast majority of Poskim [brought in footnote above] all rule it is permitted and that so is the main opinion, and so is the custom; Nitei Gavriel 3:1
[126] Chelkas Mechokei E.H. 21:1; Piskeiy Harosh; Semag L.S. 126; Rashal ibid; Chochmas Adam ibid; Misgeres Hashulchan ibid
[127] Heard from a child psychologist with decades of experience in dealing with incest and molestation cases that occur within the family
[128] Poskim brought in Nitei Gavriel 3 footnote 4
[129] See Nitei Gavriel 3:12; The Laws of Yichud [Dubov] p. 10 footnote 25
[130] Is this prohibition Biblical or Rabbinical? This prohibition is merely Rabbinical. [See Beis Shmuel ibid; Piskeiy Harosh 4:22; Nitei Gavriel 3 footnote 2]
[131] All Poskim ibid; Yerushalmi ibid; Rashi Kiddushin ibid in explanation of opinion of Rav Assi
The reason: The inclination for a mother or daughter is completely dormant and Yichud is hence allowed even permanently. However, the Yetzer for a sister although dormant is still possible, and hence the Sages limited the Yichud allowance to only a temporary basis. [See Rashi Kiddushin ibid; Pnei Yehoshua ibid; Tosafus Rosh Kiddushin ibid] Alternatively, it is not possible to decree against living alone with a mother or daughter, as opposed to a sister. [Erech Shaiy ibid]

Poskim debate the exact definition of permanent in this regard, as explained in the Q&A, although the general consensus is no more than thirty days.

> **Summary:**
> Temporary Yichud is permitted between siblings. It is thus permitted for them to live alone on a temporary basis. It is, however, forbidden for a brother and sister to live alone on a permanent basis. Those who are stringent to avoid even temporary Yichud with siblings are blessed.
>
> **Advice to parents:**[132]
> Parents are to take heed to try to avoid situations in which their children of opposite genders remain alone together for extended periods of time. This especially applies towards children of pubescent, or prepubescent age. Children should be instructed that they are never allowed to lock the door of their room when they are there with a sibling of the opposite gender.

12. Yichud with a woman and her mother/daughter in-law:[133]

It is permitted to be in Yichud with a woman and her mother in-law or daughter in-law.[134] [This refers to a woman's husband's mother, her son's wife.[135] It is permitted to be in Yichud with such a pair even at night.[136] This allowance applies even if the man is accustomed to being around women and feels comfortable around them.[137] This allowance applies even if the man is well acquainted with the women.[138] This allowance applies even if the man or woman is a Parutz [promiscuous man].[139] This allowance applies even if the two women share a great relationship.[140] This allowance applies even to live together on a permanent basis.[141] However, if the daughter in-law is no longer married to the woman's son, such as due to death or divorce, Yichud is forbidden.[142] Likewise, a future daughter in-law who is not yet married, does not have this allowance apply.[143]]

> - Practical examples: 1) It is permitted for a man to remain in the home of his friend even when his friend is out of town, if his friend's wife and the wife's mother in-law is at the home. 2) It is permitted by a Chupas Niddah for a Chasan and Kallah to remain together in their home if the Chasan's mother is present. This applies even at night, when they go to sleep. 3) It is permitted for a man to stay alone by his grandmother's home even if his aunt [Uncles wife], who is the daughter in-law of his grandmother, is present.

---

[132] Heard from a child psychologist with decades of experience in dealing with incest and molestation cases that occur within the family
[133] Michaber E.H. 22:10; Kiddushin 81a; See Taharas Yisrael 22:23; Nitei Gavriel 24:1; The Laws of Yichud p. 60
[134] The reason: As these women hate each other and will never cover up for each other. [Michaber ibid]
[135] Zechor Leavraham 10; Implication of Parach Mateh Ahron 2:95; Pischeiy Teshuvah 22:11
[136] Taz 22:9; Rashal Kiddushin 4:24; Dvar Halacha 5:23-24; Poskim in Nitei Gavriel 24:16 footnote 26; The laws of Yichud ibid
Other opinions: Some Poskim rule that at night two Shomrim are required. [Beis Moshe 22:14, brought in Nitei Gavriel ibid]
[137] Beis Shmuel 22:14; Levush 22; Dvar Halacha 5:23-24
[138] Dvar Halacha 5:23-24
[139] Taharas Yisrael 22:23; Dvar Halacha 5:23-24; Tzitz Eliezer 6:40; However, See Shevet Halevi 5:204
[140] Minchas Ish 11:28; Nitei Gavriel 24:10
[141] Perach Mateh Ahron 95; Dvar Halacha 5:23-24
[142] Dvar Halacha 5:22
[143] Nitei Gavriel 24 footnote 1

------------------Wedding------------------
13. Must a Kallah cover her hair during the Chuppah/wedding:[144]

The opinions: A woman is required to cover her hair from the time she is married and onwards.[145] It is debated amongst Poskim as to the exact definition of marriage in this regard; Does it refer to the Kiddushin, Chuppah, the Yichud room, or the actual culmination of the marriage later on in the privacy of their home? Aside for the debate brought in Poskim[146] as to what is the defining act of Nessuin, which makes a woman considered to be a Nesuah, in addition, there is dispute in Poskim[147] as to whether the covering of the hair is dependent on the status of Nessuin or not. The following are the opinions on this matter:

1. Chuppah: Some Poskim[148] rule that Nessuin is defined as the time that the Kallah stands under the Chuppah, and thus from that time and onwards she is considered married, [and is required to cover her hair like any married woman. According to this approach, seemingly a Kallah must come to her Chuppah wearing a head covering, such as a Sheitel.[149]] Furthermore, some Poskim[150] rule that the legal definition of Nessuin is irrelevant regarding the obligation to cover the hair, as this obligation begins from the Kiddushin, and today that the Kiddushin is performed under the Chuppah, she therefore becomes obligated to cover her hair from that point and onwards.

2. Yichud: Other Poskim[151] rule that Nessuin is defined as the time that the Chasan and Kallah remain together in privacy for the first time after the Chuppah, which is formally known as the Yichud room. Likewise, some Poskim[152] rule that the obligation to cover the hair begins from the Nessuin and not from the Kiddushin. [According to these joint opinions, from the Yichud room and onwards she is considered married and is required to cover her hair like any

---

[144] See Admur 339:8; Michaber and Rama E.H. 55:1; Beir Heiytiv 21:5; Pischeiy Teshuvah 21:2; Shulchan Haeizer 5:5; Nitei Gavriel Nissuin 2:58; Koveitz Oholei Torah 822-829; 1128 p. 116; Koveitz Hearos Kfar Chabad 160-162

[145] Admur 75:4; Michaber E.H. 21:2 as explained in Beis Shmuel 21:5; Michaber 115:4

[146] As brought in Michaber and Rama E.H. 55:1 and the coming footnotes, the opinions of the definition of Nissuin varies from: 1) The bedecking; 2) The Chuppah; 3) Bringing her into one's home, even without Yichud; 4) Yichud that is fit for Biya.

[147] Some Poskim rule even an Arussa must cover her head. [Chavos Yair 196; Teshuvas Yitzchak Halevi [brother of Taz] 9, brought in Beir Heiytiv 21:5; Rav Akiva Eiger E.H. 21 and Tinyana 79; Beis Meir 21; Mayim Rabim 30; Erech Shaiy Apei Zutri; M"B 75:11] Other Poskim rule only a Nesua must cover her hair. [Shvus Yaakov 1:103, brought in Beir Heiytiv 21:5; Masas Moshe E.H. 2:7; Yeshuos Yaakov E.H. 21:9; Shita Mekubetzes Kesubos 15b] Other Poskim imply that only after Beilas Mitzvah must she cover her hair. [Chasam Sofer Y.D. 195]

[148] 1st opinion in Admur 339:8; 2nd opinion in Rama E.H. 55:1; Beis Yosef 61 in name of Orchos Chaim in name of Ittur; Rosh Sukkah 2:8; See Chelkas Mechokeik 55:7 and Aruch Hashulchan 55:7-9

Badekening: Some Poskim rule that Nessuin is defined as the time that the Kallah has the sheet placed over her head, formally known as Badekening, and thus from that time and onwards she is considered married. [3rd opinion in Rama E.H. 55:1; Tosafus Yuma 13b] According to this approach, seemingly a Kallah must start wearing a head covering, such as a Sheitel, from her Badekening. However, her the Mishneh [Kesubos 2:1, brought in Chelkas Mechokeik 21:2] explicitly states that a Kallah comes out with her "Hinuma" and her hair uncovered, and hence we clearly see that this was not the stage that required covering the hair. Now, although one can argue that perhaps this only applied until the Chasan that placed the veil over her head, and once he does so, she must cover her hair [see Aruch Hashulchan 55:10] this only applied in previous times when Kiddushin was done before the Badekening. However, today that the Badekening is done before the Kiddushin and Chuppah, this form of Nissuin is no longer applicable according to any opinion, as there is no Nissuin before Kiddushin. [Chelkas Mechokeik 55:9; Aruch Hashulchan 55:10]

[149] The following Poskim emphasize a Nesua must cover her hair even if she is still a Besula: Shvus Yaakov 1:103 [in his full wording, not brought in Beir Heiytiv 21:5] that a Nesua must cover her hair even if she is still a Besula; Yehoshua 89; Masas Moshe E.H. 2:7; Yeshuos Yaakov E.H. 21:1; Shita Mekubetzes Kesubos 15b; Yad Eliyahu 79; Degul Merivava E.H. 21; This would certainly apply according to all Poskim brought in next footnote

[150] Chavos Yair 196; Teshuvas Yitzchak Halevi [brother of Taz] 9, brought in Beir Heiytiv 21:5; Rav Akiva Eiger E.H. 21 and Tinyana 79; Beis Meir 21; Mayim Rabim 30; Erech Shaiy 21; Apei Zutri; M"B 75:11; See Admur 75:4 and Michaber E.H. 21:2 that "an **Eishes Ish** is obligated to cover her hair" which implies even an Arussa!

[151] The following Poskim rule it must be Yichud that is fit for Biya: 2nd opinion in Admur 339:8; Michaber E.H. 55:1; Rambam Ishus 10; The following Poskim rule that the Yichud is not needed to be fit for Biya, and it suffices to bring her into one's home: 1st opinion in Rama E.H. 55:1 and Ran Kesubos 1a; Chelkas Mechokeik 55:6

[152] Shvus Yaakov 1:103 [in his full wording, not brought in Beir Heiytiv 21:5] that a Nesua must cover her hair even if she is still a Besula; Yehoshua 89; Masas Moshe E.H. 2:7; Yeshuos Yaakov E.H. 21:1; Shita Mekubetzes Kesubos 15b; Yad Eliyahu 79; Degul Merivava E.H. 21; Shvus Yaakov 1:103 [in his full wording, not brought in Beir Heiytiv 21:5] that a Nesua must cover her hair even if she is still a Besula; Yehoshua 89; Masas Moshe E.H. 2:7; Yeshuos Yaakov E.H. 21:1; Shita Mekubetzes Kesubos 15b; Yad Eliyahu 79; Degul Merivava E.H. 21; This would certainly apply according to all Poskim brought in previous footnotes who hold from Eirusin and onwards she must cover her hair

married woman. According to this approach, seemingly a Kallah must come out of the Yichud room wearing a head covering, such as a Sheitel.[153]]

3. Morning after: Some Poskim[154] rule that regardless of the legal definition of Nessuin, the obligation of covering the hair only begins when the Chasan and Kallah culminate their marriage after the wedding in the privacy of their home.[155] According to this approach, a Kallah must only begin wearing a head covering, the morning after the wedding.

The final ruling and custom: Some Poskim[156] maintain that the main Halachic opinion regarding the definition of Nessuin follows the 2nd approach brought above, that a Kallah is considered a Nesua only from the time of the Yichud. Nonetheless, even in their opinion, we suspect for all the definitions of Nessuin, including that she is considered a Nesua from the time of the Chuppah.[157] Likewise, the majority of Poskim[158] rule that a Kallah must begin covering her hair at the very least from the point she is defined as a Nesua and onwards. Accordingly, a Kallah should come to her Chuppah wearing a head covering, and certainly should be wearing a Sheitel after exiting the Yichud room. Nonetheless, the widespread custom amongst Jewry is not like this approach. Although, some are particular even today for the Kallah to attend the Chuppah in her Sheitel, and even more are accustomed to have the Kallah come out of the Yichud room already wearing a head covering[159], nonetheless, this is not the mainstream approach. The vast majority of Kallahs follow the third opinion, to only begin wearing a head covering from the morning after the wedding, and not beforehand.[160] Despite this, most Rabbanim[161] of Anash rule like the

---

[153] The following Poskim emphasize a Nesua must cover her hair even if she is still a Besula: Shvus Yaakov 1:103 [in his full wording, not brought in Beir Heiytiv 21:5] that a Nesua must cover her hair even if she is still a Besula; Masas Moshe E.H. 2:7; Yeshuos Yaakov E.H. 21:9; Shita Mekubetzes Kesubos 15b; Degul Merivava E.H. 21; Chavos Yair 196; Teshuvas Yitzchak Halevi [brother of Taz] 9, brought in Beir Heiytiv 21:5; Rav Akiva Eiger E.H. 21 and Tinyana 79; Beis Meir 21; Mayim Rabim 30; Erech Shaiy Apei Zutri; M"B 75:11; See Admur 75:4 and Michaber E.H. 21:2 that "an **Eishes Ish** is obligated to cover her hair" which implies an Arussa!

[154] Implication of Chasam Sofer Y.D. 195 that we cover the hair only after Beilas Mitzvah [however see Kinyan Torah 2:43 that this refers to the shaving of the head and not the head covering]; Rosh Kesubos 2:3 that hair may be uncovered the first day after Chuppah, brought in Mahariy Levi 9; Masas Moshe E.H. 2:7; See Sefer Hachaim 263; Beis Shearim Y.D. 273; See Halichos Bas Yisrael p. 80; Nitei Gavriel 34:1 and 7

The opinion of the Shvus Yaakov: Some Melaktim mention that a possible way of learning the Shvus Yaakov 1:103, brought in Beir Heiytiv 21:5, is that the matter is dependent on whether she is a Besula or Beula, however in truth, when looking in the actual words of the Shvus Yaakov ibid, he clearly writes that his discussion refers to an Arussa who is a Besula, and not a Nesua, in which case even if she is a Besula she must cover her hair. The Melaktim who wrote otherwise seemingly based their statement on the partial quote brought in the Beir Heiytiv ibid and not in the actual source. Nonetheless, the Shvus Yaakov ibid does testify to the custom that the Kallah goes with uncovered hair on the day of her Chuppah, which can be learned to imply like this approach, that until the next morning she does not have to cover her hair.

[155] The reason: Possibly the reason is because the covering of hair of a married woman is connected with the Mitzvah of Sotah, which is the source for the law of covering the hair, and since a woman cannot become a Sotah until after the Beilas Mitzvah, so too perhaps the covering of the hair obligation does not begin until then. [See Shvus Yaakov ibid *"She would go with uncovered hair the day of the wedding because there is no worry that she would be promiscuous on that day"*; See Koveitz Oholei Torah ibid] Another possible reason is because the entire obligation to cover the hair is based on the Biblical custom of Tzenius that our foremothers had, and on the fact that seeing a married women's uncovered hair is a rarity which can lead to forbidden thoughts. Thus, since on the day of the wedding it is accustomed of world Jewry to not cover the hair, this was never included in the original Biblical custom and obligation and does not cause bad thoughts. [See Mahariy levi ibid for a similar explanation justifying the allowance for the Kallah to not fully cover her hair after the Chuppah, as so is the custom, and therefore there is no Hirhur of men when this hair is uncovered, and therefore it does not need to be covered; See also Rebbe in Igros Kodesh 11:200, printed in Likkutei Sichos 8:285, that the main source for not requiring Besulos to cover the hair is because so is the custom from the time of Moshe, and the same can be applied regarding covering the hair only the day after the wedding]

[156] Beis Shmuel 55:5; Bach 55; Nitei Gavriel 58:5 footnote 6 that the main opinion is like the Michaber, that Yichud is Koneh; However see Admur 339:5 and M"A 339:11 that Chuppah is Koneh a Besula, and from the wording it is implied only that we suspect for the opinion of the Rambam that one needs Yichud to be Koneh, and not that the Rambam is the main opinion; The Rama 55:1 concludes that we do all the stages of Chuppah to cover all the opinions, and does not give any arbitration as to who the main opinion follows; See also M"A 55

[157] See Rama ibid; Admur ibid; Chelkas Mechokeik ibid

[158] Shvus Yaakov 1:103 [in his full wording, not brought in Beir Heiytiv 21:5]; Masas Moshe E.H. 2:7; Yeshuos Yaakov E.H. 21:9; Shita Mekubetzes Kesubos 15b; See Degul Merivava E.H. 21; Chavos Yair 196; Teshuvas Yitzchak Halevi [brother of Taz] 9, brought in Beir Heiytiv 21:5; Rav Akiva Eiger E.H. 21 and Tinyana 79; Beis Meir 21; Mayim Rabim 30; Erech Shaiy Apei Zutri; M"B 75:11

[159] See Nitei Gavriel 58:5 that the custom is to cover the hair after the Yichud room, and some do so already before the Chuppah;

[160] See article of Rav Hendel in Koveitz Oholei Torah ibid; Halichos Bas Yisrael p. 80; Nitei Gavriel 34:1; Rav Rafael Kahn stated to Rav Mundshine that the custom in Russia was to only cover the hair the next morning; Rav Yungreiss of the Eida Hachareidis acknowledged to Rav Mundshine that so is the Minhag; Rav Mundshine in his article states that so is the widespread custom of all Chassidic groups, including those of Hungarian descent, and that so is and was the widespread Chabad custom

Custom of Sephardim: The Sephardi custom is to only begin covering the hair the next morning. However, this is because they hold the main Kinyan of Nessuin is the Yichud [as rules Michaber 55:1] and they do not perform Yichud by the Chuppah. However, according to the Ashkenazi custom to perform Yichud by the Chuppah, they agree that Ashkenazim must come out of the Yichud room with covered hair. [See Yabia Omer1:8; Yechaveh Daas 5:62; Heard from Harav Yaakov Yosef]

[161] Rabbanim who are stringent: Rav Z.S. Dworkin [after Chuppah-brought in Nitei Gavriel 58 footnote 9; However Rav Mundshine writes that he heard from Rav Cheikin that Rav Dworkin ruled that only the next day a covering is needed; Likewise Rav Avraham Jaffee related that when

main opinion which requires the head to be covered either from the Chuppah, or at least from after the Yichud room. Practically, every Kallah is to ask her Rav for what she should do. It is worth noting the great blessing given in the Zohar for one who is scrupulous in covering the hair, and certainly being stringent in this matter helps give a great abundance of blessing to the couple and future children.

> **Summary:**
> According to the mainstream approach in Poskim, a Kallah is to cover her hair starting from under the Chuppah, or at the very least from after the Yichud room, and so is followed by many. Nonetheless, the widespread custom is to cover the hair only after the wedding, the next morning, and practically, each Kallah is to ask her Rav for guidance and direction in this matter.

14. How many people amongst the Minyan must eat bread in order to be able to recite Sheva Brachos?[162]

Sheva Brachos may only be recited after a meal in which a Chasan and Kallah are present if there is a Minyan of ten men above the age of Mitzvos in the room.[163] Of these ten men, a certain amount of them must have eaten bread during the meal in order to be allowed to recite Sheva Brachos.[164] However, the Talmud, Rishonim, and early Poskim do not express how many bread washers are needed during the meal, and we hence find a debate amongst the Poskim in this regard. The following are the opinions in this matter:

The opinions: Some Poskim[165] entertain that perhaps ten men must wash on bread during the meal in order to be allowed to recite Sheva Brachos. Other Poskim[166], however, rule that the criteria necessary to say Sheva Brachos is similar to that of saying a Zimun with Elokeinu, and hence it suffices to have seven

---

he got married in 1953, as a close student of Rav Dworkin, he asked him as to when his Kallah should begin covering her hair, and Rav Dworkin directed that the custom is to only cover the hair the next day after the Chuppah]; Rav Osdaba [from Chuppah]; Rav M.S. Ashkenazi and Rav Y.S. Yuroslavsky, brought in Hearos Ubiurim 713:23 [from Yichud room; Rav Ashkenazi states that so was the custom of all the Chassidishe families in Russia]; Rav Eliyahu Landa responded that the hair must be covered from the Yichud room and onwards, however not under the Chuppah, as the Mishneh says "Yotzeis Verosha parua"; Rav Yosef Yeshaya Braun argues vehemently against only covering the next day; See Koveitz Chasuna See Yabia Omer1:8; Yechaveh Daas 5:62; Heard from Harav Yaakov Yosef that Ashkenazim must cover the hair from after the Yichud room and onwards.

Rabbanim who are lenient: Rav Z.S. Dworkin, according to testimony of Rav Cheikin and Rav Jaffe; Rav Hendel of Migdal HaEmek, brought in Koveitz Oholei Torah ibid; Rav Y.K. Marlow, as testified by his son Rav Yossi Marlow, that by his own wedding his wife did not have her hair covered; Rav S.Z. Garelik of Kfar Chabad would perform Chuppah's with the hair of the Kallah uncovered [Heard from Rav Mondshine]

The custom of the Rebbetzin and Beis Harav: Some have a tradition that the custom followed in Beis Harav is that the Rebbetzins did not cover their hair until the next morning after the Chuppah. [Heard from Rav Y.L. Groner, that so is the tradition that he received, that his grandmother [from Beis Harav] did not cover her hair and that so was true regarding Rebbetzin Menucha Rachel.] However, there is clear testimony that the Rebbetzin Chaya Mushka covered her hair from Chuppah and onwards. [So proves article in Hearos Ubiurim 712; 825:65; 828:63 based on testimonies of people who heard this from the Rebbetzin herself, and that so was the custom of Rebbetzin Nechama Dina; However in in his early articles printed in Oholei Sheim, Rav Mondshine argued that the Rebbetzin only covered her hair the next day, as explained to him by Rav Nachman Rafael Kahn, or at the very most from after the Yichud room, but not under the Chuppah] Likewise, this was the directive she gave to the Gurary families who follow the tradition of Beis Harav, that the Kallahs should cover all their hair in the Yichud room and onwards, and so was practiced by Gurary family members. This clearly contradicts the above testimony of Rav Groner. [See Teshuros of Gurary family weddings; See Ohalei Torah ibid]

The Rebbe's approach: Some say that the Rebbe once inquired if the hair would be covered under the Chuppah [See Leket Shichichas Hapeia p. 30], although that the Rebbe answered people who asked that they should follow the Minhag Hamakom. Likewise, the Rebbe never made a public statement about this issue and was Misader Kiddushin for couples that had their hair uncovered under the Chuppah. [See Leket Shichichas Hapeia p. 30; Ohalei Torah ibid; Testimony of Rav Yehoshua Mondshine in Koveitz Ohalei Torah] A recent memoir has been published of in the name of Rav Nasan Gurary in which he testifies that the Rebbe told him in the midst of a Farbrengen that there is no Rav who would rule that you can cover the hair the next day, and that it does not need to be covered by the wedding. This testimony, however, has not been properly substantiated, and Rav Nasan Gurary himself does not remember exactly what the Rebbe said. [See Koveitz Hearos Ubiurim 1128 p. 116]

[162] See Pischeiy Teshuvah E.H. 62:8; Otzer Haposkim 17:18; Yabia Omer 3:11; Nitei Gavriel Nissuin chapter 102

[163] Michaber E.H. 62:4 *"Birchas Chasanim [i.e. Sheva Brachos] may not be recited after Birchas Hamazon unless ten adult men are present"*

[164] So is understood From the fact that Sheva Brachos may only be said after a meal over bread: See Michaber ibid who writes "Birchas Hamazon"; China Vichisda Kesubos 1 p. 112b; Shoel Vinishal 3:419 based on Tosafos Pesachim 102b; Otzer Haposkim 17:34; Shraga Hameir 1:58; Halacha Lemoshe 5; Nitei Gavriel ibid 102:1

[165] Pischeiy Teshuvah ibid in name of Zechor Leavraham

[166] Birchas Habayis 62:19; Shoel Umeishiv Telisa 1:198; Bireich Es Avraham 71:22; Leaning opinion of Pischeiy Teshuvah ibid in name of Zechor Leavraham that majority suffices

men present who washed on bread, and another three who ate other foods to an amount that requires an after blessing, in order to say the Sheva Brachos.[167] Other Poskim[168] imply that it suffices to have six men who washed on bread. Other Poskim[169] rule it suffices to have three people who washed on bread and another three who ate another food, and the other four do not have to eat at all. Other Poskim[170] rule that it suffices to have three people who washed on bread, and the remainder of the Minyan do not even have to eat anything at all.

The final ruling:[171] Practically, the custom is like the second opinion above, to follow the same laws as a Zimun with Elokeinu, and hence of the ten men, seven are to wash on bread and another three eat a Kezayis or Revius of another food or drink. All ten men must still be prior to reciting an after blessing over their foods at the time of Birchas Hamazon in order to be able to join. If one went ahead and recited an after blessing prior to Birchas Hamazon, then just as they no longer join for the Zimun of ten, so too they no longer join for the Sheva Brachos.[172] Nonetheless, it is not necessary that all ten men recite the after blessing at the same time, and some may do so after the communal Birchas Hamazon.[173]

Summary:
The laws of Sheva Brachos follow the same criteria as a Zimun of Elokeinu, and hence of the ten men, seven are required to wash on bread and another three to eat or drink at least a Kezayis or Revius of another food or beverage.

Q&A

Must the Panim Chadashos eat at the Sheva Brachos meal?[174]
There is no requirement for the Panim Chadashos to eat during the meal of Sheva Brachos, and hence so long as there are seven men who washed on bread, and three who ate other foods that require an after blessing, the Sheva Brachos may be recited [even if the Panim Chadashos simply stands nearby[175]]. [However, the guest must be someone honorable enough to the Baalei Hasimcha to make them feel rejoiced by his presence, and that they would give him food if he wanted.[176]]

Must the Chasan and Kallah wash on bread?[177]
The Chasan and Kallah are both to wash on bread during the meal in order to allow the Sheva Brachos to be recited.

May one who did not eat at the meal recite Sheva Brachos?[178]
Some Poskim[179] rule it is not necessary for the person saying the blessing to have eaten anything by the meal.[180] Other Poskim[181] rule that only those who ate bread during the meal may say the Sheva Brachos.

---

[167] Regarding the necessity to have seven men who washed and three who ate a Kezayios/Revius of other foods in order to recite Elokeinu by a Zimun-See: Admur 197:2; https://shulchanaruchharav.com/halacha/how-many-people-must-eat-to-make-a-zimun-of-ten-with-elokeinu/
The reason: As the Sages did not enact the saying of Sheva brachos unless a Zimun is recited with Hashem's name. [Birchas Habayis ibid]
[168] Leaning opinion of Pischeiy Teshuvah ibid in name of Zechor Leavraham that majority suffices; Pnei Yitzchak 1 Mareches Brachos 1 Kuf; See Yabia Omer 3:11 and Otzer Haposkim ibid who write they in truth intended to say 7 and not 6.
[169] Minchas Pitim 62; Poskim recorded in Otzer Haposkim ibid; Nitei Gavriel ibid footnote 6
[170] Halef Lecha Shlomo O.C .93; Poskim recorded in Otzer Haposkim ibid; Nitei Gavriel ibid footnote 7; See Pischeiy Teshuvah ibid in name of Zechor Leavraham who seems to question that perhaps not even a Zimun is required, and so long as ten people are in the room it suffices.
[171] Yabia Omer ibid; Sova Semachos 1:26; Nitei Gavriel ibid
[172] Nitei Gavriel 102:3; So rule regarding a Zimun: Admur 197:4; M"A 197:4; Elya Raba 197:6; M"B 197:9
[173] Nitei Gavriel 102:4; Sova Semachos p. 116; See Nessuin Kehilchasan p. 433 who questions this matter and as to whether all seven must recite Birchas Hamazon together
[174] Opinion in Rama 62:7; Ran Kesubos
[175] Chelkas Mechokeik 62:11
[176] Chelkas Mechokeik 62:11
[177] Halef Lecha Shlomo O.C .93; Tzitz Eliezer 13:99; Yabia Omer 6:9; See Kisvei Daas Kedoshim p. 84; Hanesuin Kehilchasa p. 532; Nitei Gavriel 102:5
Other opinions: Some write that a Chasan and Kallah are not required to wash on bread in order to recite Sheva Brachos. [Sova Semachos 1]
[178] See Nitei Gavriel 102:6
[179] Zechor Leavraham 2:2 questions this matter; Yaskil Avdi 8:20-28; Beir Moshe 2:118; Shraga Hameir 1:58; Rivivos Efraim 4:227
[180] The reason: So is proven from the fact that the Panim Chadashos is not required to eat.
[181] China Vechisda Kesubos 1 112b; Pnei Yitzchak 1 Mareches Brachos 1 Kuf; Cheshev Haeifod 1:9; 2:3; Yabia Omer 3:11-7

> Practically, the widespread custom is to [only] allow those who ate something during the meal to say Sheva Brachos, even if they did not eat bread.[182]

---------------Kesuba----------------

15. Using a Kesuba of a Besula for a Beula:[183]

The Sages established different Kesuba sums for a woman who is a Besula versus a Beula.[184] The Ikkur Kesuba of a Besula is 200 Zuz, while the Ikkur Kesuba of a Beula is 100 Zuz.[185] The following will discuss whether one may use the Kesuba of a Besula for a Kallah who is not a Besula.

Without knowledge of the Chasan: [It is forbidden for a Kallah who is not a Besula to withhold this information from her Chasan and have him obligate himself to a Kesuba of a Besula.[186]] If this occurred, the [entire[187]] Kesuba is invalid.[188] Accordingly, a new Kesuba of 100 Zuz must be written as soon as the Chasan is informed.[189] [Nonetheless, the Kiddushin remains valid even in such a case.[190]]

With knowledge of the Chasan: Some Poskim[191] rule that if a Chasan is informed that his Kallah is not a Besula, he may nevertheless choose to obligate himself to the Kesuba of a Besula, and hence use a regular Besula Kesuba for the wedding.[192] According to this approach, there is no obligation for a Chasan to inform the Misader Kiddushin, or anyone else for that matter, of the status of his Kallah if she is not a Beula, so long as he agrees to obligate himself to the Kesuba of a Besula.[193] However, this only applies if the Kallah did not become prohibited to a Kohen[194], otherwise, a Kesuba of a Beula must be used.[195] [Nonetheless, initially, it is proper for every couple to use the form of Kesuba that was established for

---

[182] Nitei Gavriel ibid; See Beir Moshe ibid

[183] See Eiyn Yitzchak E.H. 1:67; Igros Moshe O.C. 4:118

[184] Who is a Beula? A Beula includes any woman who was previously intimate with a man in a way that she is no longer considered a virgin, whether in or out of wedlock, and whether willingly or due to rape. Furthermore, even if she was never intimate with a man, but lost her virginity due to an accident [i.e. Mukas Eitz], she is considered a Beula in this regard and is to receive a Kesuba of 100 Mana. [Michaber E.H. 67:5; Kesubos 11b]

[185] Michaber E.H. 66:6; Mishneh Kesubos 10b

[186] Implication of Michaber E.H. 67:5; Eiyn Yitzchak ibid 15; Igros Moshe ibid; Kovetz Teshuvos of Rav Elyashiv 1:159; Even Yisrael 9:133
The reason: As the Kesuba is invalid, and it is forbidden to live with a person without a Kesuba. [Eiyn Yitzchak ibid; Rav Elyashiv ibid; See however Even Yisrael 9:133] Likewise, not telling the Chasan is considered Gneivas Daas. [Rav Elyashiv ibid; Even Yisrael ibid]
Other opinions: Some Poskim give room for the Chasan to not be informed that his Kallah is not a Besula. [See Maharsham 7:152 who gave such a Heter in a time of need, under specific circumstances and conditions; See Even Yisrael 9:133 that it is not considered to be living without a Kesuba, as the Chasan is unaware of its invalidation and will be deterred to easily divorce her]

[187] This includes both the Ikkur and Tosefes Kesuba. [Darkei Moshe 67; Beis Shmuel 67:4; See Chelkas Mechokeik 67:5 who questions why the Tosefes Kesuba is also invalid]

[188] Michaber E.H. 67:5; Kesubos 11b
The reason: As this is a classic case of Mekach Taus [a transaction performed under false pretenses], in which case we invalidate the obligation. [Beis Shmuel ibid]

[189] Rama 68:9; Tur 68; Rambam

[190] Implication of Rama ibid, Rambam and Tur; Michaber E.H. 39:5 that if he accepted the Mum after discovery, the Kiddushin is valid; Haflah in Kuntrus Achron; Eiyn Yitzchak ibid 2-15 [See there for a thorough analysis on this subject, and his conclusion that according to all the Kiddushin is valid]; Rav Elyashiv ibid; See Even Yisrael ibid
Other opinions: Some rule that the Kiddushin is invalid and needs to be redone. [Tosafus Kesubos 11, brought in Beis Shmuel 68:24; See Eiyn Yitzchak ibid]

[191] Igros Moshe O.C. 4:118; Heard in name of Rav Z.S. Dworkin regarding Baalei Teshuvah weddings, although this matter has not been confirmed

[192] Writing the term "Deoraisa": The term Deoraisa written in a Kesuba of a Besula refers to the coinage of the sum obligated, and not to the idea that the Kesuba of a Besula is Biblical. [See Rama 66:6; Beis Shmuel 66:14 and Chelkas Mechokeik 66:24 in name of Rosh] Thus, it is permitted to write this term even if she is a Beula.
Writing the word Besula: Tzaruch Iyun regarding how we can allow the term Besula to be written if it is a lie. See however Maharsham 7:152; Igros Moshe ibid.
If the Kallah was intimate with the Chasan: Some Poskim rule that when she lost her Besulim to the Chasan, then certainly the Kesuba of a Besula is to initially be written. [Shemesh Tzedakah E.H. 5, brought in Pischeiy Teshuvah E.H. 177:3; Igros Moshe ibid and E.H. 1:101; See Tur 177; Rambam Naara 8:3 and Mishneh Lamelech there] However, other Poskim rule she is to have a Kesuba of a Beula written. [Noda Beyehuda Tinyana 33; Pischeiy Teshuvah ibid; Chasam Sofer E.H. 1:133]

[193] Igros Moshe ibid extends this and says that it is even forbidden to tell them, as it serves no purpose.

[194] A woman becomes invalid to a Kohen if she had relations with a gentile, or with a relative, or any man, that she is forbidden to marry, or a Chalal. [See Michaber E.H. 6:8]

[195] Igros Moshe ibid; See Levush 66:2; Otzer Haposkim 66:145
The reason: In order to inform the public that she is invalid to a Kohen, so she does not come to marry a Kohen if she becomes a widow.

their status, and hence a Kesuba of a Beula should be used in such a case, even if the Chasan does not mind obligating himself to the Kesuba of a Besula.[196] Accordingly, some Misader Kiddushin's are accustomed to question the Chasan as to the state of the Kallah, prior to writing the Kesuba, and will not use a Kesuba of a Besula for a Beula even with the Chasan's consent.[197] If the family is embarrassed that a Kesuba of a Beula is being used due to it being read and publicized under the Chuppah, one may prearrange with the reader of the Kesuba to read the Nussach of a Besula.[198]]

Summary
A Kallah who is not a Besula must inform her Chasan of this information, and a Kesuba of a Beula is to be written. Nonetheless, some Poskim permit the Kesuba of a Besula to be written if a) the Chasan is pre-informed and nevertheless consents, and b) the Kallah has not become prohibited to marry a Kohen. Initially, however, a Kesuba of a Beula is to always be used even if the above conditions are fulfilled.

Q&A

Must the Misader Kiddushin be told that she is a Beula if he is not the person who is writing the Kesuba?

There is no need to inform the Misader Kiddushin that the Kallah is a Beula if he is a different person than the one being Misader the Kesuba.

At what stage must a Kallah inform her Chasan that she is not a Besula?[199]

This information is not to be divulged until the Chasan has shown deep interest in closing the Shidduch and getting married. Some Poskim[200] rule that it is even forbidden to divulge this information on the outset, prior to the first meeting, or prior to a serious development of the Shidduch.

A Segula for Shalom Bayis:
It is known that having a Kosher Kesuba is an imperative Segula for marital harmony. Rav Mordechai Shmuel Ashkenazi za"l, the previous Rav of Kfar Chabad, stated that over the years he noticed that couples who had the Kesuba of a Besula written when in truth the Kallah was a Beula had increased issues in Shalom Bayis, and he hence would tell couples to always use the correct status Kesuba in all cases.

---

[196] See Maharsham ibid; Heard from Rav Ashkenazi za"l, previous Rav of Kfar Chabad, as aside for the issue presented in writing a falsehood that she is a Besula, in his experience, many of the couples who he used the above Heter to write the Kesuba of a Besula, later came to him for serious Shalom Bayis challenges, and hence he stopped allowing such Kesubos to be written for a Beula, even with consent of the Chasan.

[197] So I received from Rav M.S. Ashkenazi za"l, previous Rav of Kfar Chabad, that he would ask each Chasan at the time of writing the Kesuba if the Kallah is a Besula or Beula.

[198] Maharsham 7:152

[199] Igros Moshe ibid

[200] Igros Moshe ibid

------------------Divorce------------------
16. Child support-Until what age is one Halachically obligated to support his children?[201]

A person is [Rabbinically[202]] obligated to support his sons and daughters until the age of six years old.[203] From age six and onwards, he is to support them in accordance to the institution of the Sages, until they become an adult [see Q&A for definition of adult].[204] This applies even if the father is not wealthy.[205] This applies even if the child was born out of wedlock [and certainly after a divorce].[206] [Until the child is age six], this applies even if the child has money of his own, such as through inheritance [or a trust fund set up by others on his behalf].[207] However, from age six, the father does not need to support his child if the child has his own money [that has been allocated to him through inheritance, or a trust].[208]

If the father refuses to pay: If the father refuses to support his children, [then if they are below age six, the Beis Din has authority to force him to pay, through seizing his assets and bank accounts.[209] However, if the father refuses to support his children who are above age six,] the Beis Din cannot enforce him to do so[210], however they scream at him, and shame him, and implore him to pay. If he still refuses, they [are to] proclaim to the public that this individual is cruel, as he refuses to support his children, and he is worse than a non-Kosher bird which feeds its chicks. The above, however, only applies if the husband is not wealthy, if however, the husband is considered wealthy enough to support his children from his charity funds[211], then the Beis Din forces him to support them out of charity [through seizing his assets and money], until the child becomes an adult. [The above was true in previous times, however, in 1941, the chief Rabbinate of Eretz Yisrael instituted that its courts can legally enforce a father to pay child support until age 15, even if he is not wealthy, and so is done today amongst all Batei Dinim in Eretz Yisrael.[212] Furthermore, each Beis Din has the discretion to enforce payments of child support until age 18[213], and at times even past age 18[214], in accordance to the case at hand.[215] In the event of a divorce, it is

---

[201] Michaber E.H. 71:1
[202] Ramban Shemos 21:3; Avnei Miluim 71:3
[203] Michaber ibid; Ula in Kesubos 65b
[204] Michaber ibid; Takanas Usha in Kesubos 49b

The difference between the obligation of before and after age 6/Is this Rabbinical institution an individual obligation or is it an obligation of Tzedakah? The Rabbinical institution to support children above the age of six is unlike the obligation to support children below age of six, as below age six, the giving is an absolute obligation, similar to one's obligation to pay for an item that he has purchased. However, above age six, the matter is not a complete obligation, but a social responsibility of giving charity for the benefit of one's children. Since the matter is defined as charity, therefore, a Beis Din is unable to force a parent to support his child from after age six, unless he is deemed wealthy, on at least some level. [Implication of Shach Y.D. 251:5; Taz 249:1; Avnei Miluim 71:3; so rule: Rav Elyashiv; Rav Ovadia Yosef; Rav Mordechai Eliyahu; See Psak Din of Beit Din Rabbani Ariel, case number 466314-3] Some Dayanim however maintain that the payment after age six is a complete Rabbinical obligation, and is not the status of charity. [Rav Hertzog; Rav Uziel]

[205] Beis Shmuel 71:1
[206] Michaber E.H. 71:4
[207] Michaber ibid; Tur in name of Rosh and Maharam Merothenberg
[208] Beis Shmuel 71:2; Bach

Other opinions: Some Poskim rule that an ex-husband must support all the children who live in the home of his ex-wife, as part of his Kesuba obligations. [Igros Moshe E.H. 1:106 and Y.D. 1:143; based on Ran Kesubos 28b and Bach 71] Accordingly, the obligation would apply even if the child has his own wealth. Practically, the Poskim negate this ruling. [Michaber 71:4 requires child support to be paid even if the child is born out of wedlock; Beis Shmuel 71:1 negates ruling of Ran ibid; Shevet Halevi 5:133 that the conclusion of the Igros Moshe ibid contradicts the Setimas Haposkim]

[209] Chelkas Mechokeik 71:1
[210] Michaber ibid; see Shach Y.D. 251:5

The reason: Although the Sages instituted that one is to support one's children until they become an adult, this is not an absolute obligation but a mere Rabbinical moral practice of Tzedakah. [see Taz 249:1; Shevet Halevi 5:133; Poskim brought in previous footnotes]

Other opinions by children born from marriage: Some Poskim rule that an ex-husband must support all the children that live in the home of his ex-wife, as part of his Kesuba obligations. [Igros Moshe E.H. 1:106 and Y.D. 1:143; based on Ran Kesubos 28b and Bach 71;] Accordingly, the Beis Din may force him to do so. Practically, the Poskim negate this ruling. [Michaber 71:4 requires child support to be paid even if the child is born out of wedlock, and we thus see that it has no relevance to the Kesuba; Beis Shmuel 71:1 negates ruling of Ran ibid; Shevet Halevi 5:133 that the conclusion of the Igros Moshe ibid contradicts the Setimas Haposkim]

[211] For the exact definition of wealthy, and if it follows the general definition of wealth regarding the laws of Tzedakah: See Nesivos Mishpat 25:5; Machaneh Efraim Tzedakah 1; Maharashdam Y.D. 166; Avnei Miluim 71:4
[212] See Yaskil Avdi E.H. 4:15; Hilchos Maaser Kesafim 11 footnote 371; Heard from Harav Yaakov Yosef za"l
[213] See ruling of the Moetzet Rabbanut Hareishit 21st of Sivan, 5741; 20th Marcheshvan 5746; 18th Kisleiv 5776 that they decided to raise the age of obligation from age 15 to age 18. However, this Takana did not spread amongst all areas, or amongst all Rabbanim. Rav Ovadia Yosef za"l opposed it, and hence practically, every Beis Din has jurisdiction to rule as they see fit. [Heard from Harav Yaakov Yosef zal] See next footnote however regarding a father who is wealthy

common practice to include the amounts allocated for alimony and child support within the divorce agreement, and in such a case, the father must abide by whatever agreements were established there.]

Summary:
A father is to support his children until they become an adult. Until age six, this is a complete monetary obligation which can be enforced by the Beis Din. From age six and onwards, this a Rabbinical institution which only applies if the child does not have money of his own, and in previous times could not be enforced by the Beis Din, unless the father was deemed wealthy. However, in today's times, many Batei Dinim enforce the parent to support his children until age 15 or 18, and at times even later, in accordance to the needs of the child and the wealth of the father.

Q&A

What is the definition of an "adult"? Until what age is a father to support his children in accordance to the institution of the Sages, and from Tzedakah?

Above we stated from the Shulchan Aruch that the Sages instituted that one support his child until he reaches adulthood, and if the father is wealthy, they can enforce payment until the child reaches adulthood. The question is raised regarding the age of adulthood applicable to this matter. Until what age is every father to support his child, due to the Rabbinical institution, and until what age can the Beis Din enforce a wealthy father to support his child? An adult is defined as the age that a child is able to enter the workforce and support himself.[216] Accordingly, a father is Rabbinically required to support his child, and if he is wealthy, can be forced to do so, until the child reaches an age where he can support himself. All the above is regarding the obligation to support the child until he can make his own living, however, the Mitzvah of charity applies to the father throughout the life of the child, and hence if the father is wealthy and the child is unable to properly support himself even after reaching the above-mentioned age, then the father must give charity to help support his child, irrelevant of the child's age.[217]

Secular law:
In all countries, there exist various laws regarding child support; such as: 1) Upon which parent does the responsibility fall? 2) Until what age must child support be given?[218] 3) How much money must the parent provide? The law regarding these matters differ based on country, state, jurisdiction, and family court judge. The effect that state laws have on the Halachic ruling regarding these matters, requires further research.[219] In Israel, the Chief Rabbinate maintains legislative autonomy regarding child support cases, and hence, there is no secular Israeli law that exists in contradiction to the Jewish

---

[214] As stated above, if the father is considered wealthy, and the child does not have money of his own [and cannot work, such as he is in the army, in college, etc] then we force the father to pay. [See Michaber Y.D. 251:4] The appointed Beis Din reviews this matter, and they decide whether the father is indeed deemed wealthy, and if the child is indeed deemed in need of support. They also decide the amount of monetary support to be given, and the amount that should be carried by the mother.

[215] See Psak Din of Beit Din Rabbani Ariel, case number 466314-3 for a lengthy discussion and ruling on this subject

[216] Derisha 71; Beis Shmuel 71:3; Maaseh Rokeiach on Rambam Ishus 12:14 *"The age is not 13 years of age, but until they can support themselves"*; Igros Moshe Y.D. 1:143; However, see Beis Shmuel ibid in name of Rabbeinu Yerucham who implies that the Rabbinical obligation is until adulthood [13 years of age] and past that age [until they can support themselves] it is merely an obligation of Tzedakah [and only applies if he is wealthy-see Nesivos Mishpat 25:5; However see Machaneh Efraim Tzedakah 1; Maharashdam Y.D. 166; Avnei Miluim 71:4; Beis Yaakov 71:1; Baal Haflah]. See Techumin 16 Mezonos Habanim; Psak Din of Beit Din Rabbani Ariel, case number 466314-3; See Hilchos Talmud Torah of Rav Ashkenazi p. 488 who states that older children is defined as above Bar and Bas Mitzvah, as the Sages obligated the father to support his children until that age.

[217] Michaber Y.D. 251:4; Derisha E.H. 71; Beis Shmuel 71:3; Rashba 3:292

[218] Many States in the USA require payment of child support until age 18. Others until age 19, and others until age 21; See here for a summary of law per state: http://www.ncsl.org/research/human-services/termination-of-child-support-age-of-majority.aspx

[219] Obviously, it is forbidden to go to a secular court to deal with these issues, and one must go to a Beis Din. However, the question is regarding whether the Beis Din should take into account the secular law in the administration of their Halachic verdict. Perhaps we Halachically require one to follow the law of the land regarding this matter, just as we rule regarding any monetary obligation that a person accepts upon himself, and by definition of living in a country with certain laws, he has accepted upon himself to abide by certain monetary obligations. This can be viewed similar to one's obligation to pay taxes and the like. See Igros Moshe Y.D. 2:113; Vetzaruch Iyun.

law regarding this matter. Nonetheless, the secular Israeli courts [i.e. Beit Mishpat] also have the authority to hear child support cases, and to rule in accordance to their view, which does not follow Jewish law.[220] Obviously, a Jew may only deal with these issues in a Beis Din, who follow Jewish law.

17. Must one divorce his wife if he has been married for 10 years without children?[221]

From the letter of the law, if a man has been married for ten years[222] and has not yet had children[223], then in certain circumstances[224] the couple must get divorced[225] and are forced to do so by the Beis Din.[226] Nevertheless, the age-old custom of several generations is not to be particular about matches, and hence we no longer force such a couple to get divorced when they do not have children [and rather the couple remains married[227]].[228] [Many Gedolei Yisrael, and G-d fearing Jews, have remained married after ten years despite not having children.]

---

[220] See here: http://www.mikragesher.org.il/%D7%91%D7%99%D7%AA-%D7%94%D7%93%D7%99%D7%9F-%D7%94%D7%A8%D7%91%D7%A0%D7%99-%D7%91%D7%99%D7%AA-%D7%9E%D7%A9%D7%A4%D7%98/

[221] Michaber and Rama E.H. 154:10; Rama E.H. 1:3; Mishneh and Gemara Yevamos 64a

[222] From when are the years counted? The following times are not included as part of the ten years: Business trips; illness of husband or wife; imprisoned. [Michaber 154:11; Braisa Yevamos ibid] After a miscarriage the ten years restart. [Michaber 154:12] Some Rishonim rule that the ten years are only counted in Eretz Yisrael, and hence childless couples in the Diaspora are never required to get divorced. [Hagahos Maimanis Ishus 15:4 in name of Ravayah; Tosafos; Sefer Hateruma and Raavan; Semag Assei 49; Mordechai Perek Haba Al Yivimto, brought in Biur Hagr"a 1; See Bigdei Kehuna 1, brought in Pischeiy Teshuvah E.H. 154:27] However, most Rishonim and Poskim do not differentiate between the Diaspora and Eretz Yisrael, and the ten-year count requires divorce no matter where one lives. [Implication of Rambam; Rif; Michaber ibid; Biur Hagr"a 1; See Aruch Hashulchan 154:24-25 for many proofs that it applies even in the Diaspora, and that all the Poskim agree to this] Nonetheless, if one moves from the Diaspora to Eretz Yisrael then the ten years restart. [Rashba in name of Raavad, brought in Aruch Hashulchan 154:25 and that so is the Halacha] Likewise, if one lives in Eretz Yisrael and travelled to the Diaspora, then his stay in the Diaspora does not count. [Poskim ibid]

[223] If they had children but did not fulfill Peru Urevu: Some Poskim rule that they must get divorced even if they had a child, or had children, but have not yet fulfilled the Mitzvah of Peru Urevu [i.e. boy and girl]. [Implication of Michaber ibid as understood from Rama's gloss; Rashba; Nimukei Yosef; See Aruch Hashulchan 154:23] Other Poskim, however, rule that this only applies if no children have been born. If, however, they had a child, then although they did not fulfill the Mitzvah of Peru Urevu, they do not need to divorce. [Rama 154:10; Rambam Ishus 15; Rivash 15:1] Some Poskim, however, limit this leniency only to a case that the wife can still have children, otherwise he must divorce her. [Beis Shmuel 154:24] Other Poskim, however, are lenient in all cases, and so is the custom. [Meil Tzedakah 33, brought in Pischeiy Teshuvah E.H. 154:26]

Miscarriages: Although a miscarriage restarts the ten-year count, if a woman had three consecutive miscarriages, then they are to get divorced [in even less than ten years]. [Michaber 154:12]

If he had children from a previous marriage: If the husband has children [boy and girl] from a previous marriage, then he may remain married to his wife even after ten childless years. [See Michaber 154:17]

[224] Cases of exception: If the man knows that he cannot have children, then there is no need for him to get divorce, as in any event he cannot fulfill the Mitzvah of Peru Urevu. [Rama 154:10] Some Poskim rule that if the couple desires to remain married and the Kesuba settlement is very expensive, or the wife helps support his Torah learning, then they are not required to get divorced. [Bigdei Kehuna 1, brought in Pischeiy Teshuvah E.H. 154:27]

Does this law apply in the Diaspora? See previous footnotes!

[225] Marrying a second wife: Alternatively, rather than get divorced, one can marry a second wife who can have children [and live with both wives]. [Michaber ibid] This option is not viable for Ashkenazi Jewry due to the Cherem of Rabbeinu Gershom unless the wife refuses to get divorced, in which case he may marry a second wife based on Heter Meiah Rabbanim. [see Noda Beyehuda Tinyana 102; Pischeiy Teshuvah E.H. 154:25; Aruch Hashulchan 1:25] However, it is viable for Sephardi Jewry, and so has been done in numerous cases through the Israeli Rabbinate. [See Yabia Omer E.H. 7:2] See letter in Likkutei Sichos 15:480, printed in Shulchan Menachem 6:59, written to a Sephardi man asking if he can marry a second wife being that they have not had children in ten years *"You need to receive a ruling from the Sephardi Rabbanim to allow you to take a second wife. I, as an Ashkenazi, cannot write you such an allowance. However, according to Sephardi custom, as you write, it is easier to receive an allowance. Nonetheless, you must try to appease your wife by a) explaining to her that not everyone's purpose in this world is to have children, and b) By raising other children, such as his new wife's children, Hashem considers it as if she is raising him; c) You should write a Sefer Torah in the merit of your wife."*

[226] Michaber and Rama ibid; Mishneh and Gemara Yevamos 64a that must divorce; Rav Tachlifa in Kesubos 77a that Beis Din forces him to divorce

The reason: As a man is obligated to perform the Mitzvah of Peru Urevu, and the Sages estimated that if a woman did not have children in ten years, most like she never will. [Aruch Hashulchan 154:23]

[227] Although the implied ruling of Rama/Rivash is simply that we do not force a divorce, although ideally they should get divorced [see Bigdei Kehuna 1, brought in Pischeiy Teshuvah E.H. 154:27], nonetheless, the custom is not to get divorced.

[228] Rama 1:3; 154:10; Darkei Moshe 1:3; 154:13; Rivash 15 *"Certainly from the letter of the law we prevent them from getting married, however what can we do that we never saw in our days, and never heard in many generations of a Beis Din forcing them to divorce…if we forced them all to divorce, it would increase in fights and argument, and therefore the Sages of the generations decided to ignore the union of such couples, as there is no prohibition of Erva or any other prohibition involved"*; Hagahos Maimanis Ishus 15:4 in name of Ravayah [Aviasaf] *"We no longer force to divorce even in the Israel as the Talmud states that after the destruction it would have been proper to decree not to have children and hence at the very least we do not force a divorce upon such a couple."*; Mordechai Yevamos 112, brought in Darkei Moshe 154:13, questions

Why may one remain married, if the marriage cannot bear children?

The Rebbe related the following in a letter addressed to a couple who was childless after ten years:[229] *It is written in the holy Sefarim, in particular in the Sifrei Kabbalah[230], that although one must do all that is necessary to fulfill the Mitzvah of Peru Urevu, there are certain cases of exception in which G-d exempts one from doing so. The reason for this is because he has a different purpose in his life [that G-d has destined for him].* The Shlah Hakadosh[231] writes in the name of Rav Shlomo Alkabetz that Hashem sends certain souls into the world for a specific Tikkun, or leadership positions, which exempts them from having children. Not only do they not need to have children, and will not get punished for not having children, but even if they have children, the children will not spiritually be considered as theirs for any purpose. This is why Ben Azaiy did not have children, as his purpose in this world was solely for Torah learning.

Raising other children:[232]

One who raises and educates a child, is considered as if he gave birth to them, even if one is not their biological parent. This is learned from the Torah itself, from where we see that the holy foremothers gave their husbands other wives in marriage in order to raise the children that they will bear. Accordingly, a couple who cannot have children may adopt another's child and be considered as if they gave birth to him. [However, prior to doing so, one must be aware of all the laws involved with an adopted child such as Yichud, affectionate touch etc. A Rav is to be contacted in such a case]

Maaseh Shehaya

The Baal Shem Tov can argue on the Mishneh:[233]

A Chassid once came to the Tzemach Tzedek, asking for a blessing, and the Tzemach Tzedek replied that only the Baal Shem Tov can affect such a miracle. The Tzemach Tzedek related that the Baal Shem Tov was so powerful that he could argue on a Mishneh. Which Mishneh? The Mishneh which states that after ten years of marriage without children, a divorce is necessary, and in many cases the Baal Shem Tov effected that the couple have children even after ten years.

The Rebbe convinces a couple to stay married:[234]

One morning in New York, in the early the 50's or 60's, the Rebbe took an unexpected ride with his wife the Rebbetzin. The curious Bochurim followed the Rebbe's car to see where it would be heading. You see, in the early years the Rebbe was accustomed to walk home after Davening, and when the Bochurim saw the Rebbe get into the car with his wife they knew that something was astray. After about 20 minutes of driving, the Rebbe's car pulled up to a driveway in front of a home in the Williamsburg neighborhood. The Rebbe and Rebbetzin left the car and entered the house. After the passing of a considerable amount of time, the Rebbe and Rebbetzin exited the house and returned to Crown Heights. The curious Bochurim, knowing no limits to help quench their curiosity, knocked on the door of the house to try to receive some hint as to what transpired in the home. A middle-aged couple answered the door and asked how they can be of help. The Bochurim replied that they wanted to know as for what purpose the Rebbe visited their home. "Which Rebbe?" asked the couple. "The Lubavitcher Rebbe", answered the Bochurim. "You mean that the couple who just visited my home

---

whether today one may divorce such a wife as Rabbeinu Gershom forbade divorcing a wife against her will. Mordechai Perek Haba Al Yivimto, brought in Biur Hagr"a 1

Other opinions: Some Poskim negate the reliance on the above custom and rule that one is required to divorce. [Biur Hagr"a 1 "All these claims are pushed off" Rav Yaakov Yosef that so rules Chasam Sofer and Shut Beis Yosef E.H. 14 [I did not find these sources]]

[229] Likkutei Sichos 15:480, printed in Shulchan Menachem 6:59
[230] See Zohar Vayeishev 188b; Shaar Hagilgulim Hakdama 3; Shlah Hakadosh in next footnote
[231] Shlah Hakadosh p. 381 [Parshas Ki Seitzei gloss from Rav Shlomo Alkabetz]
[232] See Likkutei Sichos 15:480, printed in Shulchan Menachem 6:59; Bigdei Kehuna 1, brought in Pischeiy Teshuvah E.H. 154:27, in end of Teshuvah; Avnei Nezer
[233] Sefer Hatzetzaim p. 123 as heard from Chassidim
[234] Heard from Rav S.Z. Labkowski, R.Y. of central T.T. Yeshiva N.Y, who was one of the Bochurim involved

was the Lubavitcher Rebbe and Rebbetzin?" asked the couple in astonishment. "Yes, indeed it was," replied the Bochurim, "and what is it that they told you?" Please come in and have a seat and we will explain. You see my wife and I are married for over ten years and we have not merited having children. We have thus seriously considered getting divorced, as is the ruling of the Shulchan Aruch. Today this respected couple came to our door, looking like a Rabbi and Rebbetzin, and persuaded us not to get divorced. The Rabbi explained that according to Halacha there is no need to get divorced today, and that even he and his wife are married for more than ten years without children, and they still remain married despite the letter of the law. The couple convinced us not to get divorced, and now I see that it was none other than the Lubavitcher Rebbe and his wife who came to visit us. All those present were left in astonishment seeing the Rebbe's and Rebbetzin's care for a couple they did not know, and how they troubled themselves to meet with them to help save their marriage.

Choshen Mishpat

---------------Beis Din----------------

1. Must a guilty defendant pay for court expenses and litigation fees according to Halacha?[1]

Fees involved in the initial Din Torah:[2] The losing party of a Din Torah is not required to reimburse the winning side for expenses involved. This applies even if he forced the winning party to come to court in a different city, [and there were traveling expenses involved]. If, however, the losing party refused to come to any Beis Din and the winning party had to pay expenses to enforce the losing party to appear, then the losing party is responsible to pay for all the expenses, [beginning from the time that he refused arbitration[3]].

Fees involved in enforcing the court order: If a defendant who was found to be monetarily liable by a Beis Din refuses to pay the plaintiff the money he is owed, then the plaintiff may receive permission from the Beis Din to take him to the civil courts in order to enforce the judgment. All expenses of the plaintiff involved in forcing the defendant to pay is added to the debt of the defendant, and he is obligated to reimburse the plaintiff.[4] This includes court fees, lawyer fees, writ of execution expenses [in Israel known as Hotzah Lepoal].[5] [It, however, does not include travel expenses to collect the money, or bank wiring expenses, and the like.[6]] However, some Poskim[7] rule that if one took the defendant to secular court, the defendant is not obligated to pay for any court fees or lawyer fees of the plaintiff, even though the plaintiff was forced to go to secular court due to the defendant's refusal to pay.[8] Practically, the main opinion follows the first approach, to hold the defendant monetarily liable for all expenses endured in enforcing him to pay the arbitrated sum to the plaintiff.[9] If, however, the defendant was taken to secular court prior to the plaintiff receiving permission from the Beis Din, then the defendant cannot be held liable for expenses.[10] [This applies even in a case that the plaintiff did not need permission to go to the secular courts.[11]]

Summary:
The losing party of a Din Torah is not required to reimburse the winning side for expenses involved, unless the losing party refused to come to any Beis Din and the winning party had to pay expenses to enforce the losing party to appear. If a defendant who was found to be monetarily liable by a Beis Din refuses to pay the plaintiff the money he is owed, then the plaintiff may receive permission from the Beis Din to take him to the civil courts in order to enforce the judgment, and all expenses of the plaintiff involved in forcing the defendant to pay is added to the debt of the defendant.

---

[1] Michaber C.M. 14:5
[2] Michaber C.M. 14:5; Tur 14; Tosafus Sanhedrin 31b; Rosh Sanhedrin 3:40; Mordechai based on Gemara
[3] Rama ibid; Maharik 11; Nemukei Yosef; Maryu; Teshuvas Harosh 108
[4] Opinion in Rama ibid; Teshuvas Harosh 73:2 and Bava Kama 10:6; [however see Hagahos Imrei Baruch 14]; Implication of Stam opinion in Michaber ibid; Aruch Hashulchan 14:12 *"If the plaintiff has a verdict from the Beis Din and the defendant refuses to comply, then if the plaintiff received permission to go to the secular courts, he may charge the defendant for all the expenses involved in doing so."*
The reason: This is either due to a fine of the Sages, or due to Din Grami.
[5] See Michaber ibid fees of "Judges and Toanim"
[6] Shach 14:10; Rashal in Yam Shel Shlomo Bava Kama 10:14; However, see Rosh Kesubos 9:27; Michaber 106:1; See Igros Moshe C.M. 2:26 Anaf 2 regarding if a stipulation for this can be made in the Shtar Borerus
[7] Yeish Mi Sheomer in Michaber ibid; Rivash 475; Teshuvas Rashba 940; Vishev Hakohen 99, brought in Hagahos Imrei Baruch 14 and Pischeiy Teshuvah 14:14 that in truth if the Beis Din does not give permission then this applies even according to Rosh ibid and if it does give permission then it applies even according to the Rashba, and hence there is no dispute. So also writes Maharshdam C.M. 35
[8] The reason: As the defendant's refusal is a mere Grama/cause of damages, and we do not obligate one to pay for Grama damages. [Rivash ibid]
[9] Rama ibid "So appears to me to be the main opinion"; Beis Yosef 14 "The Rosh's opinion appears correct"; Rameh Mepuno 89; Shach 14:13; Rashal in Yam Shel Shlomo Bava Kama 10:14; Vishev Hakohen ibid that there is no dispute if received permission from Beis Din; Maznaim Lamishpat C.M. 14:5 that the defendant cannot say Kim Li like the Rashba as it's against the ruling of the Rama, as well as that some Poskim learn even the Rashba agrees if permission was given by the Beis Din; Maharshdam C.M. 35; Aruch Hashulchan 14:12
[10] Rama ibid; Vishev Hakohen 99, brought in Pischeiy Teshuvah 14:14
[11] Gloss of Rebbe Akiva Eiger, brought in Pischeiy Teshuvah 14:13

> **Q&A**
> **If the losing party lost the case in Beis Din due to what was revealed to be a fictitious claim, can he be held liable to pay the winning party's expenses?**
> Some Poskim[12] rule that the losing party is only exempt from court expenses if his claim was accurate but simply did not find merit in court. If, however, his claim was discovered to be fictitious, and a blatant lie, then he is obligated to pay for court expenses of the winning party.

------------------Loans------------------

2. Lending money to a person who has no means of paying back:[13]

If the lender knows that the borrower does not have the means to pay back the loan, and does not plan to invest the money in a business which will bring profit, but rather wants to use it in a way that will not produce any income and will leave the lender without the means of collecting his debt, then not only is he not obligated to lend him the money, but it is even better not to do so.[14] [If however one knows that the borrower has income coming in that can cover the loan, or that he owns items that can be sold to cover the loan, then he is allowed to lend him the money.[15] Nevertheless, he is not obligated to lend him money simply on the basis that he can sell his items, if there is worry that he may not do so.[16]]

3. Repossession-Collecting possessions of a debtor in order to collect a debt:

Debt due to a loan:[17] A lender may not forcibly collect items from a debtor to repay a loan. It may only be done through a Beis Din, through a representative sent by them to collect the loan. If the lender transgressed and collected the loan on his own in a forcible manner, whether he grabbed an item from him in the street, or he entered his home (without permission), then he transgresses a negative command.[18] However, the collector sent by the Beis Din has authority to force the debtor to make a payment or provide collateral. If he plans to collect items in exchange for the debt [and sell them off to pay the debt], then he may even enter the debtor's home. However, in such a case that he is collecting items to pay the debt, he must leave the debtor with the basic needs provided under the provision of Siddur Baal Chov.

Debt due to stalled payments on merchandise, services, rent, employee, damages:[19] The above law which allows only a court representative to take possession of items from the debtor, applies specifically regarding debt incurred due to a loan. However, by other forms of incurred debt, such as delayed rent payment for a car, item or a home, or delayed payment to an employee, or delayed payment to reimburse an item one stole[20], it is permitted for the person who is owed the money to personally make the collection, and he may even enter the home of the debtor to take possession of belongings. The above, however, only applies if the debt did not turn into the status of a loan. If, however, the debt was reinsured into a loan [i.e. Zakfan Alav Bemilveh] then it follows the same laws as all debt due to loans.[21] [Practically, as soon as the final due date arrives, and the employer or renter has still not paid his

---

[12] Yeshuos Yisrael 14:5; Rav Zalman Nechemia Goldberg; See Rama 14:5 that if the defendant said that he would come to court and then did not show up that he must pay for expenses
[13] Admur Halva 5; Michaber C.M. 97:4; Tur C.M. 97:8
[14] The reason: As in the end he will need to pressure him to pay back the money and will transgress each time the prohibition of "Lo Sihyeh Lo Kenoshe." [Admur ibid]
[15] See Ahavas Chesed Dinei Halvah 1:9 that if a Mashkon is given he may lend him the money if he wants, and the same would apply to if he has items he can sell, as Admur Halvah 13 rules that so long as one has more than Sidrei Baal Chov one does not transgress "Lo Siyeh Lo Kinoshe"
[16] See Avnei Yashpei 2:119
[17] Admur Halva 7; Michaber 97:6; Mishneh Bava Metzia 113a
[18] The reason: As the verse states "Lo Savo El Beiso..." from which we learn that may not enter the home of the borrower and take his possessions, and it goes without saying that he cannot forcibly take an item from him even outside of his home. [Admur ibid]
[19] Admur Halva 14 and Gezeila 29; Michaber 97:14; Rambam Malveh 3:13; Braisa Bava Metzia 115a; Aruch Hashulchan 97:22
[20] Admur ibid; Shach 97:6
[21] Admur ibid; Michaber ibid; Gemara ibid; Sifri 142
The reason: As the verse [Devarim 24:10] states "Ki Sashe Bereiacha Masas Meuma Lo Savo El Beiso Lavot Avoto." [ibid] Masas Meuma means any debt.

obligations, the owed money's become a debt.[22] Some say, however, that it becomes a debt as soon as one makes a calculation of the total amount he is owed.[23]]

A guarantor:[24] It is permitted for a lender to enter the home of the guarantor of a loan in order to repossess collateral for his loan. If, however, the guarantor was an Eiruv Kablan[25], then he has the same status as the borrower, and it is forbidden for the lender to enter his home.

Summary:
It is forbidden for an individual to forcibly collect payment for a debt, or forcibly take items in exchange for the debt, unless the debt was <u>not</u> incurred due to a loan, and was not reinsured into a loan. It is permitted for an emissary of the Beis Din to forcibly collect a debt from the debtor, and enter his home and take possession of items in order to reimburse the loan. He must however leave the debtor with the minimum objects required in Siddur Baal Chov.

Q&A

May one obtain a writ of execution [U.S.] order or Hotzah Lepoal [Israel] to collect a debt?[26]
If the debtor refuses to pay the debt after being confirmed by the Beis Din, then it is permitted to turn to the sheriff to obtain an execution order to force the debtor to pay the debt. The representatives of the execution order have permission to enter the home of the debtor and collect valuables in order to repay the debt. They must however leave the debtor with the items provided under the codes of Siddur Baal Chov.

If one came across money, or an item that belongs to the debtor, may he take it and keep it for himself in exchange for the debt?
This is permitted in some cases, according to some Poskim[27], so long as it does not involve entering the property of the debtor or taking it from his hands.[28] Practically, in all cases one is to advise with a Rav prior to doing so.

------------------Neighbors/Bein Adam Lechaveiro----------------

4. The prohibition to create and continue a Machlokes/dispute:
It is forbidden to continue a dispute, and one who does so transgresses a negative command, as the verse[29] states "Do not be like Korach and his people".[30] This applies even if in truth one's side is correct and the

---

[22] Admur Halva 39; Rama 67:17; Aruch Hashulchan 67:8
[23] Admur ibid
[24] Admur Halva 14
[25] The difference between a regular guarantor, and an Eiruv Kablan is that a regular Areiv only agrees to hold responsibility in paying the loan in the event that the original borrower cannot pay. However, an Eiruv Kablan accepts responsibility of payment even if the original borrower has ability to pay back, and the lender has the discretion to choose who he wants to collect the loan from. [See Michaber C.M. 129:8 and 15]
[26] Shevet Halevi 10:263; See Chevel Nachalaso 4:49
[27] 1st opinion in Rama C.M. 4:1 regarding if found in the hands of others or is by him as a Pikadon; Rivash 396; See also Rama 72:17; Mahara Sasson 96; Beis Efraim C.M. 76; Chochmas Shlomo 4; Ketzos Hachoshen 4; Pischeiy Choshen 6:5
[28] <u>The reason</u>: This is permitted under the law "Oseh Adam Din Leatzmo." The Torah only forbade forcibly taking possessions or money from the debtor, such as trespassing into his house, or wrestling an item from him.
[29] Bamidbar 17:5
[30] Rav and Resih Lakish in Sanhedrin 110a; Smag 157 [Biblical-Possibly listed as Mitzvah 157]; Rambam and Ramban Sefer Hamitzvos Shoresh 8 [Rabbinical]; Marganisa Tava on Sefer Hamitzvos Shoresh 8; M"B 156:4; See Piskeiy Teshuvos 156:13
<u>Is this prohibition Biblical or Rabbinical?</u> Some Poskim learn this prohibition is Biblical and is counted as one of the 613 commands. [Smag 157; Marganisa Tava on Sefer Hamitzvos Shoresh 8; M"B 156:4 in name of Smag; Mentioned in Likkutei Sichos 18:202 footnote 3; See also Igros Kodesh 14:391 "One is to distance himself from Machlokes, which is Biblically forbidden according to all opinion"; See also Toras Menachem 5743 1:388] Other Poskim rule the verse of "Lo Yiyeh Kekorach Veadaso" is not Biblically coming to teach us against continuing a Machlokes. Rather, this prohibition is merely Rabbinical, and the verse is used as an Asmachta. [Rambam and Ramban Sefer Hamitzvos Shoresh 8] Some Poskim learn the verse of "Lo Yiyeh Kekorach Veadaso" is in truth a Biblical prohibition against arguing against the Kehuna, as did Korach, and not against all Machlokes. [Ramban Sefer Hamitzvos Shoresh Shemini 5] Other Poskim learn the above verse is not a Mitzva at all and is simply stating that one who argues against the Kehuna will not be punished like Korach was punished. [Rambam Sefer Hamitzvos Shoresh 8; Kinas Sofrim ibid; Megilas Esther ibid]

other side is guilty of wrongdoing, as even Moshe who was correct, went to make peace with Dasan and Aviram.[31] One should distance himself from it like one distances from fire.[32]

Machlokes Lesheim Shamayim-for religious matters: The above prohibition applies even to a Machlokes that is Lesheim Shamayim, for religious reasons.[33] A person should even nullify a custom or Chumra to avoid Machlokes.[34] Majority of suffering and tragedies experienced by the Jewish people come as a result of Machlokes Lesheim Shamayim.[35]

The prohibitions transgressed with Machlokes: Aside for the innate prohibition against making a Machlokes, Machlokes also leads to other prohibitions. It leads to hatred, which transgresses the command of "Do not hate your brother in your heart."[36] It also leads to various other Biblical transgressions, such as revenge, Lashon Hara, anger, physical fighting.

The punishments: One who continues a conflict is placed in excommunication.[37] A home that contains Machlokes, hosts the Satan in their home.[38] Such a home will eventually become destroyed.[39] Many good people, endeavors, and communities have been destroyed due to Machlokes.[40]

How to end a dispute:
From a letter of the Rebbe:[41] *Whenever there are two parties in argument over a matter in this physical world, it is nearly impossible for one party to be completely correct, and the other party to be completely at fault. Every party has at least some wrongdoing that needs amending. In fact, as explained in Chassidus, it is this wrongdoing that may have triggered the wrongdoing of the other, perhaps to even a greater quantity and quality, as the verse states that just as water reflects one's image so too the heart of man reflects another's heart. Many good endeavors have become sabotaged due to conflict and discord that is motivated by a desire of imaginative respect, and is at times embellished within claims of fear of heaven and matters of piety [Shpitz Chabad]. Some people, after hearing the above words, rather than make an accounting of their own soul and situation, repenting for their ways and judging the other person favorably to the point he feels humbled before him, they rather demand the above from the other party. They use this to enthusiastically preach to the other party that they should do Teshuvah, and with no less enthusiasm, they judge themselves favorably, with great scrupulousness, and demand of others that they be humble before him.*

How many times must one attempt to end a dispute?[42]
The following is ruled regarding asking forgiveness for wrongdoing, and seemingly, the same can be applied towards attempting to end a dispute: If the victim refused to forgive the offender after he approached him for forgiveness, the offender must try to appease him another two times in different ways. If the victim still refuses to forgive him, the offender is no longer obligated to try to appease him. Nevertheless, he must tell ten people that he has asked for forgiveness from the person he offended, and the victim refused to be consoled.[43]

---

[31] So was done by Moshe, who was certainly correct in his dispute; See Riy Milunil
[32] See Kav Hayashar 3; Rambam ibid
[33] Admur Igros Kodesh 32; Noda Beyehuda Kama Y.D. 1 "Today there is no real Machlokes Lesheim Shamayim"; Chasam Sofer Korach
[34] See Admur 468:11-14; See Igros Kodesh 14:391 regarding Nussach of Davening; 5:91; 16:12 and 99; 19:249 regarding wearing a Tallis as Chazan
[35] Igros Kodesh Admur Hazakein Letter 32
[36] Sheilasos of Rav Acha 131
[37] Kav Hayashar 34
[38] Zohar 1:37
[39] Derech Eretz Zuta 9
[40] Rambam in his will to his son
[41] Igros Kodesh 13:19; 3:20; 11:138
[42] Admur 606:2-3; Michaber 606:1
[43] Admur 606:2; Michaber and Rama 606:1

5. The law if a neighbor's tree is encroaching onto one's property:[44]

Cutting the branches: One whose neighbor's tree is encroaching into one's property, then if it is getting in the way of one's use of the property[45], then he may cut down the area of the tree that extends into his property and is of nuisance.[46] However, one may not cut any part of the tree that is on his neighbor's side of the property, even if it is of nuisance.[47] One may not cut more than necessary to prevent the damage, even if it is encroaching onto his side of the property.[48] The same applies towards a privately-owned tree which encroaches onto the public pathway, that its branches may be cut to allow for smooth transit.[49] [Nonetheless, if the tree is a fruit bearing tree, then it is best to have the branches cut by a gentile, in order to avoid any possible danger associated with cutting down a fruit tree.[50]]

May one keep the fruits of the tree?[51] The determining factor of ownership of a tree is the property in which its root and trunk grow, and not where its branches extend to. Thus, if a tree that grows in one property extends its branches and fruits into another property, the branches and fruit remain the property of the owner of the property in which the trunk of the tree grows. Accordingly, although it is permitted for one to cut down the encroaching branches that interfere with one's use of the property, he does not have a right to keep the fruits of the tree, and it must be given to the owner, unless he receives their explicit permission to keep the fruit. The same applies regarding the wood of the branches, that they must be given to the owner [if the owner is known to make use of them].

Cutting the roots of a neighbor's tree:[52] If the roots of a neighbor's tree are growing under one's property, it is permitted cut the roots that interfere with one's use of the property. Thus, for example, if one is making use of a 24-centimeter ditch, then he may cut all roots that interfere with that ditch. This applies even if cutting the roots may damage the tree. The roots that are cut to be returned to the owner of the tree [if the owner has a use of them], unless the roots are a 16 Ama [8 meter] distance from the tree, in which case one may keep the roots.

Summary:
The branches, fruits, and roots of a tree within 15 Amos of the tree, that encroach into one's property, remain under the legal ownership of the tree owner. One may not take the fruits or branches for himself. Nonetheless, any area that interferes with one's use of his property, may be cut in limitation to accommodate that use.

Secular Law:
While each State in the USA contains their own codes and laws regarding neighbors and trees, the general legal practice follows similar guidelines as those given by Halacha, with a few exceptions. The law: **a)** One may trim all the branches of the tree that extend into one's property, up until the property line. [According to Halacha, however, one may only cut the areas that interfere.] **b)** The

---

[44] Michaber C.M. 155:26; Mishneh Bava Basra 27b
[45] See Michaber and Mishneh ibid *"He may cut the tree up until the point where the stick of the plow reaches."* Smeh 155:64 "So it does not interfere with his plow" Michaber and Mishneh ibid "If it is a carob or fig tree which gives lots of shade, it may be cut down up until the border of one's property." Smeh 155:65 "As its shade is plentiful [and prevents sun from reaching the field]" Michaber 155:28 *"If the branches of a tree encroach onto one's roof and prevent him from repairing or renovating it, he may cut it down."*
[46] The reason: As the Torah gave permission for the victim to cut from the tree as much as necessary to remove the damage. [Smeh 155:66]
[47] See Michaber and Mishneh ibid "Until the border"
[48] See previous footnotes
[49] Michaber 155:27; Mishneh Bava Basra 27b
[50] The following Poskim rule the danger applies even to cutting branches: Beir Sheva, brought in Mishneh Lamelech Issurei Mizbeiach 7:3; Mahariy Besen 118; Beis Yitzchak 1:144; Har Tzevi 2:101-102; Teshuvos Vehanhagos 1:376; Piskeiy Teshuvos 629:12; The following Poskim rule that there is danger involved even when cutting for a justifiable reason: Sheilas Yaavetz 1:76, brought in Darkei Teshuvah 116:51; Toras Chaim on Bava Basra 26a; Makor Chesed 62 in Bava Basra ibid; Makor Chesed 62; Shivim Temarim 53:17; See Igros Kodesh 7:264
[51] Rama 167:2 *"However, if the tree grows in one property and encroaches onto another property, we follow the trunk, and it is all his"*; Michaber 155:29 and 167:2 that even if the tree is in the middle of the border and equally belongs to both of them, one may not take the fruit from the branches that extends into his property, and rather it must be equally divided. Hence, we see that the fruits always remain the property of the owner. See also Michaber 155:30 "If the roots are within a 16 Ama distance from the tree he may cut it **and give it to the owner.**"; Bava Metzia 197a
[52] Michaber 155:30; Bava Basra 26a

> fruits of the branches that extend into your property still belong to the owner of the tree. The owner is defined as whoever's property grows the trunk and roots of the tree. **c)** You cannot cut the parts of the tree that are in your neighbor's property even if the leaves and debris of the tree fly into your yard and are a nuisance to your property. **d)** One may not cut the roots of a tree that encroach into one's property if it will damage the tree. [According to Halacha, it is permitted to cut the areas that interfere.] As practical advice, always try to first resolve the issue with your neighbor, and if necessary seek legal counsel in your state.

6. The confidentiality of a conversation:[53]

A conversation between two people is considered confidential and neither party may reveal its details to others until one is explicitly told by the other person that he may reveal it.[54] [This applies even though the other person did not explicitly say to keep the conversation private.[55] This applies even if telling over the conversation to others does not transgress the prohibition of saying Lashon Hara or Rechilus, and will not bring any foreseeable damage to the other.[56] Some Poskim[57], however, explain that this only applies if it is recognizable that the conversation is meant to remain confidential, such as that the conversation took place in private quarters or that the content is of a nature that is clearly meant to be kept private. Thus, if the conversation took place in public, with more than three people present, there is no restriction against telling it over to others so long as it does not involve Lashon Hara or Rechilus.[58]]

> **Q&A**
>
> **Secretly taping a conversation:**
> Based on the above, one may not record another's conversation for the purpose of sharing it with others. However, conversations may be secretly taped for legal purposes to protect the honesty and integrity of an agreement and enforce them, if necessary, before a Rabbinical tribunal. Under no conditions, however, may they be released to the public. Those who secretly tape conversations and then release them to the public on the internet or through social media transgress several Biblical prohibitions, including Lashon Hara, Rechilus, and making Machlokes.
>
> **May one who received a letter or email from an individual reveal to others what was written?**
> See next!

---

[53] Admur 156:14; M"A 156; Semag Lavin 9; Hagahos Maimanis end of Hilchos Deios; Yuma 4b; Chikikeiy Lev Y.D. 49; Omitted in Rambam; See Sefer Chofetz Chaim in Beir Mayim Chaim 2:27

[54] The source and reason: As the verse states "Vayidaber Hashem Eilav Beohel Moed Leimor." [Yuma ibid] The word Leimor is coming to say "Lo Emor" that one should not reveal it. [Rashi ibid] Others explain that from the fact Hashem had to say "Leimor" which means "go say" we learn that under normal circumstances, one may not say. [Meiri and Ritva on Yuma ibid; Maharsha in Chidushei Agados Yuma ibid] The reason this may not be said is because one never knows how an innocent spread of a conversation can eventually lead to repercussions for those involved. [See Chofetz Chaim ibid]

Is this a prohibition or simply good advice of Derech Eretz? Some Poskim write that this matter is not an actual prohibition, but a mere act of Derech Eretz and good Middos, being that the person did not actually tell him to keep the conversation private. [Meiri ibid; suggestion in Chofetz Chaim Beir Mayim Chaim 2:27]

[55] Pashut from Poskim and Yuma ibid; Meiri ibid; Sefer Chofetz Chaim in Beir Mayim Chaim 2:27

[56] Pashut, as otherwise it is a Biblical prohibition and there is no novelty in this statement; See Sefer Chofetz Chaim in Beir Mayim Chaim 2:27 *"It is forbidden even if one cannot foresee anything negative occurring if he tells it over"*

The reason: As one never knows how an innocent spread of a conversation can eventually lead to repercussions for those involved.

[57] Sefer Chofetz Chaim in Beir Mayim Chaim 2:27 that so can be proven from the chosen verse in Yuima ibid which discusses Hashem speaking with Moshe in the Ohel Moed

[58] Sefer Chofetz Chaim in Beir Mayim Chaim 2:27

7. Reading another person's mail or emails:[59]

The famous Ashkenazi leader of the early middle ages, Rabbeinu Gershon Maor Hagoleh, instituted a Cherem [excommunication] against anyone who reads the mail of another person without permission.[60] [This Cherem spread to all sects of Jewry, Sephardim and Ashkenazim, and does not have a limitation in time. This Cherem is Halachically binding like any other law in the Torah, and according to some opinions, carries Biblical weight.[61] It is thus Halachically forbidden to read other people's mail, or any private document that belongs to them or is related to them.]

After the mail has been discarded:[62] Once, however, the mail has been discarded, it is permitted to read it.
Opening without reading:[63] It is forbidden to open the mail, even if one will not read the actual letter.
Mail of a gentile:[64] The prohibition against reading another's mail applies even against reading the mail of a gentile.

Practical applications:

Reading someone's email or messages [SMS/WhatsApp]:
Just as it is forbidden to read physical mail [i.e. snail mail] addressed to another person, so too it is forbidden to read electronic mail [i.e. email], as the prohibition was against reading information, and invasion of privacy, and not necessarily against the physical handling of another person's mail.

Accidently received another person's mail
One who received another person's mail may not open it to read. He is to notify the individual who it was intended for, or simply write "Return to Sender" or "Wrong Address" on the mail and put it in the nearest mailbox.

Investigative work for the sake of a Mitzvah or criminal investigation:[65]
It is permitted for a Beis Din, school, or parent, to look into another's mail or private documents for the sake of their Torah education. Certainly, it is permitted to do so to prevent a crime and protect oneself and others from possible monetary loss, or physical damage.

May one who received a letter or email from an individual reveal to others what was written?[66]
One who received a private letter or email from an individual is prohibited from sharing it with others, unless he receives explicit permission from the sender. Accordingly, that which people are accustomed to forward private emails or messages to other acquaintances, may only be done if one has explicit permission from the sender.

---

[59] Shut Maharam Merothenberg 1022; Kol Bo 116; Maharam Mintz 102; Beir Hagoleh Y.D. 334; Kneses Hagedola 334:5; Halachos Ketanos 1:59;173; 276; Toras Chaim Maharchash 3:46; Chikikeiy Lev Y.D. 49; Beis David [Salonica] Y.D. 158; See Encyclopedia Talmudit Erech Cherem Rabbeinu Gershom

[60] The reason: Doing so is prohibited under several grounds: 1) Stealing: Reading another's mail can be considered Shoel Shelo Midaas. [Toras Chaim ibid] 2) Migaleh Sodosav: It is forbidden to reveal the secrets of another. [Toras Chaim ibid; See Admur 156:14; Yuma 4b] 3) Rechilus: It is forbidden to search and investigate into another person's private matters. [Halachos Ketanos 1:276] 4) Ahavta Lereiacha Kamocha: Whatever one does not want done to him he should not do to others. [Chikikeiy Leiv ibid] 5) Gneivas Daas [Chikikeiy Lev ibid]

[61] See Maharik Shoresh 184; Mabit 2:46
The reason: As perhaps it has the status of a Shavua.

[62] Shut Maharam Merothenberg ibid
[63] Beis David ibid
[64] Chikikeiy Lev ibid
[65] Mishpitei Hatorah 92 based on Rashba 1:557
[66] Chikikeiy Lev ibid; See Admur 156:14; M"A 156; Semag Lavin 9; Hagahos Maimanis end of Hilchos Deios; Yuma 4b

> **Secular law:**
> Withholding someone's physical mail [snail mail]: Under U.S. federal law[67], it is illegal to intentionally stop a letter from being delivered to its intended recipient, and that may include not informing the U.S. Postal Service that you have another person's mail. If a person snatches a letter that isn't addressed to them and opens it, they are committing mail theft. Intentionally doing so is a federal crime that could potentially land one in prison for up to five years.
> Reading someone's mail or email: The Fourth Amendment to the United States Constitution provides a privacy protection in the sense that "The right of the people to be secure in their persons, houses, papers, and effects, against unreasonable searches and seizures, shall not be violated." The act of simply accessing and reading someone's mail or email, without their permission can be considered a State or Federal crime, with civil and/or criminal liability, depending on the circumstances.[68] [A major difference however in the secular law, versus Takanas Rabbeinu Gershom, is that in the secular law, it is not illegal to read a piece of mail that was left open, while according to Rabbeinu Gershom, doing so is not allowed.]

8. Jewish manners-Acknowledging the greetings of another:

It is forbidden to ignore the greetings of another, such as to ignore and not respond to another person telling them hello, good morning, Shalom Aleichem.[69] One who does so, and ignores another person's greetings, is called a robber/Gazlan.[70] Not responding to a greeting can cause enmity to spread between the two parties, which is completely avoidable if he would simply acknowledge the greeting. It is for this reason that the Sages required one to greet others, in order to increase love and peace and avoid matters that cause enmity.[71] [Thus, aside for the general social obligation of a human and Jew to act with Derech Eretz and respond to another who greets them, the Sages enacted this as a Halachic requirement, and one who does not do so will be held accountable in his final judgment.[72]]

During learning, prayer, other activities: One must respond to the greetings of another even if he is in the midst of an activity, such as in the middle of work.[73] Even if one is in the midst of prayer, he is to respond to another's greeting[74], unless one is in an area of prayer where he may no longer speak, such as between Baruch Sheamar and Shemoneh Esrei.[75] [Seemingly, one is required to respond even while learning Torah.]

How to respond:[76] One who is greeted with words, such as good morning, Shalom Aleichem, is to likewise respond with words. It does not suffice to simply nod the head.

---

[67] 18 USC Section 1702

[68] One can be sued under the federal Stored Communications Act [18 USC section 2510-2701] and for invasion of privacy; See case Jennings versus Jennings No. 27177; see also here: https://arstechnica.com/tech-policy/2012/10/reading-someones-gmail-doesnt-violate-federal-statute-court-finds/

[69] Brachos 6b "If he was given Shalom and did not repeat it back to him, he is called a Gazlan" [mentions in many talks of the Rebbe]; Yalkut Shimoni Yeshaya 2:397; Tosafus Bava Kama 73b; see also Tosafus Bava Basra 129b; Sefer Hatanya; Menoras Hamaor Ner 6:3; Raavan Brachos 132; Shibulei Haleket Mila; See Rabbeinu Bechayeh in Kad Hakemach Shalom; Chesed Lealafim 156:8; So is also evident from Mishneh Brachos 13a, Tur, Michaber and Admur 66:1 that one may answer Shalom even during Shema due to Darkei Shalom

[70] Brachos ibid

The reason: As the verse [Yeshayahu 3:14] states "Veatem Biartem Hakerem Gzeilas Heani Bivateichem" [Brachos ibid] This refers even to an Ashir, however, the Pasuk speaks of a poor person as by a poor person there is nothing to steel but his greeting [and hence that is how we know that even not returning a greeting is considered stealing]. [See Rashi ibid and Kol Eliyahu of Gr"a ibid] The reason why this is considered stealing is because one has taken the blessing that he received from the person and did not give it back. [See Hatanya ibid]

[71] Menoras Hamaor Ner 6:3; Kad Hakemach ibid; Admur ibid "One may answer due to Darkei Shalom"

[72] See Chagiga 5a *"On all the acts Hashem will bring to judgment, on all concealed matters, Shmuel says that this verse refers to one who spits in front of his friend and it became repulsive before him"*

[73] Tosafus Bava Kama 73b; see also Tosafus Bava Basra 129b

[74] Mishneh Brachos 13a, Tur, Michaber and Admur 66:1

[75] From the letter of the law this is allowed until the point of Shemoneh Esrei, as stated in Admur, Michaber, Tur and Brachos ibid, however, the custom today is not to answer once one is past Baruch Sheamar, as people are no longer Makpid if someone does not answer them while they are in the midst of Davening. [See Admur 66:1 "If the person is not Makpid don't answer him"; M"A 66:2 in name of Rishonim; Chinuch Mitzvah 420; Elya Raba 66:2; M"B 66:2 that so is the custom]

[76] Chesed Lealafim 156:8

----------------Business----------------

9. Hasagas Gevul in Torah education and occupations-Can an infringement claim be brought against a new Torah class, new Yeshiva, new Rabbi in town, and new Chabad house?

Background: Secular law in most of the modern world follows the economic philosophy of capitalism, and allows free unrestrained opening of businesses and competition, thus destroying the legal protection of a monopoly. Judaism, however, recognizes certain restrictions upon the opening of a new business if it will infringe on the income of a current business, and thus certain monopoly rights are granted to business owners under mitigating circumstances, as defined by Halacha.[77] This concept is known in Halacha as "Hasagas Gevul", or infringing onto another's property. Often, two Jewish businesses will go to a Jewish court of law, or Beit Din, in order to argue out an infringement claim, and see if the mitigating circumstances are met to allow a monopoly of that business in that area. We will now analyze if the restrictions of Hasagas Gevul apply also towards spiritual matters, such as opening a new Torah class in a community, opening a new Yeshiva, or a new Shul, or Chabad house, thus creating competition with a current running Torah classes and Torah institutions.

The law:[78] It is permitted for a Melamed who teaches children Torah to open a school in an area that already contains a Melamed who teaches children. This applies whether the intended audience of the new teacher is for students who are not yet registered in the other teacher's class, or even if the intent is to create competition and have students who are enrolled in the first class come join the second class. It is permitted for the new Melamed to open his school even right next door to the original Melamed.[79] Likewise, a Torah scholar may move to a new city and open a Torah class to the public even if the city already contains an official community Rav who teaches Torah to the public. This applies even if by doing so one slightly infringes on the income of the original Rav.[80] This applies even if the community Rav is much older than the new Rabbi.[81] [Likewise, one may do Mivtzaim and put on Tefillin on any Jew even if there is a set Shliach in the city.[82]] The above, however, only applies towards spiritual matters, such as teaching a Torah class and the like that do not infringe on the income of the other Rav.[83] However, regarding spiritual matters which serve as a source of income, the concept and restrictions of Hasagas Gevul certainly apply in Halachically mitigating circumstances, and the matter must be brought to arbitration by a Beis Din or an agreed upon Rav. These include the following cases:

1. Misader Kiddushin:[84] There are certain limitations against a person being Misader Kiddushin in a city which contains an appointed community Rav who performs the Kiddushin.
2. A Mohel:[85] One Mohel is restricted from infringing on the territorial rights of another Mohel, if the Halachically mitigating circumstances are met.

---

[77] See the two opinions of Rav Huna and Rav Huna Brei Derav Yehoshua in Bava Basra 21b; Sanhedrin 81a *"The intent of the verse which states that he did not defile his friends wife is to say that he did not infringe on another's business."*; Makos 24a *"The meaning of the verse that he did not do evil to his friend is that he did not infringe on another's business."*; Rambam Hilchos Shechienim 6:8 [rules like Rav Huna son of Yehoshua, and so rules Rabbeinu Chananel and Tosafos]; Admur Hilchos Hefker and Hasagas Gevul 10-13; Michaber and Rama C.M. 156:5-7; Beis Yosef C.M. 156; Darkei Moshe 156:3; Shut Harama 10; Pischeiy Teshuvah 156:3; Chasam Sofer 5:79; Igros Moshe C.M. 1:38

[78] Shulchan Aruch Y.D. 245:22

[79] Michaber Y.D. 245:22; Rambam Talmud Torah 2:7; Rav Yosef in Bava Basra 21b; See Sicha of Rebbe 10th Shevat 1955

The reason: The verse states "Hashem Chafetz Lemaan Tzidko Yagdil Torah Veyadir." From here we learn that it is permitted for a Melamed who teaches children Torah to open a school in an area that already contains a Melamed who teaches. [Michaber ibid; Rambam Talmud Torah 2:7] The Talmud [Bava Basra ibid] states that Ezra established that there be competition amongst Sofrim in order to increase in wisdom.

Does this apply even if it will run the first Melamed out of business: See Poskim listed in coming footnotes and Admur ibid Halacha 12 regarding if a Melamed may take the job of another Melamed; However, regarding opening a Talmud Torah, Yeshiva or Kolel, see Chazon Ish Emuna Ubitachon 3:1 that one may open a new Talmud Torah even if it causes the other Talmud Torah to close down. However, he may not try to cajole students from one Yeshiva to come to his Yeshiva. [Darkei Mishpat p. 167]

[80] Rama Y.D. 245:22; Teurmas Hadeshen 151

[81] Shach 245:14

[82] Hisvadyus 5747 2 p. 324-337

[83] See Poskim listed in coming footnotes and Admur ibid Halacha 12 regarding if a Melamed may take the job of another Melamed; However, regarding opening a Talmud Torah, Yeshiva or Kolel, see Chazon Ish Emuna Ubitachon 3:1 that one may open a new Talmud Torah even if it causes the other Talmud Torah to close down. However, he may not try to cajole students from one Yeshiva to come to his Yeshiva. [Darkei Mishpat p. 167]

[84] See Rama 245:22 regarding a visiting Rabbis [may not do Kiddushin] versus a resident Rabbi [may do Kiddushin]; See Shach 245:15 regarding a city where the custom is to be stringent even against a resident Rabbi doing Kiddushin; See Chasam Sofer 230 and Noda Beyehuda Tinyana E.H. 83 that in today's times there are limitations even by a resident Rabbi; See Pischeiy Teshuvah 245:11-12

[85] Shut Harambam 273; Koveitz Teshuvos [Rav Elyashiv] 1:213

3. <u>A Shul or Yeshiva or Beis Chabad</u>:[86] There are restrictions against opening a new Shul if this will infringe on the membership of another Shul in the vicinity, and the salary of its leaders. [Likewise, there may be restrictions against opening a new Yeshiva if this will infringe on the enrollment of another Yeshiva in the vicinity, and the salary of its staff.[87] Likewise, there are restrictions against opening a new Beis Chabad if this will infringe on the income of another Beis Chabad in the vicinity.[88]]
4. <u>A Sefarim or Judaica store</u>:[89] There are restrictions against opening a new Sefarim or Judaica store if this will infringe on the income of another store in the vicinity.
5. <u>Kashrus organization</u>:[90] There are restrictions against giving a Hechsher to a business if this will infringe on the income of another Hechsher who already gives a supervision over that product.

Conclusion:
While it is legally permitted to open a new Torah class in a community that already contains a Rav, there are restrictions against opening a Torah institution, or begin a profession of Kedusha, if it may infringe on the income of an already established institution, and in all cases the two parties are to speak with an agreed upon Rav or Beis Din for arbitration. Even in the former case which permits one to teach Torah classes in the city which contains a Rav, it is proper to speak with the Rav beforehand if the matter may cause friction.

The Rebbe on opening a new Chabad house if it will infringe on a currently established Chabad house:[91]
Free translation: *It is possible for one to build a house of Torah, a Beis Chabad, but it will not be a place where Hashem dwells. How can this be? If the home is not built according to Shulchan Aruch, and transgresses the laws of Hasagas Gevul, as this home is a Mitzvah Haba Beaveira. Hasagas Gevul causes the victim to cry to Hashem against the fact that his income was infringed and the commotion he makes prevents the Shechina from dwelling in the others home. It's obvious that everything involved in establishing a Beis Chabad must be in accordance to Shulchan Aruch, Toras Moshe, without any infractions of Hasagas Gevul. So, while we encourage the opening of many new Batei Chabad, it must be done with the sensitivity not to infringe on the territory of others. At the same time, however, we must make clear the following: There are matters to which Hasagas Gevul does not apply, such as teaching Torah and the like. Accordingly, we need to negate the mistake of the fools who cry foul play if another Jew desires to open a Beis Chabad due to the fact that he will steal his right of putting Tefillin onto people, or that he will diminish his honor and respect in the eyes of the public. Their foolishness is so great, that they don't suffice with just shutting down the other person's operations, but demands that he leave the city all together, thinking that the entire city and its suburbs all belong to him. It's obvious that regarding all the above, it must be given to a Rav to arbitrate according to Halacha, and the problems all begin when people take the law into their own hands and make their own rulings.*

---

[86] Igros Moshe C.M. 1:38; 2:40
[87] See Admur ibid Halacha 12 regarding if a Melamed may take the job of another Melamed; However, regarding opening a Talmud Torah, Yeshiva or Kolel, see Chazon Ish Emuna Ubitachon 3:1 that one may open a new Talmud Torah even if it causes the other Talmud Torah to close down. However, he may not try to cajole students from one Yeshiva to come to his Yeshiva. [Darkei Mishpat p. 167]
[88] Hisvadyus 5747 2 p. 324-337
[89] Igros Moshe C.M. 2:31
[90] Igros Moshe C.M. 2:40
[91] Hisvadyus 5747 2 p. 324-337

10. Is a signed document legally binding if one was unaware of its content?[92]

➢ Example 1: One signed a collage of bank documents affirming a loan, mortgage, bank account, or other matter of the like. Naturally, one did not take the time to read the fine print spread across all 50 pages. Is every statement and qualification mentioned in the document legally binding, or can the signatory claim that he never agreed to the conditions mentioned in the fine print?

➢ Example 2: One signed a rent contract and did not take the time to read through all the details. Can the tenant claim that certain statements are not legally binding due to him not being aware of it at the time of signing?

One who signs a document, obligates himself to all the financial matters and conditions written in that document, even if he is unaware of any of its content.[93] Thus, even if the document is written in a foreign language which the person who signed is not fluent in reading, and there are witnesses who testify that he signed prior to even reading it, nevertheless, the document is legally binding and all its content can be legally enforced.[94] Claiming that one did not understand the implication of the document is not a valid claim.[95] This applies even to the conditions written in the fine print.[96] [However, some Poskim[97] imply that the above only applies if there is no reason to assume that one did not have knowledge of the content of the document, in which case he cannot claim that he was unaware and did not agree to its content. If, however, there is enough Halachically acceptable circumstantial evidence[98] to assume that he did not have knowledge of the documents detailed content, then it is possible to invalidate a condition that it contains. However, some Poskim[99] clarify that the above leniency never applies in a case that one personally signed the document, and only applies to a case that witnesses signed in his place. Practically, the understanding of Admur[100] and other Poskim[101] is that one is always held liable to the entire content of a personally signed document, irrelevant of excuse or valid evidence of being unaware. However, some Batei Dinim use the above lenient approach in their judicial rulings, if the circumstances justify it.[102]]

---

[92] Michaber C.M. 45:3; 61:13 regarding Kesuba; Rama E.H. 66:13; C.M. 61:13; 68:2; Admur Hilchos Ribis 46 in parentheses; Beis Yosef E.H. 66; C.M. 68; 69; 147; Teshuvos Hameyuchasos Ramban 77; Shut Rashba 1:629; 1:985; 5:228; See Yabia Omer E.H. 3:13; Mishneh Halachos C.M. 7:61-13; Mishpitei Eretz 2:299; Techumin 8:164

Other opinions: Some Poskim rule that if one claims that he did not understand all the conditions on the document, we accept his claim. [Rav Meir, brought in Rashba 1:629] Others limit this only to a case where there when there is an Anana Sahadi that he was unaware. [Ruling of Rashba 1:1156 regarding the invalidation of a condition in the Kesuba due to the claim that the Kallah was unaware of its content; Kneses Hagedola C.M. 147; Maharash Laniado 18; Ginas Veradim E.H. 4:14; Rav Sharman in Techumin ibid in name of Riaz Anzil 49; Mishneh Halachos ibid; See Kneses Hagedola ibid and Dvar Moshe 2:69 and Yabia Omer 3:13 regarding this contradiction in Rashba] Other Poskim rule that we believe such a claim regarding a secondary detail in the document. [Kneses Hagedola C.M. 147; Maharash Halevi Y.D. 14] Others rule that we only accept this claim if the person did not personally sign, even if he had witnesses sign. [Shut Reb Betzalel Ashkenazi 24, author of Shita Mekubetzes; Yabia Omer E.H. 3:13]

[93] Admur ibid in parentheses; Implication of Michaber C.M. 45:3 and all Poskim ibid

The reason: As whenever one signs a document, he agrees to obligate himself to all of its content, and thus even if it was not read before him, it is legally valid. [Implication of Admur and Michaber ibid; Smeh 45:5; Shach C.M. 61:18; Ramban ibid "If he did not bother reading it and signed, he has obligated himself to all its content, even if he did not borrow"] Meaning, that when one signs a document, who relies on the author of the document and agrees to its content. [Smeh ibid and 62:23; Shach 45:5; Ramban ibid; Beir Hagoleh 45:3; Levush 45:3; Aruch Hashulchan 45:5] Alternatively, the reason is because certainly one has agreed to obligate himself to whatever is written there, as certainly they read it before him, and he trusted that person. [Rama E.H. 66:13; C.M. 68:2; Rashba 1:629; 5:228] If we were to invalidate documents based on this claim, a document would never have any legal meaning. [Beis Yosef E.H. 66; Rashba ibid] The Halachic ramification between the two reasons is if one knows for certain that the signatory was unaware of its content. According to the former reason the condition should be valid, while according to the latter reason perhaps the condition is invalid. See other opinions brought in previous footnote!

[94] Michaber C.M. 45:13; Teshuvas Ramban ibid; Beis Yosef C.M. 45; 68; 69; Teshuvas Habach 32 regarding Shtar Mamrani; Smeh 45:5; Shach 45:5; Levush 45:3; Aruch Hashulchan 45:5

[95] Michaber C.M. 61:13; Poskim ibid

[96] Rama C.M. 61:13; Beis Yosef 61; Rivash 480

[97] Implication of Rama E.H. 66:13; C.M. 68:2; Rashba 1:629 who all say that the reason we hold him accountable is because certainly he was made aware of its content. This implies that if we know for a fact that he was not made aware, then he is not held liable; Ruling of Rashba 1:1156 regarding the invalidation of a condition in the Kesuba due to the claim that the Kallah was unaware of its content; Some however rule that we only accept this claim if the person did not personally sign, even if he had witnesses sign. [Reb Baruch Ashkenazi 24]

[98] Such as it is written in fine print and is a secondary issue to the main obligation of the document, or there is an Anan Sahadi that he was unaware of its content. [See Kneses Hagedola ibid, and other Poskim brought above] Or that there are witnesses that he was told orally unlike that which was signed. [Aruch Hashulchan 45:5]

[99] Shut Reb Betzalel Ashkenazi 24, author of Shita Mekubetzes; Yabia Omer E.H. 3:13

[100] Admur ibid *"Even if he does not know anything"*

[101] So is implication of all rulings of Michaber ibid and Teshuvas Haramban, unlike the implications of Rama ibid and Rashba ibid

[102] See Mishneh Halachos ibid where he used the above leniency of Anan Sahadi to invalidate a Shtar Borerus; Article of Rav Sharman in Techumin ibid

> **Summary:**
> One who signs a financial document is held liable for all its content, even if he claims that he was unaware of its content, and we know for certain that his claim is correct. Accordingly, one must be very careful upon signing a document that he is aware of all its content and is able to hold up to its conditions, as a later claim that he was unaware will not be valid.

> **Secular law:**
> Secular law follows the same law as Halacha, that once a document has been signed, its details are binding, and a claim of being unaware of its content is not acceptable. Lack of this rule would potentially annul all contracts under the claim that one did not understand all its details, and put commerce to a halt. Accordingly, for the successful function of business, it is imperative for contracts to be viewed as binding even if one claims unawareness at the time of the signing. It is the responsibility of every contract signer to study the details of the contract or retain legal advice prior to doing so. Nonetheless, in certain countries, there are regulations placed on contract writing in order to protect consumers from entering into exaggerated terms of contract simply due to not taking the time to read the many pages and fine print.

11. Tips and Gratuity fees-Is one Halachically obligated to give a tip for a service he received, [i.e. waiter, cab driver, bartender, mover, etc.]?

A. Legal background:

It is customary in many countries to leave a tip, or gratuity fee, for those who provide certain services, in addition to paying the basic price for the service or product delivered. Around the world, this is most commonly practiced in restaurants, in which it is common practice to provide the waiter/waitress with a tip for their service. Customarily in the US, a restaurant tip is 15% of the total of the bill, and in Israel is 13% of the bill, although this matter differs amongst regions. As well, certain countries are accustomed to leave tips for cab drivers, movers, and other forms of service. In some situations, as is common in restaurants in some States in the US, the tip is considered part of the income of the waiter, and they are thus paid way below minimum wage by their employer. Thus, the tip or gratuity may be expected as part of their basic salary, even though one also pays the restaurant owner for the product delivered. Other States, and countries, however, do not allow tips or gratuity charges to infringe on one right for minimum wage, and hence all tips received are in addition to their basic salary. A recent law passed in Israel requires employers to pay minimum wage to workers, excluding tips.

Legal obligation: From a legal perspective, in some scenarios one is not obligated to provide a tip for a service, if he does not wish to do so, and the matter is left to the discretion of the client. However, in other cases, tips are considered obligatory and are able to be enforced. This is dependent on the country laws, and on whether the service provider informed the clients as to the policy of their service. For example, if a service provider clearly states to the client that the payment for the product does not include a gratuity fee, then it is a legal obligation to pay, and one can get arrested for theft for not doing so. On the other hand, if the matter was not made clear, then it is left to the discretion of the client. Many restaurants explicitly write on the menu that the listed price does not include a mandatory gratuity fee, and hence it may be obligatory and legally enforced. However, in Israel, consumer laws do not obligate one to pay more than the listed price, even on such conditions.[103]

---

[103] In Israel, the law prohibits a seller from adding further fees to a listed price, and hence legally one is not obligated to pay gratuity fees for restaurant orders, if it was not included in the listed price. [See Chok Haganat Hatzarchan law 17a] This matter has been brought to Israeli secular courts and they have heavily fined restaurants who included a service fee in the final bill, in addition to the listed price of the foods.

B. The Halacha:

According to Halacha, the conditions of payment for labor and employees follow the customs of the area, unless explicitly stated otherwise.[104] Hence, in countries that it is universally accepted to give a tip, or service fee, the employer must do so according to Halacha, unless he explicitly stipulated otherwise upon receiving the service.[105] This applies even if the customer is new in town and was not made aware of this practice. The amount given would be upon the discretion of the client, but is to be no less than the minimum accepted amount. Furthermore, even if it is not universally accepted to leave a tip, if at the time that the service was provided the client was informed that it does not include a gratuity/service fee, which must be paid in addition to the cost of the product, then he is obligated to pay it, if writing such conditions is legal in one's country. If it is not universally accepted to give a tip for a certain service, and no condition was explicitly made upon ordering the service, then one is not obligated to do so, even if the tip is considered part of the salary of the service provider, by his employer. The same applies if it is universally accepted to choose whether or not to give a tip, based on the quality of service, in which case the matter Halachically remains within one's discretion based on his assessment of the service. Nonetheless, even when one is not Halachically obligated to leave a tip, one should always take into account whether or not it will cause a Chillul Hashem, or spread of enmity for fellow Jews, and is hence to act accordingly.

Summary:
It is a Halachic obligation to leave a tip for a person who provided a service, in all cases that doing so is universally accepted in one's area, or was preconditioned prior to ordering the service. Otherwise, the matter is left to the discretion of the customer to decide based on quality of service or other factors.

Q&A
May one give a tip to a gentile who provided a service if he is not obligated to do so?[106]
Yes. Doing so does not transgress the prohibition of Lo Sichaneim.[107]

---

[104] See Michaber C.M. 331:1; Bava Metzia 83a; Rashba 2:168 that a Minhag overrides a Halacha in monetary matters; Rivash 171; 475; Chacham Tzevi 61
The reason: As whenever one hires another to do work for him all the accustomed work obligations and rights are assumed to have been agreed on and obligated on by the employer, and all business conditions set by two sides are Halachically binding. [See Michaber ibid] Accordingly, it is not the secular law that creates the Halachic obligation but rather the Minhag Hamedina. [Article of Rav Shpurn in Hayashar Vehatov ibid]
[105] See Mivakshei Torah 5760 and Tuvcha Yabiu 2:107 that Rav Elyashiv ruled not tipping a waiter is Chashash stealing; However see Asher Chanan 7:151 regarding tipping waiters that doing so is not an obligation, as by nature it is given to the discretion of the customer; Furthermore, based on the Israeli law brought above, it would seem that there is no Halachic obligation to give a tip, even if the universal practice is to do so, as the law prohibits making this an obligation, and that is the Minhag Medina.
[106] Beir Moshe 3:117; Shraga Hameir 7:155; Ateres Paz C.M. 1:3-12
[107] The reason: As Lo Sichaneim does not apply when one knows the gentile [Taz Y.D. 151:8] and giving him the present can bring one future benefit, such as for example, that the person continues providing one his service. [Beir Moshe ibid] Alternatively, Lo Sichaneim only applies when one is doing so out of one's good heart and gesture. However, when doing so out of obligation due to norms of society, then it does not apply. [Shraga Hameir ibid]

---------------**Hashavas Aveida**---------------

12. Returning lost money that one found:[108]

Finds scattered bills or coins in public area:[109] One who finds money [such as bills or coins] scattered [in a public area], and it is not inside of a purse/wallet, may keep the money for himself. This applies [irrelevant of the amount of money found[110] and applies] even if the money was found in a majority Jewish area.[111]

If the money contains a Siman/symbol of ownership:[112] The finder may keep the money for himself even if the cash contains a sign of ownership, such as the name of an individual.[113] [Certainly the number/value on a coin or bill is not considered a Siman to require one to return it to one who can testify to its value.] However, if the coin or bill contains a unique sign that is uncommon to be found, such as a cracked coin, then if found in a majority Jewish area, one is obligated to announce his finding and try and return it to the owner.[114] [Likewise, if a bill contains a unique writing that can be recognized by its owner, and is uncommon to be done to other bills, then it must be announced and returned. Thus, a Rebbe dollar that has a name and/or date written on it must be returned to its rightful owner]

If one finds money in a purse/wallet:[115] If one finds in a majority Jewish area a pouch, purse, or wallet that contains money, then one is obligated to announce his finding and try to return it to the owner.[116] This applies even if one found the money resting outside of the wallet, next to it, in a way that is evident that it fell from that wallet. The money is to be returned to whoever testifies towards a symbol found on the wallet/purse.

If one finds a pile of cash:[117] One who finds a pile of cash which was evidently consciously placed there temporarily and later forgotten, is obligated to announce his finding and try to return it to the owner, being that the money contains a symbol, such as the amount or its location. One is to return the money to the person who gives the symbol of the amount of money found, or the location.

---

[108] Admur Hilchos Metzia Upikadon 8; Michaber C.M. 262:6 and 11; Mishneh Bava Metzia 21a

[109] Admur ibid; Bava Metzia 24a
Other opinions: Some of today's Poskim say that we no longer rely on people constantly checking their pockets, and hence even money which is found is to be noted to be returned upon the arrival of Eliyahu. [See Pischeiy Choshen 2 footnote 23; Toras Haveida p. 66] Practically, the Gedolei Haposkim of today do not agree to differentiate, and it is thus permitted to keep the money. [Igros Moshe Y.D. 4:23-13; Hashavas Aveida Kehilchasa 5 footnote 7 in name of Rav Chaim Kanievsky and Chazon Ish] However, Rav Elyashiv is quoted to be of the opinion that only by large sums of money does the law still apply, while by small coins, it no longer applies. [See Sefer Hashavas Aveida Kehilchaso]

[110] See Sefer Hashavas Aveida Kehilchaso [Friedlander]

[111] The reason: As people are accustomed to check their [pockets or wallets for their] money all the time, and thus, we can assume that the owner who lost the money already discovered that it was missing and gave up hopes of finding it, prior to it being found. [Admur ibid; Smeh 262:13; Tur 262; Rebbe Yitzchak in Bava Metzia 21b; Accordingly, by the time the money was found it was already Hefker, and the finder may keep it just as he may keep anything from Hefker.] The reason we assume that the owner who discovers his money is missing will automatically give up hope of finding it is because money does not carry a unique symbol of ownership which one can testify towards, as many coins look the same. [Admur ibid; Smeh 262:28; Ramban 25b; Braisa Bava Metzia 25b] There is also no way for the owner to give a symbol of where his money was found, as when money is found scattered, it obviously fell from him without him realizing it and he thus does not know the exact area of where it fell from him. Likewise, he does not rely on a symbol of the amount of money that was lost to not give up hope on having the money returned to him, as perhaps some of it fell in one place and more in another place. [Admur ibid; Michaber 262:3 and 9; Smeh 262:19]

[112] Admur ibid; Michaber 262:13; Braisa Bava Metzia 25b

[113] The reason: As we suspect that perhaps the owner wrote his name on a number of bills/coins, and the one that was found is not the one that he lost, but rather a different one which he wrote his name on and was already spent, and really fell from the person who he gave it to, as money is customarily spent by the owner. [Admur ibid; Michaber ibid; Smeh 262:28; Ramban Bava Metzia ibid; Nimukei Yosef Bava Metzia ibid] Accordingly, the coin/bill is still considered to be without a sign even if one's name is written on it. [Ramban ibid] See Teshuvah of Igros Moshe printed in Hashavas Aveida Kehilchaso p. 54; Toras Haveida p. 9]

[114] Admur ibid; Rama 262:13; Ramban ibid; Nimukei Yosef ibid
The reason: As although all coins are meant to be spent [and hence there is room to suspect that the person who is claiming a sign of ownership really gave it to someone else as payment and it fell from their hands] nevertheless we do not suspect for this in this case [as we do not assume that people who claim to have lost an item, and give a correct symbol to be liars]. Now, this type of symbol [a crack in a coin] is uncommon to occur and thus there is no room at all to suspect [as we did regarding a name] that perhaps another coin of his also cracked [and that is the coin he lost, and not this one which fell from the person he gave it to]. [Admur ibid]

[115] Admur ibid; Michaber 262:20; Rambam 16:3; Mishneh Bava Metzia 24b-25a

[116] The reason: As a wallet or purse is an item that contains a symbol of ownership. [Admur ibid]

[117] Admur ibid; Michaber 262:11; Smeh 262:24; Mishneh Bava Metzia 24b

> **Summary:**
> One who finds money in a public area may keep it for himself and is not required to try to find the legal owner unless any of the following apply:
> 1. The money was found in a purse, wallet or bag.
> 2. The money was accidently left there rather than dropped.
> 3. The money contains a unique symbol that can be given by the owner, which is uncommon to be done to other money which the owner may have lost.

> **Secular law:**
> Laws regarding lost objects vary according to state and country. In many states, if the rightful owner is known to the finder, or can easily be discovered, taking the item for oneself can be considered theft. Some states require that all found property, including money, be given to the police in case the rightful owner cannot be found, and after a certain period of time, the money is returned to the finder if the owner could not be tracked.

------------------Renters----------------

13. Paying rent on time:

Rent of object:[118] It is an obligation to pay rent for an animal, or rent for an item, on time, and if one delays doing so, he transgresses a negative command.[119]

Rent of land/house:[120] Some Poskim[121] rule one who does not pay property rent on time does not transgress [the prohibition] against delaying payment.[122] [However, other Poskim[123] rule one does transgress the Biblical prohibition of delayed payment even by rentals of land. Practically, some Poskim[124] conclude one may be lenient regarding rental of actual land, however regarding rental of a house one is to be stringent. Others[125] however conclude that one must be stringent in all cases.]

---

[118] Admur Sechirus 11; Michaber C.M. 339:1; Rambam Sechirus 11:1; Bava Metzia 111a

[119] The reason: Just as it is a Mitzvah to pay a worker on time, and if one delays payment he transgresses a negative command, as explained above, so too it is a Mitzvah to pay rent for an animal or item on time, and if one delays doing so he transgresses a negative command. This is learned from the verse [Devarim 24:14-15] "Lo Sashok Sechar Ani Vievyon Meiachecha Oi Migercha Asher Beartzecha Bisharecha Biyomo Titen Secharo etc." What is the meaning of the word "Beartzecha/in your land", do we not hold that all body dependent Mitzvos apply both in Israel and the Diaspora? Rather, it is coming to teach that all matters [of commerce that are accustomed] in lands must be paid on time. [Admur ibid; Smeh 339:2; Braisa Bava Metzia 111b]

[120] Admur ibid; Michaber C.M. 339:1; Tur 339

[121] Rameh [Rav Meir ben Turdos Halevi Abulafia, a Rishon who lived in 1170-1244]

[122] The reason: As the verse states "Beartzecha/In your land" and not "Arztecha/Your land." [Admur ibid; Smeh 339:2; Bach 339; Beir Hagoleh]

[123] Semag Lavim 181; Yireim Mitzvah 263; Toras Kohanim Kedoshim; Biur Hagr"a brought in Shaar Mishpat and Pischeiy Teshuvah 339:1

[124] Ketzos Hachoshen 339:1, brought also in Pischeiy Teshuvah 339:1

The reason: As perhaps a house has the status of an item and not of land [See Rama and Shach 95], and by a Biblical prohibition one needs to be stringent. [Ketzos Hachoshen ibid]

[125] Shaar Mishpat, brought in Pischeiy Teshuvah 339:1, that one must suspect for the latter opinion by a Biblical prohibition; Aruch Hashulchan 339:2 that the main opinion follows the stringent opinion

------------------Borrowing----------------

14. Using or taking someone's item without permission:[126]

It is forbidden for one to use or take an item that belongs to one's friend without his permission.[127] This applies even if one only plans to use it on a mere occasion and then return it.[128] It is thus forbidden for one to visit his friend's house in order to use an item of his without his permission even on a mere occasion.

One knows for certain that the owner is not particular against one using or taking it:[129] If one knows for certain that the owner is not particular against one using his item, then it is permitted to use it without his explicit permission. [This, however, only applies to using the item and **then returning it to the owner in the same state,** such as to read from his friends Sefer when he knows for certain that his friend does not mind. However, it is always forbidden to "borrow" an item of another for the **sake of keeping it**, or returning it in a damaged state, even if one knows for certain that the owner does not mind, unless one receives explicit permission from the owner.[130]] Thus, it is forbidden to enter the orchard or garden of a friend and collect from the produce [for his personal use, such as to eat] without the owners explicit permission. This applies even if the owner of the orchard is a very close friend who loves him like his own soul and one thus knows for certain [that not only will he not mind, but on the contrary] he will rejoice and be happy when he is informed that his friend benefited from his fruit, nevertheless, since at the moment the owner is unaware of this, it is therefore considered that he is benefiting in a prohibited fashion. The same applies for all cases of the like. One is required to warn the public regarding this matter, as many people transgress this this due to lack of knowledge.[131] This, however, only applies to a matter that has not become public practice, or an accustomed allowance from the owner. If, however, a certain benefit of one's property has become public practice, such as allowing one's wife to give a small sum to charity to one asking by the door, (or the owner has agreed to the friends benefit already on several occasions), then it is permitted to benefit from the product even if he will take it from himself, and the owner does not have explicit knowledge of this, at the time.[132]

Items that people are not generally particular against being used or taken: Those items in which it is not common at all for any person to be particular against someone else using it without their permission, such as items that do not receive any loss or damage at all through being used, it is permitted to use these items without permission [and then return it to the owner without any loss occurring to it[133]].[134] Furthermore, if

---

[126] Admur O.C. 14:13 and C.M. Metzia Upikadon 27 regarding borrowing Sefarim; Metzia Upikadon Halacha 4 regarding benefiting from lost object and taking fruit of friend; Gezeila Ugeneiva 10 regarding benefiting from stolen item; Sheila Vesichirus 5 that it goes without saying that this applies to other items of Reshus; Rama O.C. 14:4; Smeh C.M. 75:6; Nimukei Yosef Tzitzis 12a in name of Ritva; See Piskeiy Teshuvos 14:10

[127] The reason: As borrowing an item without permission [i.e. Sheila Shelo Midaas Baalim] is considered stealing and is thus forbidden. [Admur C.M. Metzia Upikadon 27 in parentheses; Sheila Vesichirus 5; Metzia Upikadon Halacha 4]

[128] Admur 14:13 and C.M. Metzia Upikadon 27 regarding Sefarim; M"A 14:10

[129] Admur Sheila Vesichirus 5; Rama C.M. 292:20 regarding Pikadon of Sefarim by Talmid Chacham; Smeh 292:45

Contradiction from Metzia Upikadon Halacha 4: Admur states in Hilchos Metzia Upikadon Halacha 4 that one may never benefit from another person's item without his knowledge **even if one knows for certain that his friend will not mind**, thus contradicting his ruling in Sheila Vesichirus 5. Perhaps, however, one can suggest that the two Halachos refer to different cases and actually compliment and qualify each other. In the case that one desires to use the item and then return it to the owner with no loss occurring to it, such as reading a Sefer, then it is permitted to do so if one knows for certain that the owner does not mind, as in essence nothing has been taken/stolen, other than its use, and on this we know the owner does not mind. This is the ruling in Sheila Vesichirus 5. However, if one desires to take some of the item and consume it, such as to "borrow" a piece of paper for writing, or "borrow" a fruit for eating, then since he is in actuality taking the physical item from the owner and this item will not be returned, then it is forbidden to do so without explicit permission of the owner even if he knows for certain that the owner does not mind. This then is the ruling in Metzia Upikadon Halacha 4. Vetzaruch Iyun!

[130] Admur Metzia Upikadon Halacha 4 *"Even if one knows for certain that when he tells the owner that he took the item, the owner will rejoice and be happy due to the great love they share, it is nevertheless forbidden to benefit from it without the owner's knowledge. Thus, it is forbidden....."* Kuntrus Achron 1; See explanation in previous footnote!

Other opinions: Some Poskim rule it is permitted for one to take the item for personal keeping if one knows for certain that the owner does not mind. [Shach C.M. 358:1, brought in Admur ibid Kuntrus Achron 1]

[131] Admur Metzia Upikadon Halacha 4 and Kuntrus Achron 1; Mar Zutra in Bava Metzia 22a and Tosafos, Ramban, and Ritva there; Ketzos Hachoshen 262:1; Aruch Hashulchan 358

Other opinions: See previous footnote!

[132] Admur Metzia Upikadon Halacha 5 [parentheses in original]; Michaber Y.D. 248:6 regarding wife giving charity; Tosefta Bava Kama 11:2, brought in Rashbam Bava Basra 43b; Terumos Hadeshen 188

The reason this is allowed: As since the custom is to allow others to take it, it is not at all considered without the consent of the owner, as thus is the custom and the owner knows of the custom. [Admur ibid]

[133] Admur Metzia Upikadon Halacha 5 and Kuntrus Achron 1

it is customary to allow others to take the item for themselves without returning, such as to allow a pauper to take a small donation from one's wife, then one may take the item for himself even without the owners explicit knowledge.[135] The same applies if it is customary for an owner to allow someone to take a certain item [i.e. food] whenever he wishes, that he may do so without asking permission.[136] Nonetheless, it is a Midas Chassidus to avoid taking even such items, if the item would be completely eradicated if all of the public were to take from it freely.[137] However, by those items which minority of people are particular against them being used by others due to worry of damage[138], then it is forbidden to use them without explicit permission even if majority of people are not particular, and even if one will return it.[139] This applies even if one is positive that no damage will occur to the item at all, it is nevertheless forbidden to borrow it without permission.[140]

Summary:
It is forbidden to use someone else's item without permission, unless one is certain the owner is not particular against one doing so, or it is not common at all for any person to be particular, and one will return the item to the owner without any loss occurring to it. If, however, one intends on keeping the item, then it is forbidden to take it even if one is certain that the owner is not particular against one doing so, unless it has become the common practice for the owner to give permission for such a thing.

Q&A
May one use someone's pen without permission?[141]
If the pen is inexpensive and was left around in the open, such as in a Beis Midrash and the like, seemingly it may be used, as it can be assumed that it was left there for this purpose. If, however, it was left in the persons private area, then seemingly it is forbidden to use it even if one knows the person is not particular, as using the ink causes a loss to the item, [unless he has done so already many times in the past with permission of the owner, in which case he may assume that the owner does not mind].

May one use someone's phone without permission?
It is forbidden to do so unless one is certain the person does not mind him using it, and using it will not cost the owner any money.

May one borrow a piece of paper from a friend without permission?
No. This applies even if one is certain the person does not mind him using it, as it is forbidden to consume the item of another without his permission, unless he has done so already many times in the

---

[134] Admur Sheila Vesichirus 5; Shita Mekubetzes Bava Metzia 22b
[135] Admur Metzia Upikadon Halacha 5 and Kuntrus Achron 1; Admur Gezeila Ugeneiva 1; Michaber Y.D. 248:6 regarding wife giving charity; 359:1 regarding taking a piece of wood from friends gate to use as toothpick; Tosefta Bava Kama 11:2, brought in Rashbam Bava Basar 43b; Bava Kama 109b; Yerushalmi Dmaiy 3:2; Maggid Mishneh Gezeila Veaveida 1:2
[136] Admur Metzia Upikadon Halacha 5 in parentheses
[137] Admur Gezeila Ugeneiva 1; Michaber C.M. 359:1 in name of Yerushalmi regarding taking a twig from a wood fence that it is forbidden to do so due to Midas Chassidus as if everyone were to freely take a piece of wood, the fence would be destroyed [See Smeh 359:4; Beir Hagoleh ibid]; Yerushalmi Dmaiy 3:2; Bava Kama 11; Maggid Mishneh Gezeila Veaveida 1:2
[138] Such as Sefarim, in which the owner of the Sefarim suspects that perhaps he will spend a long time reading from it to the point that they will tear due to over usage, and therefore he is not pleased with allowing another to read from it at all. [Admur 14:10; Nimukei Yosef Tzitzis in name of Ritva]
[139] Admur Sheila Vesichirus 5; Shita Mekubetzes Bava Metzia 22b
The reason: Although majority of people are not particular due to that chance of damage is very rare, nevertheless, we do not follow the majority in this regard to say that one can assume that this owner is not particular against it being used. [Admur ibid]
[140] Admur Sheila Vesichirus 5 and Metzia Upikadon 27 in parentheses regarding Sefarim
The reason: As nevertheless, the owner of the item suspects that perhaps it may get damaged, and thus if he knew that this person was using his item, it is possible that he would be particular, and it is thus found that he has borrowed without permission of the owners [Sheol Shelo Midaas], which is considered stealing, even if one causes no damage or loss to the item at all, as explained in Hilchos Metzia Upikadon 27. [Admur ibid; Metzia Upikadon ibid in parentheses]
[141] See Gr"a C.M. 163; Minchas Yitzchak 7:130; Piskeiy Teshuvos 14:10; See Chesed Lealafim 14:5, brought in Kaf Hachaim 14:31, for a similar defense regarding Siddurim; Lehoros Nasan 6:127-128

> past with permission of the owner.
>
> **May one use a hotel's swimming pool without permission?**
> No.

15. Using someone's Sefarim without permission:[142]

It is forbidden for one to learn from Sefarim that belong to one's friend without his permission.[143] This applies even if one only plans to learn from it on a mere occasion.[144] This applies even if one is certain that no damage will occur to the Sefer while reading it.[145] It is thus forbidden for one to visit his friend's house in order to read a Sefer that is there without his permission even on mere occasion. This applies even if the Sefer belongs to a third person and was borrowed from him.[146]

One knows for certain that the owner is not particular: If one knows for certain that the owner is not particular against one using his Sefarim, then it is permitted to use it without his explicit permission.[147] Thus, one who gives Sefarim to a Torah scholar for him to hold and guard on his behalf [i.e. Pikadon], it is permitted for him to read from the Sefer even without the owner's permission, as certainly the owner gave it to him having in mind that he will learn from it.[148]

Sefarim that people are not generally particular against being used:[149] Those Sefarim of which it is not common at all for <u>any</u> person to be particular against someone else using them without their permission, it is permitted to use these Sefarim without permission. However, by those Sefarim which minority of people are particular against them being used by others due to worry of damage, then it is forbidden to be used without permission even if majority of people are not particular.[150] This applies even if one is positive that no damage will occur to the Sefer at all, it is nevertheless forbidden to borrow it without permission.[151] [Practically, today, based on this a number of leniencies have been adapted regarding using other people's Sefarim without permission as explained in the Q&A!]

> **Summary:**
> It is forbidden to use someone else's Sefer without permission, unless one is certain the person is not particular against one doing so, or it is not common at all for any person to be particular.
>
> **Q&A**
> **May one in Shul use someone else's Siddur without permission?**
> Many are accustomed to use another's Siddur without permission. Some Poskim[152] question this allowance, as Siddurim should maintain the same law as Sefarim. Other Poskim[153], however, defend

---

[142] Admur O.C. 14:10 and C.M. Metzia Upikadon 27 and Sheila Vesichirus 5; Rama O.C. 14:4; Smeh C.M. 72:6; Nimukei Yosef Tzitzis 12a in name of Ritva; See Piskeiy Teshuvos 14:10

[143] The reason: As the owner of the Sefarim suspects that perhaps he will spend a long time reading from it to the point that they will tear due to over usage, and therefore he is not pleased with allowing another to read from it at all. [Admur 14:10 and C.M. Metzia Upikadon 27; Nimukei Yosef Tzitzis 12a in name of Ritva]

[144] Admur ibid; M"A 14:10; Chesed Lealafim 14:5; M"B 14:16

[145] Admur C.M. Metzia Upikadon 27 and Sheila Vesichirus 5 regarding all objects

[146] Admur Sheila Vesichirus 5

[147] Admur Sheila Vesichirus 5; Rama C.M. 292:20 regarding Pikadon of Sefarim by Talmid Chachamim; Smeh 292:45

[148] Rama C.M. 292:20; Smeh 292:45; Admur 14:10 references to this Halacha

[149] Admur Sheila Vesichirus 5; Shita Mekubetzes Baba Metzia 22b

[150] The reason: Although majority of people are not particular due to that chance of damage is very rare, nevertheless, we do not follow the majority in this regard to say that one can assume that this owner is not particular against it being used. [Admur ibid]

[151] Admur ibid and C.M. Metzia Upikadon 27 in parentheses regarding Sefarim

The reason: As nevertheless, the owner of the item suspects that perhaps it may get damaged, and thus if he knew that this person was using his item, it is possible that he would be particular, and it is thus found that he has borrowed without permission of the owners [Sheol Shelo Midaas], which is considered stealing, even if one causes no damage or loss to the item at all, as explained in Hilchos Metzia Upikadon 27. [Admur ibid; Metzia Upikadon ibid in parentheses]

[152] P"M 14 M"Z 7; M"B 14:16

[153] Makor Chaim 14; Likkutei Maharich Birchas Hashachar; Aruch Hashulchan 14:13; Piskeiy Teshuvos 14:10

this practice, stating that today people are not at all particular against this, especially in light of how cheap and easily attainable these Sefarim are today. It is however forbidden to remove the Siddur from the Shul without permission from the owner.[154]

May one use someone else's Sefer left in a Shul without his permission?
Some Poskim[155] rule it is forbidden to use Sefarim that are found in Shul without the permission of the owner, just as is the law regarding Sefarim that are in his home. Nevertheless, since people are accustomed to do so, the owners are to declare and publicize that they allow others to use their Sefer that is left there.[156] Other Poskim[157], however, rule it is permitted to use someone's Sefer that was left in the Beis Midrash without his permission, as Sefarim are inexpensive and one can assume the owner left it there for others to use. Practically, the widespread custom today is to allow looking into someone else's Sefarim without his permission[158], although it is best for the owners to write on the Sefer that they explicitly give permission for it to be used. In all cases, it is forbidden to remove the Sefer from the Shul without permission from the owner.[159]

May one take a mere glance into someone else's Sefer to look something up, without his permission?[160]
The widespread custom today is to allow one to have a mere glance to look something up in the Sefer.

16. Borrowing a Shul's Sefer:[161]
An old edict that was founded in ancient congregations is that one may not remove a Tallis or Sefer from the Shul without asking permission from the owners. [This applies even if one can assume that the owner is not particular, nevertheless one must ask permission. The same applies regarding removing Shul Sefarim from the premises, that one must ask permission from the Gabbaim to do so, even if one can assume that they do not mind.[162] One who removes Sefarim from a Shul without permission is stealing from the Shul and from the public and causes Bittul Torah.[163]]

---

[154] Rama ibid; Admur 14:10 and 12 regarding Tallis and Tefillin
[155] P"M 14 M"Z 7; Chesed Lealafim 14:5, brought in Kaf Hachaim 14:31, that it is in truth forbidden to do so and those who do so are receiving an Aveira instead of a Mitzvah.
[156] Chesed Lealafim ibid
[157] See Rama C.M. 163 in name of Takanos Kadmonim and Biur Hagr"a there; Minchas Yitzchak 7:130; Piskeiy Teshuvos 14:10; See Chesed Lealafim ibid, brought in Kaf Hachaim ibid, for a similar defense regarding Siddurim; Lehoros Nasan 6:127-128
[158] Aruch Hashulchan 14:13
[159] Rama ibid; Admur 14:10 and 12 regarding Tallis and Tefillin
[160] Aruch Hashulchan 14:13; See Sdei Chemed Samech 15 who questions this ruling
[161] Rama C.M 163:6; Machatzis Hashekel 14:10; Chesed Lealafim 14:5; Shalmei Tzibur p. 34; Kaf Hachaim 14:32; Minchas Yitzchak 7:130
[162] See however Chesed Lealafim ibid, brought in Kaf Hachaim ibid, that the people who donate the Sefarim to the Shul library do so with intent that the Sefer remains in the Shul. This would imply that even the Gabbai cannot give permission. Vetzaruch Iyun
[163] Minchas Yitzchak ibid

------------------Stealing----------------

17. Paying owed bus fares in Israel:[164]

If the fare machine of a public transportation bus in Israel is not working, then under Israeli law as of October 2017, the company must still provide the bus service free of charge, and the customer is not required to repay the bus company for his fare, on another occasion. Accordingly, one is not required according to Halacha to pay the bus company back, irrelevant of the instructions of the driver, such as if he says to pay twice the next time. This law applies irrelevant to whether the company is Jewish, or gentile owned. This law applies only to public transportation buses who work under a license of the ministry of transportation. This Halacha is subject to change in the event that the law changes.

------------------Bal Tashchis----------------

18. The laws of Bal Tashchis:

A. The prohibition:[165]

The same way that one must be careful with his body not to cause it loss, or harm, or damage, so too one must be careful with one's possessions to not cause it loss or harm or damage.[166] Anyone who damages an item which is fit for people to benefit from, transgresses a negative command [and is liable for Rabbinical lashes[167]].[168] This prohibition applies whether the item is owned by a Jew, or gentile, or even if the item is Hefker, not owned by anyone.[169] [This prohibition is commonly known as "Bal Tashchis."]

Examples: Accordingly, anyone who breaks vessels, or tears clothing[170], or destroys a building, or stops up a spring, or causes loss to food or liquids, or makes the food become repulsive, (or throws money to waste), or damages any other item which is fit for people to benefit from, transgresses a negative command.

May one destroy items to instill fear upon others:[171] It is forbidden to destroy an item even if one's intentions is to show anger and fury in order to instill fear upon his household which are not acting properly.

B. The exceptions:[172]

Destroying an item for fixing purposes:[173] The above prohibition only applies when one desires to destroy or damage an item for the sake of ruin and destruction. If, however, one's intentions are to fix or modify,

---

[164] The law can be found on the website of the Ministry of Transportation: http:::nohal.mot.gov.il:%D7%A0%D7%95%D7%94%D7%9C%20%D7%90%D7%95%D7%98%D7%95%D7%91%D7%95%D7%A1%D7%99%D7%9D%20%D7%AA%D7%A7%D7%95%D7%9C%D7%99%D7%9D.aspx

The following was a response of a representative of the ministry of transportation regarding verification of this law: "The traveler is not required to pay the next time he travels on behalf of the previous use of transportation which was unable to collect the fare."

[165] Admur Shemiras Guf Venefesh Bal Tashchis Halacha 14; Bava Kama 91b; Kiddushin 32a; Shabbos 129a; Makos 22a; Rambam Melachim 6:10; Rambam Sefer Hamitzvos L.S. 57

[166] See Likkutei Sichos 18:465 that from this wording of Admur we learn that the two forms of destruction carry the same Halachic rulings.

[167] See Shivim Temarim 53 for explanation based on Admur ibid why one receives merely Rabbinical lashes, even though it remains Biblically forbidden.

[168] Admur ibid; Bava Kama ibid; Gilyon Maharsha Y.D. 116; Rambam Sefer Hamitzvos ibid; Tosafus Bava Metzia 32b; See Shivim Temarim 53

The source: As the verse states [Devarim 20:19] "Do not destroy the tree …" (as if the Torah warned us against destroying [the items] of gentiles of which we are waging war against them then certainly must one beware from destroying items of a Jew, or even items that are disowned.) [Admur ibid]

Other opinions: Some Poskim rule the prohibition of Bal Tashchis is merely Rabbinical. [Tiferes Yisrael 8:40; Possible way of learning Rambam Melachim ibid, and so learns in Rambam: Veheishiv Moshe Y.D. 57; Divrei Hamagia in Mishneh Lemelech on Rambam ibid; Noda Beyehuda Tinyana Y.D. 10; See however Shivim Temarim ibid who questions their assertion based on the Rambam's own ruling in Sefer Hamitzvos, from which it is clear that it carries a Biblical prohibition]

[169] Admur ibid; Noda Beyehuda Tinyana Y.D. 10 "Possibly is forbidden even if Hefker"

The reason: (As if the Torah warned us against destroying [the items] of gentiles of which we are waging war against them then certainly one must beware from destroying items of a Jew, or even items that are disowned.) [Admur ibid in parentheses]

Other opinions: Some Poskim rule the prohibition of Bal Tashchis does not apply by a Hefker item. [Possible way of learning Rosh on Midos 1:2, and so learns: Veheishiv Moshe Y.D. 57; Divrei Hamagia in Mishneh Lemelech on Rambam ibid; Noda Beyehuda Tinyana Y.D. 10]

[170] See Kiddushin 32a that implies one may tear it by the seam, as it can anyways be resewn.

[171] Admur ibid; Semak 175; Chinuch 529; See Shivim Temarim 53; Likkutei Sichos 18:465

Other opinions: Some Poskim rule it is permitted to destroy an item for the sake of showing anger and instilling fear into one's household. [Simple implication of Shabbos 105b and Rishonim who rule like this Gemara; Hagahos Maimanis Melachim 6; Tiferes Yisrael Midos 1:2; Ezras Kohanim Midos ibid; Devar Avraham 2:176; Kitzur SHU"A 190]

[172] Admur ibid Halacha 15

then one may damage it for this purpose if it is not possible to modify it in any other way. [This allowance applies even if one desires to destroy one item in order to fix or build another item, if it is not possible to do so otherwise, and the second item is of greater worth or value than the first item. For example, one may destroy or damage an item that is infringing or threatening another item, if the item under threat is of greater value than the threatening item. Similarly, one may destroy or damage an item that is in the way of another item, if the item under threat is of greater value than the threatening item.[174] Accordingly, we find that the Kohen appointed over the watchman at night was allowed to burn their clothing if they were caught sleeping, as this burning was done for his benefit, so the person prevents himself from falling asleep in the future.[175]]

Destroying an item for bodily benefit:[176] It goes without saying that it is permitted to damage or destroy an item in order to benefit one's body, such as one who burns a chair or table in order to warm himself up using them, if he has no other wood available. Another example; one may burn a cloth in order to cover the blood [of a slaughtered Chaya or bird] with the cloth's ash, in order so he be allowed to slaughter and eat the meat, if he has no other dirt/ash available, such as when he is on a ship. The same applies in all cases of the like.

An item which serves no use:[177] It is permitted to destroy an item which serves no use or benefit to people. It is permitted to damage or destroy it for even no purpose at all. This applies even if the item can serve a benefit to people, although people do not desire to trouble themselves to reap this benefit from the item, and it is hence rendered useless by the public. [Nonetheless, based on the teachings of the Arizal and Baal Shem Tov, one is to avoid damaging or destroying any item without a justifiable reason, even if the item seems to have no use, such as a mere leaf of a tree.[178]]

Summary:
It is Biblically forbidden to damage or destroy any item that can serve of benefit to man, whether the item is owned by a Jew, a gentile, or not owned at all. It is permitted to destroy an item in order to save, make room, or create, a more valuable item. It is likewise permitted to destroy an item for the purpose of bodily benefit. It is forbidden to destroy an item simply to release anger and instill fear upon others. It is permitted to destroy an item that is useless, for even no purpose at all.

Q&A
May one smash a car, fridge, monitor that is found in the dump or junkyard?
If the item can no longer serve any use for parts, then it may be destroyed for even no reason at all. If, however, the item can be used for parts, and it is common for people to trouble themselves to make use of these parts, then it is forbidden due to Bal Tashchis.

---

[173] Admur ibid; Rambam ibid; Chinuch 529; See Tzemach Tzedek 20:4
[174] Admur ibid regarding a fruit tree, and the same would apply to all cases of the like; See Likkutei Sichos 18:465
[175] Midos 1:2; See Likkutei Sichos 18:465
[176] Admur ibid; Shabbos 129a; Chulin 88b
[177] Admur ibid Halacha 16 regarding a non-fruit bearing tree and the same applies "To all cases of the like, in destroying other items"
[178] Likkutei Dibburim 1:112; Likkutei Sichos 38:135
The reason: As every creation has a Divine purpose and contains a G-dly vitality, and it is not within man's jurisdiction to destroy such creations. [Likkutei Dibburim ibid]

------------Niszkei Haguf Vihanefesh----------------

19. Destroying a tree:[179]
A. Destroying a fruit bearing tree:[180]

The prohibition and danger: It is Biblically forbidden to unjustifiably destroy a [healthy] fruit bearing tree due to the prohibition of Bal Tashchis, as explained above.[181] Furthermore, in addition to the prohibition of Bal Tashchis associated with destroying a fruit bearing tree, there is likewise a danger involved in doing so.[182] [This prohibition due to Bal Tashchis, and danger, applies both in Eretz Yisrael and in the Diaspora.[183] Likewise, the prohibition applies to all trees, whether owned by a Jew, gentile or public property.[184]] This however is with exception to those cases that the prohibition of Bal Tashchis does not apply [as explained next], in which case the danger likewise does not exist.[185] [Some Poskim[186] however learn that some danger exists even in those cases in which the prohibition of Bal Tashchis does not apply. Some Poskim[187] suggest that to avoid this danger even in the permitted cases, he is to ask a gentile to uproot the tree to avoid any possible danger. Other Poskim[188] add that to avoid this danger even in the permitted cases, one should sell his tree to a gentile through a Kinyan Kesef and Shtar, and then have the gentile uproot it. When the cutting of the tree is needed for a Mitzvah purpose, such as to expand a Shul, then even a Jew may cut it.[189]]

The permitted cases: [The following are the permitted cases in which the prohibition of Bal Tashchis and Sakana does not apply, although some rule that some level of danger still remains, as explained above:] It is permitted to destroy a fruit tree for a bodily or material benefit, as explained above. For example, if a fruit bearing tree weakens one's land and damages other trees that are better than it, then it may be cut down. [Thus, if a tree is causing damage towards crops of greater importance, such as vines, it is permitted to cut down that tree.[190]] Likewise, if one needs the space of the fruit bearing tree in order to build there[191], or if one wants to cut it down because it darkens one's window[192], then it is permitted to cut it down. [If, however, it suffices to cut off the branches that are darkening the window, rather than tear down the entire tree, then one must do so, and it is forbidden to cut down the entire tree.[193]] Likewise, if

---

[179] Admur Shemiras Guf Venefesh Bal Tashchis Halacha 16-17

[180] Admur ibid Halacha 16-17; Bava Kama 91b-92a; Bava Basra 26a; Makos 22a; Pesachim 50b; Semak 229; Rambam Melachim 6:10; Tzava of Rav Yehuda Hachassid 45 and Sefer Chassidim 53; Taz Y.D. 116:6; Beir Heiytiv 116:8; Pischeiy Teshuvah 116:6; Taz ibid writes that this law is omitted in Tur and Shulchan Aruch, however see Tur Y.D. 349-350; C.M. 383; See also Avodas Hagershoni Y.D. 116 and Shvus Yaakov 1:159 who question this assertion of Taz; See Shivim Temarim 53

[181] It is clearly evident from Admur ibid that cutting down a tree is Biblically forbidden due to Bal Tashchis, and so is understood from Makos ibid and so rules Sheilas Yaavetz 1:76; Gilyon Maharsha Y.D. 116; Rambam Sefer Hamitzvos ibid; Tosafus Bava Metzia 32b; See Shivim Temarim 53

Other opinions: Some Poskim imply that destroying fruit tree is only forbidden due to Sakana, and not due to Bal Tashchis [Taz Y.D. 116:6; The Poskim ibid question this ruling of the Taz; See Gilyon Maharasha ibid; Shivim Temarim ibid]

[182] Admur ibid Halacha 17; Taz ibid; Rav Chanina in Bava Basra 26a; See Shivim Temarim ibid; Sefer Chassidim ibid does not state why it is forbidden and makes no mention of danger

[183] Setimas Kol Haposkim; Shivim Temarim ibid p. 59 in his final conclusion, unlike his initial attempted understanding

[184] Admur ibid Halacha 14 regarding Bal Tashchis; Sheilas Yaavetz 1:76

[185] Admur ibid Halacha 17; Binyan Tziyon 1:61; Avnei Tzedek Y.D. 42-2, brought in Darkei Teshuvah 116:51; Shivim Temarim ibid p. 60a that so is implied from Gemara and Poskim; See also Michaber C.M. 155:26; Mishneh Bava Basra 27b regarding the allowance to cut the branches of a neighbors tree that is encroaching into one's property, and interferes with one's desired use, and no mention is made that by a fruit tree, one must beware due to the danger involved

Other opinions: See next!

[186] Sheilas Yaavetz 1:76, brought in Darkei Teshuvah 116:51, that so is intent of Sefer Chassidim; Toras Chaim on Bava Basra ibid and so learns Makor Chesed 62 in Bava Basra ibid; Shivim Temarim ibid and Makor Chesed 62 that the novelty of the Sefer Chassidim ibid who recorded the prohibition of cutting a fruit tree, is to teach us that the danger applies even in the permitted cases; Shivim Temarim 53:17 that one does not see a Siman Bracha even in the permitted cases, and so is implied from Pesachim 50b; See Igros Kodesh 7:264 who hints to this ruling of Sakana even in the permitted cases, even though it is clear that according to Admur it is allowed. In that letter the Rebbe instructed the asker to be stringent [despite Admur's leniency] being that in the past a negative occurrence happened to him as a result.

[187] Sheilas Yaavetz ibid; Shivim Temarim 53:16 that doing so avoids the leftover danger in the permitted cases, even according to Rebbe Yehuda Hachassid; Chaim Sheol 1:22 and Kaf Hachaim 116:84 that even in the permitted cases it is best to cut it through a gentile

[188] Beis Shlomo Y.D. 1:191; Zera Emes 2:53, brought in Darkei Teshuvah 116:51

[189] Sheilas Yaavetz 1:76; Ikarei Hadat Y.D. 14:2 and 8; Shivim Temarim 53:16

[190] Tzemach Tzedek chapter 41, brought in Pischeiy Teshuvah 116:6

[191] Admur ibid; Taz ibid; Rosh on Bava Kama 91b; Kneses Hagedola 116:31; Chaim Sheol 1:22; Chasam Sofer 102; Chochmas Adam 68:7; Bashamayim Rosh 334; Pischeiy Teshuvah ibid; Aruch Hashulchan 116:13; Kaf Hachaim 116:84

[192] Admur ibid; Chavos Yair 195; Lechem Hapanim 116:3; Beis Lechem Yehuda 116:4; Chaim Sheol 1:22; Kaf Hachaim 116:85

[193] Chavos Yair 195; Lechem Hapanim 116:3; Beis Lechem Yehuda 116:4; Chaim Sheol 1:22; Kaf Hachaim 116:85

the tree's [wood] can reap more money in use for building than it can reap in fruit production [then one may destroy it]. This ruling applies by all other cases of destruction [that one may do so for a positive purpose].[194] [Some Poskim[195] rule that in all cases of allowance, if one is able to uproot the entire tree with its soil and re-plant it elsewhere, then he is required to do so, rather than destroy the tree. In all the above cases of allowance, one must be certain that the benefit achieved through destroying the tree is greater than the loss of the tree. If one is in doubt, it is forbidden to do so.[196]]

B. Destroying a tree that cannot bear fruit:[197]

It is permitted to cut down any tree which cannot bear fruit. One may cut it down for even no purpose at all.

Old fruit tree: Likewise, an old fruit tree which only bears a small amount of fruit and is thus no longer worth the trouble to care and garden it, it is permitted to cut it down [for even no need at all]. The same law applies to destroying all other items of similar scenarios [in which the item either serves no benefit or its benefit is so minimal that it is deemed worthless]. An olive tree which produces a ¼ of a Kav of olives, and a palm tree which produces a Kav of dates, are [considered useful fruit bearing trees and are hence] forbidden to be cut down.

Summary:
It is Biblically forbidden to destroy or damage a fruit bearing tree without justifiable reason, and doing so is considered a danger. [Even when a justifiable reason is applicable, some Poskim maintain that the danger still somewhat applies. To avoid this danger according to all, even in the justifiable cases, one is to ask a gentile to cut the tree rather than have a Jew cut it down. If, however, one needs to cut if for the sake of a Mitzvah, then in the justifiable cases, one may have a Jew cut it down.] It is permitted to cut down a non-fruit bearing tree for even no reason at all.

The justifiable reasons: It is permitted to cut down a fruit bearing tree in any of the following cases:
1. The tree is weakening one's land and is damaging other trees that are better than it.
2. One needs the space of the tree for building purposes.
3. The tree is blocking the sun from one's window, [and it does not suffice to simply trim the branches].
4. The wood of the tree is worth more than its fruit production.

*[In all cases of allowance, one is to initially have a gentile cut the tree to avoid all worries of danger, and if one is able to uproot the tree with its roots and soil, and replant elsewhere, then he is obligated to do so.]

Q&A
May one ask a gentile to cut down the fruit bearing tree?
In all cases that it is forbidden due to Bal Tashchis and Sakana for a Jew to cut it down, it is likewise forbidden to ask a gentile to cut it down.[198] However, in those cases that it is permitted to cut down the tree, and one simply suspects for the aspect of danger, then it is permitted to ask a gentile to cut it down.[199]

---

[194] Admur ibid Halacha 16
[195] Chasam Sofer 102, brought in Pischeiy Teshuvah ibid
[196] Chasam Sofer ibid, brought in Pischeiy Teshuvah ibid
[197] Admur ibid Halacha 16; Rambam Melachim 6:9; Rabbeinu Yerucham 21; Bava Kama 91b; See Shivim Temarim 53:17
Other opinions: Some Poskim rule it is forbidden to cut down even a tree that does not bear fruit, for absolutely no need at all. [Kehilas Yaakov, brought in Darkei Teshuvah 116:51]
[198] Shivim Temarim 52:16; Poskim in Darkei Teshuvah 116:51
The reason: As throughout the entire Torah, whatever is forbidden to be performed by a Jew is forbidden to ask a Gentile to perform on one's behalf. [Poskim ibid; See Admur 243:1; 343:5; 450:20; Ribis 72; Sheila Usechirus 29; Michaber C.M. 338:6 [regarding muzzling animal]; Beis Shmuel E.H. 5:16; Beir Hagoleh; Shach Y.D. 141:17 and 23; Question brought in Bava Metzia 90a -see Biur Hagr"a 5:32]
[199] Shivim Temarim 52:16; See Shut Beshamayim Rosh 334, brought in Pischeiy Tesahuvah ibid, regarding if one needs the space of the tree that "Through a gentile one is not to be stringent at all"; Poskim in Darkei Teshuvah 116:51; Sheilas Yaavetz ibid; Chaim Sheol 1:22 and Kaf Hachaim 116:84 that even in the permitted cases it is best to cut it through a gentile

May one uproot a tree together with its roots/soil for the sake of replanting elsewhere?[200]
Some Poskim[201] rule it is permitted to uproot a tree together with its roots and soil with intent to replant elsewhere, even if there is no justifiable reason for doing so.[202] Other Poskim[203] however rule that one is never to uproot a tree, even with its soil with intent to replant elsewhere, unless one of the above justifiable reasons are applicable, such as one needs to use its space, in which case if one is able to uproot the tree with its soil one is required to do so, rather than destroy the tree. Practically, one may be lenient through a gentile.[204]

May one cut a branch off a fruit tree?[205]
Some Poskim[206] rule it is forbidden to break a branch off from a fruit bearing tree [without one of the above-mentioned justifiable reasons]. Other Poskim[207] however rule it is permitted to be done [in all cases].[208] Other Poskim[209] are lenient for the sake of a Mitzvah. Practically, one may be lenient for the sake of a Mitzvah through asking a gentile to cut it off.[210] [Thus, if one needs to cut branches for Sechach, Sukkah or Shavuos decorations, ideally one should cut the branches of a non-fruit bearing tree. If this is not available, then he is to ask a gentile to cut the branches.]
<u>Pruning branches off a tree for maintenance purposes</u>: It is permitted to prune branches off a fruit tree for the purpose of benefiting the health of the tree, so it grows healthy fruit, in accordance to the directives of a professional gardener.[211] However, it is forbidden to prune the branches simply for beauty purposes, to beautify the tree. Furthermore, even when pruning for purposes of maintaining the health of the fruit tree, it is best for it to be done through a gentile, such as a gentile gardener, as stated above.
<u>Cutting branches that encroach into one's property or public area</u>: One whose neighbor's tree is encroaching into one's property, then if it is getting in the way of one's use of the property.[212] The same applies towards a privately-owned tree which encroaches onto the public pathway, that its branches may be cut to allow for smooth transit.[213] Nonetheless, it is best to have the branches cut by a gentile, in as stated above.

Is a fruit tree that its fruit is not generally eaten by the populace considered a fruit tree in this regard?[214]
Yes. Thus, fruits that are not eaten due to infestation problems, or due to being of low quality, such as wild apples and pears, nevertheless contain the above-mentioned prohibition.

Is a tree that did not yet begin to produce fruit considered a fruit bearing tree?[215]
Yes.

---

[200] See Pischeiy Teshuvah 116:6
[201] Sheilas Yaavetz 1:76, brought in Pischeiy Teshuvah ibid; Shvus Yaakov 1:159; Chaim Sheol 1:23; Kaf Hachaim 116:86
[202] <u>The reason</u>: As the prohibition only applies against destroying the tree and when one uproots a tree with its roots and soil, it is as if the tree is still planted in the ground, as is evident regarding the laws of Arla. [Yaavetz ibid]
[203] Chasam Sofer 102, brought in Pischeiy Teshuvah ibid
[204] Chaim Sheol ibid; Kaf hachaim ibid
[205] See Darkei Teshuvah 116:51; Piskeiy Teshuvos 629:12
[206] Beir Sheva, brought in Mishneh Lamelech Issurei Mizbeiach 7:3; Mahariy Besen 118; Beis Yitzchak 1:144
[207] See Mishneh Lamelech Issurei Mizbeiach 7:3 in length; Beis Yaakov 140, brought in Darkei Teshuvah 116:51; Sheilas Yaavetz 1:76
[208] <u>The reason</u>: As the prohibition only applies to destroying the entire tree. [ibid]
[209] Divrei Chaim Y.D. 2:59; Beis Yitzchak ibid; Dovev Meisharim 1:134; Har Tzevi 2:102
[210] Har Tzevi 2:101-102; Teshuvos Vehanhagos 1:376; Piskeiy Teshuvos 629:12
[211] This follows the ruling of Admur ibid that one may cut down a fruit tree if it is causing damage to other fruits trees of greater value. Thus, certainly one may prune a branch off the tree for the sake of having the rest of the tree grow healthy fruit, as certain branches suck out an exorbitant amount of the trees energy and prevent it from developing good quality fruit.
[212] Michaber C.M. 155:26; Mishneh Bava Basra 27b
[213] Michaber 155:27; Mishneh Bava Basra 27b
[214] Neta Shoreik 42 and Avnei Tzedek 42-2, brought in Darkei Teshuvah 116:51
[215] Erech Shaiy, brought in Darkei Teshuvah 116:51

May Jew farm heart of palm?
It is permitted for a Jew to cut down palm trees for the sake of harvesting and selling the hearts of the palm. If the palm trees can bear fruit [i.e. dates] then it is to be cut down by a gentile, as explained above.

Miscellaneous

Miscellaneous

1. How to say Hashem's name when in reference to false gods, such as in the words "Elokim Acheirim:"

From the letter of the law, it is permitted to recite the actual name "Elohim" when it is written in reference to deities and not in reference to Hashem, such as in the words "Elohim Acheirim."[1] Furthermore, many are accustomed to specifically say "Elohim Acheirim" in reference to other gods, to emphasize that it is not Hashem and does not deserve the respect given towards Hashem's name.[2] Thus we find in many publications, and printings, that although when Elokim is in reference to Hashem it is written with a Kuf, the words "Elohim Acheirim" is written with a Hei. On the other hand, the Rebbe was accustomed to recite the words "Elohim Acheirim" with a Kuf, and explained that this is the common practice.[3] The reason for this is because if one says "Elo-him Acheirim", it may appear to others as a belittlement of Hashem's name.[4] Also, perhaps it is said so one not come to belittle a name that has true reference to Hashem. Practically, this matter is dependent on custom, and each community is to abide by their custom in this matter. As stated above, the custom of the Rebbe, and accordingly the Chabad custom, is to say Elokim Acheirim.

2. May one visit the Temple Mount?[5]

The Temple area contains Kedusha even today in its state of destruction. Accordingly, just as in Temple times there existed restricted areas of entry, so too in today's times, there are certain areas in which it is forbidden for a Jew to enter. Some of these areas are prohibited under the penalty of Kareis, as explained next.

The areas of restriction: The Temple Mount contains a number of areas with Halachic restrictions of access.[6] For example, the Halachically defined area of the Temple Mount [called the Har Habayis] is only permitted in entry for one who is pure from the impurity of a Niddah, Zav/Zava [Baal Keri[7]] and Yoledes.[8] The general area however remains permitted in entry for a Tamei Meis.[9] A Niddah, Zav/Zava, [Baal Keri] or Yoledes who enters into the Har Habayis, is liable for lashes.[10] The area of the Cheil and Ezras Nashim is only permitted in access for one who is pure of Tamei Meis.[11] A Tamei Meis who enters into the area of the Mikdash that is completely holy, such as the Ezras Yisrael and inwards, is liable for Kareis.[12] The area of the Kodesh may only be entered by Kohanim during the time of Avoda.[13] A Kohen who enters into the Kodesh not during times of Avoda, is liable for lashes.[14] The area of the Kodesh

---

[1] Implication of Rebbe in Likkutei Sichos 24:453; So is ruled regarding the name Tzeva-os that since it is also used for mundane purposes, it may be said as Tzevaos. Certainly, then this would apply to the name Elokim when it is used for a deity: See Sheivet Halevy 9:217; Kinyan Torah 3:110; Mishneh Halachos 13:198; Rebbe in Mamar "Vayehi Baetzem Hayom Hazeh" printed in Hisvadyos 1983 2:850 that the custom is to say Tzeva-os. See also Halichos Shlomo 22 footnote 32; Piskeiy Teshuvos 215:12

[2] So is accustomed in many circles of Litvish and Polish Jewry, and so has been taught throughout many Chadarim throughout the world. [See Hiskashrus 785 p. 19]

[3] Likkutei Sichos 24:453

[4] The Rebbe ibid cites the Ramban on Devarim 21:22 regarding hanging a Canaanite that it should not be done being it can be viewed as a belittlement of Hashem. This implies that one should avoid saying the name Elo-him even when in reference to a deity, being that people will mistake it for a belittlement of Hashem's name.

[5] Admur 94:1 in parentheses; M"A 560:2; Rambam Beis Habechira 6; Sefer Haterumah; Aguda; Semag; Chinuch; Ritva; Tashbatz; Kaftor Vaferach 6; Yireim 325 Tur; M"B 560:5; Likkutei Halachos Zevachim; Binyan Tziyon 2; Igros Moshe O.C. 2:113

Other opinions: Some Poskim rule that in today's times, during exile, there is no longer a Kareis prohibition involved in entering the restricted areas on the Temple Mount. [Raavad on Rambam ibid, brought in M"A ibid] Practically, we do not rule like this opinion. [M"A ibid; Binyan Tziyon ibid] Furthermore, there is room to learn that even according to the Raavad there is a prohibition involved. [However, see Radbaz 691]

[6] Rambam Hilchos Bias Hamikdash chapter 2-3

[7] See Pesachim 68a; Tamid 27b; Rashi Yevamos 7b and Zevachim 32b; Tosafus Yuma 6a; Rosh Nazir 44b; Ritva Yevamos 7b; Meiri Yevamos 3b; Yireim 277 and 391; Semag 304

Other opinions: Some Poskim rule a Baal Keri is permitted to enter the Har Habayis. [Omitted from Rambam Hilchos Beis Habechira 7:15; Bais Hamikdash 3:3; and implied from Shevisas Asur 3:3; Aruch Hashulchan Hasid 36:10 concludes this to be the view of the Rambam]

[8] Rambam 3:3

[9] Rambam 3:4; See Igros Moshe O.C. 2:113

[10] Rambam ibid 3:8

[11] Rambam ibid 3:5-6

[12] Rambam ibid 2:4

[13] Rambam ibid 2:1-2

[14] Rambam ibid 2:4

Hakedoshim may only be entered by the Kohen Gadol, and only on Yom Kippur.[15] One who is not a Kohen Gadol, or even a Kohen Gadol who enters not on Yom Kippur, is liable for death in the hands of Heaven.[16]

The location of the above areas of restriction:[17] It is difficult to measure the location of the above areas of restriction due to several reasons. First off, the original Har Habayis was 500 Ama by 500 Ama[18], while the current Har Habayis area is much larger than this.[19] Accordingly, there exists areas by today's Temple Mount that do not contain the Kedusha of Har Habayis at all, and is permitted in entry by every Jew. The problem however is that it is most difficult to ascertain the precise areas that are not included in the Halachic Har Habayis. Where do we measure the 500 x 500 Ama from, and what is the exact measurement of an Ama in this regard? Both of these matters are under dispute. The Poskim[20] debate over where the location of the Kodesh Hakedoshim is, and therefore dispute as to where the practical areas of restriction are located. The Poskim[21] also debate as to the exact measurement of an Ama. Accordingly, what may be a restricted area to one opinion, is not a restricted area to another opinion, and what is an unrestricted area according to one opinion may be a restricted area for another opinion. Nonetheless, the mainstream approach amongst Poskim[22] is that the center of the Kodesh Hakedoshim is by the rock found under the "Dome of the Rock" and from there one measures all the Amos of the Kodesh Hakedoshim, Kodesh/Heichal [100 x 100 Amos], Azara [From North to South is 135 Amos and from East to West is 187 Amos[23]], Ezras Nashim [135 x 135 Amos[24]], Cheil [10 Amos from the walls of the Beis Hamikdash, from East to West is 342 Amos, from North to South is 155 Amos, and is a total of 11 Amos from the Dome of the Rock[25]], and Har Habayis [500 x 500 Amos]. While we know the exact measurements of Amos for each area, it is unclear as to how many centimeters each Ama contains [as stated above] and it is also unclear from where on the rock the measurements should begin.

The practical ruling of Gedolei Yisrael:[26] It is evident from the Poskim that in previous generations Jews customarily would visit the Temple Mount in order to see the Makom Hamikdash.[27] Some Poskim[28] of earlier generations defended this practice, going as far as saying that even entering a questionable area at times may be permitted, due to their great passion to see the Holy of Holies. Nonetheless, in both the previous and current generation, the Poskim and Gedolei Yisrael[29] from all spectrums of Jewry, have severely warned the public not to enter the Temple Mount, including even the permitted unrestricted areas, lest he enter a restricted area and be liable for the severe penalty of Kareis. Meaning, that even if

---

[15] Rambam ibid 2:1
[16] Rambam ibid 2:3
[17] See Ir Hakodesh Vihamikdash 4:1
[18] Middos 2
[19] Today's Temple Mount is no longer square and has the following measurements: From East to West: 321 meters by its Northern side and 283 meters by its southern side, for an average of 302 Meters; From North to South is 490 by its Western side and 482 meters by its Eastern side, for an average of 482 Meters. There is thus an approximate total of 180 extra meters in today's Har Habayis. [See Ir Hakodesh Vihamikdash 4:1-2] The Eastern wall is 465 meters; the western wall is 488 meters; the northern wall is 317 meters; the southern wall is 275 meters
[20] Some say it is found by the rock that is under the Dome of the rock. [Radbaz 691; Ir Hakodesh Vihamikdash 4:4; All Poskim brought in later footnotes] Others say the rock is the area of the Mizbeaich. [See Ir Hakodesh Vihamikdash 4:4 who negates this position] Others say the Kodesh Hakedoshim is in the Southern area of the Har Habayis. [Kaftor Vaferach] See Igros Moshe O.C. 2:113
[21] Some say it is 48 cm [Shiureiy Torah p. 249; Daas Torah 35:116] Others say it is 53 cm [Darkei Teshuvah 19] Others say 54 cm [Aruch Hashulchan Y.D. 201] Others say 57 cm [Meishiv Davar 24] Others say 58 cm [Chazon Ish in Kuntrus Hashiurim 39:5; End of Kitzur SHU"A] 60 cm [Ir Hakodesh Vihamikdash 4:1-3] 63 cm [Darkei Teshuvah in name of Chasam Sofer 181; Levush Mordechai 133]
[22] Radbaz 691; Chida in 561; Chasam Sofer Y.D. 236; Chofetz Chaim Yalkut Halachos Zevachim p. 34; Chazon Ish E.H. 107; See Bach 561:5; Ir Hakodesh Vihamikdash 4:4; Pirkei Derebbe Eliezer end of chapter 30 [omitted from some Nuschaos] "Bnei Yishmael will build a building on the Heichal; The following historians: Bordo [year 333]; Eutychias [year 876]; Binyamon Todelo [year 1170]; Rav Pesachya Mirogenshburg; See Sefer Chatzors Beis Hashem of Rav Menachem Koran
[23] Middos 5:1; Radbaz ibid
[24] Middos 2
[25] There were 11 Amos between the western wall of the Heichal and the wall of the Azara/Beis Hamikdash. [Radbaz ibid] However, see that there were 10 Amos from the walls of the Beis Hamikdash to the Cheil. [Mishneh Middos 2:3]
[26] See Piskeiy Teshuvos 561:5
[27] Radbaz ibid; Meiri Shavuos 16a; However, see Minchas Yitzchak 5:1; Yabia Omer 5:26; Tzitz Eliezer 10:1
[28] Radbaz ibid [brought in Shaareiy Teshuvah 561:1] defends going on certain steps even though it is possibly part of the section of the restricted area, as a) Maybe it is not part of the restricted area and b) Even if it is, perhaps the air of the Azara was never made holy, and c) Perhaps we rule like the Raavad who holds there is no Kareis today involved in entering the Makom Hamikdash.
[29] Minchas Yitzchak 5:1; Yabia Omer 5:26; Tzitz Eliezer 10:1; Rav Elyashiv; Rav Wozner; Rav SZ"A; Rav Zevin; Rav Yaakov Landa; Rav Kook; Rav Mordechai Eliyahu; Rav Avinar; Chief Rabbi's of Israel in their respective terms including Rav Kook

we can determine without shadow of a doubt the exact areas of restriction, or of questionable restriction, and the areas that are permitted in entry according to all, nevertheless, one should not enter even these areas, as doing so would cause others who are unaware or not G-d fearing to enter the prohibited areas.[30]

Security forces entering the Temple mount:[31] It is permitted for security forces to enter the Temple Mount area, and even the Kodesh Hakedoshim, in order to prevent a life-threatening situation, such as to fight Arab terror which commonly occurs on the Temple Mount. Nonetheless, being that in many cases, the police send units up even during times that are free of danger, therefore a G-d fearing Jew is not to accept such a position. Commonly, due to this reason, there is a high percentage of non-Jewish soldiers who patrol the area, in order to avoid religious conflict.

Summary:
Gedolei Yisrael from all spectrums of Jewry prohibit visitation to the Temple Mount, including to those areas which have been determined to not be part of the Halachic Har Habayis and are not restricted in entry.

The Rebbe's approach:[32]
In a letter to Rabbi Meir Yehuda Geitz, the chief Rabbi of the Kosel, the Rebbe stated as follows:
It is obvious that in the current state of affairs in which the public is going from right to left [further away from Torah] that I am most vehemently against even the mere public discussion of the question of allowance to enter Har Habayis. [The reason for my absolute opposition is] because the moment that this discussion would begin, a number of people will visit the area, including the areas which are certainly prohibited, G-d save us, and that number will continue to grow, G-d have mercy on us. All the warnings about this issue (assuming they would be issued) will simply ignite the inclination of those people and increase the amount of people who go. Whoever brings up or participates in the discussion of this issue, and certainly one who actually goes up to Har Habayis, in addition to the sacrilege of the elders of Jerusalem, and the city of Jerusalem, it is sacrilege of the Har Habayis itself. Upashut!

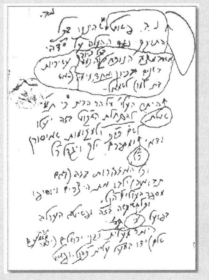

May one fly over the Har Habayis area?[33]
No. This prohibition applies likewise to a drone.[34]

---

[30] Rebbe ibid
[31] Heard from Harav Yaakov Yosef z"l
[32] Printed in Menachem Meishiv Nafshi Erech "Rav Geitz"
[33] Yabia Omer 5 Y.D. 26-9; Kinyan Torah 3:58; Piskeiy Teshuvos 561:5

3. Living or visiting Egypt?[35]

In various areas of scripture, The Torah prohibits one from living in Egypt.[36] This prohibition is counted as one of the 365 negative commands.[37]

Does the prohibition apply today? Some Poskim[38] rule that the prohibition no longer applies today.[39] Other Poskim[40], however, rule this prohibition is eternal and thus applies even today.[41]

In what scenarios does the prohibition apply: Even per the stringent opinion, some Poskim[42] rule the prohibition only applies today when traveling from Eretz Yisrael to Egypt, and not when traveling from another land to Egypt. Other Poskim[43] rule the prohibition only applies towards one who moves to Egypt for the sake of living there. However, one may visit/live in Egypt temporarily, such as for business or to learn or teach Torah and the like.[44] Furthermore, if one originally traveled there for a temporary visit/stay and ended up settling there due to financial reasons or other reasons, has not transgressed a prohibition.[45]

Final ruling: Practically, we find that many Gedolei Yisrael and G-d fearing congregations lived in Egypt, including the Rambam[46], Radbaz[47], Arizal[48], and others, thus relying on one of the Poskim recorded above each according to his reason. Thus, in conclusion, it is permitted to enter Egypt for a temporary stay, such as for business, teaching Torah, tourism, journalism, vacation and any matter of the

---

[34] The reason: As the air over the Azara was sanctified and it is prohibited for a Tamei person or item top enter that area. [Poskim ibid; See Rambam Bias Hamikdash 3:19; See Radbaz ibid that it is a doubt if the air of the Azara was made holy.]

[35] See Birkeiy Yosef E.H. 4; Chaim Sheol 1:91; Sdei Chemed Kelalim Yud 46; Likkutei Sichos 19:171, printed in Shulchan Menachem 7:156; Shut Yechaveh Daas 3:81 and Tzitz Eliezer 14:87 for a thorough discussion on this topic

[36] This prohibition is recorded three times in the Torah: Shemos 14:13; Devarim 17:16; 28:68; Sukkah 51b regarding Bnei Alexadria; Yerushalmi Sukkah 5:1; Mechilta Reb Yishmael Beshalach; Rambam Mishneh Torah Melachim 5:7

The reason: This is due to the depravity of Egypt and the fact that Hashem desired to distance us from the Egyptians and learning from their ways. [Rambam Sefer Hamitzvos Mitzvah 46; Sefer Hachinuch Mitzvah 500; Ramban Devarim 17:16]

[37] Rambam Sefer Hamitzvos Mitzvah 46; Sefer Hachinuch Mitzvah 500; Rambam Melachim 5:7

[38] Ritva Yuma 38a; Initial explanation in Smag 22; Rabbeinu Bechayeh Devarim 17:16 "It was a temporary prohibition"; Shut Deiy Hasheiv 15

[39] The reason: The reason is because the prohibition only applied in times that the indigenous Egyptians lived in Egypt, and thus today that the Egyptian people are made up of a multitude of nations due to the mixing of the multitude done by Sancheirev, therefore the prohibition no longer applies. [Smag ibid; opinion in Ritva ibid] Alternatively, the reason is because the prohibition only applied when the Jewish people lived in Eretz Yisrael, while today in exile that the Jewish people are dispersed throughout the lands, there is no difference in law regarding the various areas of the Diaspora. [Ritva ibid] Alternatively, the prohibition only applied in that generation due to the depravity of the Egyptian people, and is no longer relevant today. [Rabbeinu Bechayeh ibid]

[40] Yireim 309; Smag L.S. 227; Hagahos Maimanis Melachim 5:7; Ramban Shemos 1:13 "It is a negative command for all generations"; Kaftor Vaferach 5; Sefer Hachinuch Mitzvah 500; Beis Shmuel E.H. 4:10; Implication of Rambam Melachim 5:7 [It is clear from the Rambam ibid that he holds that the prohibition applies even today. So rules: Aruch Hashulchan Hasid Melachim 74; Rebbe in Likkutei Sichos ibid and Igros Kodesh 24:345; Tzitz Eliezer ibid; Yechaveh Daas ibid]

[41] The reason: 1) As the prohibition is dependent on the physical land, and not on the people living there, and so we see in Sukkah ibid that the people of Alexandria were punished even though his occurred after the times of Sancheirev. [Implication of 1st answer in Yireim ibid, Semag ibid, and Hagahos Maimanis ibid; See Birkeiy Yosef E.H. 4; Chaim Sheol 1:91; Minchas Chinuch Mitzvah 500; 1st suggested reason in Likkutei Sichos ibid, according to Rambam in Mishneh Torah] This reason, however is seemingly negated by the Rambam in Sefer Hamitzvos L.S. 46, who holds that the prohibition is due to the Egyptian people. [Likkutei Sichos ibid] 2) Alternatively, the reason is because the land of Egypt was not mixed by Sancheirev and hence the indigenous Egyptians live in Egypt until today. The reason for this is because the Egyptians returned to Egypt after 40 years, and hence still live there. [Yireim ibid; Semag ibid; Hagahos Maimanis ibid; Rosh in Perek Harel, brought in Michaber and Tur E.H. 4:10; Tosefta Yadayim; Ramban, brought in Harav Hamagid and Beir Hagoleh 4:10] Some Poskim, however, explicitly negate the last two reasons and stated that Sancheirev mixed up also the land of Egypt and they did not return. [Rambam Issureiy Biyah 12:25, brought in Michaber and Tur E.H. 4:10; Bach] 3) Alternatively, the reason is because a few Egyptians remained in Egypt even after the exiling of Sancheirev [Levush E.H. 4:4], and these few have a status of Kavua, and hence the prohibition remains, as their evil effect is still found. [Likkutei Sichos ibid in length, based on Rashi Yevamos 16b] See Birkeiy Yosef E.H. 4]; Chaim Sheol 1:91; Likkutei Sichos ibid

[42] Yireim ibid, brought in Ritva ibid; Smag 227; Hagahos Maimanis ibid; opinion brought in Rabbeinu Bechayeh Devarim 17:16; Beis Shmuel 4:10 in name of Mordechai; It is clear from the Rambam ibid that he holds that the prohibition applies even when arriving from other lands. [Aruch Hashulchan Hasid Melachim 74; Tzitz Eliezer ibid; Yechaveh Daas ibid]

[43] Radbaz 4:73 and on Rambam Melachim 5:7; The Radbaz negates the reason of the Yireim; Aruch Hashulchan Hasid Melachim 74; Tzitz Eliezer 14:87

[44] Rambam ibid; Sefer Hachinuch ibid

[45] Radbaz ibid

[46] Perhaps however the Rambam was forced to live there by the sultan who used his medical services, and hence he had no choice. [Kaftor Vaferach ibid; Radbaz ibid] Some say the Rambam would conclude his letters while living in Egypt with writing *"The man who transgresses three negative commands each day"* [Kaftor Vaferach ibid in name of grandson of Rambam, brought in Likkutei Sichos ibid; However see Yechaveh Daas ibid who brings Sefarim who reject this claim as a libel]

[47] See Radbaz ibid that he came to live there only temporarily for the sake of studying Torah and teaching it, and afterwards he returned to Yerushalayim

[48] Tradition states that the Arizal moved to Cairo at the age of 8, after his father passed away, and remained there until his late 30's when he moved to Safed for the remaining two years of his life.

like.[49] However, one who lives in Eretz Yisrael, may only visit Egypt for a justifiable reason, as applies in all cases that one desires to leave Eretz Yisrael for the Diaspora. Hence, one who is living in Eretz Yisrael is not to set a vacation trip for Egypt unless there is some reason to go specifically there versus Eretz Yisrael, such as sightseeing, or a cheaper bargain and one is in need of a refreshing vacation.[50]

Summary:
Some Poskim rule it is forbidden to live in Egypt even today. Practically, it is permitted to enter Egypt for a temporary stay. However, one who lives in Eretz Yisrael, may only visit Egypt for a justifiable reason.

Q&A

May one live/visit Eilat?[51]
There is a dispute amongst Poskim as to whether Eilat is considered part of the original Mitzraim in the times of Moshe. This dispute is based on whether the river of Egypt refers to the Nile and is thus west of Eilat, or whether it refers to a different river, which includes Eilat. Accordingly, some of today's Poskim discourage people who live in Eretz Yisrael from visiting Eilat, as aside for it not being part of Eretz Yisrael, it may be considered part of the original Egypt which we are prohibited from visiting.

Sparks of Kabala:[52]
The Arizal explains that the Kabalistic reason for why we no longer need to live in Egypt, and are hence prohibited from doing so, is because the entire purpose of a Jew living in an area is to elevate the Divine sparks that it contains [which fell during Sheviras Hakeilim or the sin of Adam]. Now, when the Jewish people left Egypt, they redeemed all the sparks from Egypt, taking them with them upon their exit. Accordingly, Egypt is completely empty of any sparks, and any purpose of living there. It is for this reason that the Torah prohibits one from living there, and one who returns to Egypt for no reason causes the Shechina to be exiled for no reason or purpose, and gives vitality to the already dead Kelipos.

4. Teaching your children to swim:

The Talmud[53] records an opinion that states a father is obligated to teach his son how to swim. The reason recorded in the Talmud[54] for this obligation is because on this matter "his life is dependent". This means that since it is possible that if one does not know to swim that he will drown, such as in the event of shipwreck, therefore the father is obligated to teach him to swim to prevent Sakana/danger.[55] The Rambam, Shulchan Aruch and all later Poskim however omit this ruling of the Talmud. Some Poskim[56] explain the reason for this is omission is because we do not rule like this opinion in the Gemara, but rather like the first opinion in the Gemara ibid which omits this obligation. [In conclusion, due to the lack of ruling in the Shulchan Aruch and Poskim, although teaching children to swim has Talmudic reference, it is not legally binding on the father. Nonetheless, as is the case with all matters of education, it is a moral duty of the parents to educate their children to avoid dangerous situations, and hence just as parents must teach their children how to cross the street, despite its lack of mention in Poskim, similarly they must

---

[49] Yechaveh Daas ibid
[50] Shevet Halevi 5:173
[51] Heard from Harav Yaakov Yosef z"l
[52] Peri Eitz Chaim Shaar Kerias Shema 7:3; See the English Rambam published by Moznayim which erroneously attributes further [and contradictory] statements to this source in their commentary on the Rambam's said Halacha of not living in Egypt. The author of the series has acknowledged the error and stated it would be fixed in future editions.
[53] Kiddushin 29a
[54] Kiddushin 30b
[55] Rashi Kiddushin 29a
[56] Binyan Tziyon 125

---------------Bas Mitzvah-----------------

5. Bas Mitzvah-Making a celebratory meal and party:

The old tradition of celebrating a Bar Mitzvah but not a Bas Mitzvah: The Zohar[57] states that the day of a boys Bar Mitzvah is similar to a wedding in terms of joy, and one must similarly rejoice on this day, just as one rejoices by a wedding. Accordingly, we find that throughout history a great celebratory feast, a Seudas Mitzvah, was made in honor of a boys Bar Mitzvah. The Poskim[58] discuss the significance of this meal and rule that it has the status of a Seudas Mitzvah. The reason behind this great celebration is because the child has now joined the ranks of the Jewish people who are able to serve G-d and fulfill the Divine mission of creation.[59] This is the true day of birth of a Jew.[60] Likewise, it shows one's excitement in serving Hashem. Some even write that making a celebratory meal on this day helps one merit a higher level of a Neshama.[61] We find precedent for this celebration in the Talmudic[62] statement regarding Rav Yosef, who was blind, that when he discovered that a blind person is obligated in Mitzvos, he made a celebratory meal in its honor. Certainly then, on the day that a person becomes obligated in Mitzvos, he should hold a celebration.[63] Based on this reason, it would appear that there is no reason to differentiate between the celebration of a girl's Bas Mitzvah or a boys Bar Mitzvah, as in both cases the child has now entered the ranks of the Jewish people, and it should be celebrated similar to a wedding.[64] It thus should be a day of joy, not just for the girl and her parents, grandparents, and siblings, but for all the Jewish people.[65] Nonetheless, until recent generations, the idea of a Bas Mitzvah celebration was unheard of. We find no discussion of it in Poskim, and have not received any tradition of its celebration from our ancestors, throughout our history.[66] Thus, while the Bar Mitzvah celebration and feast was accustomed throughout the ages and talked about amongst the Poskim, a Bas Mitzvah was not celebrated in those times. Seemingly, this was avoided due to reasons of modesty, in keeping with the verse "Kol Kevuda Bas Melech Penima."[67] This has all changed in the last couple of generations.

The start of the Bas Mitzvah celebrations: In the early 1900's, the conservative, and later reform, movements initiated the Bas Mitzvah celebration and spread it to the populace, as part of their campaign of gender equality between men and women.[68] Due to this, and other reasons, the Poskim[69] of that

---

[57] Zohar Chadash Bereishis 10; 15; Brought in M"A 225:4 in name of Likkutim 29; Toras Menachem 5748 3:158

[58] M"A 225:4; Rashal Bava Kama 7:37 based on Rav Yosef Keddushin 31; Degul Merivava Y.D. 391:2 in name of Rashal

[59] Yechidus 22nd Kisleiv 5746

[60] Yechidus 16th Tamuz 5747

[61] Kaf Hachaim 225:11

[62] Keddushin 31

[63] See Rashal ibid; Machatizs Hashekel 225:4

[64] Igros Moshe O.C. 2:97; Rebbe in Sefer Hasichos 5748 1:332 footnote 21; See P"M 225 A"A 5 regarding Birchas Shpotrani who asks why it is not also said by a Bas Mitzvah.

[65] Yechidus night of 15th of Tamuz 5745

[66] Ketzos Hashulchan vol. 9 p. 3; See Kaf Hachaim 225:11 that "even though we do not make a Seuda"

[67] See Ketzos Hashulchan vol. 9 p. 3; See Igros Moshe O.C. 2:97 who leaves this matter in question, although suggests that perhaps the purpose of the celebration is to publicize the child's ability to join a Minyan, and is thus not relevant to woman.

[68] The history: There were occasional attempts to recognize a girl's coming of age in eastern Europe in the 19th and 20th centuries, the former in Warsaw (1843) and the latter in Lemberg (1902). [See Marcus, Ivan G. (2004). The Jewish Life Cycle: Rites of Passage from Biblical to Modern Times.] The American rabbi, Mordecai M. Kaplan, held the first public celebration of a bat mitzvah in the United States, for his daughter Judith, on March 18, 1922, at the Society for the Advancement of Judaism, his synagogue in New York City. Change came gradually. As late as the 1930's, despite Judith Kaplan's pathbreaking example, only a handful of Conservative synagogues had adopted bat mitzvah. By 1948, however, one-third of Conservative congregations conducted them and, by the 1960s, the ceremony became the norm within Conservatism. The earliest American bat mitzvot were, ritually, not quite the same as bar mitzvot. They were usually held on Friday nights, when the Torah is not read or, if held on Saturday morning like Judith Kaplan's, the bat mitzvah girl would read from a printed Chumash, or book containing the Bible, rather than from the Torah scroll itself. The first recorded bat mitzvah at a Reform congregation occurred in 1931 but, as with the Conservative movement, the ritual did not catch on right away. By the 1950's, only one third of Reform congregations conducted them. Since the 1960s, as Reform has placed increasing emphasis on traditional rituals, bat mitzvah has grown to near universality in that movement's congregations. A number of modern Orthodox congregations have now adopted some form of bat mitzvah as well. Bat mitzvah, an innovation in 1922, is now an American Jewish institution. [Sources: American Jewish Historical Society]

[69] Zekan Ahron 1:6 [vehemently opposed it and states it transgresses grave prohibitions]; Ketzos Hashulchan vol. 9 p. 3 opposed even a family gathering; Igros Moshe O.C. 1:104 [does not go as far as to say that it is forbidden, but states that it does not involve a Mitzvah and is better off not done]; O.C. 2:97; O.C. 4:36; Otzros Yerushalayim 129 p. 461-463

generation vehemently opposed this change of tradition to start celebrating Bas Mitzvas.[70] The Rebbe, and other Halachic authorities[71], took a unique approach to this subject, which today has become the accepted custom amongst orthodox Jewry. While a girl should make note, and have a celebratory occasion in honor of her Bas Mitzvah[72], it should not be performed in an over-extravagant manner, and is not to be done with the same publicity, as is done by Bar Mitzvas.[73] It should preferably be held in the school, with her class, and her mother in attendance, and in all cases should remain small and modest.[74] The day should be utilized to further strengthen the girl's commitment to Torah and Mitzvos, and not for a vanity fair party. Obviously, one must take care that throughout the celebration, all the laws of modesty and Arayos discussed in Shulchan Aruch are abided by, such as not to have women singing in the presence of men.[75] Many elementary schools limit the celebration of the Bas Mitzvah with specified guidelines that are meant to keep it modest, affordable, and in line with tradition.

Summary:
A celebratory gathering should be held in honor of a girls Bas Mitzvah. However, it should not be performed in an over-extravagant manner, and is not to be done with the same publicity, as is done by Bar Mitzvas. It should preferably be held in the school, with her class, and her mother in attendance, and in all cases should remain small and modest. One must take care that throughout the celebration, all the laws of modesty and Arayos discussed in Shulchan Aruch are abided by, such as not to have women singing in the presence of men.

Q&A

Is a Bas Mitzvah celebratory meal considered a Seudas Mitzvah?[76]
A Bas Mitzvah celebratory meal is not considered a Seudas Mitzvah, and is similar to the status of a birthday party.

May a Bas Mitzvah celebratory meal or Kiddush take place in the sanctuary of a Shul?[77]
One may not hold a Bas Mitzvah celebratory meal in the sanctuary of a shul.[78] However, one may hold a celebratory Kiddush in the shul after Shabbos Davening, if it is common to do so in that Shul for other occasions.[79]

May one schedule a public Bas Mitzvah celebration for Friday night or Shabbos?[80]
As stated above, the Rebbe opposed public Bas Mitzvah celebrations. Nonetheless, if this has become the custom, it is best not to schedule the celebration of a Bas Mitzvah for Shabbos, in order to prevent

---

[70] The reason: First off, if our forefathers did not follow this custom, certainly there is a reason for it and we should not start a new custom. [Ketzos Hashulchan vol. 9 p. 3] Furthermore, some Poskim rule that it transgresses Bechukoseihem Lo Seileichu, as it was initiated by the reform movement who are heretics and deny the foundations of our faith. [Zekan Ahron ibid] Others say that it has no meaning and purpose in Kedusha, and hence cannot be considered a Seudas Mitzvah, and is simply like a birthday party. [Igros Moshe ibid] Likewise, many people use it today to perform parties in which Torah laws are transgressed, such as mixed singing, dancing, immodest dress and behavior, and hence even Bar Mitzvos should be nullified for this reason. [Igros Moshe O.C. 1:104; O.C. 4:36]

[71] Seridei Eish 3:93; Yechaveh Daas 2:69

[72] See Midrash Sechel Tov Vayeishev 20; Ginzei Yosef 4; Ben Ish Chaiy Rei 17; Hisvadyus 1988 vol. 3 p. 152 [146] that on the day of the birthday one is to celebrate with family and friends and have a festive Chassidic gathering, which is a Simcha Shel Mitzvah, giving praise and thanks to the Creator.

[73] See Igros Kodesh 17:237 *"Regarding the custom of Bas Mitzvah celebrations which has lately spread also to the religious world, to the point that it is almost impossible to abolish it"*; Rav Hillel Pezner received from the Rebbe in Yechidus, printed in "Bas Yud Beis Lemitzvos" chapter 3 that it should not be done similar to a Bar Mitzvah, but rather as a small and modest celebration, such as in school; Yalkut Bar Mitzvah p. 129 brings that the Rebbe told the author that one is not to make a public celebration, unless this has become the norm, in which case he should do so in a diminished fashion; In a reply to Hanhalas Beis Rivka, the Rebbe stated that it should be done either as a Mesibas Shabbos or as a Melaveh Malka. [Reshimu Shel Shana 5754 p. 113, printed in Shulchan Menachem 3:345]

[74] Ketzos Hashulchan vol. 9 p. 3; Rebbe ibid

[75] See Igros Kodesh 17:237

[76] Igros Moshe O.C. 1:104; Seridei Eish 3:93

[77] Igros Moshe O.C. 1:104; O.C. 4:36; Seridei Eish 3:93

[78] The reason: As it is not a Seudas Mitzvah, but rather a Seudas Reshus, for which even a Tnaiy upon building the Shul does not suffice. [ibid]

[79] Igros Moshe O.C. 4:36

[80] Igros Kodesh 17:237

desecration of Shabbos from occurring.

> **Sparks of Kabbalah**
> **The completion of the entrance of the G-dly soul into the body:[81]**
> The start of the entrance of the G-dly soul into a child's body is from the age that the Sages obligated the child to be educated in Torah and Mitzvos. However, the completion, and main entrance of the G-dly soul into a person is at 13 years of age for a boy, and 12 years of age for a girl. It is for this reason that they now become Biblically obligated to keep the commands, and are punished for transgression.

6. Customs associated with the day of the Bas Mitzvah:
This includes the general birthday customs, as well additional Bas Mitzvah customs.

A. Tzedakah:[82]
On the day of the Bas Mitzvah, the girl is to distribute money to charity prior to Davening Shacharis and also in the afternoon, prior to Davening Mincha. If the birthday falls on Shabbos or Yom-Tov, one is to give charity on Erev Shabbos and Erev Yom Tov, and it is proper to also give charity the day after.[83] The parents are to also distribute charity in merit of their daughter, and the same applies for the grandparents, relatives, friends, and anyone who desires the benefit of the Bas Mitzvah girl. Those who did not fulfil this custom on the day of the Bas Mitzvah, should do so on a later date, adding some money to the original amount.[84] The money should be distributed to a Chinuch institution.[85]

<u>How much to give</u>:[86] On several occasions the Rebbe instructed to give charity in numerals of 18. Some are accustomed to give in equivalent to the age that they have now reached, plus one more year. Thus, if one has turned 12 then he gives 13 to charity.

B. Davening with extra intent:[87]
On the day of the birthday one is to invest increased time and effort in one's recitation of the prayers, and meditating on the greatness of the Creator.

C. Tehillim:[88]
On the day of the birthday one is to increase in the recital of Tehillim. One is to read at least one Sefer of Tehillim.

<u>Study</u>:[89] On the day of her Bas Mitzvah, the girl is to study Psalm 13 in Tehillim.

<u>Reciting the new Tehillim</u>: On the day of one's birthday one is to begin reciting his new chapter of Tehillim after Davening that corresponds to his new age. Some have the custom to also recite their Tehillim of the previous year on the day of the birthday and they thus recite two chapters of Tehillim that day.[90] Nonetheless, the general directive is to only recite the Tehillim of the new year on the birthday.[91]

---

[81] Admur Basra 4/2; See Kaf Hachaim 225:11
[82] Yechidus 17th Shvat 5742; Minhagei Yom Huledes in Hisvadyus 1988 vol. 3 p. 152 [146]; Igros Kodesh 11/355; Sefer Haminhagim p. 186 [English]
[83] So is added in Hisvadyus ibid
[84] Yechidus 25th Tishreiy 5750
[85] Yechidus 22nd Kiseliv 5743
[86] See Hiskashrus 766 footnote 13
[87] Minhagei Yom Huledes in Hisvadyus 1988 vol. 3 p. 152 [146] letter 3
[88] Minhagei Yom Huledes in Hisvadyus 1988 vol. 3 p. 152 [146] letter 3-4
[89] Yechidus 17th Shvat 5742; Minhagei Yom Huledes in Hisvadyus 1988 vol. 3 p. 152 [146] letter 4; Igros Kodesh 3/451
[90] The Rebbeim would say a Derush also on the previous year's Tehillim on the day of the birthday. The Rebbe says that from here it is proven that also the previous year's Tehillim is relevant to the new birthday. [Mamar VeHashem Amar Hamechaseh 5737 letter 7 [Printed in Sefer Hamamrim Melukat 1 p. 210] based on Sefer Hamamrim 5680 p. 357]
[91] Answer of Rebbe to individual; See Hiskashrus 766

D. Learning Torah:[92]
On the day of the Bas Mitzvah, a girl should study more Torah than usual. It is proper to study Mishnayos on this day, as it corresponds to the words of Neshama.

E. Choosing a Mitzvah:[93]
On the day of the birthday one is to undertake a new act of piety that is within one's grasp, or a more scrupulous observance in some particular area.[94] The resolutions are to be taken in a public setting, thus making it more affective. [It is a good idea for a Bas Mitzvah girl to choose a specific Mitzvah to study in depth and choose to abide scrupulously by. She can share this Mitzvah and its details with her friends and family during the celebration.]

F. Presents:
The parents are to purchase their daughter a nice present in honor of her Bas Mitzvah.

G. Shehechiyanu:[95]
When a girl reaches 12 years of age, she is to recite Shehechiyanu on a new fruit or garment.

H. Baruch Shepatrani:[96]
The blessing of Baruch Shepatrani is not recited by the father on the day of his daughters Bas Mitzvah, even without Hashem's name.[97]

I. Doing an act of Ahavas Yisrael:[98]
On the day of the birthday one is to reach out to his fellow Jews, teach them Torah in general and Chassidus in a spirit of true Ahavas Yisrael.

The Rebbe's letter to a Bas Mitzvah girl:[99]
The following is a Free translation of a letter sent by the Rebbe to a Bas Mitzvah girl in the year 5722
Blessings and Greetings!
In response to your letter, in which you write that you have reached the age of twelve, which is the time of Bas mitzvah -May you accept upon yourself the yoke of Heaven and the yoke of the mitzvot with a whole heart. May Hashem grant you success in your studies and in your conduct, and may you grow up to be worthy of being called a "daughter of Chabad," in keeping with the desire of our holy Rebbe's, of blessed memory. May you influence your friends, too, in this direction, by speaking to them, and, even more so, by being a living example of a daughter of Israel who is educated in the ways of Chassidism. This will bring you happiness, both spiritual and material.
With blessing,

The Rebbe Rashab's letter to his granddaughter Chaya Mushka:[100]
With joy and pleasure, we congratulate you on your 12th birthday, up until 120 years. We bless you

---

[92] Kaf Hachaim 225:11; Answer of Rebbe to individual; See Hiskashrus 766
[93] Minhagei Yom Huledes in Hisvadyus 1988 vol. 3 p. 152 [146] letter 9
[94] Just as it is proper to undertake a new practice of this kind on Rosh HaShanah, so is it appropriate to undertake such a practice on one's personal Rosh HaShanah - his birthday, when his individual new year begins. [Rebbe ibid]
[95] Ben Ish Chaiy Riei 17; Kaf Hachaim 225:11; Ginzei Yosef 4; Hisvadyus 1988 vol. 3 p. 152 [146] letter 10
[96] See P"M 225 A"A 5 who raises the question; Kaf Hachaim 225:11; Ketzos Hashulchan vol. 9 p. 3;
[97] The reason: Perhaps the reason is because a father is not obligated in Chinuch of his daughter as much as a son. [P"M ibid] Alternatively, the reason is because she is still under her father's jurisdiction for certain matters, such as for Hafaras Nedarim. [Kaf Hachaim ibid; Ketzos Hashulchan vol. 9 p. 3] Alternatively, the reason is because even prior to the age of Bas Mitzvah, a girl belongs to her future husband and is hence protected from punishment of her father in his merit. [Kaf Hachaim 225:11]
[98] Minhagei Yom Huledes in Hisvadyus 1988 vol. 3 p. 152 [146] letter 7
[99] Igros Kodesh 17:310; 21:401; Likkutei Sichos 22:387
[100] Written some time before the 25th of Adar Sheini 5673

from the depths of the heart that you should be healthy and content for 120 years, to the joy and gladness of your beloved parents and us all. Today, my beloved, you have become independent in your spiritual life. We give you as a present the Chamishei Chumshei Torah, and wish you from the depths of our hearts that all of your days you should fulfill with joy all the holy commands found in it, and then the beloved G-d will guard and protect you. The holy Torah will G-d willing protect you in your lengthy and great journey in your content world, for all good spiritually and physically to no end. Congratulations from your beloved grandparents

ShulchanAruchHarav.com

1. **Largest fully resourced Practical Halacha Database on the web**
2. **Rulings of Alter Rebbe and Chabad custom**
3. **Hundreds of practical Q&A on each subject from the sea of Poskim**
4. **Perfect for the Halachic growth of you and your Ballei Battim**
5. **Daily Halacha video-Register for free**
6. **Weekly Mamar from Torah Or-Register for free**

Halacha Aids   Shabbos Aids   Semicha Aids

1. **Clear, concise, and finely detailed** practical Halacha
2. **Based on Shulchan Aruch Harav & Chabad Custom**
3. Semicha Aids: **Summary of every opinion and Halacha** in the Semicha curriculum! *Perfect for Semicha review!*

Become a Gold Member of our website and receive all our Sefarim free of charge shipped to your home immediately after publishing, in addition to helping support a Torah cause!

Become a member now at shulchanaruchaharav.com /product/support-subscription/

This Sefer is dedicated in honor of all the members and subscribers of Shulchanaruchharav.com who help support our work

To become a member and help support our work-Visit our site at shulchanaruchharav.com

Our other Sefarim available on shulchanaruchharav.com, Amazon.com and selected book stores

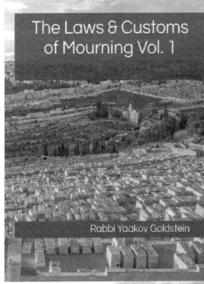
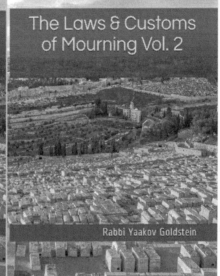

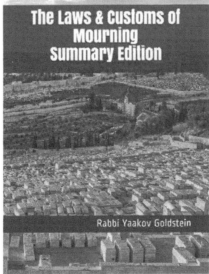

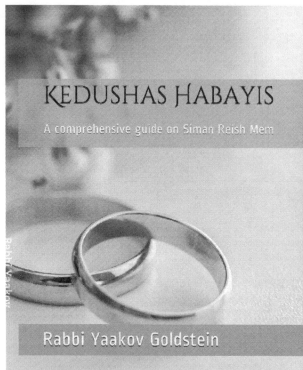
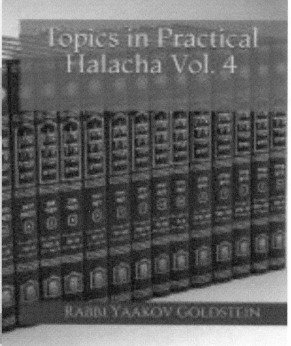

Dedication Page

> היה קורא פרק שני ברכות יז.
>
> ולא פריה ורביה ולא משא ומתן ולא קנאה ולא שנאה ולא תחרות אלא צדיקים יושבין ועטרותיהם בראשיהם ונהנים מזיו השכינה שנאמר יויחזו את האלהים ויאכלו וישתו: גדולה הבטחה שהבטיחן הקב"ה לנשים יותר מן האנשים שנא׳ ינשים שאננות קומנה שמענה קולי בנות בוטחות האזנה אמרתי א"ל רב לר' חייא נשים במאי זכיין ײבאקרויי בנייהו לבי כנישתא ובאתנויי גברייהו בי רבנן ונטרין לגברייהו עד דאתו מבי רבנן. כי הוו מפטרי רבנן מבי ר' אמי ואמרי לה מבי ר' חנינא אמרי ליה הכי עולמך תראה בחייך ואחריתך לחיי העולם הבא ותקותך לדור דורים לבך יהגה תבונה פיך ידבר חכמות ולשונך ירחיש רננות עפעפיך יישירו נגדך עיניך יאירו במאור תורה ופניך יזהירו כזוהר הרקיע שפתותיך יביעו דעה וכליותיך

> *Rav said to Rav Chiya*
>
> *"With what do women receive merit [of learning Torah]? Through escorting their children to the Talmud Torah, and assisting their husbands in learning Torah, and waiting for their husbands to return from the Beis Midrash"*

This Sefer is dedicated to my dear wife whose continuous support and sharing of joint goals in spreading Torah and Judaism have allowed this Sefer to become a reality.

May Hashem grant her and our children much
success and blessing in all their endeavors

שיינא שרה ליבא בת חיה ראשא
&
מושקא פריידא
שניאור זלמן
דבורה לאה
נחמה דינה
מנוחה רחל
חנה
שטערנא מרים
שלום דובער
חוה אסתר
בתשבע
יהודית שמחה

In memory of

Eliezer Goldstein

אליעזר בן יעקב ישראל ז"ל

May his soul be bound in the bonds of eternal life and his memory ever be for a blessing

ת.נ.צ.ב.ה

Dedicated by
Rabbi Yaakov Goldstein
The Author

In memory of the beloved Grandparents of the Author

אברהם בן יהודה
Avraham [Albert] Ben Yehuda
נלב"ע ו' תמוז תש"מ

שמחה בת יצחק
Simcha [Arlete] Bas Yitzchak
נלב"ע א' אדר א' תשע"ד

יעקב ישראל בן נתן נטע

May their souls be bound in the bonds of eternal life

ת.נ.צ.ב.ה

Dedicated by the Goldstein Family

In memory of

Gladys Szerer
שרה בת שלום ז"ל

May her soul be bound in the bonds of eternal life and her memory ever be for a blessing

ת.נ.צ.ב.ה

Dedicated by
Rabbi Roberto and Margie Szerer, New York

In memory of

פריידל באשה בת חיים שלמה
Friedel Basha bas Chaim Shlomo

משה בן שלמה
Moshe ben Shlomo

May their souls be bound in the bonds of eternal life

ת.נ.צ.ב.ה

Dedicated by the Trestman Family

In memory of our beloved Parents

בענדא שלמה בן דוד
נלב"ע כא' שבט תשע"ד

מרים יודית בת ראובן
נלב"ע י' תמוז תשנ"ג

*May their souls be bound in the bonds of eternal life
and their memory ever be for a blessing*

ת.נ.צ.ב.ה

Dedicated by
The Leiken Family

Dedicated in honor of all the members and subscribers of Shulchanaruchharav.com who help support our work

To become a member and help support our work-Visit our site at shulchanaruchharav.com

In memory of
גדלי' בן שניאור זלמן ז"ל
שניאור זלמן בן זאב ז"ל
וזוגתו יאחא רייזל בת דוד ע"ה
נתנאל בן חיים הלוי ז"ל
וזוגתו טויבא בת ירוחם פישל ע"ה

May their souls be bound in the bonds of eternal life and their memory ever be for a blessing
ת.נ.צ.ב.ה

Dedicated by
Rabbi and Mrs. Avrohom Jaffe, Manchester, England

DEDICATED BY DANIEL S. SAYANI IN HONOR OF

CHEVRA KADISHA TAHARATH JACOB ISAAC

In memory of

אברהם בן קאפעל אליעזר הכהן

AVRAHAM BEN KOPEL ELIEZER H'KOHEN

May his soul be bound in the bonds of eternal life and their memory ever be for a blessing

ת.נ.צ.ב.ה

Dedicated by his Grandson
Mr. Andrew Bales
Miami, Florida

In memory of

NOSSON BEN YAKOV KOPPEL O"H
ITA BAS AHARON O"H
AZRIEL BEN CHAIM YITZCHOK O"H

May their souls be bound in the bonds of eternal life and their memory ever be for a blessing
ת.נ.צ.ב.ה

Dedicated by
Rabbi Noach and Rivkah Vogel

In memory of

שלמה דוד בן יוסף

חנא בן שמואל חיים

אליהו בן קלמן

חי-ה לאה בת יעקב

אפרים זיסל בן מנחם מן

שרה בת מנחם יהודה

May their souls be bound in the bonds of eternal life and their memory ever be for a blessing
ת.נ.צ.ב.ה

Dedicated by
Rabbi Mat and Dr. Brachie Hoffman

לע"נ

ראובן בן גדליהו
י' ניסן ה'תשס"ב

מלכא פערל בת יעקב
כ"א חשון ה'תשנ"א

בצלאל בן מנחם מענדל
ג' ניסן ה'תשמ"ג

רחל בת פיגא
כו שבט ה'תש"נ

May their souls be bound in the bonds of eternal life and their memory ever be for a blessing

ת.נ.צ.ב.ה

נדבת
בצלאל מנחם מענדל וחי' מושקא בסמן ומשפחתם

In memory of

שטערנא שרה בת יהושע העשיל

SHTERNA SARAH BAS YEHOSHUA HESHEL

May her soul be bound in the bonds of eternal life and their memory ever be for a blessing

ת.נ.צ.ב.ה

Dedicated by her daughter
Mrs. Shainy Levin

In memory of

משה בן יהודה צבי

MOSHE BEN YEHUDA TZEVI

May his soul be bound in the bonds of eternal life and their memory ever be for a blessing

ת.נ.צ.ב.ה

Dedicated by
Daniel Schechter

In loving memory of

משה בן זלמן צבי

Moshe Ben Zalman Tzevi

Passed away on 8^(TH) Sivan 5778

May his soul be bound in the bonds of eternal life and their memory ever be for a blessing

ת.נ.צ.ב.ה

Dedicated by his grandson
Mr. Tzvi Shuchat

Made in the USA
Coppell, TX
03 October 2022

83993390R30157